Working People of California

Working People of California

Edited by
DANIEL CORNFORD

University of California Press
BERKELEY   LOS ANGELES   LONDON

University of California Press
Berkeley and Los Angeles, California

University of California Press, Ltd.
London, England

© 1995 by
The Regents of the University of California

Library of Congress Cataloging-in-Publication Data

Working people of California / Daniel Cornford, editor.
     p. cm.
    Includes bibliographical references.
    ISBN 0-520-08864-6 (alk. paper). — ISBN 0-520-08865-4 (pbk. :
alk. paper)
     1. Working class—California—History—19th century. 2. Working
class—California—History—20th century. 3. Trade-unions—
California—History—19th century. 4. Trade-unions—California—
History—20th century. 5. California—Social conditions.
    I. Cornford, Daniel A., 1947– .
    HD8083.C2W67 1995
    305.5′62′09794—dc20

                                     94-29274
                                       CIP

Printed in the United States of America
1 2 3 4 5 6 7 8 9

The paper used in this publication meets the minimum requirements of
American National Standard for Information Sciences—Permanence of
Paper for Printed Library Materials, ANSI Z 39.48–1984.

In loving memory of my mother, Jean Cornford
1924–1992

Contents

Acknowledgments

In compiling this book, and also in writing parts of it, I have received useful advice from several colleagues with expertise in both California and American working-class history. They include James Gregory, Michael Kazin, Jeffrey Lustig, Sally Miller, and Charles Wollenberg.

My colleague and friend Nancy Grey Osterud offered both moral support and shrewd advice from the inception of the book, while Jeffrey Stine provided the same, as he has since we first met in graduate school in 1976. My friend Peter Tannebaum offered constant encouragement and technical computer support at crucial times.

I of course take full responsibility for any errors of judgment or detail. In particular, it should be noted that, given the richness of the literature on California working people, very difficult choices had to be made about what to include and what to leave out.

I am very grateful to my department chair, Charles Keserich, for his continuous moral support and his awareness of the burden placed on faculty by the California State University system's heavy teaching load when combined with publishing endeavors. His sensitivity, modesty, and sense of humor make him a model department chair, especially for junior faculty.

I thank Lynne Withey of the University of California Press for her interest in the project when I first floated the idea to her in the late 1980s. I am also indebted to my editor at the University of California Press, Eileen McWilliam, for her encouragement and her prompt and efficient handling of all practical matters. In addition, I would like to thank my copyeditor, Mary Renaud, not only for her meticulous editing but also for making suggestions that substantively improved the book.

Finally, Lynn Helton, a victim of my first book, offered me constant emotional support during a difficult time in my life.

During the course of writing and compiling this book, my mother died suddenly. It is hard to comprehend the death of any loved one, especially someone so vibrant and unique. A history major herself, she nurtured my interest in the subject from my earliest years. When I returned to England for her funeral, I recovered a large notebook with some of my first, pathetic, scribbled history "essays." Interspliced among them were examples of immaculate, model note-taking in her handwriting. Her interest and support for my work never waned. It seems not so long ago that she spent two intensive twelve-hour days proofing the galleys of my first book with me. She was overjoyed when I called her with the news about my contract to publish this book. It was one of the last conversations I ever had with her. I dedicate this book to her.

Introduction

Scholarship by a new generation of social historians has transformed the writing of California history, just as the "new social history" began reshaping the study of American history in the 1960s. The essays in this volume represent some of the best recent scholarship in the field of California social history. Their focus is the experiences and activities of California working people.

While no one book can do full justice to the wide range of research on California social history, this focus on working people represents one of the most important new tendencies in the writing of California history as a whole. As David Brody and Peter Stearns have noted, the compartmentalization of social history into various subfields such as labor history, urban history, family history, women's history, demography, and ethnic study has been largely eroded.[1] In terms of working-class history, this has been a two-way process: Labor historians have broadened the scope of their work far beyond the narrow institutional aspects (usually trade unions) of working people's experience, whereas social historians have focused in microscopic fashion on the lives of working people from a "bottom up" perspective in a way that few did before the 1960s. Although a new social history of California developed somewhat belatedly, nowhere has the convergence of labor and social history produced richer yields by the mid-1990s.

This book presents a chronologically and topically balanced overview of the history of working people in California. Chronologically, the contributions range from Douglas Monroy's recent study of the California Indians to Mike Davis's account of the transformation of Fontana from a thriving blue-collar community in the 1940s to a commuter suburb of Los Angeles by the late 1980s. Topically, in addition to including new contributions on such celebrated episodes in California working-class history as the Workingmen's party of California and the San Francisco longshore strike of 1934, the book aims to redress the neglect of women and racial and ethnic minorities in traditional California history textbooks.[2]

Principles other than chronology, great events, and the representation of female and minority working people also determined the selections. Working people who were hidden from history were not merely victims of inexorable forces, but were important actors who found various ways of exerting countervailing power to protect their interests—and in doing so profoundly shaped the history of California. The means by which workers fought back were sometimes institutional, through unions and political parties, and sometimes much more subtle and complex, as Devra Weber's essay demonstrates in the case of Mexicana farmworkers.

This book is aimed not only at specialists but also at readers with little knowledge of California history. Introductory comments preceding each essay provide important background information. For readers wishing to pursue the topic further, a list of suggested readings follows each chapter.

As a general introduction to the book, it is important to examine the reasons why the new social history did not have a serious impact on the writing of California history until almost twenty years after its emergence elsewhere, in the mid-1960s. The following pages assess the work of an older generation of California labor historians, in terms of both their methodologies and their contributions to our knowledge. The discussion describes the ways in which the new social history of California is reshaping our understanding of the Golden State's history, with reference to some of the most important books, including studies by some of the contributors to this anthology. It also draws attention to significant gaps that remain in our knowledge of the state's social history.

The name Carey McWilliams recurs throughout much of this introduction. No figure looms larger in the study of California's social history. Yet he was a lawyer and journalist by training, not a historian. His most important work was published between 1939 and 1949, a period during which McWilliams wrote prolifically about California history. Four of his books were so significant that they were reprinted several times in the 1960s and 1970s.[3] McWilliams culminated a decade of astonishing productivity in 1949 with his classic *California: The Great Exception.* To this day, no book in the field of California history comes close to rivaling his synthesis.

McWilliams's interest in California social history began in the early years of the Great Depression: "The sense of social excitement was contagious," he wrote in his autobiography, "at long last that curious numbness and political paralysis of the first years of the Depression was rapidly giving way to a sense of rebellion." His experiences as head of the Division of Immigration and Housing from 1939 to 1942 in Governor Culbert Olson's "new deal" administration heightened his interest in California history: "No experience did more to shape my political point of view than this brief engagement with labor. It pushed me beyond the liberalism of the period in the direction of a native American radicalism with which I could readily identify." McWilliams also stressed that his appointment greatly deepened his interest in California's racial and ethnic minorities.[4]

In short, no work on California social history can ignore the accomplishments of McWilliams. It is most ironic that although he laid the groundwork for the new social history of California, it took almost forty years for historians to build upon it.

Since the late 1970s, the study of the California working class has burgeoned. In a 1986 review essay, Michael Kazin observed that a "widening stream of recent books and dissertations has greatly augmented knowledge of various sectors of the state's work force in different periods of its history."[5] Of the eighteen recent monographs cited by Kazin, only five had been published as books; the remainder were doctoral dissertations. Since 1986, ten of these dissertations have been published, and several have won major book prizes. Other important books and many articles have also been published since, not to mention numerous dissertations on many aspects of California social history.

Even before the 1970s, however, California's rich, complex social and labor history should have offered fertile ground for social historians. California's population has been one of the most racially diverse of any state; during the 1870s, the California Workingmen's party presented a serious challenge to the political status quo in the Gilded Age; during the Progressive Era, the labor movement in San Francisco wielded more power than labor in any other American city; the San Francisco general strike of 1934 was one of the most dramatic episodes of the turbulent 1930s. In the 1960s, the mystique associated with California since the gold rush intensified, as the Golden State became the nation's trendsetter culturally, socially, and politically.

But, despite the allure of California's history and its contemporary preeminence, the new social history of California appeared somewhat belatedly. Although during the late 1960s some California historians showed increasing interest in the study of racial and ethnic minorities,[6] the new social history did not make a major impact on the writing of California history (or, moreover, on the study of the American West) until the late 1970s and early 1980s. Indeed, Jackson Putnam stated, perhaps somewhat harshly, in a review essay published in 1989 that "California social history of the modern type is so undeveloped that it is scarcely in its infancy."[7] Certainly by the mid-1980s, the new social history of other regions— New England in particular—was much more developed than that of California, so much so that a new generation of California historians consciously sought to emulate many of the models and approaches adopted by their Eastern counterparts.

Several factors account for the slow and uneven development of the new social history. Historians of California, and also of the American West, remained mired in traditional approaches to their region's history much longer than the historians of perhaps any other region of the country.[8] Most important, historians of California and the American West were, with few exceptions, unable to exorcise the ghost of Frederick Jackson Turner.

The Turnerian straitjacket circumscribed California and Western history in various ways. By definition, it narrowed the conceptual and methodological framework that underlay the study of all regions of the American West. In a related fashion, it encouraged historians to limit the range of topics they studied. As Patricia Limerick observes: "Turner was, to put it mildly, ethnocentric and nationalistic. English-speaking white men were the stars of his story; Indians, Hispanics, French Canadians, and Asians were at best supporting actors and at worst invisible. Nearly as invisible were women, of all ethnicities."[9] The Turnerian preoccupation with agrarian settlement and "folk democracy" hardly spurred historians to study the role of labor and working people in many of the "instant cities" of the West. Turner's influence also caused historians to neglect the twentieth century. Finally, and perhaps most damaging, Turner's insistence that there was something unique about the character of the development of the American West bred a chauvinism and a parochialism among western historians that were hard to shake.

This chauvinism and parochialism were nowhere more evident than among California historians, who for many years portrayed "the state's history as a romantic anecdotal story featuring famous and heroic events: Cabrillo's voyage of discovery in 1542, the Serra Portola expedition in 1769 . . . the gold rush of 1849, the completion of the transcontinental railroad. . . ."[10] In particular, the rapid development of California following the gold rush encouraged a self-congratulatory and celebrationist perspective on the part of California historians. The increasing preeminence of California after World War II helped to perpetuate this outlook in an era when such historical provincialism was becoming increasingly anachronistic. Even Carey McWilliams, who had a very jaundiced and critical perspective on California history, insisted that the state's history was the "great exception."[11] Ironically, McWilliams, who did more than any other contemporary historian to address social issues and questions of social conflict, contributed unwittingly to the mythology that surrounded California history.

Most California historians before the 1960s wrote from an ideological perspective very different from that of McWilliams. They clung to a consensus view of history even at a time when a new generation of historians, influenced by contemporaneous events in California, was subjecting this view of American history to considerable scrutiny and criticism.

Although the writing of California history before the 1960s was dominated by traditional and conservative approaches, with studies written by and for "affluent white men . . . [who] predictably dwelt on the achievements of that group while overlooking the experiences of others,"[12] a few California historians attempted (in E. P. Thompson's famous phrase) to rescue the "inarticulate" from oblivion and the enormous condescension of posterity. Writing in the tumultuous 1930s, Carey McWilliams treated the role of labor and the state's many ethnic groups in considerable detail and with great sympathy in his classic book *Factories in the Field* (1939). In the introduction, McWilliams was quite explicit about the purpose of his book: "It is intended as a guide to the social history of California, an attempt to dispel a few of the illusions and to focus attention on certain unpleasant realities."[13]

Brilliant as McWilliams's work was, it focused primarily on the plight of California's migrant agricultural workers. When McWilliams wrote a chapter on the California labor movement as a whole ("California Labor: Total Engagement") in his book *California: The Great Exception* (1949), he was forced to rely heavily on the work of Lucile Eaves and Ira Cross. In the tradition of many labor historians until the 1960s, both Eaves and Cross were labor economists. Eaves's book *A History of California Labor Legislation* (1910) traced the roots of protective laws from the state's beginnings. Much broader in scope was Ira Cross's *History of the Labor Movement in California* (1935). To this day, Cross's work is indispensable because of the breadth and meticulousness of his research. It does, however, contain many of the limitations associated with the "old" labor history.

Cross concentrated primarily on chronicling the story of organized labor and dramatic episodes in its history. Such subjects as unskilled workers, women, minorities, and changes in the nature of work and the structure of the work force received comparatively little attention. In addition, Cross's book focused heavily on San Francisco, as he recognized in his own preface: "An attempt to do full justice to the efforts of those persons in each community who have been moved by a sincere desire to improve the lot of the working class, would require the writing of many volumes."[14] Finally, Cross's work failed to integrate California's labor history with the important history of dissenting political movements at the state and local levels.

Several useful contributions, much in the genre of Cross's work, were made to California labor history in the 1950s and the 1960s, including Grace H. Stimson, *Rise of the Labor Movement in Los Angeles* (1955); Louis B. Perry and Richard S. Perry, *A History of the Los Angeles Labor Movement, 1911–1941* (1963); Robert E. L. Knight, *Industrial Relations in the San Francisco Bay Area, 1900–1918* (1960); and Philip Taft, *Labor Politics American Style: The California State Federation of Labor* (1968). In 1966, David Selvin published *Sky Full of Storm: A Brief History of California Labor*. While this book was revised twice in the next fifteen years, it amounted to little more than a synthesis of the old, institutionally oriented labor history of Cross and his successors. Selvin did not have at his disposal much of the new California social history that might have enabled him to write a book transcending the paradigms of the old labor history.

For all its limitations, however, it would be unwise to dismiss the old institutional labor history. Indeed, as Howard Kimeldorf has recently argued, the "new labor history" overreacted to the old, and the time has come again to "bring unions back in."[15] This applies with special force to California. To be sure, the organized labor movement never embraced more than half of the nonagricultural work force of the state, and, in various periods such as the 1890s and the 1920s, its influence was minimal. Moreover, many segments of the organized labor movement held reprehensible views on race and women, were indifferent to the plight of unskilled workers, and were actively hostile to such radical movements and causes as the Wobblies, the Socialists, and the progressive agenda and activities of the Congress of Industrial Organizations (CIO). Nevertheless, from the 1850s, although its power waxed and waned, the California labor movement was a significant countervailing influence that contested vital issues at the workplace and in the legislative arena.

The union movement was a major force in San Francisco during the 1880s, and in the early twentieth century it was probably more powerful there than in any other city in America. This power diminished by the mid-1910s, but the 1930s saw the revival of the California labor movement, heralded by the San Francisco general strike of 1934. This strike is vividly described by Bruce Nelson in his contribution to this book. The outcome of the strike helped to rekindle the labor movement not only in San Francisco but also in other areas of the state.

It is essential to recognize that during the early twentieth century the American Federation of Labor (AFL) in California and its constituent unions were quite autonomous from the national AFL and the international unions.[16] In most respects, the AFL in California was more progressive than the national AFL. In San Francisco, the AFL attempted to organize unskilled workers and women workers in certain occupations and vigorously engaged in political action. As Michael Kazin's contribution to this volume indicates, even the San Francisco Building Trades Council, the aristocracy of labor, took many positions that were considerably more progressive than those of Samuel Gompers and the AFL nationally. My own work on Humboldt County shows that AFL unions launched the first international union of lumber workers and achieved remarkable success for a while. Not only did the Humboldt County labor movement engage in active and independent political efforts, but several leaders and many rank-and-file members were Socialists.[17]

Of course, AFL unions, umbrella organizations, and the California State Federation of Labor can be criticized for either excluding or neglecting various categories of workers and for failing to use their strength in San Francisco to spread unionism to other parts of the state. Several mitigating factors must be kept in mind, however. First, the California State Federation of Labor had limited funds with which to expand unionism in the early twentieth century,[18] although it did lend some measure of support to unionism elsewhere in the state. Second, even in San Francisco, the labor movement was constantly threatened by powerful employer organizations founded primarily to crush unionism.[19] Third, as the work of Eaves, Nash, and Taft in particular shows us, the AFL was quite effective as a legislative lobbying group and was responsible for passing and defending a host of important labor laws.[20] And, by the 1940s, the AFL was also active in both extending and defending many of the social welfare reforms of the New Deal era, such as unemployment insurance, affordable housing and rent control, state-supported child care facilities, and health insurance.[21]

As Carey McWilliams noted, another distinguishing feature of the California labor movement was the level of its political engagement. In the 1870s, the California Workingmen's party caused one of the greatest upheavals in the state's political history. The Workingmen's party was not just a San Francisco phenomenon but a political movement that arose (in many instances independently) in at least forty of California's fifty-two counties. Although anti-Chinese sentiment played a significant role in the life of the San Francisco Workingmen's party, it is important to appreciate, as I argue in my essay on Humboldt County, included in this volume, that factors other than anti-Chinese feeling inspired the Workingmen's party. In most California counties, the party offered a strong anti-monopoly critique of California—denouncing the role of land speculators, railroad magnates, and corrupt politicians—and called for the eight-hour day, employment on public works during hard times, free access to education for all, a state commission to regulate railroad rates, a state income tax, and other reforms that presaged those of the Populist movement fifteen years later.

The links between the organized labor movement and the vibrant California Populist movement were not as close. In the wake of the Workingmen's party challenge, the Democratic party took a fairly strong anti-monopoly position, and labor politics were (in Alexander Saxton's words) "institutionalized" in San Francisco after the demise of the Workingmen's party.[22] Elsewhere, the California Populist movement attracted considerable support from working people, including urban workers.

The saga of San Francisco labor and the Union Labor party is well known. Michael Kazin sheds fresh light on why the Union Labor party wielded such power during the early twentieth century. He offers a complex analysis of the political ideology of the labor movement and its roots in the nineteenth-century dissident tradition. Less well known is that union labor parties were formed in many other towns and cities in California and that the Socialist party received a significant vote in many towns.

After the Progressive Era, the link between labor and dissident electoral political activity was weaker, for the labor movement in the Golden State was on the defensive, as it was nationally. During the 1930s, however, working people within and outside the organized labor movement supported several radical movements or initiatives, including Upton Sinclair's End Poverty in California (EPIC) campaign, the panaceas of Francis Townsend, and the Ham 'n' Eggs initiative.[23] The social basis of these political rebellions needs further analysis, but they unquestionably had a significant working-class constituency, especially in southern California.[24]

Bitter factionalism within the California labor movement and the strict adherence of most of the state AFL leadership to the conservative national policies of the AFL prevented the organized labor movement from playing a more visible and decisive role than it might have otherwise done in the 1930s, 1940s, and 1950s. However, as Marilynn Johnson describes in her essay for this book, a coalition of labor forces made up the CIO, dissident elements in the AFL, and civil rights activists embraced a progressive social-democratic agenda in Oakland during the late 1940s and met with early electoral success. The extent to which similar alliances were forced elsewhere warrants further study. The organized California labor movement, despite having to combat a fierce anti-union offensive from the late 1930s onward, was remarkably effective in defeating a series of anti-labor electoral measures, including three "right-to-work" initiatives between 1938 and 1958.

In assessing the achievements of the old labor history and the contributions that an institutional approach can make in the future, it would be foolish to overlook the work of such historians as Eaves, Cross, and Taft. While their prose is sometimes arid and the story dull, these histories provide a useful narrative framework and are the result of painstaking primary research. Institutional labor history can be productively combined with some of the approaches of the new social history.[25] This is most ably demonstrated in the essays contributed to this book by Vicki Ruiz and Dorothy Sue Cobble. In writing about the workplace struggles of waitresses in San Francisco, for example, Cobble gives us meticulous institutional labor history while also using categories such as gender, race, and class to illuminate many facets of the waitresses' work and union experience, not the least of which was her finding that these women possessed a fierce pride in their craft.

If we are to fill some of the yawning gaps that remain in our knowledge of the history of California working people, we are going to need studies that do not neglect institutional aspects of the labor movement's history. The "old" California labor historians concentrated primarily on San Francisco in the second half of the nineteenth century and the early part of the twentieth. Notwithstanding the work of Stimson and the Perrys, we know far less about the history of the labor movement in Los Angeles, and even less about its history in countless small towns and cities throughout the state. We even lack a thorough narrative account of the history of the California labor movement, including San Francisco itself, in the period from the 1920s to the 1950s. We know a lot about certain unions, strikes, and episodes, but no one has attempted to piece the information together.

The new California history has begun to explore many noninstitutional aspects of the lives of working people. It follows the path trod in the late 1960s and early 1970s by a vanguard influenced by historians such as David Montgomery and Herbert Gutman. Nowhere was this path more clearly defined than in Gutman's groundbreaking 1973 article "Work, Culture, and Society in Industrializing America," which called for a redefinition of the parameters of labor history and, in effect, for its marriage to social history and other subdisciplines of history. Rebelling against "the traditional imperial boundaries that have fixed the territory open to American labor historians for exploration," Gutman accused an older generation of labor historians of spinning "a cocoon around American workers, isolating them from their own subcultures and from the larger national culture." The narrowly economistic assumptions of these historians "caused the study of American working class history to grow more constricted and become more detached from larger developments in American social and cultural history and from the writing of American social and cultural history itself."[26]

To unravel and explore the experience of California working people, social and labor historians began to examine the lives of these people from a much more microcosmic perspective than did the previous generation of historians. To a significant extent, this has been accomplished by focusing on the working class from the standpoint of a particular community, an occupation, or a racial or ethnic group, usually within a relatively limited time span. The old social or labor history had revealed that, regardless of the author's sympathies, studies that were sweeping in their chronological, geographical, and occupational breadth deterred the historian from tapping a diverse array of qualitative and quantitative sources that could help to analyze numerous aspects of working-class life. The use of community and case studies was, moreover, especially fruitful when applied to California history because of the state's racial heterogeneity and the size and diversity of its economy and geography.

Like their counterparts elsewhere, the new California social historians, wary of the celebrationist and consensual framework of their predecessors, also probed for evidence of social conflict, whether studying the plight of Native Americans before the gold rush or the situation of black workers in the shipyards of California during World War II. They have shown that the California working class was not simply a passive victim of teleological forces; rather, within certain limits, it played a significant role in shaping its own destiny.

This research has involved much more than simply documenting episodes of resistance. It has entailed examining in great depth the social, economic, and cultural universe of working people. Race, class, gender, and culture have been examined both as important subjects in themselves and as forces shaping patterns of working-class resistance and accommodation. James Gregory's essay in this anthology is a model of how the analysis of a subculture (in this case, that of the "Okies") can explain much about the political values and responses of working people.

The greatest achievement of the new social history of California, however, has been to enhance our knowledge of the social and cultural world of the state's racial and ethnic minorities. During the 1980s, for example, several important books began to portray California Indians as something more than victims of a demographic holocaust—differing from the earlier view so forcefully and influentially expressed by Sherburne Cook.[27] The very title of Albert Hurtado's book *Indian Survival on the California Frontier* (1988) proclaimed the author's differences with Cook. Hurtado acknowledges that contact with whites in the gold rush era resulted in a "demographic disaster," but he insists that "Indians were not merely passive victims of white rapacity. While Indian populations were rapidly declining, the survivors adapted to novel circumstances." And, he concludes, "that any Indians survived is testimony that abhorrent conditions can produce courage and strength in people, a tribute to the persistence of mankind."[28]

Hurtado examined the vital contribution of Indian labor during and immediately after the gold rush in more detail than anyone else has done to date. George Phillips also stresses the adaptability of Indian culture and the Indians' resistance to oppression.[29] The complex interplay between Indians and Hispanic and Anglo cultures and the resultant patterns of resistance and accommodation are major themes of Douglas Monroy's book *Thrown Among Strangers: The Making of Mexican Culture in Frontier California* (1990), from which he has extracted an essay for this anthology. Monroy and Hurtado both emphasize that the ruthless exploitation of California Indian labor occurred in the context of the internationalization of the California economy during the late eighteenth and early nineteenth centuries. James Rawls is also conscious of the California Indians' place in the global economy and stresses the important role of Native American labor in the gold rush era. Rawls, however, views the California Indians much more as victims and is more concerned with chronicling how and why the Europeans and Americans developed such negative images of them.[30] Rawls's approach was highly influenced by his mentor, Winthrop Jordan, whose book *White Over Black: American Attitudes Toward the*

Negro, 1550–1812 (1968) transcended the boundaries of social and intellectual history and became a model for a younger generation of historians studying race relations.

While ambitious attempts have been made toward a synthesis of California Indians' history, our knowledge of other minority groups has been enhanced primarily by case studies focusing on a particular racial or ethnic group in a community or occupational context, usually within a specific time frame. This has been especially true in the field of Chicano studies. In his book *The Los Angeles Barrio: A Social History, 1850–1890* (1979), Richard Griswold del Castillo uses a wide range of quantitative data to explore in rich detail the social history of the emergent Los Angeles barrio, with attention to the familial and occupational structure of the community. Focusing on the period from 1900 to 1930, Ricardo Romo's book *History of a Barrio: East Los Angeles* (1983) picks up the story where Castillo leaves off. Romo successfully places his subject in the wider context of Chicano history, writing one of the best accounts of the forces that impelled the massive migration from Mexico early in the twentieth century.

Complementing Romo's and Castillo's work, but even more ambitious chronologically and geographically, is Albert Camarillo's *Chicanos in a Changing Society: From Mexican Pueblos to American Barrios in Santa Barbara and Southern California, 1848–1930* (1979). Not only does this study cover almost a century, it also compares the experiences of Chicanos in Santa Barbara with those of Chicanos in San Bernardino and San Diego. The central thrust of these books has been to examine why Chicanos became a subordinate economic group while exploring the resiliency and adaptability of their culture. This is also the primary theme of George Sanchez's recent and highly acclaimed book *Becoming Mexican American: Ethnicity, Culture, and Identity in Chicano Los Angeles, 1900–1945* (1993).[31]

In choosing occupation as their primary focus, Vicki Ruiz and Patricia Zavella have greatly added to our knowledge of the lives of Chicana cannery workers as well as providing many insights into the important role that Chicanas played in the California labor movement from the 1930s.[32] Likewise, Devra Weber's book *Dark Sweat, White Gold: California Farmworkers, Cotton, and the New Deal* analyzes the experience of Chicano agricultural workers and their role in the upheavals of the 1930s. The extent and quality of research on the social history of California Chicanos in the post–World War II years do not quite match up to the work done on the preceding years, however. Useful scholarship concerning Cesar Chavez and the United Farm Workers has been published—see, for example, Cletus Daniel's essay in this volume, which provides an excellent overview—but the definitive works on the subject remain to be written.[33]

The historiography on Asians in California, especially the Chinese and the Japanese, has followed a similar trajectory. Throughout the 1960s, scholarship focused on the racism to which these groups had been subjected, from the rabid sinophobia of the California Workingmen's party to the internment of the Japanese during World War II. While some historians, such as Varden Fuller, Carey McWilliams, and Lloyd Fisher, examined the crucial role of Chinese and Japanese immigrants in California agriculture, they focused on Asian workers as part of the state's farm labor supply and, like other historians of California Asians, made relatively little attempt to examine internal social history.

Since the 1960s, several important articles and works have remedied this deficiency. Among the most significant is Sucheng Chan's *This Bittersweet Soil: The Chinese in California Agriculture, 1860–1910* (1986). Broader than its title suggests, the book places Chinese immigration in a global context, sweepingly assesses previous work in the area, and touches on the experience of urban Chinese Californians as well. By making meticulous use of manuscript census data and a host of local quantitative sources, Chan paints a microscopically detailed and rich portrayal of Chinese social and economic life in the state. As she observes in her introduction, most scholars have focused on Chinese immigration and the anti-Chinese movement in California, while most of the work on the social history of the Chinese people in California has examined the urban and nonagricultural Chinese population. Chan's contribution to this anthology highlights the important role the Chinese played in the development of the state's agriculture in the late nineteenth century. Sylvia Sun Minnick's book *Samfow: The San Joaquin Chinese Legacy* (1988), though not focused exclusively on agricultural workers, is another important study of the social history of the Chinese in California that makes careful use of local sources, especially newspapers.[34]

Comparable in scope to Sucheng Chan's work on the Chinese in California are Yuji Ichioka's *The Issei: The World of the First Generation Japanese Immigrants, 1885–1924* (1988) and John Modell's *The Economics and Politics of Racial Accommodation: The Japanese of Los Angeles, 1900–1942* (1977). Various community studies of the Japanese in California have not received the attention they deserve because they have been published by local presses. Valerie Matsumoto's book *Farming the Home Plane: A Japanese American Community in California, 1919–1982* (1993) promises to reach a much wider audience, however. Karl Yoneda's

Ganbatte: Sixty-Year Struggle of a Kibei Worker (1983) is a fascinating account of his involvement as an organizer in the Communist party and the California labor movement, shedding light on the involvement of Japanese people and other workers in such causes. Ronald Takaki's *Strangers from a Different Shore: A History of Asian Americans* (1989) and Sucheng Chan's *Asian Californians* (1991) are invaluable synthetic works; Chan's book provides an excellent annotated bibliography on the history of all Asian workers in the state.

As Rudolph Lapp notes in the bibliographic essay accompanying his general survey *Afro-Americans in California* (1987), "the research and writing of black history in California is still in its early stages of development" compared to work published on African Americans in the East and the South.[35] Although this observation applies with special force to social and labor history, several influential publications on the social history of African Americans have appeared since the late 1970s. Charles Wollenberg's work reflects a growing tendency to study the social, political, and economic history of African Americans rather than simply focusing on oppression and the struggle for racial equality.[36] His article on blacks in the Bay Area shipyards in this anthology embodies this holistic approach and has influenced other historians studying the significant role of African Americans in the California labor movement during and after World War II.

While devoting relatively little space to the labor movement, Douglas Daniels's *Pioneer Urbanites: A Social and Cultural History of Black San Francisco* (1980) was among the first and most important new social histories of African Americans. Daniels uses a wide array of sources to construct a sophisticated and dynamic portrayal of African American community formation. Of equal breadth and significance is Albert Broussard's *Black San Francisco: The Struggle for Racial Equality in the West, 1900–1954* (1993). African Americans' struggle for equality is a central theme, but the book also explores in depth the social, cultural, and political history of the African American community in San Francisco, placing developments squarely in a statewide and national context. Broussard pays close attention to the structure of African American employment and examines the difficult relationship between black workers and the Bay Area union movement from the late 1930s onward. Shirley Ann Moore's forthcoming book *To Place Our Deeds: The African-American Community in Richmond, California, 1910–1963* promises to have all the depth and breadth of Daniels's and Broussard's work.

As Gloria Lothrop has noted in a review essay, our knowledge of California women's history still lags behind what we know about women in many other states and regions.[37] Perhaps the greatest contribution to California women's history has come from the ethnic community and occupational studies of the type described above. Three valuable autobiographies and biographies have been published since Lothrop's review essay. Dorothy Healey's autobiography, *Dorothy Healey Remembers: A Life in the American Communist Party* (1990), is a lucid and detailed account by one of California's most illustrious radicals, offering especially valuable insights into the role of Communists in the labor movement and the social and political history of California in the 1930s, 1940s, and 1950s. Vivian Raineri's biography of Elaine Black, *The Red Angel* (1991), covers similar topical and chronological terrain and is equally indispensable. Ingrid Scobie's biography of Helen Gahagan Douglas, *Center Stage: Helen Gahagan Douglas, A Life* (1992), is a rather more conventional biography. Although its subject was hardly a grassroots activist, Scobie's biography says much about the overlapping ideologies of liberal women like Douglas and more radical women like Healey and Black. In recounting the story of Douglas's 1950 senatorial campaign, the book also illustrates the particularly difficult state and national context in which California liberals and radicals had to operate in the late 1940s, as well as going some way toward compensating for the recent dearth of good California political histories of the post–World War II period.

To what extent was the history of labor in California different from developments in other states and regions? Writing in 1949, Carey McWilliams had no doubt that, in terms of its "engagement" at the workplace and in the political arena, the history of California working people was exceptional.[38] He stressed that the relative isolation of California from the national labor market enhanced labor's bargaining power and that the state's early dependence on San Francisco as a port gave waterfront unions enormous power. He also argued that because the commerce and population of the state were so concentrated in two large metropolises, and because agriculture and industry were so interdependent until almost the mid-twentieth century, the urban labor movement found unusual allies ("Curious Ducklings"), including the small shopkeeping element, a "large sector of the rural population," and white-collar workers. Finally, McWilliams stressed the degree to which anti-Oriental sentiment "invested labor in California with a political power far stronger than it has ever possessed in any other state."[39]

Almost half a century later, many California social historians share much of this analysis and are able to draw on a larger body of empirical evidence than McWilliams had to support it. But not all of the sweeping generalizations made by McWilliams in 1949 have stood the test of time. Most debatable are his contentions that labor found allies among "a large sector of the rural population" and that agricultural workers became "integral parts of the labor movement."[40] For reasons that McWilliams explained better than anyone, California's rural proletariat was almost totally unorganized before the 1930s, and the urban labor movement did relatively little to reach out to agricultural workers. Even after the 1930s, at least until the United Farm Workers became established in the 1970s, farmworkers remained poorly organized. In this respect, the state's farmworkers were hardly the "great exception." The militancy and courage demonstrated by California farmworkers in their struggles during the 1930s may have clouded McWilliams's judgment.

Some of McWilliams's other explanations for the allegedly unique character of California labor history were also a little wide of the mark and have been called into question by more recent research. In saying that "there seemed to be something in the air, in the social atmosphere of San Francisco, that prompted workingmen to organize," McWilliams uncharacteristically strayed into the realm of the metaphysical. His assertion that in California "class lines and distinctions were forgotten, and a universal spirit of rough democracy prevailed" contradicted much of his own evidence and reeked of Turnerianism.[41] It is also not supported by much recent empirical work on the social structure of late-nineteenth-century California.[42] Nor does recent research support his generalizations about the importance to the labor movement of the International Workingmen's Association and the Industrial Workers of the World in the late nineteenth and early twentieth centuries.[43] Finally, McWilliams never satisfactorily explained the historical weakness of the labor movement in southern California.[44]

As Michael Kazin argues in his article "The Great Exception Revisited," we will need more state and regional studies to determine how different California actually was. Yet some of the recent findings of the new social history indicate that in some areas the social history of California may have been quite parallel to that of other states and regions. If we take, for example, the political engagement of working people during the late nineteenth century, the evidence indicates that strong, dissident third-party movements sprang up in many places, espousing an ideological program similar to that of the California Workingmen's party (although sinophobia did not find a place in their platforms, except in western states). Leon Fink has calculated that during the 1880s "Workingmen's parties of one variety or another sprung up in 189 towns and cities in thirty-four (out of thirty-eight) states and four territories."[45] While the problem of land monopoly in California heavily influenced Henry George, works such as his *Progress and Poverty* were as widely and favorably received in states such as Ohio and New York as they were in the Golden State. These radical books were not the product of Californians' propensity to flirt with utopian proposals, as McWilliams argued.

It is true that in the early twentieth century the union movement did not hold such "undisputed sway" elsewhere as it did in San Francisco for a few years. Nevertheless, the labor movement became an important force in many major eastern and midwestern towns and in western cities such as Seattle and Butte, Montana. Moreover, the kind of polarized struggles that took place between labor unions and employers' organizations in San Francisco occurred in many other cities and in many of the extractive industries of the American West.

Even if some of McWilliams's generalizations about the exceptionalism of the California labor movement are wide of the mark, however, his work in *California: The Great Exception* still provides brilliant insights into some of the distinctive aspects of the state's social history. Nowhere is this more evident than in his analysis of the social, political, and economic implications of California's agricultural economy. McWilliams was one of the first historians to chronicle the rise of a California "latifundia" in the immediate gold rush period. He also recognized the social and political consequences of this development and the unique and pervasive power that agricultural employers wielded in the state. McWilliams explained the paradox of agricultural interests exercising such broad power in one of the most urban states in the country not simply by pointing to the rise of a latifundia but also by explaining the close interdependence of agriculture with many of the state's basic industries, from food processing to transportation and utilities. As McWilliams knew from his first-hand experience as director of the California Division of Immigration and Housing, the power of such organizations as the Associated Farmers went further than their ability to crush farm labor unionism; it extended into almost every corner of California political life and created a hostile climate for working people within and outside the organized labor movement. In this connection, it is worth noting that recent works by historians such as Marc Reisner, Donald Worster, and Donald Pisani show clearly that the parameters of the power wielded by California agribusiness extended far beyond its ability to inhibit agricultural trade unionism.[46]

Only during World War II did California begin to develop an industrial base that was not essentially a spin-off of agriculture and the state's other extractive industries. During the war, the California labor movement had a brief opportunity to extend its power beyond its primary base in craft unions in San Francisco and Los Angeles and to challenge the hegemony exercised by agricultural and industrial employers since the 1910s. From 1939 to 1947, the value of California manufactured products increased by 256 percent;[47] and between the end of World War II and 1953, almost twelve thousand new plants, representing capital of $3.2 billion, were opened.[48] Total employment in manufacturing increased 67 percent between 1946 and 1958.[49]

Although the labor movement grew at a faster rate in southern California, where manufacturing employment expanded most rapidly, the state's labor movement failed to build a strong base in the manufacturing industries. Indeed, the number of manufacturing workers who were union members declined from 52 percent in 1951 to 46 percent in 1957, and non-manufacturing workers still accounted for 67 percent of total union membership in 1957. On the eve of the AFL-CIO merger, only two of the fifteen largest unions in California were affiliated with the CIO: the autoworkers, which ranked eighth, and the steelworkers, which ranked tenth.[50]

The defeat of the 1958 right-to-work initiative indicated that California labor retained some political clout. But it would be misleading to make too much of this victory. For most of the period since the late 1930s, California labor had been on the political defensive. As Marilynn Johnson's essay in this volume shows, a brief window of opportunity for the labor movement to forge a broad political coalition appeared in the 1940s. A formidable array of obstacles stifled such prospects, however.

Perhaps nowhere was the struggle between the AFL and the CIO more bitter than in California. The strength of the Communists in the northern California labor movement and the lateness of Culbert Olson's attempt at a "little new deal" for California (1938–1942) fueled virulent anti-radical sentiment within and outside the labor movement. To be sure, there existed within the AFL a liberal wing prepared to cooperate with the CIO in the political arena, but the California AFL was no longer the autonomous body it had once been, and AFL president William Green used his power to crush the dissidents.[51] With internecine warfare inside the labor movement and growing anti-Communist sentiment at the state and national levels, the political context was not conducive to the California labor movement exploiting the propitious post–World War II economic climate. By 1946, many of the dissidents within the state labor movement had been dissuaded from following any course that deviated from the policy of the national AFL and CIO leadership, which tied the labor movement's fate to that of the Democratic party even as many Democrats rushed headlong to support the anti-labor Taft-Hartley Act.

Of course, as Mike Davis indicates in the article he has contributed to this book, important enclaves of blue-collar solidarity and unionism persisted in places such as Fontana, although racism, company welfarism, and factionalism within unions served as constraints. More important still, in the case Davis describes, the failure of Kaiser to modernize its steel-making plant in the 1960s doomed Fontana.

By the 1960s, the California labor movement, just like labor nationally, had to contend both with permanent job losses in some of the old manufacturing industries and with modernization and mechanization in others such as longshoring, where the International Longshoremen's and Warehousemen's Union (ILWU) was forced to accept containerization. However, two factors held off deindustrialization in California much longer than in most of the nation's industrial centers. First, the continuation of massive defense spending preserved some existing industries such as aerospace. Second, high-tech industries created hundreds of thousands of new jobs in California, especially in Los Angeles County and Silicon Valley.[52]

California's defense-dependent industries sustained a core of blue-collar unionism in the state. But recent cutbacks in defense expenditures threaten to erode the state's manufacturing base. In 1992, the Commission of State Finance estimated that 180,000 jobs had been lost in the previous two years because of Pentagon budget cuts.[53] In 1993 defense industry employment fell by 17 percent, and between 1989 and 1993 aerospace employment alone declined from 374,000 workers to 220,000.[54]

Plant relocations and factors unrelated to the retrenchment in defense spending have also hurt the California economy. A study prepared by the Aerospace Taskforce of the Los Angeles Economic Roundtable predicts that as many as 350,000 jobs in high-tech industries may disappear.[55] All told, approximately one million jobs, most of them in manufacturing, have been lost in California since 1989. Little wonder that the proportion of California manufacturing workers who are organized has shrunk from one-third in 1973 to about 15 percent today.[56]

High-tech employment not directly related to defense industries has hardly alleviated the plight of California workers. Many of the nonprofessional workers in the industry are poorly paid. Increasingly, the unskilled work force is made up of newly arrived immigrant women workers. As Karen Hossfeld shows in her article, the union movement has for the most part taken little interest in organizing these workers. Despite the objective obstacles to unionizing them, some efforts have recently been made in Silicon Valley; even by conservative estimates, however, Silicon Valley shed almost one-seventh of its work force between 1991 and 1993, which indicates that the prospects for unionization are not bright.[57]

It is ironic that at a time when working people inside and outside the California labor movement face the most formidable challenge to their working conditions and institutions since the 1930s,[58] academic and popular interest in the history of California working people flourishes as never before. The essays in this book reflect this paradox and caution the reader not to make deterministic or fatalistic predictions about the future. At many junctures in the state's history, the destiny òf working people appeared equally—or even more—grim. Repeatedly, however, California workers faced with serious challenges have devised both institutional and extra-institutional forms of resistance to combat the tide of seemingly inexorable forces.

NOTES

1. David Brody, "Labor History in the 1970s: Toward a History of the American Worker," and Peter N. Stearns, "Toward a Wider Vision: Trends in Social History," both in *The Past Before Us: Contemporary Historical Writing in the United States,* ed. Michael Kammen (Ithaca: Cornell University Press, 1980), pp. 205–230, 252–269.

2. One of those critical of "the romantic view of California history so often enshrined in the textbooks and popular literature of a generation ago" and calling for a broader social history of California is Charles Wollenberg ("A Usable History for a Multicultural State," *California History* 74 [Summer 1985]: 203–209).

3. These four books by Carey McWilliams are *Factories in the Field: The Story of Migratory Farm Labor in California* (Boston: Little, Brown, 1939); *Southern California Country: An Island on the Land* (New York: Duell, Sloan and Pearce, 1946); *North from Mexico: The Spanish-Speaking People of the United States* (Philadelphia: J. B. Lippincott, 1949); and *California: The Great Exception* (New York: A. A. Wyn, 1949). In addition, McWilliams's book *Brothers Under the Skin* (Boston: Little, Brown, 1943) was reprinted in 1964.

4. Carey McWilliams, *The Education of Carey McWilliams* (New York: Simon and Schuster, 1979), pp. 66, 84, 100.

5. Michael Kazin, "The Great Exception Revisited: Organized Labor and Politics in San Francisco and Los Angeles, 1870–1940," *Pacific Historical Review* 55 (August 1986): 371–402.

6. Roger Daniels and Spencer C. Olin, Jr., eds., *Racism in California: A Reader in the History of Oppression* (New York: Macmillan, 1971); George E. Frakes and Curtis B. Solberg, eds., *Minorities in California History* (New York: Random House, 1971); Robert F. Heizer and Alan F. Almquist, *The Other Californians* (Berkeley: University of California Press, 1971); Roger Olmsted and Charles Wollenberg, eds., *Neither Separate nor Equal: Race and Racism in California* (San Francisco: California Historical Society, 1971).

7. Jackson K. Putnam, "The Gilded Age and Progressivism, 1880–1930," in *A Guide to the History of California,* ed. Doyce B. Nunis, Jr., and Gloria Ricci Lothrop (Westport, Conn.: Greenwood, 1989), p. 35.

8. For a critical evaluation of the major general works in California history from Bancroft to the rash of California history textbooks that began appearing in the 1960s, see Gerald D. Nash, "California and Its Historians: An Appraisal of the Histories of the State," *Pacific Historical Review* 50 (August 1981): 387–413. Nash's overall assessment of the recent general works is somewhat contradictory. On the one hand, he notes California historians' "emphasis on the uniqueness of California's experience"; on the other, he praises these historians for avoiding "parochialism" and for viewing "their subject in a broad perspective." At the same time, he notes that "California still lacks a comprehensive history of business, agriculture, or labor," not to mention "a comprehensive history of politics."

9. Patricia Nelson Limerick, *The Legacy of Conquest: The Unbroken Past of the American West* (New York: W. W. Norton, 1987), p. 21.

10. Richard B. Rice, William A. Bullough, and Richard J. Orsi, *The Elusive Eden: A New History of California* (New York: Alfred A. Knopf, 1988), p. 3. The prologue to this book, "Californians and Their History: Myths and Realities," offers a sweeping attack on the traditional approaches to California history.

11. McWilliams, *California: The Great Exception.*

12. Rice, Bullough, and Orsi, *Elusive Eden,* p. 4.

13. McWilliams, *Factories in the Field,* p. 4.

14. Ira B. Cross, *A History of the Labor Movement in California* (Berkeley: University of California Press, 1935), p. xi.

15. Howard Kimeldorf, "Bringing Unions Back In (Or Why We Need a New Old Labor History)," *Labor History* 32 (Winter 1991): 91–103. In responses to this article in the same issue of *Labor History,* some historians took issue with Kimeldorf, but most agreed that union movement history was important and believed that the move to bring unions back in had developed further than Kimeldorf acknowledged. It is worth noting that, in part, Kimeldorf's major work to date has been on the California labor movement; see Kimeldorf, *Reds or Rackets? The Making of Radical and Conservative Unions on the Waterfront* (Berkeley: University of California Press, 1988).

16. This point is made in Philip Taft, *Labor Politics American Style: The California State Federation of Labor* (Cambridge: Harvard University Press, 1968); in Michael Kazin, *Barons of Labor: The San Francisco Building Trades and Union Power in the Progressive Era* (Urbana: University of Illinois Press, 1987); and in Daniel Cornford, *Workers and Dissent in the Redwood Empire* (Philadelphia: Temple University Press, 1987).

17. Kazin, *Barons of Labor,* esp. chap. 6 (reprinted here); and Cornford, *Workers and Dissent,* chap. 8.

18. Taft states that "its regular annual income in the early decades seldom exceeded $5000 and was frequently below this amount" (*Labor Politics American Style,* p. 3).

19. On the power of employer organizations in California labor relations, see William Issel and Robert W. Cherny, *San Francisco, 1865–1932: Politics, Power, and Urban Development* (Berkeley: University of California Press, 1986); and William Issel, "Business Power and Political Culture in San Francisco, 1900–1940," *Journal of Urban History* 16 (November 1989): 52–77.

20. Lucile Eaves, *A History of California Labor Legislation, with an Introductory Sketch of the San Francisco Labor Movement* (Berkeley: University of

California Press, 1910); Gerald D. Nash, "The Influence of Labor on State Policy, 1860–1920: The Experience of California," *California Historical Society Quarterly* 42 (September 1963): 241–257; Taft, *Labor Politics American Style*.

21. Taft's book *Labor Politics American Style*, while in some respects a brief for the AFL, provides useful information on this much-neglected topic. See also Marilynn S. Johnson's essay in this volume and her book *The Second Gold Rush: Oakland and the East Bay in World War II* (Berkeley: University of California Press, 1993).

22. Alexander Saxton, *The Indispensable Enemy: Labor and the Anti-Chinese Movement in California* (Berkeley: University of California Press, 1971), p. 152. Several useful articles and chapters on California Populism have been written, but we still lack a monograph on the subject. Michael Magliari's work provides an excellent, broad overview of California Populism in a well-researched and very insightful case study; see Magliari, "California Populism, a Case Study: The Farmers' Alliance and the People's Party in San Luis Obispo County, 1885–1903" (Ph.D. dissertation, University of California, Davis, 1992).

23. Jackson Putnam's book *Old-Age Politics in California: From Richardson to Reagan* (Stanford: Stanford University Press, 1970) is still a valuable work on this subject. Royce D. Delmatier, Clarence F. McIntosh, and Earl G. Waters, *The Rumble of California Politics, 1848–1970* (New York: John Wiley, 1970), the standard California political history, is useful but in need of updating.

24. James N. Gregory, "Who Voted for Upton Sinclair? The EPIC Campaign of 1934" (paper delivered at the Southwest Labor Studies Association Conference, San Francisco, April 29, 1989).

25. On synthesizing the new and the old labor history, see David Brody, "Reconciling the Old Labor History and the New," *Pacific Historical Review* 62 (February 1993): 1–18. See also the responses to the Kimeldorf article cited in note 15.

26. Herbert G. Gutman, "Work, Culture, and Society in Industrializing America," *American Historical Review* 78 (1973): 531–587.

27. Sherburne F. Cook, *The Conflict Between the California Indian and White Civilization: The Indian Versus the Spanish Mission*, Ibero-Americana, no. 21 (Berkeley: University of California Press, 1943); Sherburne F. Cook, *The Conflict Between the California Indian and White Civilization: The American Invasion, 1848–1870*, Ibero-Americana, no. 23 (Berkeley: University of California Press, 1943).

28. Albert L. Hurtado, *Indian Survival on the California Frontier* (New Haven: Yale University Press, 1988), pp. 7, 218.

29. Works by George Phillips include *Chiefs and Challengers: Indian Resistance and Cooperation in Southern California* (Berkeley: University of California Press, 1975); and *The Enduring Struggle: Indians in California History* (San Francisco: Boyd and Fraser, 1981).

30. James J. Rawls, *Indians of California: The Changing Image* (Norman: University of Oklahoma Press, 1984); Winthrop D. Jordan, *White Over Black: American Attitudes Toward the Negro, 1550–1812* (Chapel Hill: University of North Carolina Press, 1968).

31. Useful overviews of Chicanos in California are provided in the following books: Albert Camarillo, *Chicanos in California: A History of Mexican Americans in California* (San Francisco: Boyd and Fraser, 1984); Rodolfo Acuña, *Occupied America: A History of Chicanos* (New York: Harper Collins, 1988); and Mario Barrera, *Race and Class in the Southwest: A Theory of Racial Inequality* (Notre Dame: University of Notre Dame Press, 1979).

32. Vicki L. Ruiz, *Cannery Women, Cannery Lives: Mexican Women, Unionization, and the California Food Processing Industry, 1930–1950* (Albuquerque: University of New Mexico Press, 1987); Patricia Zavella, *Women's Work and Chicano Families: Cannery Workers of the Santa Clara Valley* (Ithaca: Cornell University Press, 1987).

33. Accounts have tended to be of a rather narrative nature. Recent and useful are J. Craig Jenkins, *The Politics of Insurgency: The Farm Workers Movement in the 1960s* (New York: Columbia University Press, 1985); Linda C. Majka and Theo J. Majka, *Farm Workers, Agribusiness, and the State* (Philadelphia: Temple University Press, 1982); Margaret Rose, " 'From the Field to the Picket Line: Huelga Women and the Boycott,' 1965–1975," *Labor History* 31 (Summer 1990): 271–293. Forthcoming from the University of Oklahoma Press is Richard A. Garcia and Richard Griswold del Castillo, *Cesar Chavez: His Life and Times.*

34. Sucheng Chan, *This Bittersweet Soil: The Chinese in California Agriculture, 1860–1910* (Berkeley: University of California Press, 1986), pp. 2–3. Minnick is openly critical of a generation of scholars who found it "easier to write Chinese and ethnic history by fanning an angry flame, delineating the victims and the exploiters." In this approach, she argues, the Chinese were portrayed as "a hapless lot and devoid of spirit," while "their accomplishments appeared to be the result of Confucius, patience, and supernatural strength." See Sylvia Sun Minnick, *Samfow: The San Joaquin Chinese Legacy* (Fresno: Panorama West Publishing, 1988), pp. xvi–xvii.

35. Rudolph M. Lapp, *Afro-Americans in California* (San Francisco: Boyd and Fraser, 1987), p. 112.

36. Books by Charles Wollenberg include *All Deliberate Speed: Segregation and Exclusion in California Schools, 1855–1975* (Berkeley: University of California Press, 1976); *Golden Gate Metropolis: Perspectives on Bay Area History* (Berkeley: Institute of Governmental Studies, 1985); and *Marinship at War: Shipbuilding and Social Change in Wartime Sausalito* (Berkeley: Western Heritage Press, 1990).

37. Gloria Ricci Lothrop, "California Women," in Nunis and Lothrop, *A Guide to the History of California*, pp. 111–128.

38. McWilliams, *California: The Great Exception.*

39. Ibid., p. 140.

40. Ibid., p. 128.

41. Ibid.

42. See, for example, Neil Larry Shumsky, *The Evolution of Political Protest and the Workingmen's Party of California* (Columbus: Ohio State University Press, 1991); Ralph Mann, *After the Gold Rush: Society in Grass Valley and Nevada City, California, 1849–1870* (Stanford: Stanford University Press, 1982); Robert A. Burchell, "Opportunity and the Frontier: Wealth Holding in Twenty-Six Northern California Counties, 1848–1880," *Western Historical Quarterly* 18 (April 1987): 177–196; and Robert A. Burchell, "The Faded Dream: Inequality in Northern California in the 1860s and 1870s," *Journal of American Studies* 23 (August 1989): 215–234.

43. The influence of the International Workingmen's Association was short-lived, lasting only for the first half of the 1880s. Despite dramatic free speech fights in Fresno and San Diego and brief efforts to organize agricultural workers, the IWW (the Wobblies) never made much of an impact on California. As Kazin notes, the Wobblies in California had forty locals and five thousand members at their peak in 1914. He argues that, to a significant extent, the AFL "stole the syndical-

ists' thunder"; see Kazin, "Great Exception Revisited," pp. 390–391. This conclusion is congruent with my findings on lumber workers in the redwood region of California; see Cornford, *Workers and Dissent*, pp. 151–174. See also Cletus E. Daniel, "In Defense of the Wheatland Wobblies: A Critical Analysis of the IWW in California," *Labor History* 19 (Fall 1978): 485–509.

44. Kazin notes that before World War I the Los Angeles Central Labor Council and the Building Trades Council combined never amounted to more than six thousand members. This number represents only one-tenth of the membership of the San Francisco Labor Council and the Building Trades Council at their peak. During the 1940s and 1950s, the labor movement in southern California grew at a faster rate than in northern California; by 1957, Los Angeles had 204,000 more union members than San Francisco. At this time, however, 50 percent of the workers in San Francisco–Oakland were organized, whereas only 35 percent were organized in Los Angeles, and 37 percent in San Diego. See Kazin, "Great Exception Revisited," p. 389; and Irving Bernstein, "Trade Union Characteristics, Membership, and Influence," *Monthly Labor Review* 82 (May 1959): 533.

45. Leon Fink, *Workingmen's Democracy: The Knights of Labor in American Politics* (Urbana: University of Illinois Press, 1983), p. 26. David Montgomery also stresses the importance of independent working-class political action in the Gilded Age; see Montgomery, "To Study the People: The American Working Class," *Labor History* 21 (Fall 1980): 485–512.

46. Marc Reisner, *Cadillac Desert* (New York: Viking, 1986); Donald Worster, *Rivers of Empire* (New York: Pantheon, 1985); and Donald J. Pisani, *From Family Farm to Agribusiness* (Berkeley: University of California Press, 1984).

47. *California Blue Book, 1950* (Sacramento: California State Printing Office, 1950), p. 783.

48. *California Blue Book, 1954* (Sacramento: California State Printing Office, 1954), p. 598.

49. Maurice I. Gershenson, "Shifts in California's Industrial and Employment Composition," *Monthly Labor Review* 82 (May 1959): 509.

50. Bernstein, "Trade Union Characteristics," p. 534.

51. Taft, *Labor Politics American Style*, alludes to this interference and to the presence of AFL dissidents. More revealing is Jim Rose, "Collaboration with a Dual Union: Oakland AFL Political Practice, 1943–1947" (1990; unpublished paper in possession of the editor).

52. A good economic history of California has not been written, but the following are valuable works on the California economy during and after World War II: Gerald D. Nash, "Stages of California's Economic Growth, 1870–1970: An Interpretation," *California Historical Quarterly* 51 (Winter 1972): 315–330; Gerald D. Nash, *The American West Transformed: The Impact of the Second World War* (Bloomington: Indiana University Press, 1985); Gerald D. Nash, *World War II and the West: Reshaping the Economy* (Lincoln: University of Nebraska Press, 1990); and Joel Kotkin and Paul Grabowicz, *California Inc.* (New York: Rawson, Wade, 1982). On the importance of defense spending and the military-industrial complex to California, see Roger W. Lotchin, *Fortress California, 1910–1961: From Warfare to Welfare* (New York: Oxford University Press, 1992).

53. *San Francisco Chronicle*, October 7, 1992, and August 7, 1993; *San Jose Mercury News*, October 7, 1992.

54. *San Francisco Chronicle*, September 18, 1993.

55. Cited in Mike Davis, "Who Killed Los Angeles? Part Two: The Verdict Is Given," *New Left Review* 199 (May-June 1993): 29–54.

56. Ibid.

57. Useful recent newspaper accounts of working conditions in Silicon Valley include "Laboring in the Silicon Jungle," *San Francisco Examiner*, April 25, 1993; and "Heavy Load for Silicon Valley Workers," *San Francisco Examiner*, May 23, 1993. On recent efforts to organize workers in Silicon Valley, see "The Underside of High-Tech: Silicon Valley Immigrant Workers Fight Sweatshop Conditions," *The Bay Guardian*, January 27, 1993. On the decline of high-tech jobs in Silicon Valley, see *San Francisco Chronicle*, July 7, 1993, and July 29, 1993.

58. The November 18, 1991, issue of *Time* magazine was a special issue devoted to "California: The Endangered Dream." The situation has worsened since the publication of this issue. Statistics compiled by the U.S. Commerce Department's Bureau of Economic Analysis revealed that California ranked 47th in the growth of personal income between March 1991 and March 1993 (*San Francisco Chronicle*, July 23, 1993).

1

WORKERS IN CALIFORNIA
BEFORE 1900

1 Brutal Appetites
*The Social Relations of the
California Mission*

Douglas Monroy

EDITOR'S INTRODUCTION

Nowhere in North America was the labor of Native Americans more important than in California, first to the European settlers and then to the Yankees. In most other areas of North America, Europeans and Yankees benefited only indirectly from Indian labor via involvement in trade. Moreover, despite labor shortages and a willingness to deprive Indians of their lands and exterminate them if necessary, relatively few attempts were made in North America to coerce or enslave Native American labor.

In California, however, the story was different. A whole set of circumstances made Native Americans by far the most important source of labor in California from the 1770s until the early 1850s, circumstances ranging from a scarcity of alternative sources of labor, at least until the gold rush brought flocks of white settlers in the 1850s; to the geographic isolation of California, which both limited the number of Hispanic, European, and American settlers and circumscribed the Native Americans' ability to flee and resist; to the desire of Spanish missionaries to "civilize" the Indians. Between 1769 and the secularization of the missions in 1834, approximately sixty thousand Indians worked in the missions. Following the secularization of the missions, a majority of the California Native Americans worked on the large ranchos of the californios. A system of debt peonage and vagrancy laws tied most Indians to the land, although they were technically "free."

The conquest of California by the United States in 1846 did little to alter the status of the Indian. Apprenticeship laws, kidnappings, and vagrancy statutes resulted in the de facto slavery of thousands of Indians. Other Indians found themselves sucked into the increasingly thick web of capitalist market relations that had begun during the Mexican California period (1821–1846) and that accelerated dramatically after the gold rush. With their traditional means of subsistence increasingly undermined, they were forced to work in growing numbers as wage laborers for whites in the mines and the fields.

In this extract from his book *Thrown Among Strangers: The Making of Mexican Culture in Frontier California,* Douglas Monroy describes how the Spanish looked down on the Indians because of the natives' apparent lack of a work ethic. He argues that both the Europeans and the Anglo-Americans failed to appreciate the extent to which abundance and Native American spiritual values engendered a system that "produced only as much as the need for food and shelter demanded, with a work rhythm the environment dictated."

Accordingly, the Spanish believed that to convert the Indians into *gente de razón,* the work habits and social mores of the natives would have to be transformed. Beginning in the 1770s, the padres attempted to impose this transformation in the missions by purging the Native Americans of their libertine values—for example, by clothing and sexually segregating them.

At the same time, the missionaries attempted to impose a European work discipline on their neophyte work force. The mission sundials and clocks symbolized this determination to introduce a new regime. Confined, restrained, and disciplined, the Indians became highly productive workers, toiling in all facets of a very diverse mission agricultural economy. They also worked as nonagricultural laborers and even as artisans. The missions became the centerpiece of the California economy, providing food and other commodities to the pueblos and presidios. The padres also hired out their Indian work force to the presidios and to members of the *gente de razón.*

During the early nineteenth century, as the hide and tallow trade with New England began to flourish, the California mission economy became increasingly linked to the world economy. Monroy painstakingly demonstrates this but argues that "the relationship between the producers, the neophytes, and those who controlled production, the Catholic fathers, remained fundamentally constant."

Although Monroy stresses that a variety of factors lured or forced many coastal Indians into the missions and that many Native Americans accommodated themselves to the new regime, he also shows that Indians resisted in a number of ways, from running away to other forms of noncooperation. In the concluding segment of his selection, he recounts several instances in which Indians attacked their padres and collectively attempted to overthrow the missionary order.

◆　　◆　　◆

The native people of California followed the ways of their ancestors and, in return, they survived. For them, acting in history meant the repetition of these ancient ways. Repeating their ceremonial dances connected their bodies to these historical cycles and to their ancestors, and interwove their flesh and their spirits with the cosmos. Time existed as a line on a cylinder in which they emphasized that which could and should be repeated for the cosmos to continue. Their myths, their sacred history, told them how to be. They had to exist in the ways they always had, or, in Mircea Eliade's words, practice "the cyclical recurrence of what has been before, in a word, eternal return." Little did they know, or could they know, that a tribe of strangers from a place called Iberia, who had already visited them but gone away, was growing increasingly worried about incursions by a people from Russia. Decisions made as a result of these fears would quickly shred the delicate fabric their ancestors had so carefully woven over thousands of years. They would be thrown into a European conception of linear history, complete with its notion of progress. Now the passage of time would take these native people to new places in their relationship to the cosmos.[1]

Europeans and Anglo-Americans consistently perceived Indians as lazy. Juan Bautista de Anza, in a typical Spanish characterization of the people he encountered in California, referred to a "free tribe that is indolent by nature." These people were obviously neither indolent nor free. But their work rhythms gave this impression to all who observed them from an accumulationist perspective. Indians worked intermittently rather than steadily, as survival and nature, rather than a daily schedule or clock, demanded. Most of their food was seasonal; acorns ripened and grasshoppers were abundant in a wingless stage only at particular times. Moreover, ritual may have required that certain animals be killed only at the time deities prescribed, as was true with other tribes. At these junctures people exerted themselves steadily and intensely in a disciplined fashion to procure their livelihoods. The men hunted, and the women gathered and stored food for lean times. Then they rested and loafed. In addition, their ecosystem could not tolerate intensive, accumulationist exploitation—there were only so many animals and oak trees. For this "affluence without abundance" they worked less than people with a plethora of labor-saving devices, maybe ten to fifteen hours a week excluding rituals, and produced only as much as the need for food and shelter demanded, with a work rhythm the environment dictated.[2]

The Spanish would make the Indians into *gente de razón,* or people of reason. The phrase encapsulates the wholeness of the Spanish vision for the Indians of California. Of course, to a Spaniard, to be *de razón* meant to be Catholic, Castilian-speaking, settled into tax-paying towns, working in agriculture, and loyal to his majesty, the king of Spain. But even more fundamentally, to be *de razón* meant that one's reason, with some help from the fear of God, would produce an individual who internalized the need to manage, or even renounce, instinct for the good of the social organization. Human reason, moreover, provided the basis for humans technologically to work their will *over* nature. By contrast, for Indians, human reason studied nature—which included magic. Such reflection then prepared people to act so as to function *with* nature. Nature constantly engaged in biological reproduction and encouraged humans to do likewise. The Indians, apparently, engaged in plenty of such "natural" procreative activity, to the great trepidation of the Christian padres. The Indians' actions did not seem at all rational to the other culture. Evidently undisciplined Indian instinct, the playground of the devil, seemed to rule the Indians, rather than reason. An anonymous pundit discerned the issue in Alta California nicely, remarking, "Such, then, is the issue: if its inhabitants are addicted to independence."[3] It was the lot of the Franciscan priests to break the Indians of their addiction to what the Spanish perceived as the Satanic offshoot of liberty and independence—libertinage.

The padres regarded the Indians as children. They were *sin razón* to the Franciscans, people who had not attained the age of reason (about seven years), and thus their dependent little ones. "They are our children," Father Serra wrote to the viceroy, "for none except us has engendered them in Christ. The result is we look upon them as a father looks upon his family. We shower all our love and care upon them." The *llavera,* or woman in charge of keys for the Indian women's *monjerio,* or dormitory, remembered how Padre Zalvidea "cared much for his mission children, as he called the Indians he himself had converted to Christianity." "No matter how old they are," confirmed Padre Juan Calzada, guardian of the College of San Fernando, in 1818, "California Indians are always children."[4] Moreover, by reducing Indians to Christianity and settled agricultural ways, the padres ripped from under them their economic and cultural supports. Traditional hierarchies were apparently destroyed as the Indians, despite their previous status in their clans, all became as children—not only in the view of the European Franciscans but in their physical and emotional dependence on the mission system as well. In trying to wean Indians from the bosom of mother nature and rear them to become civilized Christians, the padres only succeeded in infantilizing them.

The padres had all the obligations and duties of fathers toward children as well as the rights and privileges. They could arbitrarily regulate the activities of their dependents according to their desires for their children's development. As Don José del Carmen Lugo remembered, "The minor faults which the Indians committed, the kind that the father of a family would punish, these padres could correct themselves." Pablo Tac, a Luiseño Indian, recalled his experience at the mission with the padres: "None of the neophytes can go to the garden or enter to gather the fruit. But if he wants some he asks the missionary who immediately will give him what he wants, for the missionary is their father." The padres were to be loving and stern, with love forthcoming when the Indians internalized, or at least complied with, the fathers' wishes. They monitored their children constantly. In the sacristy of Mission San Gabriel one can see a large, round, framed mirror with a sign saying, "Used by the padres during mass to watch the movements of the Indians." The medieval mind generally perceived those who had not reached the age of reason as innately licentious and unconstrained, even more sinful than the adult sons of Adam. Padre Tapis of Mission Santa Barbara punished Indian transgressions of European mores "with the authority which Almighty God concedes to parents for the education of their children." "They are treated with tolerance," affirmed Father President Lasuén in 1801, "or dealt with more or less firmly . . . while awaiting the time when they will gently submit themselves to rational restraint."[5]

The first step in reining in the Indians' unbridled spontaneity and wildness was their reduction and confinement to missions, where they could be parented and taught the Catholic faith. Those "who live dispersed and vagrant in that extensive land," as Viceroy Bucareli perceived them, would have to be settled and clothed on their way to civilization. Recall that in Serra's view the Indians must first be clothed "for decency and modesty," especially the frail sex. Fathers Gil y Taboada and Zalvidea of San Gabriel replied to the Interrogatorio that "although they are much addicted to nudity, we make every effort to have them go decently covered. The dress which for the present is given for that purpose is the frazada or blanket, a short tunic which we call the *Cotón*, and a narrow cloth which serves as covering and which we call the *taparabo* or breechcloth for men. For the women, a blanket, tunic, and a skirt." Now that the Indians appeared on their way toward looking like Spaniards, or at least not like naked savages, they would have to sound like Spaniards too.[6]

The missionaries presented the Castilian language to the Indians in mixed ways and with mixed results. The padres largely, though not always, made a serious effort both to learn the native languages and to teach Spanish to the Indians. Adult Indians did not take quickly to the new idiom, if at all, so special efforts were made to teach the children their prayers in Spanish. At the same time, at least at San Gabriel, the mission "has the catechism in the respective idioms of the natives or tribes of which its population is composed; but they are not approved by the Bishops, because not only is it difficult but well nigh impossible for the Bishops to find an interpreter who could revise them; for even composing them the missionaries found it a matter of much labor and patience." Padre Zalvidea, who wrote these words, was probably one of the few with any facility in an Indian language. The llavera of the mission remembered that he taught the Indians to pray "in their own language." In 1811 each mission received an *interrogatorio*, or questionnaire, from the Spanish government; the replies about language vary. At San Fernando "there are those who understand Spanish, but they speak it imperfectly." At Santa Barbara "several neophytes understand Spanish somewhat," and at San Luis Rey "many of the Christians, especially the men, speak and understand Spanish, although not perfectly." These are statements of padres with an interest in demonstrating the success of their teaching. The father president summed up the situation: "Some speak Spanish, although with much difficulty." One Indian, whose narrative of mission life survives, did learn Spanish. However, typical of such "successes," he was raised in the mission. On the whole, it would appear that the adult Indians did not learn the language with which to learn the Word.[7]

The friars at San Luis Rey asserted, with a sureness suspect when considered against other friars' statements about Indian indolence, that "the new Christians regulate themselves by the clock of the mission; and for timing their rest, meals, and work, we sound the bell." Each mission had a clock and usually two bells, the larger one to note the time for prayers and devotions and the smaller one the temporal duties. At Mission San Carlos excavators in the 1920s uncovered a sundial on which "all around the dial, carved in stone, were objects and figures indicating, apparently, the various duties to be performed by the neophytes at the hour marked by the shadow of the gnomon." There came to be, in other words, a new regulator of activities for the neophyte Indians, one they neither comprehended nor internalized.

Time for such people had been rather circular, or, more accurately, cylindrical, as we have already seen. The important events were repeatable ones. Time was not linear, with every event leading to some new place in history, nor abstractly represented, with minutes and hours dividing days, or weeks dividing months. The seasons were the important events, and they came, went, and came back again in the same fashion each time. Padre Serra had an alarm clock at Mission San Carlos, and the padres at Santa Clara received "a wooden clock with little bells for hours and quarter hours." These clocks, powerful symbols of European work discipline, did not sound meaningfully in the ears of the neophytes. "They satiate themselves today, and give little thought to tomorrow," whined Padre Lasuén. "If they are put to work, nobody goads them on. They sit down; they recline; they often go away, and come back when it suits them." The strength of the old habits and practices earned the Indians a reputation for laziness in the world of the timepiece.[8] This reputation they would carry with them through the European phase of their history. It would further justify the Spanish view that only force could hold them in the missions because they were brutal (in the Latin sense of the word, that is, irrational and insensible) and the later Yankee Protestant view that they deserved to die.

The Indians had to adapt themselves not only to an entirely new conception of time discipline. Tools have a power of their own, and they press people to transform their sense of, and relationship to, nature. Consider, for example, the making of a plow from a tree. Tree, as the Indians understood it, was a spirit-inhabited being that gave acorns or other fruits, provided fuel, and welcomed birds. The deities had arranged its nature that way and given it a spirit that encouraged it to act in the world with those purposes. To make tools from it, people had to transform their sense of tree. Its mechanical and technical potentialities had to be separated from its literally animated pith. If it became the (or any) tree, simply a thing, then its wood could be used without fear of retribution from any spirits. This is not to say that Christian Europe had cast out thoroughly all the pagan spirits from peasant consciousness by this time. Nonetheless, the European spirit world, embodied and unified in the Christian concept of the one true God, transcended earthly life and objects; it had despiritualized the world. Europeans encountered simply a tree, which they could use without fear of retribution from the spirit world for acting inappropriately toward it and its prescribed function. Making use of technology—or more accurately the Iberians' prototechnology or handicrafts, which had at least the potential to improve the material quality of life for the California Indians—required a metamorphosis of the Indian relationship to nature and all its beings.

The Indian relationship to animals is particularly important in this regard and will help clarify this idea. Animals and humans, their spirits and their flesh, together formed the Indian creature world. All beings, two-legged, four-legged, and winged, coexisted in the spirit part of the world. This notion gave the Indians of California and the rest of the Americas a certain oneness with animals. The oneness was not always harmonious because they often preyed on one another, but it was a oneness the Europeans had lost or transcended. For the latter, the laws of science came to govern all anatomies, which they increasingly perceived as simply mechanical because the influence of the spirits, especially that of the Devil, had become mere shadows in the light of the one true God. Animals, then, came to have otherness for Europeans when they rigorously separated mind and spirit from their own bodies and denied animals a spiritual nature. Christian Europe perceived all bodies as only corporeal, the human soul as ethereal, and animals as having no souls or spirits. Not only does this view divide the self into two sometimes-warring parts, but it also changes people's relations to animals. Humans and animals no longer coexisted in the European spirit world as they still did for the people of the California coast before 1769. Animals were no longer companions but others that humans could utilize as they did the trees. (Curiously enough, the founder of the padres' order, Saint Francis of Assisi, in some ways sought to restore human and animal companionship. All were God's creatures to Saint Francis, but he distinguished between "irrational animals" and "human beings made in the image of God." Only the latter had souls, though they all could be "brothers.") In Genesis 1:28 God told humans to "rule over the fish in the sea, the birds of heaven, and every living thing that moves upon the earth." For Indians, though, their essential oneness with these creatures in the spiritual world required that they maintain a certain equality with animals in the material world.

Thus, for Indians to use an ox-driven wooden plow required a tremendous transformation of their orientation toward the cosmos. The ox and the tree lost the old spirits that had animated them and formed part of their essence. The mass production of animals for food and as trade items, such as occurred with the huge mission cattle herds, further alienated people from an interconnected and companionate relationship to animals, except to keep them as dependent pets. Many of the Europeans' tools and skills could well have advantaged the Indians, but they could not find a place in the firmly held Indian worldview. The sacristy of Mission San Gabriel displays cabinets that the neophytes constructed with fantastically carved drawer handles depicting grotesque heads. Though such images were not uncommon in Iberian cathedrals, we cannot help but wonder what spirits still animated these drawers and knobs even after instruction in European religion and wood handicrafts. Such custom, habit, and story, so long in their formulations, could not have been transformed without considerable consequences, including the resistance and destruction of tribal peoples. Indeed, tools only fatally confused and disordered the California Indian world.[9]

Tools developed initially in cultures only when someone, in the words of Lewis Mumford, "performed the stunning act of dissociating" a function such as lifting from its essence as something that only arms performed. Levers could do lifting only when lifting was dissociated from what usually did it, thus allowing something else to fulfill that particular function. The Indian view of nature's beings as animated stood between them and the use of the Europeans' tools. Those without technics could not control and manipulate the environment because it was not separated from humankind but animated with genuinely kindred spirits. Thus the environment, and each of its constituents, was endowed with the same caprices and unruly fears and urges that humans had. Technology, which insists upon arrangement, regularity, and, most important, a sense that humans can work their own productive will on, rather than with, nature, cannot manage a disorderly and inconsistent world. It requires that the body be accessible to manipulation by authority for specified operations and not be susceptible to spirits or desires. In a way, then, Father Peyri was correct when he wrote that "apathy reigns over the Indians." At least I think we can understand why he believed this.[10]

The padres brought to the Indians an institution ideally suited to enable them to make the leap to a mechanical mind-set. The mission, with its thoroughgoing efforts to restrain the bodily appetites, could have provided the discipline necessary for the separation of the world into physical and animated spheres if the Indians were willing to accept such a division. Loathing and then denying the body reinforced its split from the mind, making it easier to allow machines, in Mumford's words, "to counterfeit this or that action of the body." The teachings of the church about the sinful nature of the flesh, so susceptible to devilish influence, meshed nicely with the demands of technical transformation in which objects must be dissociated from their spirits, desires, whims, and animation. Christianity helped in this regard when it ejected the spirits that animated all things and replaced them with a single omnipotent Spirit. Moreover, though the ways of this new God often proved inscrutable, at least He had a great plan, which His law regulated, and He had created an orderly world. Bringing the Indians the Word, the padres believed, would free them from their animist view of the world and help them understand its regular and consistent essence. Padre Lasuén showed dim awareness of this situation: "Here then we have the greatest problem of the missionary: how to transform a savage race such as these into a society that is human, Christian, civil, and industrious. This can be accomplished only by 'denaturalizing' them. It is easy to see what an arduous task this is, for it requires them to act against nature." But nature and its spirits did prove stronger than the Europeans' earnest efforts—the Indians usually took to neither God nor industry.[11]

Herein ultimately lies the meaning of *de razón* as well. To become like the Europeans, the Indians would have to achieve the same split of body and mind that their civilizers accepted. The mind must control the body both for religion and for technology. Reason must control appetite and nature. Padre Venegas stated the problem with the Indians from the *de razón* point of view thoroughly if not sympathetically: "Their characteristics are stupidity and insensibility; want of knowledge and reflection; inconstancy, impetuosity and blindness of appetite; an excessive sloth and abhorrence of fatigue; an incessant love of pleasure, and amusement of every kind, however trifling or brutal; in fine, a most wretched want of everything which constitutes the real man, and renders him rational, inventive, tractable, and useful to himself and society." Yes, they were as children to the Europeans—not yet grown to the age of reason wherein the mind would successfully (usually) battle the body for control and subjugate its desires to the need both for internally disciplined productive activity and for the appropriately humble relationship to God so that His plan would be revealed.[12]

The resistance or indifference of the Indians to this particular form of reason and European-style maturation was attributed either to their brutish nature or to the workings of the Devil, or to both. This explanation for their apparent unwillingness to adopt the conquerors' ways produced and justified coercion of the Indians. Padre Lasuén, upset at a failure to increase troops at the presidios, wrote in 1797 that if the authorities

withdraw or altogether remove soldiers from the limited garrisons . . . they may lose everything. The majority of our neophytes have not yet acquired much love for our way of life; and they see and meet their pagan relatives in the forest, fat and robust and enjoying complete liberty.

They will go with them, then, when they no longer have any fear and respect for the force, such as it is, which restrains them.

Even that most notable of soldier-loathers, Padre Serra, noted "that the presidio needs more people to contain the uneasy and pernicious disposition of these natural Christians and heathens."[13] The first restraint, and likely the most important one the fathers imposed on their Indio children, was the severe limitation of their sexuality.

In California the priests confronted their antithesis. The fathers were usually sexually restrained, punctual, monotheistic, sedentary, and bent on accumulating wealth for the missions. In their minds, of course, what they did was virtuous, and what the Indians did, largely the opposite, was sinful. The Indians were everything the Europeans (with the exception of many soldiers) had been trying to transcend or repress. By terrorizing and generally restricting women who realized Satan's will through their "insatiable lust," the Europeans conquered "carnal lust." Sexuality was a fearful, if not devilish, issue for these fathers. They confronted primitive and apparently uncontrolled and infantile beings who represented that over which their civilization thought it had triumphed. The California padres, like virtually all European fathers, knew what to do with people whose alleged sexuality threatened their sense of restraint and civilization. They controlled them with seeming kindness, infantilized them, and then coerced them to discipline their sexual relations. The priests unilaterally transferred their role of loving, kind, protective European father, and ruthless castigator of their errant, incontinent, and lesser charges, to the California Indians. Indeed, not only would the subjugation of the Indians' physical intimacy elevate Indians to their standards and inculcate a body-mind duality, but also the padres could overcome any of their own ambivalence about their own victory over desire through the rigorous control of someone else—their Indian children.

The padres enforced sexual restraint with lock and key. Few things were locked up in Spanish California, but an exception was the securing of unmarried Indian women, and sometimes men, in the missions. The model for this practice was the locking up of daughters by their fathers. Class tensions do not seem to have produced sufficient anxiety among property holders that they felt the need to make fast their private property, though the missions secured supplies from the neophytes. There seem to have been enough material goods on the bounteous California coast to supply all and limit the fear of losing goods. Instead, the padres feared too much sex, or at least sex Christian marriage had not confined. The padres divided up traditional Indian families to take control of them. They knew from experience that children raised in the mission were much more likely to become Hispanicized than their parents, who were largely set in their libertine ways. Wives and husbands lived in a ranchería very near the mission with their little children. The llavera at Mission San Gabriel, Eulalia Pérez, remembered how "the girls [*mujercitas*] were brought to the monjerio when they were seven to nine years of age, and were tended there until they left to marry." Indian girls were socialized to European ways in "what was commonly called the monjerio," as another woman recalled from the era, "under the care of an older Indian woman who was like the matron. She watched them carefully . . . and never lost sight of them." A very few settler women, well-trained Indian women, or, later on, sometimes soldiers' wives served as *la madre abadesa* (abbess). She had the job of keeping the young Indias "secure from any insult." They could not come out until the morning; the llavera made sure that the door was locked and then gave the key to the padre.[14]

Properly confined, restrained, disciplined, and denaturalized—in short, reduced—the Indians could now engage in actual production in the missions. Unlike in the Rio Grande Valley, where the natives had evolved a sophisticated agricultural system in which surpluses were produced and stored and which the intruders could appropriate, in California the initial Spanish colonizers had to depend on their supply system from San Blas, on the coast of central Mexico, for sustenance until the missions could start producing. Anza's first expedition to San Gabriel (1774) found the priests and guards existing on only three corn tortillas and some herbs a day. On that journey Padre Francisco Garcés, formerly of Mission San Javier del Bac in Tucson, noted in his diary, "We found the mission in extreme poverty, as is true of all the rest. . . . We were sorry on both sides, the fathers at having so little to give, either of animals or provisions, and we at having brought nothing to relieve them of their want." By the time of Anza's second expedition (1776), Padre Font reported milk, cheese, and butter from "fat cows," a small flock of sheep, hogs, and some chickens at San Gabriel. "I do not remember having eaten fatter or finer mutton," he wrote. Nature had taken its course with the few livestock that boats had carried from the lower to the upper California missions. Fortunately, the missions soon started producing a bounty from the hospitable California soil. Once the land could be planted in corn, beans, and wheat, not only could the missionaries supply themselves and the neophytes with an abundance of food, but so too could the presidios partake of the plenty.

Now, moreover, food, which was utterly crucial to the conversion effort, could be offered to the heathens consistently. The Indians would not wander off when the handouts were over, and the padres would not have to fear starving the rest of the mission inhabitants. The generosity of California's coastal soil and temperate climate compensated for the lack of willing and able neophyte producers, who were now hesitatingly and falteringly engaging in sedentary agriculture on land over which the Indians had roamed and gathered their sustenance only a few years previously.[15]

Initially, the soldiers assigned to the missions were to provide both the labor necessary to get the enterprises under way and a model of de razón work habits. Hispanicized Indians from Baja California assisted them in this task and functioned, in Bancroft's words, "as servants of all work in the new missions." One of the military guards also held the position of *mayordomo* (Serra's 1773 trip to Mexico established the right of missions to employ such a soldier) and directed the labors of the neophytes. Under the mayordomo were the *caporales*, who were "selected from the more intelligent Indians who understood a goodly part of the Spanish language." These caporales interpreted and transmitted orders and, once they approached a state of *razón*, "assisted . . . the mayordomo in the policing and the work generally." Besides sowing, tending gardens and fruit orchards, and raising livestock, the Indians had to begin construction of the edifices that would house and train them until they could be settled into pueblos of their own. The first buildings were no more than lean-tos, at least at San Gabriel and Santa Barbara. Then in the 1780s the Indians were directed in the raising of structures with walls made of willow poles filled in with mud and tule-thatched roofs. Sharpened poles formed a stockade surrounding the structures. In 1792 the government in Mexico sent twenty artisans to further train Indians (even those de razón) in masonry, carpentry, tailoring, and leatherworking. Their instruction had some effect on the productive abilities of the missions, though most of the skilled mechanics returned to Mexico in 1800. By 1795 the various artisans and workers of Mission San Gabriel had raised the edifice to half its intended height with stone and mortar, and by 1801 it had a vaulted, albeit cracked, roof. (An earthquake in December 1812, however, knocked all this down.) Learning European skills was a long process for the Indians, one that was never completed.[16]

It is difficult to discern precisely how much work the mayordomos and priests got out of the neophytes. In 1799 investigators for Governor Borica reported that the Indians worked from six to nine hours a day, depending on the season, and more at harvesttime. The padres maintained that the neophytes worked only four to six hours a day, with only half of them working at any given time. The Indians soon learned passive resistance to this rudimentary industrial discipline. Father Lasuén noted that "the healthy are clever at feigning sickness, and they know that they are generally believed, and . . . even when there is only a doubt, the missionary will always give them dispensation from work." Generally, the neophytes' workday began about two hours after sunrise, following breakfast and the assignment of tasks. Between eleven o'clock and noon they ate, and then they rested until two o'clock. At five o'clock came worship and the end of work. The Indians worked six to eight hours a day, thirty to forty hours a week, at an easy pace that did not require undue strain. The men herded the "half-wild stock," plowed, tended, and harvested crops, and labored in the mission workshops. "The women," la Pérouse observed, "have no other employment than their household affairs, the care of their children, and the roasting and grinding of corn." Though most of these tasks were "both tedious and laborious," in the adventurous Frenchman's words, it seems clear that the quantity of work was not injurious to the Indians.[17]

But the missions produced—ah, but they produced! Simultaneously they introduced the novice Christians to European methods of production and relationship to nature, on the one hand, and assumed responsibility for provisioning the far northern frontier of New Spain, on the other. Once in motion, the missions relieved San Blas from responsibility for supplying the presidios with food. Mission San Gabriel, the "Queen of the Missions," emerged as the largest producer in California under the direction of the tormented Padre Zalvidea. The mission's obraje, or workshop, had looms, forges, and facilities for carpentry and the production of bricks, wheels, carts, plows, yokes, tiles, soap, candles, earthenware, adobes, shoes, and belts. By 1800 the obrajes wove California wool into clothing for the neophytes, and there was enough soap to keep everyone clean, if they chose to use it. Some leather goods still had to be imported from Mexico, however. The mission ranchos raised cattle, pigs, chickens, geese, and sheep. Fruit trees, grapevines (which yielded a claret and a brandy famous in all of Hispanic America), wheat, corn, potatoes, beans, garbanzos, lentils, squash, watermelon, and cantaloup all grew in abundance. The magnitude and diversity of production, based in agriculture but expanding into light artisanal manufacturing, might lead one to believe that the missions were indeed securing California by successfully occupying and inhabiting the remote territory.[18]

The statistics are striking. According to Bancroft, between 1783 and 1790 the number of mission horses, mules, and cattle increased from 4,900 to 22,000, while sheep, goats, and swine increased from 7,000 to 26,000. Between 1790 and 1800 these numbers trebled. In 1783 the missions produced 22,500 bushels of grain, in 1790, 37,500, and in 1800, 75,000. By 1810, a year of decline, the missions counted 116,306 head of cattle, 16,782 horses, and 1,561 mules. By 1821 there were 149,730 head of cattle, 19,830 horses, and 2,011 mules. In 1819 Mission San Fernando, in the shadow of Mission San Gabriel, had 12,800 cattle. At the time of the disestablishment of the missions in 1834, the Queen of the Missions had 163,578 vines, 2,333 fruit trees, 12,980 head of cattle, plus 4,443 "cattle loaned to various individuals," 2,938 horses, and 6,548 sheep.[19]

The harvest of cattle and other agricultural products outpaced that of Christians. For example, in 1785 there were only one and a third head of cattle to each neophyte. Six years later the ratio increased to three to one, and by 1800 to four to one. By 1810 there were 6.2 head of cattle to each mission Indian, and by 1820, 7.3, a monumental feat of both nature and the padres. The soil and climate of California produced more than the various inhabitants could consume.[20]

Although most contemporaries of the missions seemed to believe that the Indians were well fed, there is conflicting evidence about the quality and quantity of nutrition the Indians realized from mission largess. Mission San Gabriel, reported the friars at the turn of the century, "gives them sufficient time so that they have three meals of corn, wheat, beans, and meat a day. Likewise, in their respective seasons is given them an abundance of cheese, milk, melons, peaches, and all other kinds of Spanish fruits." The llavera of the mission confirmed the padres' optimistic estimation of their charges' diets. Breakfast was usually pozole (boiled barley and beans) and meat; lunch consisted of pozole with meat and vegetables, and atole, and meat. On holidays they got chocolate. The rancheros, José del Carmen Lugo, José María Amador, and Carlos Híjar, agreed that the Indians were well fed. "Everything was given to them in abundance, and they always went away satisfied but lazy, for they did not like to go to work," declared the latter. "This sort of food," la Pérouse added, "of which the Indians are extremely fond . . . , they eat without either butter or salt, and it would certainly to us be a most insipid mess." The neophytes supplemented this European-style food with their traditional nuts and berries, which the fathers reluctantly allowed them to gather from the wild.

By contrast, Sherburne Cook refers to the Indians' diet as "suboptimal, . . . a level of nutrition probably insufficient for ordinary maintenance and certainly below the optimum necessary to provide a high resistance to infection." He estimates a daily intake of only two thousand to twenty-one hundred calories. (In comparison, slaves in the American South consumed about a thousand more calories a day, but this was in 1859, the height of slavery. Moreover, slaves were generally larger and worked harder than the neophytes.) Cook asserts that the missionized Indians foraged because "conversion frequently outran cultivation." In other words, the padres had to let the Indians have their native foods or they would be hungry and run away. E. B. Webb agrees that injections of such food into the diet kept them from fleeing but emphasizes that it was an "occasional vacation." Cook's otherwise brilliant book is here problematic, in my opinion. As we have seen, the quantity of food produced changed over the brief history of the missions. In this matter Cook is ahistorical. For example, his statistics for beef consumption derive from 1796. Only ten years later cattle production increased 50 percent and 15 years later 100 percent. Furthermore, different missions produced different quantities of food, depending on the environment and the fortitude of the padres. Cook does not address caloric consumption in the mature missions, and it actually appears to have differed only insignificantly from that of comparable groups. The point, though, is that the California environment and the diligence of the padres enabled the stabilized missions to adequately feed their neophytes.[21]

The missions produced plenty of surplus food, which needed some outlet if production were to continue. Some went to the presidios as early as the late 1770s, and some went to trade. The missions were surely the most successful producers in Alta California by 1800. The fledgling ranchos, the tiny pueblos such as Los Angeles, and the presidial fields did not produce nearly as much. For example, in 1782 Los Angeles could contribute only $15 to support Spain's war with England, whereas Mission San Gabriel gave $134. The year 1810, however, marks an important watershed in mission-presidial economic relations. In September of that year Padre Hidalgo's famous "Grito de Dolores," the call to take up arms for the independence of Mexico, caused such chaos that few or no supplies could make their way north to the far frontier. After that time the presidios thoroughly depended on the missions for food, though it is important to remember that the missions depended on the presidios for a market through which to earn much-needed exchange credits.

The vast majority of Indians working at the presidios were actually hired from the missions. They received a small wage, usually about two reales a day, credited to the mission account, and food and clothing, in exchange for all types of labor including field work, personal service, adobe making, general repair and maintenance and other construction work, and blacksmithing. Skilled neophytes earned a little more, and sometimes pay was only one and a half reales a day. The first decade of the nineteenth century appears to have been the heyday of the mission as labor contractor for the presidios. There is some evidence of decline in the practice after 1810 in the mission account books, but it may only reflect the increasing inability of the presidios to pay. In 1815 Padre Zalvidea wrote to Comandante de la Guerra, "The governor's letter was received offering [illegible] and the fifty Indians that the Sergeant of the Los Angeles garrison requested are on their way." Indian labor was still crucial to the military after 1810 even if it could not pay for it on a regular basis. The padres initiated a practice of great significance for the history of California after the mission period when they hired out their surplus mission Indians to the gente de razón. By the turn of the century there were few de razón families without an Indian servant. The labor of Indians on the ranchos left an indelible stamp on the history of production in California, and the padres facilitated this organization of work. Suffice it to say that hiring out of Indians provided an important source of income for the missions close to a pueblo or presidio.[22]

The padres considered such income central to the continuation of their mission. The number of souls saved still measured the success of their enterprise, but the fathers nevertheless sought to save some money too. The crown's laxity in delivering its annual allotments to both the missions and the presidios encouraged them to test out more reliable sources of support. Of course, the events following 1810 intensified this desire for financial independence from the crown—indeed, made it into a requirement. The American and British trading ships that began to appear off the coast, especially after 1796, suited the padres' needs for hard cash and provided an outlet for their surplus production. As early as 1794 Governor Borica was sufficiently concerned about smuggling to wrest promises from the padres that they would not engage in such trade. It became customary for American vessels, especially those involved in the fur trade, to materialize in several ports on their way down the coast to replenish their supplies and see if anyone had anything to sell. William Shaler, a genuine Connecticut Yankee, stealthily appeared in the courts of several missionaries. His journal contains this advice and information:

> For several years past, the American trading ships have frequented this coast in search of furs, for which they have left in the country about 25,000 dollars annual, in specie and merchandise. The government has used all their endeavors to prevent this intercourse, but without effect, and the consequence has been a great increase of wealth and industry among the inhabitants. The missionaries are the principal monopolizers of the fur trade,

but this intercourse has enabled the inhabitants to take part in it. At present, a person acquainted with the coast may always procure abundant supplies of provisions.

Earnest producers of valuable surpluses in service of the faith, the padres were no match for this son of Calvin when it came to marketing and commerce. Robert Archibald notes that "some twenty or at least one-half of the pious padres were in his debt. Of these, only four had honored their notes."[23]

The missions provided for more than the local economy. The padres brought California into the world market through their trade with New England. Despite their dependence on the paternalism of the Spanish crown for their very existence, the friars itched for freer trade relations with those outside the realm, even though the restrictive trade requirements of Spanish mercantilism were integral aspects of this system that had fostered missionization in the first place. This desire for freedom from such mercantile and colonial fetters is familiar from the American and Latin American revolutions. The friars had a much more amenable trade situation with the end of Spanish mercantilism in 1821; ironically, however, they had remained largely loyal to Spain during Mexico's struggle for independence and had refused to take an oath of obedience to the constitution of 1824. But financially strapped Mexico did impose customs duties, which in turn encouraged the friars to smuggle even by means of ships engaged in legitimate trade. Juan Bandini, a Spaniard who journeyed to Peru, where he started his family before establishing himself as a ranchero in southern California, describes how trade generally operated in the 1820s:

> The commerce of the ships which resort to this coast is entirely confined to the missions; that with private individuals being of little importance. As soon as a vessel arrives at a port the captain puts himself in communication with the minister of the neighboring mission; the latter asks for a list of the articles for sale, selects those that are needed, such as iron, carpenters tools, dyes, hand mills to grind wheat . . . , cotton clothes, thread as well as gaudy colored bandanas of the cheapest quality, also such articles as may be necessary for the use of churches, stills to make brandy and copper boilers to render the tallow and make soap, kitchen utensils and tableware.

The missionaries brought Christianity to the Indians and the world market to California, especially after 1822. José del Carmen Lugo remembered how "when I was twelve or fourteen years old I used to see carretas loaded with hides and tallow headed for the ships at San Pedro." It was mainly these hides and tallow that the padres exchanged for manufactured goods, at the rate of two dollars (about fourteen reales) for each arroba (twenty-five pounds) of tallow and each cowhide. This trade with the Yankees was seductive indeed. "The missions produced grain in great quantities," Lugo noted, "but they had to feed their numerous neophytes. Later the missions increased production near the ports, because they were in a position to sell their surpluses such as hides and tallow." It is probably impossible to know what proportion of this trade was aboveboard, though Bandini asserted that "the duties collected [at the port] . . . are never sufficient . . . , and as they [the mission] control all branches of business and are exempt from all taxes it is not to be wondered but that the public funds are short." [24]

Some of the produce of the lands held in trust for the Indians was now transformed into commodities. Whereas initially production was only for subsistence, now some was for gain. California previously had a barter economy, but because of the increasing volume of trade with foreigners, money was now becoming the medium of exchange. The missions were clearly the economic mainstay of Alta California. They supplied the military and the townspeople, the trade of their surpluses brought in manufactured goods, and it was they who were the earnest and vital producers. The priests kept precise records in their leather-bound account books. They paid close attention to their transactions with the presidios. Usually the balance in their books favored the missions over the presidios, and they received a signed warrant for payment from the *habilitado general*, or paymaster, in Mexico City. When payment was not forthcoming, the balance was carried over to the next year. When they could not collect the debts of persons with whom they had traded, they would often send a collector and pay him a commission. The missions functioned as banks, allowing one to discharge his debt to another by having the mission pay out and charging it to his mission account. The mission paid either from its small cash reserves or in kind. They protected their monopolies. For example, Lugo asserted that the fathers, out of egoism, would not let the ranchos have orange and lemon seeds.[25] Providing an outlet for the products of Indian labor, their increasing trade also strengthened the Indian labor system at the missions, which brought to California economic independence and security from foreign intrusion. Lurking in the background, however, were the decline of the neophyte population and the continuous unfolding of liberalism, which would bring freedom, if not equality, to the mission Indians.

Narratives such as the following often give the impression that events happened quickly: the Indians were baptized, and the soldiers outraged them; they had to change their relationship to animals, but the old spirits still had some effect; the padres smuggled, and the capitalist world market embraced the missions. Actually, much time passed between events. It is vital to remember that on most days not much happened. Although the padres did indeed draw California into the capitalist market, and that very market encouraged production for gain beyond the Indians' subsistence, in no way can we say that the prevailing social relations were correspondingly transformed. What prevailed on a daily basis can tell us much more about the nature of human interaction at the missions than can inclusion in the world marketplace. Yes, the involvement in the world capitalist system had important effects on California society, and this incorporation of mission production even strengthened their system. However, the relationship between the producers, the neophytes, and those who controlled production, the Catholic fathers, remained fundamentally constant. This relationship, moreover, made an indelible mark on the future of California.

Not surprisingly, the padres' actions to discipline the Indians to enhance production and instill faith provoked resentment and rebelliousness. Sherburne Cook calculates that 10 percent of the neophytes ran away at one point or another and that 40 percent of the runaways made good on their efforts. Fleeing was only one sign that many Indians did not take to their new environment. A social scientist may incline toward abstractions and generalizations about why an Indian would take flight, but it is important to remember that Indians reacted in concrete ways to concrete situations; they did not philosophize about, and then respond to, their situation. A number of *huidos* [escapees] from Mission San Antonio de Padua, south of Monterey, were questioned after their capture about why they absconded. The most typical response was that they "had been flogged for leaving [including simply wandering off] without permission." Many left when a loved one died. The comment "Twice, when he went out to hunt food or to fish, Father Danti had him whipped" exemplifies nicely the dynamics of punishment and flight. This neophyte most likely just wanted something of his customary food to eat. He could understand no reason why he should not hunt or fish. To the padre, his action was treason and apostasy. Freely accepting baptism and subjecting himself to the king of Spain, the former heathen had accepted certain obligations, which he was now fleeing. Punishment seemed entirely appropriate to the padre and confounding or despotic to the Indian. Thus, the chosen forms of chastisement could never have their intended effect of deracinating the natives, who perceived them as arbitrary. The Indian decided to decamp in response to his baffling situation. Returned to the fold, he was, of course, whipped.[26]

On occasion neophytes attacked the fathers. The initial revolts at San Diego and Toypurina's efforts at San Gabriel attempted to expel an unwanted interloper and restore the old ways. Later struggles revolved around the already-established social relations between the feudal and Catholic fathers and their neophyte Christian charges. Events at San Gabriel in late 1810 illustrate a transitional form of revolt containing aspects of both sorts of insurrection. As many as eight hundred men, mostly gentiles, poised themselves to strike at the mission in November. Had they attacked, they easily would have wiped out Mission San Gabriel. Yet the new ways had by this time irrevocably altered Indian life. The raid intended not only to end the mission but also to redress grievances of the Franciscan entrada. It seems that both neophytes and gentile Indians cooperated in the pilfering of the mission storehouses. Some had been caught and imprisoned for what the Indians likely considered just expropriation of goods. Besides, they were probably hungry, given the interlopers' pressures on their food supply. Thus agitated, instead of eliminating the productive mission they made off with three thousand sheep (which were recaptured). Two contradictory impulses motivated this action: to eradicate the Spanish priests, and to appropriate the mission as a source of food. This sort of rebelliousness, existing within the mission structure, now prevailed. Acts of revenge took place within the mind-set of an institutionalized mission. Nazario, for example, Padre Panto's cook, used *cuchasquelaai*, an herb, to poison the "rigorous disciplinarian" of Mission San Diego, who died six months later in 1812. He was not the first priest to be so afflicted either. In 1801 at Mission San Miguel, north of San Juan Capistrano, Padre Francisco Pujol died of a violent illness. His two companions, padres Carnicier and Martínez, survived their seizures, for which several Migueleños claimed credit.[27]

One striking episode provides a window (somewhat opaque, given the lack of records and the passage of time) into the dynamics of the padres' discipline and punishment of Indians. In 1812 several of the neophytes plotted revenge on Father Andrés Quintana (of the cat-o'-nine-tails), who had journeyed from his home in Álava, Spain, to California, where in 1805 he assumed his duties at Mission Santa Cruz. It is unclear whether the Indians responded to fears of a new iron strap to punish fornication and theft, which the padre had ordered, or were getting even for his brutal whipping of the neophyte Donato. What is clear, though, is the dynamic of the punishment spectacle. The ritual, intended as a lesson for the group, this time catalyzed the neophytes' solidarity, and the violence this time boomeranged. Between nine and sixteen Indians conspired to smother the padre so that the death would look natural. They began their revenge by first crushing one of his testicles after ambushing him on his way to administer the last rites to the Indian gardener, who was feigning death. They shut him in his rooms, squeezed out his breath, and unlocked the monjerio. Then "the young people of both sexes gathered and had their fun," as one Indian recalled. The essential castration of the padre was the first step toward the superabundant restoration of the Indians' sexual mores. From the Indian point of view the padre received a punishment befitting the crime he committed against them.

The denouement of the story is also interesting. One of the Indians, Lino, took a break from his diversion with one of the women to make sure the father was actually dead. Lino found him recovering and then with some of the others "crushed the Padre's other testicle," finally killing him. The death of the priest raised suspicions. In the investigation, according to some accounts, the padre's stomach was cut open to see if he had been poisoned, but "because of modesty they did not discover" his altered condition. A few years later several Indian women, squabbling, were overheard accusing one another's husband of the deed. The assassins were arrested and tried in 1816. Though the authorities in Mexico took Quintana's cruelty into account (testimony was given that he had beaten two neophytes almost to death), five of the culprits received two hundred lashes and sentences of two to ten years at hard labor at the Santa Barbara or San Diego presidio. Lino died in 1817, and only one of the convicts is said to have lived through his punishment.[28]

Such patricide occurred infrequently, yet Quintana's case best illuminates the underlying tensions of the Indian-padre relationship. (The Indian informant about these events at Santa Cruz reported, however, that the neophytes stoned Quintana's successor, Padre Alba.)[29] Does the uniqueness of the Indian actions toward the unfortunate, but unconsciously trouble-seeking, cleric relegate the instance to footnotes or anecdotes about Old California? No; such episodes isolate, clarify, and condense the fermenting tensions that everyday activities and Indian apathy concealed. These stresses characterize most societies and historical epochs and seem to move history. Remaining generally submerged, they flare up at rather random moments in events worthy of note.

What the Indians at Santa Cruz did after emasculating the father was included in an event in 1824, this time to the south, at Mission Santa Barbara. In February of that year Chumash neophytes directed a revolt against the soldiers of missions Santa Inez, La Purísima, and Santa Barbara. The trouble started at Santa Inez when Corporal Cota ordered a neophyte flogged. The ritual of chastisement reversed itself again when the oneness of the Indians, rather than the reassertion of the Europeans' power, emerged from the violent ceremony. The transgressor's companions attacked the soldiers and padres, and while the soldiers successfully defended themselves and the ministers, the neophytes burned mission buildings. The revolt quickly spread to La Purísima and Santa Barbara but remained confined to actions against the soldiers, who retaliated viciously, at least at Santa Barbara. The soldiers sacked the Indians' houses and killed indiscriminately. The various tensions of the soldiers of Mexican California that had been simmering since 1810, especially the loss of a steady payroll and supply system, now erupted. There seems to be little doubt that the revolt happened in a context of soldiers' increasing demands for Indian-produced necessities and their escalating abuse of Indians. Padre Antonio Ripoll of Santa Barbara cried over the news of the rebellion of his children. Though the target of the Chumash revolt differed from that of the Santa Cruz episode, both insurrections disclosed tensions that existed within the social relations of mission society. At least one incident of the Chumash revolt was similar to events at Santa Cruz. During the revolt, Father Ripoll reported, the neophyte Andrés "separated the exchanged wives and returned them to their proper husbands." Five witnesses testified after the revolt that carnality reigned. The official report states, "When the Christians arrived in the valley they exchanged their women for those of the gentiles without distinction as to married and unmarried women, for they were all mixed up among the Indians." As difficult as it may be to discern precisely what happened, clearly two different understandings of conjugal relations existed at Mission Santa Barbara.[30]

In other words, at both Mission Santa Cruz and Mission Santa Barbara the neophyte Indians associated insurrection against the Europeans with rebellion against the sexual discipline the missions had instituted. Revolt encompassed restoration of the sexual license their culture validated. The imposition of European productive, spiritual, and sexual ways, together with the introduction of European diseases, produced various Indian responses. They responded with apathy toward the clock and labor, apostatized and fled the Word of God, and occasionally revolted against punishment for such flights and sexual transgressions. They emerged thoroughly diseased from this harsh and bewildering journey. These Indian adaptations, defiances, and ruinations distill for us the significant social tensions of California mission culture and society. Not only were the neophytes diseased and, in the eyes of the padres, incapable of discipline and indolent, but they were now genuinely threatening too. It is only in hindsight that we know that these instances of revolt did not portend general insurrection. Californians orally relating their memoirs to one of Bancroft's assistants in the 1870s attributed the Chumash revolt to a carefully planned conspiracy. The continuation of the mission effort proved more and more doubtful, regardless of the increasing population pressures on the land.[31]

The end of the missions was contained in their beginning, when the soldiers brought diseases and the priests sought to upset the Indians' delicate balance with nature and replace it with their particular notions of subduing and replenishing the earth. Formally, however, the mission period came to a close during the years of the secularization, 1833 to the early 1840s. The social relations that mission California produced in those few years derived from many factors—Iberian political and religious imperialism, patriarchal relations between Spanish fathers and Indian children, the conflict over the relationship of humans to labor and nature, and disease. Clearly, production in California entailed much more than providing (converted) producers with tools to work the landscape and then markets for the products of their labor. We see here how a culture emerges as well. The sometimes explosive, sometimes degenerating interplay of conquering proselytizers and native heathens, the efforts of each to adapt to or force the other's acquiescence, and the unfolding of history produced this curious syncretic culture of Alta California. The Spaniards had the best of intentions; they meant to bring reason and salvation to the Indians. Instead, they shredded their native culture and infested them with fleas and microbes. Then the padres buried the Indians.

NOTES

1. Mircea Eliade, *Cosmos and History: The Myth of the Eternal Return* (New York, 1959), 88–89; Calvin Martin, "Time and the American Indian," and Richard Drinnon, "The Metaphysics of Dancing Tribes," both in *The American Indian and the Problem of History*, ed. Calvin Martin (New York, 1987), 192–220 and 109–11.

2. Sherburne F. Cook, *The Conflict Between the California Indian and White Civilization* (Berkeley and Los Angeles, 1976), 99; Marvin Harris, *Cows, Pigs, Wars, and Witches: The Riddles of Culture* (New York, 1975), 126–30; A. L. Kroeber, *Handbook of the California Indians* (Washington, D.C., 1925), 652; Marshall Sahlins, "The Original Affluent Society," in *Stone Age Economics* (Chicago, 1974), 1–32.

3. Statement "de un particular," Prov. Int. Tom. 23, Wright Collection, Archivo General de México (henceforth AGM).

4. Fray Junipero Serra to Carlos Francisco de Croix, August 22, 1778, in *Writings of Junipero Serra*, ed. Antoine Tibesar (Washington, D.C., 1966), 3:252–53; Eulalia Pérez, "Una Vieja y Sus Recuerdos" (1877), Bancroft Library, 6; Padre

Calzada is quoted in C. Alan Hutchinson, "The Mexican Government and the Mission Indians of Upper California, 1821–1835," *The Americas* 21 (April 1965), 340–41.

5. José del Carmen Lugo, "Life of a Rancher," *Historical Society of Southern California Quarterly* 32 (September 1950), 227; Pablo Tac, "Conversion of the San Luiseños of Alta California," ed. Ninna Hewes and Gordon Hewes, *The Americas* 9 (July 1952); Fermín Lasuén, *Writings of Fermín Lasuén*, ed. and trans. Finbar Kenneally (Washington, D.C., 1965), 2:202; E. B. Webb, *Indian Life at the Old Missions* (Los Angeles, 1952), 149.

6. Juan Bojores, "Recuerdo sobre la Historia de California" (1877), Bancroft Library, 9; Bucareli to Arriaga, Mexico City, January 27, 1773, in *Anza's California Expeditions*, ed. and trans. Herbert Eugene Bolton (Berkeley, 1930), 5:53; Serra to Bucareli, August 17, 1775, in Serra, *Writings*, 2:306; the San Gabriel padres are quoted in Webb, *Indian Life*, 43.

7. Gil y Taboada and Zalvidea are quoted in Webb, *Indian Life*, 47; Pérez, "Una Vieja," 20; the responses to the "Contestación" are in Cook, *Conflict*, 143–44; Lorenzo Asisara's narrative is in José María Amador, "Memorias sobre la Historia de California" (1877), transcript by Thomas Savage, Bancroft Library.

8. Webb, *Indian Life*, 32–38 (the padres from San Luis Rey are quoted on page 36); Lasuén, *Writings*, 2:202, 207.

9. This discussion derives from John Berger, "Why Look at Animals," in his *About Looking* (New York, 1980), 1–13; Barry H. Lopez, *Of Wolves and Men* (New York, 1978), 98–113; Stanley Diamond, *In Search of the Primitive: A Critique of Civilization* (New Brunswick, 1981), 8–9; Carolyn Merchant, *The Death of Nature: Women: Ecology, and the Scientific Revolution* (San Francisco, 1982), 99–215; *The Little Flowers of St. Francis*, ed. and trans. Raphael Brown (Garden City, N.J., 1958), 88–91, 321–22.

10. Lewis Mumford, *Technics and Civilization* (New York, 1934), 31–33, 107–12; Michel Foucault, *Discipline and Punish: The Birth of the Prison* (New York, 1979), 135–56; Fray Antonio Peyri to Juan Bandini, December 25, 1828, Stearns Papers, Huntington Library.

11. Mumford, *Technics and Civilization*, 33–36; Lasuén, *Writings*, 2:202.

12. Padre Venegas is quoted in Alexander Forbes, *California: A History of Upper and Lower* (London, 1839), 184.

13. Lasuén to Fray Antonio Nogueyra, January 21, 1797, in Lasuén, *Writings*, 2:6; Serra to Lasuén, January 12, 1780, in Serra, *Writings*, 3:418.

14. Pérez, "Una Vieja," 16; Apolinaria Lorenzana, "Memorias de La Beata" (1878), Bancroft Library, 7–8; "Font's Complete Diary of the Second Anza Expedition," in Bolton, *Anza's California Expeditions*, 4:181–82; José del Carmen Lugo, "Vida de un Ranchero" (1877), Bancroft Library, 100; Carlos N. Híjar, "California in 1834: Recollections" (1877), Bancroft Library, 33; Amador, "Memorias," 90; Hubert H. Bancroft, *California Pastoral, 1769–1848* (San Francisco, 1888), 232; Webb, *Indian Life*, 27–28; Nellie Van de Grift Sanchez, *The Spanish Period* (Chicago, 1926), 306; Antonia Castañeda, "Comparative Frontiers: The Migration of Women to Alta California and New Zealand," in *Western Women: Their Land, Their Lives*, ed. Lillian Schlissel, Vicki Ruiz, and Janice J. Monk (Albuquerque, 1988), 290.

15. "Diary of Juan Bautista de Anza," in Bolton, *Anza's California Expeditions*, 2:205; "Garcés' Diary from Tubac to San Gabriel," in Bolton, *Anza's California Expeditions*, 2:347; "Font's Complete Diary," in Bolton, *Anza's California Expeditions*, 4:178; Robert Archibald, *The Economic Aspects of the California*

Missions (Washington, D.C., 1978), 11; Webb, *Indian Life*, 40–41, 168–71; Cook, *Conflict*, 142.

16. Hubert Howe Bancroft, *History of California* (1884: San Francisco, 1963), 1:613–16; Lugo, "Life of a Rancher," 225–26; Archibald, *Economic Aspects*, 145; Webb, *Indian Life*, 100, 130–31; Lasuén to Don José Arguello, November 20, 1792, to Don Diego de Borica, January 26, 1796, and January 29, 1796, in Lasuén, *Writings*, 1:258–59, 369–71; Amador, "Memorias," 194.

17. Bancroft, *History of California*, 1:591–92; Lasuén, *Writings*, 2:207; Sanchez, *Spanish Period*, 305; Cook, *Conflict*, 91–94; J. F. G. de la Pérouse, *A Voyage Round the World, Performed in the Years 1785, 1787, and 1788* (London, 1807), 2:197.

18. Archibald, *Economic Aspects*, 11, 159; Zephyrin Engelhardt, *San Gabriel Mission and the Beginnings of Los Angeles* (San Gabriel, 1927), 58, 71–74; Lugo, "Vida de un Ranchero," 98–99, 113; Bancroft, *History of California*, 1:617–18; J. M. Guinn, *Historical and Biographical Record of Southern California* (Chicago, 1902), 41.

19. Bancroft, *History of California*, 1:387–88, 577; Archibald, *Economic Aspects*, 179; Guinn, *Historical and Biographical Record*, 50.

20. The following table, compiled from data in Archibald, *Economic Aspects*, 154–79, compares the number of cattle and the number of Indians living in the California missions.

Year	Number of Neophytes	Number of Cattle	Neophytes:Cattle
1785	5,123	6,813	1:1.33
1791	8,425	25,180	1:2.99
1795	11,025	31,167	1:2.83
1800	13,688	54,321	1:3.97
1805	20,372	95,035	1:4.67
1810	18,770	116,306	1:6.20
1815	19,467	139,596	1:7.17
1820	20,473	149,489	1:7.30

21. The San Gabriel padres are quoted in Webb, *Indian Life*, 41; Pérez, "Una Vieja," 18; Lugo, "Vida de un Ranchero," 100; Amador, "Memorias," 188; Híjar, "California in 1834," 34; la Pérouse, *Voyage Round the World*, 2:197; Cook, *Conflict*, 40–48; Richard Sutch, "The Care and Feeding of Slaves," in Paul A. David, Herbert G. Gutman, Richard Sutch, Peter Temin, and Gavin Wright, *Reckoning with Slavery: A Critical Study on the Quantitative History of American Negro Slavery* (New York, 1976), 261–67; Neal Salisbury, *Manitou and Providence: Indians, Europeans, and the Making of New England, 1500–1643* (New York, 1984), 31–32.

22. Archibald, *Economic Aspects*, 103–4; Engelhardt, *San Gabriel Mission*, 94–95; Fray José María de Zalvidea to de la Guerra y Noriega, San Gabriel Mission, October 18, 1815, José de la Guerra y Noriega Papers, Huntington Library; Bancroft, *History of California*, 1:614.

23. Archibald, *Economic Aspects*, 130–32; Hutchinson, "Mexican Govern-

ment," 335; Tomás Almaguer, "Interpreting Chicano History: The World-System Approach to Nineteenth-Century California," *Review* 4 (Winter 1981), 473–77 (Shaler is quoted on page 475).

24. Archibald, *Economic Aspects*, 130, 185; Bancroft, *History of California*, 2:195, 3:89–90; Juan Bandini to Eustace Barron, December 8, 1828, Stearns Papers, Box 4; Lugo, "Life of a Rancher," 229–30.

25. Archibald, *Economic Aspects*, 63–65; Lugo, "Vida de un Ranchero," 78.

26. Cook, *Conflict*, 58–61, 70.

27. William Mason, "Indian-Mexican Cultural Exchange in the Los Angeles Area, 1781–1834," *Aztlán* 15, no. 1 (Spring 1984), 136–37; Bancroft, *History of California*, 2:323–24, 345; Irving Berdine Richman, *California Under Spain and Mexico, 1535–1847* (Boston, 1911), 219–20.

28. The story of Quintana and his neophytes relies largely on the recollection of Amador, "Memorias," 67–77, which includes the narrative of the neophyte Lorenzo Asisara; Bancroft, *California Pastoral*, 596; José María Estudillo to Fray Marcelino Marquinez, October 15, 1812, California Historical Documents Collection, Huntington Library; Zephyrin Engelhardt, *The Franciscans in California* (Harbor Springs, Mich., 1897), 376; Bancroft, *History of California*, 2:387–89; Foucault, *Discipline and Punish*, 60–65.

29. Amador, "Memorias," 74.

30. Ibid.; Ripoll to Father President Vicente Francisco Sarría, Santa Barbara, May 5, 1824, in "Fray Antonio Ripoll's Description of the Chumash Revolt at Santa Barbara in 1824," ed. and trans. Maynard Geiger, *Southern California Quarterly* 52 (December 1970), 354; "Testimony, June 1, 1824," de la Guerra Documents, quoted in Cook, *Conflict*, 108; Bancroft, *History of California*, 2:527–37; Webb, *Indian Life*, 51; Angustias de la Guerra Ord, *Occurrences in Hispanic California*, ed. and trans. Francis Price and William H. Ellison (Washington, D.C., 1956), 7–9.

31. Bancroft, *History of California*, 2:527.

FURTHER READING

Archibald, Robert. *The Economic Aspects of the California Missions.* 1978.

Cook, Sherburne F. *The Conflict Between the California Indian and White Civilization.* 1976.

Costo, Rupert, and Jeanette Costo, eds. *The Missions of California: A Legacy of Genocide.* 1987.

Heizer, Robert F., and Albert B. Elsasser. *The Natural World of the California Indians.* 1980.

Hurtado, Albert. "California Indians and the Workaday West: Labor, Assimilation, and Survival." *California History* 69 (Spring 1990): 2–11.

———. *Indian Survival on the California Frontier.* 1988.

"Indians of California." Special issue. *California History* 71 (Fall 1992).

Kroeber, Theodora. *Ishi in Two Worlds.* 1961.

Monroy, Douglas. *Thrown Among Strangers: The Making of Mexican Culture in Frontier California.* 1990.

Phillips, George Harwood. *Chiefs and Challengers: Indian Resistance and Cooperation in Southern California.* 1975.

—————. *Indians and Intruders in Central California, 1769–1849.* 1993.

Rawls, James J. *Indians of California: The Changing Image.* 1984.

Weber, David J. *The Mexican Frontier, 1821–1846: The American Southwest Under Mexico.* 1982.

2 Chinese Livelihood in Rural California

The Impact of Economic Change,
1860–1880

Sucheng Chan

EDITOR'S INTRODUCTION

The first Chinese immigrants came to California shortly after the discovery of gold. At the end of 1849, only a few hundred Chinese people lived in the state, but in the early 1850s the rate of Chinese immigration accelerated dramatically, with 20,000 people arriving in 1852 alone.

By 1860, the Chinese constituted by far the largest component of the foreign-born population of California. The 1860 census counted 35,000 Chinese people in California, almost one-tenth of the state's population. Chinese immigration continued at a steady rate during the 1860s and 1870s. All told, 322,000 Chinese people entered the United States between 1850 and 1882, when the Chinese Exclusion law was passed. Approximately three-quarters of them settled in California, and in 1880 they made up 9 percent of the state's population and 16 percent of San Francisco's inhabitants. The young age of most Chinese immigrants meant that their participation rate in the California labor force was very high.

Beginning with the Foreign Miners' Tax in 1850, the Chinese were frequently the victims of white vigilante and even quasi-"legal" violence. During the 1850s, efforts were made in the state legislature to halt Chinese immigration. At the local level, "pigtail ordinances" and measures excluding the Chinese from public schools were passed. Anti-Chinese sentiment reached fever pitch in the mid-1870s in the context of one of the most severe economic depressions in the state's history. By the late 1870s, all major political parties were taking strong anti-Chinese positions, and pressure from California congressmen, in particular, resulted in passage of the Chinese Exclusion Act of 1882.

Most studies of the Chinese in California have focused on the virulent anti-Chinese movement, with only passing reference to how Chinese people obtained their livelihood. To the extent that this question of livelihood has attracted the interest of historians, attention has been concentrated on the Chinese occupational structure in urban settings, especially San Francisco. But as Sucheng Chan points out in the following article, up until 1880 a majority of California Chinese lived outside San Francisco, many of them in rural areas of the state.

Chan meticulously reconstructs the occupational structure of the Chinese in three of California's more rural counties between 1860 and 1880. Her work shows that the Chinese labor force in California was both diverse and dynamic. Until the 1860s, most rural Chinese worked as independent miners, entrepreneurs, professionals, and artisans. By the late 1860s, discriminatory practices and changing socioeconomic conditions began to proletarianize the Chinese, forcing them to become wage laborers who increasingly had to take the most menial and low-paying jobs.

By 1880, an increasing number of Chinese were working as tenant farmers, common laborers, and factory hands. Chan paints a particularly detailed portrait of the Chinese involvement in agriculture, which contributed dramatically to the transformation of California agriculture in the late nineteenth century from cattle and wheat farming to an agricultural economy based more on the cultivation of fruits and vegetables. In his book *Factories in the Field*, Carey McWilliams concluded that if it had not been for the contribution of Chinese agricultural labor, this transition would have been delayed by twenty-five years.

◆   ◆   ◆

The historical literature on Chinese Americans is quite uneven in the topics covered, in the geographic focus of the studies, and in scholarly quality. Since American reaction to Chinese immigration was negative, much scholarly effort has been devoted to explaining the causes of the anti-Chinese movement, which culminated in Chinese exclusion in 1882. Major monographs by Mary Roberts Coolidge, Elmer Clarence Sandmeyer, Gunther Barth, Stuart Creighton Miller, Robert McClellan, and Alexander Saxton have offered different explanations for the anti-Chinese movement.[1] Delber L. McKee investigated how the federal government implemented the exclusionary legislation and the reaction of China and Chinese Americans to it, while Fred W. Riggs traced the political process which led to the repeal of the various exclusion laws in 1943.[2] These works necessarily focus on those whom Roger Daniels has called the "excluders" rather than on the "excluded," so even though they illuminate the temper of the times, they provide little insight into the attitudes of the Chinese themselves—why they came, how they perceived the United States, and what their communities were like.

Available studies of Chinese immigrant communities fall into two categories: those that treat Chinatowns as a special type of community with features distinct from Anglo-American ones and those that describe facets of particular communities. In both instances, communities are analyzed mainly in terms of their institutional structure. The works of Rose Hum Lee, Stanford M. Lyman, S. W. Kung, Betty Lee Sung, Francis L. K. Hsu, and Jack Chen—though differing vastly in scholarly sophistication and tone—share the common characteristic of being general surveys of Chinese American life.[3] Chinatowns are treated as a distinct type of community, so that regardless of where a Chinatown is located, its social structure is implied to be similar to that of any other Chinatown. Studies of individual Chinatowns, in contrast, have greater temporal and geographic specificity. Some of the early writings portrayed the more exotic or lurid aspects of San Francisco's Chinatown.[4] More recent studies describe either San Francisco's Chinatown or analyze certain aspects of New York's Chinatown.[5] Two exceptions to the typological approach and the heavy emphasis on San Francisco or New York are James W. Loewen's investigation of the Chinese in the Mississippi Delta and Melford Weiss's analysis of the Chinese in "Valley City," California.[6] Loewen's work is unique because, unlike other authors who elucidate the social structure of Chinese American communities in terms of institutional patterns brought over from China, he considers the pattern of racial segregation peculiar to the South to be a more important influence than Chinese cultural and social heritage on the Delta Chinese community.

The reliance on San Francisco data by so many authors has created a false impression that all Chinese communities in America are merely smaller replicas of the one in San Francisco and that the Chinese American historical experience is quite homogeneous. Although the importance of San Francisco as the cultural, social, political, and economic center of "Chinese America" is beyond dispute, the city and county of San Francisco never contained the majority of the Chinese-ancestry population in California, much less in the United States. Throughout the second half of the nineteenth century, the largest proportion of Chinese immigrants lived in the rural counties of California. During the first two decades of Chinese immigration, an overwhelming proportion of the Chinese population located in the mining counties, first in the southern mines, and after the mid-1860s in the northern mines. From the 1870s through the 1890s, quite a large contingent worked in the Trinity and Klamath mining regions.

As a settlement center, San Francisco achieved genuine demographic preeminence only in the 1880s and 1890s when two factors fostered the city's emergence as the premier city of "Chinese America": 1) the development of manufacturing industries, which provided employment for Chinese; and 2) the anti-Chinese movement, which caused many Chinese to flock to the city's segregated Chinatown in search of security. Even in 1880 and 1890, only 20.6 percent and 24.0 percent, respectively, of the total Chinese population in the United States lived in San Francisco, while 50.6 percent and 43.4 percent, respectively, lived in California outside of San Francisco.[7] For that reason, a balanced view of the Chinese American historical experience cannot overlook the rural segment of the Chinese immigrant population.

Although more Chinese lived in rural California than in any other part of the country throughout the nineteenth century, there has been no overall study of the Chinese in rural America. Glimpses of rural life are available only in travellers' accounts[8] and in a few studies of Chinese labor, such as those by George Seward and Ping Chiu.[9] The paucity of primary sources is one reason for the lack of studies of the Chinese in rural America. Newspapers published in the rural counties seldom mentioned the Chinese, and when they did, the news was of the sensational sort or dealt with the pros and cons of continued Chinese immigration.[10] Some documents in Chinese have been salvaged, but these provide only episodic evidence on Chinese economic and social life in rural California, and it is difficult to judge how representative the individual cases may be.[11] The dearth of written sources cannot be remedied by the use of oral history interviews, since no persons who could tell us something about life in the nineteenth century are still alive.

For systematic information, the two most useful archival sources are the U.S. manuscript population census and the county archival documents, which are available in the office of the county recorder in every county in California.[12] These sources provide information on the demographic composition and occupational structure of Chinese communities in rural California, even though they tell nothing about the subjective aspects of the Chinese experience. This study of the Chinese occupational structure in three rural California counties is based on such census and county archival records.

Sacramento, Yuba, and San Joaquin counties were chosen for study because they contained three of the most important Chinatowns outside of San Francisco in the nineteenth century—Sacramento, Marysville, and Stockton. Only the Chinatown in Oroville, Butte County, was of equal importance. However, since conditions in Butte and Yuba counties were quite similar, the inclusion of Butte County in this study would have been redundant.[13] In looking at Sacramento, Yuba, and San Joaquin counties, it is possible to shed new light on the Chinese clustered in the larger rural Chinatowns as well as those scattered throughout the countryside.

The historical importance of Sacramento and Marysville has been imprinted upon the collective memory of Chinese Americans through the language they use. To this day, Chinese Americans call San Francisco "Dai Fou" (Big City), Sacramento "Yee Fou" (Second City), and Marysville "Sam Fou" (Third City). Stockton has not been deemed significant enough for inclusion in this terminological ranking, but it and San Joaquin County are part of this study because initial large-scale Chinese entry there was due to the development of agriculture, and not to mining and trading as in Sacramento and Yuba counties. An examination of developments in San Joaquin County makes it possible to determine whether the original economic magnet attracting Chinese to a locality had any impact on the subsequent development of the pattern of Chinese livelihood there.

The years 1860–1880 have been chosen for analysis because they represent a period of significant change and development for the Chinese population in California. In the first two decades of Chinese immigration, the majority of the Chinese in rural California worked as independent miners and entrepreneurs. Only from the late 1860s onward did an increasing number begin to earn their living as wage laborers. This fact is worth emphasizing because the Chinese have been depicted all too frequently as "cheap labor" and little more. Such a depiction distorts historical reality. The Chinese in rural California initially engaged in a wide range of occupations, many of which did not involve wage labor. Changing socioeconomic conditions in the American West, along with racial discrimination—rather than Chinese "willingness" to be cheap labor—were responsible for proletarianizing the Chinese population.

In this study, occupations have been grouped under four categories on the basis of function: primary extraction and production, which includes farming, fishing, and mining; manual labor, which includes agricultural as well as nonagricultural labor; personal service, which includes employment as servants, cooks, and prostitutes; and entrepreneurs, professionals, and artisans, which includes all persons earning a living through the sale of merchandise or the practice of a trade or profession.

Between 1860 and 1880, tenant farming, paid farm labor, nonagricultural labor, and personal services replaced gold mining and independent entrepreneurship as the foundation of economic life for the Chinese in rural California. In the process, more and more Chinese became dependent on white employers for their livelihood, both in the towns and in the rural areas. In 1860, artisans, professionals, and entrepreneurs made up the largest proportion of the Chinese population in the rural Chinatowns, while miners—who represented almost all of the persons in the category "primary extraction and production"—were numerically dominant in the hinterland. A decade later, the absolute number as well as relative percentage of persons engaged in primary extraction and production had declined because of the exodus from the mines, while the number in nonagricultural labor and personal services had increased greatly. The number of artisans, professionals, and entrepreneurs remained about the same. In 1880, though mining occupied even fewer persons, an increasing number of Chinese farmers accounts for the rise in the absolute number of persons in primary extraction and production, particularly in Sacramento County. The number of persons in agricultural and nonagricultural labor increased, while the number in personal services and in independent enterprises remained about the same.

These longitudinal changes show that the Chinese communities were able to support a fairly consistent number of entrepreneurs throughout this period, but the economic opportunities open to the rest of the Chinese population depended on changes in the larger economy. Discriminatory actions and legislation also increasingly restricted the range of Chinese economic activities, as a hierarchical division of labor along racial lines became firmly institutionalized on the Pacific Coast. Unlike the American South, where the line of cleavage was drawn between black and white, in California the dichotomy was between Chinese and white. As the nineteenth century progressed, Chinese were relegated in increasing numbers to menial, low-paid, and low-status jobs.

Occupational Structure, 1860

The gold rush had a greater impact on the Chinese population in California than it did on other ethnic groups in the state. Throughout the mining era, a larger proportion of the Chinese engaged in mining than did their counterparts among other ethnic groups. In 1860, 70.4 percent of all gainfully employed Chinese above the age of fifteen were miners, compared to 31.6 percent among non-Chinese gainfully employed persons.[14] Moreover, the Chinese remained in mining longer than the non-Chinese population. White miners had begun their exodus from the mines by the mid-1850s, but Chinese miners began to drift out only after 1863.[15] As late as 1900, small clusters of aging Chinese miners were still listed in the manuscript population census.

Chinese miners worked mainly placer claims, so they were found primarily along streams and rivers. An analysis of the locational distribution of Chinese miners in Yuba County indicates that in 1860, Chinese miners were concentrated most heavily along the Yuba River and its tributaries. The number of Chinese miners was largest in Long Bar, North-east, Foster Bar, and Slate Range townships—townships through which the Yuba, Middle Yuba, and North Yuba rivers flow. In contrast, few Chinese miners were found in Rose Bar, Parks Bar, and New York townships, where a range of mountains is located. There were gold deposits in these latter townships, however, for the number of white miners in them was large.[16] In these mountainous areas, the gold deposits were in hardrock quartz claims, and Chinese miners did not have the capital to purchase the necessary heavy equipment to work such deposits, nor did they feel secure enough to invest in expensive machinery that they might be forced to abandon.

In the 1860s, most of the Chinese miners along the Yuba River and its tributaries were independent prospectors and not laborers for mining companies. They frequently formed their own companies consisting of up to forty partners.[17] Many Chinese miners in Yuba County obtained their claims through preemption rather than through purchase. Preemption claims did not have to be bought; the claimants only had to file the necessary documents in the county recorder's office and put up markers to show the boundaries of their claims. The ability of Chinese miners to file preemption claims is worth noting, for it has been commonly assumed that because of anti-Chinese sentiment in the mines, Chinese immigrants had to resort to buying worked-over claims abandoned by white miners.[18]

The earliest Chinese preemption claims appeared in Yuba County records in 1856. Ah Louie and Company claimed 240 feet at Buckeye Bar along the Yuba River, while Sham Kee claimed 4,200 feet eight miles outside of Marysville City, also along the Yuba River.[19] Records of prices paid by Chinese miners for claims they purchased indicate the approximate amount of money that they saved when they were able to obtain claims through preemption. In 1856, Ah Chung and Company purchased two claims of sixty feet each from Frederick Antenheimer (the Yuba County tax collector) and John Lawrence for $620. The purchase price included two wheelbarrows and running planks.[20] In the following year, Antenheimer and Ferdinand Furning sold two claims measuring ninety feet each to Ah Locke and Thin Shue for $695, and threw into the bargain two frame houses, two pumps, and miscellaneous mining tools.[21] Those Chinese who were able to obtain claims through preemption therefore saved hundreds and perhaps even thousands of dollars.

Contrary to the situation in some counties where Chinese miners were driven away from good claims that they had located, quite a number of Chinese miners along the Yuba River in both Yuba and Sierra counties were allowed to work the same locations year after year. In January 1869, four different Chinese companies filed multiple preemption claims at Missouri Bar on the Yuba River. Hong Fook Kong and Company, with ten partners, filed ten claims of 100 feet each, which they renewed annually between 1870 and 1874. Then they disappeared from the county records until March 1878, when they filed thirty-two claims with thirty-two partners. By 1879, however, the larger group had splintered, and Hong Fook Kong and Company was once again composed of ten partners filing ten claims. These claims were renewed in 1880 and 1881.[22]

Three other groups also worked the same stretch of the Yuba River during the twelve-year period between 1869 and 1881. In Key and Company, with six partners, filed six claims contiguous to Hong Fook Kong and Company's claims, stretching upriver for 600 feet.[23] Jim and Company, with four partners, filed four claims upriver from In Key and Company's claims.[24] Both companies followed the same pattern of claims renewal as Hong Fook Kong and Company. The fourth group, Ah King and Company, had six partners who filed claims which were not contiguous to the other three companies during the same period of time. Perhaps that is why in 1878, when they filed thirty-two claims with thirty-two partners (a different group of persons from the thirty-two in the Hong Fook Kong Company), three of the partners were not individuals but corporate entities: Hong Fook Kong and Company, In Key and Company, and a fifth group called Ah Kong and Company.[25] It may be surmised that certain Chinese miners were buying shares in other people's claims in different localities. This second example of a company enlarging its membership also showed that such larger groupings had a tendency to splinter, for by 1879 Ah King and Company was back to six partners.

Mining was an extremely important source of livelihood for the Chinese in Yuba County. Almost 80 percent of the Chinese there in 1860 were miners, whereas only 21.4 percent of the non-Chinese population were miners. The Chinese constituted 35.9 percent of all the miners in the county, but they made up only 13 percent of the total population. In California as a whole, 29.4 percent of all miners in 1860 were Chinese, while 9.2 percent of the total population were Chinese.

The economic and social importance of gold mining in 1860 led to a bifurcated social structure in rural Chinese immigrant communities. There were a large number of miners who did not grow their own food except for fresh produce cultivated in some corner of their mining grounds. To supply the needs of these miners for food and personal services, there appeared a small group of Chinese entrepreneurs, most of whom lived in the towns in the mining counties, or in cities such as Sacramento, Marysville, and Stockton—the three major supply posts and transportation nodes of the entire mining region.

The occupational structure of the Chinese population in the three cities differed sharply from that found among the Chinese in the hinterlands. In each of the three cities, persons engaged in merchandising and various trades made up the largest portion of the Chinese population. Sacramento City, being the largest of the three with a Chinese population of 980, had the greatest range of occupations, with artisans, professionals, and entrepreneurs constituting 49.4 percent of the city's Chinese population. Marysville, second in importance as an urban center in the Sacramento Valley with a Chinese population of 227, had 34.8 percent of its Chinese population earning a living as merchants, professionals, and artisans. Stockton, located at the northern end of the San Joaquin Valley, being relatively farther away from the center of activities in the southern mines, was less crucial as a supply post and consequently had the least differentiated occupational structure, the bulk of its Chinese population of 115 persons being laundrymen.[26]

Next in importance to the urban entrepreneurs, artisans, and professionals were persons engaged in personal service, which included cooks, servants, waiters and dishwashers, and prostitutes.[27] So employed were 20.8 percent of the Chinese population in Sacramento, 41.4 percent in Marysville, and 29.6 percent in Stockton. By far the largest number of persons in this grouping were prostitutes, with 113 in Sacramento, 75 in Marysville, and 18 in Stockton. In 1860, there were as yet few Chinese servants.

The remaining occupational categories were relatively unimportant. Individuals engaged in mining, truck gardening, and fishing ranged from

8.7 percent of the Chinese population in Stockton to 11.9 percent in Marysville and 16.3 percent in Sacramento. Manual laborers ranged from half a percent in Stockton to 5 percent in Sacramento. Finally, approximately 10 percent of the Chinese population in each city was unemployed in 1860.[28] Chinese living outside city limits in Sacramento and Yuba counties were almost all miners. (There were only nine Chinese living outside of Stockton in San Joaquin County in 1860.) Chinese farm laborers had not yet become an important element in the rural landscape in 1860. Varden Fuller and Carey McWilliams have stated that Chinese had entered the harvest labor market to work as migratory farm laborers in significant numbers by the late 1850s,[29] but census data do not support their assertions. Even though the 1860 census was taken between June and August, and both Sacramento and San Joaquin counties, in particular, had thriving wheat-growing areas, no Chinese farm laborers were enumerated in the census of the three counties. Census data indicate that the Chinese who first worked on farms were cooks, with 18 in Sacramento County, 35 in Yuba County, and 8 in San Joaquin County.

In terms of the integration of the Chinese immigrant population into the larger society, the miners were certainly very much a part of the mining economy, although contemporaneous accounts indicate that, for the most part, the Chinese miners kept to themselves for the sake of safety.[30] Other than miners, the only Chinese who interacted with whites were cooks, servants, and laundrymen, because they were dependent on white employers for their livelihood. Some prostitutes also served white customers, but it is not known how many did so.[31] Mining and personal service, then, were the two main avenues for sporadic social interaction between Chinese and whites in the 1860s.

Occupational Structure, 1870

In the decade between 1860 and 1870, four significant developments in the larger California economy influenced the occupational structure of the rural Chinese immigrant population: the decline of mining, the emergence of San Francisco as a manufacturing center, the growth of intensive agriculture, and the completion of the transcontinental railroad. Through immigration, the Chinese population had increased during the decade. Mining absorbed a far smaller absolute number as well as percentage of the Chinese population, but other opportunities for earning a living in light manufacturing, agriculture, and common labor became available.

Gold mining declined enormously in importance as a source of livelihood for the rural Chinese population in California between 1860 and

1870. In 1860, there had been 24,282 Chinese among a total of 82,573 miners in the state, but by 1870, of the some 43,000 miners left in California, about 16,000 were Chinese. Compared to a decade earlier when miners made up over 70 percent of the Chinese population in California, they now constituted only about a third.[32]

A significant divergence had developed between the economy of San Francisco and the rest of the state by 1870. Such a trend was clearly observable as it affected the Chinese immigrant population. In San Francisco, 27.2 percent of the gainfully employed Chinese worked in light manufacturing. Four industries—cigar and tobacco manufacturing, the boot and shoe industry, woolen mills, and the sewing trades—employed over 2,300 Chinese workers. In contrast, in all of rural California, only 174 persons, or only 0.7 percent of the gainfully employed Chinese adults, worked in light manufacturing, 96 of whom were in the shoe industry, 48 in the cigar industry, 28 in the sewing trades, with 1 each in a woolen mill and in an iron foundry.[33] Fifteen of the shoemakers lived in Sacramento City, 6 in Marysville, and 1 in Stockton. Of the cigar makers, 35 worked in Sacramento City and 3 in Marysville. Eleven of the individuals engaged in the sewing trades lived in Sacramento, while 8 lived in Yuba County.[34] Thus, although Sacramento and Marysville also had nascent light manufacturing industries, the number of Chinese employed in this sector was miniscule compared to San Francisco.

After manufacturing, independent businesses and various professions absorbed the largest number of Chinese in San Francisco. These trades provided a livelihood to 25.8 percent of the gainfully employed Chinese in the city. Nonagricultural manual laborers made up 24.8 percent of the gainfully employed, while those in personal service constituted 14.8 percent. Only 6 percent of the San Francisco Chinese population were in primary extraction and production, and over three-fifths of them were miners visiting the city. The only important resident group in primary production was 145 fishermen.[35]

In rural California, on the other hand, over 17,000 of the 37,000 Chinese remained in primary extraction and production—a sector that supported 46 percent of them. Miners numbered some 16,000; truck gardeners and farmers some 1,000; while 151 fishermen made up the rest of this group. Next in numerical importance were almost 6,000 nonagricultural laborers; slightly over 3,000 providers of personal service; and almost 3,000 artisans, professionals, and entrepreneurs. Even though labor-intensive agriculture was developing, in 1870 only a little over 2,000 Chinese in rural California as a whole worked as agricultural laborers.[36]

The three counties in this study differ from rural California seen as a whole: a much larger percentage of their Chinese population had entered agriculture by 1870. Sacramento County led the state in the transformation of its agriculture from extensive grain cultivation to intensive fruit and hop growing. In 1870, Sacramento County ranked first in the state in the value of its orchard products, and fifth in the value of its market garden products. Truck gardening had been an important means of livelihood for the Sacramento Chinese as far back as the 1850s. By 1870, although truck gardening continued to be important, Chinese agriculturalists had begun to move out of small-scale truck gardening inside the city of Sacramento into large-scale tenant farming in the Sacramento Delta. While 35 Chinese truck gardeners and 4 farmers resided within city limits (compared to 110 truck gardeners cultivating plots within city limits a decade earlier), 37 truck gardeners and 26 farmers now tilled the soil in the Sacramento Delta.

The presence of Chinese farmers in the Sacramento Delta was first documented narratively in a newspaper account in 1869 and statistically in the 1870 manuscript agriculture census.[37] In 1873, the first lease was officially recorded between two Chinese tenants, Chou Ying and Wee Ying, and George D. Roberts, president of the Tide Land Reclamation Company, which had employed many Chinese to drain the peat islands of the delta. Chou Ying and Wee Ying leased 551 acres in three tracts on a mixed cash-rent and share-crop basis. On one tract, they paid eight dollars per acre, while on the other two tracts, they were to give the landlord a fourth of the crops. However, the lease stipulated that if the tenants chose to grow Chinese vegetables, then the landlord did not wish to have any of the crops; instead, a cash rent of ten dollars per acre would be paid.[38]

In the late 1870s, other Chinese tenants leased plots ranging from 160 acres to 200 acres for rents ranging from fifteen dollars per acre for unimproved land to eighty dollars per acre for land with growing orchards. Most of these leased farms were in the so-called backswamps of the peat islands, where the danger of floods was much greater. White owner-operators usually retained farms along the elevated natural levees for their own cultivation.[39] It is difficult to compare the rent paid by Chinese tenants to that paid by white tenants, for the former usually leased farms on a cash rental basis, while almost all the latter leased them on a share-cropping basis.

Chinese had also begun to work as farm laborers by 1870, but they were found in significant numbers only in Sacramento and San Joaquin counties, with 567 and 224 persons, respectively. The largest concentration of Chinese farm laborers in Sacramento County was in Sutter, Franklin, and Georgiana townships—the three townships along the Sacramento River in the delta portion of the county. The only other cluster of Chinese farmworkers was in the hopfields of American and Center townships, along the American River. In these areas, approximately a third of them lived in the households of white farmers, while the remainder lived in their own households. Since the number of Chinese farmers was still relatively small, it can be assumed that almost all the Chinese agricultural laborers worked for white farmers in 1870.[40] In San Joaquin County, the Chinese farm laborers were also in the delta region. No Chinese farm laborers were enumerated in Yuba County, but Marysville had sixty Chinese truck gardeners.[41]

The completion of the transcontinental railroad in 1869 disgorged thousands of Chinese workers into the labor market all over the western states. Many of these discharged workers returned to California, where most of them sought work as nonagricultural common laborers. Their presence was especially noticeable in Marysville and Stockton. In the former city, common laborers made up 45.6 percent of the Chinese population, while in the latter, the figure was 44.3 percent.[42] Levee building and maintenance, road-building, and other hard construction work probably engaged most of these persons. If this was indeed the case, then Chinese laborers were responsible for building many of the roads, ditches, levees, and bridges in these areas.

By 1870, a tripartite division of labor had emerged within the Chinese immigrant population: independent miners and agriculturalists, independent urban entrepreneurs earning their living largely within ethnic enclaves, and a numerically growing group of wage-earners who depended on employment from the larger society for their livelihood.

The number of persons in primary extraction and production varied according to locality. This group represented less than 5 percent of the total Chinese population in the three cities. In the countryside, there were no Chinese miners or farmers in San Joaquin County, while in Sacramento County outside of Sacramento City, miners, farmers, truck gardeners, and fishermen made up 43.7 percent of the Chinese population, and in Yuba County outside of Marysville, 64.8 percent of the Chinese were in agriculture or mining.

Proportionately (but not in absolute numbers), artisans, professionals, and entrepreneurs had declined in importance in the three cities by 1870. Moreover, within this grouping, some subtle but significant changes had occurred during the 1860–1870 decade. Practitioners of certain skilled trades, such as bakers, cabinetmakers, and carpenters, had all but disappeared, most probably because better organization by whites had driven the handful of Chinese in these occupations in the 1860s out of them. On the other hand, occupations requiring a small amount of capital investment had grown in importance. The number of boardinghouse keepers increased, reflecting the emergence of Sacramento, Marysville, and Stockton as important stopping places for transient Chinese migrant laborers. The number of professional gamblers had also increased dramatically, perhaps indicating that some individuals had discovered a profitable way to earn a living by exploiting their fellowmen's need for recreation. Chinese had also carved a niche for themselves as vegetable vendors manning stationary stalls (in contrast to peripatetic Chinese vegetable peddlers, long a familiar sight on the California scene). Lastly, Chinese appeared for the first time in 1870 in a number of semiskilled trades, such as brick, barrel, and candle making.

Persons dependent on white employers for their livelihood had increased greatly in number. They included farm laborers, nonagricultural common laborers, wage-earners in light manufacturing, and a growing number of persons providing personal service.[43] Together with laundrymen whose customers were mainly white, this group embraced the majority of the Chinese population in all three cities and in rural Sacramento County. In rural Yuba County, they made up a third of the Chinese population, while in rural San Joaquin County, they included almost the entire Chinese population.

If employment by whites is viewed as a channel for interaction with the larger society, then the Chinese population in rural California in 1870 was in more frequent interaction with the white population than a decade earlier. Although such interaction was mainly in the form of employer-employee relations, and even though such social relations were hardly a good basis for providing genuine understanding between the two groups, it nonetheless cannot be said that the Chinese lived only in their own segregated world by the beginning of their third decade of settlement in California.

Occupational Structure, 1880

Between 1870 and 1880, two major trends and one minor one can be detected in the evolution of the occupational structure of Chinese communities in rural California. First, while the relative percentage of persons engaged in primary extraction and production remained about the same as ten years earlier, the composition of this group changed. The absolute number of miners in Sacramento and Yuba counties remained more or less constant, but because the overall Chinese population had increased considerably, the percentage of miners in the total population declined. An increasing number of farmers, particularly in Sacramento and San Joaquin counties, compensated for the decrease in the number of miners. Agriculture had become a very important source of livelihood as well as a channel for upward social mobility for the rural Chinese population.

Second, both the absolute number as well as the percentage of common laborers fell significantly in Marysville and Stockton. This was probably because a large number of the discharged railroad workers had by now found employment in other lines of work. Some no doubt had returned to China, while others had become farm laborers.

Third, a small number of Chinese had begun to work in factories in Sacramento, Yuba, and San Joaquin counties. The majority of them worked in woolen mills in the cities of Sacramento, Marysville, and Stockton. In the latter city, a handful of Chinese also worked in a paper mill. But these numbers are so small that it cannot be argued that a trend was developing. Sacramento City was the only place in rural California where Chinese entry into manufacturing and factory production was clearly visible—there, thirty-four Chinese cigar makers and twenty-eight woolen mill workers resided. There were also forty-four persons engaged in the sewing trades, but it is not clear how many worked as independent artisans and how many worked in sewing factories.[44]

By 1880, Chinese immigrants were working in agriculture as owner-operators, small-scale tenants, large-scale tenants, farm laborers, fruit and vegetable peddlers, commission merchants, and farm cooks. (The small-scale tenants are differentiated from the large-scale ones because the *scale* of operations made a great difference in the *mode* of operation: the former usually cultivated vegetables and berries, employing few, if any, hired hands; while the latter most commonly grew potatoes, onions, beans, and deciduous fruit, employing large numbers of seasonal laborers.) In the 1880s, tenant farmers and farm laborers became the two most numerous groups of Chinese immigrant agriculturalists.

The Sacramento–San Joaquin Delta and the bottomlands along the Sacramento and Feather rivers were the two regions where Chinese settlers first farmed in California on a large scale. The patterns of agriculture undertaken in these two areas contrast strikingly with each other. In the Sacramento–San Joaquin Delta, Chinese tenant farmers cultivated both Irish and sweet potatoes, onions, and beans. (Asparagus, the crop which made the delta world-famous, did not become important commercially until the turn of the century.) These crops were grown because they were most suitable for the soil and climatic conditions of the delta and not because they required a lot of hand labor. Thus, it was the availability of fertile land, and *not* because the Chinese were allegedly willing to provide "cheap labor," which drew Chinese immigrants into agriculture in the delta. In 1880, there were 537 Chinese farmers in that part of the delta which lies within the boundaries of Sacramento and San Joaquin counties. A smaller number were found in the section of the delta located in Contra Costa, Yolo, and Solano counties. They had been drawn there because the peat soil was so fertile that three crops could be grown each year. In short, the delta was a popular area because the potential profit to be made was great, but it was also a high-risk area because of periodic floods.[45] Chinese who were willing to take those risks were entrepreneurs in the true sense of the word.

Along the bottomlands of the middle stretch of the Sacramento River and along the Feather River, a different pattern of agriculture evolved with Chinese participation. There, labor-intensive fruit growing was undertaken alongside the cultivation of vegetables on a field (rather than market garden) scale. White landowners had already planted orchards in the area around Marysville prior to the Chinese entry into agriculture. However, many new orchards were planted with Chinese labor beginning in the mid-1870s.

The Chinese developed a symbiotic relationship with the landowners. Those Chinese who planted orchards for their landlords were employed not as farm laborers but as tenant farmers. Landowners leased several hundred acres at a time to Chinese tenants who were then required to prepare the ground for planting, and sometimes even to supply the saplings needed. These tenants, in turn, had responsibility for recruiting the requisite labor supply during the planting, thinning, weeding, and harvesting seasons. While the orchards were growing, the Chinese de facto were renting the land between the growing saplings for their own use. They grew berries and vegetables between the rows of trees. In some instances, a graduated rental payment calibrated to the life cycle of the fruit trees was set up. When the trees were young, and their roots had not yet spread, the tenants paid a relatively high rent for use of the land between the trees. Then by the third and fourth years, when the trees' roots had spread out far enough to be injured if the land in between were plowed for other crops, the rent would be decreased because the land could no longer be used for other crops. At the same time the trees had not yet begun to bear fruit so no income could be obtained from the land. By the fifth and sixth years, when the trees began to bear and the Chinese tenants could sell the fruit, their rent increased again. In this manner, the Chinese acted simultaneously as tenants who leased land to grow crops of their own and as caretakers for the growing orchards.[46]

By 1880, agriculture had become economically important to the state and to the rural Chinese immigrant communities. In rural Sacramento County, 1,123 out of a population of 3,278 Chinese (over a third of the population) depended on agriculture for their livelihood. The only other occupations of almost equal numerical importance were mining, with 1,070 persons, and nonagricultural manual labor, with 711 persons. In rural San Joaquin County, 723 persons (three-fifths of the total population) depended on agriculture for a living.[47]

Chinese involvement in California agriculture in both the Sacramento–San Joaquin Delta and the bottomlands along the Sacramento and Feather rivers was also important in the 1880s because the nature of Chinese tenancy helped to determine the pattern of Chinese interaction with the larger society. Chinese large-scale tenants always needed seasonal help, which they recruited from the rural Chinatowns. The white landowners usually had no direct dealing with these seasonal laborers. The tenants made the decision on how many workers to hire, how much to pay them, and how long to keep them. In other words, the tenants assumed all the managerial responsibility for cultivating the land. In some instances, landlords continued to live on their farms, while in other cases, they were absentee. The tenant farmers acted as middlemen who funneled jobs to their compatriots, on the one hand, and labor and managerial expertise to white landowners, on the other hand. County archival records indicate that many of these Chinese tenants operated hundreds and sometimes even thousands of acres[48]—a scale of agriculture undreamed of in the Pearl River Delta of Kwangtung Province from which most of them had emigrated. Agriculture was one of the most important channels for upward social mobility among rural Chinese immigrants in nineteenth-century California.

The tenant farmers were not the only ones to use their position for upward social mobility. Those who worked for them also hoped that their association with the tenants would eventually give them a share of the agricultural dividends. The mechanism for accomplishing this was the partnership system used by Chinese immigrants in urban enterprises as well as in agriculture. County archival records provide the names of many agricultural companies known as "yuen" (garden) in Chinese. Individuals' names were frequently listed alongside the companies' names, so that we know the number of partners in each outfit. Each partner signed his own name in Chinese characters on the county documents. The manuscript population census provides corroborating evidence on the emerging practice of forming partnerships: in the 1870 census, the majority of Chinese farm laborers lived in their own households, but by 1880 in the two areas under examination, the majority of Chinese farmworkers lived in the households of Chinese tenant farmers, where some members were explicitly listed as partners, while others were designated laborers. The farm laborers were taken into the tenant farmers' households not only as workers, but also as potential partners. The practice was still discernible in the 1900 manuscript census.[49]

Next to agriculture in attracting Chinese came nonagricultural common labor, followed by personal service occupations. In the three cities, entrepreneurs, artisans, and professionals were still important, ranging from 26.4 percent of the Chinese population in Marysville to 36 percent of the population in Sacramento.[50]

In terms of interaction with white employers, a portion of the farm laborers, all the nonagricultural common laborers, most of those in personal service, factory workers, and laundrymen were the most important groups. In Sacramento City in 1880, 70 percent of the Chinese were dependent on white employers for their livelihood. In the rest of Sacramento County, the proportion was 44 percent. In Marysville, 67 percent of the total Chinese population depended on white employment, while 31 percent did so in the rest of Yuba County. In Stockton and the rest of San Joaquin County, the proportions were 29 percent and 78 percent, respectively. Thus, by 1880, the rural Chinese population was highly dependent on the economy outside their own ethnic communities for subsistence. Moreover, they had made a full transition from being independent producers to wage-earners.

By way of conclusion, a number of propositions may be advanced. Generally speaking, structural changes within the California economy were the major determinants of change in the occupational structure of the Chinese population in rural California. Although racism also had a great effect because it restricted the range of occupations open to the Chinese, its impact is more difficult to measure. At a more refined level of analysis, regional variations are discernible. By comparing San Francisco with interior cities such as Sacramento and Marysville on the one hand and with the rural hinterland on the other hand, it appears that the degree and pattern of integration of the Chinese labor force into the overall economy depended on several factors: a region's initial economic base, its degree of urbanization, and its degree of industrialization. One pattern emerged in localities where the initial economy was based on mining but which soon turned to agriculture: in the countryside, few Chinese became wage-earners until the 1870s, while in the towns, as time passed, the larger and more urban the setting, the greater was the number of Chinese dependent on white employment. A second pattern was found in localities such as San Joaquin County where there had been no mining. There, the rural Chinese depended almost entirely on white landowners and other employers for their livelihood from the beginning of their settlement in the region. San Francisco showed yet another pattern of development. In this city, the industrial center of the state, small-scale Chinese manufacturers competed with whites to employ the community's Chinese residents.

Finally, it is clear that at no time in the 1860–1880 period was the Chinese population completely segregated into ethnic enclaves, but neither was it fully integrated into the larger economy and society. Consequently, the Chinese fitted into two social stratification systems, which overlapped but were not coincidental with each other. However, given the nature of the data presented here, it is not possible to specify exactly how these two systems affected each other because occupational divisions and rankings represent only one aspect of society. A full understanding of any society's social structure must take into account the perceptions, attitudes, and patterns of noneconomic social interaction of many different persons and groups. Thus, to provide a broader understanding of the historical evolution of race relations in rural California, theories about the process of labor differentiation during different stages of economic development must be combined with theories about how human consciousness is molded.

NOTES

1. Mary Roberts Coolidge, *Chinese Immigration* (New York, 1909), shows how the fragile balance in the political strength of the Democratic and Republican parties in the post–Civil War period—in California as well as in the nation—led politicians to appeal to anti-Chinese sentiment to win votes, with lower-class whites participating most actively in anti-Chinese activities. Elmer Clarence Sandmeyer, *The Anti-Chinese Movement in California* (Urbana, 1939), states that the anti-Chinese movement had multiple causes, but singles out racial antagonism and the fear of economic competition as the most important. Gunther Barth, *Bitter Strength: A History of the Chinese in the United States, 1850–1870* (Cambridge, Mass., 1964), argues that as sojourners the Chinese had only a limited goal in coming to the United States—to earn money—so they were viewed as unassimilable by Americans who considered their presence to be a "threat to the realization of the California vision"—the belief that the most perfect form of American civiliza-

tion was "destined to culminate on the shore of the Pacific." Stuart Creighton Miller, *The Unwelcome Immigrant: The American Image of the Chinese, 1785–1882* (Berkeley and Los Angeles, 1969), challenges the thesis that the anti-Chinese movement was a peculiarly California phenomenon by demonstrating that Americans in other parts of the country had held negative stereotypes of the Chinese long before any Chinese immigrants set foot on American soil. Robert McClellan, *The Heathen Chinee: A Study of American Attitudes Toward China, 1890–1905* (Athens, Ohio, 1971), also discusses the negative images of the Chinese in American literature, showing how Americans based their evaluations of the Chinese on "private needs and not upon the realities of Chinese life." Alexander Saxton, *The Indispensable Enemy: Labor and the Anti-Chinese Movement in California* (Berkeley and Los Angeles, 1971), traces the "ideological baggage" of the anti-Chinese movement to different strands of thought which shaped the Democratic and Republican parties, as well as the labor movement. By emphasizing the white workingmen's sense of displacement and deprivation in the latter half of the nineteenth century, Saxton chronicles how the anti-Chinese movement aided the skilled-crafts component of the labor movement to consolidate its own position, on the one hand, while uniting skilled and unskilled workers in a common anti-Chinese cause, on the other hand. The Chinese were perceived to be tools of monopolists, so hostility against Chinese was in part displaced hostility against those with money and power.

2. Delber W. McKee, *Chinese Exclusion Versus the Open Door Policy, 1900–1906: Clashes over China Policy in the Roosevelt Era* (Detroit, 1977); and Fred W. Riggs, *Pressures on Congress: A Study of the Repeal of Chinese Exclusion* (New York, 1950).

3. Rose Hum Lee, *The Chinese in the U.S.A.* (Hong Kong, 1960); Stanford M. Lyman, "The Structure of Chinese Society in Nineteenth-Century America" (Ph.D. dissertation, University of California, Berkeley, 1961); Stanford M. Lyman, *Chinese Americans* (New York, 1974); S. W. Kung, *Chinese in American Life: Some Aspects of Their History, Status, Problems, and Contributions* (Seattle, 1962); Betty Lee Sung, *Mountain of Gold: The Story of the Chinese in America* (New York, 1967); Francis L. K. Hsu, *The Challenge of the American Dream: The Chinese in the United States* (Belmont, Calif., 1971); and Jack Chen, *The Chinese of America* (San Francisco, 1980).

4. Among the more respectable nineteenth-century eyewitness accounts of San Francisco's Chinatown are William W. Bode, *Lights and Shadows of Chinatown* (San Francisco, 1896); Iza Duffis Hardy, *Through Cities and Prairie Land: Sketches of an American Tour* (Chicago, 1882); William H. Irwin, *Pictures of Old Chinatown by Arnold Genthe* (New York, 1908); Benjamin E. Lloyd, *Lights and Shades in San Francisco* (San Francisco, 1876); and Helen H. Jackson, *Bits of Travel at Home* (Boston, 1878). Later accounts of nineteenth-century Chinese life include Alexander McLeod, *Pigtails and Gold Dust: A Panorama of Chinese Life in Early California* (Caldwell, 1947); and Charles Morley, "The Chinese in California, as Reported by Henryk Sienkiewicz," *California Historical Society Quarterly,* XXXIV (1955), 301–316.

5. Victor G. and Brett de Bary Nee, *Longtime Californ': A Documentary Study of an American Chinatown* (New York, 1972); Chia-ling Kuo, *Social and Political Change in New York's Chinatown: The Role of Voluntary Associations* (New York, 1977); Peter Kwong, *Chinatown, New York: Labor and Politics, 1930–1950* (New York, 1979); and Bernard Wong, *Chinatown: Economic Adaptations and Ethnic Identity of the Chinese* (New York, 1982).

6. James W. Loewen, *The Mississippi Chinese: Between Black and White* (Cambridge, Mass., 1971); and Melford S. Weiss, *Valley City: A Chinese Community in America* (Cambridge, Mass., 1974).

7. The word "lived" is used only for convenience. Since the Chinese population in the American West in the nineteenth century was a highly mobile one, given the nature of the work they did, census counts of the Chinese population represent the demographic distribution only at particular points in time.

8. Glimpses of the Chinese in rural California may be found in several kinds of travellers' accounts: articles written by reporters sent out by eastern newspapers that appeared in serial form, sections on the Chinese in books written by contemporary observers, and occasional references to the Chinese in unpublished diaries and reminiscences. There is also scattered mention of the Chinese in local histories.

9. George F. Seward, *Chinese Immigration: Its Social and Economic Aspects* (New York, 1881); and Ping Chiu, *Chinese Labor in California, 1850–1880: An Economic Study* (Madison, 1967).

10. In the four scrapbooks of newspaper clippings on the Chinese collected by Hubert Howe Bancroft's assistants, only a dozen or so items out of several thousand are non-judgmental in tone. See *Bancroft Scraps*, vols. 6–9, Bancroft Library, University of California, Berkeley.

11. Among the most complete runs of manuscripts in Chinese are the business records of Chung Tai, a general merchandise firm in North San Juan, Nevada County; the business records of Wing On Wo, a firm in Dutch Flat, Placer County; and disinterment lists from the Chinese cemetery at Fiddletown, Amador County. The first two items—and less complete records of other Chinese stores and several gambling houses in rural California—are at the Bancroft Library, University of California, Berkeley, while the third item is in the Chinese American History Archives, Asian American Studies Library, University of California, Berkeley.

12. For a discussion of the value of county archival documents for researching Chinese American economic and social history, see Sucheng Chan, "Using California County Archives for Research in Chinese American History," *Annals of the Chinese Historical Society of the Pacific Northwest*, I (1983), 49–55.

13. Besides, a study of the Chinese in Butte County has already been published: Susan W. Book, *The Chinese in Butte County, California, 1860–1920* (San Francisco, 1976).

14. The 1860 census counted 34,933 Chinese, of whom 433 were below age fifteen. I am making the assumption that the 34,500 Chinese above age fifteen were gainfully employed. Of these, 24,282 were miners. There were 58,291 non-Chinese miners among 184,692 gainfully employed non-Chinese adults. U.S. Bureau of the Census, *Eighth Census of the United States: Population, 1860* (Washington, D.C., 1864), 26 and 35.

15. Chiu, *Chinese Labor in California*, 25–26.

16. Based on my tally of miners in Yuba County, the townships with relatively large numbers of Chinese miners were Long Bar Township with 494 Chinese and 250 non-Chinese miners, North-east Township with 161 Chinese and 226 non-Chinese miners, Foster Bar Township with 271 Chinese and 245 non-Chinese miners, and Slate Range Township with 272 Chinese and 538 non-Chinese miners. The townships with few Chinese were Rose Bar Township with 13 Chinese and 568 non-Chinese miners, Parks Bar Township with 27 Chinese and 196 non-Chinese miners, and New York Township with 64 Chinese and 407 non-Chinese miners. U.S. Bureau of the Census, "Eighth Census of the United States: Population, 1860" (Manuscript census for Yuba County, California).

17. The figure is based on the maximum size of Chinese miners' households enumerated in the 1860 manuscript population census and on the number of partners listed in a random sample of records of mining claims and leases of mining grounds in California's mining counties.

18. Saxton, *The Indispensable Enemy*, 53.

19. Yuba County, California, "Preemptions" (Marysville, 1856–1865), 1: 349 and 353. (All citations from county archival records will give the first page of the document only. All Chinese names are spelled as they appear in the county records. No consistent transliteration is used because it is not possible to do so without knowing what the Chinese characters are.)

20. Ibid., unnumbered pages.

21. Ibid.

22. Yuba County, California, "Preemptions" (Marysville, 1865–1881), 2: 198, 204, 217, 224, 231, 236, 307, 329, 352, and 384.

23. Ibid., 2: 198, 204, 217, 224, 230, 235, 352, and 383.

24. Ibid., 2: 198, 205, 216, 224, 231, 236, 328, 351, and 384.

25. Ibid., 2: 199, 204, 217, 225, 232, 237, and 306.

26. My tally and computation are from U.S. Bureau of the Census, "Eighth Census of the United States: Population, 1860" (Manuscript census for Sacramento, Yuba, and San Joaquin counties, California). It should be noted that my tallies do not always coincide with the figures given in the published census; after discovering numerous computation errors in the published census, I decided to trust my own counts.

27. Prostitutes have been included in the "personal service" category because their function is to satisfy the personal, sexual needs of their customers. Others may disagree with my reasoning and choose to list them either as "laborers," since their work provides profits for pimps and brothel owners, or as "professionals"— prostitution being referred to as the "oldest profession."

28. My tally and computation are from U.S. Bureau of the Census, "Eighth Census of the United States: Population, 1860" (Manuscript census for Sacramento, Yuba, and San Joaquin counties, California).

29. Varden Fuller, "The Supply of Agricultural Labor as a Factor in the Evolution of Farm Organization in California," in U.S. Senate Committee on Education and Labor, *Hearings Pursuant to Senate Resolution 266*, 76 Cong., 3 sess., Part 54, Exhibit A (1940), 19777–19898; and Carey McWilliams, *Factories in the Field: The Story of Migratory Farm Labor in California* (Boston, 1939).

30. Accounts of acts of violence against Chinese miners—some resulting in death—as reported in local newspapers were sometimes reprinted in the San Francisco press. For example, the *San Francisco Bulletin* (Dec. 18, 1856) reprinted an item from the *Shasta Republican* stating that "hundreds of Chinese" had been "slaughtered in cold blood" during the last five years by "desperados," and that Francis Blair was the first white man ever to be hanged for murdering Chinese. The *San Francisco Bulletin* (May 19, 1857) reprinted an item from the Auburn *Placer Press* reporting that Chinese miners at Kelly's Bar had been robbed by men with double-barreled guns; the writer noted that though the Chinese recognized the robbers as men who had previously robbed them at Dutch Ravine, they could not hope for justice since Chinese testimony was not accepted in court.

31. Lucie Cheng Hirata, "Free, Indentured, Enslaved: Chinese Prostitutes in Nineteenth-Century America," *Signs: Journal of Women in Culture and Society*, V (1979), 13, states that the "higher-class" prostitutes served only Chinese customers, while the "lower-class" ones served a mixed clientele of Chinese and whites. Hirata based her assertion on undocumented and somewhat casual remarks

in Charles Caldwell Dobie, *San Francisco's Chinatown* (New York, 1936), 195, 242–243.

32. There are problems with figures for the 1870 census. Chinese are listed discretely in U.S. Bureau of the Census, *Ninth Census of the United States: Population, 1870* (Washington, D.C., 1872), 722, Table XXX, column 19, but the figures there do not match those tallied by either Ping Chiu or me. Ping Chiu, who cited the same page from the same source, stated that there were 30,330 miners in 1870, of whom 17,363 were Chinese. He probably misread the published figure of 36,339 as 30,330, but there is no indication how he arrived at the figure of 17,363 since the published number was 9,087. (Chiu, *Chinese Labor in California*, 27.) According to my own count, there were 15,283 Chinese miners in the following counties: Del Norte, Klamath, Siskiyou, Trinity, and Shasta (in the Trinity-Klamath mining region), Plumas, Butte, Sierra, Yuba, Nevada, and Placer (in the northern mining region), El Dorado, Amador, Calaveras, Tuolumne, and Mariposa (in the southern mining region), and Sacramento. There were doubtless scattered clusters of Chinese miners in other counties which were not investigated; therefore, 16,000 Chinese miners is a reasonable estimate. I have used an estimated total of 43,000 miners because the number of non-Chinese miners of listed nationalities was 25,734 (sum of the nationalities listed in columns 8–18 of Table XXX cited above), the unlisted residue was 1,518, and the number of Chinese miners I counted was about 16,000. This total is about 7,000 more than the published figure of 36,339.

33. My computation has been adapted from U.S. Bureau of the Census, *Ninth Census of the United States: Population, 1870*, 722, 799. Those who use figures from the 1870 published census should realize that the subtotals given for each economic sector do not coincide with the sum of the individual occupational categories because residual categories—each containing only a small number of individuals—were not included.

34. My tally is from U.S. Bureau of the Census, "Ninth Census of the United States: Population, 1870" (Manuscript census for Sacramento, Yuba, and San Joaquin counties, California).

35. My computation is based on U.S. Bureau of the Census, *Ninth Census of the United States: Population, 1870*, 799.

36. Ibid.

37. The *Sacramento Bee* (Nov. 11, 1869) noted the presence of a "Chinese colony" whose members were successfully "cultivating the ground on a cooperative plan" on land leased from J. V. Simmons. The reporter stated that there were two white women married to two of the Chinese farmers in this group. U.S. Bureau of the Census, "Ninth Census of the United States: Productions of Agriculture, 1870" (Manuscript census for California) lists fourteen Chinese farmers—three in Franklin Township and nine in Georgiana Township, Sacramento County, and two in Merritt Township, Yolo County. These farmers grew Irish and sweet potatoes as well as vegetables on farms ranging from 25 to 340 acres in size.

38. Sacramento County, California, "Leases" (Sacramento, 1853–1923), B: 95.

39. The tenure status of farmers was given in U.S. Bureau of the Census, "Tenth Census of the United States: Productions of Agriculture, 1880" (Manuscript census). By matching the names of owner-operators against plat maps of Sacramento County in the California State Archives, it is possible to determine the locations of owner-operated farms—almost all of which were found on the natural levees along the rims of the delta's islands and mainland tracts.

40. My tally and computation are from U.S. Bureau of the Census, "Ninth Census of the United States: Population, 1870" (Manuscript census for Sacramento

County, California).

41. Ibid. (Manuscript census for San Joaquin and Yuba counties).

42. Ibid.

43. As indicated in the manuscript census, Chinese servants and cooks in rural California almost invariably lived either in the households of white families or in their own households. For that reason, I think I am justified in assuming that almost all of them worked for white employers. Kwong, *Chinatown, New York*, 38, made a statement which is puzzling: "They had little capital, yet wanted work that would avoid dependence on either white employers or workers. Service jobs—as laundrymen, domestic servants, workers in Chinese restaurants—fitted these requirements." In my view, domestic servants cannot be lumped together with laundrymen and restaurant workers because a very large portion of Chinese servants worked for white employers. The situation in San Francisco and New York may have differed from rural California because of a smaller percentage of live-in servants. Not having analyzed the San Francisco and New York manuscript census data, I cannot say if this was in fact the case. If it was, then such urban day-servants would indeed have interacted with their white masters less since they did not live in their employers' households.

44. My tally and computation are from U.S. Bureau of the Census, "Tenth Census of the United States: Population, 1880" (Manuscript census for Sacramento, Yuba, and San Joaquin counties).

45. "Slickens" (sediment) from hydraulic mining in the 1860s through 1880s raised riverbeds and greatly increased the probability of floods, while simultaneously ruining the topsoil of the flooded areas. The Sacramento–San Joaquin Delta is an inverted delta which provides the only outlet to the sea for both the Sacramento and San Joaquin rivers. The peat islands and tracts of the delta were constantly subjected to flooding. When natural or man-made levees broke, the centers of the islands, known as the backswamps, would flood first since they were lower than the surrounding levees, and they sometimes took years to drain. Crop losses during certain years were total.

46. This information has been drawn from numerous leases in Yuba, Sutter, and Tehama counties.

47. My tally is from U.S. Bureau of the Census, "Tenth Census of the United States: Population, 1880" (Manuscript census for Sacramento and San Joaquin counties).

48. In the Sutter-Yuba basin, the average size of farms leased by Chinese tenants ranged from 94 acres in 1881 to 842 acres in 1875. The Chinese tenant who operated on a larger scale for a longer period of time than any of his compatriots was Chin Lung, who farmed the San Joaquin Delta from the 1890s until the end of World War I.

49. In 1880, 60 percent of the Chinese farm laborers in Sacramento County and 30 percent of those in San Joaquin County lived in the households of Chinese farmers; in 1900, the percentages were 52 and 82, respectively. These percentages are based on my tally and computation from U.S. Bureau of the Census, "Tenth Census of the United States: Population, 1880" and "Twelfth Census of the United States: Population, 1900" (Manuscript census for Sacramento and San Joaquin counties). No tally can be done for 1890 since the 1890 manuscript census was destroyed in a fire in the U.S. Department of Commerce building in 1921.

50. My tally and computation are from U.S. Bureau of the Census, "Tenth Census of the United States: Population, 1880" (Manuscript census for Sacramento, Yuba, and San Joaquin counties).

FURTHER READING

Barth, Gunther. *Bitter Strength: A History of the Chinese in the United States, 1850–1870.* 1964.

Beesley, David. "From Chinese to Chinese American: Chinese Women and Families in a Sierra Nevada Town." *California History* 67 (September 1988): 168–179.

Chan, Sucheng. *Asian Americans: An Interpretive History.* 1991.

———. *Asian Californians.* 1991.

———. *This Bittersweet Soil: The Chinese in California Agriculture, 1860–1910.* 1986.

"The Chinese in California." Special issue. *California History* 57 (Spring 1978).

Chiu, Ping. *Chinese Labor in California, 1850–1880: An Economic Study.* 1967.

Daniels, Roger. *Asian America: Chinese and Japanese in the United States Since 1850.* 1988.

———. *The Politics of Prejudice: The Anti-Japanese Movement in California and the Struggle for Exclusion.* 1977.

Friday, Chris. "Asian American Labor and Historical Interpretation." *Labor History* 35 (Fall 1994): 524–546.

Lydon, Sandy. *Chinese Gold: The Chinese in the Monterey Bay Area.* 1985.

Minnick, Sylvia Sun. *Samfow: The San Joaquin Chinese Legacy.* 1988.

Takaki, Ronald. *A Different Mirror: A History of Multicultural America.* Chapter 8. 1993.

———. *Strangers from a Different Shore: A History of Asian Americans.* 1989.

Young, Zo Kil. *Chinese Emigration into the United States, 1850–1880.* 1979.

2

WORKERS AND GROUP IDENTITY

3 Dishing It Out

Waitresses and the Making of Their Unions in San Francisco, 1900–1941

Dorothy Sue Cobble

EDITOR'S INTRODUCTION

The contagious spread of trade unionism in early-twentieth-century San Francisco was not confined to skilled male workers; unskilled and semi-skilled workers also achieved a considerable degree of organization. As early as 1902, there were two thousand organized culinary workers in San Francisco, a significant and growing number of them female waitresses. The waitresses of San Francisco founded the first California affiliate of the Hotel Employees and Restaurant Employees International Union (HERE) in 1901. Subsequently, the problems of operating in a union with men led the San Francisco waitresses to form one of the first separate locals in the country in 1906.

The fortunes of HERE, and those of the women within the union, waxed and waned in the early decades of the twentieth century. By the late 1930s, however, the majority of hotels and motels were union houses, and 95 percent of the twenty-five hundred restaurants were organized.

In this extract from her book *Dishing It Out: Waitresses and Their Unions in the Twentieth Century*, Dorothy Sue Cobble explores the vicissitudes of women's trade unionism from the early twentieth century until World War II. She argues that from the outset waitresses defined their goals in explicitly self-conscious ways, announcing their intention to "further the rights of working women" and to bring about economic and political equality with men. Like male waiters, they had a deep sense of craft identity that was crucial to the success of their organizing efforts. During the 1930s, Cobble contends, the success of the longshoremen's strike, in particular, helped to galvanize both male and female restaurant workers. With its eighteen thousand members, the union also helped to organize some of San Francisco's largest downtown department stores.

◆　◆　◆

[Where] waitresses' unions are strong, the business is on a high plane, the hard work fairly paid and the working women who are engaged in it are self-respecting and respected by all who know them. They are distinctly high class, and so it can be here, if the girls will get together and work.

　—Anonymous journalist writing for the *Independent* in 1908

We are all working as we never did before, and our days and hours are forgotten. Our feet are sore, our bones ache, our throats are tired, but we feel great because we are getting something done.

　—Gertrude Sweet, International organizer, HERE, April 13, 1937

The historic barriers to female unionism before the 1930s were formidable: women's lack of permanent wage status, the ambivalence emanating from a trade union movement overwhelmingly male, the class tensions between female wage earners and their elite sisterly allies, and the objective difficulties in organizing "unskilled" workers with little strike leverage.[1] Moreover, as recent scholars have argued, many women workers may have preferred to exert collective power in ways other than unionization.[2] Yet waitresses not only chose unionization as their vehicle for expressing militancy, but they also managed to build all-female union institutions in these early years that provided them with an impressive degree of power and dignity.

Waitresses turned to unionization as early as the 1880s, forming separate all-female unions as well as locals that included male waiters and other food service crafts. With the help of the Federated Trades Council of San Francisco and the International Workingmen's Association, San Francisco waitresses organized a separate local on May 25, 1886, while Los Angeles waitresses united with male culinary workers in requesting that the White Cooks, Waiters and Employees Protective Union of the Pacific Coast charter a mixed-gender and craft local. Many of these earliest locals affiliated briefly with the Knights of Labor, but by the mid-1890s most had either disbanded or cast their lot with the newly emerging American Federation of Labor (AFL).[3]

In April of 1891, the AFL chartered the Waiters and Bartenders National Union with an initial membership of 450. The Waiters and Bartenders

National Union, later to change its name to the Hotel Employees and Restaurant Employees International Union (HERE), made little progress until the first years of the twentieth century: in 1899 the total membership of the union had not passed a thousand. By World War I, however, membership climbed to sixty-five thousand: HERE had established itself as a permanent fixture in the industry.[4] The Industrial Workers of the World also experimented with organizing the "foodstuff" industry in this era but with notably meager results. IWW culinary locals sprang up in a few Western IWW-dominated mining and lumbering towns, and the IWW inspired strikes in New York and other immigrant centers, but their organizations were short-lived and geared primarily to male waiters and cooks.[5]

Choosing Separatism

Substantial gains in organizing female culinary workers did not occur until after the founding of separate HERE-affiliated waitress organizations. The first permanent waitress union, Local 240 in Seattle, received its charter on March 31, 1900. Over the next decade, HERE waitress organizations took root in at least a half dozen other communities. By the World War I era, at the height of the movement for separate female organizations, more than seventeen permanent waitress locals existed, and approximately 70 percent of organized HERE waitresses belonged to separate locals.

The impetus for separate gender organization among women workers has been poorly understood by scholars. Although many unions barred women from membership or relegated them to second-class citizenship, separate-gender organization was not merely a product of nor a reaction to the discrimination of male workers. In many industries, the sex segregation of work decreed that membership in locals organized by trade or department would be either predominantly one sex or the other. Moreover, although a consensus on separatism as a strategy never existed among working women, in certain periods and in certain trades, women themselves pushed for separate-sex organizations.[6]

Waitresses had strong affinity for separatism. They initiated numerous separate locals before the 1930s, and their commitment to separatism sustained many of these locals into the 1970s. In part, their preference for separatism derived from their ethnic and cultural orientations. As Susan Glenn has suggested, Americanized, native-born women tended to be greater supporters of separatism because of their unencumbrance with the strong community and class ties of recent immigrant women and their closer connection with the native-born variety of feminism rooted in the separate-spheres traditions of American middle-class womanhood.[7] The

particular workplace experiences and family status of waitresses also nour-
ished their inclinations to organize autonomous, all-female locals—locals
that could address "female" concerns and provide women with an "initiating," leadership role.

The desire of waitresses for separate organization prevailed over the
mixed-gender model suggested by the organization of food service work.
In contrast to many workplaces where divisions along sex and craft lines
were synonymous, female and male servers belonged to the same craft.
Simply following the craft logic of the food service workplace would have
resulted in a mixed-sex craft division in which waiters and waitresses belonged to the same craft local. The formation of separate waitress locals
necessitated a rationale beyond craft identity: the legitimacy of gender
concerns had to be put forward.

Moreover, female culinary workers faced opposition from male unionists who supported integrating women into mixed-sex locals or organizing
them into separate but subordinate branches of the male local. A separate,
autonomous female local would create problems. Some men feared conflict
over wage scales, work rules, and distribution of jobs; others were reluctant to lose dues-paying members.[8] The International union pursued neutrality: it officially encouraged organization by craft "regardless of race,
color, sex, or nationality" but allowed for the formation of separate organizations based on race and sex. Section 49 of the 1905 HERE Constitution
read: "there shall not be more than one white or colored local of the same
craft in any city or town, except waitresses who may obtain a charter." In
short, women workers had to take the initiative in establishing their own
locals, and they did so.[9]

Organized male culinary workers seldom erected formal constitutional
barriers to the entry of women, but their reluctance to organize women
retarded the growth of waitress organizations and at times was as much of
an obstacle as the hostility of employers. Women HERE members from
their first days of union participation appealed to their male counterparts
for organizing support, but the majority of men resisted these calls to action until the 1930s.

The problems of operating within mixed locals led San Francisco waitresses to conclude that their interests as women trade unionists would be
better served through separate-sex organizations where they could define
their own organizational goals and practices. Much to the surprise of the
waiter officials of San Francisco's Local 30, not only the bartenders but
"the waitresses too" began "asking for an organization" in 1901. By April,
sixty-three waitresses had formed a branch of the waiters' union; five

years later, having "decided that a separate organization was desirable," they petitioned their male co-workers for "a local of their own." Once the waiters voted approval, the new two hundred and fifty member local installed its first officers on February 21, 1906.[10]

The San Francisco local enjoyed continuity and vigor in its principal leaders. The waitresses elected Minnie Andrews as president and first business agent. Andrews guided the local through its first decade, later becoming one of the first women organizers on the International staff. Louise Downing LaRue—a firebrand agitator for women's suffrage and a veteran officer of the mixed culinary locals in St. Louis and San Francisco—took a leading role as did Maud Younger, a native-born San Francisco heiress (known locally as the "millionaire waitress") who devoted her life to suffrage and social reform. By the 1920s and 1930s, the reins of leadership passed to Montana-born Frankie Behan, a 1922 transfer from Seattle who served as an officer into the 1950s, and Lettie Howard, who devoted thirty-nine years to the union, broken only by her absence in 1919 when she helped organize waitresses in Los Angeles. There were others such as Julia Marguerite Finkenbinder, Elizabeth Kelley, and Laura Molleda, almost all of whom were native born and of Northern European background.[11]

The first waitress locals encountered considerable obstacles in sustaining their fledgling organizations. In addition to the ambivalence of their own culinary brothers, they faced bitter feuds with employers, condescension from middle-class "uplift" or moral reform groups, and divisions in their own ranks. Nevertheless, many locals weathered these trials and established themselves permanently in the industry.

Typically, female locals faced their greatest battles with employers after they demonstrated significant bargaining power. Employers often underestimated the organizational potential of their female employees and, taken by surprise, were forced to grant concessions. These initial union victories, however, sparked employer counterorganization and open-shop campaigns.

The San Francisco waitresses in their first two decades experienced cycles of advance followed by employer backlash and defeat. After the union began pressing for the ten-hour day in 1901, the local Restaurant Keepers Association gained the backing of the San Francisco Employer Association and precipitated a strike. After enjoining union picketing, the owners held out for six months, operating their restaurants with scab labor. The union lost considerable membership—union waitresses had trouble getting jobs, and some were forced to leave town or assume false names—but the local followed the strike defeat with a remarkable period of rebuilding. In part, the unprecedented surge in membership resulted from the waitresses' decision to pursue "more subtle means than direct action," according to one early authority on the union. The Waitress Union dedicated itself to an educational campaign that brought results in both working conditions and increased membership. Although many restaurants refused to bargain or sign agreements, by May of 1902, a handful of establishments instituted working conditions in conformity with the standard 1902 Waitress Wage Scales and Working Agreement: employment of union members only; six-day week; and $8 a week for day work, $9 for night work. In December 1903, the waitresses survived a second open-shop campaign and lockout by the employers. With the assistance of Mayor Eugene Schmitz, recently elected by San Francisco's Union Labor party, they emerged victorious with a new one-year agreement that reduced hours to nine a day.[12]

By the time the separate waitress charter became official in 1906, union waitresses had signed up a majority of their co-workers. Relying on "silent picketing" to foil court injunctions and the new union strategy of "monthly working buttons" worn conspicuously by all union waitresses—an idea that can "accomplish . . . what the Union label has secured for the printers and other craftsmen"—the local steadily increased its numbers and influence, even adding cafeteria waitresses to its ranks after 1910.[13] In 1916, however, when San Francisco culinary workers struck for the eight-hour day, the employers regained the upper hand. The strike, dubbed a "complete failure" by more than one analyst, was called off after three months, but not before membership defections left the Waitress Union reeling. In particular, the cafeteria women disregarded the strike order and remained on the job. As a result, the Waitress Union lost the cafeteria workers and did not regain them until the 1930s.[14]

Some waitress locals disappeared completely during these years. In New York City, Waitresses' Local 769 had the support of the Women's Trade Union League (WTUL) and such well-known reformers as San Francisco's Maud Younger, but it went under in 1908 after only a few years of activity.[15] In 1912 and 1913, the International Hotel Workers Union, a syndicalist-inspired, independent organization, agitated among New York's hotel and restaurant workers, drawing in a few waitresses. IWW organizers Elizabeth Gurley Flynn and Joseph Ettor, who lent their talents to the organization, urged novel tactics such as exposing adulterated food and "scientific sabotage"—defined variously as dropping trays of food on the floor, spilling "gravy on the shirt-fronts of well-dressed patrons," and confusing orders—but few if any concessions were wrested from employers. The WTUL picked up the refrain for a separate waitress union in 1914, but a credible organization was not in place until 1919.[16]

Waitress unionism revived during World War I. Long-established HERE locals gathered steam, and new HERE units such as Local 729, representing the employees of the Harvey eating houses, sprang to life. In Minneapolis, department store waitresses held out for $9 a day and a guaranteed return to their posts in the tea room, preferring "to be silent picket[s] and pace the sidewalk with [their] message than be turned into inexperienced and inefficient glove or ribbon sales[women]."[17]

Most locals incurred losses in the labor turmoil following the war, but by the mid-twenties membership resumed its upward spiral. By 1927, female membership in HERE had more than quadrupled from pre–World War I figures. Women now represented more than a fifth of the total membership of the International union, a sizable leap from 5.4 percent in 1910 and 9.3 percent in 1920,[18] and for the first time, women outnumbered men in some of the mixed culinary unions, prompting workers in the industry to label these communities "girls' towns."[19] These changes resulted partially from the resiliency of the female unions during this period and the feminization of food service work; the declining vitality of the male-dominated locals also contributed to the changing sex ratio.

The advent of Prohibition and the employer campaigns of the 1920s cut deeply into the male membership of HERE. Having peaked in 1918, the number of male culinary unionists dropped precipitously after the passage of the 18th Amendment and plunged downward throughout the 1920s, hitting bottom in 1933. The 18th Amendment, in effect nationwide by January 1920, wrecked the all-male bartending constituency within the union. Numerous waiter and cook locals also folded up for lack of membership and finances. After the passage of Prohibition, employers who previously had been sympathetic to unionism because of the higher profit margins accompanying liquor service adopted tough bargaining stances. Speakeasies, operating in a subterranean fashion, did not yield to traditional organizing methods. The public attention generated by unionization usually resulted in the bar or restaurant closing.[20] In addition to these industry-specific problems, the union faced a climate inhospitable to any brand of unionism. The American Plan destroyed locals across the country, and employers' liberal use of court injunctions, yellow-dog contracts, and employer-dominated culinary associations stymied union advance at point after point.[21]

In addition to facing the hostility of employers and the lackluster support of potential allies, waitress unionists contended with internal divisions

among their own ranks. Before the New Deal, some white waitresses—
fully 90 percent of the trade in this period—reached out to black and Asian
women, but on the whole, their attitude was ambivalent and even hostile.
Female culinary activists were neither more nor less progressive on this issue than their brother unionists.

Most white waitress officials, like their male counterparts, encouraged
black women either to form separate black waitress locals or to join mixed-
gender all-black locals. Separate locals of black waitresses sprang up in
Philadelphia in 1918 and in Atlantic City in 1919.[22] A small number of
waitress locals also accepted black women, at least temporarily. The
Chicago waitresses in their earliest days organized black women and white
into the same local, and the Butte Women's Protective Union (WPU)
prided itself in "not drawing the color line"—in 1907 three of their members were from "the colored race." But most, like San Francisco, restricted
union membership to "white women only" until the 1930s.[23]

In contrast to the ambiguous policy toward blacks, culinary unionists
preached a stridently unambivalent message to Asian workers: they were
unwelcome in the industry and in the union. The stated International position was that "no member of our International be permitted to work with
asiatics, and that no house card or bar card or union button be displayed in
such a place." For years, the frontispiece of the national culinary magazine
proclaimed, "Skilled, Well-paid Bartenders and Culinary Workers Wear
Them [union buttons]. Chinks, Japs, and Incompetent Labor Don't." Indeed,
one of the most promising organizing strategies in this period was to gain
sympathy for union labor by advertising the link between union-made products and white labor. Local unions frequently reported successful boycotts of
restaurants employing Asian help and the subsequent implementation of
contracts requiring the discharge of all Asian workers. Restaurant owners
simply were not allowed to bring their Asian employees into the union.[24]

Female culinary activists shared these prejudices against Asian workers. Waitress organizer Delia Hurley spent a considerable amount of her
time speaking to unionists in other trades, beseeching them to honor
HERE boycotts of restaurants employing Chinese and Japanese help. "We
laid special stress on the injury these people were doing our organization,
and that the members of our local were being dispensed with . . . through
the inability of proprietors . . . to compete with these chinks." In Butte,
where in the 1890s a successful union-led boycott of establishments employing Chinese had reduced the numbers of Chinese in the service trades,
the WPU still refused house cards to the popular Chinese "noodle par-
lours" in the 1920s and insisted that white girls seek employment only in

non-Asian restaurants. Women HERE leaders spoke fervently against a resolution introduced in the 1920s by San Francisco's Hugo Ernst that would have allowed admittance of Asians who were American citizens. Ernst's resolution was resoundingly defeated.[25]

Nonetheless, because only a small proportion of waitresses were black or Asian, the exclusionary policies practiced by most female locals did not interfere substantially with the successful organizing of white waitresses. Exclusionary waiter and cook unions suffered more from unorganized nonwhite competitors than did waitress locals because employers who hired black and Asian front-service personnel preferred men. In fact, in the short run, racial exclusionary policies may have solidified the ranks of white waitresses and hence facilitated their organizing.

Divisions among waitresses based on marital status, economic circumstance, and age hampered the organization of white waitresses more than cultural or ethnic divisions. Time and again, veteran organizers complained of the antiunion attitudes of the part-time married workers, the young waitresses, and the summer-only workers. After years of organizing, Hurley realized "the injury being done our organization by a certain set of women workers, viz, the short day workers, of whom most are married women who pretend they are only using their spare time, and have no desire to do anything that would further the interest of women workers." Another waitress organizer defined the problem as the naiveté of younger women who, upon first entering the trade, considered their work outside the home to be temporary. The new workers are young and "don't feel much responsibility for what happens to other people, and they don't look far ahead. 'It isn't worthwhile to join the union,' they say, 'because we will soon get married and quit working.' That's what they think now. A lot of them come back later, and want a job, and then they see what it means to the older women who still must work." According to a waitress business agent in Atlantic City, two classes of women undermined standards there: the school teachers working temporarily over the summer and "the kind . . . very popular with the men folks" that she chose not to describe by name.[26]

Nevertheless, waitress organizations suffered less from this problem than women's locals in other trades. The majority of waitresses not only worked year-round and full-time but also perceived their work status as permanent and their work as essential to their economic survival and that of their families. This economic stake in their work underlay their trade identification and made it one of the more significant allegiances in their lives. Moreover, the impact of part-time and summer workers was minimized by their peripheral status in the trade. Significantly, the short-hour girls were married or living at home, whereas the long-hour girls were self-supporting single or divorced women.[27] This segregation of the industry by family and economic status meant that waitresses with "problem attitudes" were concentrated in certain peripheral sectors and were not a factor in organizing campaigns involving year-round hotels or full-service restaurants in which the staff was predominantly long-hour employees. "One-meal girls" did not compete directly with the long-hour waitresses and rarely were used as replacements in strike situations; in large part, they were not available or did not desire full-time employment.

In sum, although waitress solidarity was strained and sometimes broken by internal dissension, waitresses succeeded in forging sufficient unity to sustain unionism. In some circumstances, the union-oriented majority ignored the dissenters in their ranks and organized despite the disinterest of their "problem" co-workers. In other situations, white waitresses chose to exclude their Asian and black co-workers and organized in opposition to their nonwhite sisters. Nevertheless, in some notable instances, such as in Chicago, the ties of craft and gender overcame the differences of race, ethnicity, age, and family status, uniting all the sisters in the craft.

Victories on the Political Front

Unlike their brother AFL unionists, waitresses devoted a considerable portion of their energies to the pursuit of protective legislation in the pre–New Deal era. Many actively lobbied for maximum hour legislation and minimum wage laws.[28] Thus, they were not adverse to parting ways with the larger labor movement and asserting what they perceived as the particular interests of their craft and of their sex. They were pragmatists, however, rather than ideologues. The survival of their organization took precedence over advancing the interests of working-class women as a whole. Moreover, their position on protective legislation was determined by the economic, political, and social circumstances in which they operated rather than deriving from an overarching, universal belief concerning the role of the state. Where they perceived the law as beneficial to their trade, their support held firm. In other less propitious instances, they condemned protective laws. In short, waitresses were neither voluntarist nor antivoluntarist in regard to legislative matters, but adjusted their philosophy to the exigencies of their particular situation. By winning victories in the legislative arena, waitress locals demonstrated their effectiveness as reform organizations and created among unorganized waitresses a new respect for the power of collective activity.

Waitresses needed little prompting to join the movement for maximum hour legislation that peaked in the decade before World War I. Indeed, although middle-class women's organizations spearheaded the campaign nationwide, waitresses and their sisters in working-class female organizations took the lead in states such as Washington, California, and Illinois. Waitress activists initiated legislative reform, shepherded bills through their state legislatures, and in many cases celebrated ensuing victories.[29]

In California, working women such as Hannah Nolan of the Laundry Workers' Union, Margaret Seaman of the Garment Workers, and Louise LaRue of the Waitresses were the chief speakers in favor of passage of the 1911 hours bill. Their principal arguments centered on preserving the health of working women, reducing the percentage of workers with tuberculosis, and protecting women's child-bearing functions. When the hotel proprietors challenged the law in court, winning a victory in the California lower courts, Louise LaRue responded: "We are sorry he [the lower court judge] isn't a woman and had to walk 10 to 12 hours a day and carry several pounds . . . , then perhaps he would realize that not half of the women who work in dining rooms are in condition physically to become mothers of the future generation."[30]

In contrast to the enthusiasm shown over maximum hour laws, waitresses were less certain of the advantages of minimum wage legislation. The majority of locals supported it, but some vacillated, dramatically shifting their stance toward wage legislation in the course of their activities.[31] The twists and turns in the positions taken by waitresses in California clearly reveal how economic concerns undergirded waitress union policy.

After initially opposing the concept, California waitresses came to favor minimum wage laws by the 1920s. When the San Francisco Labor Council voted against the minimum wage in 1913, the loudest opposition came from delegates representing women workers: garment workers, waitresses, and laundry workers. San Francisco waitresses did not dispute the arguments of minimum wage proponents that the health of working women and their competency as future mothers would be enhanced; they simply found the protection of their own trade union organization more compelling. Joining in the general negative consensus of male unionists from AFL president Samuel Gompers to local AFL officials, they argued that "any minimum established by law would certainly be lower than that established by the unions, thus tending to undermine the union scales." Such legislation, they reasoned, "would prove a detriment to the only practical method of improving the conditions of the working women, namely organization." Significantly, waitresses also feared that a minimum wage for women would mean female job loss because women "are fitted to perform, without previous experience and study, but very few avocations" and must rely on situations where "job training is provided, but little in the way of cash compensation."[32]

Ignoring the objections raised by both unions and employers, the California public voted in favor of the legislation in a 1913 referendum election, and soon thereafter organized labor began vying with employers over the control of the Industrial Welfare Commission (IWC)—the five-person board given jurisdiction over maximum hours, minimum wages, and working conditions. Waitresses' Local 48 joined with the San Francisco Labor Council, Millinery Workers, Laundry Workers, Bakery Workers, League of Women Voters, and the YWCA to form the Committee for Enforcement of the Minimum Wage. Much to their surprise, they found they could obtain acceptable standards and that the commission was committed to aggressive enforcement of those standards. They also discovered that state regulation of minimum standards neither inhibited organizing sentiments nor depressed union wage scales. In fact, after the IWC passed its first wage order governing hotel and restaurant employees in 1919, organized labor negotiated one of its better contracts. The first IWC minimum, set higher than the current union wage scale, could be used effectively as a public indictment of the low wage rates in the service trades.[33]

Union support of protective legislation enhanced labor's appeal among its own members as well as among the unorganized. Because wage-and-hour orders were less frequently violated by union employers, that fact became one more argument in favor of organizing. In houses that employed members of the Waitresses' Union the law was never violated, Bee Tumber, a prominent Southern California waitress officer, pointed out in 1924. "The girls receive their wages in real money instead of 'charge offs' for meals [and] laundry." They have "good food served them," and above all it is "possible to have improper conditions remedied by the representative of the union." Organized workers received the protection of the collective bargaining agreement and the advantage of an outside organization that would ensure legislative standards were met.[34]

Although the majority of California organized labor continued to oppose the minimum wage, by the mid-1920s the waitress organizations broke publicly with their brother unionists. When the state supreme court heard arguments concerning the constitutionality of the legislation, Waitresses' Local 639 in Los Angeles, along with other female wage-earner organizations, filed briefs in support of the law. Waitresses had seen how government regulation could work for them, not against them. They moved from being leading opponents of government interference with wages to being staunch defenders.[35] In short, rather than relying on abstract principles in forming their positions, waitresses stayed close to the lessons taught by experience.

Before the 1930s, then, waitress unionists made limited but significant breakthroughs in both the collective bargaining and legislative arenas. Relying primarily on their own tenacity, ingenuity, and organizational strength, their accomplishments were piecemeal in scope and were often lost in bitter strikes or hostile court decisions. But unlike women in many other trades, waitresses established permanent institutions dedicated to the uplift of their craft. After 1930, assisted by a radically different social climate and a labor movement aggressively extending its organizational sway, waitresses finally wrested a decent standard of living from their employers and extended those standards to large numbers of female service workers.

Described in 1930 as little more than "an association of coffin societies," the labor movement confounded critics by its unprecedented expansion over the next two decades, adding fifteen million members by the early 1950s.[36] Culinary workers were not immune to the union fever: HERE nearly doubled its membership in 1933, the first heady year of New Deal legislation favoring unionization. Membership spurted ahead during the sit-downs of 1936 and 1937, and again during the war years. By the end of the decade HERE membership topped four hundred thousand, with a quarter of all hotel and restaurant workers organized.

As the International union matured into a substantial power within the hotel and restaurant industry, its membership became increasingly female. The percentage of women within the union doubled after 1930, climbing to 45 percent by 1950. Waitress locals aggressively reached out to unorganized waitresses in hotels, cafeterias, drugstores, and department stores; many waiters' locals opened their doors to female servers for the first time; and the new industrial hotel locals swept in large numbers of waitresses, chambermaids, female cashiers, checkers, and kitchen workers. By the late 1940s, more than two hundred thousand female culinary workers were organized, with close to a quarter of these within separate waitress organizations.[37]

The upsurge of unionism among waitresses undoubtedly was linked to larger societal forces that affected all workers: the more favorable public policy toward labor, the breakthroughs in organizing tactics and strategy on the part of the Congress of Industrial Organizations (CIO), and the enhanced bargaining leverage of workers during World War II. But this general picture cannot fully explain the growth of waitress unionism. After all, other groups of women workers, notably from the clerical and retail sector, failed in bringing permanent, widespread unionization to their industry.

The recovery of organized strength among culinary workers occurred first among male workers, primarily bartenders, and waiters. The repeal of Prohibition in December 1933 boosted male membership as restaurants added the serving of hard liquor and as soda fountains, creameries, and lunch stands metamorphosed into taverns and cocktail lounges. *Catering Industry Employee,* HERE's national journal, proudly announced that union house and bar cards "swing in perfect rhythm with the ceiling revolving fans of local beer gardens. Banned during prohibition days because their presence would uncover the close links between speakeasies and the Bartenders' Union, the displays . . . now hold prominent places."[38]

HERE organizing campaigns also benefited from the passage of the National Industrial Recovery Act in 1933. Like the mining and garment unions, HERE sought to influence New Deal legislation and exploit the situation for organizing purposes. In the case of the restaurant code, HERE lobbied National Recovery Administration (NRA) chief Hugh Johnson, threatened a strike if the codes were not revised upward, and testified at hearing after hearing along with the Amalgamated Food Workers (AFW), the Food Workers Industrial Union (FWIU), the Women's Trade Union League (WTUL), and the Women's Bureau.[39]

The NRA codes sparked organization in the culinary industry because they raised hopes of improved wages and working conditions, yet failed miserably in delivering on these promises. The problem was twofold: the codes themselves, largely determined by employers, were substandard; and employers violated even these barest of employee protections because the government gave little evidence of either having the will or the ability to uphold code standards. According to San Francisco waiter official Hugo Ernst, if employers in that city adopted the governmental standards, working conditions would be "as bad as those thirty years ago."[40]

The Fruits of Solidarity

In San Francisco, waitresses enjoyed not only a long tradition of separate-sex organizing among workers and city residents, but also a solid union consciousness that resurfaced with a vengeance in the 1930s.[41] Waitresses' Local 48 organized first in restaurants patronized by union clientele, spread its drives to restaurants outside working-class neighborhoods, swept up cafeteria, drugstore, and tea-room waitresses, and then embraced waitresses employed in the large downtown hotels and department stores. By 1941, waitresses in San Francisco had achieved almost complete organization of their trade, and Local 48 became the largest waitress local in the country. Their success resulted from a combination of factors: an exceptionally powerful local labor movement; sympathetic, fair-minded male co-workers within the Local Joint Executive Board (LJEB); and the existence of a waitress organization committed first and foremost to organizing and representing female servers.

In the early 1930s, Local 48 confronted unrelenting employer pressure for wage reductions and lowered standards. Delighted by the meager standards set by the NRA codes, restaurateurs replaced their union house cards with the Blue Eagle insignia (indicating compliance with government recommendations), lowered wages, and reverted to the fifty-four-hour week.[42]

In response, Local 48 informed the owners that the five-day, forty-hour week was the union standard, and, in conjunction with the other culinary crafts, they picketed some 284 restaurants in 1933 alone. They sidestepped restrictive local picketing ordinances by "selling" labor newspapers in front of targeted eating establishments during peak business hours. The attorney for one distraught employer complained to the judge that "the women walked back and forth in front of the plaintiff's restaurant, and prominently displayed newspapers bearing the headline in large black letters 'Organized Labor' and 'Labor Clarion,' and each of said women called out repeatedly in a loud, shrill, penetrating voice, at the rate of 30 to 40 times a minute, 'organized labor' 'organized labor.'"[43]

Culinary workers also resisted wage cuts in the hotels. After two years of reductions totaling 20 percent, the cooks struck the leading hotels in April 1934. The San Francisco LJEB considered calling a general strike of all culinary workers in San Francisco, but Edward Flore, assisted by federal mediators, convinced employers to submit the cooks' dispute to an arbitration board.[44]

Less than two months after the first discussion of an industrywide strike, culinary union members voted 1,991 to 52 to join the emerging citywide shutdown on behalf of striking maritime workers. Outraged over the death of two workers—one of whom was a cook and member of Local 44—during a bloody clash between police and picketers who had gathered in support of striking longshoremen, the San Francisco labor movement brought business to a standstill for three days. In the end, they secured collective bargaining in the maritime industry. The solidarity and militancy displayed by the culinary locals was typical. The International union wired sanction for an industrywide sympathy strike, and culinary crews

walked out 100 percent at midnight on Sunday, July 15. The few nonunion
houses that dared open the following Monday morning closed their doors
after "a little persuasion." Only two restaurants on Third Street where
strikers ate—operated by people "apparently very close to the labor movement"—were in operation.[45]

Relying on the labor unity that prevailed among San Francisco unions
in the aftermath of the 1934 General Strike, the waitresses' local doubled
its membership over the next four years. They received general assistance
from the Teamsters, the needle-trades workers pressured the kosher bars
into compliance, and the printers, streetcarmen, longshoremen, and maritime trades organized the restaurants and bars adjacent to their work sites.
Culinary spokespeople acknowledged their dependence: "There is a much
better spirit of cooperation than formerly and the Culinary Workers have
profited from it. We are indebted to the Maritime Unions and . . . in fact all
the unions pull with us whenever we go to them with our troubles, thus
our brothers did not give their lives for nothing."[46]

During the heady days of 1936 and 1937, organizing reached a fever
pitch stimulated by the successful sit-down strikes in auto and other industries and the Supreme Court's favorable ruling on the constitutionality
of the Wagner Act. San Francisco waitresses moved from their base in
small independent restaurants to tackle campaigns in drugstore and 5 and
10 cent store lunch counters; in cafeterias and self-service chains; and in
department store restaurants and the dining rooms of the major San Francisco hotels. The most significant breakthrough came as a result of the San
Francisco hotel strike of 1937. The strike, which brought union recognition and a written contract covering workers in fifty-five hotels, inaugu-
rated a new chapter in culinary unionism in San Francisco. With the backing of the San Francisco Labor Council (SFLC) and the promise from such
pivotal unions as the butchers, bakers, teamsters, musicians, and stationary engineers not to cross the lines, three thousand hotel employees, one-
third of whom were women, walked out on May 1, shutting down fifteen
San Francisco hotels simultaneously.[47]

From the outset, the strikers were exceptionally well organized. "The
union moved with military precision," wrote the federal mediator, "set up
their strike headquarters [and] organized their picket squads, each squad
consisting of one representative of each of the unions involved." As workers came off the job, they were handed printed cards bearing strike and
picket instructions. Picket duty lasted for four continuous hours; failure to
picket meant loss of one's job once the strike was settled. Margaret Werth,
the waitress business agent assigned to the hotels, organized militant

waitress picket lines and achieved notable results with her waitress parade and beauty contest. After eighty-nine days of effective mass picketing that closed off the hotels to food delivery and arriving guests, a back-to-work settlement was signed involving fifty-five San Francisco hotels. The unions gained wage increases of 20 percent for most employees, equal pay for waiters and waitresses, preferential hiring with maintenance of membership, the eight-hour day, and union work rules for all crafts. For a generation of food service workers, the curtain rang down on the open-shop era with resounding finality.[48]

After this victory, the union soon reached a separate four-year agreement with the majority of small hotels in the city. Next they secured recognition from the Owl Drug Company chain, operating eleven stores in San Francisco with culinary departments; the major resident clubs of San Francisco; the Clinton's Cafeteria chain; and, after fourteen years on the union's unfair list, the Foster System, which consisted of thirty-two luncheon restaurants. "Please rush fifty house cards," Hugo Ernst, president of the San Francisco LJEB, wrote the International in 1937. "All Foster new houses will open up with a display of the house cards and other places too . . . demand the cards."[49]

The unionization of San Francisco's large downtown department stores also meant new members for Local 48. In October 1934, the LJEB moved into action against the Woolworth and Kress's 5 and 10 cent stores, placing them on the "We Don't Patronize" list, picketing, and distributing thousands of handbills house-to-house in working-class districts "to acquaint workers with the slave conditions that prevail." The Retail Clerk officials warned the LJEB that "it costs too much money to organize these national chains" and that they "would not consider wasting money on them," but the culinary workers continued picketing.[50]

Victory came in the spring of 1937 when Woolworth and twenty-five other department and specialty stores signed on with the newly chartered Department Store Employees, Local 1100, Retail Clerks International Union, AFL.[51] Initially, the retail local represented the food service workers in the stores as well as the sales employees because Ernst, supporting an industrial approach to organizing, had waived jurisdiction over the lunchroom employees. In 1940, however, Local 48 successfully demanded that the food service workers in department stores be part of their union.[52]

The infant department store and hotel unions faced major trials in their first few years such as the department store strike of 1938 and the hotel strike of 1941, but unionization had come to stay. Every eating establishment of any consequence had a union agreement. The Retail Creamery

Association, composed of fifty ice cream and fountain stores, signed on with the waitresses in 1940, granting a wage scale and working conditions on a par with the waiters. A year later, the union negotiated an agreement with the Tea Room Guild (some twenty employers), winning the closed shop, a forty-hour, five-day week, vacations with pay, and employer responsibility for providing and laundering uniforms.[53] By 1941, culinary union membership in San Francisco approached eighteen thousand. A majority of the hotels and motels were operating as union houses, and 95 percent of the estimated 2,500 restaurants in San Francisco were organized.[54]

Tactics: Reason, Humor, and Muscle

The organizing and bargaining tactics employed by San Francisco culinary unionists from the late 1930s to the 1950s represent the apogee of union power and creativity. With the majority of the industry union, many shop owners now voluntarily recognized the union. In 1941 alone, seventy-three restaurant owners sent the LJEB requests for union cards. Evidently, many employers judged the house or bar card announcing their union status essential to a steady flow of customers in union-conscious San Francisco. To promote patronage in unionized eateries, the culinary unions fined members for eating in nonunion restaurants and bought "a steady ad in the [San Francisco] *Chronicle* advertising the various union labels." They also appointed a committee specifically to devise "ways and means to advertise our Union House Card."[55]

In some cases, unionization appealed to employers who desired stability in an industry characterized by extreme open entry and a high rate of business failures. Citywide equalization of wage rates protected establishments from cut-throat competitors and chain restaurants that could slash wages and prices in one location until the independent competition capitulated. Employers recognized this function of culinary unionism and on more than one occasion approached the LJEB with names of nonunion houses that should be organized. "We, the undersigned, respectfully request your assistance" began one employer plea to the LJEB. "Attempts have been made to get [unfair] places to join us . . . these attempts have failed completely. We understand that union houses are protected against cut-throats and we wonder why we have been neglected."

Culinary unionists also realized that thorough organization was necessary to protect the competitive position of union houses. In the union campaign to organize tea rooms, for example, all but a few had signed up by the summer of 1939. The union pursued those recalcitrants, insisting they were "unfair competition for the others." Reasoning along similar lines, the LJEB refused to issue house cards to employee-owned, cooperative enterprises although they met wage scales and working conditions. Their lower prices, the LJEB pointed out, were "a menace" to the union restaurants of the city. From 1937 through the 1950s, when organization among San Francisco restaurants remained close to 100 percent, many employers willingly complied with this system of union-sponsored industry stabilization and cooperation.[56]

Employers who failed to recognize the good business sense of unionization were asked to justify their refusal before the united board of culinary crafts. If this interrogation proved fruitless, the employer was reprimanded to a higher body: the executive council of the SFLC or a conference of retail and service unions including the Bakery Drivers, Milk Wagon Drivers, Bakers, and other involved parties. When these oral persuasions went unheeded, the restaurant faced increasing pressure through the council's "We Don't Patronize" list. Few employers could withstand the business losses of withdrawn union patronage when approximately one-fifth of San Francisco's entire population belonged to a labor organization. The Duchess Sandwich Company, for instance, explained that they refused to "force unionism" on their employees and declined to recognize the culinary workers. After less than a month on the council's unfair list, the co-owners of the company wrote that "we have given further consideration to your request that we take the initiative in bringing our employees into the Culinary Workers Organization. . . . We will be glad . . . to work out ways of bringing our plant into complete union membership . . . [and] to get away from the penalties which have piled up on us as a result of your putting us on the unfair list."[57]

When necessary, culinary unionists turned to picketing, creative harassment of shop owners and their clientele, and innovative strike tactics. Traditional strikes, whether by skilled or semiskilled culinary workers, rarely had much impact on businesses that could use family members or find at least one or two temporary replacements. In response, locals often picketed without pulling the crew inside. In these cases, picketing could be successful even if the potential union members working inside were indifferent or hostile to unionism. If picketing persuaded customers to bypass the struck restaurant or halted delivery of supplies, the employer usually relented. With the unity prevailing among San Francisco labor following the 1934 General Strike, culinary unionists experienced few problems stopping deliveries. Influencing customers was a far more difficult proposition.

Mass picketing intimidated prospective customers, but even in the heyday of union rank-and-file activism the LJEB had trouble generating large groups of pickets for so many scattered, isolated locations.[58] To supplement and reinforce weak picket lines, the San Francisco culinary unions devised masterful public relations techniques. The 1941 department and variety store pickets, for instance, attended the Stanford-UCLA football game and passed out "score cards" asking the captive public to help them "hold that line." Using the extended metaphor of football, the leaflets explained that "when Hi prices and Hi taxes throw their full power against left tackle—that's where the pocketbook is kept—only higher wages can plug the hole, and stop the play."[59]

Other attention-grabbing devices used by the same strikers in 1938 and again in 1941 included "Don't-Gum-up-the-Works gum" given out up and down Market Street, boats cruising the Bay during the Columbus Day celebration to advise "Do Not Patronize," and costumed picket lines. The costume variations were endless: Halloween pickets, women on skates, and even Kiddie Day picket lines. One picketer engaged a horse and buggy and trotted around San Francisco carrying a large placard that read "this vehicle is from the same era as the Emporium's labor policy." During the 1941 department store strike when a prize was offered for the picketer with the best costume, a young lunch counter striker won with a dress covered entirely with spoons; on her back she carried a sign reading "Local 1100 can dish it out but can the Emporium take it?" The 1938 dimestore strikers called themselves "the million dollar babies from the 5 & 10 cent stores." Carmen Lucia, an organizer for the Capmakers International Union who assisted the strikes, recalled, "I had them dressed up in white bathing suits, beautiful, with red ribbons around them, and [they'd] bring their babies on their shoulders." Strikers' children handed out leaflets reading "Take our mothers off the streets. Little Children Like to Eat."[60]

A community contingent reinforced the continuous flow of propaganda from the strikers. One group, developed out of the 1938 strike, called itself the Women's Trade Union Committee. Open to union women and wives of union men, the committee, chaired by waitress Frances Stafford, devoted itself to "educating women who have union-earned dollars to spend, as to where and how to spend them." During strikes, the committees escalated their "educational tactics." One devised a tactic called the "button game": shoppers were to go to stores in the busy hours, fill their carts with merchandise, and then demand a clerk wearing the union button. In eating places, supporters relied on somewhat different tactics. Helen Jaye, a San Francisco waitress in the 1930s, recalled one approach: "The people who came into the cafeteria . . . were members of the ILGWU and they . . . gave him [the owner] the very dickens. I remember a couple of men [took] their trays up to the cash register and just dumped them on the floor."[61]

The Compromise of Collective Bargaining

Faced by this intimidating array of union tactics and the more favorable legal and political climate for labor, employers revised their approach to unions in the 1930s and in the process profoundly reshaped labor relation practices in the hotel and restaurant industry. Small and large employers now formed employer associations whose primary goal was the establishment of formal industrywide collective bargaining. In addition to stabilizing the industry and reducing competition, they hoped to end once and for all the insidious union "whip-saw technique" whereby the union insisted on dealing with each employer separately, playing one against the other. They also sought an end to the system in which union workers unilaterally determined their wages and working conditions and then struck for employer compliance. In other words, rather than oppose unionization altogether, employers banded together to contain the power of unions through institutionalized collective bargaining.[62]

The union, on the other hand, desired the extension of its old system of unilaterally determined wage scales and enforcement of standards on a house-by-house basis. Before 1937, individual culinary locals met and voted on the conditions that would govern their craft. These wage scales and working rules were not discussed with the employer; they were arrived at by the mutual consent of the members of each separate local. The individual crafts then submitted their proposals to the LJEB for approval (if a LJEB existed). The board, on behalf of its member trades, presented the standards to individual employers. Employers agreeing to the union wage scales and working conditions earned the privilege of displaying a union house card. A single-page "Union Labor License Agreement," signed by both the union and the employer, bound the "union card employer" to hire only union "members in good standing dispatched from the office of each respective union" and to pay employees "not less than the rate of wages . . . adopted by the LJEB." It was "expressly understood" that the LJEB reserved "the right to alter or modify or change the said scales from time to time." Wages and conditions of employment, then, were determined by the union "on a unilateral non-bargaining basis" and could be changed overnight at the whim of the unions.[63]

In 1937, the employers banded together and began organizing to subvert the old system. At a mass meeting of the restaurateurs, called by attorney David Rubenstein, they empowered the Golden Gate Restaurant Association (GGRA) to act as their negotiating body. The majority of small luncheonettes and cafeterias formed a separate but similarly inclined organization, the Dairy Lunch and Cafeteria Owners Association (DLCOA). Rubenstein, chosen to head both organizations, needled apathetic owners still outside the associations by constant warnings of the dire consequences of inaction. "They are picking us off one by one," he railed. "If you fail to attend [association meetings] and are squeezed to the wall like a soft tomato, blame none but yourself."[64]

For three years, neither the GGRA nor the DLCOA made headway in moving the LJEB toward industrywide collective bargaining.[65] Desperate, the restaurant employers turned for assistance to Almon Roth, president of the San Francisco Employer's Council. The council had solidified its reputation during the 1938 department store strike, helping the employers win a single master agreement on an open-shop basis.[66] When the culinary unions issued their 1941 wage cards, directing significant wage increases for the first time since the 1920s, Roth responded, "the terms and conditions set forth in the cards which you have presented . . . are not satisfactory." Sixty-seven of the larger downtown restaurants instituted a 25 percent wage cut and reverted to the six-day week, eight-hour day.[67]

In the end, after a two-month lock-out in the summer of 1941, the employers gained their primary objective, a signed master agreement, but at the cost of acceding to union wage demands and a closed-shop clause. The LJEB compromised by signing one standard five-year contract covering the sixty-seven downtown restaurants, the tea rooms, dairy lunches, and cafeterias "with the right each year to re-open the contract and strike on wages but not on working conditions." The house card system continued, but the agreements signed by employers no longer required them to abide by wage scales determined solely by the LJEB. At the insistence of the employers, bilateral bargaining had come to San Francisco's restaurant industry.[68]

Association bargaining on a bilateral basis was more easily achieved in the hotel than in the restaurant industry. The few large hotel owners could coordinate and agree much more readily than could an unwieldy group of some hundred small restaurant entrepreneurs, some renowned for their flamboyance and boundless egos. Hotel employers also had no prior history of union-dominated unilateral bargaining to overcome. The hotel owners established industrywide association bargaining in their first encounter with the unions in 1937. In a second round of negotiations in 1941, the Hotel Employers Association and the union deadlocked over the union proposal for a closed shop and preferential hiring through the union hiring hall. The ensuing hotel strike, called on August 30, 1941, convinced hotel employers that the open-shop era was an irretrievable heirloom of history. When back-to-work orders were finally issued by the National War Labor Board in April 1942, after eight grueling months, the union had proven itself a formidable opponent.[69]

Thus, by the early 1940s, an accord was achieved in the San Francisco hotel and restaurant industry that opened a new era of surprising stability and cooperation.[70] Union power had been extended over a wider terrain, yet at the same time employers had modified and diluted that power by forging a new bilateral bargaining system. The next major strike was not to occur until the 1980s, when the carefully crafted system of the 1930s began unraveling.

NOTES

1. Chapter epigraphs quoted from "Story of a Waitress," *Independent,* 18 June 1908, 1381; and Gertrude Sweet to Robert Hesketh, 13 April 1937, Reel 416, Local Union Records, Hotel Employees and Restaurant Employees International Files, Washington, D.C. (hereafter LUR, HERE Files).

On barriers to female unionism, see, for example, Ruth Milkman, "Organizing the Sexual Division of Labor," *Socialist Review* 49 (January-February 1980): 95–150; Alice Kessler-Harris, "Where Are the Organized Women Workers?" *Feminist Studies* 3 (Fall 1975): 92–110; and Nancy Schrom Dye, *As Equals and as Sisters: Feminism, the Labor Movement, and the Women's Trade Union League of New York* (Columbia, 1980).

2. See, for example, Dana Frank, "Housewives, Socialists, and the Politics of Food: The New York City Cost of Living Protests," *Feminist Studies* 11 (Summer 1985): 255–85; and Patricia Cooper, *Once a Cigar Maker: Men, Women, and Work Culture in American Cigar Factories, 1900–1919* (Urbana, 1987).

3. Ira B. Cross, *A History of the Labor Movement in California* (Berkeley, 1935), 177 and 33n.; Grace Heilman Stimson, *Rise of the Labor Movement in Los Angeles* (Berkeley, 1955), 66; Matthew Josephson, *Union House, Union Bar: A History of the Hotel and Restaurant Employees and Bartenders International Union, AFL-CIO* (New York, 1956), 7–12; Robert Hesketh, "Hotel and Restaurant Employees," *American Federationist* 38 (October 1931): 1269–71; "Brief History of Our Organization," *The Federation News,* 25 January 1930; Henry C. Barbour, "Wages, Hours, and Unionization in Year-Round Hotels," unpublished study, School of Hotel Administration, Cornell University, 1948, 115–16; Paul Frisch, "Gibraltar of Unionism: The Development of Butte's Labor Movement, 1878–1900," *The Speculator* (Summer 1985): 12–20. For a discussion of the relation between the Knights of Labor and culinary workers, see *Mixer and Server* (periodical; hereafter *MS*), April 1904, 5–7.

4. Since 1981 the official name of the union has been the Hotel Employees and Restaurant Employees. For official HERE membership figures, see the HERE Officers' Report, 1947, 17–18, HERE Files. The major published accounts of the history of the International include Josephson, *Union House, Union Bar;* Jay Rubin and M. J. Obermeier, *Growth of a Union: The Life and Times of Edward Flore* (New York, 1943); Morris A. Horowitz, *The New York Hotel Industry* (Cambridge,

1960), 21–65 passim; and John P. Henderson, *Labor Market Institutions and Wages in the Lodging Industry* (East Lansing, 1965), 129–59.

5. An examination of the IWW Collection, Walter Reuther Library, Wayne State University (hereafter IWW, WRL-WSU), and various IWW newspapers such as *Industrial Worker* and *Solidarity* revealed only scattered organizing efforts among culinary workers. For references to IWW culinary organizing outside New York before World War I, see "To the Workers Who Feed the World," Box 174; 10 October 1906–15 September 1911, General Executive Board Minutes, Box 7, file 1; "Address to the Hotel and Restaurant Workers," *Industrial Union Bulletin*, 4 January 1908, Box 156; Foodstuff Workers Industrial Union, Local 460, Box 69—all in IWW, WRL-WSU. Also see *Industrial Worker*, 21 May 1910, 13 August 1910, 24 September 1910, 11 June 1910, 18 June 1910; *Solidarity*, 28 June 1913, 16 August 1913; and Guy Louis Rocha, "Radical Labor Struggles in the Tonopah-Goldfield Mining District, 1901–22," *Nevada Historical Society Quarterly* 20 (Spring 1977): 10–11. For IWW organizing in New York, see note 16.

6. Early discussions of gender separatism include Belva Mary Herron, "The Progress of Labor Organizations Among Women, Together with Some Considerations Concerning Their Place in Industry," *University Studies* 1 (May 1905): 443–511; Alice Henry, *The Trade Union Woman* (New York, 1915); Alice Henry, *Women and the Labor Movement* (New York, 1923); and Teresa Wolfson, *The Woman Worker and the Trade Unions* (New York, 1926). For more recent analyses, see Roger Waldinger, "Another Look at the ILGWU: Women, Industry Structure, and Collective Action," and Alice Kessler-Harris, "Problems of Coalition-Building: Women and Trade Unions in the 1920s," both in *Women, Work, and Protest: A Century of Women's Labor History*, ed. Ruth Milkman (Boston, 1985), 86–138; and Susan Glenn, *Daughters of the Shtetl: Life and Labor in the Immigrant Generation* (Ithaca, 1990).

7. In *Daughters of the Shtetl*, ch. 6, Glenn notes that her work draws on Mary Jo Buhle's distinction between native-born varieties of feminism and urban-immigrant varieties. See Buhle, *Women and American Socialism, 1870–1920* (Urbana, 1981), chs. 2, 3, passim.

8. In "The Progress of Labor Organizations Among Women," 66, Herron suggests that men prefer mixed locals in trades in which direct competition exists; separatism is advocated where competition is minimal. In the culinary industry, sex segregation lessened direct competition but did not eliminate it. Hence, it is not surprising that men were divided in their attitudes toward separatism.

9. *MS*, May 1902, 5; June 1905, 84.

10. Lillian Ruth Matthews, *Women in Trade Unions in San Francisco* (Berkeley, 1913), 76; *MS*, April 1901, 6; April 1906, 28; *San Francisco Labor Clarion* (hereafter *SFLC*), 23 January 1906; *San Francisco Examiner*, 3 April 1901.

11. *Catering Industry Employee* (HERE's national journal; hereafter *CIE*), June 1900, 7; April 1940, 35; August 1946, 37; April 1947, 40; October 1948, 37; *SFLC*, 9 January 1903, 4 December 1904, 7 July 1905, 23 January 1906, 1 May 1908, 10 July 1908, 1 January 1909, 24 February 1911, 25 June 1915, 24 August 1928, 22 February 1946, 5 December 1947; *San Francisco Call*, 5 July 1909. For additional details on LaRue and Younger, see Susan Englander, "The San Francisco Wage-Earners' Suffrage League: Class Conflict and Class Coalition in the California Women's Suffrage Movement, 1907–1912," master's thesis, San Francisco State University, 1989, ch. 3.

12. *San Francisco Examiner*, 4 May 1901, 6 May 1901; *MS*, November 1902, 35; *San Francisco Chronicle*, 12 August 1917; *SFLC*, 18 December 1903; Robert E. L.

Knight, *Industrial Relations in the San Francisco Bay Area, 1900–1918* (Berkeley, 1960), 67–72, 136; Matthews, *Women in Trade Unions in San Francisco*, 78; Ed Rosenberg, "The San Francisco Strikes of 1901," *American Federationist* (1902): 15–18.

13. *SFLC*, 18 August 1905, 27 October 1905, 19 June 1906, 10 August 1906, 6 September 1907, 26 March 1909, 13 August 1909, 27 August 1915; Knight, *Industrial Relations in the San Francisco Bay Area*, 164–65; Louise Margaret Ploeger, "Trade Unionism Among the Women of San Francisco," master's thesis, University of California, 1920, 107–8.

14. *SFLC*, 19 May 1916, 21 July 1916, 11 August 1916, 25 August 1916; Ploeger, "Trade Unionism Among the Women of San Francisco," 108–11.

15. See John B. Andrews and Helen Bliss, *A History of Women in Trade Unions, 1825 to the Knights of Labor*, 61st Cong., 2d sess., 1911, Senate Document 645, 147, for New York City female culinary membership from 1902–9. See Gary M. Fink, ed., *Biographical Dictionary of American Labor* (Westport, 1984), 56–57, 599–600, for a description of Maud Younger's activities. Dye, *As Equals and as Sisters*, 61–65, 76–80; "Story of a Waitress."

16. Offshoots of the New York movement also appeared in Buffalo, Boston, Philadelphia, and elsewhere. For IWW organizing in New York City, see Frank Bohn, "The Strike of the New York Hotel and Restaurant Workers," *International Socialist Review* 13 (February 1913): 620–21; "Workers of the World Now Run Affairs for New York Waiters," *Square Deal* 12 (February 1913): 29–32, 87; *Solidarity*, 14 and 21 February 1914; 15 June 1912, 2; 15 February 1913, 4; Hugo Ernst, "The Hotel and Restaurant Workers," *American Federationist* 53 (June 1946): 20–21, 29; New York Hotel and Motel Trades Council, *The Story of the First Contract* (New York, 1974), 19–25; *New York Times* (hereafter *NYT*), 8, 10, 14, 20, 31 May 1912; 2, 4, 22 June 1912; 4 July 1912; 13–14, 25 January 1913; 1–2 February 1913; 14–15 May 1914; 9, 21, 28 December 1915; 29 October 1918; 7 and 27 December 1918.

17. Organizing can be traced in *SFLC*, 16 November 1917, 21 June 1918, 7 March 1919, 4 August 1919; *NYT*, 7 and 27 December 1918; "Department Store Waitresses Win Increase," *Life and Labor Bulletin*, July 1918, 141.

18. For IWW organizing attempts during World War I and the 1920s, see "Wake Up! Hotel, Restaurants, and Cafeteria Workers," n.d. [ca. 1920s], Box 177, IWW, WRL-WSU; Charles Devlin, "Help Organize Hotel, Restaurant, and Domestic Workers," *One Big Union Monthly* 2 (February 1920): 49; Charles Devlin, "Who Does Not Work Neither Shall He Eat," *One Big Union Monthly* 2 (August 1920): 56–57; "Who Will Feed Us When Capitalism Breaks Down?" *One Big Union Monthly* 2 (November 1920): 40–42; "The Servant Girl Rediscovered," *One Big Union Monthly* 2 (January 1920): 53–54; L. S. Chumley, "Hotel, Restaurant, and Domestic Workers," 1918, Box 163, IWW, WRL-WSU.

19. Ernst categorizes Denver in this fashion; see *MS*, July 1923, 38. The term also is used by Max Kniesche in "Schroeder's Cafe and the German Restaurant Tradition in San Francisco, 1907–1976," an interview by Ruth Teiser conducted in 1976 for the Regional Oral History Office, Bancroft Library, University of California, Berkeley (UCB).

20. Interview with Charles Paulsen conducted by the author, 28 July 1983, Cincinnati; Rubin and Obermeier, *Growth of a Union*, 164–80.

21. Following World War I, employers linked the open-shop concept with Americanism by dubbing it the "American Plan." The "yellow-dog contract" was a pledge by the employee that he or she would not join or support a union. Some

employers required these contracts from all newly hired workers. For a general account that includes particulars on HERE, see Irving Bernstein, *The Lean Years* (Boston, 1960), 85, 117, 336. See also Lawrence Nelson to Lena Mattausch, 28 January 1922, letter stuck in Local 457 Minutebook, 1916–22, Local 457 Files, Butte, Montana.

22. *MS*, November 1918, 19–20; July 1919, 79. HERE also chartered black "domestic worker" unions in this period. See Elizabeth Haynes, "Negroes in Domestic Service in the U.S.," *Journal of Negro History* 8 (October 1923): 435.

23. *MS*, October 1907, 35; Emily Barrows, "Trade Union Organization Among Women in Chicago," master's thesis, University of Chicago, 1920, 156; Esther Taber, "Women in Unions: Through Trade Union Organization Waitresses Have Secured Marked Improvement in Conditions," *American Federationist* 12 (December 1905), 927; Waitresses' Local 48 Constitution and By-Laws, n.d., Bancroft Library, UCB.

24. *CIE*, April 1935, 6. The International did allow local unions to admit Asian workers (although their right to transfer from one local to another was denied); front cover, *MS*, April 1905; *CIE*, July 1925, 31; February 1937, 54.

25. *MS*, November 1905, 30; May 1917, 41; *Proceedings*, 1923 Convention, HERE Files, 131. Ernst also favored organizing Japanese culinary workers. See *SFLC*, 18 August 1916. The Butte response is illuminated in the following: Frisch, "Gilbraltar of Unionism," 14–15; Rose Hum Lee, *The Growth and Decline of Chinese Communities in the Rocky Mountain Region* (Ph.D. diss., Department of Sociology, University of Chicago, 1947; rept., New York, 1978), 104–16, 187; Local 457 Minutebook, 21 June 1918, Local 457 Files; Local 457 Minutebook, 8 January 1926 and 5 March 1926, Box 14-1, Women's Protective Union Collection (WPUC), 174, Montana Historical Society, Helena, Montana.

26. *MS*, May 1917, 23; July 1919, 79; four-page typed manuscript by Ethel M. Smith, "The Union Waitress Interprets," n.d., 2, Reel 2, C-2, Papers of the Women's Trade Union League and Its Principal Leaders (microfilm edition; hereafter WTUL Papers), Radcliffe College, Arthur and Elizabeth Schlesinger Library, Cambridge, Mass.; William Whyte, *Human Relations in the Restaurant Industry* (New York, 1948), 192.

27. Frances Donovan, *The Woman Who Waits* (Boston, 1920), 134; Chumley, "Hotel, Restaurant, and Domestic Workers."

28. Although the labor movement had taken the lead in the nineteenth-century drive for shorter hours, by the early twentieth century its response was more ambivalent. The AFL's voluntaristic viewpoint discouraged state interference and touted free collective bargaining as the better method for improving working conditions, especially for adult men. They objected less to maximum hour legislation than to minimum wage legislation, however, because wage rates fluctuated much more rapidly than did standards for hours, and the minimum wage might more easily become the maximum. The historic struggle for hours legislation in the nineteenth century also ameliorated the AFL's voluntaristic sentiment in regard to hours; no such legacy existed in relation to wage legislation. For a discussion of the relation between the labor movement and protective legislation, see Susan Lehrer, *Origins of Protective Labor Legislation for Women, 1905–1925* (Albany, 1987), 144–83.

29. For an overview of the campaigns to secure protective legislation, see Elizabeth Brandeis, "Organized Labor and Protective Labor Legislation," in *Labor and the New Deal*, ed. Milton Derber and Edwin Young (Madison, 1961); Barbara A. Babcock et al., *Sex Discrimination and the Law: Causes and Remedies* (Boston, 1975); and Judith Baer, *The Chains of Protection: The Judicial Response to*

Women's Labor Legislation (Westport, 1978). For the seminal role of middle-class organizations, especially on the East Coast, see U.S. Department of Labor, Women's Bureau, *History of Labor Legislation for Women in Three States*, Bulletin no. 66, by Clara Beyer (Washington, D.C., 1929); and Consumers' League of New York City, *Behind the Scenes in a Restaurant: A Study of 1017 Women Restaurant Employees* (New York, 1916).

30. Consumers' League of New York City, *Behind the Scenes in a Restaurant*, 36; *MS*, April 1909, 55; July 1911, 34; U.S. Department of Labor, Women's Bureau, *History of Labor Legislation for Women in Three States*, 123; *SFLC*, 3 February 1911, 3; Earl C. Crockett, "The History of California Labor Legislation, 1910–1930," Ph.D. diss., University of California, Berkeley, 1931, 12–14.

31. Nancy Dye discusses similar divisions among working-class women in the WTUL in Dye, *As Equals and as Sisters*, 146–52. She notes that sex-specific minimum wage laws were harder to justify than similar hours legislation because "there was no physiological reason for women to earn a specified wage." By the 1920s, however, the working-class women within the league united in favor of protective legislation, emphasizing the social and economic conditions that necessitated protection.

32. *Coast Seamen's Journal*, 22 January 1913, 6; *SFLC*, 20, 27 December 1912, 2; U.S. Department of Labor, Women's Bureau, *History of Labor Legislation for Women in Three States*, 130–31n; Crockett, "The History of California Labor Legislation," 12–14.

33. California (State) Industrial Welfare Commission, *Fifth Biennial Report for 1922–24* (1927), 12; California (State) Industrial Welfare Commission, *What California Has Done to Protect the Women Workers* (Sacramento, 1929); Ploeger, "Trade Unionism Among the Women of San Francisco," 115–19; California (State) Industrial Welfare Commission, *Fourth Biennial Report for 1919–20* (1924), 130.

34. *MS*, August 1924, 18–19.

35. California (State) Industrial Welfare Commission, *Fifth Biennial Report for 1922–24*, 18; handwritten notes, Box 4, File "Calif. DIW Misc.," San Francisco Labor Council Records, Bancroft Library, University of California, Berkeley (hereafter SFLC R, BL-UCB); Crockett, "The History of California Labor Legislation," 72–73, 90–94.

36. Quote from Henry Pelling, *American Labor* (Chicago, 1960), 178. For labor union membership growth during the 1930s and World War II, see Marten Estey, *The Unions: Structure, Development, and Management* (New York, 1981), 11–12.

37. The Hotel Employees and Restaurant Employees did not record the membership totals for individual crafts; thus, the exact number of organized waitresses can only be estimated. Nonetheless, the membership figures for waitress locals provide some guidance.

38. Philip Taft, "Brief Review of Other Industries," in *How Collective Bargaining Works*, ed. Harry A. Mills (New York, 1942), 924; *CIE*, August 1933, 28.

39. *CIE*, January 1935, 25; Josephson, *Union House, Union Bar*, 193–98. The participation of the left-wing unions, AFW and FWIU, is mentioned in Grace Hutchins, *Women Who Work* (New York, 1934). For an account of the involvement of the Women's Bureau, see the correspondence between Edward Flore and Mary Anderson, File "HERE," Box 865, RG-86, NA.

40. See the Restaurant Industry Basic Code, submitted by the National Restaurant Association, approved 10 August 1933; Hugo Ernst to John O'Connell, 20

December 1933, F-"Culinary Misc.," Box 8, SFLC R, BL-UCB; Lafayette G. Harter, Jr., "Master Contracts and Group Bargaining in the San Francisco Restaurant Industry," master's thesis, Stanford University, 1948, 42.

41. For an overview of San Francisco's union traditions, see Michael Kazin, *Barons of Labor: The San Francisco Building Trades and Union Power in the Progressive Era* (Urbana, 1987), ch. 1.

42. *CIE*, September 1933, frontispiece; October 1933, 28; February 1934, 21; LJEB Minutes, 20 December 1933, Local 2 Files, San Francisco, HERE Files.

43. LJEB Minutes, 20 December 1933, Local 2 Files; typed ms., "Findings of Fact and Conclusions of Law," B. J. Della Valle v. Cooks, Waitresses and Miscellaneous Employees, 4, File "Cooks vs. Valle," Box 7, SFLC R, BL-UCB.

44. LJEB Minutes, 15 May 1934, Local 2 Files; File 170−9742, RG-280, NA.

45. LJEB Minutes, January 1933−December 1934, in particular, 13 July 1934, Local 2 Files; interview with William G. Storie conducted by Corinne Gilb, UCB, 24 January, 31 March, 7 April, 1959, 53; *SFLC*, 3 August 1934. For accounts of the General Strike, see Irving Bernstein, *The Turbulent Years: A History of the American Worker, 1933−1941* (Boston, 1969), 252−98; and Bruce Nelson, *Workers on the Waterfront: Seamen, Longshoremen, and Unionism in the 1930s* (Urbana, 1990), ch. 5.

46. David Selvin, *Sky Full of Storm* (San Francisco, 1975), 50; interview with Lou Goldblatt conducted by Lucy Kendall for the California Historical Society, n.d.; *CIE*, October 1934, 33; September 1935, 15; Membership Records, HERE Files.

47. Only one hotel in San Francisco was unionized at this point, the Whitcomb Hotel. Ernst to James Vahey, 5 March 1935, File "HERE," Box 8, SFLC R, BL-UCB; *CIE*, October 1934, 33; March 1936, 33; *SFLC*, 8 January 1937; LJEB Minutes, 3 October 1933, 21 January 1936, 15 January 1937, 6 April 1937, 15 April 1937, 1 May 1937, Local 2 Files; Van Dusen Kennedy, *Arbitration in the San Francisco Hotel and Restaurant Industries* (Philadelphia, 1952), 13; telegram, Matthewson to Hugh Kerwin, 19 April 1937 and 28 May 1937, Case file 182−2408, RG−280, NA. Local 283, chartered in March of 1937, demanded recognition and working conditions comparable to the other organized crafts. George O. Bahrs, *The San Francisco Employers' Council* (Philadelphia, 1948); *CIE*, June 1937.

48. Josephson, *Union House, Union Bar*, 264−69; "Summary Report," Matthewson to Kerwin, 28 July 1937; "Final Report," 28 July 1937, by Matthewson; telegram, Matthewson to Kerwin, 17 July 1937. All in Case file 182−2408, RG-280, NA. LJEB Minutes, 15 April 1937, Local 2 Files; transcript, "Award of Fred Athearn, Arbitrator, to the San Francisco LJEB and San Francisco Hotel Operators," San Francisco, 1937, Local 2 Files; Harter, "Master Contracts and Group Bargaining in the San Francisco Restaurant Industry," 52−64; Kennedy, *Arbitration in the San Francisco Hotel and Restaurant Industry*, 13−14, 29−32, passim; press release, 22 December 1937, and Ernst to Clarence Johnson, 4 January 1938, LJEB Correspondence Folder, Local 2 Files.

49. LJEB Minutes, 27 August 1937, Local 2 Files; *SFLC*, 10 December 1937. Arbitration Proceedings between the San Francisco LJEB and Owl Drug Co. before George Cheney, Union Opening Brief, 16 December 1943, SFLC R, BL-UCB, 2−3; S.F. clubs to LJEB, October 1937, and Ernst to Hesketh, 9 December 1937, LJEB Correspondence Folder, Local 2 Files.

50. Warren G. Desepte to C. C. Coulter, 10 February 1935, 26 February 1935, 30 August 1936, 11 September 1936, Reel 1, Retail Clerks International Union Records, Wisconsin State Historical Society, Madison, Wisconsin; Ernst to O'Connell, 13 October 1934, File "HERE," Box 8, SFLC R, BL-UCB.

51. In part because of the actions of local AFL unionists like Ernst, San Francisco department stores remained within the AFL, unlike those in New York and other major cities.

52. Strike Board Minutes, 9 November 1940, Local 2 Files. For further details, see Dorothy Sue Cobble, "Sisters in the Craft: Waitresses and Their Unions in the Twentieth Century," Ph.D. diss., Stanford University, 1986, 199–201.

53. Local 48 EB Minutes, 19 July 1938, and Local 48 MM Minutes, 20 April 1938, Local 2 Files; *CIE*, February 1940, 26–27.

54. *B/G Organizer Bulletin*, 11 October 1941; Union Brief and Exhibits, Arbitration Proceedings between the San Francisco LJEB and the Hotel Employers' Association before Edgar Rowe, 18 August 1942, 2, Local 2 Files.

55. LJEB Minutes, 15 October 1936 and 17 June 1941, Local 2 Files.

56. Petition, 13 September 1937, San Francisco Employers to Ernst; Ernst to O'Connell, 21 July 1939, LJEB Correspondence Folder, and LJEB Minutes, 16 October 1934 and 6 November 1934, Local 2 Files.

57. Ernst to SFLC Delegates, 15 March 1933 and 25 July 1933, and T. K. Bronson to O'Connell, 9 October 1939, File "HERE," Box 8, SFLC R, BL-UCB; Duchess Sandwich Co. President to C. T. McDonough, 14 December 1940, LJEB Correspondence Folder, Local 2 Files.

58. LJEB Minutes, 4 June 1940 and 16 July 1940, Local 2 Files.

59. *Department Store Strike Bulletin*, 3 October 1941, and "Score Card," San Francisco Strikes and Lockouts Collection, Box 1, BL-UCB.

60. *Department Store Strike Bulletin*, 3 November 1941; 18 November 1941; interview with Carmen Lucia conducted by Seth Widgerson and Bette Craig, Wayne State University, Oral History Project, 1978.

61. Stafford to SFLC, 16 December 1938, File "Local 1100," Box 15, SFLC R, BL-UCB; *CIE*, January 1939, 43; interview with Helen Jaye conducted by Lucy Kendall for the California Historical Society, 23 March 1981.

62. In imitation of union practices, employer members who refused to abide by group decisions were fined, harassed, and shunned. See Josephson, *Union House, Union Bar*, 295–96.

63. Interview with William G. Storie, 154; Kennedy, *Arbitration in the San Francisco Hotel and Restaurant Industry*, 11; Bahrs, *The San Francisco Employers' Council*, iii; binder entitled "House Card Agreements 1938–1946," Local 2 Files; interview with Paul St. Sure conducted by Corinne Gilb, March-June 1957, Institute of Industrial Relations Oral History Project, UCB, 487–89.

64. Rubenstein to Ernst, 18 November 1937, 20 November 1937, and leaflet signed by David Rubenstein, n.d. [ca. November 1937], LJEB Correspondence Folder, Local 2 Files.

65. LJEB Minutes, 2 August 1938, 6 June 1939, 5 March 1941, and Rubenstein to LJEB, 26 February 1938, LJEB Correspondence Folder, Local 2 Files.

66. Bahrs, *The San Francisco Employers' Council*, 10; LJEB Minutes, 6 May 1941, 20 May 1941, 10 June 1941, Local 2 Files. Interview with William G. Storie, 154–56.

67. Interview with William G. Storie; Andrew Gallagher to John Steelman, 3 July 1941 and n.d. [ca. July 1941], Case File 196–6257A, RG-280, NA; Harter, "Master Contracts and Group Bargaining in the San Francisco Restaurant Industry," 67; and Edward Eaves, "A History of the Cooks and Waiters' Unions of San Francisco," Ph.D. diss., University of California, Berkeley, 1930, 98.

68. Interview with William G. Storie; LJEB Minutes, 25 August 1941, Local 2 Files. This first master restaurant contract subsequently became the universally

accepted scale for organized restaurants whether or not they belonged to the association. Copies of both the old and new house card agreements can be found in the binder entitled "House Card Agreements 1938–1946," Local 2 Files.

69. For a detailed account of the 1941 San Francisco hotel strike, consult Josephson, *Union House, Union Bar*, 293–96; and Harter, "Master Contracts and Group Bargaining in the San Francisco Restaurant Industry," 73–101. See also Case File F–196–2066, RG-280, NA. In other cities, hotel employers also turned to association bargaining. Gertrude Sweet wrote the International of this new employer technique, much feared by the unions. Sweet to Hesketh, Reel 416, LUR, HERE Files.

70. For further comments on the remarkable stability of San Francisco culinary labor relations and the unprecedented use of arbitration machinery, see Kennedy, *Arbitration in the San Francisco Hotel and Restaurant Industry*, 1–19, 100–109; and Harter, "Master Contracts and Group Bargaining in the San Francisco Restaurant Industry," 128–33.

FURTHER READING

Cobble, Dorothy Sue. *Dishing It Out: Waitresses and Their Unions in the Twentieth Century.* 1991.

———. "'Drawing the Line': The Construction of a Gendered Work Force in the Food Service Industry." In *Work Engendered: Toward a New History of American Labor,* edited by Ava Baron, pp. 216–242. 1991.

———. "'Practical Women': Waitress Unionists and the Controversies over Gender Roles in the Food Service Industry." *Labor History* 29 (Winter 1988): 5–31.

Deverell, William, and Tom Sitton, eds. *California Progressivism Revisited.* 1994.

Eaves, Lucile. *A History of California Labor Legislation, with an Introductory Sketch of the San Francisco Labor Movement.* 1910.

Englander, Susan. *Class Coalition and Class Conflict in the California Woman Suffrage Movement, 1907–1912: The San Francisco Wage Earners' Suffrage League.* 1992.

Healey, Dorothy, and Maurice Isserman. *Dorothy Healey Remembers: A Life in the American Communist Party.* 1990.

Hundley, Norris C. "Katherine Phillips Edson and the Fight for the California Minimum Wage, 1912–1923." *Pacific Historical Review* 29 (August 1960): 271–285.

Katz, Sherry J. "Dual Commitments: Feminism, Socialism, and Women's Political Activism in California, 1890–1920." Ph.D. dissertation, University of California at Los Angeles, 1991.

———. "Frances Nacke Noel and 'Sister Movements': Socialism, Feminism, and Trade Unionism in Los Angeles, 1909–1916." *California History* 67 (September 1988): 180–189.

Kraft, James P. "The Fall of Job Harriman's Socialist Party: Violence, Gender, and Politics in Los Angeles, 1911." *Southern California Quarterly* 70 (Spring 1988): 43–68.

Laslett, John H. M., and Mary Tyler. *The ILGWU in Los Angeles, 1907–1988.* 1989.

Matthews, Lillian Ruth. *Women in Trade Unions in San Francisco.* 1930.

Nash, Gerald D. "The Influence of Labor on State Policy, 1860–1920: The Experience of California." *California Historical Society Quarterly* 42 (September 1963): 241–257.

Schaffer, Ronald. "The Problem of Consciousness in the Woman Suffrage Movement: A California Perspective." *Pacific Historical Review* 45 (November 1976): 469–493.

4 Okies and the Politics of Plain-Folk Americanism

James N. Gregory

EDITOR'S INTRODUCTION

In the early decades of the twentieth century, California agriculture expanded greatly. In 1900, there were 72,000 farms in the state, valued at a total of $708 million. By 1925, California boasted 136,400 farms, worth more than $3 billion. This growth was spurred by the spread of irrigation, which enabled farmers to cultivate fruits and vegetables on a large scale in the arid Central Valley. The era of "factories in the field" had truly arrived.

The rapid expansion of California agriculture, especially seasonal crops, called for a large, migratory agricultural proletariat. To an extent, this need was met by Japanese, Mexican, Filipino, and other minority workers. During the 1920s, however, the Alien Land Acts and other factors greatly reduced the number of Japanese workers in California agriculture. Mexican immigrants, in particular, helped to make up the shortfall, but even their increasing numbers failed to meet the labor demands of California agriculture. During the 1920s and 1930s, these demands were met from a more indigenous source.

While California agriculture continued to expand during the interwar period, this was not the case in many other states. Low prices, foreign competition, mechanization, soil erosion, drought, pestilence, and New Deal farm programs all combined to drive millions of farmers off the land in this period. No area of the country was as hard hit as the American Southwest. By 1950, 23 percent of all people born in Oklahoma, Texas, Arkansas, and Missouri lived outside the region. These states lost 50 percent of their agricultural work force between 1910 and 1950.

During the 1920s and 1930s, more than 550,000 Southwesterners migrated to California, primarily to Los Angeles and the Central Valley, where

a significant number ended up as part of California's agricultural proletariat. In the 1940s, upward of 600,000 more "Okies," lured especially by
the prospect of work in California's booming wartime industries, joined the
exodus from the Southwest.

Jim Gregory's book *American Exodus: The Dust Bowl Migration and Okie
Culture in California* provides the most detailed and authoritative account
we have of the migration of people from the Southwestern states of Oklahoma, Texas, Arkansas, and Missouri, examining both the causes and the
character of this mass migration. Gregory also explores in depth the profound social, cultural, and political impact that this Okie migration had on
California in the 1930s and 1940s. Specifically, he examines the nature of
the Okie subculture in California and how Southwesterners adapted to life
in their newly adopted state.

In this extract from his book, Gregory argues that a very distinctive
Okie subculture existed in California, "derived largely from the outlooks,
habits, and institutions of Southwestern 'plain folk,' a broad social category encompassing most rural and blue-collar whites." Okie culture was
an amalgam of many components, including late-nineteenth-century populism and early-twentieth-century fundamentalism.

A "cult of toughness" helped condition the response of the Okies to
California. Although their political traditions encouraged them to support
some radical causes in the 1930s, their patriotism, racism, individualism,
and "toughness" made them indifferent, even hostile, to trade unionism.
Later, in the context of World War II, when many Okies got jobs in California's cities, they became much more receptive to trade unionism. But
Okies in rural areas remained as indifferent or hostile to agricultural
unionism in the 1940s as they had been in the 1930s. Gregory probes the
reasons for this through his analysis of Okie culture.

The patterns of alienation built up in the 1930s encouraged the process of
cultural adaptation that gave California its Okie subculture. Regional cultural differences that in other circumstances had meant little took on expanded significance in this one. Although some Southwesterners consciously abandoned distinguishing characteristics, others fell back on the
cultural resources of their upbringing, creating community systems laced
with values and institutions of Southwestern origin. The primary locus of

this subculture was the San Joaquin Valley, but in weakened form it also developed in the metropolitan areas, especially during the 1940s when new waves of migrants created for the first time substantial enclaves of Southwesterners in the cities.

Some definitions are needed. The term subculture is quite elastic, which is useful in this case. A subculture is a social formation with a distinctive set of norms and values that offers members a significant sense of identity and locus for social interaction. Subcultures come in many forms, based on ethnicity, class, religion, political ideology, peer group, even consumer interests. But the Okie subculture does not fit neatly into any one of these categories. Depending upon where we look and also what time periods we examine, the formation seems to take on different shapes.[1]

Social science has never supplied the right tools for categorizing the process of cultural adjustment that accompanied the Dust Bowl migration. Initially it was not seen as a cultural process at all. Apart from the concern that the migrants came from a "backward" area, few contemporaries gave much thought to questions of regionalism, assuming that differences between native-stock Americans were minor, that culture carried social consequences only when linguistic, political, religious, or moral traditions were sharply differentiated. Trained social scientists were especially reluctant to find significance in the regional backgrounds of the migrant population. In the usual view class and its many complications alone defined the group.

Anthropologist Walter Goldschmidt best expressed this assessment. After close consideration he concluded that the migrants were not really a group in any coherent sense. A "disorganized aggregate" sharing conditions of poverty and hostility, they lacked "mechanisms by which they could be organized into a community." Though he described in detail the separate Okie neighborhoods, social life, and religious institutions, he assumed these to be transitory developments attributable to the vicissitudes of class. To the extent that the migrants demonstrated divergent values and customs, a history of rural disadvantage or more recent poverty was to blame. Otherwise, the newcomers seemed to share in the basic standards of the host society and appeared most anxious to win acceptance within it.[2]

Stuart Jamieson saw matters differently and, for his time, singularly. In 1942 the Berkeley-trained labor economist published the results of his study of Olivehurst, one of several Okie communities in the Sacramento Valley. Struck by the similarities between the social position of the "new American migrants" and the foreign immigrant groups they had largely replaced in the agricultural labor force, he observed that the newcomers take on the "appearance of a distinct 'ethnic group.'" Despite cultural backgrounds that are "fundamentally the same" as their hosts', he argued, the economic and social context contributed to the migrants' "quasi-segregation" and had the "effect of perpetuating some old traditions and customs of the settlers," among which he listed speech, dress, paternalistic family relations, and religious institutions.[3]

Although he was essentially alone with this formulation in the 1940s, a time when conventional definitions of ethnicity envisioned only national, religious, and racial groups, the redefinition of ethnicity in the last few decades has made his argument increasingly plausible.[4] Indeed, it is consistent with what regional sociologists John Sheldon Reed and Lewis Killian have been saying recently about the ethnicity of white Southerners. In a long list of books and articles published since 1972, Reed catalogues the similarities between Southern whites and conventionally recognized ethnic minorities, stressing the region's persecution complex, enduring sectional identity, and persisting differences in social, personal, and religious values. Killian introduced some of the same points in his 1970 book *White Southerners*, which was published in Random House's Ethnic Groups in Comparative Perspective series. He also examined the process of Southern out-migration and argued that it was among the "hillbillies" of Chicago and other northern cities that the evidence of minority group behavior was strongest. Caught in an urban context of stereotypes and hostilities not much different from that experienced by their Okie cousins, the working-class Southern whites Killian studied engaged in a process of group formation and cultural retention typical of ethnic minorities.[5]

It is a tempting argument, but there are some complications, at least in the case of the California migrants. The issue of group definition is one. Until recently, few Southwesterners of the middle class identified themselves as Okies. On the other hand, a number of people from states other than the Southwest associated with and were perceived to be Okies; and some today embrace the term. There is something similarly fuzzy and flexible about the cultural materials, the institutions and symbols, that in time gave the group a sense of community and identity. These, too, have not been consistently and exclusively Southwestern.

While in the end it may be valuable to talk about Okie ethnicity, it is important first to deconstruct the experience, to understand that the subculture has operated in several guises. Being an Okie for some Southwesterners is a straightforward matter of regional heritage, and for them the ethnic concept is relevant. They celebrate their state origins and proudly proclaim symbols and distinguishing cultural elements of that background. If ethnicity refers to a sense of peoplehood rooted in a perception of common history and ancestry, some Okies qualify.[6]

But for other participants the subculture expresses something different, either experiential pride (as veterans of the migrant experience) or, most interesting, allegiance to a set of social-political perspectives that might be labeled plain-folk Americanism. This ideological persuasion was part of the cultural system of the Southwest—or more properly of a particular class of Southwesterners—but it was not exclusive to that region. Other white Americans, particularly other rural Protestant-stock Americans, shared many of these interests and values, and still others later found them attractive. Here it is harder to talk about ethnicity, since regionalism was not the central issue. In this guise the Okie subculture was an ideological community of uncertain and, indeed, expanding dimensions. For those who identified with this version of the community, being an Okie was a matter of experiences, standards, and values.

A Framework of Understandings

California's Okie culture derived largely from the outlooks, habits, and institutions of Southwestern "plain folk," a broad social category encompassing most rural and blue-collar whites. As in other parts of the South, the social structure of the trans-Mississippi states divided most obviously into three basic categories: blacks; whites of the business, professional, and land-wealthy strata; and the majority white population of modest means. Some scholars insist on subdividing this last group into its wage-working, tenant farmer, and yeoman components, while others confuse the issue with labels like "poor white" or "redneck." Those distinctions are not helpful here. Tied together in many instances by kinship, rural and formerly rural working-class Southwesterners shared a wide range of life-ways, values, and outlooks. Most of all they shared a seasoned political culture.[7]

Southwestern plain folk claimed a set of social and political commitments that had once flourished widely in nineteenth-century America. Heirs to anti-monopoly and citizen-producer ideas that in earlier periods had guided both agrarian and working-class radicalism, they stood also in the shadow of generations of white Protestants who had fought to preserve the Republic's ethnic and religious integrity. These perspectives tracked through a long line of neo-populist campaigns aimed at rural and working-class audiences. From the days of the powerful Farmers' Alliance, through the resurrected radicalism of Huey Long, "Alfalfa Bill" Murray, and "Ma" Ferguson, those constituencies responded best to shirt-sleeved campaigners who talked about the dignity of hard work and plain living and promised deliverance from the forces of power, privilege, and moral pollution, near and far.[8]

Southwestern plain folk brought these and other outlooks to California and made them the basis for their subculture. What they built, however, was not merely a replica of what they left behind. The Okie subculture evolved through a process of cultural negotiation involving many participants. Partly a dialogue between Southwesterners and their new California setting, there was also a speaking role for non-Southwesterners who associated with the migrant population. The resulting synthesis expressed some of the familiar ways of the Southwest, but other elements were changed or newly emphasized.

The subcultural construction occurred in stages. It was not until the 1940s that the more obvious institutions—churches, saloons, and country music—began to solidify and make an impact on the surrounding society. Until then the subculture was harder to locate. In the 1930s, the group was taking shape informally and more or less unintentionally in the neighborhoods, camps, and job sites where migrants gathered. Through the act of socializing, men and women discovered common understandings and worked out the new meanings that would give the group its sense of identity and cohesion.

We are fortunate to have a source which identifies some of the more important values that were affirmed in those interactions. The "Pea-Patch Press" was Charles Todd's name for the collection of newspapers emanating from the FSA (Farm Security Administration) camps during the last years of the 1930s. *Tow-Sack Tattler, Pea-Pickers Prattle, Covered Wagon News, Voice of the Migrant*—the colorful, free-form titles say much about the style of these tiny mimeographed publications which were supported by camp fees and published whenever someone volunteered to serve as editor. The format was usually wildly eclectic. More community bulletin board than newspaper, they published a hash of contributions from residents and management. Letters, recipes, poems, jokes, stories, editorials, complaints, homilies, political opinions, discussions of current issues, reports of camp gossip, notices of meetings, lists of rules and regulations, jeremiads by camp managers—whatever was available went out in the next issue.[9]

Many of the contributions were original, but residents also sent in remembered bits of verse, Bible passages, riddles torn from other publications, anything that seemed meaningful enough to share. It is this participatory aspect which makes the camp newspapers so valuable. We hear from children, parents and grandparents, men and women, union activists and Pentecostal worshippers, those who liked California and those who hated it. They wrote not only about issues but also about day-to-day life. We witness their attempts at entertainment, their approach to humor, their sense of propriety. In letters, poems, and gossip notes, they argued and agreed about community standards, about morals, about right and wrong as they wrestled with the meaning of their California experience and reminded themselves what was important in life.

Were these camp residents typical of the broader population of Okies? Those who lived in the camps were often poorer, more transient, newer to California than residents of the migrant subdivisions where the lasting social networks were being strung. But any distinctions between the populations of these settings were minor and temporary. Residents of camps and Little Oklahomas came from the same background, occupied the same farmworker class, and faced similar adjustment challenges. In both settings large numbers of mostly Southwestern newcomers explored the basic business of living together. The difference is that the camp residents left us a record of the process.

Cult of Toughness

Reading that record for its core values, one concern stands out. A favorite poem expressed it.

> If the day looks kinder gloomy
> An' the chances kinder slim;
> If the situation's puzzlin',
> An' the prospect awful grim,
>
> An Perplexities keep pressin'
> Till all hope is nearly gone
> Just bristle up and grit your teeth,
> An' keep on goin' on.[10]

The message of persistence, determination, of "try, try again" defined one of the essentials of what the migrants considered good character. Learned in school, in church, from parents and friends, courage and determination were the special forte of these plain people. Struggle, they assured themselves, was what they and their ancestors did best. Persistence was more than the key to success—there could be no dignity, manhood, or self-esteem without it. No other theme was expressed as frequently or as passionately as the need to never let up, never quit, to always "keep on goin' on." Winnie Taggart shared her composition "Migratory Grit" with fellow residents of the Brawley camp near the pea fields in the Imperial Valley:

Forget the grouch, erase the frown.
Don't let hard luck get you down.
Throw up your head, thrust out your chest,
Now at a boy! Go do your best.
                . . .
It's hard to laugh, and be at ease,
When the darned old peas all start to freeze.
But a pea tramps always full of grit,
He never does sit down and quit.
                . . .
To laugh, should be the pea tramp's creed
For that is what we greatly need.
It does not take great wealth to laugh
Just have the grit to stand the gaff.[11]

These calls for courage, determination, and "grit" reflected a preoccupation with toughness that became one of the cornerstones of the Okie subculture. The values involved were in no way unique to the migrants, but in the process of emphasizing and reinforcing them, they were beginning to forge the normative standards of the group and a myth that would anchor expressions of group identity.[12]

Toughness meant, first of all, an ability to accept life's hardships without flinching or showing weakness, a standard applied to both males and females. Displays of weakness were actively discouraged in the camp newspapers. "Complainers," "grumblers," "gripers," and "whiners" came in for frequent criticism. "All's not well that is the talk; / A grumbler being the worst of the lot," one poet chided.[13] "'Taint no use to sit an' whine," cautioned another version of "Keep On A-Goin'."[14] "Now come on everybody, quit that complaining," a letter writer at the Indio camp in the Coachella Valley urged. "Every cloud has a silver lining. If you don't like things here in camp and the relief you get, be nice enough to keep it to yourself."[15]

Toughness also meant a willingness to fight, metaphorically for women, in all senses of the word for men.

It takes a little courage;
And a little self-control;
And a grim determination;
If you want to reach the [goal];

It takes a deal of striving;
And a firm and stern-set chin.
No matter what the battle,
If you really want to win.

You must take a blow and give one.
You must risk and you must lose
And expect within the battle
You must suffer from a bruise.

But you mus[t]n't wince or falter.
Lest a fight you might begin.
Be a man and face the battle.
That's the only way to win.[16]

An Arvin camp resident thought his fellow campers might benefit from that untitled poem, perhaps remembered from childhood, a personal credo now being shared. Its message was a familiar one in the migrant communities. It mentions goals but is mostly about struggles and manliness. A man has courage and self-control, he fights his own battles, facing each with "stern-set chin." And, significantly, he prepares not so much to win as to lose, steeling himself to "suffer from a bruise."

Another poem, labeled "A Man's Creed," repeats the same themes:

Let this be my epitaph
Here lies one who took his chances
In the busy world of men
Battled luck and circumstances
fought and fell and fought again
Won sometimes, but did no crowing
Lost sometimes, but did not wail
Took his beating but kept going
And never let his courage fail.[17]

In both of these contributions a man's creed is courage, not as a means to something but as a goal itself. What is important is the ability to fight and fall and fight again, to take a "beating" and keep going. There is an understanding of life here that lies outside the Franklinesque formulas of aspiration and success that are the core of middle-class American culture.

These invocations speak to a worldview in which struggle is the only verity, in which society is divided not into winners and losers but into those who fight and those who quit, men and cowards. They speak to a system of honor which, Bertram Wyatt-Brown and others suggest, may be a special feature of the culture of Southern whites. More definitely we can say that these values flourish outside the middle-class mainstream of twentieth-century American society, in working-class and rural contexts where symbols of prestige are hard to come by, where money and occupation cannot be everything. This was a context Okies knew well.[18]

Physical courage was a central part of the creed, and not just for males. Both children and adults were expected to know how and be willing to fight. Fist fights occurred frequently in the camps, in the schools, and in nearby saloons and were a continual source of concern to camp authorities, among others. Most involved males, but girls also fought with surprising frequency.

Young people have a "strange code," the Shafter camp manager complained in his regular column. "A young lady was called into my office for fighting and she said she had to fight or the other children would call her chicken."[19] He need only have read his own camp newspaper to begin to understand that the "code" was promoted by parents as well as the younger generation. Aside from crime or base immorality, no more serious charge could be leveled at another person than the charge of cowardice. "The world will forgive you for being blue, sometimes forgive you for being green, but never forgive you for being yellow," a Yuba City camp philosopher intoned.[20]

The words were meant to be taken seriously, and elsewhere were backed up with punishing ridicule. A boy who walked away from a school fight was mercilessly taunted as a crybaby in the Arvin camp newspaper: "Bill Jones got his feelings hurt in the school room the other day, he went home to get his [baby] bottle but his mother was not home so he came back crying."[21]

The migrants' support for the values of toughness and courage which made up that "strange code" can also be seen in the enormous popularity accorded the sports of boxing and wrestling. Amateur bouts were staged weekly at many of the FSA camps and quickly proved to be the best attended of the camps' many recreational activities, attracting Okies living outside the camps as well as residents. On some nights, crowds of up to 500 people would assemble to watch what the Shafter *Covered Wagon News* described as "plenty of good fighting and lots of action."[22] The matches featured contests between boys of several age levels up to the early twenties and nearly always included at least one pair of girls.

The Shafter paper's description of a fight between two teenage girls shows something of both the enthusiasm for the sport and the importance attached to displays of toughness:

> A rough and tumble exhibition was put on by Mildred Searcy and Aldyth Aust, two of our promising young ladies. Mildred sure protected her pretty face all during the two rounds, and bucked like a ram with her head. Both girls displayed good sportsmanship by taking their punishment with a smile.[23]

That fighting between girls should be sanctioned in this way suggests a significant departure from the standards of comportment absorbed by generations of middle-class American women. Nevertheless, as the passage itself implies, fighting was primarily a test of male honor. For women, toughness had more to do with the ability to shoulder burdens, withstand pain, and bear up under life's trials. Female toughness was preeminently a matter of fortitude.

In several respects the migrants' cult of toughness represented an adjustment of old values to a new setting. In their efforts to deal with the formidable challenges of resettlement, the migrants appear to have emphasized courage and determination even more than they had back home. Beyond that, these values took on new social implications. At home toughness was a matter of individual concern; in California it became a badge of group pride, something that Okies believed made them collectively special.[24]

To listen to former migrants today is to encounter again and again this proprietorial claim to toughness. It takes various forms, emerging sometimes in proud tales of Okie fighting prowess. In his book *Okies*, a collection of short stories, Kern County native Gerald Haslam, a second-generation Okie on his father's side, sees fighting as one of the major themes of the group experience. His male characters are frequently locked in combat, proving their courage and manhood to themselves and each other, rising to each challenge instinctively, obsessively, even as they sometimes wish they could turn a cheek and walk away. In the story "Before Dishonor," a battered "good old boy" moves from one teeth-shattering fight to another as other males test the truth of the "Death Before Dishonor" tattoo on his forearm. "There's things a kid does just haunts a man," the protagonist says of the tattoo he must defend. For Haslam it is all part of a particular system of honor which haunts and therefore helps to define Okies.[25]

If Haslam is intrigued by the Okie reputation for violence, he is not alone. Many of his contemporaries and elders relish stories about fighting, particularly accounts of fights between resilient Okies and insolent Californians. The understanding is that Okies were singularly proficient with their fists, more than a match for their native detractors. "About the time they'd say, 'Okie,' I'd put my fist in their mouth," Byrd Morgan recalls.[26] Charles Newsome uses the same proud tone in telling of his school-yard fights:

> As the Missourians always said, "It was show me time." . . . Well, the Okie was the one that could show them so that's why there were a lot of little tough Okie kids running around the schools because they had to be tough.[27]

James Lackey was an adult when he arrived in California, and evidently a good fight never came his way. But he witnessed many and sees courage as an Okie trait. "I've never seen an Okie run from trouble at all. If you corner an Okie he's going to fight."[28] Hadley Yocum likewise takes pride in the fights won by others. "I'll tell you one thing," says the former Arkansas and Oklahoma sharecropper, whose land holdings now make him a millionaire, "the native Californians weren't no match for the boys coming from Oklahoma when it came to fist fights."[29]

This celebration of combat skills is part of the mythology of the Okie subculture. By mythology I do not mean the claims are untrue—indeed, there are good reasons to believe most of them—but rather that, true or not, such ideas form an important element in the framework of the group's identity.[30]

The toughness myth extends beyond physical combat, however. In its most important manifestation, Okies find meaning in the belief that they or their parents or grandparents were part of a special encounter with suffering, a special exercise in perseverance and hard work, a special triumph over adversity.

Listen to Francis Walker, who looks back proudly on the years she and her family spent in the cotton fields of the San Joaquin Valley. "The Okies were invincible, they won, they are here, they own land, houses—and are comfortable," she insists.[31] "Okies were resilient," echoes Dee Fox, a third-generation Okie whose pride in her heritage comes from "hearing all the stories" from her grandparents and parents.[32] Okies "were willing to work," says Charles Newsome, "they'd work long hours trying to get ahead" while the "big shots" who settled the area earlier "had learned to live on a silver spoon and . . . didn't know how to compete."[33]

Okies are people "who tried to stay alive and managed," explains Lester Hair, who was born in Arizona as his parents made their way west from Texas in 1924. And struggle, he continues, gives them a sense of pride "that is more important to that person than anything else."[34] Hard times, hostile treatment, persistence, and struggle—"*that's what made Okies out of us,*" concludes Texas-born Bernie F. Sisk, who worked his way out of the fruit orchards to become congressman from Fresno County.[35] Whether all this struggle was in fact unique is unimportant; the belief that it was continues to shape a group identity.

A Shifting Populism

Related values of a more political nature also helped the newcomers feel themselves part of a special enterprise. The process turned on their understandings of American heritage and character. As they took a close look at the residents and the reigning values of their new state, they found a basis for rethinking their inferiority complex. California had some significant flaws. Maybe the migrants were not the ones who should be making the concessions and changes.

Plain-folk Americanism found its central bearings in a neo-populist perspective that understood but two great social classes, producers and parasites. Once key to a far-reaching radical critique of the economic order, the perspective had been changing political coloration since the turn of the century as adherents added anti-Communism, racism, nativism, and the resilient individualism evident in the toughness code to their list of political priorities. By the 1930s, many plain folk embraced an ideological construction which seemed to cross the conventional boundaries of Northern (and Californian) politics. Ever sympathetic to appeals on behalf of the common man or against the "interests," they responded with equal vigor to symbols that recalled a white Protestant and intensely patriotic vision of Americanism. This parochial populist combination matched neither the business conservatism nor the urban liberalism that had become dominant in California's Depression-era political life. A lens through which the migrants judged their surroundings, it became as well one of their contributions to their new state.[36]

The outlook was evident in the camp newspapers, in the way camp residents dealt with questions of ambition, privilege, and equality. Invocations to personal ambition were curiously muted. For all the talk of determination and fighting, no Andrew Carnegie models appeared on these pages; few indeed were the discussions of competitive striving. This is striking when we consider the didactic nature of many of the contributions and the fact that they were often aimed at the younger generation. Reading closely we can see that particular standards of ambition were being employed. Exhorting one another to be the best they could be, contributors urged also that limits be recognized. Be your own man, proud but no better than anyone else—this was what contributors seemed to want for themselves and their children.

What occupational references there were suggest unfamiliarity with and some distrust of white-collar work. Bankers seem to have been hated, businessmen mostly ignored, bureaucrats and intellectuals widely lampooned. A joke about an "old Texas farmer" who uses common sense to outsmart a pretentious college professor reveals a sense of distance from the world of higher education. Underlying these evaluations was a basic belief in the primacy of manual labor. Real work meant creating with one's hands either in the fields or in the factories, ideally in a setting where one was independent, "his own boss."[37]

Clearer than the migrants' occupational discriminations was their intolerance of social snobbery or elitism. Residents frequently blasted those who put on uppity airs, acted "high hat," or who tried to become "better than other people." "In Oklahoma and Texas where we folks come from one person ain't no better than another," an angry Shafter camp resident wrote after learning that elected camp council members were to be henceforth exempt from the task of cleaning bathrooms.[38]

Outsiders found that a democratic demeanor was essential to any sort of effective dealings with Okies. Eleanor Roosevelt passed the test. After she paid a brief visit to the Shafter camp, the newspaper exuded: "No more gracious lady, no kindlier lady have we folks ever seen. When she talked with us she was so common, so plain, so sincere. Said a man in Unit Five, 'She is plain like all of us—not stuck up or stuffed.'"[39]

On the other hand, some of the camp managers, most of them young college graduates, ran afoul of the migrants' standards. Oklahoma-born Wiley Cuddard, Jr.,* criticized the string of previous managers at the Arvin camp—all "educated men, who have never done any real work"—for acting like "Dictators." The last one, he said, was "the professor type, he didn't associate with the people enough, too much business about him." Cuddard had nothing but praise, however, for the new manager, Fred Ross: "he is an educated man but when he came here he acted as one of the boys. . . . He didn't act one bit better than his staff or the people in the camp. And he's always got time to say a few words to you."[40]

This commitment to social equality and resentment of pretension and authority had implications for the migrants' adjustment. Strictures against social snobbery dampened status ambitions that otherwise might have lured young people out of the working class and hence out of the Okie milieu. Here may be one of the factors in the high drop-out rate among high school students. If the camp newspapers are any guide, young people were taught at home to set modest life goals. Mrs. V. E. Langley passed along this piece of advice to residents of the Brawley camp in the Imperial Valley:

> We all dream of great deeds and high positions. . . . Yet success is not occupying a lofty place or doing conspicuous work; it is being the best tha[t] is in you.
>
> Rattling around in too big a job is worse than filling a small one [to] overflowing. Dream aspire by all means; but do not ruin the life you must lead by dreaming pipe dreams of the one you would like to lead. Make the most of what you have and are. Perhaps your trivial, immediate task is your one sure way of proving mettle.[41]

"The secret of happiness is not doing what one likes, but in liking what one has to do," a Yuba City camp resident argued.[42] That was the message also of a popular poem entitled "Be What You Is" that appeared in print in several different newspapers:

> If you're just a little tadpole
> Don't try to be a frog
> If you're just a tail
> Don't try to wag the dog
> You can always pass the plate
> If you can't exhort and preach
> If you're just a little pebble
> Don't try to be the beach.
> Don't be what you ain't
> Jes' be what you is.
> For the man who plays it square
> Is a-goin to get "his."[43]

Reinforced by the teachings of some of the churches they attended and also by important themes in country music, messages of restrained ambition doubtless helped to sustain the class integrity of the Okie group.

This sort of class consciousness also had political implications. Politics loomed large in the catalogue of fears inciting native hostility. Residents assumed the newcomers to be Democrats and, worse, probably radical Democrats. They were not far from the mark. Missouri, north Oklahoma, and parts of the Arkansas Ozarks knew something of the Republican party, but most Southwesterners had been raised in areas that acknowledged only one legitimate party. And since the onset of the Depression, major elements of that Democratic party had become reacquainted with radical-sounding rhetoric and proposals which harkened back to the 1890s. Leading Southwestern politicians such as Thomas Gore and "Alfalfa Bill" Murray of Oklahoma, Jim and Miriam ("Pa" and "Ma") Ferguson of Texas, Hattie Carraway of Arkansas, and, of course, the broadly influential Huey Long of Louisiana had greeted the economic crisis of the 1930s with a resurrected language of angry opposition to Eastern money and corporate greed, with dramatic calls for federal action to rein in the rich and redistribute wealth, and with renewed commitment to the cause and dignity of plain, hard-working folks—in short with a neo-populism (a debilitated populism, says historian Alan Brinkley) that found an eager if perhaps not entirely credulous audience among the region's distressed rural and working-class populations.[44]

Percentage Voting for Democratic Candidates and Ham 'n' Eggs Initiative, for Arvin Precincts and Statewide California

Electoral Contest	Arvin	Statewide
1934 gubernatorial (Sinclair v. Merriam)	54%	38%
1936 presidential (Roosevelt v. Landon)	75%	67%
1938 gubernatorial (Olson v. Merriam)	71%	52%
1940 presidential (Roosevelt v. Willkie)	65%	57%
1939 Ham 'n' Eggs	65%	34%

SOURCES: *Arvin Tiller*, Nov. 6, 1939; Voter Registration and Election Results Arvin Area, Goldschmidt Records, San Bruno; Michael P. Rogin and John L. Shover, *Political Change in California* (Westport, 1969), 123, 132; Robert E. Burke, *Olson's New Deal for California* (Berkeley, 1953), 33, 112.

The same disposition shows itself in the voting habits of many of the migrants who settled in California. Using the largely Okie town of Arvin as a gauge, we can see what worried Republicans and conservative Democrats. Arvin, from 1934 through the end of the decade, voted more strongly Democratic and much more in favor of liberal and radical Democratic candidates than the state as a whole. While Californians rejected the 1934 candidacy of Upton Sinclair, Arvin voted for him. Four years later, when Culbert Olson won the governor's mansion with 52 percent of the statewide vote, Arvin residents gave him 71 percent of theirs. Olson's blasts against big business, his calls for public ownership of utilities, and his endorsement of a watered-down version of Sinclair's "production for use" proposal may have bothered a good number of Californians, but those familiar with the anti-corporate, government-as-savior tone of Southwestern electioneering were not among them.

The best indication of the neo-populist mind set of the new voters was Arvin's showing on the oddly named Ham 'n' Eggs initiative of 1939. Losing two to one statewide, it won by the same margin in Arvin amidst indications that the proposal was especially dear to the hearts of much of the migrant population. Ham 'n' Eggs was a radical welfare scheme derived from the earlier formulations of Dr. Francis Townsend, the famous Long Beach geriatric crusader. Among other things it called for the distribution of $30 in special scrip every Thursday to each needy Californian over the age of fifty. Like the Townsend plans, the goal was to assist the elderly while stimulating the economy through massive currency expansion.[45]

Denounced as crackpot economics not only by financial experts and conservative politicians but also by much of the liberal and left community, including Upton Sinclair, the initiative nevertheless seems to have inspired more enthusiasm and political activity than any other issue to come before the Okie group in the 1930s. Letters to camp newspapers and the established press called out their endorsement, often revealing a profound mistrust of the experts who opposed it: the self-same bankers alleged to have brought on and profited from the Depression. "Ham and eggs everybody," Arkansan Henry King urged fellow residents of the Arvin camp. "Do you believe it will work, the money Gods say it wont. . . . [Don't] believe those dirty rich liars that say Ham and Eggs wont work. . . . Ham and eggs wont work if the rich can help it." [46]

In addition to playing to the migrants' suspicions of bankers, corporations, and pretentious wealth, Ham 'n' Eggs found a responsive echo in the neo-populist fondness for currency manipulation schemes. Financial conspiracies were responsible for the economic crisis, financial wizardry would resolve it. Bill Hammett was the kind of voter who found Ham 'n' Eggs compelling. Although his comments were made several years before the initiative appeared, his political philosophy suggests the sort of down-home radicalism that earned the ballot measure so much support among resettled Southwesterners:

> I ain't no communist . . . I hold the American flag's just as good here and now as when Betsy Ross finished her stitchin' and handed it over to George Washington. What's good over in Russia don't mean it's good for us. I ain't edicated enough to know whether it's Epic plan or Townsend plan or whatever, but if there's plenty folks ready and willin' to raise food and other folks are still starvin', don't take no college edication to know there's somethin' cloggin' the gin feed.[47]

Labor's Dilemma

If the migrants' worldview could take them in radical directions, it also, as the orthodox left discovered, took them in conservative ones. The plain-folk ideology circulating in the migrant communities was tinged with much else beside the old populism of their forefathers. When Okies talked of social equality, they usually meant equality for whites and often only native-stock whites. When they sorted out their pantheon of enemies, they frequently figured Communists to be more dangerous than bankers. And when faced with organizational opportunities that might yield collective benefits, they typically fell back instead on habits of individualism and family self-sufficiency. The 1930s marked something of a midpoint in the transformation of the political culture of Southwestern plain folk. The insurgent potential had been steadily draining away. Even as many Southwesterners continued to use a class-based terminology of the plain versus the powerful, more persuasive commitments to patriotism, racism, toughness, and independence were pointing towards the kind of conservative populism that George Wallace would articulate three decades later.

Suggestions of this trend can be seen in the migrants' response to the two left-wing unions which tried to recruit them in the closing years of the 1930s. The United Cannery, Agricultural, Packing and Allied Workers of America, a Congress of Industrial Organizations union better known by its acronym UCAPAWA, and the Workers Alliance, which called itself the "union of the unemployed," together tried to organize the migrants in their twin roles as farmworkers and relief recipients. Neither was very successful. The plain people's consciousness which found expression in the Ham 'n' Eggs vote fit much less well with the programs and campaigns of radical organized labor.

Strictly speaking, the Workers Alliance was a pressure group rather than a union. A loosely structured organization that enjoyed the support of both the Socialist and Communist parties, it was the chief successor to the militant Unemployed Councils of the early 1930s. Chapters first appeared in the agricultural areas of California in 1936 and quickly began to pick up members among the Okie population dependent upon relief. Sending grievance committees to lobby local relief authorities while backing those efforts with petitions and public demonstrations, the organization gained a reputation for influence and with it a small but significant following in many of the camps and communities. Helpful, too, was the fact that Workers Alliance stewards sometimes controlled the distribution of jobs on WPA projects. Even migrants who disapproved of the organization's radical politics sometimes found it useful to join. "Seems you've might near got to belong . . . to get what's coming to you," one man complained as he contemplated signing up.[48] Membership figures are hard to judge, but it seems likely that chapters in Arvin, Bakersfield, Madera, and Marysville could each claim the support of several hundred members by early 1939, while smaller chapters operated in several other locales.[49]

UCAPAWA first appeared in the migrant communities in late 1937. Part of the newly independent CIO, it pulled together several tiny food-processing and farm-labor locals left over from the campaigns of the early 1930s. Its leaders sought first to build a strong base in the canneries and packing houses (a sector rapidly falling to the American Federation of Labor) but at the urging of state CIO leaders agreed to undertake as well the formidable task of organizing the state's vast armies of seasonal farm-workers. UCAPAWA's commitment to the project, however, was inconsistent and greatly hindered by a shortage of financial resources and skilled organizers. Unsure whether it should be setting up dues-paying locals or organizing strikes, the union mostly drifted behind events. Workers Alliance activists took charge of most of the organizing, converting their chapters into UCAPAWA locals during harvest seasons, and at times initiating walkouts for which UCAPAWA leaders were not fully prepared.[50]

Serious strike activity began in the fall of 1938 with a spontaneous walkout by several hundred Kern County cotton pickers, many of them residents of the Shafter FSA camp. Emboldened by the reputation of the mediagenic CIO and angered by the drastic wage cuts that accompanied the federally sponsored acreage cutbacks, a militant minority, consisting of Okies and Hispanics, had initiated the action. The union dispatched organizers to try to broaden and discipline the strike, but after some exhilarating efforts at coaxing other workers from the fields using automobile picket caravans, the strike collapsed, helped to its early end of the mass arrest of some one hundred picketers.[51]

The next year saw a wave of similar walkouts in other crops as cadres of activists spread the union enthusiasm up and down the state. One or two of the strikes resulted in wage increases, but most, like the Kern strike, floundered after dramatic beginnings, either because most workers refused to strike or because other migrants appeared to take the jobs of those who did.[52]

The cotton harvest of 1939 promised to be the major test. UCAPAWA tried a new strategy. Counting on the support of the recently installed Olson administration and the public sympathy engendered by the publication of The Grapes of Wrath, leaders were hoping to win bargaining concessions from growers without a strike. But when industry representatives ignored the recommendations of the governor's Wage Rate board, the scene was set for confrontation.

The union concentrated efforts in Madera County, where a strong Workers Alliance local had been preparing for months. Initial reports were encouraging. A majority of cotton pickers in the area responded to the strike call, and hundreds gathered in the county park for assignment to picket caravans. Despite some early arrests, observers counted the strike 75 percent effective in the first week in that county, though efforts to inspire walkouts elsewhere in the cotton belt fizzled badly.[53]

The Madera momentum was also about to end—the Associated Farmers saw to that. On the strike's ninth day, a mob of several hundred growers attacked a rally of union supporters with clubs, pick handles, and tire irons. Other beatings and arrests followed as local officials cooperated with efforts to break the strike. With the governor unwilling to intervene and most of the leaders in jail or driven from the county, UCAPAWA's most significant farm-labor strike came to a close. The defeat ended serious efforts to organize field workers. Activists maintained some of the locals and kept the threat of further campaigns alive for another year or so, but union headquarters had lost interest and now turned its energies elsewhere.

It is unwise to make too much of UCAPAWA's poor showing. Substantial obstacles stood in the way of any attempt to organize the farm-labor force, an occupational sector that remains largely nonunion to this day. The timing of the UCAPAWA campaign was particularly bad, coinciding with a dramatic drop in farm employment and a growing surplus of workers. The combination made many migrants angry, but left others desperate for work and unable to make the sacrifices a strike demanded.

Slim Phillips's case is indicative of the choices many faced. He had just arrived in California, was out of money, and had not yet heard of the strike when a grower stopped him on the highway and offered him work. He accepted but moments later encountered a carload of strikers. "We want to get a little better price on this cotton," they told him.

> So I says we ain't got nothing to eat. If you got the price of something to eat why we can talk business with you, otherwise, we is gonna starve. We just didn't have no money. That was all there was to it. We was broke.[54]

Given the desperation of people like Phillips, the aggravating labor market conditions, not to mention the difficulties of coordinating farm-labor strikes against the obstinate and very powerful agricultural industry in California, UCAPAWA's failure is anything but surprising. Still, one can ask whether the values and disposition of the migrants had something to do with the campaign's problems. Many observers thought so, concluding in the final analysis that Southwesterners were not good union material, that, as Charles Todd put it, they were "immune to the wiles of the organizer."[55] Later writers have also followed this lead. Walter Stein argues that the migrants were unfamiliar with unions and too individualistic to support the campaign. Comparing the UCAPAWA experience with the more encouraging results of the earlier Cannery and Agricultural Workers Industrial Union drive among mostly Mexican field workers, he observes that "precisely because Okies were rural Americans with that streak of individualism, they were less malleable material for union organizers than were Mexicans. Rugged individualism and collective action do not mix well."[56]

Can this be correct? The Western South, historian Lawrence Goodwyn assures us, had once thrilled to the cooperative strategies of the Farmers' Alliance and then with equal vigor had supported the programs of the People's party. Even more distinctively, in the years immediately prior to World War I, Oscar Ameringer, Kate Richards O'Hare, and Thomas "Red" Hickey had built the nation's largest Socialist party membership on the foundation of former Populists. Enjoying the support of thousands of tenant farmers, miners, timber workers, and urban sympathizers, the movement had garnered over a third of the vote in many of Oklahoma's poorer counties, and substantial numbers as well in western Arkansas and northern Texas. Now a mere twenty years later was it possible that migrants from this region were too individualistic to contemplate joining a union?[57]

The story is more complicated than that. First, it is important to understand that not all migrants responded alike to the union campaign. A sizable minority did join or support these organizations. Many of the activists who agitated in the fields and camps, triggered the walkouts, and mounted the picket caravans were Okies, as were the hundreds and occasionally thousands who responded to their calls. Though definitely in the minority, the number of union supporters was by no means negligible. Just how many there were is not clear, but three small surveys perhaps provide a clue. Approximately one-quarter of the 60 men James Wilson interviewed were UCAPAWA members or supporters; 30 percent of Lillian Creisler's 100 Modesto respondents, not all of whom were farmworkers, belonged to some sort of union; and 39 percent of Walter Hoadley's 117-family Salinas area sample said they might like to join a union, though UCAPAWA was not specifically mentioned. To estimate, then, that one out of every three at least sympathized with the union would not be irresponsible.[58]

Many belonging to this pro-UCAPAWA segment seem to have had prior experience with either unions or radical causes. Arthur Brown,* active in UCAPAWA in Kern County, learned his unionism working in the oil fields of Oklahoma. Carrie Morris and her husband, mainstays of the Marysville local and leaders of several walkouts, claimed thirty years of unionism in various industries before coming to California. Likewise, the president of the Wasco local, who looked back on careers in both mining and railroad work, liked to tell visitors that he had "been a Union man all my life." Given the number of farmworkers who had previously worked in nonagricultural jobs, these backgrounds were not unusual.

Some 28 percent of residents in Modesto's Little Oklahoma claimed previous union experience.[59]

Other sympathizers came to UCAPAWA via the Southwest's radical movements. Like Jim Ballard, an Arkansas tenant farmer who grew up reading the Socialist weekly *Appeal to Reason,* some of the people settling in California were veterans of the prewar Socialist campaigns. Others, too young to have participated in the glory days of the Debsian movement, had been involved in such Depression-era leftist ventures as the Southern Tenant Farmers' Union, the Oklahoma-based Veterans of Industry (an organization of the unemployed), or, for that matter, the Workers Alliance, which had chapters in the Southwest as well as California. Tex Pace, editor of the Visalia camp *Hub,* is a good example. His penchant for items about Commonwealth Labor College at Mena, Arkansas, suggests his roots in the radical subculture of his home region.[60]

These radicals, however, no longer enjoyed the sympathy that would have once made them welcome in a large percentage of the region's rural households. The two decades since World War I had indeed seen a major transformation in political consciousness. The patriotic fervor and uncompromising repression of the war and Red Scare years had begun the process. Next came the nativist, fundamentalist, and moral reform crusades of the 1920s. The Ku Klux Klan attained for a time major influence in the region, taking power in Texas and Arkansas and coming close in Oklahoma. The experience helped even Klan opponents learn to equate radicalism with treason, anti-Communism with Americanism.[61]

The region's farm population had been especially affected. Even though the Klan found more enemies than friends among the region's plain folk, the organization's preeminent lesson took hold in the 1920s. Henceforth, patriotism would remain the foremost proposition for the majority of Southwestern farm folk. All other impulses, including their continued interest in economic justice, would be subject always to qualms about the proper activities for loyal Americans. For the organized left, this proved an insurmountable burden. Still a force in the Southwest's cities, oil fields, and mining camps, radicals usually encountered an aroused and suspicious majority opinion in rural and small-town settings. Despite the turmoil and discontent that the 1930s brought to the region's farm population, patriotic concerns channeled most energies away from the radical left, sometimes into the election campaigns of neo-populist candidates such as Murray and Carraway, sometimes into apathy.[62]

It was to be the same in California. Chief among the obstacles that the unionists faced were the strong anti-Communist sentiments of many of their fellow migrants. Both UCAPAWA and the Workers Alliance were vulnerable on that score. As grower representatives and major newspapers never tired of pointing out, both organizations had important links to the Communist party. For people like Oklahoman Clint Powell,* there was nothing more to be said. Probably unaware that he was inverting the Populists' famous challenge to raise less corn and more hell, he refused to have anything to do with a "damned red outfit" which "just raises more hell than anything else." [63]

Even migrants who otherwise claimed to be interested in unionization were sometimes deterred by the Communism issue. An old-timer who felt that unionization was definitely "in my interests" nevertheless insisted that "it won't do us a bit of good unless it's 100 per cent, and unless all the radicals are killed off." "The radicals," he continued, "are so unreasonable, it hurts rather than helps us." [64] A twenty-seven-year-old Oklahoman who felt "we need some form of pullin' together to prevent goin' into slavery" was also wary. Though he thought UCAPAWA "is the best thing we've got now to keep wages up," he was not a member. "I don't knock on the CIO but I do say let's be careful lest we join an organization that's influenced by some foreign government." [65]

The scope and vehemence of this concern seem unusual for the late 1930s. Most sectors of the American public probably shared the migrants' antipathy towards Communism, but not in the same measure. At least in urban settings, the CIO found its Communist allies more help than liability, as tens and hundreds of thousands of industrial workers ignored red-baiting campaigns and picked up the union card. But anti-Communism had become a more serious proposition in heartland regions like the Western South where the nativist-fundamentalist fires of the 1920s had burned so brightly. [66]

Religious and racial concerns also had something to do with UCA-PAWA's difficulties. The evangelical churches that claimed the attention of a significant minority of the migrant group often spoke against union membership, sometimes quite vehemently. "They get up and tell the people that the CIO is wrong, and that those who are wearing the CIO badges have the mark of the 'beast' upon them," a UCAPAWA leader charged, and he suspected the preachers were "paid by the ranchers." [67] They did not need to be bribed. Many of these churches belonged to Pentecostal or Holiness sects that taught that all forms of political action were wrong because they distracted from the pursuit of individual salvation. Worldliness of any kind was to be avoided. Even the conservative American Federation of Labor "had trouble with these holy rollers." A frustrated Cannery

Workers Union official complained, "They have screwy ideas. Some of them don't want to belong to any organization and will quit their jobs rather than join a union. Their preachers won't let them belong to any organization, but their own." [68]

Again, it had not always been so. Evangelical groups had played a different role in the era of Southwestern radicalism before World War I, says historian Garin Burbank. The Socialist movement, he argues, gained the support of preachers and deeply religious farm folk who found a resonance between the promises of Socialism and chiliastic Christianity. [69] But that link had largely dissolved by the 1930s. Among the ministers and religious-minded migrants who came to California one finds only scattered examples of sympathy for radicalism: a Nazarene minister active in the Olivehurst chapter of the Workers Alliance; a Pentecostal preacher known as Brother Theodore, who reconciled his belief in Socialism by saying, "Ah have to seek the truth, Brother, an' after ah've found that truth then ah've gotta preach it"; and Lillie Dunn, who discovered Jesus at age thirteen and the Communist party twelve years later and never found the two in conflict. [70] They were exceptional. Most of the migrants involved in the union campaign were not necessarily irreligious, but rarely were they closely involved in a church. [71]

UCAPAWA's policy of racial inclusion may have also limited its appeal to white Southwesterners. Like most left-wing CIO organizations, the union insisted that workers of all colors and national origins be included, though not always within the same local. Bowing to the logic of language groups, UCAPAWA divided them into Spanish- and English-speaking locals. Still, the fact that Hispanic farmworkers, some of them veterans of the 1933 strikes, played prominent roles in some strikes kept certain whites on the sidelines. Even more troublesome was the presence of a small number of black unionists. The Wasco local evidently defied headquarters and discouraged interested blacks from attending most functions. The local's president denied this and assured Walter Goldschmidt that all races were welcome, but his wife interrupted to insist, "You can't equalize me with no nigger—I don't care what." [72]

The issue of individualism remains to be considered. Much depends on the definition, whether an ideology or a condition is meant. The notion that rural Southwesterners were "rugged individualists" unfamiliar with the rudiments of cooperation is another one of the mistaken stereotypes generated by a society that was uncomfortable with its rural shadow. Here is the *New York Times* quoting a Farm Security Administration official's characterization of the migrants: "These are men who got a shotgun and guarded a stalk of cotton that was hanging over the fence so that the farmer on the other side of the fence wouldn't pick it." "They're the greatest individuals on earth," he went on. "They'd die in a factory."[73] This is nonsense. Okies were neither loners nor frontiersmen, and they did as well as anyone else in the factories. Cooperation was certainly nothing new. The churches that many supported and attended before coming to California were proof of that.[74]

On the other hand, it was true that plain-folk culture gave considerable emphasis to issues of self-reliance and personal or family autonomy, and true that even today symbols of independence rank highly in the honor scheme of the Okie group. That makes the union question complicated, because it is not necessarily true that unionism and the spirit of independence are incompatible. Over the years a good deal of American labor activism has been generated in defense of principles of self-reliance, manhood, and personal integrity. From railroadmen in the 1880s to teamsters in the 1980s, the collective discipline of unionism seems often to be marshaled in favor of symbols of pride and independence.[75]

The notion that Okies were unprepared for or ideologically opposed to unions breaks down as soon as industries other than agriculture are considered. In the oil fields and canneries, or in the shipyards and aircraft factories that many entered during World War II, Southwesterners showed little reluctance and in some cases considerable enthusiasm for workplace organization. Confronting faceless corporations, they were readily persuaded that the exercise of group power was not only practical but honorable.

But a union of farmworkers seemed a different proposition. Farming was too sacred an endeavor for the tactics of the factory. Whatever their current social station, the majority of these former farmers could not but remain loyal to the enterprise of their ancestors. And whatever their current economic interests, they thus found it hard not to identify with their employers.

UCAPAWA faced an impossible public relations problem. Organizers tried to convince the newcomers that California agriculture was not what they were used to, that independent farming was a fiction in an industry controlled by giant concerns, and that in any event the union had no quarrel with the small growers. "All the farms around here are financed, and the finance companies wouldn't allow but so much [for wages], and they couldn't pay more," explained a Missourian who found the lessons persuasive. It galled him that "a bunch of these Chamber of Commerce,

White Collar fellows, who never farmed in their lives, go up to Fresno every year and set the prices." [76]

But even as many of the migrants agreed with the union's characterization of the system as "monopoly agriculture," it was difficult for UCAPAWA to break the bonds of sympathy that these former farmers often felt for their particular California employers. Many are the stories of workers who stuck by their bosses during the strikes because "he was a good fellow." Ed Crane, who allows that "I never was too much on strikes," worked through several in the 1930s. "If I'm working for a person I owe my allegiance to my employer until it becomes patently unfair and then I'll go somewhere else to go to work. That's been my theory of the whole thing." [77]

Particularly if they worked for a grower of modest scale, the migrants were quick to identify with him. A young father from Kansas was barely feeding his family on his 25 cents per hour wage. But though he knew it "is a little too low, a man should have 30 cents," he was not complaining. "Under present prices these California farmers are payin' about all they can stand fer wages. . . . Last year a good many farmers went broke." [78] Martin Childs* sympathized with the aims of the union but was too much of a farmer at heart to fully accept the logic of opposing interests implicit in the union strategy. "The ranchers have done pretty well [by us]," he allowed. "Our main drawback is too many people. We've rustled pretty hard in my family and got quite a bit of work. They seem to pay a reasonable fair price. Some folks don't think they do, but I figure they pay a reasonable fair price." [79]

And with less frequency the same logic worked for even the wealthiest of growers. James Lackey is today a stalwart member of the pipefitters' union, but in the late 1930s he made his home on the gigantic DiGiorgio ranch, most famous of the "factories in the field." And he had no interest in the union: "I didn't see anybody taking advantage of anyone. . . . It was friendly and the bosses were good. In fact I talked to the old man DiGiorgio, the one that owned it, and little Joe. . . . they was just like common people. All the bosses were swell." Here was the unions' dilemma. A farmer (even a millionaire California grower with international corporate interests), if he acted like a man of the soil and treated his employees with dignity, was more of a kindred spirit than were some of the allies the unions proposed: nonwhites, Communists, educated middle-class sympathizers. [80]

The significance of all this for the UCAPAWA campaign was limited. Farm-labor unionism in the late 1930s was defeated by market conditions that would have undermined even the most determined constituency. But the migrants' response helps us to see both the variation in their political orientations and the majority trend. If we seek the central tendency in this emerging subculture, we will find it among those who were suspicious of the left and impressed with gestures of independence and toughness even while they retained a faith in programs that promised economic justice. This was a political culture in transition, lodged somewhere between the agrarian radicalism of an earlier era and the flag-waving conservatism of the next. And for the moment it found at best an awkward home in California, fitting only partly under the very liberal banner of California's Democratic party.

True Americanism

Nativism and racism were aspects of the value system of Southwestern plain folk which figured also in the subculture taking shape in California. For all their aggravation at the hands of middle-class white society, nothing bothered the newcomers more than California's system of racial and ethnic relations. It was one of the features of their new surroundings that convinced them that California's standards, not their own, needed changing.

Settlement in California imposed a number of unfamiliar ethnic encounters on migrants from the Western South. Coming from a region where blacks and in some settings Hispanics were the only significant minorities and where white Protestant supremacy was an unquestioned fact of life, the greater diversity and somewhat more tolerant habits of California offered a serious challenge.[81]

Some found themselves working for Italian, Scandinavian, Portuguese, Armenian, or perhaps even Japanese growers; others for Hispanic labor contractors or once in a while a black contractor. They competed for jobs with Hispanic and Filipino workers, sometimes finding that these groups were preferred by certain growers. All this was confusing. "We thought we were just 100 percent American," recalls Martha Jackson, who arrived in California as a teenager in 1937. "I had never heard of an Armenian, I had never met an Italian and I never had seen Chinese or Japanese or Mexican people. . . . We thought their grandparents didn't fight in the Civil War or Revolution."[82]

The new encounters were especially difficult because of the contempt Okies experienced at the hands of so many white residents. Accustomed to a social structure which guaranteed them ethnic privileges, they read California's arrangements as an inversion of accustomed patterns. "I have not noticed the California critics condemning the Filipinos, Japanese, or any other foreigners," William Siefert wrote to Fresno's major newspaper. "But when United States born citizens come here, they say we cut wages and lower their standard of living."[83]

"Just who built California?" another writer asked rhetorically before revealing his ignorance of California's ethnohistory:

> Certainly not the Chinese, Japanese, Hindus, etc., that you let stay inside her borders. . . . The aliens are perfectly welcome, but the real citizens must stay out. . . . Not one word of protest did I hear [about foreigners]. But let a citizen from the East come out here and try to make a home and be a respectable person and one hears plenty.[84]

James Wilson encountered similar complaints among the migrants he interviewed in Kern County. Among those who would speak freely of their feelings of discontent, several blamed Mexicans, Japanese, and Filipinos, all of whom, one Oklahoman claimed, "git the cream of the crop, they git the jobs." "That is where a lot of our trouble is," he continued, "the country is too heavily populated with foreigners . . . the farmers ain't got no business hirin' them fer low wages when we native white American citizens are starvin'."[85] It was bad enough, Clyde Storey* maintained, that Californians refused to "treat you like a white man," but to encounter a sign reading "No White Laborers Need Apply" at the ranch belonging to former President Herbert Hoover was in his mind the most painful irony of all.[86] A young Oklahoman summarized the fear that pressed heavily on the self-esteem of many migrants: "they think as much of a 'Nigger' uptown here as they do white people."[87] It was not true, of course, but the decline in their own social position, combined with what most Southwesterners saw as a substantial elevation in the rights of racial and ethnic minorities, perhaps made it seem so.

Without question the most troubling feature of the California ethnic system for Southwesterners centered on interactions with blacks. A tiny black population shared the farm-labor occupational strata with Okies in the San Joaquin Valley. Excluded even from the FSA camps, living mostly in isolated enclaves in some of the larger towns, blacks, as always, suffered far more serious economic and social discrimination than any whites. Still, they enjoyed certain opportunities not common to the Southwest, and these offended the sensibilities of the newcomers. The superiority of white over black was the bottom line of plain-folk culture, and any change in the status of black people was very deeply felt.[88]

The most obvious breach in segregation etiquette occurred in the schools, some of which admitted black students to the same classrooms as whites.

Ruth Woodall Criswell recalls the resulting trauma in her household. It was "the first time in my life I'd ever gone to school with anyone except just white children." Her parents "could hardly reconcile themselves to the fact. At first they didn't seem to mind so much about the Mexican and Chinese but the blacks bothered them."[89]

Noting that "they are niggers back home but colored people here," one of Goldschmidt's informants confessed similar worries. "I thought it would be awful to send our children to school with niggers, but they aren't so bad. The children like the niggers alright—they don't bother any. These niggers around here don't bother us any if you let them alone."[90]

Alvin Laird was one of many Southwestern parents who became embroiled with school officials over the issue. He claims (though it is hard to believe) that education authorities in the Imperial Valley tried to enroll his children in an "all-colored school." "My children ain't going to go over there," he told the officials, and rather than send them he kept them out of school until the family moved north to the San Joaquin Valley. There were problems in the new setting as well. After his daughter was blamed for an altercation with a black teenager, he confronted the school principal, announced that his daughter would not apologize, and threatened that if the youth "don't leave my daughter alone I'll have one of them boys of mine to whop him so you won't know him when he comes to school."[91]

Parents' anxieties were played out in a sometimes violent fashion by the younger generation. Charles Newsome remembers with some embarrassment his first days at an elementary school in Tulare County.

> The teacher assigned me and told me to go sit in this desk . . . it was right behind the only colored kid in the class. So I was a little smart ass Okie and I had never had much school with them so no way was I going to get behind no colored kid . . . I told her "Teacher, I don't sit behind no nigger." So when recess time came naturally that's when a fight got started.[92]

The fighting became more serious in the upper grades. High school teachers sometimes blamed Okie youths for persecuting black students, and knifings and serious brawls were reported.[93] Not all of this was the fault of whites. Juanita Price, one of the few black Oklahomans to come west during the 1930s, recalls some of the violence in the Bakersfield area and blames it on both sides:

> When the white Southerners came here a lot of them got whippings from black people . . . the blacks had a little hostility in them and when they came out to California they thought the situation was different so they could just whip a white fella and forget it. And many fights went on. The

blacks had said all their lives, "one of these days I'm going to whip me a white kid," and they'd whip one. It was just stupidity.

Some of it was also bloody. She tells of one particularly violent incident. "Tex's Bar," an Okie hangout in Bakersfield, prominently displayed a "NO NIGGERS" sign on the door. When a black man walked in one day, the owner tried to throw him out. The would-be customer then pulled a knife and "cut him up real bad."[94]

All this needs to be qualified. Racial tolerance was not unknown in the Western South, and some migrants warmly endorsed more equitable racial relations. Despite the example of the Wasco UCAPAWA local, racial liberalism was especially pronounced among the minority who participated in unions and radical politics. And others also came to accept the sorts of inter-ethnic contact that California imposed. James Wilson listened as a group of young cotton choppers discussed their employer, a black labor contractor:

HARVEY JOHNSON*:	That "Nigger" guy is a nice boss, better than a lot of white men.
BILL BROWN*:	But I wouldn't let anybody know I was workin' fer a "Nigger."
HENRY JOHNSON*:	He said to me the other day, "Will you please cut the weeds over behind those beets?" He said "Please."
BOYD JONES*:	They think as much of a "Nigger" uptown here as they do white people. I don't even like fer one of them to ask me fer a cigarette. Another thing, they drink out of the same cup.
ANGUS DOW*:	I don't mind drinkin' out of the same cup if he'll set it down and let it set fer five minutes.
HARVEY JOHNSON*:	I've been in ten states and don't like them yet.[95]

As the conversation indicates, this was a process which would take time. Even as some whites were learning new lessons, others clung tenaciously to racial animosity. And if we are looking again for central tendencies, it would have to be said that racism remained the subculture's dominant voice. Many Southwesterners found purpose in speaking out against rather than for interracial understanding.[96]

This became quite evident in the 1940s, when the racial composition of California underwent a fundamental change. Black migration accelerated dramatically during World War II, nearly quadrupling the state's Afro-American population by 1950. Where Okies and blacks met there was continual tension. Sociologist Katherine Archibald observed the conflict in a Bay Area shipyard. Blacks were resented by most whites, she noted, but especially by Okies, who "found it hard to accept the casual contact between Negro men and white women to which Northern custom had become indifferent—sitting together on streetcars and buses, standing together before lunch counters or pay windows, working side by side in the same gangs."[97] Grumbling that "it's the niggers who are taking over California," Okies talked loudly, she added, about lynchings and other bloody remedies. "What you need round here," one Southwesterner told her, "is a good old-fashioned lynching. Back in my home state we string a nigger up or shoot him down, every now and then, and that way we keep the rest of them quiet and respectful."[98]

Apparently it was not all talk. Violent incidents, including cross burnings and even murders, occurred in both the Bay Area and Los Angeles, settings where defense work brought the two groups of Southerners together. At the end of the war a brief florescence of Ku Klux Klan activity in southern California was linked to Southwestern whites.[99]

Southwesterners enjoyed no monopoly on racism, of course. Nor did California, with its legacy of anti-Asian sentiment, need instructions in white supremacy. Black newcomers met resistance from many quarters. But some white Southwesterners brought a heightened militancy to the subject. Both because interracial contacts at work and school were new and because their self-esteem at this juncture was so fragile, vigorous racism became a prominent feature of the Okie response to California. Charles Newsome remembers the transference. "The people out here [Californians] looked down on the Okies but the Okies looked down on other people too at the time."[100]

An outlet for frustration, racism was in subtle ways also a source of group identity—something that made at least some Okies feel special and distinct. While many white Californians shared the migrants' racist outlook, the fact that some features of California law and custom were different than back home allowed certain newcomers to conclude that there was much that was wrong with the state and its citizenry. And some, as we see in Archibald's report, styled themselves guardians of white supremacy, dispensing advice on how to deal with blacks. Here, sadly, was another understanding and shared purpose, another piece of the subcultural framework.

Native Sons

If the debasement of California's nonwhites had therapeutic and group definitional implications, the migrants' concept of Americanism figured more ambiguously in relations with the state's whites, most of whom possessed old-stock credentials not much different than their own. Mostly, Americanism provided a bridge. That so many of the Californians were "Americans" minimized the migrants' defensive reactions and sustained their interest in assimilation, which as we have seen was one compelling strategy of adjustment. But for some members of the group, expectations about the behavior of proper Americans also provided ammunition for criticizing their native hosts. And while this endeavor was but a weak reflection of the disdain Okies knew was directed their own way, it offered some measure of emotional conciliation and group definition.

Southwesterners used several devices to turn the tables on Californians, the simplest of which were snide labels of their own, including "Calies," "native sons," and the curious favorite, "prune pickers," which played on the bathroom humor associated with the sticky, sweet dried fruit. A stereotype accompanied the labels, the thrust of which was that Californians were selfish, arrogant, "privileged characters" who thought they were better than everyone else. As one novice poet put it:

> Some of the Californians go around, with their nose stuck up;
> Like when it would rain, They'd use it for a cup.[101]

This view of rude and haughty natives was often coupled with the notion that Californians had grown soft and lazy, and furthermore that their resentment of the migrants was rooted in jealousy and fear. "If it weren't for Texas, Oklahoma, and Arkansas, there wouldn't be much to California, would there?" a migrant hitchhiker lectured Charles Todd. He figured that everybody else in the state had forgotten the meaning of real work.[102]

As have-nots often do, the migrants also enjoyed suggestions that Californians' lofty social positions rested upon lowly origins and ill-gotten or unearned wealth. A popular ditty that apparently pre-dated the Dust Bowl migration delighted Okies with its irreverent view of the California pedigree.

> The miners came in forty-nine,
> The whores in fifty-one;
> And when they bunked together
> They begot the native son.[103]

The author of a letter to the *Modesto Bee* had different suspicions about California bloodlines. Establishing his own credentials as a "native son of the U.S.A." whose "father and grandfather served in the Civil War," he addressed his challenge "to the native son who owns your big dairies, your big vineyards, your big orchards, look up the records and get the facts. . . .

The few I have worked for, I have been informed, got their starts from their fathers, who happened not to be native sons."[104] Here was the plain folks' critique in a nutshell: "big" farms, too big and too cushy; unearned wealth and social position; and possibly immigrant backgrounds. It was quite a brief.

Still, these attempts at denigration, unlike those directed at nonwhites, were not particularly serious. Few Okies really entertained feelings of superiority over white Californians. Most of the jibes were simply attempts to reassure themselves and regain some composure. Nevertheless, the process had bearing on the emerging subculture. In clarifying their definitions of proper Americanism and in laying special claim to that heritage, the migrants were developing an identity capable of sustaining a group experience that initially owed its existence to external forces of class and prejudice.

We will let Ernest Martin restate the proposition that underlay the group identity. An Oklahoman who came to California as a child, grew up in the valley, then moved to Los Angeles and became a minister and religious scholar, he speaks boldly and with insight about the cultural and cognitive parameters of the Okie experience. They considered themselves "the best Americans in the world," he recalls. "To our people their way of life was America. New York isn't America . . . we were America."[105]

There is no simple statement of regional pride. The Okie subculture was anchored in a group concept that is not reducible to the ethnic formula that scholars sometimes employ in relation to other groups of Southern white out-migrants. Instead of a particularistic definition of the group based on state origins, many Southwesterners laid claim to a nativist conception of national community. Plain-folk Americanism was in some respects a regional enterprise—white Southerners were its core proponents in California—but it also spoke to and for whites of many other backgrounds. Hence, the curious dynamics of the Okie subculture. Southwesterners drew together and gained feelings of pride and definition from this ideological system but never manifested the exclusivity, the insularity, of an ethnic subsociety. Plain-folk Americanism gave their community a different thrust, outward and expansive, open to other whites who embraced the proper values. These heartlanders had come to California with something not just to save but to share.

This would become increasingly clear in the decades to come. The 1940s would simultaneously reduce the structures of social and economic isolation and encourage the proliferation of key cultural institutions. Country music and evangelical churches would become important emblems of the

Okie group in the post-Depression decades. And each would function in the dual manner we have been observing, on the one hand solidifying elements of group pride, while also carrying messages of wider appeal that helped to spread the Okie cultural impact far beyond the formal boundaries of the Southwestern group.

NOTES

1. My definition of subculture follows Milton M. Gordon, *Assimilation in American Life* (New York, 1964), 39. For a rich discussion of the uses and possible definitions, see Edward Merten, "Up Here and Down Home: Appalachian Migrants in Northtown" (Ph.D. diss., University of Chicago, 1974), 180–99; J. Milton Yinger, "Contraculture and Subculture," *American Sociological Review* 25 (1960), 625–35.

2. Walter Goldschmidt, *As You Sow* (Glencoe, 1947; reprint ed., Montclair, N.J., 1978), 60–61, 70. Few other scholars even raised the question of Okies as a separate cultural group. Most concerned themselves strictly with the parameters of economic adjustment, as in the work of Paul Taylor, his students Lillian Creisler and Walter Hoadley, Carey McWilliams, and the Bureau of Agricultural Economics investigators. James Wilson collected wonderful material on the social attitudes and religious outlooks of the migrants in his two studies, but offered little interpretation of its significance.

3. Stuart M. Jamieson, "A Settlement of Rural Migrant Families in the Sacramento Valley, California," *Rural Sociology* 7 (March 1942), 50–51, 57. Writing in 1947, Paul Faulkner Tjensvold also commented on the Southern cultural characteristics of the migrants and noted that some of these were being maintained in California. "An Inquiry into the Reasons for the Post-Depression Migration from Oklahoma to Kern County in California" (MA thesis, University of Southern California, 1947), 45.

4. The ethnic formulation was sharply criticized at the 1947 meeting of the American Sociological Association. In a panel on the state of ethnic research, UCLA sociologist Leonard Bloom suggested that Okies had the characteristics of an ethnic group. Other panelists dismissed the idea, one suggesting that Bloom might as well include "Townsendites [or] the Aimee McPhersonites" under the ethnic heading. "Concerning Ethnic Research," *American Sociological Review* 13 (April 1948), 171–82. The standard understanding of ethnicity in that period is found in W. Lloyd Warner and Leo Srole, *The Social Systems of American Ethnicity* (New Haven, 1945), 28.

In contrast, recent ethnic studies tend to employ a more elastic definition that accepts the possibility of new or "emergent" ethnic groups. See, for instance, William L. Yancy, Eugene P. Ericksen, and Richard N. Juliani, "Emergent Ethnicity: A Review and Reformulation," *American Sociological Review* 41 (June 1976), 391–403; Abner Cohen in *Urban Ethnicity* (New York, 1974), ix–xxiv; Donald L. Horowitz, "Ethnic Identity," in Nathan Glazer and Daniel P. Moynihan, eds., *Ethnicity: Theory and Experience* (Cambridge, 1975), 111–40; Jonathan D. Sarna, "From Immigrants to Ethnic: Toward a New Theory of 'Ethnicization,'" *Ethnicity* 5 (Dec. 1978), 370–77; Kathleen Neils Conzen, "Immigrants, Immigrant Neighborhoods, and Ethnic Identity: Historical Issues," *Journal of American History* 66 (Dec. 1979), 603–15.

5. Works by John Shelton Reed include *The Enduring South: Subcultural Per-

sistence in Mass Society (Chapel Hill, 1972); *Southerners: The Social Psychology of Sectionalism* (Chapel Hill, 1983); *Southern Folk, Plain and Fancy: Native White Social Types* (Athens, Ga., 1986). Lewis M. Killian, *White Southerners* (New York, 1970), 143–44; also Merten, "Up Here and Down Home," 311–13. Their ideas have been seconded by George Brown Tindall, *The Ethnic Southerners* (Baton Rouge, 1976), 1–21; and, most important, by the *Harvard Encyclopedia of American Ethnic Groups*, Stephan Thernstrom, Ann Orlov, and Oscar Handlin, eds. (Cambridge, 1980), 944–48.

6. This definition follows the one proposed by R. A. Schermerhorn, *Comparative Ethnic Relations: A Framework for Theory and Research* (Chicago, 1970), 12, and employed by Werner Sollars in his review of "Theory of American Ethnicity . . . ," *American Quarterly* 33 (1981 Bibliography issue), 257–83. Other uses of the term are surveyed in Wsevolod W. Isajiw, "Definitions of Ethnicity," *Ethnicity* 1 (July 1974), 111–24.

7. We cannot pretend to any unanimity on the issue of social structure in either the Southwest or the greater South. The lumpers and the splitters have been going at it continuously since the days of Frederick Law Olmstead. Here I am following John Reed's sensible suggestion of a two-race, two-class model in *Southern Folk, Plain and Fancy*, 23.

8. Dewey Grantham, *Southern Progressivism: The Reconciliation of Progress and Tradition* (Knoxville, 1983), 87–107; Lawrence Goodwyn, *Democratic Promise: The Populist Moment in America* (New York, 1976); Raymond Arsenault, *The Wild Ass of the Ozarks: Jeff Davis and the Social Bases of Southern Politics* (Philadelphia, 1984); Alan Brinkley, *Voices of Protest: Huey Long, Father Coughlin, and the Great Depression* (New York, 1982), esp. 47–53; V. O. Key, *Southern Politics in State and Nation* (New York, 1950), 261–68; James R. Green, *Grass-roots Socialism: Radical Movements in the Southwest, 1895–1943* (Baton Rouge, 1978), 396–437; Worth Robert Miller, "Oklahoma Populism: A History of the People's Party of Oklahoma Territory" (Ph.D. diss., University of Oklahoma, 1984); John Thompson, *Closing the Frontier: Radical Response in Oklahoma, 1889–1923* (Norman, 1986).

9. Charles Todd, "The Pea-Patch Press," typescript in Charles Todd Collection. The best collection of the FSA newspapers resides in the Documents Library, University of California, Berkeley, but the Farm Security Administration Collections at San Bruno (National Archives, Pacific Sierra Division) and at the Bancroft Library contain additional issues. Sheldon S. Kagan, "Goin' Down the Road Feelin' Bad: John Steinbeck's *The Grapes of Wrath* and Migrant Folklore" (Ph.D. diss., University of Pennsylvania, 1971), makes some interesting comments on the literary quality, the humor, and the political values revealed in the camp newspapers.

10. *Westley Worldbeater* (May 22, 1942). For other versions of this poem, see *Covered Wagon News* (Shafter) (July 13, 1940); *Thornton's Camp Paper* (Fall 1940).

11. *Camp Echo* (Brawley) (Jan. 13, 1939). Also recorded by Margaret Valiant in her Migrant Camp Recordings, Archive of Folk Culture, Library of Congress. "Root Hog or Die" by Bill Jackson in Todd-Sonkin Recordings is another example of the same theme. (Todd-Sonkin Recordings and field notes, Charles L. Todd and Robert Sonkin, Migrant Recordings, 1940 and 1941, Archive of Folk Culture, Library of Congress.)

12. Two recent works explore the toughness theme in American culture: Elliot J. Gorn, *The Manly Art: Bare-Knuckle Prize Fighting in America* (Ithaca, 1986); Rupert Wilkinson, *American Tough: The Tough-Guy Tradition and American*

Character (New York, 1986). Roland Marchand, *Advertising the American Dream* (Berkeley, 1985), 285–333, shows that many of these images were appearing in the advertising of the 1930s.

13. "A Grumbler," *Weed Patch Cultivator* (Arvin) (Nov. 11, 1938).

14. *Thornton's Camp Paper* (Fall 1940).

15. *Migratory Clipper* (Indio) (March 9, 1940). See also "The Optimist" in *Voice of the Migrant* (Marysville) (Dec. 15, 1939); "Depression" in *Covered Wagon News* (Shafter) (July 27, 1940); "Old Mrs. So and So," *Tow-Sack Tattler* (Arvin) (Sept. 8, 1939).

16. *Tow-Sack Tattler* (Arvin) (Nov. 11, 1939).

17. *Covered Wagon News* (Shafter) (Aug. 24, 1940).

18. Bertram Wyatt-Brown, *Southern Honor: Ethics and Behavior in the Old South* (New York, 1982). I would also strongly recommend Merten's chapter on honor in "Up Here and Down Home," 142–79.

19. *Agri-News* (Shafter) (Aug. 11, 1939). Also *Tow-Sack Tattler* (Arvin) (Oct. 25, 1940).

20. *Voice of the Agricultural Worker* (Yuba City) (May 28, 1940).

21. *Tow-Sack Tattler* (Arvin) (Oct. 28, 1939). See also Oct. 20 and Nov. 11, 1939, issues. For an example of the stoic attitude expected of children, see Todd-Sonkin field notes, 6.

22. Sept. 8, 1939. The popularity of the matches and the social pressure to fight are recalled by Oscar "Scotty" Kludt in his interview by Michael Neely, Fresno, May 1, 1981, Odyssey Program, 22. See also Lawrence I. Hewes, Jr., Report Before the Special Committee Investigating the Interstate Migration of Destitute Citizens, San Francisco, Sept. 25, 1940, mimeographed copy in FSA Collection, Box 10, Bancroft. If the coverage in the *Bakersfield Californian* (Kern County's major daily) is any indication, professional wrestling was also extremely popular. And it was hardly accidental that some of the featured wrestlers sported names like "Bob Montgomery, the Arkansas blond caveman" and "Otis Clingman, the popular Texas cowboy."

23. *Agri-News* (July 21, 1939).

24. In his discussion of honor and fighting among Chicago's Southern whites, Merten, "Up Here and Down Home," 289, also observes that these values became exaggerated in the new setting. There is a rich literature on the Southern use of violence as an expression of masculine honor. In addition to the studies already cited, see John Shelton Reed, *One South: An Ethnic Approach to Regional Culture* (Baton Rouge, 1982), 139–53; Sheldon Hackney, "Southern Violence," *American Historical Review* 74 (Feb. 1969), 906–25; Raymond D. Gastil, *Culture Regions of the United States* (Seattle, 1975), 97–116; H. C. Brearley, "The Pattern of Violence," in William T. Couch, ed., *Culture in the South* (Chapel Hill), 678–92; Evon Z. Vogt, *Modern Homesteaders: The Life of a Twentieth Century Frontier Community* (Cambridge, Mass., 1955), 158–59; Elliot J. Gorn, "'Gouge and Bite, Pull Hair and Scratch': The Social Significance of Fighting in the Southern Backcountry," *American Historical Review* 90 (Feb. 1985), 18–43.

25. Gerald Haslam, *Okies: Selected Stories* (Santa Barbara, 1975), 60.

26. Interview by Stacey Jagels, Oakhurst, May 2, 1981, Odyssey Program, 23.

27. Interview by Michael Neely, Visalia, March 23, May 12, 1981, Odyssey Program, 38.

28. Interview by Stacey Jagels, Bakersfield, March 31, April 2, 1981, Odyssey Program, 43.

29. Interview by Stacey Jagels, Hanford, June 2, 1981, Odyssey Program, 24.

30. My thoughts on group myths have been informed by Michaela di

Leonardo's recent exploration of Italian-American ethnic identity in *The Varieties of Ethnic Experience: Kinship, Class, and Gender Among California Italian Americans* (Ithaca, 1984). She notes that Italians hold a number of assumptions about group characterological and behavioral traits, some of which are clearly not unique to the group. Regardless, the assumptions themselves have significance. It is the belief in distinctiveness that constitutes one of the essentials of the group relationship. Related points about the content of ethnic identity are made by Talcott Parsons, "Some Theoretical Considerations on the Nature and Trends of Change of Ethnicity," in Glazer and Moynihan, *Ethnicity: Theory and Experience*, 64–66; Fredrik Barth, introduction to *Ethnic Groups and Boundaries: The Social Organization of Culture Difference* (Oslo, 1969), 11–16).

31. Gerald Haslam, "The Okies: Forty Years Later," *The Nation* 220 (March 15, 1975), 302. See also her Jan. 1975 letter to Haslam in Charles Todd Collection.

32. Mark Jones, "Dust Bowl Clan Marks 44 Years in West," *Los Angeles Times* (Aug. 2, 1981).

33. Interview, 38.

34. Interview by author, Reedley, April 31, 1985.

35. George Baker, "66, The Road Back in Time," *Sacramento Bee* (Jan. 1, 1978) (emphasis added).

36. Redneck Populism might be another term for what I am describing. Several recent studies have guided my thinking about plain folks' political values, most important among them Robert Emil Botsch's excellent *We Shall Not Overcome: Populism and Southern Blue-Collar Workers* (Chapel Hill, 1980); Arsenault, *The Wild Ass of the Ozarks*; J. Wayne Flynt, *Dixie's Forgotten People: The South's Poor Whites* (Bloomington, 1979). Useful but marred by its condescending tone is Julian B. Roebuck and Mark Hickson III, *The Southern Redneck: A Phenomenological Class Study* (New York, 1982).

37. *The Hub* (Visalia) (Sept. 13, 1940); *Covered Wagon News* (Shafter) (March 12, 1940); *Tow-Sack Tattler* (Arvin) (Sept. 8, 1939). See also Eric H. Thomsen, "Maverick Universities or How the Migrant Gets an Education" (speech before the San Francisco Public School Forum, Jan. 29, 1937), in FSA Collection, carton 2, Bancroft; James West (Carl Withers), *Plainville U.S.A.* (New York, 1945), 135–36, 212–13; Vogt, *Modern Homesteaders*, 143–45. These occupational valuations were basically similar to those described by Bruce Palmer, *Man Over Money: The Southern Populist Critique of American Capitalism* (Chapel Hill, 1980), 9–19.

38. *Agri-News* (Aug. 25, 1939).

39. *Covered Wagon News*, quoted in Todd, "Pea-Patch Press," page numbers omitted.

40. An asterisk indicates that a pseudonym is used for the individual who was interviewed. James Bright Wilson, "Social Attitudes of Migratory Agricultural Workers in Kern County, California" (MA thesis, University of Southern California, 1942), 178–79. Walter Stein discusses the problem of relations between the migrants and camp managers in "A New Deal Experiment with Guided Democracy: The FSA Migrant Camps in California," Canadian Historical Association, *Historical Papers 1970*, 132–46.

41. *Camp Echo* (Brawley) (Dec. 9, 1939).

42. *Voice of the Agricultural Worker* (Yuba City) (May 28, 1940).

43. *Weed Patch Cultivator* (Arvin) (Nov. 11, 1938); *Voice of the Migrant* (Marysville) (Feb. 23, 1940). "The Future" in *Tow-Sack Tattler* (Arvin) (Nov. 17, 1939) is a little less cautious, counseling neither ambition nor passivity, but suggesting the importance of "choosing the right tools for life's work."

44. Brinkley, *Voices of Protest*, 165–68; Keith L. Bryant, Jr., *Alfalfa Bill Murray* (Norman, 1968), 177–213, and "Oklahoma and the New Deal" in John Braeman, Robert H. Bremner, and David Brody, eds., *The New Deal: The State and Local Levels* (Columbus, 1975), 172–73, 183; Harry S. Ashmore, *Arkansas: A Bicentennial History* (New York, 1978), 137–46; David Ellery Rison, "Arkansas During the Great Depression" (Ph.D. diss., University of California, Los Angeles, 1974), 57–62; Key, *Southern Politics in State and Nation*, 261–68; Green, *Grassroots Socialism*, 396–437; Norman D. Brown, *Hood, Bonnet, and Little Brown Jug: Texas Politics, 1921–1928* (College Station, Texas, 1984); Lionel V. Patenaude, *Texans, Politics, and the New Deal* (New York, 1983), 86–120; Donald W. Whisenhunt, *The Depression in Texas: The Hoover Years* (New York, 1983), 197–229; George Norris Green, *The Establishment in Texas Politics: The Primitive Years, 1938–1957* (Westport, 1979), 13–14. For Missouri's different political habits, see John H. Fenton, *Politics in the Border States* (New Orleans, 1957), 126–70.

45. Lillian Creisler, "'Little Oklahoma' or the Airport Community: A Study of the Social and Economic Adjustment of Self-Settled Agricultural Drought and Depression Refugees" (MA thesis, University of California, Berkeley, 1940), 60; Walter Evans Hoadley, "A Study of One Hundred Seventy Self-Resettled Agricultural Families, Monterey County, California, 1939" (MA thesis, University of California, Berkeley, 1940), 138. The Ham 'n' Eggs movement is described in Jackson K. Putnam, *Old-Age Politics in California: From Richardson to Reagan* (Palo Alto, 1970), 89–114; Robert E. Burke, *Olson's New Deal for California* (Berkeley, 1953); Carey McWilliams, *Southern California: An Island on the Land* (New York, 1946), 303–8.

46. *Tow-Sack Tattler* (Arvin) (Oct. 28, 1939). Also *Tent City News* (Gridley) (Sept. 23, 1939); *Bakersfield Californian* (Oct. 9, 1939); Lloyd Stalcup and Mr. Becker interviews, Todd-Sonkin Recordings.

47. California State Relief Administration, M. H. Lewis, *Migratory Labor in California* (San Francisco, 1936), 140. Hammett is given the pseudonym Clay Bennett in this source.

48. Wilson, "Social Attitudes of Migratory Agricultural Workers," 343.

49. Stuart M. Jamieson, "The Origins and Present Structure of Labor Unions in Agriculture and Allied Industries in California," Exhibit 9576, La Follette *Hearings*, Part 62, p. 22540; Jamieson, "A Settlement of Rural Migrant Families in the Sacramento Valley," 57–59; Jamieson, *Labor Unionism in American Agriculture* (Washington, D.C., 1945), 119; Fred Snyder, "Jobless Hordes in California Offer an Opportunity for Adroit Campaign of Skillful Radical Propaganda," *San Francisco Examiner* (Feb. 28, 1939, also March 1, 2, 5, 1939); Norman Lowenstein, "Strikes and Strike Tactics in California Agriculture: A History" (MA thesis, University of California, Berkeley, 1940), 113; *Tow-Sack Tattler* (Arvin) (Oct. 16, 1939); *Farmer-Labor News* (Feb. 19, 1937); *The Rural Worker* (Nov. 1936).

50. On the formation of UCAPAWA and the beginnings of its California campaign, see 1936 and 1937 issues of *The Rural Worker* and the *CIO News—Cannery Workers Edition*. Accounts of the campaign can be found in Walter J. Stein, *California and the Dust Bowl Migration* (Westport, 1973), 220–82; Devra Anne Weber, "The Struggle for Stability and Control in the Cotton Fields of California: Class Relations in Agriculture, 1919–1942" (Ph.D. diss., University of California, Los Angeles, 1986), 312–402; Cletus E. Daniel, *Bitter Harvest: A History of California Farmworkers, 1870–1941* (Ithaca, 1981), 276–85; Linda C. Majka and Theo J. Majka, *Farm Workers, Agribusiness, and the State* (Philadelphia, 1982), 113–35.

And for an insider's view, see the Dorothy Healey interview by Margo McBane, March 7, 1978, Women Farmworkers Project.

51. *CIO News — Cannery Workers Edition* (Oct. 22, Dec. 5, 1938); Weber, "The Struggle for Stability and Control in the Cotton Fields of California," 354–58; Clarke A. Chambers, *Farm Organizations: A Historical Study of the Grange, the Farm Bureau, and the Associated Farmers, 1929–1941* (Berkeley, 1952), 72–73.

52. La Follette Committee, *Report*, 78th Congress, Part 8, pp. 1476–80; Lowenstein, "Strikes and Strike Tactics," 107–9.

53. The strike can be followed in the *Bakersfield Californian* (Sept. 22–Oct. 28, 1939). Weber, "The Struggle for Stability and Control in the Cotton Fields of California," 368–402, provides the newest and richest account. Others include Bryan Theodore Johns, "Field Workers in California Cotton" (MA thesis, University of California, Berkeley, 1948), 117–46; La Follette Committee, *Report*, 78th Congress, Part 8, pp. 1492–1527; and *Hearings*, Part 51, pp. 18633–773; Chambers, *Farm Organizations*, 72–81.

54. Todd-Sonkin Recordings, Visalia, Aug. 13, 1941. See the union's report of the difficulty of recruiting "half starved workers" in *UCAPAWA News* (April 1940).

55. Charles L. Todd, "California, Here We Stay!" typescript (New York, 1946?) in Charles Todd Collection; Ben Hibbs, "Footloose Army," *Country Gentleman* (Feb. 1940), 5, reprint in Migrant Labor Collection, Bakersfield Public Library; *New York Times* (March 6, 1940); Wilson, "Social Attitudes of Migratory Agricultural Workers," 358; California Governor's Committee to Survey the Agricultural Labor Resources of the San Joaquin Valley, *Agricultural Labor in the San Joaquin Valley: Final Report and Recommendations* (Sacramento, 1951), 289. It is interesting to follow organized labor's evaluation of Okies as potential unionists in *Farmer-Labor News* and *UCAPAWA News*. Through 1939 the journals were blindly optimistic, bending over backward to deny stories that "you can't organize the Oklahomans into the union" (*Farmer-Labor News* [April 23, 1937]). The tune changed after the cotton strike. In early 1941, Clyde Champion, chief UCAPAWA organizer, told Goldschmidt that the Okies were hopeless: "These people from Oklahoma aren't very class-conscious. It isn't in their background" (*As You Sow*, 71). See also *UCAPAWA News* (April 1940).

56. Stein, *California and the Dust Bowl Migration*, 264–65. He elaborated on this theme in his paper "Cultural Gap: Organizing California's Okies in the 1930's," presented at the Southwest Labor History Conference, Stockton, Calif., April 25, 1975. Cautioning that some Okies were strong unionists, Sheila Goldring Manes, on the basis of interviews with former organizers, essentially agrees with Stein's assessment; see "Depression Pioneers: The Conclusion of an American Odyssey, Oklahoma to California, 1930–1950, A Reinterpretation" (Ph.D. diss., University of California, Los Angeles, 1982), 388–94. The most thorough study to date of the UCAPAWA cotton campaign is Devra Weber's "The Struggle for Stability and Control in the Cotton Fields of California." She prefers not to engage directly the question of Okie sympathy, correctly emphasizing the systemic obstacles to union success and stressing in particular the strategic importance of an integrated cotton industry response. UCAPAWA's more successful campaign among Hispanic cannery workers is the subject of Vicki L. Ruiz, *Cannery Women, Cannery Lives: Mexican Women, Unionization, and the California Food Processing Industry, 1930–1950* (Albuquerque, 1987).

57. Goodwyn, *Democratic Promise*. On the Socialist campaigns, see Oscar Ameringer, *If You Don't Weaken: The Autobiography of Oscar Ameringer* (New

York, 1940); Green, *Grass-roots Socialism;* Garin Burbank, *When Farmers Voted Red: The Gospel of Socialism in the Oklahoma Countryside, 1910–24* (Westport, 1976); Manes, "Depression Pioneers," 186–222; Thompson, *Closing the Frontier.*

58. Wilson, "Social Attitudes of Migratory Agricultural Workers," 324–59; Creisler, "'Little Oklahoma,'" 40; Hoadley, "A Study of One Hundred Seventy Self-Resettled Agricultural Families," 112.

59. Wilson, "Social Attitudes of Migratory Agricultural Workers," 347; *UCAPAWA News* (Feb. 1940); Mr. P. N., Wasco field notes of Walter Goldschmidt, 1941 (in Goldschmidt's possession, Dept. of Anthropology, University of California, Los Angeles); Creisler, "'Little Oklahoma,'" 40.

60. Dellar Ballard interview by Margo McBane, Mary Winegarden, and Rick Topkins, Lindsay, July 19, 1978, Women Farmworkers Project; *Hub* spring 1940 issues. See also the anonymous interview with a former UCAPAWA organizer in the Women Farmworkers Project series; Mr. C. C., Wasco field notes.

61. Charles C. Alexander, *The Ku Klux Klan in the Southwest* (Lexington, 1965); Green, *Grass-roots Socialism,* 345–408; Burbank, *When Farmers Voted Red,* 160–89.

62. Green, *Grass-roots Socialism,* 397, calls the 1930s the "Indian Summer" of Southwestern radicalism. The only significant rural stirrings occurred in the Arkansas Delta, where the Southern Tenant Farmers Union built a short-lived biracial organization. See Donald Grubbs, *Cry from the Cotton: The Southern Tenant Farmer's Union and the New Deal* (Chapel Hill, 1971); Jamieson, *Labor Unionism in American Agriculture,* 264–71; Manes, "Depression Pioneers," 239–44; James R. Scales and Danney Goble, *Oklahoma Politics: A History* (Norman, 1982), 214–17; Jacqueline Gordon Sherman, "The Oklahomans in California During the Depression Decade, 1931–1941" (Ph.D. diss., University of California, Los Angeles, 1970), 45–47.

63. Wilson, "Social Attitudes of Migratory Agricultural Workers," 333.

64. Robert Girvin, "Migrant Workers Thinkers," *San Francisco Chronicle* (March 10, 1937).

65. Wilson, "Social Attitudes of Migratory Agricultural Workers," 339 (Freeman*). For examples of anti-Communism in the FSA camps, see *Covered Wagon* (Indio) (March 4, 1939); letter from J. H. Ward to Earl R. Becker in FSA Collection, Box 22, San Bruno; Stein, *California and the Dust Bowl Migration,* 268–69.

66. Peter Friedlander, *The Emergence of a UAW Local, 1936–1939: A Study in Class and Culture* (Pittsburgh, 1975), 97–110, found differences in the response of Catholic and Protestant workers (some Southerners) in a Detroit auto parts plant. More generally on the response to Communists, see Bert Cochran, *Labor and Communism: The Conflict That Shaped American Unions* (Princeton, 1977), 82–102; Harvey Klehr, *The Heyday of American Communism: The Depression Decade* (New York, 1984), 223–51.

67. Wilson, "Social Attitudes of Migratory Agricultural Workers," 331–32.

68. James Bright Wilson, "Religious Leaders, Institutions, and Organizations Among Certain Agricultural Workers in the Central Valley of California" (Ph.D. diss., University of Southern California, 1944), 316.

69. Burbank, *When Farmers Voted Red.* Also on the relationship between Protestantism and radicalism, see Herbert Gutman, "Protestantism and the American Labor Movement: The Christian Spirit in the Gilded Age," in Gutman, *Work, Culture, and Society in Industrializing America* (New York, 1976), 79–117.

70. Jamieson, "A Settlement of Rural Migrant Families in the Sacramento Valley," 57; medical case history No. 33, FSA Collection, carton 2, Bancroft; interview

with Lillie Ruth Ann Counts Dunn by Judith Gannon, Feb. 14, 16, 1981, Bakersfield, Odyssey Program.

71. See Wilson, "Social Attitudes of Migratory Agricultural Workers." Of the eight informants involved with the union, only one was a church member. Nevertheless, all believed in God and considered themselves Christians.

72. Wasco field notes; Stein, *California and the Dust Bowl Migration*, 270. Cletus Daniel, *Bitter Harvest*, 185, discusses racial tensions between Okies, blacks, and Mexicans in the 1933 CAWIU campaign.

73. *New York Times* (March 6, 1940); Paul S. Taylor, "Again the Covered Wagon," *Survey Graphic* 24 (July 1935), 349; Katherine Douglas, "Uncle Sam's Co-op for Individualists," *Coast Magazine* (June 1939).

74. The argument that rural Southwesterners were committed individualists who operated best within minimal community structures gains some support from anthropologist Evon Vogt's *Modern Homesteaders*, a study of an Okie community in New Mexico.

75. See the discussion of manhood in Nick Salvatore, *Eugene V. Debs: Citizen and Socialist* (Urbana, 1982), 25–26.

76. Mr. D. H., Wasco field notes.

77. Edgar Crane interview by Judith Gannon, Shafter, April 7, 1981, Odyssey Program, 10–11.

78. Wilson, "Social Attitudes of Migratory Agricultural Workers," 319.

79. Ibid., 320. Also, Tom Higgenbothan interview, Aug. 18, 1940, Todd-Sonkin Recordings; Goldschmidt, *As You Sow*, 167.

80. Interview by Stacey Jagels, March 31, April 2, 1981, Bakersfield, Odyssey Program, 33. A revealing interview with a grower who realized the importance of treating his workers with respect can be found in Goldschmidt Records, Box 66, San Bruno. Several former migrants interviewed by the Odyssey Program tell of remaining loyal to employers in the face of union pressure. See interviews with Grover C. Holliday, 48–49; Velma May Cooper Davis, 14–15; James Harrison Ward, 35; Alvin Laird, 21–22; and Clara Davis interview by author, Bakersfield, Sept. 17, 1979.

81. California's system of racial relations is surveyed in Roger Daniels and Harry H. L. Kitano, *American Racism: Exploration of the Nature of Prejudice* (Englewood Cliffs, N.J. 1970), esp. 35–72. Useful too are Roger Daniels and Spencer C. Olin, Jr., eds., *Racism in California* (New York, 1972); Charles M. Wollenberg, *All Deliberate Speed* (Berkeley, 1976); Lawrence de Graaf, *Negro Migration to Los Angeles, 1930–1950* (San Francisco, 1974).

82. Martha Lee Martin Jackson interview by Stacey Jagels, Clovis, March 10, 1981, Odyssey Program, 22.

83. *Fresno Bee* (March 22, 1938). Also printed in *Modesto Bee* (March 23, 1938).

84. *Modesto Bee* (March 9, 1938).

85. Wilson, "Social Attitudes of Migratory Agricultural Workers," 149–50, 310.

86. Ibid., 150, 316. See also *The Hub* (Visalia) (May 24, 31, June 12, 1940); Tom Collins, Reports of the Marysville Migrant Camp, 1935, in Paul S. Taylor Collection, Bancroft Library.

87. Wilson, "Social Attitudes of Migratory Agricultural Workers," 143.

88. On the FSA camps' unofficial policy of racial exclusion, see Tom Collins letter to Eric Thompson, Oct. 12, 1936, in FSA Records, Box 20, San Bruno. Examples of racist humor in the camp newspapers include *Covered Wagon* (Indio) (Dec. 10, 1938); *Tow-Sack Tattler* (Arvin) (Sept. 28, 1939, Nov. 22, 1940); *Tent City News* (Nov. 25, 1939). Todd-Sonkin Recordings provide other examples.

89. Interview by Stacey Jagels, Oildale, Feb. 24, 26, 1981, Odyssey Program, 12.
90. Mrs. L. R., Wasco field notes.
91. Interview by Judith Gannon, Porterville, Jan. 24, 1981, Odyssey Program, 11, 18.
92. Interview by Michael Neely, Visalia, March 23, May 12, 1981, Odyssey Program, 35–36.
93. Evelyn Rudd, "Reading List—Design for Living," typescript in Goldschmidt's Wasco field notes.
94. Interview by Stacey Jagels, Bakersfield, Jan. 26, 29, 1981, pp. 25–27.
95. Wilson, "Social Attitudes of Migratory Agricultural Workers," 143. Goldschmidt, *As You Sow*, 68, records a similar vignette about a popular black labor contractor. Evidence of amicable relations between Okies and Hispanics is more readily found. Margaret Valiant's Migrant Camp Recordings, Library of Congress, contain examples of these two groups interacting at FSA camps in the Imperial Valley. See also Bill Jackson's interview in Todd-Sonkin Recordings.
96. Gerald Haslam writes sensitively about the continuing pattern of racial hostility in "Oildale" and "Workin' Man's Blues" in *Voices of a Place* (Walnut Creek, Calif., 1987), 56–64, 78–97.
97. Katherine Archibald, *Wartime Shipyard: A Study of Social Disunity* (Berkeley, 1947), 70–71.
98. Ibid., 75.
99. James Richard Wilburn, "Social and Economic Aspects of the Aircraft Industry in Metropolitan Los Angeles During World War II" (Ph.D. diss., University of California, Los Angeles, 1971), 185; Lawrence Hewes, *Boxcar in the Sand* (New York, 1957), 213.
100. Newsome interview, 36.
101. *The Covered Wagon* (Indio) (April 22, 1939). Other examples: the poem "Sooner's Luck" in Todd-Sonkin Recordings; *Marysville Camp News* (July 16, 1938). Alvin Laird and Charles Newsome tell "prune-picker" stories in their Odyssey Program interviews.
102. Todd-Sonkin field notes. See also *Voice of the Agricultural Worker* (Yuba City) (Dec. 3, 1940).
103. Archibald, *Wartime Shipyard*, 55.
104. *Modesto Bee* (March 29, 1938). Also *Camp Echo* (Brawley) (Dec. 2, 1939).
105. Interview by Judith Gannon, South Pasadena, April 5, 1981, Odyssey Program, 34.

FURTHER READING

Burke, Robert E. *Olson's New Deal for California*. 1953.
Dunbar-Ortiz, Roxanne. "One or Two Things I Know About Us: Okies in American Culture." *Radical History Review* 59 (Spring 1994): 4–35.
Goldschmidt, Walter. *As You Sow*. 1947.
Gregory, James N. *American Exodus: The Dust Bowl Migration and Okie Culture in California*. 1989.
Lange, Dorothea, and Paul S. Taylor. *An American Exodus: A Record of Human Erosion*. 1939.
Larsen, Charles E. "The EPIC Campaign of 1934." *Pacific Historical Review* 27 (May 1958): 127–148.

Marsden, George M. *Fundamentalism and American Culture*. 1982.

Mitchell, Greg. *The Campaign of the Century: Upton Sinclair's Race for Governor of California and the Birth of Media Politics*. 1992.

Morgan, Dan. *Rising in the West: The True Story of an "Okie" Family from the Great Depression Through the Reagan Years*. 1992.

Mullins, William H. *The Depression and the Urban West Coast*. 1991.

Putnam, Jackson K. *Old-Age Politics in California: From Richardson to Reagan*. 1970.

Stein, Walter J. *California and the Dust Bowl Migration*. 1973.

Steinbeck, John. *The Grapes of Wrath*. 1939.

Zimmermann, Tom. "'Ham and Eggs Everybody!'" *Southern California Quarterly* 62 (Spring 1980): 1–48.

5   James v. Marinship

Trouble on the New Black Frontier

Charles Wollenberg

EDITOR'S INTRODUCTION

In 1940, African Americans made up almost 11 percent of the total population of the United States but were only 1.8 percent of California's
population. Beginning in the 1920s, however, structural and cyclical factors began to displace millions of black and white agricultural workers
from the South. The boom created by World War II led to the first massive
migration of African American people to California. Between the spring of
1942 and 1945, 340,000 black migrants poured into California. By 1950,
African Americans made up 4.7 percent of the state's population; and by
1980, they constituted 7.7 percent.

   A significant number of the wartime African American migrants were
skilled workers. A survey taken in San Francisco during World War II revealed that the migrant group contained five times as many skilled workers
as the national average for African Americans. More than three-quarters
of the new migrants worked in industry, and they were nearly evenly divided between skilled and unskilled workers. During the early months of
the war, discriminatory hiring practices severely limited black employment. Executive Order 8802, however, and the vigorous activities of Region 12 of the Fair Employment Practices Commission (FEPC), combined
with the booming demand for wartime labor, eventually resulted in the
large-scale employment of black workers.

   Although many large employers desisted from their most blatant discriminatory practices, the majority of AFL unions were slow to drop their racial
barriers. As Charles Wollenberg shows, the International Brotherhood of

Boilermakers, Iron Shipbuilders and Helpers of America forced African Americans to join segregated auxiliary locals. In 1943, black workers at a Bay Area shipyard protested this practice and refused to pay their dues. The union then withdrew their work clearances, and the company barred them from their jobs. The FEPC investigated the complaint but did not have the power to make changes. The case was taken to the California Supreme Court. In *James v. Marinship* (1945), the court declared that segregated unions in a closed shop were unconstitutional and ordered an end to the practice.

Wollenberg's article examines this important episode. He also notes that the 1945 court victory was followed by a series of others. But these decisions came at a time when employment in the shipyards was declining dramatically. Despite the outlawing of discriminatory practices, economic opportunities for African Americans after World War II were very limited.

◆　◆　◆

Nathan I. Huggins, now a distinguished Harvard historian, was one of 4846 black residents of San Francisco in 1940. He was then in junior high school and remembers "how small a community we were. . . . How self-satisfied everyone was, despite discrimination in almost every line of employment, pervasive restrictive covenants, and powerlessness in city politics." Huggins also remembers "how ambivalent everyone was about the wave of blacks from the South, brought to man new jobs in the war industries. The old [black] residents saw the new as crude, rough and boisterous. They lacked the manners and sense of decorum of San Francisco." But the newcomers made good wages and formed what Huggins calls "the basis of black business in the city." Blacks no longer could be ignored, and "complacency disappeared. Racial tensions rose." Huggins notes that many of the old black residents wished the newcomers "would all go back where they came from."[1] But they stayed and laid the foundations of most black neighborhoods and communities that still exist in the San Francisco region.

The great World War II migration is the most important event in the history of black people in the Bay Area. The region became a new black frontier, the Afro-American population growing from less than 20,000 in 1940 to over 60,000 in 1945. The number of blacks in San Francisco more than quadrupled during the war, while that in Richmond and Vallejo grew by ten times. By 1945, blacks had replaced Asians as the Bay Area's largest non-white minority and the chief target of prejudice and discrimination.[2]

In some respects, the huge migration was typical of earlier movements of non-whites to California. Like Asians and Mexicans, wartime blacks came to fill a labor shortage. But while previous minorities came as foreign immigrants and were forced into unskilled, low-paid employment, wartime blacks were American citizens recruited to fill high-wage industrial jobs created by the national emergency. About seventy percent of the employed black newcomers worked in one industry—the shipyards. Blacks made up less than three percent of the region's shipyard labor force in 1942, but that figure rose to seven percent in the following year and to more than ten percent by the end of the war.[3]

Shipyard work was largely in skilled, unionized crafts. Most Bay Area craft unions traditionally had been "lily-white," excluding both Asians and blacks, but during the war the unions suddenly had to face the possibility of large numbers of non-white members. To admit black workers violated long-standing membership rules and traditions, but to refuse to do so left unions open to charges of the very kind of undemocratic behavior against which America was supposed to be fighting. Moreover, if unions enforced membership restrictions against blacks, they would deprive shipyards of thousands of workers in the midst of a national emergency and regional labor shortage.

In spite of their significance, neither the wartime black migration nor the labor conflicts it engendered have received much historical attention. Recent works on California black history have concentrated on the pre–World War II years, and studies produced during the 1940s naturally lack historical perspective.[4] The article presented here seeks to redress this scholarly imbalance by concentrating on the wartime struggle between black workers and the Boilermakers union, which resulted in the California Supreme Court's landmark decision in the case of *James v. Marinship.* The conflict at Marinship was a microcosm of the tensions produced by the great demographic movements of World War II. In ethnic relations, as in so many other areas, the war fundamentally changed American society.

Marinship was one of the "instant" wartime shipyards created by the United States Maritime Commission. The Commission owned the yards but contracted with private companies to build and operate the plants. The first and largest such enterprise in the Bay Area was the giant Kaiser complex in Richmond. W. A. Bechtel Company of San Francisco had previously been involved in several joint business ventures with Kaiser (such as the Boulder Dam project) and had also been contracted to operate Maritime Commission yards, including Calship in southern California.

On March 2, 1942, the Commission asked Bechtel to establish a new plant on San Francisco Bay. One week later Kenneth Bechtel was in Washington with a proposal for a yard on the Marin County shoreline of Sausalito, just across the Golden Gate Bridge from San Francisco. On June 27, less than four months after the contract was awarded, Marinship laid its first keel. Initially, the yard produced "liberty ships," cargo vessels also manufactured by Kaiser. In 1943 Marinship shifted to production of prefabricated tankers, and by late 1944 the yard was launching a ship per week. By fall of 1945, Marinship had built ninety-three vessels.[5]

Bechtel originally estimated that 15,000 workers were needed to keep the yard operating twenty-four hours a day, seven days a week. In January, 1943, Marinship in fact had about 20,000 employees, and by mid-1944 the workforce had grown to 22,000. Recruiting workers was difficult in the midst of the war with ten million people in the armed forces. Marinship competed for labor with Kaiser and several other Bay Area shipyards and defense contractors. In addition to a few experienced shipbuilders, the company recruited women, teenagers, retired people, "Okies" from rural California, and newcomers from all parts of the country. Included among the industrial migrants were blacks, chiefly from states on the western rim of the South (Louisiana, Texas, Arkansas, and Oklahoma). By mid-1943, blacks were by far Marinship's largest minority group, nearly ten percent of all employees in a multi-ethnic workforce which included some Asians and Latin Americans. The company carried out a massive training effort, taking paternalistic pride in the "indoctrination program which taught colored recruits who had never held a responsible job before, as well as those from the so-called underprivileged portions of the country, good work habits."[6]

The massive influx of war workers created a major housing crisis in the Bay Area. Government restrictions limited construction of new private homes, but public housing alleviated some of the demand. Public projects were hastily erected throughout the region, including Marin City, planned in just three days for a 200-acre site immediately north of the Marinship yard. The project was built by Bechtel with Maritime Commission funds and operated by the Marin County Housing Authority. By the end of 1943, Marin City had a population of 5500 Marinship workers and their families.[7]

Under the leadership of Miles C. Dempster, Chief of Project Services, the Housing Authority attempted to make Marin City a model community.

Although it was unincorporated territory under county control, an elected City Council was established to advise county authorities. The council published a weekly newspaper, the *Marin Citizen,* and cooperated with USO and the Travelers Aid organization to provide social services. Dempster was proud of his agency's nondiscrimination policy, for unlike other Bay Area housing projects, Marin City rented accommodations on a first-come-first-served basis without regard to race. Dempster admitted that this sometimes led to inter-racial conflict and complaints from "prejudiced whites." He responded to the complaints by pointing out that "these black men are Americans. They are needed just as you are—to build ships." The City Council had both black and white members, and, according to Dempster, "gradually the color prejudices lost ground." The *Christian Science Monitor* reported that Marin City proved that "white people and Negroes can live side by side—and get along." But a former Housing Authority official admitted that if the white majority were given the power to eject blacks from the project, they probably would do so.[8]

The bulk of Marinship workers were unable to get Marin City or other Marin County accommodations and so commuted to the yard by car, bus, or ferry from San Francisco.[9] Private housing was tight for everybody, but particularly for blacks. Many Bay Area neighborhoods had restrictive covenants attached to deeds which prohibited sale or rental of homes to minorities. Residents and real estate firms practiced less formal but equally effective tactics to keep other neighborhoods and communities all-white. As a result, blacks unable to obtain public housing were crowded into those few areas that traditionally were open to minority residents.

Such an area was San Francisco's Fillmore District, home of most black Marinship workers. Before 1942, the Fillmore had a few hundred black families scattered throughout an essentially multi-ethnic, working-class neighborhood. Shortly after the attack on Pearl Harbor, several thousand residents of the Fillmore's "Japantown" were relocated to government camps by presidential order, and this opened up inexpensive housing just as the influx of black workers began. Even so, there was not enough space available. By 1943 about 9000 blacks were crowded into an area previously occupied by 5000 Japanese Americans, and city health officials classified over fifty-five percent of black housing in the Fillmore as substandard.[10] In 1945 the Fillmore was still a multi-ethnic neighborhood, but Lester Granger of the National Urban League warned it could become "another Harlem." Granger explained that San Franciscans were adopting "the social stereotypes of the East, and they want Negroes to stay in the Fillmore."[11]

While there were no legal barriers to housing discrimination, federal defense contracts did prohibit job discrimination on the basis of race, religion, and national origin. The Kaiser yards initially attempted to hire only whites in skilled trades, but protests from C. L. Dellums, vice president of the Sleeping Car Porters union, and other local black leaders forced the company to reverse that policy. By the time Marinship began hiring in 1942, blacks were being recruited at all Bay Area yards. In mid-1943 the region faced a labor shortage of 50,000 people, and any able-bodied man or woman, white or black, could get a shipyard job. Blacks and women advanced rapidly to journeyman status in welding and other trades but received few promotions to supervisory positions. Within particular job categories, workers received equal pay and benefits, regardless of race or sex.[12]

Bay Area shipyard workers usually labored together peacefully and efficiently, but racist (and sexist) attitudes were certainly present in the yards. Katherine Archibald, a Berkeley student who was employed at the Moore Company in Oakland, believed most of her white co-workers shared a "race hatred that was basic." When she tried to explain to a woman from Oklahoma that prejudice against blacks was similar to the prevalent "anti-Okie" feeling, the woman accused Archibald of inferring that Oklahomans were "no better than a nigger." Another worker responded to Archibald's plea for tolerance with the comment, "Well a nigger may be as good as you are, but sure ain't as good as me." But Archibald noted that few whites made such statements directly to blacks. A white welder explained, "if you call him that ['nigger'], he's liable as not to pick up a piece of pipe and break your head with it." According to Katherine Archibald, such fears usually kept an effective, if uneasy, racial peace at Bay Area shipyards.[13]

If Archibald was right about the prejudices of a majority of her white co-workers, the chief shipyard union, the International Brotherhood of Boilermakers, Iron Shipbuilders and Helpers of America, accurately reflected the views of most its members. The Boilermakers represented about seventy percent of the workers at Bay Area shipyards under terms of a Master Agreement between Pacific Coast shipbuilders and the AFL Metal Trades Council. The agreement established a closed shop, specifying that "all workers . . . shall be required to present a clearance card from the appropriate union before being hired." If existing union members could not be found for job openings, new workers could be hired but were still required "to secure a clearance card . . . before starting work."[14] The Boilermakers, then, had used the wartime labor shortage to achieve one of the most important union goals: control of job access. But wartime conditions had also created a multi-ethnic workforce that directly threatened the union's long tradition of white-only membership.

The Boilermakers' racial policy was shared by many, though not all, AFL craft unions. In the Bay Area, the union movement had a heritage of anti-Asian activity, and many unions also discriminated against blacks. In 1910 San Francisco black leaders persuaded a bare majority of the city's labor council to recommend that unions end restrictions against black membership, but little effort was made to enforce the resolution. The fact that employers sometimes used blacks as strikebreakers hardly promoted the cause of racial tolerance. Nevertheless, some AFL affiliates, including the Shipyard Laborers Union representing unskilled maintenance and construction workers at the yards, had long championed nondiscriminatory membership policies. In the 1930s, the new CIO unions, particularly the Longshoremen, not only had black members, but also actively supported civil rights causes in the Bay Area and elsewhere.[15]

The Boilermakers modified their national racial policies in 1937. Prior to that, blacks had been totally banned from membership, but the union's 1937 convention authorized the establishment of all-black "auxiliaries." As the term implies, the auxiliaries were not full union locals, and their members did not have full membership rights. Instead, the new structures were subordinate to regular, white locals which controlled auxiliary policies and treasuries. Auxiliaries had no independent grievance procedures, nor could they hire their own business agents. Auxiliary members had no vote on local union matters and no representation at national conventions. They also received smaller union insurance benefits than white members.[16]

Bay Area Boilermaker locals avoided direct confrontations over the issue of auxiliary membership during the first year of the war simply by issuing clearances to black shipyard workers without requiring them to join the union or pay dues. But by February, 1943, the black segment of the workforce was too large to ignore. East Bay locals formed auxiliaries and required blacks to join and pay dues equal to those paid by whites as a condition of employment. The National Association for the Advancement of Colored People filed a complaint against this policy with the National Labor Relations Board, but while the NLRB criticized the auxiliary membership status, it did not ban it outright. Meanwhile, most black workers at Kaiser and other East Bay yards apparently paid their auxiliary dues. According to the NAACP magazine *Crisis*, the black worker "knew jim crow, segregation and second-class citizenship when he saw it," but he paid his dues anyway, in "much the same manner as he took a rear seat on a bus in Memphis. . . . He regarded the payments as a necessary bribe for the privilege of working at a job that paid more than he ever dreamed."[17]

On the west side of the bay, Boilermakers Local 6, with jurisdiction over the Bethlehem and Western Pipe yards in San Francisco as well as Marinship in Sausalito, chartered Auxiliary A-41 on August 14, 1943. The local announced that henceforth black workers must join and pay dues to the auxiliary in order to receive their union work clearance.[18] The announcement provoked organized opposition by the San Francisco Committee Against Segregation and Discrimination, made up of several local blacks and led by Joseph James. James, in his early thirties at the time, grew up on the east coast, studied music at Boston University, and pursued a promising singing career in New York. He came to San Francisco in 1939 to appear in the "Swing Mikado" at the Treasure Island Exposition and settled in the Fillmore after the fair closed. He was hired at Marinship in 1942, and in two months advanced from welder's helper to journeyman, normally a six month process. By mid-1943 James was a member of a "flying squad" of expert welders used for special jobs. He was also an active member of the NAACP, a recognized black spokesman at the yard, and, with all this, still managed to keep up his singing career. His performances were a staple at Marinship launchings and ceremonies.[19]

On August 21, 1943, just a week after the establishment of Auxiliary A-41, the company employee magazine, the *Marin-er*, devoted much of its issue to a discussion of race relations at Marinship. Management obviously was concerned about racial tensions, particularly following major race riots in Detroit, Los Angeles, and other American cities earlier that summer. The special issue of the magazine was prepared with the assistance of a "Negro Advisory Board" headed by Joe James. James also wrote the lead article, "Marinship Negroes Speak to Their Fellow Workers," calling on his readers "to turn our hatred, instead of against each other, against the forces of fascism." An editorial condemned discrimination and proclaimed that the war was being fought "to prove for all time the dignity and rights of the individual man regardless of race, creed or color."[20]

Marinship soon found itself in the middle of a struggle to establish those very principles in the Boilermakers union. After three months, at least half of the approximately 1100 blacks in jobs under Boilermaker jurisdiction at Marinship still refused to join Auxiliary A-41. On November 24, 1943, the union ordered management to fire 430 black workers unless they paid their auxiliary dues in twenty-four hours and warned an additional 150 workers that they soon faced similar treatment.[21] That evening about 350 people met in San Francisco under the aegis of the Committee Against Segregation and Discrimination to decide on an appropriate response. Joe James told the meeting that their fight was not to destroy the Boilermakers but to strengthen the union by insisting that blacks be granted full and equal membership rights. C. L. Dellums reiterated the point, and the participants voted unanimously to continue boycotting the auxiliary.[22]

On Friday, November 26, about thirty blacks on the afternoon shift were refused permission to work, the company explaining that the union had withdrawn their work clearances. Throughout the ensuing controversy, Marinship insisted it was simply an innocent bystander, required to enforce its collective bargaining contract in a dispute between black workers and the union. However, by agreeing to dismiss blacks, the company accepted the legality of the union action. Legalisms aside, Marinship must have feared that resisting the Boilermakers' wishes might result in a strike that would interrupt production.

More workers were barred at the beginning of the graveyard shift on November 26, and by Saturday morning, November 27, hundreds of black men and women had gathered at Gate 3 of the yard to protest the lay-offs. Eventually, the crowd grew to about 800 and was described by the San Rafael *Daily Independent* as "Marin's greatest labor demonstration and most critical situation to arise since the San Francisco 'general strike' in the summer of 1934." Sheriff's deputies and Highway Patrolmen arrived with nightsticks and tear gas, "ready for any emergency." But two black deputies from Marin City assured the County Sheriff they could keep order, and, reported the *Independent*, they "succeeded admirably." Joe James and three other black committee members, Preston Stallinger, Edward Anderson, and Eugene Small, met with company officials and then addressed the crowd with divided counsel. James, Stallinger, and Anderson urged those who still had union clearance to return to their jobs while continuing to boycott the auxiliary. But Small called on blacks "to stand pat and not return to work" until they had won full union membership.[23]

How many workers took Small's advice is a matter of dispute. The San Francisco *Examiner* reported that 1500 walked off their jobs, but that figure is larger than the total number of Marinship blacks in jobs under Boilermaker jurisdiction. The *American Labor Citizen*, voice of the Bay Area Metal Trades Council, assured its readers that the trouble was caused by a handful of malcontents and that a "vast majority of Negro workers" remained on the job. Whatever the number of strikers, it concerned Admiral

Emory S. Land of the Maritime Commission. Initially, Land urged workers to join the auxiliary under protest, but when this plea failed, the admiral asked the company to suspend the lay-offs. California Attorney General Robert Kenny made a similar request, pointing out that if ship production slowed, "more American boys are going to die, both white American boys and black American boys."[24] However, the company again insisted that under its collective bargaining agreement it was obligated to bar workers without union clearance.

Local 6 business agent Ed Rainbow argued that the closed shop agreement was recognized by the federal government and that blacks understood Boilermaker policy when they took shipyard jobs. The *Labor Citizen* charged that black workers who "laid down their tools" had caused all the trouble, and the paper saw nothing wrong with blacks joining auxiliaries "composed of their own people." Both Rainbow and the Metal Trades organ claimed that Local 6 had no choice in the matter, since it was simply following national union policy.[25] In at least one previous instance, however, Rainbow had bent national rules. In 1942 he refused clearance for six white woman welders at Marinship, citing male-only provisions of the Boilermaker constitution. One woman became "very impolite and abrupt," and Rainbow eventually reconsidered. Thousands of white women were later accepted as full Local 6 members, and the woman who had protested so vociferously became a union shop steward. Rainbow was quoted saying he would "rather get hit by a baseball bat than to become embroiled with a pack of women who wanted to work."[26]

The business agent probably soon had similar feelings about Joe James and his supporters. By Sunday, November 28, 160 blacks, including James, lost their work clearances, and that evening about 1000 people attended a committee meeting in a Fillmore District church. Eugene Small again called for a labor boycott, telling the *Independent* that blacks were considering taking jobs "not involving union membership." But James and other leaders argued the fight was against segregation, not trade unions. Eventually, the meeting approved legal action. The next morning, committee attorneys filed suit in Federal District Court on behalf of James and seventeen other black workers, asking reinstatement by Marinship and $115,000 damages from the Boilermakers. Judge Paul St. Sure issued a temporary restraining order, suspending the lay-offs pending formal hearing of the suit.[27]

The company announced it would halt further lay-offs but refused to rehire the 160 idle workers until they received union clearance. It took another court order to achieve this, and even then, Local 6 held out until Friday, December 3. On that morning, "a crowd of waiting Negro workers" were at union headquarters in San Francisco. They gathered "before the grilled windows where permits are issued," and finally, after about four hours, "the little white slips of paper started to come through." "Now we can get back to work," Joe James announced, and during the weekend, committee sound trucks toured the Fillmore and Marin City urging blacks to return to their jobs.[28]

The formal hearing occurred on December 12 in a courtroom crowded with black spectators. Committee attorneys George Anderson and Herbert Ressner were accompanied by NAACP Chief Counsel Thurgood Marshall and Bartley Crum of the National Lawyers Guild. Anderson argued that if blacks could be forced into separate auxiliaries, so could American Indians like Ed Rainbow, Irish Americans (Judge Michael Roche) or Armenian Americans (defense attorney Charles Janigian). But the union refused to respond to this point, contending instead that federal courts had no jurisdiction and that the case should be dismissed. Judge Roche referred the dismissal motion to a three-judge panel, and until the panel made its decision, the temporary restraining order remained in force. On January 6, 1944, the judges announced they were granting the union's motion and dismissing the case. "The plaintiff's action," the court explained, "does not arise out of the federal constitution or any federal statutes."[29]

The dismissal automatically ended the restraining order, and Local 6 announced it would withdraw union clearance for workers who had not paid auxiliary dues by Friday, January 14. But on that day committee attorneys returned to court, this time before Marin Superior Judge Edward I. Butler of San Rafael. The committee now based its suit on state rather than federal law, and Judge Butler issued another temporary order restraining the lay-offs. The order was served just fifteen minutes before a work shift was to change at Marinship. The company already had removed black workers' time cards from the rack, but clerks hurriedly replaced the cards, and the shift changed without incident.[30]

While the case was being argued in court, the Boilermakers' auxiliary policy also was being investigated by the President's Fair Employment Practices Commission. President Roosevelt established FEPC in the summer of 1941 in response to a plan by a group of prominent blacks, led by Sleeping Car Porters Union head A. Philip Randolph, to stage a massive march on Washington to protest discrimination in defense employment and the federal government. Only after Roosevelt agreed to form a federal commission to monitor enforcement of non-discrimination policies in federal contracts and government civil service did Randolph call off the march. The President's order allowed FEPC to hold hearings, write reports, and issue orders and recommendations. But the commission had no independent authority to punish wrong-doers either by criminal, civil, or administrative penalties or by canceling contracts.[31]

In mid-November, 1943, the commission held hearings in Portland and Los Angeles to investigate complaints about Boilermaker auxiliaries by black workers in Pacific Northwest and southern California shipyards. Yard operators, including Kaiser and Bechtel, argued they were caught in the middle of a fight between blacks and the union. The Boilermakers simply refused to testify before the commission. During the Marinship strike later that month, FEPC Chairman Malcolm Ross asked union and management to delay lay-offs until the commission issued its report. Nothing came of Ross's request, and on December 14, 1943, FEPC announced a decision that was a blow to the union cause. The Boilermakers were ordered to "eliminate all membership practices which discriminate against workers because of race or color," and five employers, including Bechtel's Calship, were prohibited from enforcing closed shop provisions which contributed to such discrimination. However, the employers appealed the decision, and the appeal procedure, necessitating new briefs and hearings, took a year to complete. In the meantime, the commission suspended its order.[32]

Malcolm Ross hoped he could persuade the Boilermakers to change their membership policies at the union's International Convention, scheduled for the end of January, 1944, in Kansas City. This also was the hope of those attending a mass meeting in Oakland on January 23. C. L. Dellums, Joe James, and committee attorney George Anderson were among the speakers at the Oakland gathering. Business agents for the Stage Riggers and Pile Drivers described their unions' open membership rules, and Ray Stewart, a white Boilermaker, contended that "abolishing auxiliaries will benefit the union as much as the Negro." Apparently, Stewart spoke for at least some of his white co-workers. East Bay Boilermakers Local 681 had passed a resolution requesting the convention to allow full membership "without regard to race, color, creed, national origin or sex." Of six thousand signatures gathered at Bay Area shipyards in support of the resolution, about seventy-five percent came from white workers.[33]

The convention received a similar appeal from twenty-two prominent black citizens. AFL President William Green criticized job discrimination in general terms from the convention floor, and delegates heard much the same thing from President Roosevelt via telegram.[34] But incoming Boilermaker President Charles MacGowan already had made his position clear. "One of the greatest causes contributing to the failure of the Negro to advance farther," MacGowan explained, "is the professional Negro."[35] MacGowan had invited Malcolm Ross to the convention, and the FEPC chairman described his experiences in Kansas City with something less than enthusiasm: "So it happened that a bureaucrat, minced up into little pieces, was served during a several hour ceremony to the International officers and heads of lodges as a hors d'oeuvre to whet appetites for the main racial dish."[36]

Much the same thing happened to Local 681's resolution. In the end, the convention liberalized membership rules only to the extent that auxiliaries were allowed to elect delegates to future conventions and to local metal trades councils. In addition, blacks henceforth would receive equal union insurance benefits. But auxiliaries remained something less than full union locals and blacks something less than full union members.[37] The convention did break precedent by allowing a black auxiliary leader, William Smith from Richmond, to address the delegates. Smith welcomed the rule changes and promised whites "we will do our best to be worthy of your trust." That statement must have reinforced President MacGowan's conviction that the auxiliary problem was "not within the membership but with professional agitation attempting to make a cause where none exists."[38]

This was not the view of Judge Butler of the Marin Superior Court. On February 17, 1944, Butler announced his decision in what now was known as the case of *James v. Marinship*. Butler ruled that the Boilermakers' policy of "discriminating against and segregating Negroes into auxiliaries is contrary to public policy of the state of California," and he prohibited the union from requiring blacks to join auxiliaries as a condition of employment. The judge also barred Marinship from laying off workers who refused to pay auxiliary dues. As far as Butler was concerned, if the Boilermakers wished to retain closed shop privileges, they must "admit Negroes as members on the same terms and conditions as white persons."[39]

Both union and management appealed this decision to the California Supreme Court, and it took nearly a year for the state's highest court to decide the case. In the meantime, the Boilermakers did not accept blacks as full members, but the union could not require auxiliary membership as a condition of employment at Marinship. Judge Butler's decision did not apply to other yards, but during 1944, cases similar to the Marinship suit were brought in various Bay Area courts. Continued attempts by FEPC Chairman Ross to achieve a voluntary settlement failed, so the matter was

not resolved until the State Supreme Court announced its final decision on
January 2, 1945.

The court's unanimous opinion, written by Chief Justice Phil Gibson, was
a decisive defeat for the Boilermakers. The union had argued that it was
not guilty of discrimination, since blacks were paid equal wages and had
equal, though separate, status in auxiliaries. The justices did not dispute
the contention of equal wages, but found that it was "readily apparent that
the membership offered to Negroes is discriminatory and unequal." The
union also contended the case was moot because various federal agencies,
particularly the FEPC, were investigating the matter. The court responded
that since the commission's powers were limited, "it is not a complete or
adequate administrative remedy."[40]

The Supreme Court agreed with Judge Butler that the auxiliary practice
violated the California statute that held racial discrimination "contrary to
public policy." The union had argued that this statute applied only to discrimination in public places and services, not to voluntary associations
such as labor organizations. But Gibson concluded that when such an organization achieves a closed shop contract controlling access to labor, it af-
fects an individual's "fundamental right to work for a living" and thus the
union occupies a "quasi-public position." The court explained that it was
not outlawing the concept of closed shop *per se*, but that "an arbitrarily
closed union is incompatible with a closed shop."[41]

The court also refused to let management off the hook. Marinship asserted that it was simply enforcing terms of a federally approved labor
contract and could not be held responsible for union discrimination. But
Justice Gibson pointed out that the company had "full knowledge of the
dispute and at least indirectly assisted the union in carrying out discrimination." By the same token, Local 6 could not argue that it only enforced
national union policies over which it had no control. "The true rule is, of
course, that the agent is liable for his acts."[42]

The San Francisco *Chronicle* hailed the decision as confirmation of the
principle of "no representation, no dues." The *Marin Citizen* said the ruling "should be welcomed by every believer in genuine trade unionism,"
while the Communist *People's World* emphasized that the court had outlawed discrimination, not the closed shop. Joe James made the same point,
contending that his supporters had waged the battle "strictly on a pro-
union basis." By this time, James had been elected president of the San

Francisco NAACP branch and proclaimed that the organization was "in the forefront of every fight against open shop proposals."[43]

James also thanked white workers who had supported his cause. He explained that both the NAACP and the Committee Against Segregation and Discrimination were inter-racial groups, and that many whites had signed petitions, donated money, and discussed the issues with their fellow workers. At Moore shipyard, Katherine Archibald reported that the union's initial 1943 victory in federal court "aroused the rejoicing of several of my [white] colleagues." But the final decision of the State Supreme Court in 1945 gave blacks "status as a people in the eyes of their white companions." There might be mutterings of discontent, "but the decision was respected and the conviction grew that the law at least . . . was on the side of the black man." One white worker conceded, "I guess we can't keep hold of all the jobs."[44]

A few days before the court decision was announced, the FEPC released its final ruling on the appeals of the five shipyard cases in southern California and the Pacific Northwest. As expected, the commission reaffirmed its order of a year earlier that black workers could not be fired or denied employment for refusing to pay auxiliary dues. During the trial of the James case, commission chairman Ross found it ironic that union and management argued that the case was moot since it was being handled by FEPC. This, said Ross, was "a solemn plea, coming from parties who had informed FEPC that it had no authority and could go jump in the lake." Ross believed the court decision "went far beyond" the commission ruling and "knocked the pins from under the defense of the shipyards and the Boilermakers."[45]

The union announced it would obey the decision and abolish its California auxiliaries. But in their place, the Boilermakers intended to form "separate but equal" local lodges. Blacks would be given full membership rights but would be required to join all-black locals. However, black Boilermakers could transfer only to black locals, thus limiting their job mobility within the union. Whether this would have passed the judicial test will never be known, since the union made serious efforts to establish "separate but equal" locals for only a short time. A 1948 study found that all Boilermaker lodges in the Bay Area were racially integrated.[46]

James v. Marinship, then, produced important changes in Boilermaker membership practices. Ironically, very few blacks were ultimately able to take advantage of that fact. In 1944, Local 6 had 36,000 members, including about 3000 blacks theoretically in segregated auxiliaries. In 1948, the local was racially integrated but had only 1800 members of whom just 150 were black.[47] Even by the time of the Supreme Court decision, work was declining in Bay Area shipyards. The Allies clearly were winning the war, and the government began cutting back contracts. Between January, 1944, and January, 1945, total Bay Area shipyard employment fell from about 240,000 to 200,000. Black employment in the yards continued to increase slightly during that year (from 24,000 to 26,000), but after January, 1945, the black workforce also rapidly declined. It was 20,000 in July, 12,000 in September, and an "insignificant number" by mid-1946.[48]

At Marinship total employment in April, 1945, was about half of what it had been a year before. In May, Marin City housing was opened to non-Marinship workers for the first time. Company fortunes seemed to improve with the signing of new contracts to build barges for the invasion of Japan, but the Japanese surrender in August ended work on that project. The Maritime Commission asked Bechtel to continue running the yard, but the company refused, explaining that in peacetime it would not operate a government enterprise "in competition with privately-owned plants." Bechtel also declined to buy the yard, so on May 16, 1946, Marinship formally closed. Most significant work had ended several months earlier.[49]

The meaning of the decline in Bay Area shipbuilding for the black workforce is graphically described in Cy Record's story, "Willie Stokes at the Golden Gate," published in 1949. Willie came to the Bay Area from Arkansas during the war and got a job as a welder at Kaiser, ultimately earning $10 a day. After the war, he was laid off, and by June 1946 was fortunate to be making $6.40 a day as an unskilled laborer. A year later he was unemployed. Stokes found it "funny almost. One day you are an essential worker in a vital industry (they said that in speeches every time they launched a ship) and the next you were a surplus unskilled laborer, essential to no one." One sympathetic employer explained, "in most cases your wartime experiences will mean very little. During the war, wage costs weren't important and the system of classification by skills was all out of whack . . . the government was footing the bill." Now businesses were hiring only workers with high school diplomas, a credential Willie Stokes did not possess. In fact, a 1950 study found that only about twenty percent of black wartime migrants to the Bay Area over twenty-five years old had graduated from high school; half had not even finished the eighth grade.[50]

It was a classic case of "last hired, first fired." During the war, about seventy-five percent of black heads of households in San Francisco were classified as skilled industrial workers, the great majority in the shipyards. By 1948 only about twenty-five percent of black workers were still in industrial jobs, while over half were employed as unskilled laborers or service workers. More than fifteen percent of Bay Area black men were unemployed in 1948, nearly three times the state-wide rate for all persons. Only in government and clerical jobs had blacks managed to hold their wartime vocational gains, but the number of people in these categories was small. The United States Department of Employment noted that "as long as Negroes are commonly regarded as marginal labor, they will suffer very heavy unemployment when sufficient white labor is available."[51]

In this situation, it was hardly surprising that some blacks left the Bay Area after the war, including Joe James, who returned to New York to pursue his singing career. Yet an estimated eighty-five percent of the wartime migrants stayed, their numbers increased by their newborn children and by new, post-war migrations from the South. By 1950 San Francisco's black population had grown to over 40,000, by 1960 to nearly 75,000. As Lester Granger had warned, much of the Fillmore became a black "ghetto," as did Marin City, surrounded by some of the most prosperous white suburbs in America.[52]

Back in 1945 Joe James believed he had identified a pattern in California's treatment of minority migrants: "we need them, we use them, when we are through with them, we banish them."[53] Wartime blacks were needed and used, but not banished. Thousands of Willie Stokeses still live in the Bay Area, as do their children and grandchildren. They, along with growing numbers of Latinos and Asians, may soon give California a "Third World" population majority. In San Francisco many of the old, white craft unions have declined along with the industries they serve. The largest union in the city today is the Hotel and Restaurant Workers, and its members are mostly of Asian, Afro-American, and Latin American origin.

The problems of black poverty, unemployment, and lack of economic opportunity identified after World War II have become chronic for a large portion of the region's non-white population. Of course, this situation is by no means unique to the Bay Area. But the area's experience is unusual in that the beginnings of its large black population are so directly tied to the short-term boom in a single industry. As long as the wartime shipyards operated at or near capacity, blacks had access to well-paying jobs. In the midst of the national emergency and regional labor shortage, they even won the legal principle of equal membership in exclusive craft unions. But the precipitous decline of the shipyards after the war was an economic disaster from which the region's black population has never fully recovered. Even the protests, civil rights legislation, and anti-poverty measures of the 1960s did not produce economic opportunity comparable to World War II.

Nathan I. Huggins is correct when he says that wartime migration created the Bay Area's first black bourgeoisie, for only with the migration was there enough population to support black lawyers, doctors, teachers, and entrepreneurs. But Douglas Daniels makes the equally important point that the war also created the region's first black proletariat.[54] During the 1940s, these workers won battles that established important legal principles, but they have yet to win an equitable share of the region's wealth and power.

NOTES

1. Nathan I. Huggins, "Foreword," in Douglas Henry Daniels, *Pioneer Urbanites: A Social and Cultural History of Black San Francisco* (Philadelphia, 1980), xiv–xv.

2. Joseph James, "Profiles, San Francisco," *Journal of Educational Sociology* (November, 1945), 168; Neil Wynn, *Afro-Americans and the Second World War* (London, 1976), 61; Cy Record, "Willie Stokes at the Golden Gate," *Crisis* (June, 1949), 176; Charles Johnson, *Negro War Workers in San Francisco, A Local Self-Survey* (San Francisco, 1944), 2–4.

3. Johnson, *Negro War Workers*, 63; Record, "Willie Stokes," 177.

4. One recent work that does deal with the migration is Edward France, *Some Aspects of the Migration of the Negro to the San Francisco Bay Area Since 1940* (San Francisco, 1974). For recent works dealing with the pre-war black experience, see Daniels, *Pioneer Urbanites;* Rudolph Lapp, *Blacks in Gold Rush California* (New Haven, 1977); and Lawrence de Graaf, "City of Black Angels: Emergence of the Los Angeles Ghetto," *Pacific Historical Review* (August, 1970), 323–352. Best of the 1940s studies are Johnson, *Negro War Workers;* Record, "Willie Stokes"; and James, "Profiles."

5. Richard Finnie, *Marinship: The History of a Wartime Shipyard* (San Francisco, 1947), 1–7; Marinship Corporation, *Marinship* (Sausalito, 1944), 20; Sausalito *News*, March 19, 1942.

6. Finnie, *Marinship*, 39–54; Davis McEntire and Julia R. Tarnopol, "Postwar Status of Negro Workers in the San Francisco Area," *Monthly Labor Review* (June, 1950), 613; James, "Profiles," 168.

7. Finnie, *Marinship*, 62–68; Persis White and Sarah Hayne, "Marin City, A Social Problem to Marin County," in Mills College, *Immigration and Race Problems* (Oakland, 1954), 318–334.

8. Marin *Citizen*, February 23, 1945; unidentified article in "Race Relations on the Pacific Coast," Carey McWilliams papers, v. 5, Bancroft Library; Johnson, *Negro War Workers*, 33.

9. Finnie, *Marinship*, 69.

10. Johnson, *Negro War Workers*, 20–30; James, "Profiles," 168–173; Horace Clayton, "New Problems for the West Coast," Chicago *Sun*, October 14, 1943.

11. San Francisco *Chronicle*, September 19, 1945.

12. C. L. Dellums, *International President of the Brotherhood of Sleeping Car Porters and Civil Rights Leader*, oral history, Regional Oral History Office, Ban-

croft Library (Berkeley, 1973), 97–99; James, "Profiles," 169; Johnson, *Negro War Workers*, 63; France, *Some Aspects*, 67–68.

13. Katherine Archibald, *Wartime Shipyard, A Study in Social Disunity* (Berkeley, 1947), 59–74.

14. *Master Agreement Between the Pacific Coast Shipbuilders and the Metal Trades Department, AFL* (Seattle, 1941), 4–6.

15. Daniels, *Pioneer Urbanites*, 31–42; Robert Knight, *Industrial Relations in the San Francisco Bay Area, 1910–1918* (Berkeley, 1960), 213, 303, 315, 339, 361; James, "Profiles," 169; Johnson, *Negro War Workers*, 18, 70.

16. Thurgood Marshall, "Negro Status in the Boilermakers Union," *Crisis* (March, 1944), 77; Herbert Northrup, *Organized Labor and the Negro* (New York, 1944), 213–214; Ray Marshall, *The Negro Worker* (New York, 1967), 61.

17. Record, "Willie Stokes," 177; Johnson, *Negro War Workers*, 71; Ray Marshall, *Negro Worker*, 62.

18. *James v. Marinship*, 25 Cal., 2nd, 726 (1945); Johnson, *Negro War Workers*, 71.

19. *Marin-er* (October 16, 1942), 1; (August 21, 1943), 4; *American Labor Citizen*, December 6, 1943; *People's World*, January 6, 1945.

20. *Marin-er* (August 21, 1943), 4–6.

21. San Francisco *Chronicle*, San Francisco *Examiner*, *People's World*, November 24, 1943.

22. *People's World*, *Chronicle*, November 25, 1943.

23. San Rafael *Daily Independent*, November 27, 1943; *Chronicle*, *Examiner*, November 28, 1943.

24. *Chronicle*, *Examiner*, November 28, 1943; *American Labor Citizen*, December 6, 1943.

25. *American Labor Citizen*, December 6, 1943; *People's World*, November 30, 1943.

26. Finnie, *Marinship*, 213–214.

27. *Daily Independent*, November 29, 30, 1943; *People's World*, *Chronicle*, November 30, 1943; Sausalito *News*, December 2, 1943.

28. *Daily Independent*, *Chronicle*, *Marin Citizen*, December 3, 1943; *People's World*, December 4, 1943.

29. *Daily Independent*, December 13, 14, 1943, January 6, 1944; *People's World*, December 14, 15, 1943, January 7, 1944; *Marin Citizen*, December 17, 1943, January 7, 1944.

30. *Daily Independent*, January 12, 14, 1944; *People's World*, January 13, 15, 1944; *Marin Citizen*, January 21, 1944.

31. For background on FEPC, see Robert Weaver, *Negro Labor: A National Problem* (New York, 1946), 131–152; Herbert Garfinkel, *When Negroes March* (Glencoe, Ill., 1959), 38–75; Richard Dalfiume, *Desegregation of the U.S. Armed Forces: Fighting on Two Fronts* (Columbia, Mo., 1969), 115–123; Neil Wynn, *The Afro-American and the Second World War* (London, 1976), 38–48.

32. Fair Employment Practices Commission, "Press Release" (San Francisco, December 14, 1943); "Decision on Re-hearing, Cases 43, 44, 49, 50, 54" (Washington, 1945) 1–2; *Final Report* (Washington, 1946), 19–21.

33. *People's World*, January 17, 20, 25, 27, 1944; *California Eagle*, January 20, 27, 1944.

34. *People's World*, February 8, 9, 14, 1944.

35. *Boilermakers Journal* (November, 1943), 295.

36. Malcolm Ross, *All Manner of Men* (New York, 1948), 147.

37. *Boilermakers Journal* (March, 1944), 73–79; *People's World*, February 1, 14, 1944; *Marin Citizen*, February 11, 1944; Weaver, *Negro Labor*, 228–229.

38. *People's World*, February 14, 1944; *American Labor Citizen*, March 27, 1944.

39. *Chronicle, Marin Citizen*, February 18, 1944; *People's World*, February 18, 19, 1944; *California Eagle*, February 24, 1944.

40. *James v. Marinship*, 737, 744–745.

41. Ibid., 731–740.

42. Ibid., 742, 745. The decision also settled the similar cases affecting other Bay Area yards instituted after Judge Butler's ruling.

43. *Chronicle*, January 3, 4, 1945; *Marin Citizen*, January 5, 1945; *California Eagle*, January 4, 1945; *People's World*, January 3, 4, 5, 6, 1945.

44. Archibald, *Wartime Shipyard*, 92, 96–97; *People's World*, January 12, 1945.

45. Ross, *All Manner of Men*, 150–151; FEPC, "Decision on Re-hearing," 1–11; *Final Report*, 21.

46. Fred Stripp, "The Relationships of the San Francisco Bay Area Negro-American Worker with the Labor Unions Affiliated with the American Federation of Labor and the Congress of Industrial Organizations," Th.D. thesis, Pacific School of Religion (Berkeley, 1948), 164–169; Weaver, *Negro Labor*, 230.

47. Stripp, "Relationships," 166.

48. Record, "Willie Stokes," 177.

49. *Marin Citizen*, March 30, May 4, 1945; Finnie, *Marinship*, 361–371.

50. Record, "Willie Stokes," 175–179; McEntire and Tarnopol, "Postwar Status," 613.

51. Record, "Willie Stokes," 179.

52. Ibid., 187; *Chronicle*, September 19, 1945, June 16, November 17, 1947, August 29, 1948; Tom Rose and John Kirich, *The San Francisco Non-White Population, 1950–1960* (San Francisco, n.d.), 3–4; White and Hayne, "Marin City"; Ottole Krebs, "The Post-War Negro in San Francisco," in *American Communities*, v. 2 (Mills College, Oakland, 1949), 549–586.

53. James, "Profiles," 176.

54. Huggins, "Introduction," and Daniels, "Preface," in Daniels, *Pioneer Urbanites*, xv, xvii.

FURTHER READING

Archibald, Katherine. *Wartime Shipyard: A Study in Social Disunity.* 1947.

Broussard, Albert. *Black San Francisco: The Struggle for Racial Equality in the West, 1900–1954.* 1993.

Crouchett, Lawrence, Lonnie G. Bunch III, and Martha Kendall Winnacker, eds. *Visions Toward Tomorrow: The History of the East Bay Afro-American Community, 1852–1977.* 1989.

Daniels, Douglas Henry. *Pioneer Urbanites: A Social and Cultural History of Black San Francisco.* Chapter 10. 1980.

de Graaf, Lawrence. *Negro Migration to Los Angeles, 1930–1950.* 1974.

France, Edward E. *Some Aspects of the Migration of the Negro to the San Francisco Bay Area Since 1940.* 1974.

Harris, William H. "Federal Intervention in Union Discrimination: FEPC and West

Coast Shipyards During World War II." *Labor History* 22 (Summer 1981): 325–347.

Johnson, Charles. *The Negro Worker in San Francisco.* 1944.

Johnson, Marilynn S. *The Second Gold Rush: Oakland and the East Bay in World War II.* 1993.

———. "Wartime Shipyards: The Transformation of Labor in San Francisco's East Bay." In *American Labor in the Era of World War II,* edited by Sally M. Miller and Daniel Cornford. 1995.

Lemke-Santangelo, Gretchen. "African American Migrant Women in the San Francisco Bay Area." In *American Labor in the Era of World War II,* edited by Sally M. Miller and Daniel Cornford. 1995.

McBroome, Dee. "Catalyst for Change: Wartime Housing and African Americans in California's East Bay." In *American Labor in the Era of World War II,* edited by Sally M. Miller and Daniel Cornford. 1995.

———. *Parallel Communities: African Americans in California's East Bay, 1850–1963.* 1993.

Moore, Shirley Ann. *To Place Our Deeds: The African-American Community in Richmond, California, 1910–1963.* Forthcoming.

Smith, Alonzo, and Quintard Taylor. "Racial Discrimination in the Workplace: A Study of Two West Coast Cities During the 1940s." *Journal of Ethnic Studies* 8 (1981): 34–54.

Trotter, Joe William. "African-American Workers: New Directions in U.S. Labor Historiography." *Labor History* 35 (Fall 1994): 495–523.

Wollenberg, Charles. *Marinship at War: Shipbuilding and Social Change in Wartime Sausalito.* 1990.

3
WORKERS ON STRIKE

6 Racial Domination and Class Conflict in Capitalist Agriculture

The Oxnard Sugar Beet Workers'
Strike of 1903

Tomás Almaguer

EDITOR'S INTRODUCTION

By the early twentieth century, a profound transformation had taken place in California's economy, with agriculture superseding mining as the state's most important industry. From the gold rush until the early 1870s, relatively few Californians had been employed in agriculture; mining continued to be the most important source of employment through the 1860s. Aside from the lure of the mines, several factors retarded the expansion of California agriculture during these early years. First, until the completion of the transcontinental railroad in 1869, California was relatively cut off from the national market. Second, the ongoing legal disputes about ownership of the lands covered by the Spanish and Mexican land grants discouraged farmers from migrating to California and discouraged farmers within the state from expanding and diversifying their production.

California agriculture was dominated by cattle farming until the early 1860s, when wheat farming began to supplant cattle raising as the major agricultural activity. Although wheat remained California's most important crop until almost the end of the nineteenth century, a major change in the nature of California agriculture began in the 1870s, as increasing numbers of farmers engaged in fruit growing, a much more intensive form of agricultural production. This change was facilitated by the resolution of most of the Spanish and Mexican land grant disputes; the development of irrigation and land reclamation plans; the completion of the transcontinental railroad and the spread of interstate and intrastate railroad networks; and the availability of Chinese labor to work in this labor-intensive form of agriculture.

The intensification and expansion of California agriculture required a large agricultural proletariat. But as a result of the Chinese Exclusion Act of

183

1882, the Chinese population of California dwindled dramatically. During the early twentieth century, two other ethnic groups, the Japanese and the Mexicans, began to predominate in the agricultural labor force. In 1903, an alliance of more than 1,200 Mexican and Japanese farm workers conducted one of the first successful strikes of California agricultural workers.

Tomás Almaguer provides an account of this strike, describing the complexity of the relationships among workers, labor contractors, and employers. The success of the Japanese-Mexican Labor Association (JMLA) forced the American Federation of Labor in California to confront the issue of organizing minority and agricultural workers. Samuel Gompers, president of the national AFL, agreed to issue a charter making the JMLA an AFL affiliate on the condition that Asians were excluded. The JMLA refused to accept this condition for joining the AFL.

◆ ◆ ◆

In February 1903 over 1,200 Mexican and Japanese farm workers organized the Japanese-Mexican Labor Association (JMLA) in the southern California community of Oxnard. The JMLA was the first major agricultural workers' union in the state composed of different minority workers and the first to strike successfully against capitalist interests.[1] In addition to being significant to labor history, the Oxnard strike also has sociological importance. The strike raises issues such as the historical interplay between class and racial stratification, the importance of these factors in labor organizing, and variations in Anglo-American racial attitudes at the time. Emerging as one of the many "boom towns" in California at the turn of the century, Oxnard owed its existence to the passage of the 1897 Dingley Tariff Bill, which imposed a heavy duty on imported sugar, and the introduction of the sugar beet industry to Ventura County. The construction of an immense sugar beet factory in Ventura County by Henry, James, and Robert Oxnard, prominent sugar refiners from New York, drew hundreds into the area and led to the founding of the new community. The sugar beet factory quickly became a major processing center for the emerging U.S. sugar beet industry, refining nearly 200,000 tons of beets and employing 700 people by 1903.[2]

The developing Ventura County sugar beet industry had an important social impact on the new community. One major repercussion was the racial segregation of Oxnard into clearly discernible white and non-white social worlds. The tremendous influx of numerous agricultural workers quickly led to the development of segregated minority enclaves on the east side of town. The Mexican section of Oxnard, referred to as "Sonora-town," was settled by Mexican workers who migrated into the area seeking employment.[3] Arriving in the early 1900s, the Mexican population was viewed by the Anglo population with disdain. The local newspaper, for example, disparagingly reported on the Mexican community's odd "feasting," "game playing," and "peculiar customs." Mexicans were seen as a "queer" people who could be tolerated so long as they kept to themselves.[4]

Also segregated on the east side of town, adjacent to the Mexican colonia, was the "Chinatown" section of Oxnard. This segregated ethnic enclave was even more despised by the local Anglo population than "Sonora-town." Chinatown was described in the Oxnard *Courier* as consisting of numerous "measley, low, stinking and dirty huts with all kinds of pitfalls and dark alleys where murder can be committed in broad daylight without detection."[5] Despite widespread anti-Oriental sentiment in the local community, the Asian population grew to an estimated 1,000 to 1,500 people in less than a decade after the founding of Oxnard.

Ventura County residents greatly disapproved of the impact that the minority population of Oxnard had on the social character of the county. Popular opinion blamed the minority population for all the detested vices (such as gambling, liquor, drugs, and prostitution) existing in Oxnard. One prominent Anglo pioneer described Oxnard at the time as a "very disreputable town," primarily inhabited by "riff raff" and "Mexicans." Corroborating this description, one visitor of Oxnard in 1901 described the community as a "characteristic boom town," with "many saloons" and numerous "Mexicans and others loitering around."[6]

Thus, two very different social worlds emerged in Oxnard during its early years. On the east side of town were the Mexican and Chinese enclaves, whose presence contributed to Oxnard reputedly having a "damning influence on her neighbors." The Anglo residents on the west side of town, in contrast, consisted of "upstanding" German and Irish farmers and several Jewish families.[7] "While the east side of town was a rip-roaring slum," according to one local historian, "the west side was listening to lecture courses, hearing WCTU [Women's Christian Temperance Union] speakers, having gay times at the skating rink in the opera house, [and] putting on minstrel shows. . . ."[8]

Underlying the segregated social worlds existing in Oxnard was the organization of the community along distinct racial and class lines. Along the class axis there existed a small class of large-scale entrepreneurs (such as the Oxnard brothers and the major growers); an intermediate stratum of farmers and independent merchants operating small-scale concerns; and a large working class composed of skilled and unskilled wage workers tied to the local agricultural economy.

Closely paralleling this class structure was a racial stratification system that divided Oxnard into white and non-white spheres. The most obvious outward feature of this racial stratification was the residential segregation of the community. Also important, however, was the organization of the local labor market along racial lines. Anglo-Americans, for example, in the main constituted the upper class stratum of large-scale entrepreneurs and major agriculturalists. The 1900 federal manuscript census for Ventura County shows that nearly 95% of all farmers in the county were Anglo-American. In addition, white men completely monopolized the middle strata of the local class structure and held the best jobs in the low white-collar, skilled, and unskilled labor stratum.[9] At the Oxnard sugar beet factory, for example, only Anglo-American men were employed as permanent staff. All of the major department heads, foremen, supervisors, office, and maintenance staff were white men. The only exceptions to this were the few white women employed as secretaries and stenographers.[10]

Members of the minority population in Oxnard, in contrast, were overwhelmingly employed as unskilled laborers and were the primary source of contracted farm labor in the area. Nearly 50% of the Mexican and Japanese population and over 65% of the Chinese in the county were farm laborers in 1900. Another 18 to 33% of these groups were unskilled laborers in the same year.[11]

Only a small segment of the minority population in the county was in the middle strata of the local occupational structure. The most important segment of this strata in Oxnard was made up of the minority labor contractors. The existing racial and class stratification system in the county placed these contractors in a unique position. On the one hand, the class position of contractors resulted in their having class interests that conflicted with those of their working-class compatriots. These contractors, for example, received a sizeable portion of the wages earned by those working under their supervision and thus benefitted directly from the exploitative contract labor system. At the same time, however, ties of ethnic solidarity led some labor contractors to protect their workers from abuses at the hands of unscrupulous farmers. In return for securing employment and receiving a portion of their workers' wages, labor contractors actively bargained to secure an equitable wage for their laborers and to ensure that they toiled under fair working conditions.

The existence of a racial-class stratification system that was not completely symmetrical had important consequences for the contending forces involved in the 1903 Oxnard strike. While racial status and class position were closely related, there did exist some fluidity in the stratification system. The particular location of minority labor contractors in the local class structure played a key role in the 1903 strike.

The development of the sugar beet industry in Ventura County led to a precipitous increase in the demand for seasonal farm laborers in Oxnard. Initially, sugar beet farmers in Oxnard relied upon Mexican and Chinese contracted laborers. The decline in the local Chinese population and the utilization of Mexicans in other sectors of agriculture, however, led to the recruitment of Japanese farm laborers to fill this labor shortage. Japanese farm laborers were first employed in the Oxnard sugar beet industry in 1899. By 1902 there were nine Japanese labor contractors meeting nearly all the seasonal need for farm laborers in the area.[12]

In the spring of 1902, however, a number of prominent Jewish businessmen and bankers in Oxnard organized a new contracting company, the Western Agricultural Contracting Company (WACC). Among the first directors and principal organizers of the company were the presidents of the Bank of Oxnard and the Bank of A. Levy and two of the most important merchants in Oxnard. The major sugar refiner in the county, the American Beet Sugar Company, also played an instrumental role in supporting the formation of the WACC.[13]

The initial purpose in forming the WACC was to provide local farmers with an alternative to the Japanese labor contractors in the area. Anglo farmers and the American Beet Sugar Company feared that these contractors would use their control of the local labor market to press for wage increases and improvements in working conditions. Under the leadership of Japanese contractors, Japanese farm laborers had already engaged in work slowdowns and strikes to secure concessions from Anglo farmers elsewhere in the state.[14] Thus, Anglo businessmen formed the WACC in order to end reliance on Japanese labor contractors, stabilize the local sugar beet industry, reduce labor costs to local farmers, and provide a profitable return to investors. Since the businessmen and bankers behind the WACC already worked closely with local beet farmers, they easily secured contracts with them and quickly became the major suppliers of contracted labor in the area.

Undermining the position of Japanese labor contractors and gaining control of approximately 90% of the contracting business by February 1903, the WACC forced all minority labor contractors to subcontract through their company or go out of business.[15] Through this arrangement, minority contractors and their employees were both forced to work on terms dictated by the WACC. The commission formerly received by minority contractors was reduced severely through this subcontracting arrangement, and they could no longer negotiate wages directly with local farmers. The minority farm laborers employed on this basis also were affected negatively. In addition to paying a percentage of their wages to the minority contractor who directly supervised them, they also paid a fee to the WACC for its role in arranging employment. Furthermore, the WACC routinely required minority workers to accept store orders from its company-owned stores instead of cash payment for wages. Overcharging for merchandise at these stores was common.

To facilitate its operation, the WACC established two different divisions to supervise the recruitment and assignment of minority laborers. All the labor contractors and farm laborers employed by the WACC worked through these two major departments. The so-called "Jap department," located in the Chinatown section of Oxnard, was under the supervision of Inosuke Inose. Inose had formerly worked for the American Beet Sugar Company and had been one of the Japanese labor contractors in the area. Inose's association with the ABSC led to his selection as the head of the Japanese department. In addition to serving as department supervisor, Inose also managed the WACC's Japanese-American Mercantile Store. Supervising the WACC's Mexican department was Albert Espinosa. Little is known about Espinosa other than his being an experienced beet worker who had won the confidence of the WACC's directors.[16]

Most of the Japanese farm laborers and labor contractors working in Oxnard were extremely dissatisfied with having to subcontract through the WACC. Mexican farm laborers in the area and the other numerous minority laborers recruited from other parts of the state also expressed displeasure with the new system. In direct response, a large group of disgruntled Japanese laborers and contractors organized a grievance meeting in Oxnard during the first week of February 1903. At this meeting a group of sixty Japanese contracted laborers recruited from San Francisco by Inosuke Inose complained bitterly about the operation of the WACC's Japanese department. The workers claimed that working conditions and wages promised by the WACC and Inose had not been met. Instead of paying each worker a ten-hour-day's wage of $1.50, Inose gave them a piecework rate returning them considerably less. The workers thinned beets at $3.75 per acre instead of the prevailing piecework rate of $5.00 to $6.00 per acre.[17]

The grievances of these disgruntled workers provided the key impetus for forming a union made up of Japanese and Mexican farm workers and contractors in Oxnard. At a subsequent meeting held on February 11, 1903, approximately 800 Japanese and Mexican workers organized the Japanese-Mexican Labor Association, electing as officers Kosaburo Baba (president), Y. Yamaguchi (secretary of the Japanese branch), and J. M. Lizarras (secretary of the Mexican branch). Among the charter members of the JMLA were approximately 500 Japanese and 200 Mexican workers.[18] The decision to form this union and challenge the WACC marked the first time the two minority groups successfully joined forces to organize an agricultural workers' union in the state. This was no minor achievement, as the JMLA's membership had to overcome formidable cultural and linguistic barriers. At their meetings, for example, all discussions were carried out in both Spanish and Japanese, with English serving as a common medium of communication.

Although the JMLA was primarily a farm workers' union, it actually was composed of three distinct groups: labor contractors, contracted laborers, and boarding students who were only temporary workers. Japanese labor contractors and, to a lesser extent, boarding students provided the leadership for the new union. Kosaburo Baba, the union's president, was one of the labor contractors displaced by the WACC. It is also likely that J. M. Lizarras, the JMLA's Mexican secretary, was a labor contractor. The Japanese secretary of the union, Y. Yamaguchi, is identified in one Japanese-language source as a boarding student recruited from San Francisco.[19]

Although it cannot be determined with certainty, it is likely that some of the Japanese leaders of the union, particularly the boarding students, were influenced by the Japanese Socialist Movement. This movement flourished in Japan after the Sino-Japanese War of 1894–95 and had a following among some of the Issei population who immigrated to California after that date. It is known, for example, that by 1904 there existed two Socialist groups among the Issei in California: one based in San Francisco and the other in Oakland. Originally organized as "discussion-study societies," these groups were led by prominent socialists such as Katayama Sen, who helped organize the short-lived San Francisco Japanese Socialist Party in February 1904.[20]

The major purpose of the Japanese-Mexican Labor Association was to end the WACC's monopoly of the contract labor system in Oxnard. By eliminating the WACC's control, the JMLA sought to negotiate directly with local farmers and to secure better wages. Since the formation of the

WACC, the prevailing rate of $5.00 to $6.00 per acre of beets thinned had been reduced to as low as $2.50 per acre. The new union wanted to return to the "old prices" paid for seasonal labor. By eliminating the WACC from the contracting business, the JMLA also sought to end the policy of enforced patronage. One of the WACC's company stores—the Japanese-American Mercantile Store—routinely overcharged for items by more than 60%. Japanese contracted laborers patronizing the store, for example, paid $1.20 for a $0.75 pair of work overalls.

In order to secure their demands, the JMLA membership agreed to cease working through the WACC and its subcontractors. This decision was tantamount to calling for a strike.[21] In striking, the JMLA threatened seriously the success of the local sugar beet crop because its profitability rested on the immediate completion of the thinning operation. This labor-intensive process required that workers carefully space beet seedlings and allow only the strongest beet plants to remain. Unlike the harvest, where timeliness was not as crucial, beet thinning required immediate attention in order to ensure a high-yield crop.

Although the JMLA was largely concerned with wages and the policy of enforced patronage, there is evidence that the leadership of the union saw their struggle in broad class terms. The reforms demanded by the union struck at the heart of the existing relationships between major capitalist interests in the county. Chief among these was that between the business-men and bankers who owned the WACC, the American Beet Sugar Com-pany, and the major sugar beet farmers in the area. All these special inter-ests were benefitting from the exploitative use of the minority farm laborers working through the WACC. Although Anglos were primarily guilty of exploiting Japanese and Mexican laborers, individuals such as Inosuke Inose and those minority contractors still subcontracting through the WACC were also seen as adversaries. Thus, the JMLA did not simply define their struggle in racial terms. Eloquent testimony of the JMLA's position is captured vividly in one news release issued by the Japanese and Mexican secretaries of the union. In putting forth the union's demands, Y. Yamaguchi and J. M. Lizarras wrote:

> Many of us have families, were born in the country, and are lawfully seek-ing to protect the only property that we have—our labor. It is just as nec-essary for the welfare of the valley that we get a decent living wage, as it is that the machines in the great sugar factory be properly oiled—if the ma-chines stop, the wealth of the valley stops, and likewise if the laborers are not given a decent wage, they too, must stop work and the whole people of this country suffer with them.[22]

Reacting to the JMLA with hostility and mistrust, the Oxnard *Courier* posed the issue of the union's demands as "simply a question of whether the Japanese-Mexican laboring classes will control labor or whether it will be managed by conservative businessmen." There was no particular reason for local farmers to prefer dealing with the JMLA, the *Courier's* editor asserted, when there existed "reliable American contractors" who could provide labor at lower costs. Furthermore, the editor continued, "if an organization of the ignorant, and for the most part alien, contract labor is allowed to over-power an American company, the farmers will find themselves in a state of dependence on irresponsible contractors." To support this claim, the editor noted that it was primarily a small number of Japanese and Mexican contractors who were "the real inspiration of the union."[23]

In another editorial, the *Courier* contended that only a union "in the hands of intelligent white men" could provide the "enlightened management" needed to run such an organization and to provide the "mental and moral uplifting and material advancement" of the Japanese and Mexican laborers in Oxnard. The JMLA would not succeed, therefore, because it was essentially a minority union "in the hands of people whose experience has been only to obey a master rather than think and manage for themselves. . . ."[24]

Reacting to the organization of the JMLA, the American Beet Sugar Company made clear that it would do everything in its power to ensure that the new union did not disrupt the smooth operation of the sugar beet industry in Oxnard. It immediately informed the union that the company was fully in support of the WACC. In outlining the company's position, the manager of the American Beet Sugar Company, Colonel Driffill, stated to the union:

> I have heard that you have a scale of prices which is detrimental to the interests of the farmers, and the interests of the farmers are our interests, because if you raise the price of labor to the farmers and they see that they cannot raise beets at a profit, we will have to take steps to drive you out of the country and secure help from the outside—even if we have to spend $100,000 in doing so.[25]

The only segment of the local Anglo population expressing any support for the JMLA consisted of a few merchants in Oxnard. Their support of the minority union, however, was not based on humanitarian concerns. Instead, self-interest was the motivating factor. These merchants were anxious to see the WACC's enforced patronage policy ended so minority workers could freely patronize their businesses.[26]

By the first week in March, the JMLA had successfully recruited a membership exceeding 1,200 workers, or over 90% of the total beet work force in the county. The JMLA's recruitment drive resulted in the WACC losing nearly all of the laborers it had formerly contracted. The growing strength of the JMLA greatly alarmed beet farmers in the area, for nothing like the new union had been organized in Ventura County or, for that matter, anywhere else in southern California.

One of the first public displays of the JMLA's strength was exhibited at a mass demonstration and parade held in Oxnard on March 6, 1903. Describing the event, the Oxnard *Courier* reported that "dusky skinned Japanese and Mexicans marched through the streets headed by one or two contractors and beet laborers four abreast and several hundred strong." Although impressed by their numbers, the *Courier* described the JMLA's membership as "a silent grim band of fellows, most of them young and belonging to the lower class of Japanese and Mexicans." [27]

Unwilling to allow this exhibition of strength to go unchallenged, the WACC initiated an effort to undercut the solidarity of the JMLA and regain its position as the major supplier of contracted labor in Oxnard. During the second and third weeks of March, the WACC helped form an alternative, minority-led union. In supporting the organization of the Independent Agricultural Labor Union (IALU), the WACC sought to undercut the organizational successes of the JMLA and use the IALU to help regain its former dominance. The WACC believed it wiser to support a non-threatening, conservative union than face complete ruination at the hands of the JMLA.

Inosuke Inose of the WACC and "some of the most influential and best-educated of the Japanese residents of Oxnard" were among the initial board of directors of the IALU. The IALU described itself as a union striving "to secure and maintain harmonious relations between employers and employees of agricultural labor. . . ." Seeing this as its primary purpose, the IALU sought to defend its members from "any person or organization" preventing them from working "for wages and for such persons as shall be mutually satisfactory. . . ." [28] Thus, the IALU's purpose was not to eliminate the abusive treatment of minority laborers but to help regain the stability of the sugar beet industry in the area.

Immediately after its formation, the IALU began working in conjunction with the WACC to meet the pressing labor needs of local farmers. These efforts were, of course, seen by the JMLA as a strikebreaking tactic. Describing the ensuing tension, one county newspaper reported that "Oxnard is up against labor turmoil, and bloodspots are gathering on the face of the moon as it hovers over the sugartown. The Japanese-Mexican labor union has inspired an enmity and opposition that threatens to terminate in riot and bloodshed. . . ."[29] This proved to be prophetic, as an outburst of violence occurred a few days after the IALU was organized.

Occurring on March 23, 1903, in the Chinatown section of Oxnard, the violent confrontation was triggered when members of the JMLA attempted to place their union banner on a wagon loaded with IALU strikebreakers being taken to a ranch of a local farmer. The union's insignia consisted of a white banner with a red rising sun and pair of clasped hands. Superimposed over this insignia were the letters "J.M.L.A."

One newspaper described the ensuing confrontation in the following way: ". . . [A] fusillage of shots was fired from all directions. They seemed to come from every window and door in Chinatown. The streets were filled with people, and the wonder is that only five persons were shot." When the shooting subsided, two Mexican and two Japanese members of the JMLA lay wounded from the erupting gunfire. Manuel Ramirez was shot in the leg, and two Japanese workers were struck, one in the arm and the other in the face. Another Mexican, Luis Vasquez, was dead, shot in the back.[30]

Responsibility for the violent confrontation was placed on the JMLA. The Los Angeles *Times*, for example, reported that "agitation-crazed striking Mexicans and Japanese" had attacked "independent workmen" and precipitated a "pitched battle" in which dozens had been wounded and "thousands gone wild." The *Times* charged that "loud-mouthed and lawless union agitators" had directly triggered the violence. More specifically, it was the "trouble-making" Mexican leadership of the JMLA that had inflamed the "ignorant peons" into action, and "most of the firing was done by Mexicans." Even the Japanese laborers, seen as being "inclined to be peaceable," were "excited by their leaders" and fell victim to their exhortations "a good deal like sheep."[31]

Although more restrained than the *Times*, the Oxnard *Courier* also blamed the union for precipitating the confrontation. The local weekly summed up the situation in the following way:

> Naturally the riot and its causes have been a topic of general conversation on the streets [of Oxnard]. In most cases the union adherents are blamed for resorting to illegal and forceful methods to prevent men who are willing from working for the Western Agricultural Contracting Company. It is this that is primarily responsible for the riot. The attempt to place a union label where it was not wanted is at the root of the disturbance, and in reality the union has only itself to blame for the riot. . . .[32]

There was scarcely a newspaper account of the "riot" in Oxnard that did not blame the union for igniting the outburst. The only weekly that did not directly blame the JMLA was the Ventura *Independent*. This newspaper's editor, S. Goodman, argued that:

> The root of the evil lies in the fact that ten men for every single job were shipped into the sugar beet territory [of Ventura County], bringing together a restless irresponsible element, only lacking in leadership to make all kinds of trouble. . . .
>
> In the riot of Monday last, the Contracting Company is a measure at fault. Had someone of authority in the employment of the company, possessing a cool head, superintended the sending out of laborers, the restless element could have been subdued and all trouble averted.[33]

Outraged over the biased coverage of the March 23rd confrontation, the JMLA issued its own public statement. It was subsequently published in only two newspapers: the Los Angeles *Herald* and the Oxnard *Courier*. The newspaper that the JMLA was principally responding to, the Los Angeles *Times*, refused to publish the following release:

> Owing to the many false statements printed in the Los Angeles *Times* about our organization, and the murderous assaults made upon the union men last Monday afternoon, we ask that the following statement of facts be printed, in justice to the thirteen hundred men whom the Japanese-Mexican Labor Association represents.
>
> In the first place, we assert, and are ready to prove, that Monday afternoon and at all times during the shooting, the Union men are unarmed, while the nonunion men sent out by the Western Agricultural Contracting Company were prepared for a bloody fight with arms purchased, in many cases, recently from hardware stores in this town. As proof of the fact that the union men were not guilty of violence, we point to the fact that the authorities have not arrested a single union man—the only man actually put under bonds, or arrested, being deputy Constable Charles Arnold. Our union has always been law abiding and has in its ranks at least nine-tenths of all the beet thinners in this section, who have not asked for a raise in wages, but only that the wages be not lowered, as was demanded by the beet growers. . . .
>
> We assert that if the police authorities had done their duty, many arrests would have been made among the occupants of the company's house, from which the fatal volleys of bullets came. In view of the fact that many disorderly men have recently been induced to come to Oxnard by the Western Agricultural Contracting Company, and that they took part in the assaults of Monday afternoon, we demand that the police no longer neglect their duty, but arrest those persons who plainly participated in the fatal shooting.[34]

Shortly after the shooting, Charles Arnold was arrested for the murder of Vasquez, and a coroner's inquest held to determine his guilt or innocence. The conflicting testimony of 50 eyewitnesses was heard at the inquest. A number of witnesses testified that Arnold did not shoot Vasquez and, in fact, that they had not even seen him raise a gun. One witness testified that an examination of Arnold's weapons after the shooting showed that they were fully loaded and had not been fired.

Testifying against Arnold were a number of Mexican witnesses claiming to have seen Arnold fire at JMLA members. Among these witnesses was Manuel Ramirez, a victim of the shooting, who testified that it was a Japanese strikebreaker in the WACC wagon who had shot him in the leg. Despite the evidence presented to the all male Anglo jury, it soon became apparent to JMLA members that Arnold would be cleared. At the close of the second day of hearings, for example, the county coroner notified the jury that another round of testimony was needed so that more Japanese witnesses could be heard. Angered by this request, the jury protested further continuation and stated that they were "prepared to render a verdict without further evidence." After a brief adjournment, the inquest reconvened and Arnold was cleared of any complicity in the death of Luis Vasquez.[35]

Outraged at what they believed to be a gross miscarriage of justice, members of the JMLA stepped up their efforts to win the strike. Following the March 23rd confrontation, the union took the offensive and escalated militant organizing activities. In one incident, the Oxnard *Courier* reported that "a gang of 50 Mexicans, many of them masked, visited a contracting company camp on Chas. Donlon's ranch, cut the guy ropes of the tent and made the crew of some 18 men desert and come to town. . . ." A similar incident occurred at a labor camp on another local farmer's property near Oxnard.[36]

Soon thereafter, Andres Garcia, the foreman on Charles Arnold's ranch, was fired upon and nearly killed by an unknown assailant. One county newspaper speculated that the assailant mistook Garcia for Arnold, the man originally charged with Luis Vasquez's murder. Since being cleared of the charge, Arnold had openly expressed opposition to the JMLA and hired nonunion laborers to work on his ranch.[37]

In response to further strikebreaking efforts, the JMLA organized laborers being brought to Oxnard and succeeded in winning them over to the union's side. In doing so, the union stationed men at the nearby Montalvo railroad depot and met the newly recruited laborers as they arrived in the county. In one incident reported by the Ventura *Free Press*, a local rancher attempted to circumvent JMLA organizers by personally meeting incoming laborers and scurrying them off to his ranch. Before arriving at his ranch, however, the farmer was intercepted by a group of JMLA members who unloaded the strikebreakers and convinced them to join the union.[38] In discussing the success of the JMLA in organizing potential strikebreakers, one county newspaper summarily noted that "by the time these men reached Oxnard they were on the side of the union and against the Western Agricultural Contracting Company."[39]

The success of the JMLA in maintaining their strike led to a clearcut union victory. In the aftermath of the violent confrontation in Chinatown, representatives of local farmers, the WACC, and the JMLA met at the latter's headquarters in Oxnard to negotiate a strike settlement. Representing the farmers were Colonel Driffill (manager of the American Beet Sugar Company's Oxnard factory), T. H. Rice, P. S. Carr, Charles Donlon, and L. S. Rose. The WACC representative was the company's president, George E. Herz. The JMLA negotiating team was led by J. M. Lizarras, Kosaburo Baba, Y. Yamaguchi, J. Espinosa, and their counsel, W. E. Shepherd.[40] Also representing the union were Fred C. Wheeler and John Murray, socialist union organizers affiliated with the Los Angeles County Council of Labor, the California State Federation of Labor, and the AFL.

J. M. Lizarras forcefully presented the JMLA's demands at the initial meeting. Insisting that the union wanted to bargain directly with local farmers, Lizarras threatened that the union would take all of their members out of the county, thereby ensuring the loss of the entire beet crop, if their demands were not met.[41]

John Murray chastised farmers at this meeting for not quickly coming to terms with the JMLA. He impressed upon them that they should be thankful that the union was not striking for more than it was demanding.[42] Fred Wheeler also addressed the assembly. In restating the JMLA's demands, he pointed out to local farmers that "you have the beets and we have the labor and want to work directly with you. We are members of the American Federation of Labor and are here to stay. It is bread and butter to us and we will deal directly with farmers."[43] As will be seen, Wheeler's statement, giving farmers the impression that the JMLA was affiliated with the AFL, was premature.

The first sign of JMLA winning the strike occurred when the WACC partially acceded to the JMLA's demand to negotiate contracts directly with local farmers. The WACC offered the JMLA the right to provide labor on 2,000 of the 7,000 acres of farm land it had under contract. In return, the WACC requested that the JMLA order its men back to work and agree not to unionize men working for the WACC on the remaining farm land. This offer was flatly rejected by JMLA negotiators, who insisted that they would not end their strike until the WACC's monopoly was broken and all farmers agreed to contract directly with them. At one point in the negotiations the JMLA mockingly offered a proposal whereby each party would receive the right to provide labor to local farmers in proportion to the number of men they represented. Spokespersons for the JMLA noted that they represented 1,300 men while the WACC had only sixty men under contract.[44] The union's strong showing at this initial session led one local county newspaper to report that the JMLA "showed a strong front, clearly demonstrating to the ranchers that they controlled the labor necessary to do their work, and without their services beet crops must perish."[45]

On the second day of negotiations, Lizarras and Yamaguchi met with representatives of local farmers and the WACC at the American Beet Sugar Company factory in Oxnard. During this session the union firmly stood by its demand and gained the first important concession in the negotiations. It was an agreement from the farmers' committee to establish a minimum wage scale of $5.00, and a high of $6.00, per acre for the thinning of beets by union laborers. This was nearly double what the WACC was paying laborers before the strike.[46]

On March 30, 1903, the tumultuous Oxnard sugar beet workers' strike ended with the JMLA winning a major victory. The agreement reached included a provision forcing the WACC to cancel all existing contracts with local sugar beet growers. The only exception to this was the 1,800 acre Patterson ranch, which was owned by the same family that operated the American Beet Sugar Company. This ranch remained the only farm to which the WACC would continue to provide labor. Thus, the final settlement meant that the WACC relinquished the right to provide labor to farmers owning over 5,000 acres of county farm land.[47]

The success of the Oxnard strike of 1903 raised a number of important issues for the labor movement. For years, trade unions were opposed to organizing minorities in industry and were even less interested in organizing agricultural workers. The JMLA's victory, however, forced the union movement to confront the issue of including agricultural workers in its ranks. It also forced white unions to clearly articulate their position on the organization of Japanese and Mexican workers.[48]

The issue of admitting Mexican and Japanese workers to the trade union movement became an important issue in both northern and southern California after the JMLA victory. In reporting local union discussion on whether or not to organize Asian workers in Oakland, the Oakland *Tribune*, for example, noted that the "recent strike of about 1,000 Japs and Mexicans at Oxnard against starvation wages and hard-treatment has brought the matter to the front."[49]

The official attitude of organized labor toward the JMLA was, from the very beginning, mixed and often contradictory. Certain local councils, for example, supported the JMLA and further organizing of Japanese and Mexican workers. This tendency, led by prominent union socialists, also supported organizing all agricultural workers and including farm labor unions in the AFL. Most union councils and high-ranking AFL officials were, on the other hand, opposed to any formal affiliation with the JMLA. This position was based, in part, on organized labor's anti-Asian sentiment and its general opposition to organizing agricultural laborers.

Despite union opposition to minority labor and agricultural workers' unions, Fred C. Wheeler and John Murray convinced the Los Angeles County Council of Labor (LACCL) to adopt a resolution favoring the unionization of all unskilled laborers regardless of race or nationality. Shortly after the March 23rd confrontation in Oxnard, the LACCL unanimously adopted a resolution supporting the JMLA. This resolution, the San Francisco *Examiner* noted, represented "the first time that a labor council had put itself on record as in any way favoring Asiatic labor."[50]

Although the LACCL's resolution supported organizing minority workers already in the United States, it also reaffirmed the local's staunch opposition to further Asian immigration. Thus, an important element of self-interest played a role in the LACCL's decision to support the JMLA.[51] The LACCL's resolution expressed the contradictory views of the radical elements of the trade union movement concerning the organization of Japanese workers. Behind its public support of the JMLA, the LACCL acknowledged that Japanese and Mexican workers could successfully organize on their own and, therefore, it was in the interest of the trade union movement to include them in its ranks. Additionally, if left unorganized, these racial minority workers could become strikebreakers and pose a serious threat to the white labor movement in southern California.

That self-interest played a key role in the passage of this resolution was later acknowledged by P. B. Preble, secretary of the Oakland Federated Trades Council and a high-ranking member of the AFL. In a candid interview with the Oakland *Tribune*, Preble discussed the LACCL resolution in the following terms:

> This is one of the most important resolutions ever brought to the attention of the [AFL] Executive Council. It virtually breaks the ice on the question

of forming Orientals into unions so keeping them from "scabbing" on the white people. . . .

    Down there [southern California] the white workingmen have been plumb up against it from Japs and Mexicans who were being imported wholesale. . . . Down there, the Union has succeeded in putting this important company out of business, and the men are now selling their labor at the Union scale, without any cutting by middle men being done.[52]

The message was clear. The success of the JMLA forced the white trade union movement to either include or specifically exclude Mexican and Japanese workers from its ranks. In Preble's words, it became an issue only "when the forces of circumstances demand it."[53]

    While left elements in the trade union movement supported the JMLA, labor's principal organization—the AFL—was essentially hostile. Although the AFL convention of 1894 formally declared that "working people must unite to organize irrespective of creed, color, sex, nationality or politics," the reaction of the Federation leadership to the JMLA belied this stated purpose.[54] Following the JMLA victory in March 1903, J. M. Lizarras—secretary of the Mexican branch of the union—petitioned the AFL Executive Council for a charter making the JMLA the first agricultural laborers' union to be admitted into the AFL.

    Upon receiving the JMLA's petition, which was submitted under the name of Sugar Beet and Farm Laborers' Union of Oxnard, Samuel Gompers granted the union a charter but stipulated a prohibition on Asian membership. In his letter notifying Lizarras of his decision, Gompers emphasized that:

It is . . . understood that in issuing this charter to your union, will under no circumstance accept membership of any Chinese or Japanese. The laws of our country prohibit Chinese workmen or laborers from entering the United States, and propositions for the extension of the exclusion laws to the Japanese have been made on several occasions.[55]

    Evidence suggests that the San Francisco Council of Labor contacted Gompers and expressed their vehement opposition to the JMLA's request for a charter. Although the LACCL publicly supported the JMLA, the prevailing union movement's opposition to Asian labor, which Gompers shared, undoubtedly influenced this decision.[56]

    Left elements in the AFL reacted bitterly to Gompers' decision. In discussing the AFL's refusal to grant the requested charter, the *American Labor Union Journal* from Chicago charged that Gompers had "violated the express principles of the A.F. of L." and that it would "be impossible, so long as this ruling is sustained, to organize wage workers of California . . .

for there are between forty and fifty thousand Japanese in this state, and nothing can be effectively done without their cooperation."[57] Despite the objections of a few locals and councils, there is little evidence to suggest that most unions expressed anything but tacit approval of Gompers' decision.

Gompers' refusal to grant an AFL charter allowing Japanese membership was vehemently denounced by the Mexican branch of the JMLA. Outraged at Gompers' action, the Mexican membership of the union directed Lizarras to write Gompers what is undoubtedly the strongest testimony of the solidarity reached between the Mexican and Japanese farm workers of Oxnard. On June 8, 1903, Lizarras returned the issued charter to Samuel Gompers with the following letter:

> Your letter . . . in which you say the admission with us of the Japanese Sugar Beet and Farm Laborers into the American Federation of Labor can not be considered, is received. We beg to say in reply that our Japanese brothers here were the first to recognize the importance of cooperating and uniting in demanding a fair wage scale. . . .
>
> They were not only just with us, but they were generous when one of our men was murdered by hired assassins of the oppressor of labor, they gave expression to their sympathy in a very substantial form. In the past we have counseled, fought and lived on very short rations with our Japanese brothers, and toiled with them in the fields, and they have been uniformly kind and considerate. We would be false to them and to ourselves and to the cause of unionism if we now accepted privileges for ourselves which are not accorded to them. We are going to stand by men who stood by us in the long, hard fight which ended in a victory over the enemy. We therefore respectfully petition the A.F. of L. to grant us a charter under which we can unite all the sugar beet and field laborers in Oxnard, without regard to their color or race. We will refuse any other kind of charter, except one which will wipe out race prejudices and recognize our fellow workers as being as good as ourselves. I am ordered by the Mexican union to write this letter to you and they fully approve its words.[58]

In refusing to join the AFL without the Japanese branch of the union, the JMLA ultimately closed the door to any hopes of continuing its union activities in Oxnard. The AFL decision not to admit all members of the JMLA undoubtedly contributed to the union eventually passing out of existence. A systematic review of newspaper accounts of labor activities in Ventura County through 1910 failed to uncover further mention of the JMLA after its success in April 1903. No other evidence could be found concerning further JMLA activities or the exact date that the union ceased to exist. What appears to have happened is that the union continued operating for a few years and eventually disbanded. By 1906 there existed further discontent on the part of sugar beet workers in Oxnard, but no mention is made of the JMLA.[59]

For years after the Oxnard strike, AFL hostility toward organizing Japanese workers and farm laborers persisted. Not until 1910 did the AFL Executive Council attempt to organize farm workers as an element of the Federation. These efforts, however, accomplished very little. According to one authority, the AFL's activities after 1910 were explicitly "designed to favor white workers at the expense of Orientals."[60] Finally, during the war years, the Federation's efforts to organize farm laborers were abandoned altogether.[61]

Beyond its significance for labor history, the Oxnard sugar beet workers' strike also has sociological importance. The strike, for example, provides us with important clues into the nature of class and race relations in California at the turn of the century. As in other parts of the state, the capitalist economy emerging in Oxnard gave birth to a class structure in which racial divisions closely paralleled class divisions. The overrepresentation of Mexicans and Japanese as contracted farm laborers and unskilled workers, and of Anglo-Americans as farmers and businessmen, in Oxnard reveals the important convergence of racial and class stratification lines during this period. The class structure in Oxnard was not, however, a static one that approximated a caste system. Instead, a modicum of fluidity existed, and some minorities successfully made inroads into the middle strata of the local class structure. Among the most important members of this stratum in Oxnard were the numerous minority labor contractors, who served an intermediary function in the procurement of farm labor. Labor contractors were both the benefactors and exploiters of the men who worked under their direction. The peculiar position of these contractors in the minority community undoubtedly contributed to their playing a leadership role in the formation of the JMLA.

In the final analysis, it was the displacement of these minority contractors by local Anglo elites that led to the unification of minority contractors and farm laborers in a common cause. An alliance based on ethnic solidarity and common, short-term interests provided the impetus in forming the JMLA and overcoming the existing differences in the class position of minority labor contractors and farm laborers. Whether the JMLA merely wanted to return to the state in which minority contractors provided labor for local farmers or whether it truly sought to operate as a traditional union cannot be determined with certainty. The paucity of available information on the JMLA after the strike makes it impossible to know the extent to which the JMLA actually functioned as a union or if it merely became an instrument used by minority contractors to regain their dominance of the local market. Regardless of the motives of the various elements in the JMLA or which of many forms the union took after the strike, it appears that local agribusiness elites ultimately regained the upper hand and made it impossible for the JMLA to continue to function. Whether internal divisions between farm workers and labor contractors within the JMLA played a role in its demise is not known. In any event, the unique class alliance and bonds of ethnic solidarity that underlay the JMLA proved to be short-lived.

The experience of the JMLA with organized labor at the time also clearly reveals differences in the racial attitudes of Anglo-Americans. Mexican and Japanese workers were not perceived as posing the same threat to the white working class. Differences between these two groups in racial and political-legal status, religion, language, and previous competition with white labor shaped the way that the AFL reacted to the JMLA's petition for a Federation charter. Gompers' attitude toward the Japanese branch of the JMLA clearly illustrated that white racism at the time was not a monolithic structure that affected all minority groups in precisely the same way. Instead, important differences existed in the way Anglo-Americans viewed and discriminated against different minority groups.

Anglo-American attitudes toward the Japanese were essentially an extension of their earlier view of the Chinese. Like the Chinese, the Japanese were seen as a direct threat to the jobs, wages, and working conditions of white labor. Furthermore, the non-white, alien status of the Japanese also contributed to their being seen as a threat to the preservation of the white race and American cultural standards and ideals.[62]

Mexican workers, on the other hand, were not perceived at the time as posing the same threat to white labor. A number of factors account for this important difference. Foremost among these was the legal status of Mexicans as U.S. citizens and their racial status as a "white" population. The Treaty of Guadalupe Hidalgo in 1848 had extended all U.S. citizenship rights to Mexicans and socially defined them as "free white persons." Also important in mitigating Anglo racism toward Mexicans was the latter's perceived assimilability. Unlike Asians, who were viewed as uncivilized "pagan idolators," Mexicans were viewed as a Christian population possessing a culture that was not as completely foreign as that of the Asian groups. In addition, economic factors tempered anti-Mexican sentiment at this time. The late entry of Mexicans into the capitalist labor market in California resulted in their not openly competing with Anglo workers for jobs. Additionally, Mexicans were concentrated largely in the rural backwaters of southern California, away from the urban manufacturing centers where white working-class opposition to minority laborers emerged first. Finally, the Mexican population was relatively small. There were, for example, fewer Mexicans than Japanese in California at the time of the Oxnard strike. All of these factors contributed directly to the existing differences in Anglo attitudes toward the Mexican and Japanese populations.

The Oxnard strike vividly captured these differences in racial attitudes. Anglo reaction toward these two groups in Oxnard and Samuel Gompers' reaction to the JMLA request for an AFL charter provide clear examples of this. In both cases, reaction to the Japanese was more vehement and hostile than that toward the Mexican. Further Mexican immigration and direct competition with Anglos in later years would, however, lead to an anti-Mexican sentiment that was just as intensely racist as that against the Japanese in 1903. Thus, racism must be viewed in historical terms as a form of group domination that is shaped by the interaction of social, political, economic, and demographic factors. It was the unique interplay of these factors in California at the turn of the century that accounts for the different reaction of Anglos to the Japanese and Mexican membership of the JMLA.

NOTES

1. Despite its significance to labor history, there exists only one published article on the Oxnard sugar beet workers' strike of 1903, John Murray's first-hand account. See John Murray, "A Foretaste of the Orient," *International Socialist Review*, 4 (August 1903), 72–79. For brief references to the Oxnard strike and its significance to the labor movement, see the following Federal Writers' Project reports: *Oriental Labor Unions and Strikes — California Agriculture* (Oakland, 1939?), typewritten, 11–13; *Unionization of Migratory Labor, 1903–1930* (Oakland, 193–?), typewritten, 3–4. For discussions of the Oxnard strike within the context of minority labor history, see Juan Gómez-Quiñones, "The First Steps: Chicano Labor Conflict and Organizing, 1900–1920," *Aztlan: Chicano Journal of the Social Sciences and Arts*, 3 (1972), 13–49; Karl Yoneda, "100 Years of Japanese Labor History in the U.S.A.," in Amy Tachiki, Eddie Wong, and Franklin Odo, eds., *Roots: An Asian American Reader* (Los Angeles, 1971), 150–158.

2. Torsten Magnuson, "History of the Beet Sugar Industry in California," *Historical Society of Southern California, Annual Publication* 11, Part 1 (1918), 76; Dan Gutleben, "The Oxnard Beet Sugar Factory, Oxnard, California," unpublished manuscript in Ventura County Historical Museum Library; Elizabeth Ritter, *History of Ventura County, California* (Los Angeles, 1940), 141; Thomas J. Osborne, "Claus Spreckels and the Oxnard Brothers: Pioneer Developers of California's Beet Sugar Industry, 1890–1900," *Southern California Historical Quarterly*, 54 (1972), 119; Sol N. Sheridan, *Ventura County, California* (San Francisco,

1909), 48; Oxnard *Courier*, Jan. 4, 1902, Feb. 21, 1903.

3. Oxnard *Courier*, Sept. 11, 1903; William T. Dagodag, "A Social Geography of La Colonia: A Mexican-American Settlement in the City of Oxnard, California" (MA essay, San Fernando Valley State College, 1967), 5.

4. Oxnard *Courier*, Mar. 22, 1902, April 4, 1902.

5. Oxnard *Courier*, Mar. 23, 1906.

6. Transcript of interview with Mrs. Reginald Shand, Moorpark, California, Aug. 25, 1960, in Thomas R. Bard Collection, Huntington Library, San Marino, California; W. W. Brown, "The Journal of W. W. Brown: 1901–1902," *Ventura County Historical Society Quarterly*, 15 (Oct. 1969), 15.

7. Oxnard *Courier*, Feb. 11, 1910; W. H. Hutchinson, *Oil, Land, and Politics: The California Career of Thomas Robert Bard* (Norman, OK, 1956, 2 vols.), II, 96; Vera Bloom, "Oxnard: A Social History of the Early Years," *Ventura County Historical Society Quarterly*, 4 (Feb. 1956), 19.

8. Bloom, "Oxnard," 19.

9. For a detailed quantitative study of this racial and class stratification, based on data drawn from the federal manuscript census schedules, see Tomás Almaguer, "Class, Race, and Capitalist Development: The Social Transformation of a Southern California County, 1848–1903" (Ph.D. diss., Univ. of California, Berkeley, 1979).

10. Oxnard *Courier*, Oct. 11, 1902.

11. Almaguer, "Class, Race, and Capitalist Development," 247.

12. Nanka Nikkeijin Shōgyō Kaigisho, *Nan Kashū Nihonjinshi* [hereafter referred to as *History of the Japanese in Southern California*] (Los Angeles, 1956), 54–55; Kashiwamura Kazusuke, *Hoku-Bei Tōsa Taidan* [hereafter referred to as *A Broad Survey of North America*] (Tokyo, 1911), 223–224; Oxnard *Courier*, Oct. 11, 1903.

13. Oxnard *Courier*, Feb. 28, 1903; *A Broad Survey of North America*, 223; *History of the Japanese in Southern California*, 54–55.

14. See, for example, U.S. Congress, Senate, Committee on Immigration, *Abstract of the Report on Japanese and Other Races in the Pacific and Rocky Mountain States* (Washington, DC, 1911), 53–55; Varden Fuller, *The Supply of Agricultural Labor as a Factor in the Evolution of Farm Organization in California Agriculture*, U.S. Congress, Senate, Committee on Education and Labor, Seventy-Sixth Congress, 3rd Session, Hearings . . . Pursuant to Senate Resolution 266, Part 54, Agricultural Labor in California (Washington, DC, 1940), 831; Masukazu Iwata, "The Japanese Immigrant in California Agriculture," *Agricultural History*, 36 (1962), 27; Yamato Ichihashi, *Japanese in the United States: A Critical Study of the Problems of the Japanese Immigrants and Their Children* (Stanford, 1932), 176–177; Roger Daniels, *The Politics of Prejudice: The Anti-Japanese Movement in California and the Struggle for Japanese Exclusion* (New York, 1968), 8–9; H. A. Millis, *The Japanese Problem in the United States: An Investigation for the Commission on Relations with Japan, Appointed by the Federal Council of The Churches of Christ in America* (New York, 1915), 111–112.

15. *A Broad Survey of North America*, 224; Oxnard *Courier*, Feb. 28, 1903.

16. Oxnard *Courier*, Mar. 27, 1902, Feb. 28, 1903.

17. Ibid., Feb. 7, 14, 1903; San Francisco *Examiner*, Mar. 27, 1903.

18. *History of the Japanese in Southern California*, 53; *A Broad Survey of North America*, 225; Oxnard *Courier*, Mar. 27, 1903; Ventura *Free Press*, Mar. 6, 1903; Ventura *Weekly Democrat*, Feb. 27, 1903.

19. *A Broad Survey of North America*, 223–225. Also see *History of the*

Japanese in Southern California, 53.

20. Yuji Ichioka, "A Buried Past: Early Issei Socialists and the Japanese Community," *Amerasia Journal,* 1 (July 1971), 3.

21. Oxnard *Courier,* Mar. 7, 14, 1903; Ventura *Independent,* Mar. 5, 1903; Ventura *Free Press,* Mar. 7, 27, 1903.

22. Los Angeles *Herald,* Mar. 29, 1903; Oxnard *Courier,* Mar. 28, 1903.

23. Oxnard *Courier,* Mar. 7, 28, 1903.

24. Ibid., Mar. 28, 1903.

25. Murray, "A Foretaste of the Orient," 73–74.

26. Ventura *Weekly Democrat,* Feb. 27, 1903; Ventura *Free Press,* Mar. 6, 1903.

27. Oxnard *Courier,* Mar. 7, 1903.

28. Ventura *Daily Democrat,* Mar. 27, 1903; Ventura *Free Press,* Mar. 27, 1903; Los Angeles *Herald,* Mar. 27, 1903.

29. Ventura *Daily Democrat,* Mar. 1, 1903.

30. Ibid., Mar. 24, 26, 27, 1903; Los Angeles *Herald,* Mar. 24, 1903; Oxnard *Courier,* Mar. 28, 1903; Ventura *Free Press,* Mar. 27, 1903; Santa Barbara *Morning Press,* Mar. 24, 1903; San Francisco *Call,* Mar. 24, 25, 1903; San Francisco *Examiner,* Mar. 26, 1903.

31. Los Angeles *Times,* Mar. 24, 25, 1903.

32. Oxnard *Courier,* Mar. 28, 1903.

33. Ventura *Independent,* Mar. 26, 1903.

34. Los Angeles *Herald,* Mar. 29, 1903; Oxnard *Courier,* Mar. 28, 1903. Also see Murray, "A Foretaste of the Orient," 76–77.

35. Oxnard *Courier,* April 4, 1903; Ventura *Daily Democrat,* Mar. 31, 1903.

36. Oxnard *Courier,* Mar. 28, 1903. Also see Los Angeles *Times,* Mar. 24, 1903.

37. Ventura *Daily Democrat,* Mar. 31, 1903; Los Angeles *Times,* April 1, 1903; Los Angeles *Times and California Mirror,* April 4, 1903; Ventura *Independent,* April 2, 1903.

38. Ventura *Free Press,* Mar. 27, 1903.

39. Ibid.

40. Ventura *Daily Democrat,* Mar. 27, 1903; Los Angeles *Times,* Mar. 26, 1903.

41. Los Angeles *Times,* Mar. 26, 1903.

42. Ibid., Mar. 27, 1903.

43. Oxnard *Courier,* Mar. 28, 1903.

44. Oxnard *Courier,* April 4, 1903.

45. Ventura *Daily Democrat,* Mar. 26, 1903.

46. Los Angeles *Times,* Mar. 27, 1903.

47. Ventura *Free Press,* April 3, 1903; Oxnard *Courier,* April 4, 1903; Ventura *Weekly Free Democrat,* April 3, 1903; Oakland *Tribune,* April 11, 1903.

48. Stuart Jamieson, *Labor Unionism in American Agriculture,* United States Department of Labor, Bureau of Labor Statistics, Bulletin No. 836 (Washington, DC, 1945), 5.

49. Oakland *Tribune,* April 1, 1903.

50. San Francisco *Examiner,* Mar. 26, 1903.

51. Oakland *Tribune,* April 21, 1903.

52. Ibid.

53. Ibid.

54. *Proceedings, AFL Convention, 1894,* 25.

55. Samuel Gompers to J. M. Lizarras, May 15, 1903, as cited by Murray, "A Foretaste of the Orient," 77–78.

56. Los Angeles *Citizen,* Feb. 7, 1930.

57. *American Labor Union Journal,* June 25, 1903, as cited by Phillip S. Foner, *History of the Labor Movement in the United States* (New York, 1947–1965, 4 vols.), IV, 277.

58. J. M. Lizarras to Samuel Gompers, June 8, 1903, as cited by Murray, "A Foretaste of the Orient," 78. Also see Foner, *History of the Labor Movement,* III, 277.

59. On Feb. 2, 1906, a new organization called the "Cooperative Contracting Company" placed an advertisement in the Oxnard *Courier* identifying itself as an alternative to existing contracting companies in Oxnard. While it was not a union, the new company did claim to represent the interests of "Japanese laborers" in Oxnard. Their advertisement read as follows:

> We Japanese laborers who have been in Oxnard for years, wish to make contracts for the harvesting of sugar beets direct with the growers. Don't make your agreement with other contractors, because for years we laborers have been depressed by them. Contractors' ill-treatment of laborers is the growers' loss directly. We trust them no more. We can and will do better work than has ever been done here.

60. Jamieson, *Labor Unionism,* 57–58. Also see Lewis L. Lorwin and Joan A. Flexner, *The American Federation of Labor: History, Policies, and Prospects* (Washington, DC, 1933), 11; Federal Writers' Project, *The Migratory Agricultural Worker and the American Federation of Labor to 1938 Inclusive* (Oakland, 1939?), typewritten; Federal Writers' Project, *Oriental Labor Unions and Strikes;* Federal Writers' Project, *Unionization of Migratory Labor.*

61. Jamieson, *Labor Unionism,* 58.

62. For two excellent discussions of the role of white labor in the anti-Chinese and anti-Japanese movements, see Alexander Saxton, *The Indispensable Enemy: Labor and the Anti-Chinese Movement in California* (Berkeley, 1971); and Daniels, *The Politics of Prejudice.*

FURTHER READING

See also the lists of suggested readings for chapters 7 and 9.

Acuña, Rodolfo. *Occupied America: A History of Chicanos.* 1988.

Almaguer, Tomás. *Racial Fault Lines: The Historical Origins of White Supremacy in California.* 1994.

Barrera, Mario. *Race and Class in the Southwest: A Theory of Racial Inequality.* Chapters 2 and 3. 1979.

Camarillo, Albert. *Chicanos in a Changing Society: From Mexican Pueblos to American Barrios in Santa Barbara and Southern California, 1848–1930.* 1979.

Cardoso, Lawrence A. *Mexican Emigration to the United States, 1897–1931: Socioeconomic Patterns.* 1971.

Friday, Chris. "Asian American Labor and Historical Interpretation." *Labor History* 35 (Fall 1994): 524–546.

———. *Organizing Asian American Workers: The Pacific Coast Canned Salmon Industry, 1870–1942.* 1994.

Gamio, Manuel. *The Mexican Immigrant: His Life Story.* 1931.

Gómez-Quiñones, Juan. "The First Steps: Chicano Labor Conflict and Organizing,

1900–1920." *Aztlan: Chicano Journal of the Social Sciences and Arts* 3 (Spring 1972): 13–49.

Gonzales, Gilbert G., and Raul Fernandez. "Chicano History: Transcending Cultural Modes." *Pacific Historical Review* 63 (Nov. 1994): 469–498.

Hallagan, William S. "Labor Contracting in Turn-of-the-Century California Agriculture." *Journal of Economic History* 40 (1980): 757–776.

Higgs, Robert. "Landless by Law: Japanese Immigrants in California Agriculture to 1941." *Journal of Economic History* 38 (1978): 205–225.

Ichioka, Yuji. *The Issei: The World of the First Generation Japanese Immigrants, 1885–1924.* 1988.

Iwata, Masakazu. "The Japanese in California Agriculture." *Agricultural History* 36 (1962): 25–37.

———. *Planted in Good Soil: A History of the Issei in United States Agriculture.* 1992.

"Japanese Americans in California." Special issue. *California History* 73 (Spring 1994).

McWilliams, Carey. *Factories in the Field: The Story of Migratory Farm Labor in California.* 1939.

Modell, John. *The Economics and Politics of Racial Accommodation: The Japanese of Los Angeles, 1900–1942.* 1977.

Reis, Elizabeth. "Cannery Row: The AFL, the IWW, and Bay Area Cannery Workers." *California History* 64 (Summer 1985): 174–191.

Reisler, Mark. *By the Sweat of Their Brow: Mexican Immigrant Labor in the United States, 1900–1940.* 1976.

Sanchez, George J. *Becoming Mexican American: Ethnicity, Culture, and Identity in Chicano Los Angeles, 1900–1945.* 1993.

Strong, Edward K. *The Japanese in California.* 1933.

Wilson, Robert A., and Bill Hosokawa. *East to America: A History of the Japanese in the United States.* 1982.

Wollenberg, Charles. "Working on El Traque: The Pacific Electric Strike of 1903." *Pacific Historical Review* 42 (August 1973): 358–369.

Yoneda, Karl G. "100 Years of Japanese Labor History in the U.S.A." In *Roots: An Asian American Reader,* edited by Amy Tachiki, Eddie Wong, and Franklin Odo, pp. 150–158. 1971.

———. *Ganbatte: Sixty-Year Struggle of a Kibei Worker.* 1983.

7   Raiz Fuerte
Oral History and Mexicana
Farmworkers
Devra Weber

EDITOR'S INTRODUCTION

The number of Mexicans in California increased fourfold during the 1920s. By 1930, there were approximately 250,000 Mexicans in California, with 75,000 Mexican migrants making up the largest group of minority workers laboring in California's "factories in the field." As Cletus Daniel observed in his book *Bitter Harvest*, "With few exceptions, the challenges that farmworkers mounted against the authority of agricultural employers before 1930 were unorganized, spontaneous reactions to abnormally poor wages or conditions by a small group of workers employed on a single 'ranch' or in a single locality."

During the 1930s, however, as wages declined and conditions deteriorated, California's agricultural proletariat launched a series of strikes that for the first time challenged the hegemony of the growers. In 1933 alone, 37 strikes took place, involving 48,000 farmworkers; the years between 1933 and 1939 saw a total of 156 strikes by agricultural workers in the state. In no area of the country did agricultural workers make a more determined effort to organize than in California.

Mexican workers played an especially important role in this insurgency. In the late 1920s, mutual aid societies acted as de facto trade unions. In 1928, for example, a group of Mexican workers founded the Workers Union of the Imperial Valley, which conducted a brief though unsuccessful strike. Two years later, Mexican workers in the Imperial Valley struck again, led by the Mexican Mutual Aid Association. These workers received support from the Communist-led Agricultural Workers Industrial League. Although initially a certain amount of tension and suspicion existed between these two organizations, their shared concerns led to the formation of the Cannery and Agricultural Workers Industrial Union (CAWIU) in 1931.

In 1933, the CAWIU led 24 strikes in California. The initial success of the union spurred California agribusiness to take extreme measures to crush the organizing drive among the farmworkers. Using tactics that Carey McWilliams dubbed "farm fascism" in his book *Factories in the Field*, the Associated Farmers of California made especially extensive use of vigilante action against the union. Local and state authorities were only too happy to cooperate with the farm employers, and many of the CAWIU's leaders were prosecuted under the 1919 Criminal Syndicalism Act, which resulted in the union's demise.

The institutional history of the CAWIU has been ably told by Cletus Daniel and other historians, but we know relatively little about the role and perceptions of rank-and-file workers who joined the union. This is especially true for Mexican women who became members. Oral histories can play an important role in filling this gap. Despite the fallibility of memory, oral histories can provide insights into the culture, values, and consciousness of rank-and-file workers, who are often invisible in more conventional, written historical sources.

In this selection, Devra Weber skillfully uses an oral history interview to address some of these issues as she focuses on the role played by Mexican women in a 1933 strike by cotton workers in a small San Joaquin Valley town. The recollections of her principal subject, Mrs. Valdez, show that the consciousness of Mexican workers was shaped by a sense of nationalism and collective values embedded in *raiz fuerte* (strong roots). This consciousness derived in part from their belief that the United States had appropriated California and the rest of the Southwest from Mexico and in part from a legacy of ideas generated by the Mexican revolution earlier in the century. Mrs. Valdez stressed the crucial role played by women in managing their households during the strike as well as their important activity on the picket lines. Above all, the women strikers' determination to feed their families conditioned their militancy and contributed greatly to the success of the strike.

◆ ◆ ◆

Mexicana field workers, as agricultural laborers, have been remarkable for their absence in written agricultural history. Most studies have focused on the growth of capitalist agriculture and the related decline of the family farm. Concern about the implications of these changes for American culture, political economy, and the agrarian dream has generally shaped the questions asked about capitalist agriculture. If freeholding family farmers were the basis of a democratic society, capitalist and/or slave agriculture was its antithesis. Studies of capitalist agriculture have thus become enclosed within broader questions about American democracy, measuring change against a mythologized past of conflict-free small farming on a classless frontier.

When considered at all, agricultural wage workers have usually been examined in terms of questions framed by these assumptions. Rather than being seen in their own right, they have usually been depicted as the degraded result of the family farm's demise. The most thoughtful studies have been exposés, written to sway public opinion, which revealed the complex arrangement of social, economic, and political power perpetuating the brutal conditions of farmworkers. As was the case with the history of unskilled workers in industry, the written history of farmworkers became molded by the pressing conditions of their lives. The wretchedness of conditions became confused with the social worlds of the workers. Pictured as victims of a brutal system, they emerged as faceless, powerless, passive, and, ultimately, outside the flow of history. Lurking racial, cultural, ethnic, and gender stereotypes reinforced this image. This was especially true for Mexican women.[1]

These considerations make oral sources especially crucial for exploring the history of Mexican women.[2] Oral histories enable us to challenge the common confusion between the dismal conditions of the agricultural labor system and the internal life of workers. They enable us to understand, as Jones and Osterud suggest, the relationship for Mexicanas between the economic system of agriculture and community, politics, familial and cultural life. Oral histories help answer (and reconceptualize) fundamental questions about class, gender, life and work, cultural change, values and perceptions neglected in traditional sources. They also provide an insight into consciousness.[3]

In conducting a series of oral histories with men and women involved in a critical farmworker strike in the 1930s, I began to think about the nature of gender consciousness. How does it intersect with a sense of class? How does it intersect with national and ethnic identity? In the oral histories of Mexican women, their sense of themselves as workers and Mexicans frequently coincided with that of the men and drew upon similar bonds of history, community, and commonality. Yet the women's perceptions of what it meant to be a Mexican or a worker were shaped by gender roles and a consciousness that frequently differed from that of the men. This seemed to correspond to what Temma Kaplan has defined as "female consciousness." According to Kaplan,

> Female consciousness, recognition of what a particular class, culture and historical period expect from women, creates a sense of rights and obligations that provides motive force for actions different from those Marxist or feminist theory generally try to explain. Female consciousness centers upon the rights of gender, on social concerns, on survival. Those with female consciousness accept the gender system of their society; indeed such consciousness emerges from the division of labor by sex, which assigns women the responsibility of preserving life. But, accepting that task, women with female consciousness demand the rights that their obligations entail. The collective drive to secure those rights that result from the division of labor sometimes has revolutionary consequences insofar as it politicizes the networks of everyday life.[4]

This essay will explore how oral histories can help us understand the consciousness of a group of Mexican women cotton workers (or companeras of cotton workers) who participated in the 1933 cotton strike in California's San Joaquin Valley. One was a woman I will call Mrs. Valdez.

Mrs. Valdez and the 1933 Cotton Strike

Mrs. Valdez came from Mexico, where her father had been a *sembrador,* a small farmer or sharecropper, eking out a livable but bleak existence. She had barely reached adolescence when the Mexican revolution broke out in 1910. With the exception of a sister-in-law, neither she nor her immediate family participated in the revolution.[5] As is the case with many noncombatants, her memories of the revolution were not of the opposing ideologies or issues, but of hunger, fear, and death.[6] Fleeing the revolution, the family crossed the border into the United States. By 1933, she was twenty-four, married with two children, and lived in a small San Joaquin Valley town.

The agricultural industry in which she worked was, by 1933, California's major industry. Cotton, the most rapidly expanding crop, depended on Mexican workers who migrated annually to the valley to work.[7] Large cotton ranches of over 300 acres dominated the industry. Here workers lived in private labor camps, the largest of which were rural versions of industrial company towns: workers lived in company housing, bought from (and remained in debt to) company stores, and sent their children to company schools. Work and daily lives were supervised by a racially structured hierarchy dominated by Anglo managers and foremen; below them were Mexican contractors who recruited the workers, supervised work, and acted as the intermediary between workers and their English-speaking employers.

With the depression, growers slashed wages. In response farmworkers went on strike in crop after crop in California. The wave of strikes began in southern California and spread north into the San Joaquin Valley. While conducted under the banner of the Cannery and Agricultural Workers Industrial Union (CAWIU), the strikes were sustained largely by Mexican workers and Mexican organizers. The spread and success of the strikes depended on the familial and social networks of Mexican workers as much as, if not more than, the small but effective and ambitious union. The strike wave crested in the cotton fields of the San Joaquin Valley when 18,000 strikers brought picking to a standstill. Growers evicted strikers, who established ad hoc camps on empty land. The largest was near the town of Corcoran, where 3,500 workers congregated. The strikers formed mobile picket lines, to which growers retaliated by organizing armed vigilantes. The strikers held out for over a month before a negotiated settlement was reached with the growers and the California, United States, and Mexican governments.

Mexicanas were a vital part of the strike, and about half of the strikers at Corcoran were women. They ran the camp kitchen, cared for children, and marched on picket lines. They distributed food and clothing. Some attended strike meetings, and a few spoke at the meetings. And it was the women who confronted Mexican strikebreakers. In short, women were essential to this strike, though they have been largely obscured in accounts of its history. Mrs. Valdez went on strike and was on the picket lines. She was not a leader, but one of the many women who made the strike possible.

Voice and Community

Before examining her testimony, a word is in order about voice and tone as a dimension of oral histories. How information is conveyed is as important as what is said and can emphasize or contradict the verbal message. Conversation and social interaction are a major part of women's lives, and gesture and voice are thus particularly crucial to their communications. The verbal message, the "song" of a story, is especially important for people with a strong oral tradition which, as Jan Vansina has pointed out, has meaning as art form, drama, and literature. Oral histories or stories are often dramatic, moving with a grace and continuity that embody analytical reflections and communicate an understanding of social relations and the complexities of human existence.

Mrs. Valdez structured the telling of her oral history in stories or vignettes. Most sections of her oral history had distinct beginnings and endings, interrupted only if I interjected a question. She developed characters, villains and heroes, hardship and tragedy (but little comedy). How this story was constructed and its characters developed embodied her assessment of the conflict.

As she told her story, the characters developed voices of their own, each with separate and distinct tones and cadence perhaps reflecting their personalities to an extent, but more generally expressing Mrs. Valdez's assessment of them and their role in the drama. Strikebreakers, for example, spoke in high-pitched and pleading voices: the listener understood them immediately as measly cowards. Her rendition of the strikers' voices offered a clear contrast: their words were given in sonorous, deep, and steady tones, in a voice of authority that seemed to represent a communal voice verbalizing what Mrs. Valdez considered to be community values.

Mrs. Valdez's sense of collective values, later embodied in collective action either by strikers as a whole or by women, was expressed in what I would call a collective voice. At times individuals spoke in her stories: the grower, Mr. Peterson; her contractor, "Chicho" Vidaurri; and the woman leader "la Lourdes." But more often people spoke in one collective voice which transcended individuality. This sense of community as embodied in a collective voice became a central feature of her narrative and permeated everything she said about the strike. This manner of telling underscored the sense of unanimity explicit in her analysis of solidarity and clear-cut divisions.[8] How she told the story underlined, accentuated, and modified the meaning of the story itself.

Beyond her use of different voices, Mrs. Valdez's narrative contains substantial non-verbal analysis of the "facts" as she remembered them. Her voice, gestures, and inflections conveyed both implications and meanings. She gestured with her arms and hands—a flat palm hard down on the table to make a point, both hands held up as she began again. Her stories had clear beginnings and often ended with verbal punctuations such as "and that's the way it was." She switched tenses around as, in the heat of the story, the past became the present and then receded again into the past. Vocal inflections jumped, vibrated, climbed, and then descended, playing a tonal counterpoint to her words.

Mrs. Valdez's memories of the 1933 strike focused on two major concerns: providing and caring for her family and her role as a striker. How she structured these memories says much about her perceptions and her consciousness as a woman, a Mexican, and a worker: it is striking to what extent her memories of the strike focused on the collectivity of Mexicans and, within this, the collectivity of Mexican women.

Mrs. Valdez's sense of national identity, an important underpinning to her narrative, reflects the importance of national cohesion against a historic background of Anglo-Mexican hostility.[9] Mrs. Valdez vividly recounted the United States' appropriation of Mexican land in 1848 and the Treaty of Guadalupe Hidalgo which ceded the area to the United States. She drew from stories of Mexican rebellion against U.S. rule in California and the nineteenth-century California guerrillas Tiburcio Vasquez and Joaquin Murieta: the knowledge that Mexicans were working on the land which once belonged to Mexico increased her antagonism towards Anglo bosses. Mrs. Valdez may well have felt like another interviewee, Mrs. Martinez, who upon arriving at the valley pointed it out to her son and told him, "Mira lo que nos arrebataron los bárbaros."[10]

Most of these workers had lived through the Mexican revolution of 1910–1920, and they utilized both the experience and legacy within the new context of a strike-torn California. The military experience was crucial in protecting the camp: often led by ex-military officers, Mexican veterans at the Corcoran camp formed a formidable armed security system. Mrs. Valdez remembers that during the strike stories of the revolution were told, retold, and debated. The extent to which Mexicans employed the images and slogans of the revolution helped solidify a sense of community. Workers named the rough roads in the camp after revolutionary heroes and Mexican towns. Even Mrs. Valdez, whose individual memories of the revolution were primarily of the terror it held for her, shared in a collective memory of a national struggle and its symbols: she disdainfully compared strikebreakers with traitors who had "sold the head of Pancho Villa."[11]

Mrs. Valdez expressed a sense of collectivity among Mexicans. There were, in fact, many divisions—between strikers and strikebreakers, contractors and workers, people from different areas of Mexico, and people who had fought with different factions of the revolution or Cristero movement. Yet conflict with Anglo bosses on what had been Mexican land emphasized an identification as Mexicans (as well as workers) that overshadowed other divisions.

The Community of Mexican Women

Mrs. Valdez remembered a collectivity of Mexican women. By 1933, Mexican women worked alongside men in the fields. Like the men, they were paid piece rates and picked an average of two hundred pounds per ten-hour day. Picking required strength, skill, and stamina. As one woman recalled:

> But let me describe to you what we had to go through. I'd have a twelve foot sack . . . I'd tie the sack around my waist and the sack would go between my legs and I'd go on the cotton row, picking cotton and just putting it in there. . . . So when we finally got it filled real good then we would pick up the [hundred pound] sack, toss [!] it up on our shoulders, and then I would walk, put it up there on the scale and have it weighted, put it back on my shoulder, climb up on a wagon and empty that sack it.[12]

As Mrs. Valdez recounted, women faced hardships in caring for their families: houses without heat, which contributed to disease; preparing food without stoves; and cooking over fires in oil barrels. Food was central to her memory, reflecting a gender division of labor. Getting enough food, a problem at any time, was exacerbated by the depression that forced some women to forage for berries or feed their families flour and water. Food was an issue of survival. As in almost all societies, women were in charge of preparing the food, and Mrs. Valdez's concern about food was repeated in interviews with other women. Men remembered the strike in terms of wages and conditions; women remembered these events in terms of food. Men were not oblivious or unconcerned, but women's role in preparing food made this a central aspect of their consciousness and shaped the way they perceived, remembered, and articulated the events of the strike.

Mrs. Valdez's memory of leadership reflects this sense of female community. After initially replying that there were no leaders (interesting in itself), she named her labor contractor and then focused on a woman named Lourdes Castillo, an interesting choice for several reasons. Lourdes Castillo was an attractive, single woman who lived in Corcoran. She wore makeup, bobbed her hair, and wore stylish dresses. Financially independent, she owned and ran the local bar. Lourdes became involved with the strike when union organizers asked her to store food for strikers in her cantina.

In some respects, Lourdes represented a transition many Mexican women were undergoing in response to capitalist expansion, revolution, and migration. When the revolution convulsively disrupted Mexican families, women left alone took over the work in rural areas, migrated, and sometimes became involved in the revolution. "Soldaderas," camp followers in the revolution, cooked, nursed, and provided sexual and emotional comfort. Some fought and were even executed in the course of battle. This image of "la soldadera," the woman fighting on behalf of the Mexican community, was praised as a national symbol of strength and resistance.

Yet it was an ambivalent image: praised within the context of an often mythicized revolution, the "soldaderas" were criticized for their relative sexual freedom and independence. The term "soldadera" became double edged. When used to describe an individual woman, it could be synonymous with "whore."

Gender mores in the United States differed from those in rural Mexico. Some changes were cosmetic manifestations of deeper changes: women bobbed their hair, adopted new dress and makeup. But these changes reflected changes in a gender division of labor. Women, usually younger and unmarried, began to work for wages in canneries or garment factories, unobserved by watchful male relatives. Some women became financially independent, such as Lourdes, and ran bars and cantinas. Financial independence and a changing gender division of labor outside the house altered expectations of women's responsibilities and obligations. Yet these women still risked the disapprobation of segments of the community, male and female.

According to Mrs. Valdez, during the strike Lourdes was in charge of keeping the log of who entered and left the camp and spoke at meetings. She was also in charge of distributing food.[13] Lourdes thus reflects women's traditional concern about food while at the same time she epitomized the cultural transition of Mexican women and the changing gender roles from pre-revolutionary Mexico to the more fluid wage society of California. It was precisely her financial independence that enabled her to store and distribute the food. Perhaps Mrs. Valdez's enthusiastic memories of Lourdes suggests Mrs. Valdez's changing values for women, even if not directly expressed in her own life.

While Mrs. Valdez described the abysmal conditions under which women labored, the women were active, not passive, participants in the strike. Women's networks that formed the lattice of mutual assistance in the workers' community were transformed during the strike. The networks helped form daily picket lines in front of the cotton fields. Older women still sporting the long hair and rebozos of rural Mexico, younger women who had adapted the flapper styles of the United States, and young girls barely into their teens rode together in trucks to the picket lines. They set up makeshift child care centers and established a camp kitchen.

With the spread of the conflict, these networks expanded and the women's involvement escalated from verbal assaults on the strikebreakers to outright physical conflict. When after three weeks growers refused to settle, women organized and led confrontations with Mexican strikebreakers. According to Mrs. Valdez, the women decided that they, not the men, would enter the fields to confront the strikebreakers.[14] They reasoned that strikebreakers would be less likely to physically hurt the women.

In organized groups, the women entered the field, appealing to strikebreakers on class and national grounds—as "poor people" and "Mexicanos"—to join the strike. Those from the same regions or villages in Mexico appealed to compatriots on the basis of local loyalties, denouncing as traitors those who refused.

Exhortations turned to threats and conflict. The women threatened to poison one man who had eaten at the camp kitchen—an indication again of the centrality (and their power over) food. But women had come prepared. Those armed with lead pipes and knives went after the strikebreakers. One ripped a cotton sack with a knife. Others hit strikebreakers with pipes, fists, or whatever was handy. Although strikers had felt that the women would not be hurt, the male strikebreakers retaliated, and at least one woman was brutally beaten:

> Las mismas mujeres que iban en los troques . . . que iban en el picoteo. Adentro, les pegaron. Les rompieron su ropa. Les partieron los sombreros y los sacos y se los hicieron asina y todo. Y malos! Ohh! Se mira feo! Feo se miraba. Y nomas miraba y decia "no, no." Yo miraba la sangre que les escurria. [She imitates the strikebreakers in high-pitched, pleading tones:] "No les peguen, déjenlos, no les peguen." [Her voice drops as the voice of the strikers speaks:] "Que se los lleve el esto . . . Si a nosotros nos esta llevando de frio y de hambre pos que a ellos también. No tienen, vendidos, muertos de hambre!" [Her voice rises as the strikebreakers continue their plea:] "Pos nosotros vivemos muy lejos, venimos de Los Angeles . . . tienes que saber de donde, que tenemos que tener dinero pa' irnos." [Her voice lowers and slows as it again becomes the voice of the strikers:] "Si . . . nosotros también tenemos que comer y también tenemos familia. *Pero no somos vendidos!*"[15]

This passage underlines the importance of the female collectivity. The women went in because it was women's business, and they acted on behalf of the community. Mrs. Valdez implied that the men had little to do with the decision or even opposed it. "Porque las mujeres tenemos más chanza. Siempre los hombres se detenian más porque son hombres y todo. Y las mujeres no. Los hombres no nos pueden hacer nada. No nos podian hacer nada pos ahi vamos en zumba."[16]

The issues of confrontation focused around food. This underlines a harsh reality—strikebreakers worked to feed their families; without food, strikers would be forced back to work. Her memory reflects the reality of the confrontation but also her understanding of the central issue of the strike. Mrs. Valdez recalls the strikebreakers justifying themselves to the women in terms of the need to feed their families. But the striking women's ultimate rebuke was also expressed in terms of this need: "Si . . . nosotros también tenemos que comer y también tenemos familia. *Pero no somos vendidos!*"[17] Food remained central in her memories. Discussions about the strike and strike negotiations were all couched in relation to food. Her interests as a Mexican worker were considered, weighed, and expressed within the context of her interests as a woman, mother, and wife.

As the strike wore on, conditions grew harsher in the Corcoran camp. Growers lobbed incendiaries over the fence at night. Food became hard to get, and at least one child died of malnutrition.[18] In response to public concern following the murder of two strikers, the California Governor overrode federal regulations withholding relief from strikers under arbitration and, over the protestations of local boards of supervisors, sent in trucks of milk and food to the embattled camp. Mrs. Valdez remembers nothing of federal, state, or local government or agencies, but she remembered the food: ". . . rice, beans, milk, everything they sent in."

At a meeting where Lourdes addressed strikers, food, or lack of food, was juxtaposed against their stance in the strike:

> Pa' [Lourdes] decirles que pasaran hambre.
> "Mira," dice . . . "aunque alcanzemos poquito pero no nos estamos muriendo de hambre," dice. "Pero no salga. Pero NINGUNO a trabajar . . . aunque venga el ranchero y les diga que, que vamos y que pa' ca. No vaya ninguno!" dice.
> "Miren, aunque sea poquito estamos comiendo . . . pero no nos hemos muerto de hambre. Ta viniendo comida . . . nos estan trayendo comida."
> [Mrs. Valdez interjected:] Leche y todo nos daban . . . Si. Y a todos ahi los que trabajaban diciendo que no fueran con ningún ranchero. Que no se creeran de ningún ranchero. Que todos se agarraban de un solo modo que nadien, todos parejos tuvieran su voto, parejos. . . .[19]

Mrs. Valdez was clear about the effects of a united front on both sides, but if one grower broke with the others the rest would follow. [The collective voice speaks:] "No. Y no que no. No. Si nos paga tanto vamos. Y al pagar un ranchero tenían que pagar todos lo mismo. Tenían, ves."[20]

Unity and the centrality of women were carried over into her recollection of the final negotiations:

> El portuguese [a growers' representative] . . . le dijera que ahí iban los rancheros . . . a tener un mitin en el campo donde estaban todos ahí campados con la Lourdes Castillo y todo.

"Si," dice. "Ahí vamos a juntarnos todos los rancheros. Y vamos a firmar. Les vamos a pagar tanto. Y vamos a firmar todos para que entonces, si, ya vayan cada quien a sus campos a trabajar."

"Si," dice [the strikers' representative], "pero no menos de un centavo. No. No salimos hasta que tengan un . . . sueldo fijo. Todos vamos. Pero de ahí en más ni uno vamos. *Ni uno* salimos del camps." Y todo.[21]

The strike was settled, the ranchers had been beaten, and wages went up.

The Structure of Memory

Mrs. Valdez's account of the strike and women—how she structured her memories—tells us more about why Mexicanas supported the strike than interviews with leaders might have. Without the perceptions of women such as Mrs. Valdez it would be more difficult to understand strike dynamics.

Of particular interest is the fact that she remembers (or recounts) a collectivity among Mexican strikers. In her telling, workers speak in a collective voice and act as a united group. She remembers little or no dissent. In her account, *all* the workers on the Peterson ranch walked out together to join the strike, *all* the women were on the picket lines, and *all* the strikers voted unanimously to stay on strike. Growers, also a united group, spoke with one voice as a collective opposition. The lines between worker and grower were clearly drawn. According to Mrs. Valdez, it was this unity that accounted for the strike's success.

But within this collectivity of Mexicans was the collectivity of women. Mrs. Valdez focused on female themes and concerns about food, caring for their families, and, by extension, the greater community. Women were the actors on the picket line, made decisions about the strike, and acted as a unit. It is perhaps this sense of female collectivity and the concern around the issue of food that accounts for why Lourdes was considered a leader, though she is never mentioned by men in their accounts. Mrs. Valdez stated flatly that the women were braver—men played little part in her narrative. She remembered female leadership, female participation, female concerns, and a largely female victory. While other interviews and sources may disagree (even among women), it does suggest Mrs. Valdez's reality of the strike of 1933.

What Mrs. Valdez didn't say suggests the limitations of oral narratives. She either did not know, recall, or choose to recount several crucial aspects of the story: like many other strikers, she remembered nothing of the CAWIU, or of Anglo strike leaders mentioned in other accounts. This was not uncommon. The role of the New Deal and the negotiations of the governments—Mexican, United States, and Californian—play no part in her narrative. The visit by the Mexican consul to the camp; visits by government officials; threats to deport strikers—she recounted nothing about the negotiations that led to the settlement of the strike.

Her memory of the strike thus is limited. But the fact that Mrs. Valdez's memories were so similar to those of other women indicates that hers is not an isolated perception. There are also many points at which the memories intersect with those of the men. We thus may be dealing with a community memory made up of two intersecting collective memories: the collective memory (history) of the group as a whole, and a collective memory of women as a part of this.

Conclusion

Oral narratives reflect people's memory of the past: they can be inaccurate, contradictory, altered with the passage of time and the effects of alienation. In terms of historical analysis, Mrs. Valdez's oral history used alone raises questions. Was there really such unity in face of such an intense conflict? There were, obviously, strikebreakers. Were there no doubts, arguments? In part she may have been making a point to me. But it may be also indicative of her consciousness, of the things important to her in the event. Mrs. Valdez also remembers a largely female collectivity. Certainly, from other sources, it is clear men played a crucial role as well. Yet her focus on women provides information unavailable in other sources, and provides a point of view of women. It suggests which issues were important to the female collectivity, how and why women rallied to the strike, and how they used their networks within the strike.

So how may an oral history be used? Seen on its own, it remains a fragment of the larger story. Oral narratives must also be read critically as texts in light of the problem of alienation, especially in the United States, where various forms of cultural and historical amnesia seem so advanced. Used uncritically, oral histories are open to misinterpretation and may reinforce rather than reduce the separation from a meaningful past. This is especially true of the narratives of those people usually ignored by written history. Readers may lack a historical framework within which to situate and understand such narratives. The filters of cultural and class differences and chauvinism may also be obstacles. Some may embrace these narratives as colorful and emotional personal statements while ignoring the subjects as reflective and conscious participants in history.

In the case of the Mexican women farm laborers considered in this essay, oral testimonies are not a complete history nor can they, by themselves, address the problems of historical amnesia. Used with other material and read carefully and critically, however, such narratives prove crucial to a re-analysis of the strike. They need to be interpreted and placed within a historical framework encompassing institutional and social relations, struggle, and change. But when this is done, testimonies like that of Mrs. Valdez become a uniquely invaluable source. Used critically, they reveal transformations in consciousness and culture; they suggest the place of self-conscious and reflective Mexican women—and farm laboring women in general—in the broader history of rural women in the United States.

NOTES

1. Portions of this essay appear in Devra A. Weber, "Mexican Women on Strike: Memory, History, and Oral Narrative," in *Between Borders: Essays on Mexicana/Chicana History*, ed. Adelaida del Castillo (Encino, California: Floricanto Press, 1990), 161–174.

2. I use the term used by the women themselves. They called themselves Mexicans. Although all had lived in the United States over fifty years, all but one identified themselves as Mexicanas by birth, culture, and ethnicity. The one woman born and raised in the United States, and a generation younger, referred to herself interchangeably as Mexicana and Chicana.

3. Lu Ann Jones and Nancy Grey Osterud, "Breaking New Ground: Oral History and Agricultural History," *Journal of American History* 76 (September, 1989), 551–564.

4. Temma Kaplan, "Female Consciousness and Collective Action: The Case of Barcelona, 1910–1918," *Signs* (Spring, 1982), 545.

5. The sister-in-law is an interesting, if fragmentary, figure in Mrs. Valdez's memory. From Mrs. Valdez's account, the sister-in-law left her husband (Mrs. Valdez's brother) to join a group of revolutionaries, as a companera of one of them. When she returned to see her children, she threatened to have the entire family killed by her new lover. It was in the wake of this threat that the family fled to the United States.

6. That these were the main concerns of many Mexicans does not undermine the importance of the revolution in their lives, nor the extent to which the images and symbols of the revolution *later* became symbols of collective resistance, on both a class and national scale.

7. By 1933, the overwhelming majority of Mexican workers did not migrate from Mexico but from settled communities around Los Angeles or the Imperial Valley, adjacent to the Mexican border. Some came from Texas. The point is that they were not the "homing pigeons" described by growers who descended on the fields at harvest and cheerfully departed for Mexico. They were residents, and some of the younger pickers were United States citizens.

8. I want to emphasize that this is *her* analysis. I would disagree with the picture of solidarity; disputes among strikers would, I think, bear this out. Nevertheless, the point is that Mrs. Valdez's historical analysis tells us a great deal about her con-

ception of the strike—and perhaps her conception of what I should be told about it.

9. In Mexico, Mexicans tended to have a greater sense of identity with the town or state they came from than with the country as a whole. These identities are still strong, as are the rivalries which exist between them. It has been argued that the Mexican revolution helped create a sense of national consciousness. One of the primary reasons was its opposition to foreign interests. For those who migrated north, across the Rio Bravo, the sense of opposition to Anglo Americans was even greater. It was on the border areas, after all, where the corridors of resistance developed, and where many have argued the sense of Mexican nationalism was strongest.

10. "Look at what the barbarians have stolen from us." Interview by author with Guillermo Martinez, Los Angeles, April 1982.

Note: Having encountered strong objections (not from the *OHR*) to using the original Spanish in such a text, a word of explanation is in order. Translating another language—especially if the language is colloquial and therefore less directly translatable—robs the subjects of their voice, diminishing the article as a consequence. This is especially true if, as in this case, the language is colloquial and, to those who know Spanish, manifestly rural and working class. The original text gives such readers an indication of class and meaning unavailable in a translation. It also underscores the value of bridging monolingual parochialism in a multilingual and multicultural society. In any event, full English translations for all quotations will be provided in the notes.

11. After his death, Villa's corpse was disinterred and decapitated. His head was stolen in the 1920s, and the incident became a legend.

12. Interview by author with Lydia Ramos. All names used here are pseudonyms.

13. It is unclear whether Lourdes did keep the log. In a brief interview, Lourdes confirmed that she spoke at meetings and distributed food.

14. It is unclear exactly who made this decision. Roberto Castro, a member of the central strike committee, said the strike committee decided that women should enter the fields to confront strikebreakers because the women would be less likely to be hurt. The women remembered no such decision, and said that they made the decision themselves. It is hard to fix definitively the origins of the idea, but this may not matter very much; even if the strike committee made the decision, the action was consistent with spontaneous decisions by women that both antedated and followed this strike. Mexican women in Mexico City and other parts of the republic had taken part in bread riots in the colonial period. They had fought in the revolution. And in California, later strikes, in the 1930s, but also as recently as the 1980s, were punctuated by groups of Mexican women invading the fields to confront strikebreakers both verbally and physically. In short, it was a female form of protest women used both before and after the strike.

15. "The same women who were in the trucks, who were in the . . . picket line . . . these women went in and beat up all those that were inside [the fields] picking cotton. . . . They tore their clothes. They ripped their hats and the [picking] sacks. . . . And bad. Ohhh! It was ugly! It was an ugly sight. I was just looking and said, 'No, no.' I watched the blood flowing from them."

[She imitates the strikebreakers' voice in a high-pitched, pleading tone:] "Don't hit us. Leave them [other strikebreakers] alone. Don't hit them."

[Her voice drops as the collective voice of the strikers speaks:] "Let them be set upon . . . If we are going cold and hungry then they should too. They're cowards . . . sellouts. Scum."

[Her voice rises as the strikebreakers continue their plea:] "Because we live far away, we come from Los Angeles. . . . We need to have money to leave. . . ."

"Yes," she says [her voice lowers and slows as it again becomes the voice of the strikers:] "We also have to eat and we also have family," she says. *"But we are not sellouts!"*

16. "Because women take more chances. The men always hold back because they are men and all. But the women, no. The men couldn't make us do anything. They couldn't make us do anything [to prevent us from going] and so we all went off in a flash."

17. "Yes . . . We also have to eat and we also have family. *But we are not sellouts!"*

18. As the local district attorney admitted after the strike, conditions in the strikers' camp were no worse than those of the cotton labor camps. Growers did use the bad conditions, however, to pressure the health department to close the strikers' camp as a menace to public health.

19. "She [Lourdes] was telling them that they might have to go hungry for awhile.

" 'But look,' she said . . . 'they are bringing us food. We'll each get just a little, but we're not going to starve,' she says. 'But don't leave. But don't ANYBODY go to work. Even if a rancher comes and tells you "come on, let's go," don't anybody go,' she says.

" 'Look, even if it's a little bit, we're eating. But we aren't starving. They're bringing us food.'

[Mrs. Valdez interjected:] "They brought us milk and everything. Everybody that was working [in the strikers' camp] were told not to go with any rancher. They were told not to believe any rancher. But everyone had to stand together as one. Everyone had an equal vote [in what was decided] . . . equal."

20. [The collective voice speaks:] " 'No. And no [they said]. No. No. If you pay us this much, then we go. And if one [rancher] pays [the demand], then all the ranchers have to pay the same.' They had to, you see."

21. "The Portuguese [a growers' representative] told [the strikers' representative] that the ranchers . . . were going to have a meeting at [the strikers' camp] with 'la Lourdes.' 'Yes,' he says. . . . 'We're going to pay you so much. All of us are going to sign so that then all of you can return to your camps to work.'

'Yes,' said [the strikers' representative]. 'But not a cent less. No. We won't go until we have a set wage. Then all of us go. But if there is something more [if there is more trouble] NONE of us go. Not even ONE of us leaves the camp.' "

FURTHER READING

See also the lists of suggested readings for chapters 6 and 9.

Anderson, Rodney. *Outcasts in Their Own Land: Mexican Industrial Workers, 1906–1911.* 1976.

Balderama, Francisco. *In Defense of La Raza: The Los Angeles Mexican Consulate and the Mexican Community, 1929–1936.* 1982.

Clark, Marjorie Ruth. *Organized Labor in Mexico.* 1934.

Del Castillo, Adelaida R., ed. *Between Borders: Essays on Mexicana/Chicana History.* 1990.

Frisch, Michael. "American History and the Structures of Collective Memory: A

Modest Exercise in Empirical Iconography." *Journal of American History* 75 (March 1989): 1130–1155.

Frisch, Michael, ed. *A Shared Authority: Essays on the Craft and Meaning of Oral and Public History*. 1990.

Fuller, Varden. *Labor Relations in Agriculture*. 1955.

Gluck, Sherna, and Daphne Patai, eds. *Women's Words: The Feminist Practice of Oral History*. 1991.

Gómez-Quiñones, Juan. *Mexican American Labor, 1790–1890*. 1994.

Gonzales, Gilbert. "The Mexican Citrus Pickers' Union, the Mexican Consulate, and the Orange County Strike of 1936." *Labor History* 35 (Winter 1994): 48–65.

Grele, Ron. *Envelopes of Sound: The Art of Oral History*. 1985.

Guerin-Gonzáles, Camille. *Mexican Workers and American Dreams: Immigration, Repatriation, and California Farm Labor, 1900–1939*. 1994.

Gutiérrez, David G. *Walls and Mirrors: Mexican Americans, Mexican Immigrants, and the Politics of Ethnicity*. 1995.

Haas, Lisbeth. *Conquests and Historical Identities in California, 1769–1936*. 1995.

Hart, John M. *Anarchism and the Mexican Working Class, 1860–1913*. 1978.

Portelli, Allesandro. *The Death of Luigi Trastulli and Other Stories: Form and Meaning in Oral History*. 1991.

Taylor, Paul S. *Labor on the Land: Collected Writings, 1930–1979*. 1981.

Thelen, David. "Memory in American History." *Journal of American History* 75 (March 1989): 1117–1129.

Weber, Devra. *Dark Sweat, White Gold: California Farmworkers, Cotton, and the New Deal*. 1994.

8   The Big Strike

Bruce Nelson

EDITOR'S INTRODUCTION

No group of workers has played a more important role in the labor history
of California than its seafaring and longshore workers. From the founding
of the Coast Seamen's Union in 1885 to the launching of the International
Longshoremen's and Warehousemen's Union (ILWU) in 1937, longshoremen and sailors were in the vanguard of the California labor movement.
During the 1880s and 1890s, the seafaring workers gave crucial support to
the embryonic and fragile California labor movement, first lending assistance to the Knights of Labor and then helping to sustain trade unionism
during the depression of the 1890s. They were also a vital force in securing
the "undisputed sway" of trade unionism in San Francisco during the Progressive Era.

Several factors account for the militancy of the seafaring workers. First,
the harsh conditions and treatment that sailors experienced aboard ships
made their lives, in the words of Andrew Furuseth's biographer Hyman
Weintraub, "a purgatory of unending hell." On shore, the control that the
"crimp," or boardinghouse keeper, had over hiring reduced sailors to a
state of debt peonage. Second, as Bruce Nelson observes in his book *Workers on the Waterfront*, sailors "lived on the fringes of society and had little
or no recourse to the family, church, ethnic, and other institutions that
served the purpose of reconciling working people to the hegemony of the
employing class or of creating a subculture that reinforced an alternative
value system." Third, during their worldwide voyages, seamen were exposed to a wide range of social and political systems at various ports of call.
The recollections of seafaring activists indicate that their political consciousness was shaped significantly by events as diverse as famines in

China, the brutality of colonialism in India, and the syndicalism of British and Australian seamen and dock workers. Finally, the seafaring work force was relatively homogenous on the West Coast, especially in California, where men of Scandinavian origin predominated.

Seafaring workers were not, however, eternally militant and always capable of sustaining strong trade unions. To begin with, these workers had to contend with the opposition of highly organized anti-union shipowners. In addition, considerable jurisdictional factionalism existed among the seafaring unions. On the West Coast, a serious gulf between the sailors and the longshoremen led to the creation of separate unions in the early twentieth century.

Factionalism, a depressed economy, and the almost total control over hiring that employers achieved with their "Blue Book union" after a major strike in 1919 seriously undermined maritime trade unionism in the 1920s and the early 1930s. By 1933, however, the maritime workers, pushed to the limit by employers and encouraged by New Deal legislation, began to assert themselves.

The leadership of the International Longshoremen's Association (ILA) and the International Seamen's Union (ISU) was cautious and conservative. But on the West Coast (and especially in San Francisco), the rank-and-file workers were restless. Dissident elements within the Sailors' Union of the Pacific (SUP)—the largest affiliate of the ISU—and those within the ILA demanded improvements in working conditions, wages, and the hiring system. Harry Bridges, a leading activist within the ILA, soon became the spokesman for a host of dissident workers. At the same time, former Wobblies and Communists who belonged to the rival Marine Workers Industrial Union (MWIU) helped to rekindle the spark of maritime trade unionism on the San Francisco waterfront.

Bruce Nelson tells the story of how these mounting tensions exploded into the 1934 longshoremen's strike—one of the most dramatic events in California labor history. He argues that while Harry Bridges and the MWIU helped spark and organize the walkout, the strike was in essence a rank-and-file insurgency of longshoremen who defied the conservative leadership of their AFL unions. However, Nelson contends, when the AFL leadership saw that the writing was on the wall, they moved, with some success, to coopt control of the strike.

When two workers were killed on "Bloody Thursday," the outpouring of support for the strike was widespread and spontaneous. Eventually, however, mass arrests of strikers, vigilante action, a viciously hostile news-paper campaign, and the desertion of the teamsters from the strike per-suaded the longshoremen to submit their dispute to arbitration and end the strike. They secured significant concessions in the agreement that fol-lowed, and the outcome of the strike set the stage for a resurgent Califor-nia trade union movement later in the 1930s. Figuring prominently in this renaissance would be the ILWU, founded in 1937 and led by Harry Bridges, which, to a significant extent, represented a coalescence of the forces that had helped to organize the 1934 strike.

◆   ◆   ◆

Every year, in early March, Andrew Furuseth sent an anniversary mes-sage to the Sailors' Union of the Pacific to commemorate its founding in 1885. In 1929, when the union's fortunes were at an all-time low, Furu-seth's letter to the few diehard members and their guests burned with a zeal that was peculiarly out of character with the times. *"I wish we could all of us be saturated with the spirit of the crusader,"* he said. "Let us make this meeting a Pentecostal one, and go away from it with the determina-tion to achieve, to live up to the highest and best that is in us."[1]

Five years and two months later, maritime workers erupted with the "spirit of the crusader" and waged one of the great battles in the history of the American working class. Even by the standards of 1934, one of the most extraordinary years in the annals of labor, the Big Strike fully mer-ited the adjective its partisans assigned it.[2] This eighty-three-day drama transformed labor relations in the Pacific Coast maritime industry and ushered in an era of militant unionism that caught Andrew Furuseth and the leadership of the International Seamen's Union completely by sur-prise. In fact, the character of this upheaval was such that it alarmed Fu-ruseth as much as it did the employers. Although the Big Strike ended on an ambiguous note, and in its immediate aftermath was sometimes charac-terized as a defeat for labor by friend and foe alike, the insurgent maritime workers armed themselves with the lessons of the strike and applied these lessons to their workaday world with stunning results.

Before discussing the contours of this Pentecostal era, we must examine the major characteristics and lessons of the Big Strike, because they became a major part of the foundation on which the new order was constructed. One of the problems in presenting these lessons is that even a sober and restrained portrayal may appear as one-sided and romanticized as a crude proletarian novel. But in this case the real world is more dramatic than fiction. To be sure, there was complexity and unevenness. For example, the vital port of Los Angeles remained open throughout the strike; and a substantial number of seamen never joined the ranks of the strikers, in some cases because their ships anchored in the outer harbors and refused to let the men debark, in other cases because they consciously decided to stay aboard the vessels. But in the final analysis, these and other examples of weakness failed to overshadow or undermine the strike's central characteristics.

Among the many threads that were a part of the Big Strike's dynamism, four stand out as crucial: first, the strikers' militancy, steadfastness, and discipline in the face of an adversary who wielded an arsenal of weapons ranging from private security forces and vigilantes to the bayonets and machine guns of the National Guard; second, a solidarity that swept aside old craft antagonisms and culminated in a general strike; third, a rank-and-file independence and initiative that came to mean frequent defiance of AFL norms and officials; and finally, in the face of an increasingly hysterical and violent wave of anti-Communist propaganda, a willingness to assess the Red presence in the strike independently, from the workers' own standpoint, and a growing tendency to view Red-baiting as an instrument of the employers.

The strike began on May 9 with the longshoremen's coastwide walkout. Within days seamen and other maritime workers swelled the picket lines, and teamsters refused to handle scab cargo. As the magnitude of the conflict became apparent, Assistant Secretary of Labor Edward McGrady rushed to San Francisco and presided over several efforts to reach a compromise. Two such agreements were concluded, one on May 28 and another on June 16. But both were negotiated by top AFL officials who had no authority to represent the strikers, and they were emphatically repudiated by the rank and file. The strikers' rejection of the mid-June agreement convinced the shipowners that reason was of no avail, and they developed a plan to open the port of San Francisco by force. On July 3 the waterfront became "a vast tangle of fighting men" as seven hundred police tried to move scab cargo through the picket lines. Two days later, on what became known as Bloody Thursday, all hell broke loose. The *Chronicle* called it "War in San Francisco!" as "blood ran red in the streets." At the end of the day, two workers—longshoreman Howard Sperry and strike sympathizer Nick Bordoise, a Communist—lay dead; National Guard troops were erecting barbed-wire fortifications on the waterfront; and armored personnel carriers replaced the pickets.[3]

It appeared that labor was defeated, but on July 9 a massive funeral procession for Sperry and Bordoise paraded up Market Street, and the uncanny power of this event crystallized sentiment for a general strike. With a renewed surge of confidence, the general strike began in both San Francisco and Oakland on July 16. However, the strike apparatus was in the hands of AFL conservatives, and they were able to terminate the general walkout after four days. Shorn of their most vital allies, the maritime workers had little choice but to agree to place their demands before the presidentially appointed National Longshoremen's Board. After eighty-three days, the men returned to work on July 31.

From the beginning of the walkout, the strikers displayed awesome courage and militancy. In the first few days there were violent outbursts up and down the coast, as employers hired large numbers of strikebreakers and tried to maintain business as usual behind a protective shield of police. In Oakland, according to newspaper reports, four hundred strikers stormed the gates of the municipal pier, "drove police before them and staged a hand to hand battle with 72 strike breakers." In Portland, "a mob of 400 striking longshoremen threw one policeman into the water and severely beat others" in an attack on a ship housing scabs.

The most dramatic confrontation occurred in Seattle, where a timid and conservative ILA (International Longshoremen's Association) leadership stood by as employers put strikebreakers to work on every pier. In response on May 12 a flying squad of six hundred Tacoma longshoremen, along with several hundred strikers from Everett and "all of the militant men we could find in Seattle," stormed the docks. The army of two thousand men battered down pier doors, swept police aside, and halted work on eleven ships where strikebreakers had been handling cargo. The flying squad also paid visits to other cities, with so much success that a shipowner spokesman complained: "Within a few days all work at Pacific Northwest ports had to cease owing to violence by strikers and to lack of police protection. The strikers took over entire control of the waterfront."[4]

The high point of this militancy came on Bloody Thursday in San Francisco, when an army of police tried to reopen the port by terrorizing the maritime strikers into submission. According to the eyewitness account of a "small investor" named Donald Mackenzie Brown,

> Struggling knots of longshoremen, closely pressed by officers mounted and on foot, swarmed everywhere. The air was filled with blinding gas. The howl of the sirens. The low boom of the gas guns. The crack of pistol-fire. The whine of the bullets. The shouts and curses of sweating men. Everywhere was a rhythmical waving of arms—like trees in the wind—swinging clubs,

swinging fists, hurling rocks, hurling bombs. As the police moved from one group to the next, men lay bloody, unconscious, or in convulsions—in the gutters, on the sidewalks, in the streets. Around on Madison Street, a plain-clothes-man dismounted from a radio car, waved his shotgun nervously at the shouting pickets who scattered. I saw nothing thrown at him. Suddenly he fired up and down the street and two men fell in a pool of gore—one evidently dead, the other, half attempting to rise, but weakening fast. A gas bomb struck another standing on the curb—struck the side of his head, leaving him in blinded agony. The night sticks were the worst. The long hardwood clubs lay onto skulls with sickening force, again and again and again till a face was hardly recognizable.

Late in the afternoon, when "the police were mopping up the remaining combatants," Brown walked by the ILA headquarters. There "two men were helping a staggering picket away from the fray. He was stripped to the waist showing a gaping bullet hole in his back." Henry Schmidt later recalled a grim moment that may have involved the same striker. During a lull in the battle, near the ILA hall, "I noticed a man in front of me, and I figured that's a cop and he's got a shooting iron ready for action. Then I noticed another man in front of him. There was absolutely no reason for this policeman to do anything, but he raised his rifle, or whatever it was, and he shot this striker in the back. He went down like a load of lead."

For most of the day, even the sadistic violence and superior technical equipment of the police could not deter the strikers. Brown, the businessman, was overawed by the workers' "insane courage." "In the face of bullets, gas, clubs, horses' hoofs, death; against fast patrol cars and the radio, they fought back with rocks and bolts till the street was a mass of debris. . . . They were fighting desperately for something that seemed to be life for them."[5]

Bloody Thursday was an epic moment, but it was by no means unique. Class warfare has punctuated the American industrial landscape for more than a century. What may be even more noteworthy than the militancy of the strikers and the violence of their adversaries is the staying power and growing discipline that the maritime workers demonstrated over a period of nearly three months. Perhaps the most remarkable example of this steadfastness occurred in Los Angeles and its adjacent port city of San Pedro, where the strikers persevered and increased their numbers in spite of the weakness of their unions and the blatantly obvious role of the police as instruments of capital. The passage of the National Industrial Recovery Act had forced the Los Angeles employers to temper their long-standing crusade for the open shop, but the coming of the strike rekindled their zeal for the methods that had earned Los Angeles its reputation as "scab city."

When 97 percent of the longshoremen who voted in a representation election chose the ILA, waterfront employers signed a contract with the company union that had received the votes of only thirty-two men. Representatives of the Merchants' and Manufacturers' Association helped to enlist thousands of strikebreakers, many of whom were housed in stockades along the waterfront. The Los Angeles Police Department assigned some seven hundred officers to the harbor area, and they were aided by hundreds of special deputies and private security guards. The $145,000 required to maintain this police army came not from the city but from the employers themselves. In fact, these ties between the police and the large employers in Los Angeles became so lucrative for the former that after a subsequent maritime strike, a police official recommended that "each executive from each oil company in the harbor district should be invited and entertained at our police range for lunch . . . and there presented with a police badge in recognition of their splendid cooperation and in furtherance of their friendly relationship [with] our department."[6]

Between the police and the maritime strikers, however, there was anything but a friendly relationship. One observer characterized the Los Angeles Intelligence Bureau, or "Red squad," as "unbelievably sadistic," and even the *Los Angeles Daily News* belatedly acknowledged the "definite campaign of brutality and terrorism indulged in by the police red squad in the confines of the harbor department jail." The *Nation* reported that approximately five hundred arrests were made in the port of San Pedro during the course of the strike. The fate of Thomas Sharpe, a member of the International Seamen's Union, was by no means exceptional. His statement about his ordeal is worth quoting at some length because Sharpe's case symbolizes not only the method and rationale of the authorities, but also the extraordinary staying power of the workers in the face of a sustained campaign of terror. Sharpe reported:

> On Monday the 16th of July, I went on picket duty on Terminal Island. We were not out to do violence. . . . We had no clubs or weapons of any kind. . . . I went across the street, where I saw a man dressed as an unemployed seam[a]n, standing against the wall with a police riot club hanging besides his right leg. . . . He grabbed me by the arm and walked me across the street to the police car. . . . This man I learned from the description I have from other seamen at the hospital who were beat and tortured by him was Strand of the "red squad."

Strand took the young seaman to the police station and pushed him into a dark hallway where, Sharpe reported, he hit me on the right shin bone with his riot club, which was a solid wooden club about two feet long and 1¼ inches thru. I fell to the floor and every muscle in my body went limp. While I was on the floor he beat me unmercifully. The only thing that was said was, I'm going to run all the reds out of San Pedro if I have to break their damn necks. I answered that I ain't no red. He then grabbed my right foot and hit me eight or nine times, again and again on the same shin bone with his club. Then he twisted the right foot until the bones he had splintered with his club cracked and came thru the flesh, severing an artery. It started [to] hemorrhage and the blood simply poured out of me.

Sharpe remained either in the hospital or in jail, with a cast on his leg and another on his shoulder (also broken in the beating), until August 14, nearly one full month after his incarceration, when he was taken into court and the charges against him were dismissed.[7]

As grim as the Sharpe incident was, and there were innumerable examples of lone strikers being arrested, or kidnapped, and beaten, a far more massive and deadly confrontation had occurred on May 14 at a stockade that housed a large number of strikebreakers. A twenty-year-old longshoreman named Dick Parker died that night of a gunshot wound in the heart. The *Los Angeles Times* claimed that a mob of strikers rushed the stockade, set it on fire, and jeopardized the lives of police and private security guards who were protecting the facility. Parker was shot, said the *Times*, while "leading some 300 strikers in their attack." (Tom Knudson, a forty-five-year-old ILA member, died later of injuries sustained in the incident.)[8]

The newspaper of the marine workers maintained, however, that "the police opened fire on a large crowd of pickets . . . before any of the men could take a step toward the armed fortress." One participant, striking seaman Bob McElroy, who was standing no more than ten feet from Parker when he was shot, recalled in later years that the demonstration had begun as "an impromptu thing. . . . There was no provocation, no commotion, no threats, no nothing—just a gun going off and Parker going down." At a special coroner's inquest, McElroy and others identified a former Los Angeles police officer who was serving as a private security guard at the scab stockade as the man who shot Parker. But there was no indictment and trial. Dick Parker, who had joined the ILA only a few hours before his death, became the first martyr of the Big Strike.[9]

In spite of the beatings, the arrests, and the two killings, in spite of the fact that they were never able to shut down the vast Los Angeles harbor, the ranks of the strikers remained solid and the scale of their activity increased. Whereas there had been only about three hundred pickets on the docks in the early days of the strike, their numbers increased to about eighteen hundred as seamen and teamsters joined the picket lines. One striking seaman reported in early July that "open meetings are held daily and the crowds are so large that loud speakers are necessary." This growing combativeness and unity led a Sailors' Union activist to declare soon afterward that "the 1934 strike did more to solidify the longshoremen and the seafaring men of San Pedro than anything that was ever done before."[10]

The most dramatic examples of the strike's increasingly disciplined militancy occurred in San Francisco. On Bloody Thursday, in the "Battle of Rincon Hill," the strikers conducted themselves with remarkable precision and imagination in the face of three successive assaults by policemen, who according to Henry Schmidt were "using their firearms freely and laying down a barrage of tear gas bombs." And in the famed funeral procession in which labor honored Sperry and Bordoise, tens of thousands of marchers demonstrated a unity of purpose and a solemn dignity that left friend and foe alike awestruck. The *Chronicle* reported that in life Sperry and Bordoise "wouldn't have commanded a second glance on the streets of San Francisco, but in death they were borne the length of Market Street in a stupendous and reverent procession that astounded the city." Other eyewitnesses spoke of "an oncoming sea" and "a river of men flowing . . . like cooling lava." One participant noted "an ominous silence among spectators and marchers alike. . . . The sound of thousands of feet echoed up that hollow canyon—nothing else. . . . It was a magnificent sight—those careworn, weary faces determined in their fight for justice thrilled me. I have never seen anything so impressive in all my life." As he marched up Market Street, Roy Hudson was also struck by "the *silence*—you could hear it—not a placard, not a slogan, complete and utter silence. You could *hear* what was in the atmosphere." Even an employer spokesman sensed it, acknowledging the event as "the high tide of united labor action in San Francisco."[11]

This high tide was the culmination of many waves of solidarity that had broken down the traditional barriers of craft and nationality. It began in the ranks of the longshoremen themselves. They had cast aside the Blue Book; they had built an aggressive rank-and-file movement—so aggressive that one conservative union official characterized it as "mob rule." Their pent-up fury had exploded on May 9 and in succeeding days, driving strikebreakers from the docks or forcing them to take refuge behind massive police lines. Now, particularly in San Francisco, they faced an issue that had contributed to their defeat in previous strikes. Would the union offer the hand of solidarity to black longshoremen? And would black workers honor the picket lines?[12]

Unlike the Eastern and Gulf ILA locals, which provided black long-shoremen with a secure but subordinate place within the union, Pacific Coast longshore unions had always excluded blacks. In San Francisco, facing the unremitting hostility of the Riggers and Stevedores, black workers had found that strikebreaking was the only way they could gain employment on the waterfront. In the 1916 and 1919 strikes they had been "an important factor in defeating the unions." Of course, the shipowners had eagerly recruited them then, but by 1926 black longshoremen were employed on only a few docks. Labor economist Robert Francis noted in early 1934 that "today there are not more than fifty black men working on the San Francisco waterfront."

In late 1933 the local 38–79 executive board had expressed a mild interest in "working with the colored boys of San Francisco and the bay District." But as Sam Darcy acknowledged, for the most part the ILA displayed a "passive attitude towards the question of Negro workers, and in some cases, actual antagonism towards including them in the Union." Although "the rank and file militants of the I.L.A. made a sincere effort to unite black and white workers," only a handful of black longshoremen joined the union before May 9.[13]

In the first few days of the strike employers recruited nearly a thousand scabs in San Francisco. The majority, according to one participant, were white-collar workers and college students, including a sizable contingent from the University of California football team. The ranks of the strike-breakers also included several hundred black men, and the violent flare-ups along the Embarcadero sometimes had racial overtones.[14]

However, as Henry Schmidt recalled, there was a vitally important breakthrough early in the strike that was to set the tone for the future of race relations on the San Francisco docks. Schmidt had gone down to the Luckenbach pier, where most of the regular black longshoremen were employed; along with a black union member he had called on them to join the strike. "On the same afternoon or the next day," he remembered, "these Negro brothers came to the then union headquarters at 113 Steuart Street. I can still see them coming up the stairs and entering the premises. . . . Somebody raised the question, 'Why didn't you come earlier to join up?' And they replied, 'We didn't know that you wanted us.'"[15]

An even greater wave of solidarity began to gather momentum on the very first day of the strike, as seamen walked off the ships and joined the

longshore picket lines. The seamen's involvement, however, was complicated by the condition and outlook of their unions. Veteran ISU (International Seamen's Union) official Walter Macarthur acknowledged that the
Sailors' Union officials were helpless and that "the seamen found themselves entirely at a loss for leadership or advice." Harry Bridges claimed in
retrospect that the ISU affiliates "were forced to strike because of the pressure of the MWIU [Marine Workers Industrial Union]." Bridges's recollection was supported by Bill Caves, an outspoken deck sailor who played
an important—and controversial—role in the Big Strike. Caves maintained that "the whole attitude of the SUP [Sailors' Union of the Pacific]
officials during the 1934 strike was to stay aboard the ships," and that "it
was only the militant action of the MWIU that forced the issue."[16]

Although not entirely accurate, these charges have considerable merit.
The ISU affiliates on the Pacific Coast were in a sorry state before the Big
Strike engulfed them. The Sailors' Union had weathered the long drought
better than the marine cooks' and firemen's unions, but the news from the
SUP was hardly encouraging. The Seattle branch seldom attracted more
than a dozen members to its weekly meetings, and Portland was able to
muster one quorum in the six months that preceded the 1934 strike. As for
San Pedro, it "seem[ed] to be going to hell altogether." When a local
official took sick, the union was unable to find anyone to replace him. Even
the San Francisco headquarters usually acknowledged that "things here
are slow," and sometimes "exceedingly slow."

In explaining the union's moribund condition, the SUP leadership
pointed the finger at the seamen themselves. George Larsen, the Sailors'
Union secretary and chief spokesman, lamented that the majority "don't
seem interested in any kind of organization." When the Portland SUP
agent reported a growing sentiment among the men that "the union
should do something," Larsen pointed to the international officials' long-
standing effort to bring about change through the NRA (National Recovery Administration) shipping code hearings in Washington and blamed
the lack of results on "the majority . . . who sail outside of the union." "Let
the men understand that it is because of lack of organization among us that
we are faced . . . [with] low wages, miserable working conditions, and in-
tolerable employment conditions. Let them be reminded that in vessels
where men are doing the hardest kind of physical labor, namely in many
steamschooners, no raise has taken place since they were reduced to the
starvation point some two years ago. . . . the answer is, come into the
union." When the Portland official reported again that "the men would
like to se[e] the Union take some action," Larsen exploded: "The trouble is

not with the union, it rests with [the men]. . . . The only way to wake them up is with a big stick."[17]

Begrudgingly, the Sailors' Union spokesman acknowledged that the longshoremen had demonstrated "sense enough to get into one organization" and prepare for "concerted action." But whenever the dockworkers moved beyond mere preparation, Larsen reacted with fear and pessimism. "I can see a bunch of trouble ahead," he declared during the San Francisco stevedores' wildcat against Matson and the Blue Book. "I think the men have been ill advised." Increasingly, he was convinced that the source of these disturbances was the "considerable number of Communists" in the San Francisco ILA. "Should it come to a strike and a finish fight," he wrote in late March, "I am afraid the longshoremen will be the losers." As for the seamen, he recognized that some of them would join the walkout, but "there is little that we can do about it."[18]

When the longshoremen struck on May 9, the ISU Pacific District leadership took an ambiguous position, advising union members to stay aboard ship in those few cases where "the unions have recognition or an understanding with the owners." On all other ships, the ISU stressed the question of "liberty." Larsen wrote to Portland on May 11: "Let the men be told that none of the steam schooners recognize any of our unions, and that therefore, they are at liberty to quit. . . . But the unions are not demanding it, that is to say it is not mandatory."[19]

The Portland steam schooner men acted unanimously two days before Larsen offered them the option. They deserted the ships on May 9 and joined the longshore picket lines, thus serving as the advance guard of a spontaneous walkout that caught the ISU leadership by surprise. Larsen had blasted the nonunion seamen for losing faith in themselves. But apparently many of them had lost faith only in the capacity of the ISU affiliates to take decisive action. When the longshoremen showed the way, they followed.

The Marine Workers Industrial Union took immediate steps to give the seafarers' walkout a more organized character. The MWIU's membership on the West Coast was probably smaller than that of the SUP. But the Marine Workers had one major advantage, namely, a core of activists who were eager to strike and to build closer ties between the men on the ships and those along the shore. In fact, MWIU members began supporting the longshore strike even before the stevedores walked off the job. On May 8 the S.S. *Oakmar* pulled into San Francisco Bay and her entire crew struck in anticipation of the longshoremen's action. One seaman recalled that "every man aboard of her was a member of the M.W.I.U." On May 12, the union held a well-attended conference; the assembled delegates called a formal strike for eight o'clock that evening and put forward their own set of demands. The crews of seventeen ships responded to the MWIU's strike call, and within a few days the men on practically every vessel coming into San Francisco joined the longshoremen on the picket lines.[20]

It is probable, however, that the seamen's spontaneous determination to strike was more important than the MWIU's leadership in triggering many of the actions that occurred. The deck department of the S.S. *President Hoover*, for example, walked off the ship in San Francisco and immediately pressured the SUP officials to call a strike. There had been a self-appointed organizer aboard this Dollar line vessel. But as it turned out, his role was secondary at best. Harold Johnson, a Communist seaman, recalled that "my duty was to recruit people into the MWIU, the Young Communist League, and the Communist Party. I didn't succeed." In fact, he acknowledged, "I was a constant pain in the ass." Indeed, when the ship pulled into San Francisco on the first day of the strike and a number of crew members looked to Johnson for leadership, instead of taking time to help spearhead an organized walkout, the young zealot simply packed his seabag and walked off the ship, alone.

The next day the *President Hoover* sailed to San Pedro, returning to San Francisco a few days later. This time the entire deck crew walked off together, led by able-bodied seaman Bill Caves. A stereotypical sailor, Caves had joined the navy at age seventeen and had been sailing ever since. Now in his forties, he was muscular, literate, and outspoken to the point of belligerence. He took great pride in the fact that he had broken every one of his knuckles in various brawls. (He was also a homosexual who along with half a dozen other crew members on the *Hoover* was being treated for syphilis.) Although somewhat erratic, Caves "radiated excitement." By virtue of his charisma and experience, he was far better able than the politically zealous but unseasoned Harold Johnson to help crystallize the anger and determination of his fellow seamen.[21]

The MWIU's initiative, the catalytic role of natural leaders like Bill Caves, and the massive—often spontaneous—upsurge of rank-and-file seamen hastened the inevitable. The Sailors' Union took a formal strike vote on May 15. Coastwide only 146 men cast ballots, with 131 of them voting to "hit the bricks." (The vast majority of seamen were not union members when they walked of the ships and were thus ineligible to participate in the strike vote.) Within a week all seafaring unions on the Pacific Coast, including those representing licensed officers, were on strike, and George Larsen could declare: "Most of the men going to sea have faith in the union, let's show them their faith is not misplaced. We must stick and win." [22]

With the seamen on the picket lines, the teamsters quickly became crucial to the strike's continued momentum. If they had been willing to haul scab-unloaded cargo, the maritime workers' position would have been undermined. But in spite of repeated warnings from their leadership about the sanctity of contracts, the rank-and-file truck drivers refused to handle goods that were bound to or from the docks. [23]

The high point of the strike's extraordinary solidarity was the San Francisco general strike. Although it is impossible to identify the exact number of workers who participated, it probably exceeded a hundred thousand, encompassing not only San Francisco but Oakland and Alameda County as well. Sam Darcy commented that initially "the General Strike was effective beyond all expectations. Not only had the overwhelming bulk of organized workers joined the strike, but many thousands of unorganized workers" also walked out. Of perhaps greater significance than the numbers was the attitude of the rank-and-file participants. Longshoreman Germain Bulcke lived several miles from the San Francisco waterfront, and with no streetcars running, he had a long walk to his picket duty at Pier 35. "But it was a very happy feeling," he recalled. "I felt like I was walking on air." Mike Quin claimed that in the city's working-class neighborhoods, "an almost carnival spirit" prevailed. "Laboring men appeared on the streets in their Sunday clothes, shiny celluloid union buttons glistening on every coat lapel. Common social barriers were swept away in the spirit of the occasion. Strangers addressed each other warmly as old friends." [24]

Meanwhile, across the bay, as employer representative Paul St. Sure recalled, momentum was building, until "with dramatic suddenness everything was down in Oakland." The Amalgamated Streetcar Workers met in the early hours of the morning, after the trolley system's daily shutdown at 2 A.M., to consider what action to take. Employers were confident that this vital artery would remain in operation, because the company had recently granted a voluntary wage increase and its work force included many "old-timers . . . loyal to the company." Imagine the employers' shock, then, when the Streetcar Workers passed a resolution that committed the union to walk out in sympathy with the waterfront and general strikes "and called upon the employees of the Key System and workers of the community to take over the transit company as a mass transportation system for working people." At that moment, St. Sure remembered, the East Bay business community became convinced that "there was a revolution in progress. . . . frankly we were frightened . . . [because] the streetcar workers, who had no direct connection with the strike . . . were actually proposing taking over the property; . . . we felt this was the first step in [a] class conflict that might lead to anything."[25]

Where did such resolutions come from? In spite of all the hysteria about imminent revolution and Communists on the march, George Larsen of the Sailors' Union readily admitted that the strike was not led by Communists—they "are loudmouthed but not in control"—nor even by trade union officials like himself, "for they are swept along by [the workers'] deep resentment against the shipowners." Instead Larsen pointed to the centrality of rank-and-file anger and initiative. Perhaps no other dimension of the Big Strike was more vital than the energy and determination radiating from thousands of anonymous workers. The case of Ed Darling, an oiler on the S.S. *Washington,* may not be entirely representative, but the strike could not have succeeded without the spirit of militant activism that he exemplified. Ed Darling was in many ways a typical seaman. He had been sailing in the navy or the merchant marine for twenty-three years by 1934. Although he was a high-school dropout who admitted to spending most of his money on "women and whiskey," he was also an avid music enthusiast who never missed an opera or a symphony when he had the opportunity in port. *Fortune* chronicled the story of his involvement in the Big Strike:

> When he heard about the strike, he jumped the ship in Marshfield, Oregon, and beat it up to Portland in a boxcar. In Portland he promptly got a thirty day suspended sentence for attacking a scab, which made it necessary for him to leave the city. Thereupon he went to Seattle, where he picketed fourteen to sixteen hours a day, tossed rocks at the engineers and firemen who tried to move freight along the waterfront, and greased the railroad tracks so that the engines couldn't move. From a woodworking factory he helped to steal 300 clubs that had just been turned out for the police and vigilantes. He was gassed and clubbed frequently and lost all his upper teeth in a fight with a scab. Then one day . . . he met the man who had knocked out his teeth, and in an attempt to break a bone for every tooth he had lost, he battered the scab so fearfully that he was afraid to stay in Seattle. The remaining month of the strike he spent on veteran's relief in Portland, doing nothing to excite the attention of the police.[26]

Ed Darling was one of those men who, like Henry Schmidt, had been praying for a showdown with the shipowners. But there were many others who discovered only during the course of the strike that they had the will and the confidence to combat the employers. One stevedore admitted, "I have always been afraid of strikes," but declared that his experience on the picket lines "proves to me what power the workers have if they will only use it." The shipowners "have treated us as if we were not human," he said, "and now that the strike is [on] I can't see how in hell they got away with it for so long. We must have been asleep; we should have given it to them long ago. Well, we have the power now; if they don't behave themselves we will take the ships and run them to suit ourselves."[27]

Such a statement may reflect a touch of picket line bravado or, if taken literally, may have represented only a small minority of the strikers. But like the Streetcar Workers' resolution, it is also indicative of the festive, irreverent, and spontaneously radical sentiments that come to the fore in a crisis of this magnitude. In this situation it was inevitable that the conflict between the insurgent strikers and their conservative officials would often reach a fever pitch. Secretary of Labor Frances Perkins declared that "the officers of the unions have been swept off their feet by the rank and file movement." Likewise, Paul Eliel, a spokesman for the Industrial Association, commented with alarm on the declining authority of San Francisco Teamster President Mike Casey. Once known as Bloody Mike, Casey was by now a solidly entrenched member of the AFL hierarchy, and he was on friendly, even intimate, terms with the employers. Because the forces of capital relied heavily on AFL representatives like Casey to settle the strike in a way that would minimize the damage to the employers' interests, it was painful for Eliel to admit that "as strong a man as Michael Casey has absolutely lost control of the Teamsters' Union and he is unable to lead it any more. He used to be able to drive it."[28]

Appropriately, however, it was the longshoremen who provided the most vivid example of the conflict between rank-and-file insurgency and AFL conservativism. The pivotal figures in this conflict were Henry Bridges and ILA President Joseph P. Ryan. Whereas Ryan's was a familiar name in the councils of business, government, and the American Federation of Labor, Bridges was so obscure at the beginning of the strike that one veteran MWIU leader who had spent considerable time on the San Francisco waterfront in 1931 and 1932 couldn't even remember who he was. "You know him," Harry Hynes reminded Tommy Ray as they followed the strike news in a New York gin mill. "Australian Harry! He works on the Matson dock and plays the horses."

At first glance, Bridges was hardly an appealing candidate for the leadership of an insurgent movement. He lacked the surface charm of Walter Reuther, the impressive bulk and prophetic aura of John L. Lewis, the rough-edged proletarian hue of Joe Curran. To some observers, the only thing that seemed to distinguish him was his long nose. *Fortune* spoke of his "hawk eyes and nose and long spidery arms." Journalist George West found him "physically unimpressive" and said he had "no 'personality,' no charm, no radiation." Frances Perkins remembered him as "a small, thin, somewhat haggard man in a much-worn overcoat." Richard Neuberger spoke of his "monastic simplicity," but unlike Perkins he also perceived the cocksure personality who "swaggers like a racetrack bookie."[29]

As for the longshoremen, although they good-naturedly called him the Nose, they did not judge Bridges by his looks. Author Charles Madison correctly noted that he became the stevedores' spokesman through his unique "ability to verbalize their yearnings and concretize their goal." In fact, it is remarkable how often longshoremen and outsiders alike referred to the effectiveness of his use of language. His style was simple and direct. His speeches were "cold," "clean," "clear," "rapid-fire," "precise," with every word "like the blow of a hammer," building an orderly and readily comprehensible edifice for his listeners. One observer described how he captivated a meeting of two thousand maritime workers in Portland "with a few masterful words." In spite of strong opposition from the Portland ILA officials, "he presented his case with such brilliance that the audience rose to give him a unanimous vote of confidence."[30]

Fellow longshoreman John Olsen remarked that "he had a certain charisma that nobody else seemed to have. There are certain men . . . who have the ability to present something so that you understand it, and you feel a part of it." Olsen recalled one particular case in San Francisco "when we had a big meeting, and . . . all the officials of the old ILA were there opposing Harry. They all spoke first. Harry finally got up and said . . . , 'It's me against all of them.' [Then] he took something out of his pocket, and he read it. When he got through talking, he had the whole meeting on his side. He had that ability to draw you to him that very few men have."

Even men who were far removed from the stevedores' rough-and-tumble environment were struck by this quality in Bridges. Paul Eliel marveled at his "extraordinary presentation" before the National Longshoremen's Board in July 1934. He said that "speaking without notes and extemporaneously," Bridges "showed not only an unusual command of the subject matter but of the English language as well." After his testimony, said Eliel, "employers were able for the first time to understand something of the hold which he had been able to establish over the strikers both in own union and in the other maritime crafts." Likewise, Harvard Dean James M. Landis concluded that Bridges's testimony at his first deportation hearing "was given not only without reserve, but vigorously as dogma and faiths of which the man was proud. . . . It was a fighting apologia that refused to temper itself to the winds of caution."[31]

The same qualities that inspired admiration in Eliel and Landis were infuriating to many on the employers' side. For men who were used to the friendly, even deferential posture of a Ryan or a Scharrenberg, Bridges's self-assurance appeared arrogant, his faint smile seemed a sneer, his scorn for bourgeois amenities and his refusal to shy away from controversy became the mark of treason. Admiral Emory Land of the War Shipping Board recalled that Bridges never came to Washington "without insisting on having an appointment with me. And it was always one of the most unhappy appointments I ever had. Naturally, we never agreed on any single thing. . . . He always had a snarl on his upper lip. I've always said he had a crooked brain. He was an out-and-out Commie."

Louis Adamic rightly observed that the shipowners were "mentally and emotionally paralyzed" by their hatred of Bridges. In an editorial that represented the employers' view as much as Hearst's, the *San Francisco Examiner* once characterized "the line-up in the waterfront labor situation" as

Harry Bridges vs. responsible union labor
Harry Bridges vs. the shipping industry
Harry Bridges vs. San Francisco, the Pacific Coast, the entire American seaboard.
Put in one phrase—the issue is:
COMMUNISM VS. AMERICAN LABOR.

The shipowners convinced themselves that they loathed Bridges because he was a Communist. But, in part, at least, their hatred derived from the fact that this upstart dockworker often proved a superior foe. George West described him as a "lightning thinker" and a "master of repartee." "Facing the shrewdest of corporation lawyers," he said, Bridges "makes them seem soft and a little helpless by comparison."[32]

Of course, in the eyes of the longshoremen and the other maritime workers, these very same qualities made "Limo" an effective leader and, ultimately, a folk hero. As one "Stevie" put it, "Harry Bridges is a 100% union man. . . . He's a man in a million. A union man at heart, not a faker. Maybe I admire him because they call him a radical. If Harry Bridges is a radical, I am a radical too." Even a self-proclaimed "Conservative Longshoreman" expressed similar sentiments, declaring, "Anybody can see . . . that Bridges knows what he is talking about. He stands ready to offer leadership to our local, something we have always lacked, and what's more, he is ready to fight for what he believes to be right. I have changed my mind about that man. He is not too radical for me now. He is a good trade unionist." [33]

It is important to emphasize that Bridges as leader was very much a product of the rank-and-file movement. He did not create the burst of energy that drove the maritime workers forward during the 1934 strike. Nor was he solely responsible for the continuing upsurge that would transform conditions on the waterfront and give the Pentecostal era its special dynamism. Without the determination of the Ed Darlings and thousands of anonymous rank and filers, even the most skillful and dedicated leaders would have been helpless. As one longshore activist declared, "It was collective action that won the strike, not a few individuals." [34]

It is also true that Bridges was neither as malevolent as the shipowners imagined him nor as perfect as many of the longshoremen portrayed him. Like any human being, he had faults. He was notoriously irascible, and his warmest admirers agreed that he had trouble delegating authority. These traits may have contributed to his inordinate capacity to make enemies, even among those who had once been his close allies in the union movement. According to Richard Neuberger, "Bridges demands tolerance for himself but is inclined to be intolerant of others." Darcy recalled that he was "very jealous of anyone he thought might excel him in leadership," and that he often "tried to belittle the role of other people." Herbert Resner, a left-wing attorney who knew Bridges well up until 1950, found him "notoriously lacking in . . . human kindness." My purpose, however, is not to provide an all-sided portrait of Bridges's personality and career, but rather to analyze the qualities that enabled him to become the leading spokesman for his fellow maritime workers during the thirties. Among these men, whether they were radical or conservative, Bridges was widely regarded as the embodiment of the best in themselves and their movement. As a marine fireman put it, "We like Bridges because he is rank and file." [35]

No one could accuse Joe Ryan of being rank and file, although *Fortune* did concede that he "still goes down to the waterfront to visit with his boys—after a pleasant dinner" at a New York restaurant. Whereas Bridges wore inexpensive clothes and was obviously indifferent about his appearance, Ryan dressed "with splendor," wearing painted neckties and pinstriped, elegantly tailored double-breasted suits on his massive, 200-pound frame. "Next to myself," he used to say, "I like silk underwear best." Another of his favorite sayings was "What does I.L.A. stand for? Why it means 'I Love America!'" Irving Bernstein has aptly characterized him as "an old-style Tammany politician who . . . strayed into the labor business."

Ryan began stevedoring around 1910. Several years later an injury and his gift for blarney combined to end his career as a working longshoreman. Elected to local union office in 1913, he made his way up the ILA hierarchy until he achieved the rank of international president in 1927. During his long reign, there were no authorized strikes on the New York waterfront, even though conditions for the majority of dockworkers were abominable. He fortified his regime by courting politicians and hiring criminals. Under the aegis of the Joseph P. Ryan Association, his friends sponsored annual testimonial dinners that raised large sums of money for his personal and political use. Among the honorary chairmen of the 1931 dinner, which raised $8,000 to send the Ryan family on a vacation trip to Europe, were New York Governor Franklin D. Roosevelt, former Governor Alfred E. Smith, and New York City Mayor James J. Walker.

Ryan also had many friends at the other end of the social spectrum. Matthew Josephson characterized the Brooklyn waterfront in particular as "a racketeers' jungle run wild." A congressional subcommittee concluded that Ryan had used his position as head of the New York State Parole Board to make ILA headquarters "the court of last resort for all shady aspirants and claimants along the waterfront, as well as the fountainhead of protection . . . for vicious criminals in key waterfront posts." Refuting Ryan's claim that his motive was the rehabilitation of ex-convicts, the committee declared that "the waterfront is not where a man can 'go straight'—it is where he can keep crooked." Finally, the ILA president was forced to fall back on the hackneyed ruse of fighting communism on the docks, telling the committee that "some of those fellows with the bad criminal records were pretty handy out there when we had to do it the tough way." [36]

With the employers, however, Ryan always preferred to do it the easy way. Although he had no authority to negotiate any binding agreements on behalf of the Pacific District union membership, the ILA president came to the West Coast and made several highly publicized efforts to settle the strike on terms that fell far short of the men's demands. In mid-June he participated in a series of carefully orchestrated maneuvers that resulted in an alleged settlement of the strike. The so-called Saturday Agreement met some of the stevedores' demands and compromised on others, but it was negotiated by ILA and Teamsters union officials who had no authorization to represent the longshoremen. In fact, their elected representatives were excluded from the proceedings. When the agreement was signed, the press immediately declared the strike over, before the men had had a chance to examine the terms of the settlement or vote on the matter. The Sunday *Chronicle* ran the banner headline "S.F. Strike Ends; Port Open Monday" and featured a picture of a smiling Ryan on the telephone, saying "Hello Seattle! It's All Over Boys."

But the longshoremen overwhelmingly rejected the pact. In the ports of San Francisco, Portland, and Tacoma, they refused even to vote on it. The *Chronicle* was forced to admit that "the proposal [was] shouted down by a thunder of 'noes.'" Why this emphatic rejection of an agreement where the employers compromised significantly on the longshoremen's demands? Because the pact made no provision for resolution of the seamen's grievances. This was fine with diehard craft unionists like Ryan and Furuseth, but to the aroused rank and file it was a betrayal of the solidarity that had become one of the strike's most powerful weapons.[37]

The climactic moment in this escalating confrontation between the strikers and their conservative officials came when Ryan attended the San Francisco ILA meeting and attempted to explain his actions to the three thousand longshoremen who were packed into the hall. The growing clamor from the audience made it clear that he was in deep trouble. Suddenly, Pirate Larsen leaped onto the stage, pointed an accusing finger at the ILA president, and shouted, "This guy's a fink and he's trying to make finks out of us. Let's throw him out!" As Henry Schmidt recalled, "Pirate brought the house down."

From that moment on, Joseph P. Ryan—international president of the ILA, former president of the New York City Central Labor Council, crony of governors, mayors, and millionaire employers—was a dead letter on the West Coast. Before returning to the more hospitable confines of the East, however, Ryan took a parting shot at the rank-and-file stevedore who had replaced him as principal spokesman for the men. "Bridges does not want this strike settled," he declared. "My firm belief is that he is acting for the communists."[38]

It had quickly become standard procedure in many quarters to attribute the strike and the grim determination of the strikers to the machinations of the Reds. Only ten days into the conflict, Assistant Secretary of Labor Edward McGrady, his efforts at mediation rebuffed, had declared in frustration: "San Francisco ought to be informed of the hold of the Red element on the situation. A strong radical element within the ranks of the longshoremen's union seems to want no settlement of this strike." Two days later, the president of the San Francisco Chamber of Commerce eagerly followed McGrady's lead, stating matters in far more apocalyptic terms. "The San Francisco waterfront strike," he declared, "is out of hand. It is not a conflict between employer and employee—between capital and labor—it is a conflict which is rapidly spreading between American principles and un-American radicalism. . . . There can be no hope for industrial peace until communistic agitators are removed as the official spokesmen of labor and American leaders are chosen to settle their differences along American lines." [39]

Even as sanguine an employer spokesman as Paul Eliel tended to view the strike in these terms. Although he avoided the apocalyptic frame of reference, he was frankly alarmed about the broad practical implications of the waterfront strike. In a letter to the National Labor Board, he said:

> The I.L.A. in San Francisco at the present time, is absolutely and unequivocally in the hands of a group of Communists. You know I am not a Redbaiter and I more or less laugh at these Communist scares. In the present instance, however, I am convinced that the I.L.A. has definitely been taken by a Communist group.
>
> Now the difficulty of the employers accepting a closed shop with the I.L.A. in view of this existing leadership of the I.L.A. here is that *such a crowning of the achievements of the strike committee would, it is believed, affect the entire crop-harvesting situation most adversely.* In addition, it would constitute a definite threat to the leadership of the more conservative labor men in San Francisco whose control of their unions is tottering. [40]

The control of the "conservative labor men" was indeed tottering, and in the maritime unions it was about to collapse. But Eliel was wrong in reducing the motive force in this drama to communism. To be sure, the Communist party played an active and important role in the strike, placing its newspaper, legal apparatus, and other elements of its institutional network at the disposal of the strikers. There were influential Communist cadres in several of the AFL unions, and the Communist party recruited many new members during the strike, especially among the maritime workers. Darcy estimated that there were perhaps six or eight Communists among the members of the ILA strike committee in San Francisco. The extent of the Party's influence on Harry Bridges was a matter of controversy and litigation for many years. One Communist later remarked that he "enjoyed intimate ties with the Party, usually on his own terms." And even as devout an anti-Communist as John Brophy acknowledged that Bridges "was not one to be captured or used, but had his own ideas and ambitions." Bridges himself readily acknowledged his substantial agreement with the program and political line of the Party, but denied being a member. In any case, it is symbolic of the significant and open relationship of the Communist party to the strike that during the funeral procession for the martyrs of Bloody Thursday, Darcy and Mrs. Bordoise, wife of slain Communist Nick Bordoise, rode in one car at the head of the line of march, while Bridges and Mother Mooney, whose son Tom was the nation's most famous "class war prisoner," rode in another.[41]

It is clear, if only by inference at times, that the Communist presence in the strike gave it a more disciplined and organized character and a more effective leadership, especially among the longshoremen. But the scope and dynamism of the upheaval far exceeded the ability of the rather insignificant number of Communists to control or direct it. The fact is that the Big Strike was an authentic rank-and-file rebellion that had long been waiting to happen. It drew upon deep wellsprings of discontent that required leadership and direction but did not submit easily to manipulation. There was a spontaneous impulse toward solidarity and discipline that was quite evident in the Battle of Rincon Hill, in the stirring funeral march for Sperry and Bordoise, and in other events where masses of workers flowed together "like cooling lava" in uncanny demonstrations of self-direction and self-discipline that left even their own leadership amazed. This was perhaps clearest in the funeral procession, which Paul Eliel wrongly characterized as "a brilliant and theatric piece of propaganda." For what stands out about this event is the self-discipline and determination that characterized the spontaneous participation of thousands of workers. They, and not its planners, made the event into a living piece of propaganda. Indeed, they made it the general strike in embryo. And they made good on their promise that if no police were present on the streets that day, the workers would maintain a dignified order that the police could only have disrupted. As Sam Darcy recalled in later years, "What was amazing was the organizational job those workers did that day. Every spot was organized along the [route of march], and it all came from the ranks. They worked out the details themselves."[42]

What is more significant than the degree of Communist involvement in the Big Strike is the fact that the constant barrage of Red-baiting made communism an issue among the strikers, or at least forced them to take an increasingly clear stand on the question of Communist participation in the strike. While several unions responded to the anti-Red campaign by issuing statements condemning communism, the growing trend in the ranks was to view Red-baiting as another in the arsenal of weapons that the employers used to divide and conquer the workers.[43]

The issue of communism caused particularly bitter conflict within the AFL seamen's unions, largely because of the presence of the MWIU. From the day they voted to join the strike, the ISU leadership resisted every move to build a united front with the Marine Workers Union. In fact, they suspected that anyone who advocated such unity must be a Red himself. But to the rank-and-file seamen, the issue was not ISU versus MWIU or Americanism versus communism. To them the issue was the maritime strikers versus the shipowners, and the MWIU was, in the eyes of many seamen, a legitimate marine workers' organization that was making a solid contribution to the winning of the strike. As one MWIU picket put it: "Up to this very minute no one has crammed a communist license down my throat nor have I been forced to change my religion or politics. The main issue is the strike; the main point is solidarity and a continuous picket line."[44]

The issue of the united front came to a head in mid-June. On the fourteenth, the ISU walked out of the daily conference of striking maritime unions because the MWIU, with the support of the longshoremen, had been seated at the meeting. The following evening the ISU joint strike committee issued a press statement condemning communism in general and the MWIU in particular. But the stevedores' rejection of the Saturday Agreement sparked a wave of insurgency among the rank and file of the ISU. On the evening of the seventeenth, right after the tumultuous longshore meeting—the "thunder of 'noes'"—in San Francisco, a thousand seamen held a gathering where ISU strike committee chairman Bill Caves delivered a ringing speech condemning the ISU officials for refusing to unite with the MWIU. Sam Telford, a leader of the Marine Workers Union, spoke at the meeting, to a loud welcome, and the evening concluded with cheers for the united front. The next day George Larsen suspended Caves from the strike committee, whereupon his office "was stormed by an angry mob." That evening, in a close vote, the Sailors' Union membership repudiated Larsen's action and restored Caves to his position of leadership. Meanwhile, the Seattle ISU voted unanimously that "there should be no distinction made between MWIU and ISU men" on the picket lines; and a striker from San Pedro reported on the growing fraternization between MWIU members and the rank and file of the ISU on the Southern California waterfront.[45]

In addition to its triumphant moments, the Big Strike had other dimensions and was shaped by other events that threatened to undermine its splendid achievements. Toward the end of the upheaval, two factors in particular began to corrode the morale that had sustained the strikers through more than two months of bitter conflict. One was the manner in which the general strike ended, leaving the question of whether this massive outpouring of solidarity constituted a triumph for labor, an inconclusive stalemate, or a victory for the employers. The other was the systematic campaign of terrorism by police and vigilantes that accompanied the general strike. To what extent did this campaign represent a division in the ranks of the workers themselves? To what extent did it place militant labor on the defensive and signify a period of repression and retreat? These questions haunted the waterfront as the strike entered its final days.

The campaign of vigilante and police terror began with the general strike, but was preceded by a mounting wave of provocation by the media, the employers, and government officials. For example, on June 21 the *Chronicle* began an article on American Legion Week with the declaration that "San Francisco trains its guns on communism today!" A few days later the *Foc'sle Head* reported that "American Legion gangsters are cruising around the streets beating up lone pickets." On the eve of the terror campaign, California Governor Frank Merriam insisted that "a more active and intensified drive to rid this State and nation of alien and radical agitators should be undertaken *by the workers themselves* if they are to enjoy the confidence of the people." General Hugh Johnson, the mercurial chief of the National Recovery Administration, was even more direct. In a speech at the University of California, he demanded that the "subversive element" in the ranks of labor "must be wiped out. They must be run out like rats."[46]

On July 17, the same day that Johnson placed the imprimatur of the federal government on vigilante terror, there was a massive raid on the Marine Workers Industrial Union hall, the most visible symbol of the Red presence on the waterfront. National Guardsmen with machine guns mounted on trucks cordoned off an entire block. Police then entered the hall, arrested eighty-five people, and systematically destroyed everything in sight. The reign of terror continued for nearly a week and spread to many of the smaller cities and agricultural communities in northern and central California. Newspapers openly applauded the actions of vigilantes who smashed up target after target and left bleeding victims whom the police then arrested for vagrancy. In one instance, a Finnish workers' hall was "reduced to kindling, while the helpless workers watched their thousand-dollar library, their theater with its two grand pianos, all their equipment that spelled years of sacrifice, reduced to rubble." In another instance an eyewitness reported that "the Workers' Center in Oakland . . . was blood-spattered from wall to wall; the stairways that led to the street was actually slippery with coagulated blood." In San Jose a group of vigilantes—approvingly described by a local newspaper as "armed with bright new pick-handles, their faces grim, eyes shining with steady purpose"— terrorized thirteen suspected Communists and ran them out of the country. The *San Jose Evening News* exulted that "the mongoose of Americanism dragged the cobra of communism through the good Santa Clara Valley orchard dirt last night." [47]

The *San Francisco Chronicle* claimed that the activity of these "citizen vigilantes" represented a move by "conservative union labor . . . to purge its ranks of Communists." The *San Francisco Examiner* reported that "police started the raids . . . but were superseded by an infuriated band of men, reported to be union strikers." Most unions, however, vehemently denied any involvement in the terror, and there were carefully documented charges that the police and their anonymous accomplices acted under the direction of the Industrial Association. Mike Quin, a contemporary who in 1936 wrote what remains the best full-length account of the strike, declared that many of the vigilantes were "strikebreakers brought in from Los Angeles by the Industrial Association to run the scab trucks on the waterfront. A lesser number were businessmen, bank managers, and adventurous members of the industrialists' white-collar staffs." Lorena Hickok, a representative of the Roosevelt administration who was in California at the time, was told that most of the vigilantes were American Legionnaires. But it is probable that the vast majority of the raiders were policemen. Robert Cantwell of the *New Republic* reported that the raids were badly stage-managed, since the so-called "workers looked very much like police dressed like workers"; and Communist leader Sam Darcy, who had good reason to inquire, recalled, "We establish beyond question that policemen were being dressed as longshoremen to carry through the vigilante raids." [48]

Significantly, the "vigilant citizens" generally steered clear of the waterfront. With the exception of the raid on the MWIU hall and a brief episode at the ILA soup kitchen, the police and their accomplices avoided frontal assaults on the maritime strikers, their leaders, and their various headquarters. Sam Darcy maintained that in spite of the arrest of many Communist party members (more than three hundred alleged Communists were arrested in one day), "those of our comrades who were on the front line trenches of the maritime and general strikes hardly suffered at all as a result of the terror, because they were, so to speak, 'hidden' among the masses and [had] the confidence and support of large numbers of workers."[49]

The police-vigilante campaign was, nonetheless, ominous. But it is possible that the manner in which the general strike ended was even more destructive of morale on the waterfront. For more than a month before it began, the maritime workers had regarded this consummate act of labor solidarity as their ultimate weapon and had believed that it would force the employers to meet their basic demands. Hence, when it ended inconclusively, accompanied by banner headlines that shouted "General Strike Crushed by Determined Citizens" and "Bridges Admits Failure of Plot to Starve City into Defeat," the strikers inevitably fell prey to a certain amount of confusion and demoralization.[50]

The general strike was not a Red plot to starve the city into submission. Rather, it was the culmination of a massive outpouring of solidarity from within the ranks of labor. It had gained its initial momentum from the growing united front of longshoremen, seafarers, and teamsters, and had been fed by the intransigence of the employers and the violence of the police. In the wake of Bloody Thursday, and the military occupation of the waterfront, the solemn, massive funeral march in which labor paid tribute to its fallen comrades made the general strike a virtual certainty.[51]

Contrary to the *Chronicle*'s exultant headline, the "determined citizens" of San Francisco did not "crush" the general strike. Even the widespread and officially condoned vigilante activity did not bring about its demise. When the strike ended, many businessmen and public officials regarded Hearst general counsel John Francis Neylan as man of the hour. Neylan was chief guardian of William Randolph Hearst's interests on the West Coast, and he orchestrated the newspaper campaign that drowned the general strike in a sea of hostile—and largely false—propaganda. In a private letter, Neyland expressed the opinion that "I have been given entirely too much credit. . . . The plain truth is, the whole community is deeply indebted to the reputable labor leaders." Without their "courageous and intelligent action," he wrote, "we would have been faced with an extremely complicated situation, leading to bloodshed and the spread of the general strike idea to other communities."[52]

When the longshoremen and their allies first raised the idea of a general strike, most of San Francisco's established labor leaders regarded it as a "radical menace." They continued their opposition until the momentum of events threatened to overwhelm them. As Secretary of Labor Perkins informed President Roosevelt, "The conservative leaders of all of the San Francisco unions urged against the general strike. They were overwhelmingly outvoted by the rank and file members who were emotionally very much stirred by the situation." In the case of the teamsters, Mike Casey acknowledged that "nothing on earth could have prevented that vote. In my thirty years of leading these men, I have never seem them so worked up, so determined to walk out."

At the crucial moment, however, the labor leaders showed enough political sense to change direction and seize control of a movement they could no longer thwart. As one union official confided to a friend, "It was an avalanche. I saw it coming so I ran ahead before it crushed me." The top AFL officials simply designated themselves leaders of the Labor Council's strike strategy committee and then used all of their institutional power to maneuver the strike movement to serve their own purposes. The key figure in this regard was George Kidwell of the Teamsters, a man with a reputation for liberalism, pragmatism, and keen intelligence. Once he recognized the inevitability of a general walkout, Kidwell concluded that it could be the instrument for taking the entire strike situation in San Francisco out of the volatile and stubborn hands of the maritime workers. He developed a twofold agenda: first, to force both the employers and the marine unions to accept arbitration; and second, to turn an avalanche of class feeling into an orderly and limited expression of sympathy. Thus, from the beginning of the general strike, Kidwell and the other members of the strategy committee sought to defuse the potential for open class warfare and to bring the drama to a rapid, orderly conclusion. On the third day, a Sailors' Union spokesman complained that "our General Strike seems to be dissolving under our feet. . . . The strike is now being run by other Unions, and the conservatives, having all the voting power, seem to be attempting to force us back to work immediately." After four days, by a surprisingly close vote of 191 to 174, the Labor Council delegates terminated the general strike.[53]

San Francisco Mayor Angelo Rossi danced around his office for joy at the news and declared, "I congratulate the real leaders of organized labor on their decision." ILA President Ryan in turn congratulated Rossi "as one good pal to another." In Sacramento, Governor Merriam gave thanks that "the sane, intelligent, right-thinking leadership in the labor organizations has prevailed over the rash counsel of communistic and radical agitators." But the maritime workers were in no mood to celebrate. For them all that remained was the uneasy feeling that their ultimate weapon had never been fully tested and the gratuitous recommendation of the Central Labor Council that they accept the arbitration they had been rejecting all along.[54]

The premature and inconclusive termination of the general strike left the maritime workers in a difficult position. After nearly two and a half months on strike, literally thousands of arrests, at least six deaths, and hundreds of serious injuries, the men and their families were still holding the line. But their allies were gradually cutting the ties of solidarity that had been the strike's lifeblood. When the teamsters voted to return to work unconditionally, the maritime strikers were once again on their own. Paul Taylor, a scholar whose work combined objectivity with strong sympathy for agricultural and marine workers in California, sat in the ILA hall with a number of longshore strike leaders as they anxiously awaited the outcome of the teamsters' vote. "The big shabby room was depressing," Taylor reported, "and the three [or] four men sitting around were depressed. Ralph Mallen the head of the Publicity committee sat by the phone. He looked tired and beaten. In the three months he had aged years. . . . There was no confidence now, only silence and painful waiting." Although they stated that they felt "more strengthened . . . today than at any time during the entire maritime strike," their strategic alternatives were now severely limited and their morale was being tested as never before.[55]

In these circumstances, the employers' long-standing offer of arbitration to the longshoremen began to appear more palatable. The men had maintained that they would never arbitrate the hiring hall issue and that they would not return to work until the seamen's grievances were resolved. But when in the immediate aftermath of the general strike the National Longshoremen's Board conducted a coastwide ballot on the question of submitting the stevedores' dispute to arbitration, 6,504 longshoremen voted yes and only 1,515 voted no. Even in the storm center of San Francisco, the yes ballots carried by a three to one margin. Only the lumber port of Everett, Washington, rejected arbitration, by the margin of a single vote.

The longshoremen's decision to accept arbitration left the seamen in the lurch and jeopardized the magnificent unity that the marine workers had forged during the strike. Following the stevedores' vote, there was a growing rumble of bitterness among the seamen. Long-standing craft antagonisms that had been swept aside in a matter of days now threatened to reappear and to engulf the maritime strikers in "all the muck of ages" once again.[56]

Matters seemed ready to come to a head on July 29, the eighty-second day of the strike, at a packed meeting in the Sailors' Union hall in San Francisco. A parade of officials came before the angry seamen and tried to explain why the vanguard body of the strikers seemed to be abandoning their more vulnerable comrades to an uncertain fate. In this procession two men stood out as a vivid symbols of the different realities, programs, and outlooks that had been part of the seamen's experience and that confronted them with alternative choices now. One of these men was Harry Bridges; the other, Andrew Furuseth. Bridges had emerged as the strike's leading spokesman; he was a powerful force among longshoremen and seamen. But on this day, in these circumstances of reemerging craft jealousies, it appeared that Old Andy might well have the last word.

Furuseth, the grizzled eminence of the seafaring world, appeared almost ghostlike with his gaunt countenance and shock of white hair. In spite of numerous eccentricities, he remained a quintessential representative of traditional AFL unionism. The seamen of this generation knew him more as a legend than as a real person. But some of them were no doubt aware that he had favored arbitration and opposed the general strike movement, along with his friends in the top echelon of the San Francisco Labor Council. Although these conservative officials were widely regarded as sell-outs and fakers, many sailors retained a large measure of respect for "the Old Man of the Sea." Only a few days earlier, in San Pedro, he had addressed a mass meeting of eight to nine hundred seamen, and one official reported that "when Andrew got through you could hear the cheers from here to Los Angeles. . . . man after man came forward and shook Andrew by the hand."[57]

At this moment, perhaps the crucial contrast between Bridges and Furuseth lay in their differing attitudes toward craft unionism. Furuseth had staked his entire career on keeping the seamen free of entangling alliances, and his bitterest battles had been with the longshoremen. Bridges, on the other hand, had been a leading adherent of broad maritime unity throughout the strike, and along with the *Waterfront Worker* he had strongly opposed the longshoremen's decision to accept arbitration. He remained one of the most forceful spokesmen in favor of a Pacific Coast marine federation that would embrace not only the maritime crafts, but teamsters, machinists, scalers, and all other workers whose labor brought them into contract with ships and cargo.

After more than three decades of craft separation, the militants' dream of maritime unity had emerged as a powerful reality during the strike. But now that the longshoremen had in effect voted to abandon the seamen, the specter of long-standing craft antagonisms reappeared. The stevedores, the largest and strongest of the maritime crafts, had firm assurances that they would receive a serious hearing before the presidentially appointed arbitration board. What was more important, they had displayed the kind of muscle that would compel significant concessions from the arbitrators. But the seafarers were divided into more than half a dozen organizations; they had only recently received the promise that their demands would be arbitrated; and the terms of their dispute with the shipowners lacked the clear and sharp visibility that had characterized the conflict between longshoremen and employers from the very beginning. In short, the seamen were widely regarded as a mere auxiliary to the main event. As one of their numbers put it, with bitter frustration, "We had nothing to say because it was well known all over that the longshoremen's strike was going on, but who ever heard of a seamen's strike!"[58]

This was the scenario as Bridges faced the sailors' union meeting. Characteristically, he came right to the point. "I think the longshoreman is ready to break tomorrow," he told the seamen. "They have had enough of it. They have their families to support. They are discouraged by the teamsters' going back to work. They didn't get enough support from the [central labor] council. Up to this minute, as far as I know, there may have been about twelve desertions. But . . . it doesn't take many men. A hundred or two would do the trick. . . . In this case unless you stick 100% the majority doesn't count."

Would the seamen stand their increasingly isolated ground and then accuse the longshoremen of scabbing because a hundred or two stevedores were about to break ranks and compel a retreat? "It will be terrible," said Bridges, "if we go back tomorrow and the sailors stay out." The only answer? "We must go back together and on good terms. If the longshoremen go back and the sailors stay out that will break the unity of the whole thing. That is the best thing we have in our hands. Unity!"

Bridges recognized that recent events had put the maritime workers on the defensive. "The shipowners have got us backed up," he said, "and we are trying to back up step by step . . . instead of turning around and running." Without apologizing or pandering, he acknowledged that the seamen had good reason to be angry about the stevedores' unilateral decision. "I don't know how you fellows are going to take this," he said. "It's going to be a tough pill to swallow." After a final plea for unity, even in retreat, Bridges yielded the floor to Andrew Furuseth.[59]

Old Andy, a veteran of nearly fifty years of maritime unionism, undoubtedly had never heard of Harry Bridges prior to the 1934 strike. But in spite of Bridges's courage and forthrightness, the ISU president could hardly have held him in high regard. For Bridges represented two things that Furuseth despised: longshoremen and radicalism. Now that the dockworkers had voted to go their own way, Furuseth saw an opportunity to pursue the course he had been following for decades. In a rambling speech that was vintage Furuseth, he quoted scripture—"How often shall we forgive an erring brother?"—and forgave the "erring" seamen for quitting the ISU after the collapse of the 1921 strike. He exclaimed that the moment had arrived to restore the integrity and power of the legislation for which he had campaigned endlessly. How? By embracing the ISU and its leadership, by refusing to cooperate with the fink halls—the employer-controlled hiring halls—that had been the most vivid symbols of the ISU's impotence, and by trusting in the goodwill of the government. "This is a federal question," he said. "The government is for us. The government feeds the men in San Pedro. They will feed them here if it becomes necessary." He passed along the personal assurances of NRA chief Johnson that "as soon as the general strike was out of the way and . . . the soldiers were out of San Francisco, . . . he himself would fight like a tiger for the seamen."

Furuseth then referred briefly to the long series of jurisdictional and tactical disputes that had characterized relations between seamen and dockworkers. He implied that the longshoremen's vote to return to work was an act of "damned cowardice," but emphasized that "they have acted as a trade union has got a right to act." Their decision "leaves the longshoremen free to act for themselves and us to act for ourselves. It leaves us to our own affairs."[60]

Here was the nub of the matter. The ILA's action had created exactly the opening that Furuseth wanted, namely, to disengage the seamen from the longshoremen and to break up the intercraft unity that he viewed with such alarm and distrust. Soon after the longshoremen's courageous rejection of the Saturday Agreement because it failed to resolve the seamen's grievances, Furuseth had arrived in San Francisco and stated to the press: "Something's got to be done quickly to get [the seamen] back on their ships. While they're in port right now they must vote on submitting their differences to arbitration." He made this plea at a time when maritime unity had reached unprecedented heights. Now, however, in the wake of Bloody Thursday, the military occupation of the waterfront, and the conservatives' successful move to end the general strike, the longshoremen were somehow guilty of "damned cowardice" when they voted to follow the same course that Old Andy had recommended for the seamen a month earlier.[61]

On any other day the seamen might well have alternated between shouts of outrage and chuckles of irreverent amusement at much of Furuseth's speech. He asked them to trust a government whose support of the shipowners and disregard of their own most basic needs was one of the most obvious, and painful, facts of seafaring life. His reference to General Johnson's concern for the seamen must have sounded hollow at best at a time when the NRA administrator's bitter denunciation of the general strike as "bloody insurrection" and "a menace to government" was still ringing in their ears. Moreover, Old Andy's gesture of forgiving the seamen for abandoning the ISU could hardly have invoked a sentiment of gratitude among men who had left the union because they had long regarded it as impotent or worse. The maritime strike had created the opportunity, and the necessity, to reshape the moribund ISU into a real weapon in the hands of the seamen. But they had spontaneously walked off the ships, or had followed the MWIU's lead, and the ISU had belatedly joined them on the picket lines. Finally, Furuseth's denunciation of the longshoremen for their "damned cowardice" would ordinarily have been regarded as a vile slander upon courageous comrades who had paid a high price, including the death of at least four ILA members, for their determination to bring a new era to the waterfront.[62]

But on this day there was widespread confusion and a growing sense of betrayal. Old craft jealousies and antagonisms were plainly evident in remarks that the stevedores were about to "crawl back" to work, and that "we will win where the longshoremen couldn't." Moreover, Furuseth carried the hour not only by feeding the fires of negativism but also by concluding with a masterful appeal to the seamen's militancy and anger. The old man who only a few days ago had seemed to merit the mantle of ridicule implicit in the nicknames Andy the Weeping Willow, Andy Feroshus, and Andy Forsake-us now came forward with a proposal for what was to be the strike's final moment of symbolism. He suggested an act of defiance that "will go like fire" and "wake up everybody." "What do you think my proposition is? It is horrible and yet it is the most beautiful you can ever think of. . . . We are going to build a fire. Alongside of that fire we will have a can of petroleum and each man who has got a fink hall book will come along there and he will dip it into that petroleum and throw it on the fire. . . . The newspapers will know about it. The associated press will know all about it. The pictures will be shown on screens all across the country."[63]

With one stroke, Furuseth captured the seamen's imaginations, rescued them from their apparent obscurity, and seized the initiative from the longshoremen and Bridges. The meeting adjourned after a unanimous yes to the question "Are you willing to stay as you are absolutely until the International Seamen's Union orders you back to work?" Furuseth, who during the height of the strike had sought to persuade the seamen to go back to work alone, now seemed in no hurry to return to the ships. The unifying thread in the old man's apparently puzzling course was his obsessive determination to separate the seamen from entangling alliances with other crafts in general and longshoremen in particular. For the moment, Old Andy had indeed had the last word.[64]

The next day seamen in San Francisco gathered in a vacant lot near the Sailors' Union hall, built a huge bonfire, and joyously burned the hated fink books. The press reported that Furuseth "insisted on attending the ceremony, but his frail condition, due to a recent illness," kept him from taking an active part. While he watched the ritual from a nearby embankment, "solicitous [union] members brought him glasses of water."[65]

On July 31, however, the necessity imposed by the stevedores' decision caught up with the seamen. Fortified by the ritual of consigning the fink hall to a fiery grave, and by several conciliatory gestures from the shipowners, the seafarers joined the longshoremen in returning to work. After eighty-three days, the Big Strike was over.

NOTES

1. Silas B. Axtell, comp., *A Symposium on Andrew Furuseth* (New Bedford, Mass.: Darwin Press, 1948), p. 81.

2. The term was popularized by Mike Quin in *The Big Strike* (Olema, Calif.: Olema Publishing Co., 1949). On the extraordinary eruptions of 1934, see Irving Bernstein, *The Turbulent Years: A History of the American Worker, 1933–1941* (Boston: Houghton Mifflin, 1970), pp. 217–317. For narratives of the 1934 maritime and general strike, see Bernstein, *Turbulent Years*, pp. 252–98; Charles P. Larrowe, "The Great Maritime Strike of '34," Pt. 1, *Labor History* 11 (Fall 1970): 403–51, and Pt. 2, *Labor History* 12 (Winter 1971): 3–37, hereafter cited as Larrowe-1 and Larrowe-2; and Quin, *The Big Strike*.

3. Quin, *The Big Strike*, pp. 104–5, San Francisco Chronicle, July 6, 1934, p. 1.

4. *San Francisco Chronicle*, May 12, 1934, p. 2; May 18, 1934, p. 17; *Los Angeles Times*, May 13, 1934, p. 6; Ronald Magden and A. D. Martinson, *The Working Waterfront: The Story of Tacoma's Ships and Men* (Tacoma, Wash.: International Longshoremen's and Warehousemen's Union, Local 23, 1982), p. 110; Michael Egan, "'That's Why Organizing Was So Good': Portland Longshoremen, 1934: An Oral History" (senior thesis, Reed College, 1975), p. 51; Roger D. Lapham, "Pacific Maritime Labor Conditions as They Affect the Nation" (address to the Chamber of Commerce of the United States, Washington, D.C., Apr. 30, 1936), in Roger Lapham, "An Interview on Shipping, Labor, San Francisco City Government, and American Foreign Aid," conducted by Corinne L. Gilb, San Francisco, January–August 1956 (transcript in the Bancroft Library, University of California, Berkeley), p. 412. Egan's Reed thesis includes an interview with Harry Pilcher, an Everett longshoreman and Communist party member, who participated in the events on the Seattle waterfront. Pilcher recalled (p. 51): "By Friday [the third day of the strike] they had scabs on every dock in Seattle. Us fellows from Everett and

Tacoma got together and we rounded up all of the militant men we could find in Seattle. And Saturday morning we hit the docks in force. . . . I'd say at least a thousand unemployed came down and backed us up. . . . we got through that Saturday and there wasn't any scabs left on the Seattle waterfront."

5. Donald Mackenzie Brown, "Dividends and Stevedores," *Scribner's* 97 (Jan. 1935): 54–55; Henry Schmidt, *Secondary Leadership in the ILWU, 1933–1966* (oral history project conducted by Miriam F. Stein and Estolv Ethan Ward, 1974–81, Berkeley Regional History Office, Bancroft Library, University of California, Berkeley), p. 99.

6. Jerold S. Auerbach, *Labor and Liberty: The La Follette Committee and the New Deal* (New York: Bobbs-Merrill, 1966), pp. 177–78; Ivan F. Cox to Robert F. Wagner, Feb. 5, 1934, carton 11, San Francisco Labor Council, AFL-CIO, Correspondence and Papers, 1906–65, Bancroft Library, University of California, Berkeley, hereafter cited as SFLC papers; Louis B. Perry and Richard S. Perry, *A History of the Los Angeles Labor Movement, 1911–1941* (Berkeley: University of California Press, 1963), pp. 366–67; U.S., Congress, Senate, Subcommittee of the Committee on Education and Labor, *Report, Violations of Free Speech and Rights of Labor,* Report no. 1150, 77th Cong., 2d sess. (Washington, D.C.: Government Printing Office, 1942), pt. 2, pp. 131, 134–35; hereafter cited as La Follette Committee, *Report.*

7. *Los Angeles Daily News* quoted in Larrowe-1, p. 410; Lew Levenson, "California Casualty List," *Nation,* Aug. 29, 1934, pp. 243–45; [American League Against War and Fascism (Los Angeles Committee)] *California's Brown Book* (Los Angeles: American League Against War and Fascism, 1934), pp. 4–5.

8. *Los Angeles Times,* May 16, 1934, sec. 2, pp. 1, 10.

9. *Voice of the Federation,* June 28, 1935, p. 4; interviews with Bob McElroy, May 31, 1979, and Feb. 3, 1981.

10. Perry and Perry, *History of the Los Angeles Labor Movement,* p. 367; *Foc'sle Head,* July 2, 1934, p. 2; *Voice of the Federation,* June 14, 1935, p. 2.

11. Schmidt quoted in *Voice of the Federation,* June 21, 1935, p. 4; *San Francisco Chronicle,* July 10, 1934, p. 1; Frederic Chiles, "General Strike: San Francisco, 1934—An Historical Compilation Film Storyboard," *Labor History* 22 (Summer 1981): 457; Quin, *The Big Strike,* p. 129; anonymous recollection in Case Files, Coast 1934, 1934 Strike Personal Interviews, ILWU Archives, Anne Rand Research Library, San Francisco; interview with Roy Hudson, Oct. 29, 1981; Paul Eliel, *The Waterfront and General Strikes, San Francisco, 1934: A Brief History* (San Francisco: Hooper Printing Co., 1934), p. 128.

12. [George Larsen] to P. B. Gill, Apr. 26, 1934, Seattle correspondence, 1934, SUP Central Archive, Sailors' Union of the Pacific Headquarters, San Francisco.

13. Francis, "History of Labor on the San Francisco Waterfront," pp. 12, 182–83; ILA Local 38–79, executive board minutes, Oct. 9, 1933, ILWU Archives; Sam Darcy, "The Great West Coast Maritime Strike," *Communist* 13 (July 1934): 671–72.

14. Charles P. Larrowe, *Harry Bridges: The Rise and Fall of Radical Labor in the United States* (New York: Lawrence Hill, 1972), p. 38; Theodore Durein, "Scabs' Paradise," *Reader's Digest* 30 (Jan. 1937): 21; Herbert R. Northrup, *Organized Labor and the Negro* (New York: Harper and Brothers, 1944), pp. 152–53; *San Francisco Chronicle,* May 10, 1934, p. 4; May 13, 1934, p. 3; May 16, 1934, p. 3.

15. Schmidt, *Secondary Leadership in the ILWU,* p. 228. In an interview with the author on Oct. 14, 1981, Schmidt recalled, "All of a sudden, fourteen or fifteen black [longshore]men walked into the office and said, 'Well, we're here. Do you want us?'"

16. Walter Macarthur to Mr. Michelson, Jan. 31, 1936, carton 1, Walter Macarthur, Correspondence and Papers, c. 1905–44, Bancroft Library, University of California, Berkeley, hereafter cited as Macarthur papers; Bridges quoted in Larrowe-1, p. 416; Caves's statement appears in a letter he wrote on Aug. 26, 1938; in "Case of Ferdinand Smith, Vice-President of National Maritime Union of America [Sept. 23, 1938]," p. 17, in ILWU files relating to seamen and maritime unions, carton 12.

17. [George Larsen] to P. B. Gill, Apr. 26, 1934; Nov. 17, 1933; Nov. 23, 1933; George Larsen to John A. Feidje, Dec. 12, 1933; to Carl E. Carter, Feb. 17, 1934; Apr. 6, 1934; Apr. 20, 1934; Carl E. Carter to George Larsen, Mar. 29, 1934, SUP Central Archive, Portland correspondence, 1934.

18. [George Larsen] to John A. Feidje, Oct. 12, 1933; [George Larsen] to Carl E. Carter, Mar. 1, 1934; Mar. 15, 1934; Apr. 6, 1934, SUP Central Archive, Portland correspondence, 1934.

19. "Minutes of Meeting of District Committee[,] International Seamen's Union of America," May 9, 1934, SUP Central Archive, 1934 strike file; [George Larsen] to C. E. Carter, May 11, 1934, SUP Central Archive, Portland correspondence, 1934.

20. *Waterfront Worker*, Oct. 22, 1934, p. 7; May 21, 1934, p. 3; *San Francisco Chronicle*, May 13, 1934, p. 3; Darcy, "The Great West Coast Maritime Strike," p. 670.

21. Interview with Harold Johnson, Aug. 4, 1984.

22. SUP, minutes of headquarters meeting, San Francisco, May 15, 1934; [George Larsen] to P. B. Gill, May 24, 1934, SUP Central Archive, Seattle correspondence, 1934.

23. On the teamsters, see Robert McClure Robinson, "A History of the Teamsters in the San Francisco Bay Area, 1850–1950" (Ph.D. diss., University of California, Berkeley, 1951), pp. 223–63; Paul Eliel, *The Waterfront and General Strikes*, p. 50. Eliel stated: "Had it not been for this stand of the Teamsters' Union the strike of longshoremen would undoubtedly have collapsed within a week or ten days at the most."

24. Sam Darcy, "The San Francisco Bay Area General Strike," *Communist* 13 (Oct. 1934): 995; Bulcke quoted in Joseph Blum and Lisa Rubens, "Strike," *San Francisco Sunday Examiner and Chronicle, California Living Magazine*, July 8, 1984, p. 12; Quin, *The Big Strike*, p. 148. The San Francisco newspapers generally refrained from offering an exact estimate of the number of participants in the general strike. The number of organized workers on strike in San Francisco appears to have been close to fifty thousand. The press did estimate that between forty-two and forty-seven thousand workers struck in the East Bay. However, these figures almost certainly did not include the apparently significant number of unorganized workers who also walked off the job. Therefore, the Communists' estimate of some hundred and twenty-five thousand participants may well be accurate. See William F. Dunne, *The Great San Francisco General Strike: The Story of the West Coast Strike—The Bay Counties' General Strike and the Maritime Workers' Strike* (New York: Workers' Library, 1934), p. 3.

25. J. Paul St. Sure, "Some Comments on Employer Organizations and Collective Bargaining in Northern California Since 1934," an interview conducted by Corinne Gilb for the Institute of Industrial Relations Oral History Project, University of California, Berkeley, 1957, pp. 69–70, 72–73.

26. George Larsen to Andrew Furuseth, May 18, 1934, SUP Central Archive, 1934 strike file; "Seven Seamen," *Fortune* 16 (Sept. 1937): 123.

27. *Waterfront Worker*, May 21, 1934, p. 4.

28. Frances Perkins to Franklin D. Roosevelt, July 15, 1934, in Franklin D. Roosevelt, Papers as President, Official File, 1935–45, 407-B, box 11, Franklin D. Roosevelt Library, Hyde Park, N.Y., hereafter cited as FDR Official File; Quin, *The Big Strike*, pp. 98–99; Eliel quoted in Larrowe-1, p. 444.

29. Interview with Al Richmond, Sept. 17, 1982; "The Maritime Unions," *Fortune* 16 (Sept. 1937): 132; George P. West, "Labor Strategist of the Embarcadero," *New York Times Magazine*, Oct. 25, 1936, p. 7; Frances Perkins, *The Roosevelt I Knew* (New York: Viking Press, 1946), p. 316; Richard L. Neuberger, "Bad-Man Bridges," *Forum* 101 (Apr. 1939): 198–99.

30. Charles A. Madison, *American Labor Leaders: Personalities and Forces in the Labor Movement*, 2d ed. (New York: Frederick Ungar, 1962), p. 409; Estolv E. Ward, *Harry Bridges on Trial* (New York: Modern Age Books, 1940), p. 105; *Voice of the Federation*, Apr. 23, 1936, p. 3.

31. Interview with John P. Olsen, San Francisco, Oct. 22, 1981; Eliel quoted in Larrowe-2, pp. 17–18; Landis quoted in Ward, *Harry Bridges on Trial*, p. 230.

32. Emory Scott Land, "The Reminiscences of Emory Scott Land," Oral History Collection, Columbia University, 1963, p. 191; Louis Adamic, *My America, 1928–1938* (New York: Harper and Brothers, 1938), p. 375; *San Francisco Examiner*, Aug. 30, 1935, p. 8; West, "Labor Strategist of the Embarcadero," p. 7.

33. *Waterfront Worker*, Feb. 11, 1935, p. 6; Oct. 15, 1934, p. 6.

34. John P. Olsen quoted in Chiles, "General Strike: San Francisco, 1934," p. 465.

35. Bruce Minton and John Stuart, *Men Who Lead Labor* (New York: Modern Age Books, 1937), p. 199; Neuberger, "Bad-Man Bridges," p. 199; interview with Sam Darcy, Harvey Cedars, N.J., Dec. 19, 1979; "Herbert Resner: The Recollections of the Attorney for Frank Conner," in *The Shipboard Murder Case: Labor Radicalism and Earl Warren, 1936–1941*, ed. Miriam Feingold Stein (interviewer) (Berkeley: Regional Oral History Office, Bancroft Library, University of California, 1976), pp. 13–14; *Voice of the Federation*, July 19, 1936, p. 4.

36. "The Maritime Unions," p. 137; Matthew Josephson, "Red Skies over the Waterfront," *Collier's*, Oct. 5, 1946, pp. 17, 89–90; Bernstein, *Turbulent Years*, p. 266; Charles P. Larrowe, *Shape-Up and Hiring Hall: A Comparison of Hiring Methods and Labor Relations on the New York and Seattle Waterfronts* (Berkeley: University of California Press, 1955), pp. 16–17; U.S., Congress, Senate, Committee on Interstate and Foreign Commerce, *Waterfront Investigation: New York– New Jersey*, 83d Cong., 1st sess., Report no. 653 (Washington, D.C.: Government Printing Office, 1953), pp. 7–13.

37. *San Francisco Chronicle*, June 17, 1934, pp. 1, 2; June 18, 1934, p. 1.

38. Quin, *The Big Strike*, pp. 84–85; Henry Schmidt interview; *San Francisco Chronicle*, June 29, 1934, p. 1.

39. Quin, *The Big Strike*, pp. 52–53.

40. Eliel quoted in Larrowe-1, pp. 43–44.

41. Darcy interview; Joseph R. Starobin, *American Communism in Crisis, 1943–1957* (Cambridge, Mass.: Harvard University Press, 1972), p. 258; John Brophy, *A Miner's Life*, ed. John O. P. Hall (Madison: University of Wisconsin Press, 1964), p. 275. Brophy was the CIO's first director and, after John L. Lewis, the person most crucial to the organization during its formative stages. A deeply religious Roman Catholic, Brophy eventually became a staunch anti-Communist. In 1938, however, he stridently attacked those who raised the cry of "Communist" within the CIO, lambasting the "social and intellectual bankruptcy of their methods" and

even accusing them of treason. *Labor Herald,* Aug. 25, 1938, p. 2, in John Brophy, Papers, 1917–63, Department of Archives and Manuscripts, Catholic University of America, Washington, D.C.

42. Eliel, *The Waterfront and General Strikes,* p. 128; Darcy interview.

43. Even the San Francisco ILA local passed an anti-Communist resolution, in response to strong pressure from the Labor Council. The resolution declared that any ILA member who refused "to disavow all connections with the Communist element on the waterfront . . . shall be held to trial on charges of insubordination and if found guilty shall be expelled from Local 38–79." Although the resolution was "unanimously concur[r]ed in" at a membership meeting, it seems to have had no effect on the strike committee's close working relationship with the MWIU, the International Labor Defense, and other Communist-led organizations and individuals. Ivan F. Cox to John O'Connell, June 26, 1934, in SFLC papers, carton 11.

44. *Foc'sle Head,* June 28, 1934, p. 2.

45. *Foc'sle Head,* May 18, 1934, p. 1; June 22, 1934, pp. 1, 2; July 2, 1934, p. 2; "A Synopsis of the Events Leading up to and Following the Attempt to Suspend W. W. Caves, from the Office of Chairman of the Strike Committee, Sailors' Union of the Pacific," SUP Central Archive, 1934 strike file; interview with Bob McElroy, May 31, 1979. Eventually Caves was removed from the strike committee. The minutes of a special meeting on June 24 recorded the decision "to suspend W. W. Caves from the strike committee, because he has not been around for three days, and because his attitude and general disposition seems to inject a spirit of dissension in the committee." SUP Strike Committee, minutes of special meeting, San Francisco, June 24, 1934, SUP Central Archive, 1934 strike file.

46. *San Francisco Chronicle,* June 21, 1934, p. 4; *Foc'sle Head,* June 25, 1934, p. 1; Johnson and Merriam quoted in *Nation,* Aug. 29, 1934, p. 228 (emphasis added).

47. Miriam Allen De Ford, "San Francisco: An Autopsy on the General Strike," *Nation,* Aug. 1, 1934, p. 122; ibid., p. 113; John Terry, "The Terror in San Jose," *Nation,* Aug. 8, 1934, p. 162.

48. *San Francisco Chronicle,* July 18, 1934, p. 1; *San Francisco Examiner,* July 18, 1934, p. 1; "Who Owns the San Francisco Police Department?" *Nation,* Aug. 29, 1934, pp. 228–29; Quin, *The Big Strike,* pp. 162–63; Lorena Hickok to Aubrey W. Williams, Aug. 15, 1934, in *One Third of a Nation: Lorena Hickok Reports on the Great Depression,* ed. Richard Lowitt and Maurine Beasley (Urbana: University of Illinois Press, 1981), p. 305; Robert Cantwell, "War on the West Coast: I. The Gentlemen of San Francisco," *New Republic,* Aug. 1, 1934, p. 309; Sam Darcy to author, May 12, 1981. There may have been some workers, even a few strikers, involved in the reign of terror. With sorrow and anger, the *Waterfront Worker* acknowledged the apparent truth of the rumor that "some I.L.A. men were in the posse that helped smash the workers meeting places." *Waterfront Worker,* Sept. 14, 1934, p. 2; Oct. 1, 1934, p. 7.

49. Darcy, "The San Francisco Bay Area General Strike," p. 999.

50. *San Francisco Chronicle,* July 19, 1934, p. 1. Three days earlier the *Chronicle* (July 16, 1934, p. 2) had reported that Bridges recommended the "immediate establishment of food distribution depots in every section of the city." "If the people can't get food," the paper reported Bridges as saying, "the maritime workers and longshoremen will lose the strike."

51. Paul Eliel stated that as the last marchers broke ranks, "a general strike, which up to this time had appeared to many to be a visionary dream of a small group of the most radical workers, became for the first time a practical and realizable objective." Eliel, *The Waterfront and General Strikes,* p. 128.

52. John F. Neylan to F. C. Atherton, Aug. 16, 1934, in John Francis Neylan, Correspondence and Papers, c. 1911–60, Bancroft Library, University of California, Berkeley, box 56. On the role of the San Francisco newspapers in the general strike, see Earl Burke, "Dailies Helped Break General Strike," *Editor and Publisher*, July 28, 1934, p. 5; and Evelyn Seeley, "War on the West Coast: II. Journalist Strikebreakers," *New Republic*, Aug. 1, 1934, pp. 310–12.

53. John A. O'Connell to William Green, July 2, 1934, SFLC papers, carton 31; Frances Perkins to Franklin D. Roosevelt, July 15, 1934, in FDR Official File, 407-B, box 11; Casey quoted in Paul S. Taylor and Norman Leon Gold, "San Francisco and the General Strike," *Survey Graphic* 23 (Sept. 1934): 409; interview with Sam Kagel, July 18, 1984; "Henry Melnikow, and the National Labor Bureau: An Oral History," interview conducted by Corinne Lathrop Gilb, Institute of Industrial Relations, University of California, Berkeley, 1959, pp. 181–82, 189, 197–98; Carl Lynch to Strike Committees, I.S.U. of A., July 18, 1934, SUP Central Archive, 1934 strike file.

54. Quin, *The Big Strike*, pp. 176–77, 179.

55. Paul S. Taylor, "The San Francisco General Strike" (typescript, n.d.), p. 16, in Paul S. Taylor, material relating to agricultural and maritime strikes in California, 1933–42, Bancroft Library, University of California, Berkeley, carton 3; Quin, *The Big Strike*, p. 180.

56. Larrowe, *Harry Bridges*, p. 87; the phrase "all the muck of ages" is from Karl Marx and Friedrich Engels, *The German Ideology*, quoted in Martin Glaberman, *Wartime Strikes: The Struggle Against the No-Strike Pledge in the UAW During World War II* (Detroit: Bewick Editions, 1980), p. 126.

57. John Cooper to George Larsen, July 26, 1934, SUP Central Archive, 1934 strike file.

58. "Proceedings, Special Meeting, Sailors' Union of the Pacific, Maritime Hall Building, San Francisco, July 29, 1934," carton 6, p. 1, Paul Scharrenberg, Correspondence and Papers, Bancroft Library, University of California, Berkeley; hereafter cited as SUP, "Proceedings . . . July 29, 1934."

59. Ibid., pp. 4–5.

60. Ibid., pp. 8, 11–13.

61. *San Francisco Chronicle*, June 30, 1934, p. 2.

62. Johnson quoted in ibid., July 18, 1934, pp. 1, 5.

63. SUP, "Proceedings . . . July 29, 1934," pp. 14–15; the nicknames ridiculing Furuseth appeared in the *Foc'sle Head*, June 29, 1934, p. 1; July 12, 1934, p. 2.

64. SUP, "Proceedings . . . July 29, 1934," p. 14.

65. *San Francisco Chronicle*, July 31, 1934, p. 7.

FURTHER READING

Cherny, Robert. "The Making of a Labor Radical: Harry Bridges, 1901–1934." *Pacific Historical Review*. Forthcoming.

Eliel, Paul. *The Waterfront and General Strikes, San Francisco, 1934: A Brief History*. 1934.

Finlay, William. *Work on the Waterfront: Worker Power and Technological Change in a West Coast Port*. 1988.

Kimeldorf, Howard. *Reds or Rackets? The Making of Radical and Conservative Unions on the Waterfront*. 1988.

————. "World War II and the Deradicalization of American Labor: The ILWU as a Deviant Case." *Labor History* 33 (Spring 1992): 248–278.

Larrowe, Charles P. *Harry Bridges: The Rise and Fall of Radical Labor in the United States.* 1972.

Mills, Herb, and David Wellman. "Contractually Sanctioned Job Action and Workers' Control: The Case of San Francisco Longshoremen." *Labor History* 28 (Spring 1987): 167–195.

Nelson, Bruce. *Workers on the Waterfront: Seamen, Longshoremen, and Unionism in the 1930s.* 1988.

Quam-Wickham, Nancy. "Who Controls the Hiring Hall? The Struggle for Job Control in the ILWU During World War II." In *The CIO's Left-Led Unions,* edited by Steve Rosswurm, pp. 47–67. 1992.

Quin, Mike. *The Big Strike.* 1949.

Schwartz, Harvey. "Harry Bridges and the Scholars." *California History* 59 (Spring 1980): 66–79.

————. *The March Inland: Origins of the ILWU Warehouse Division, 1934–1938.* 1978.

Torigian, Michael. "National Unity on the Waterfront: Communist Politics and the ILWU During the Second World War." *Labor History* 30 (Summer 1989): 409–432.

Weintraub, Hyman. *Andrew Furuseth, Emancipator of the Seamen.* 1959.

Wellman, David. *The Union Makes Us Strong: Radical Unionism on the San Francisco Waterfront.* 1995.

9 A Promise Fulfilled

Mexican Cannery Workers in
Southern California

Vicki Ruiz

EDITOR'S INTRODUCTION

During the interwar period, most Mexicans who came to the United States settled in southern California, with two-thirds of California's Mexican population residing in five southern counties. Los Angeles itself, which in 1900 had a Mexican population of no more than five thousand, had approximately one hundred fifty thousand residents of Mexican birth or heritage in 1930. By 1940, only Mexico City could claim a greater number of Mexican inhabitants.

Although almost 40 percent of Mexicans in California in 1930 were agricultural workers, another large group—nearly one-third—worked in manufacturing, including an even higher proportion of Mexican women. At that time, the food processing industry employed more Mexican women than any other industry.

As the californios became increasingly marginalized and proletarianized in the late nineteenth century, Mexican women's contribution to the family wage through their seasonal labor in agriculture and food processing became more and more essential, as Albert Camarillo, Pedro Castillo, and Richard Griswold del Castillo have shown. Founded in the 1860s, the cannery industry became an important source of women's employment. During the late 1880s, women of Mexican descent began to enter the food processing plants in significant numbers. In 1900, sixteen thousand women labored in California canneries and packing houses, and by the 1930s three-quarters of California's seventy-five thousand cannery workers were women. In southern California, a significant number of these workers were Mexican, especially in Los Angeles, where Mexican women made up 23.5 percent of the total cannery work force.

Although short-lived, the successes of the Cannery and Agricultural Workers Industrial Union in the early 1930s demonstrated the benefits of unionism to many Mexican, Filipino, and Anglo cannery workers. In 1937, a group of union organizers, disillusioned by the AFL's apathy toward the cannery workers, founded the United Cannery, Agricultural, Packing and Allied Workers of America (UCAPAWA) under the auspices of the newly founded CIO.

In this essay, Vicki Ruiz examines the progress of UCAPAWA, with special focus on the Cal San strike of 1939 and the role Mexican women played in the strike. Ties of kinship and ethnicity had resulted in the evolution of a "cannery culture" at the plant. Although men made up only one-quarter of the cannery workers, they were also a part of the cannery culture because of their ethnic and family ties. The cannery workers at Cal San succeeded in attracting community support for their demands and made many gains after the strike.

Women organizers, such as Luisa Moreno and Dorothy Healey, played crucial roles in building UCAPAWA. Some were radicals; in her book *Cannery Workers, Cannery Lives*, Ruiz states that at least seven women leaders were members of the American Communist party. Whatever their political persuasion or gender, the leaders of UCAPAWA strove to build a union that maximized rank-and-file participation.

By World War II, women made up half of the membership of UCAPAWA. Moreover, in the majority of UCAPAWA locals, women held more than half of the staff and administrative positions. During the early 1940s, the union was successful not only in raising wages significantly but in securing benefits for women in their contracts, such as "equal pay for equal work" clauses and maternity leaves with no forfeiture of seniority.

After World War II, UCAPAWA (reorganized in 1946 as the Food, Tobacco, Agricultural and Allied Workers Union of America [FTA]) was confronted with serious challenges. Jurisdictional battles with the AFL's rival Teamsters Union intensified, while the employers increasingly collaborated with the Teamsters. UCAPAWA did not have the financial resources to match this alliance. In addition, a red-baiting campaign against several UCAPAWA leaders proved effective, and the passage of the anti-labor Taft-Hartley Act in 1947 compounded the union's problems.

By 1949, when the FTA was expelled from the CIO for its alleged pro-Communist line, the membership and the vitality of the union had dwindled. Nevertheless, as Ruiz concludes in this article, the history of

UCAPAWA "demonstrates that Mexican women, given sufficient opportunity and encouragement, could exercise control over their work lives, and their family ties and exchanges on the line became the channels for unionization."

◆ ◆ ◆

Since 1930 approximately one-quarter of all Mexican women wage earners in the Southwest have found employment as blue collar industrial workers (25.3 percent in 1930, 25.6 percent in 1980).[1] These women have been overwhelmingly segregated into semi-skilled, assembly line positions. Garment and food processing firms historically have hired Mexicanas for seasonal line tasks. Whether sewing slacks or canning peaches, these workers have generally been separated from the year-round, higher paid male employees. This ghettoization by job and gender has in many instances facilitated labor activism among Mexican women. An examination of a rank and file union within a Los Angeles cannery from 1939 to 1945 illuminates the transformation of women's networks into channels for change.

On August 31, 1939, during a record-breaking heat wave, nearly all of the four hundred and thirty workers at the California Sanitary Canning Company (popularly known as Cal San), one of the largest food processing plants in Los Angeles, staged a massive walk-out and established a twenty-four-hour picket line in front of the plant. The primary goals of these employees, mostly Mexican women, concerned not only higher wages and better working conditions, but also recognition of their union—the United Cannery, Agricultural, Packing and Allied Workers of America, Local 75—and a closed shop.

The Cal San strike marked the beginning of labor activism by Mexicana cannery and packing workers in Los Angeles. This essay steps beyond a straight narrative chronicling the rise and fall of UCAPAWA locals in California. It provides a glimpse of cannery life—the formal, as well as the informal, social structures governing the shop floor. An awareness of the varying lifestyles and attitudes of women food processing workers will be developed in these pages. No single model representing either the typical female or typical Mexicana industrial worker exists. Contrary to the stereotype of the Hispanic woman tied to the kitchen, most Mexican women, at some point in their lives, have been wage laborers. Since 1880, food processing has meant employment for Spanish-speaking women living in California, attracted to the industry because of seasonal schedules and extended family networks within the plants.[2]

During the 1930s, the canning labor force included young daughters, newly married women, middle-aged wives, and widows. Occasionally, three generations worked at a particular cannery—daughter, mother, and grandmother. These Mexicanas entered the job market as members of a family wage economy. They pooled their resources to put food on the table. "My father was a busboy," one former Cal San employee recalled, "and to keep the family going . . . in order to bring in a little more money . . . my mother, my grandmother, my mother's brother, my sister and I all worked together at Cal San."[3]

Some Mexicanas, who had worked initially out of economic necessity, stayed in the canneries in order to buy the "extras"—a radio, a phonograph, jazz records, fashionable clothes. These consumers often had middle-class aspirations and, at times, entire families labored to achieve material advancement (and in some cases, assimilation), while in others, only the wives or daughters expressed interest in acquiring an American lifestyle. One woman defied her husband by working outside the home. Justifying her action, she asserted that she wanted to move to a "better" neighborhood because she didn't want her children growing up with "Italians and Mexicans."[4]

Some teenagers had no specific, goal-oriented rationale for laboring in the food processing industry. They simply "drifted" into cannery life; they wanted to join their friends at work or were bored at home. Like the first women factory workers in the United States, the New England mill hands of the 1830s, Mexican women entered the labor force for every conceivable reason and for no reason at all. Work added variety and opened new avenues of choice.[5]

In one sense, cannery labor for the unmarried daughter represented a break from the traditional family. While most young Mexicanas maintained their cultural identity, many yearned for more independence, particularly after noticing the more liberal lifestyles of self-supporting Anglo co-workers. Sometimes young Mexican women would meet at work, become friends, and decide to room together. Although their families lived in the Los Angeles area and disapproved of their daughters living away from home, these women defied parental authority by renting an apartment.[6]

Kin networks, however, remained an integral part of cannery life. These extended family structures fostered the development of a "cannery culture." A collective identity among food processing workers emerged as a result of family ties, job segregation by gender, and working conditions. Although women made up seventy-five percent of the labor force in California canneries and packing houses, they were clustered into specific departments—washing, grading, cutting, canning, and packing—and their earnings varied with production levels. They engaged in piece work while male employees, conversely, as warehousemen and cooks, received hourly wages.[7]

Mexicana family and work networks resembled those found by historian Thomas Dublin in the Lowell, Massachusetts, mills in the ante-bellum era. California canneries and New England cotton mills, though a century apart, contained similar intricate kin and friendship networks. Dublin's statement that women "recruited one another . . . secured jobs for each other, and helped newcomers make the numerous adjustments called for in a very new and different setting" can be applied directly to the Mexican experience. Mexican women, too, not only assisted their relatives and friends in obtaining employment but also initiated neophytes into the rigor of cannery routines. For instance, in the sorting department of the California Sanitary Canning Company, seasoned workers taught new arrivals the techniques of grading peaches. "Fancies" went into one bin; those considered "choice" into another; those destined for fruit cocktail into a third box; and finally the rots had to be discarded. Since peach fuzz irritated bare skin, women shared their cold cream with the initiates, encouraging them to coat their hands and arms in order to relieve the itching and to protect their skin from further inflammation.[8] Thus, as Dublin notes for the Lowell mills, one can find "clear evidence of the maintenance of traditional kinds of social relationships in a new setting and serving new purposes."[9]

Standing in the same spots week after week, month after month, women workers often developed friendships crossing family and ethnic lines. While Mexicanas constituted the largest number of workers, many Russian Jewish women also found employment in southern California food processing firms.[10] Their day-to-day problems (slippery floors, peach fuzz, production speed-ups, arbitrary supervisors, and even sexual harassment) cemented feelings of solidarity among these women, as well as nurturing an "us against them" mentality in relation to management. They also shared common concerns such as seniority status, quotas, wages, and child care.

Child care was a key issue for married women, who at times organized themselves to secure suitable babysitting arrangements. In one cannery, the workers established an off-plant nursery and hired and paid an elderly woman who found it "darn hard . . . taking care of 25 to 30 little ones." During World War II, some Orange County cannery workers, stranded without any day care alternatives, resorted to locking their small children in their cars. These particular workers, as UCAPAWA members, fought for and won management-financed day care on the firm's premises, which lasted for the duration of World War II.[11] Cooperation among women food processing workers was an expression of their collective identity within the plants.

At Cal San many Mexican and Jewish workers shared another bond— neighborhood. Both groups lived in Boyle Heights, an East Los Angeles working-class community. Although Mexican and Jewish women lived on different blocks, they congregated at street car stops during the early morning hours. Sometimes friendships developed across ethnic lines. These women, if not friends, were at least passing acquaintances. Later, as UCAPAWA members, they would become mutual allies.[12]

Cannery workers employed a special jargon when conversing among themselves. Speaking in terms of when an event took place by referring to the fruit or vegetable being processed, workers knew immediately when the incident occurred, for different crops arrived on the premises during particular months. For instance, the phrase "We met in spinach, fell in love in peaches, and married in tomatoes" indicates that the couple met in March, fell in love in August, and married in October.[13]

Historians Leslie Tentler and Susan Porter Benson, studying women workers on the east coast, have also documented the existence of female work cultures. However, unlike the women Tentler studied, Spanish-speaking cannery workers were not waiting for Prince Charming to marry them and take them away from factory labor. Mexican women realized that they probably would continue their seasonal labor after marriage. Also in contrast, Benson, delineating cooperative work patterns among department store clerks from 1890 to 1940, asserted that women experienced peer sanctions if they exceeded their "stint," or standard sales quota.[14] Mexican cannery workers differed from eastern clerks in that they did not receive a set salary, but were paid according to their production level. Collaboration and unity among piece rate employees attested to the strength of the cannery culture. Although increasing managerial control at one level, gender-determined job segmentation did facilitate the development of a collective identity among women in varying occupations and of diverse ethnic backgrounds.

Of these work-related networks, the cannery culture appeared unique in that it also included men. Making up twenty-five percent of the labor force, men also felt a sense of identity as food processing workers. Familial and ethnic bonds served to integrate male employees into the cannery culture. Mexicans, particularly, were often related to women workers by birth or marriage. In fact, it was not unusual for young people to meet their future spouses inside the plants. Cannery romances and courtships provided fertile *chisme*, which traveled from one kin or peer network to the next.[15]

The cannery culture was a curious blend of Mexican extended families and a general women's work culture, nurtured by assembly line segregation and common interests. Networks within the plants cut across generation, gender, and ethnicity. A detailed examination of the California Sanitary Canning Company further illuminates the unique collective identity among food processing workers. Cal San, a one plant operation, handled a variety of crops—apricots and peaches in the summer, tomatoes and pimentoes in the fall, spinach in the winter and early spring. This diversity enabled the facility, which employed approximately four hundred people, to remain open at least seven months a year.[16]

Female workers received relatively little for their labors as a result of the seasonal nature of their work and the piece rate scale. In the Cal San warehouse and kitchen departments, exclusively male areas, workers received an hourly wage ranging from fifty-eight to seventy cents an hour. On the other hand, in the washing, grading, cutting, and canning divisions, exclusively female areas, employees earned according to their production level.[17] In order to make a respectable wage, a woman had to secure a favorable position on the line, a spot near the chutes or gates where the produce first entered the department. Carmen Bernal Escobar, a former Cal San employee, recalled:

> There were two long tables with sinks that you find in old-fashioned houses and fruit would come down out of the chutes and we would wash them and put them out on a belt. I had the first place so I could work for as long as I wanted. Women in the middle hoarded fruit because the work wouldn't last forever and the women at the end really suffered. Sometimes they would stand there for hours before any fruit would come down for them to wash. They just got the leftovers. Those at the end of the line hardly made nothing.[18]

Although an efficient employee positioned in a favorable spot on the line could earn as much as one dollar an hour, most women workers averaged thirty to thirty-five cents. Their male counterparts, however, earned from $5.25 to $6.25 per day.[19]

Though wages were low, there was no dearth of owner paternalism. Cal San's owners, George and Joseph Shapiro, took personal interest in the firm's operations. Both brothers made daily tours of each department, inspecting machinery, opening cans, and chatting with personnel. Sometimes a favored employee—especially if young, female, and attractive—would receive a pat on the cheek or a friendly hug; or as one informant stated, "a good pinch on the butt." [20]

While the Shapiros kept close watch on the activities within the cannery, the foremen and floor ladies exercised a great deal of autonomous authority over workers. They assigned them positions on the line, punched their time cards, and even determined where they could buy lunch. Of course, these supervisors could fire an employee at their discretion. One floor lady earned the unflattering sobriquet "San Quentin." Some workers, in order to make a livable wage, cultivated the friendship of their supervisors. One favored employee even had the luxury of taking an afternoon nap. Forepersons also hosted wedding and baby showers for "their girls." While these "pets" enjoyed preferential treatment, they also acquired the animosity of their co-workers. [21]

The supervisors (all Anglo) neither spoke nor understood Spanish. The language barrier contributed to increasing tensions inside the plant, especially when management had the authority to discharge an employee for speaking Spanish. Foremen also took advantage of the situation by altering production cards of workers who spoke only Spanish. One foreman, for example, was noted for routinely cheating his Mexicana mother-in-law out of her hard-earned wages. Some women sensed something was wrong but either could not express their suspicions or were afraid to do so. Bilingual employees, cognizant of management's indiscretions, were threatened with dismissal. [22] In general, low wages, tyrannical forepersons, and the "pet" system prompted attempts at unionization. In 1937 a group of workers tried to establish an American Federation of Labor union, but a stable local failed to develop. Two years later Cal San employees renewed their trade union efforts, this time under the banner of UCAPAWA-CIO. [23]

The United Cannery, Agricultural, Packing and Allied Workers of America has long been an orphan of twentieth-century labor history even though it was the seventh largest CIO affiliate in its day. Probable reasons for this neglect include the union's relatively short life—1937–1950—and its eventual expulsion from the CIO on the grounds of alleged communist domination. UCAPAWA's leadership was left-oriented, although not directly connected to the Communist Party. Many of the executive officers and organizers identified themselves as Marxists, but others could be labeled New Deal liberals. As one UCAPAWA national vice-president, Luisa Moreno, stated, "UCAPAWA was a *left* union, not a communist union." Union leaders shared a vision of a national, decentralized labor union, one in which power flowed from below. Local members controlled their own meetings, elected their own officers and business agents. National and state offices helped coordinate the individual needs and endeavors of each local. Moreover, UCAPAWA's deliberate recruitment of Black, Mexican, and female labor organizers and subsequent unionizing campaigns aimed at minority workers reflected its leaders' commitment to those sectors of the working class generally ignored by traditional craft unions.[24]

This CIO affiliate, in its policies and practices, closely resembled the nineteenth-century Knights of Labor. Like the Knights, UCAPAWA leaders publicly boasted that their organizations welcomed all persons regardless of race, nationality, creed, or gender. Both groups fostered grass roots participation as well as local leadership. Perhaps it was no coincidence that the official UCAPAWA motto "An Injury To One Is An Injury To All" paraphrased the Knights' "An Injury To One Is The Concern Of All."[25]

In California, UCAPAWA initially concentrated on organizing agricultural workers, but with limited success. The union, however, began to make inroads among food processing workers in the Northeast and in Texas. Because of its successes in organizing canneries and packing houses, as well as the inability of maintaining viable dues-paying unions among farm workers, union policy shifted. After 1939, union leaders emphasized the establishment of strong, solvent cannery and packing house locals, hoping to use them as bases of operations for future farm labor campaigns.[26] One of the first plants to experience this new wave of activity was the California Sanitary Canning Company.

In July 1939, Dorothy Ray Healey, a national vice-president of UCAPAWA, began to recruit Cal San workers. Healey, a vivacious young woman of twenty-four, already had eight years of labor organizing experience. At the age of sixteen, she participated in the San Jose, California, cannery strike as a representative of the Cannery and Agricultural Workers Industrial Union (C&AWIU). Healey had assumed leadership positions in both the C&AWIU and the Young Communist League.[27]

Dorothy Healey's primary task involved organizing as many employees as possible. She distributed leaflets and membership cards outside the cannery gates. Healey talked with workers before and after work, and visited their homes. She also encouraged new recruits who proselytized inside the plants during lunch time. As former Cal San employee Julia Luna Mount remembered, "Enthusiastic people like myself would take the literature and bring it into the plant. We would hand it to everybody, explain it, and encourage everybody to pay attention." Workers organizing other workers was a common trade union strategy, and within three weeks four hundred (out of 430) employees had joined UCAPAWA. This phenomenal membership drive indicates not only worker receptiveness and Healey's prowess as an activist but also the existence of a cannery culture. Membership cards traveled from one kin or peer network to the next. Meetings were held in workers' homes so that entire families could listen to Healey and her recruits.[28]

The Shapiros refused to recognize the union or negotiate with its representatives. On August 31, 1939, at the height of the peach season, the vast majority of Cal San employees left their stations and staged a dramatic walk-out. Only thirty workers stayed behind, and sixteen of these stragglers joined the picket lines outside the plant the next day. Although the strike occurred at the peak of the company's most profitable season and elicited the support of most line personnel, management refused to bargain with the local. In fact, the owners issued press statements to the effect that the union did not represent a majority of the workers.[29]

In anticipation of a protracted strike, Healey immediately organized workers into a number of committees. A negotiating committee, picket details, and food committees were formed. The strikers' demands included union recognition, a closed shop, elimination of the piece rate system, minimal wage increases, and the dismissal of nearly every supervisor. Healey persuaded the workers to assign top priority to the closed shop demand. The striking employees realized the risk they were taking, for only one UCAPAWA local had secured a closed shop contract.[30]

The food committee persuaded East Los Angeles grocers to donate various staples such as flour, sugar, and baby food to the Cal San strikers. Many business people obviously considered their donations to be advertisements and gestures of goodwill toward their customers. Some undoubtedly acted out of a political consciousness, since earlier in the year East Los Angeles merchants had financed El Congreso De Pueblos Que Hablan Español, the first national civil rights assembly among Latinos in the United States.[31] Whatever the roots of its success, the food committee sparked new strategies among the rank and file.

Early in the strike, the unionists extended their activities beyond their twenty-four-hour, seven days a week picket line outside the plant. They discovered a supplementary tactic—the secondary boycott. Encouraged by their success in obtaining food donations from local markets, workers took the initiative themselves and formed boycott teams. The team leaders approached the managers of various retail and wholesale groceries in the Los Angeles area urging them to refuse Cal San products and to remove current stocks from their shelves. If a manager was unsympathetic, a small band of women picketed the establishment during business hours. In addition, the International Brotherhood of Teamsters officially vowed to honor the strike. It proved to be only a verbal commitment, for many of its members crossed the picket lines in order to pick up and deliver Cal San goods. At one point Mexicana union members became so incensed by the sight of several Teamsters unloading their trucks that they climbed onto the loading platform and quickly "depantsed" a group of surprised and embarrassed Teamsters. The secondary boycott was an effective tactic—forty retail and wholesale grocers abided by the strikers' request.[32]

Action by the National Labor Relations Board further raised the morale of the striking employees. The NLRB formally reprimanded the Shapiros for refusing to bargain with the UCAPAWA affiliate. However, the timing of the strike, the successful boycott, and favorable governmental decisions failed to bring management to the bargaining table. After a two and a half month stalemate, the workers initiated an innovative technique that became, as Healey recalled, "the straw that broke the Shapiros' back."[33]

Both George and Joseph Shapiro lived in affluent sections of Los Angeles, and their wealthy neighbors were as surprised as the brothers to discover one morning a small group of children conducting orderly picket lines on the Shapiros' front lawns. These malnourished waifs carried signs with such slogans as "Shapiro is starving my Mama" and "I'm underfed because my Mama is underpaid." Many of the neighbors became so moved by the sight of these children conducting what became a twenty-four-hour vigil that they offered their support, usually by distributing food and beverages. And if this was not enough, the owners were reproached by several members of their synagogue. After several days of community pressures, the Shapiros finally agreed to meet with Local 75's negotiating team.[34] The strike had ended.

A settlement was quickly reached. Although the workers failed to win the elimination of the piece rate system, they did receive a five cent wage increase, and many forepersons found themselves unemployed. More important, Local 75 had become the second UCAPAWA affiliate (and the first on the west coast) to negotiate successfully a closed shop contract.[35]

The consolidation of the union became the most important task facing Cal San employees. At post-strike meetings, Dorothy Healey outlined election procedures and general operating by-laws. Male and female workers who had assumed leadership positions during the confrontation captured every major post. For example, Carmen Bernal Escobar, head of the secondary boycott committee, became "head shop steward of the women."[36] Soon UCAPAWA organizers Luke Hinman and Ted Rasmussen replaced Dorothy Healey at Cal San. These two men, however, concentrated their organizing energies on a nearby walnut packing plant and, thus, devoted little time to Cal San workers. In late 1940, Luisa Moreno, a UCAPAWA representative, took charge of consolidating Local 75. Like Dorothy Healey, Moreno had a long history of labor activism prior to her tenure with UCAPAWA. As a professional organizer for the AF of L and later for the CIO, Moreno had unionized workers in cigar making plants in Florida and Pennsylvania.[37]

Luisa Moreno helped insure the vitality of Local 75. She vigorously enforced government regulations and contract stipulations. She also encouraged members to air any grievance immediately. On a number of occasions, her fluency in Spanish and English allayed misunderstandings between Mexicana workers and Anglo supervisors. Participation in civic events, such as the annual Labor Day parade, fostered worker solidarity and union pride. The employees also banded together to break certain hiring policies. With one very light-skinned exception, the brothers had refused to hire blacks. With union pressure, however, in early 1942 the Shapiros relented and hired approximately thirty blacks. By mid-1941, Local 75 had developed into a strong, united democratic trade union, and its members soon embarked on a campaign to organize their counterparts in nearby packing plants.[38]

In 1941, Luisa Moreno, recently elected vice-president of UCAPAWA, was placed in charge of organizing other food processing plants in southern California. She enlisted the aid of Cal San workers in consolidating Local 92 at the California Walnut Growers' Association plant, and Elmo Parra, president of Local 75, headed the Organizing Committee. Cal San workers also participated in the initial union drive at nearby Royal Packing, a plant which processed Ortega Chile products. Since ninety-five percent of Royal Packing employees were Mexican, the Hispanic members of Local 75 played a crucial role in the UCAPAWA effort. They also organized workers at the Glaser Nut Company and Mission Pack. The result of this spate of union activism was the formation of Local 3. By 1942, this local had become the second largest UCAPAWA union.[39]

Mexican women played instrumental roles in the operation of Local 3. In 1943, for example, they filled eight of the fifteen elected positions of the local. They served as major officers and as executive board members. Local 3 effectively enforced contract stipulations and protective legislation, and its members proved able negotiators during annual contract renewals. In July 1942, for example, *UCAPAWA News* proclaimed the newly signed Cal San contract to be "the best in the state." Also, in 1943, workers at the Walnut plant successfully negotiated an incentive plan provision in their contract. The local also provided benefits that few industrial unions could match—free legal advice and a hospitalization plan.[40]

Union members also played active roles in the war effort. At Cal San, a joint labor-management production committee worked to devise more efficient processing methods. As part of the "Food for Victory" campaign, Cal San employees increased their production of spinach to unprecedented levels. In 1942 and 1943, workers at the California Walnut plant donated one day's wages to the American Red Cross. Local 3 also sponsored a successful blood drive. Throughout this period, worker solidarity remained strong. When Cal San closed its doors in 1945, the union arranged jobs for the former employees at the California Walnut plant.[41]

The success of UCAPAWA at the California Sanitary Canning Company can be explained by a number of factors. Prevailing work conditions heightened the union's attractiveness. Elements outside the plant also prompted receptivity among employees. These workers were undoubtedly influenced by the wave of CIO organizing drives being conducted in the Los Angeles area. One woman, for example, joined Local 75 primarily because her husband was a member of the CIO Furniture Workers Union.[42] Along with the Wagner Act, passage of favorable legislation, such as the Fair Labor Standards Act, the Public Contracts Act, and the California minimum wage laws (which set wage and hour levels for cannery personnel), led to the rise of a strong UCAPAWA affiliate.[43] Workers decided that the only way they could benefit from recent protective legislation was to form a union with enough clout to force management to honor these regulations.

World War II also contributed to the development of potent UCAPAWA food processing locals, not only in southern California, but nationwide. To feed U.S. troops at home and abroad, as well as the military and civilian population of America's allies, the federal government issued thousands of contracts to canneries and packing houses.[44] Because of this increased demand for canned goods and related products, management required a plentiful supply of content, hard-working employees. Meanwhile, the higher-paying defense industries began to compete for the labor of food processing personnel. Accordingly, canners and packers became more amenable to worker demands than at any other time in the history of food processing. Thus, during the early 1940s, cannery workers, usually at the bottom end of the socio-economic scale, had become "labor aristocrats" as a result of wartime exigencies.[45]

They were in an atypical position to gain important concessions from their employers in terms of higher wages, better conditions, and greater benefits. As UCAPAWA members, women food processing workers utilized their temporary status to achieve an improved standard of living.[46]

Of course, the dedication and organizing skills of UCAPAWA professionals Dorothy Ray Healey and Luisa Moreno must not be minimized. While Healey played a critical role in the local's initial successes, it was under Moreno's leadership that workers consolidated these gains and branched out to help organize employees in neighboring food processing facilities. The recruitment of minority workers by Healey and Moreno and their stress on local leadership reflect the feasibility and vitality of a democratic trade unionism.

Finally, the most significant ingredient accounting for Local 75's success was the phenomenal degree of worker involvement in the building and nurturing of the union. Deriving strength from their networks within the plant, Cal San workers built an effective local. The cannery culture had, in effect, become translated into unionization. Furthermore, UCAPAWA locals provided women cannery workers with the crucial "social space"[47] necessary to assert their independence and display their talents. They were not rote employees numbed by repetition, but women with dreams, goals, tenacity, and intellect. Unionization became an opportunity to demonstrate their shrewdness and dedication to a common cause. Mexicanas not only followed the organizers' leads but also developed strategies of their own. A fierce loyalty developed as the result of rank and file participation and leadership. Forty years after the strike, Carmen Bernal Escobar emphatically declared, "UCAPAWA was the greatest thing that ever happened to the workers at Cal San. It changed everything and everybody."[48]

This pattern of labor activism is not unique. Laurie Coyle, Gail Hershatter, and Emily Honig in their study of the Farah Strike documented the close bonds that developed among Mexican women garment workers in El Paso, Texas. Anthropologist Patricia Zavella has also explored similar networks among female electronics workers in Albuquerque, New Mexico, and food processing workers in San Jose.[49] But while kin and friendship networks remain part of cannery life, UCAPAWA did not last beyond

1950. After World War II, red-baiting, the disintegration of the national union, Teamster sweetheart contracts, and an indifferent NLRB spelled the defeat of democratic trade unionism among Mexican food processing workers. Those employees who refused to join the Teamsters were fired and blacklisted. The Immigration and Naturalization Service, moreover, deported several UCAPAWA activists, including Luisa Moreno.[50] In the face of such concerted opposition, Local 3 could not survive. Yet, the UCAPAWA movement demonstrates that Mexican women, given sufficient opportunity and encouragement, could exercise control over their work lives, and their family ties and exchanges on the line became the channels for unionization.

NOTES

1. Vicki Ruiz, "Working for Wages: Mexican Women in the American Southwest, 1930–1980," Southwest Institute for Research on Working Women, Paper No. 19 (1984): 2.

2. Albert Camarillo, *Chicanos in a Changing Society* (Cambridge, MA: Harvard University Press, 1979), pp. 92, 137, 157, 221; Pedro Castillo, "The Making of a Mexican Barrio: Los Angeles, 1890–1920" (Ph.D. dissertation, University of California, Santa Barbara, 1979), p. 154; Ruiz, "Working for Wages," p. 17.

3. Paul S. Taylor, "Women in Industry," Field Notes for his book *Mexican Labor in the United States, 1927–1930*, Paul S. Taylor Collection, Bancroft Library, Berkeley, CA; Heller Committee for Research in Social Economics of the University of California and Constantine Panuzio, *How Mexicans Earn and Live* (University of California Publications in Economics, 13, No. 1, Cost of Living Studies V) (Berkeley, CA: University of California, 1933), pp. 12, 15. Interview with Julia Luna Mount, November 17, 1983, by the author. The term *family wage economy* first appeared in Louise Tilly and Joan Scott, *Women, Work, and Family* (New York, NY: Holt Rinehart and Winston, 1978).

4. Taylor, Field Notes.

5. Taylor, Field Notes; Caroline F. Ware, *The Early New England Cotton Manufacture* (Boston, MA: Houghton Mifflin Company, 1931; rpt. ed., New York, NY: Johnson Reprint Corporation, 1966), pp. 217–219.

6. Douglas Monroy, "An Essay on Understanding the Work Experience of Mexicans in Southern California, 1900–1939," *Aztlan* 33 (Spring 1981): 70; Taylor, Field Notes.

7. U.S., National Youth Administration, State of California, *An Occupational Study of the Fruit and Vegetable Canning Industry in California*, Prepared by Edward G. Stoy and Frances W. Strong, State of California (1938), pp. 15–39 (hereafter referred to as *N.Y.A. Study*). My thoughts on the development of a cannery culture derive from oral interviews with former cannery and packing house workers and organizers, and from the works of Patricia Zavella, Thomas Dublin, and Louise Lamphere.

8. Thomas Dublin, *Women at Work: The Transformation of Work and Community in Lowell, Massachusetts, 1826–1860* (New York, NY: Columbia University Press, 1979), pp. 41–48; interview with Carmen Bernal Escobar, February 11, 1979, by the author; Mount interview; letter from Luisa Moreno dated March 22, 1983, to the author.

9. Dublin, *Women at Work,* p. 48.

10. Mount interview; Escobar interview.

11. "Interview with Elizabeth Nicholas," by Ann Baxandall Krooth and Jaclyn Greenberg, published in *Harvest Quarterly,* Nos. 3–4 (September–December 1976): 15–16; interview with Luisa Moreno, August 5, 1976, by Albert Camarillo.

12. Howard Shorr, "Boyle Heights Population Estimates: 1940" (unpublished materials); David Weissman, "Boyle Heights—A Study in Ghettos," *The Reflex* 6 (July 1935): 32; Mount interview; interview with Maria Rodriguez, April 26, 1984, by the author. Note: Maria Rodriguez is a pseudonym used at the person's request.

13. Interview with Luisa Moreno, July 27, 1978, by the author.

14. Leslie Woodcock Tentler, *Wage Earning Women: Industrial Work and Family Life in the United States, 1900–1930* (New York, NY: Oxford University Press, 1979), pp. 71–75; Escobar interview; Susan Porter Benson, " 'The Customers Ain't God': The Work Culture of Department Store Saleswomen, 1890–1940," in *Working Class America,* ed. Michael H. Frisch and Daniel J. Walkowitz (Urbana, IL: University of Illinois Press, 1983), pp. 197–198.

15. *N. Y. A. Study,* pp. 15–39; Castillo, "Making of a Mexican Barrio," p. 54; Moreno interview, July 1978; Rodriguez interview, April 1984. Note: *Chisme* means gossip.

16. California Canners' Directory (July 1936), p. 2; Escobar interview; *UCAPAWA News,* September 1939; *Economic Material on the California Cannery Industry,* prepared by Research Department, California CIO Council (February 1946), p. 18; California Governor C. C. Young, Mexican Fact-Finding Committee, *Mexicans in California* (October 1930) (San Francisco, CA: California State Printing Office, 1930; reprinted by R and E Research Associates, San Francisco, CA, 1970), pp. 49–54, 89; interview with Dorothy Ray Healey, January 21, 1979, by the author; Escobar interview; letter from Luisa Moreno dated July 28, 1979, to the author.

17. U. S., Department of Labor, Women's Bureau, *Application of Labor Legislation to the Fruit and Vegetable Preserving Industries* (Bulletin of the Women's Bureau, No. 176) (Washington, D.C.: Government Printing Office, 1940), p. 90; Escobar interview; *N. Y. A. Study,* pp. 15–39.

18. Escobar interview; Rodriguez interview.

19. Escobar interview; *N. Y. A. Study,* pp. 15–39.

20. Escobar interview; Mount interview.

21. Escobar interview; Healey interview.

22. Escobar interview.

23. Victor B. Nelson-Cisneros, "UCAPAWA and Chicanos in California: The Farm Worker Period," *Aztlan* 6 (Fall 1976): 463.

24. Interview with Luisa Moreno, September 6, 1979, by the author; Healey interview; Moreno interview, August 1976; Moreno interview, July 1978; *Report of Donald Henderson, General President* to the Second Annual Convention of the United Cannery, Agricultural, Packing and Allied Workers of America (San Francisco, CA, December 12–16, 1938), pp. 14, 22, 32–33; *Proceedings,* First National Convention of the United Cannery, Agricultural, Packing and Allied Workers of America (Denver, CO, July 9–12, 1937), p. 21; *New York Times,* November 24, 1938; *Proceedings,* Third National Convention of United Cannery, Agricultural, Packing and Allied Workers of America (Chicago, IL, December 3–7, 1940), pp. 60–66.

25. Philip S. Foner, *Women and the American Labor Movement* (New York,

NY: The Free Press, 1979), pp. 190–194, 197–198, 211–212; Susan Levine, "Labor's True Woman: Domesticity and Equal Rights in the Knights of Labor," *Journal of American History* 70 (September 1983): 323–339; Sidney Lens, *The Labor Wars* (Garden City, NY: Anchor Books, 1974), p. 65; *Constitution and By-Laws*, as amended by the Second National Convention of the United Cannery, Agricultural, Packing and Allied Workers of America, Effective December 17, 1938, pp. 2, 26–27.

26. Sam Kushner, *Long Road to Delano* (New York, NY: International Publishers, 1975), pp. 90–91; Nelson-Cisneros, "UCAPAWA and Chicanos in California," pp. 460–467, 473; *Proceedings*, Third UCAPAWA Convention, p. 10; *Executive Officers' Report*, pp. 9–10.

27. Nelson-Cisneros, "UCAPAWA and Chicanos in California," p. 463; Healey interview; *UCAPAWA News*, October 1939.

28. Healey interview; Escobar interview; *UCAPAWA News*, September 1939; Mount interview.

29. Escobar interview; Healey interview; *UCAPAWA News*, September 1939; *Los Angeles Times*, September 1, 1939.

30. Healey interview; Escobar interview.

31. Escobar interview; Moreno interview, August 1976; Albert Camarillo, *Chicanos in California* (San Francisco, CA: Boyd & Fraser, 1984), pp. 61–63.

32. *UCAPAWA News*, September 1939; *UCAPAWA News*, December 1939; Escobar interview.

33. *UCAPAWA News*, September 1939; Healey interview.

34. Healey interview; *UCAPAWA News*, September 1939; *UCAPAWA News*, December 1939.

35. Healey interview; Escobar interview; *UCAPAWA News*, December 1939.

36. Escobar interview; Healey interview; Moreno letter, July 1979.

37. Moreno interview, September 1979; Moreno interview, August 12–13, 1977, with Albert Camarillo; Escobar interview; Moreno interview, July 1978.

38. Escobar interview; Moreno interview, September 1979; Moreno letter, July 1979.

39. *UCAPAWA News*, August 25, 1941; Moreno interview, September 1979; Moreno letter, July 1979; *UCAPAWA News*, November 17, 1941; *UCAPAWA News*, December 1, 1941.

40. *UCAPAWA News*, February 1, 1943; *UCAPAWA News*, July 15, 1942; *UCAPAWA News*, December 15, 1943; *UCAPAWA News*, June 15, 1942; *UCAPAWA News*, July 1, 1944.

41. *UCAPAWA News*, April 10, 1942; *UCAPAWA News*, April 1, 1943; *UCAPAWA News*, March 11, 1942; *UCAPAWA News*, May 15, 1943; *FTA News*, January 1, 1945; Moreno interview, September 1979; Moreno letter, July 1979.

42. Escobar interview. For more information concerning other CIO campaigns, see Luis Leobardo Arroyo, "Chicano Participation in Organized Labor: The CIO in Los Angeles, 1938–1950," *Aztlan* 6 (Summer 1975): 277–303.

43. Women's Bureau Bulletin, *Application of Labor Legislation*, pp. 3–8, 102–103.

44. Vicki L. Ruiz, "UCAPAWA, Chicanas, and the California Food Processing Industry, 1937–1950" (Ph.D. dissertation, Stanford University, 1982), pp. 164, 194.

45. The term *labor aristocracy* first appeared in E. J. Hobsbawm's *Labouring Men: Studies in the History of Labour* (New York, NY: Basic Books, Inc., 1964). Other historians have refined the applicability and criteria for the term.

46. Ruiz, "UCAPAWA, Chicanas," pp. 151–176.

47. Sara Evans has defined "social space" as an area "within which members of an oppressed group can develop an independent sense of worth in contrast to their received definitions as second-class or inferior citizens." *Personal Politics* (New York, NY: Vintage Books, 1980), p. 219.

48. Escobar interview.

49. Laurie Coyle, Gail Hershatter, and Emily Honig, "Women at Farah: An Unfinished Story," in *Mexican Women in the United States*, ed. Magdalena Mora and Adelaida Del Castillo (Los Angeles, CA: Chicano Studies Research Publications, 1980); Patricia Zavella, "Support Networks of Young Chicana Workers," paper presented at the Western Social Science Association Meeting, Albuquerque, New Mexico, April 29, 1983; Patricia Zavella, "Women, Work, and Family in the Chicano Community: Cannery Workers of the Santa Clara Valley" (Ph.D. dissertation, University of California, Berkeley, 1982).

50. For more information on the Teamster take-over, see Ruiz, "UCAPAWA, Chicanas," pp. 206–243.

FURTHER READING

See also the lists of suggested readings for chapters 6 and 7.

Daniel, Cletus E. *Bitter Harvest: A History of California Farmworkers, 1870–1941.* 1981.

DeWitt, Howard A. "The Filipino Labor Union: The Salinas Lettuce Strike of 1934." *Amerasia Journal* 5 (1978): 1–22.

Galarza, Ernesto. *Merchants of Labor: The Mexican Bracero Story.* 1964.

García, Mario T. "Americans All: The Mexican-American Generation and the Politics of Wartime Los Angeles, 1941–1945." *Social Science Quarterly* 65 (June 1984): 278–289.

———. *Memories of Chicano History: The Life and Narrative of Bert Corona.* 1994.

Gonzalez, Gilbert G. "Labor and Community: The Camps of Mexican Citrus Pickers in Southern California." *Western Historical Quarterly* 22 (August 1991): 289–312.

Guerin-Gonzales, Camille. "Conversing Across Boundaries of Race, Ethnicity, Gender, and Region: Latino and Latina Labor History." *Labor History* 35 (Fall 1994): 547–563.

Healey, Dorothy, and Maurice Isserman. *Dorothy Healey Remembers: A Life in the American Communist Party.* 1990.

Matthews, Glenna. "The Fruit Workers of the Santa Clara Valley: Alternative Paths to Union Organization During the 1930s." *Pacific Historical Review* 54 (February 1985): 51–70.

McWilliams, Carey. *Factories in the Field: The Story of Migratory Farm Labor in California.* 1939.

Monroy, Douglas. "Anarquismo y Communismo: Mexican Radicalism and the Communist Party in Los Angeles During the 1930s." *Labor History* 24 (1983): 34–59.

Reisler, Mark. *By the Sweat of Their Brow: Mexican Immigrant Labor in the United States, 1900–1940.* 1976.

Ruiz, Vicki L. *Cannery Women, Cannery Lives: Mexican Women, Unionization, and the California Food Processing Industry, 1930–1950.* 1987.

Taylor, Paul S. "Foundations of California Rural Society." *California Historical Society Quarterly* 24 (September 1945): 193–228.

———. *Mexican Labor in the United States.* 1928.

Weber, Devra. *Dark Sweat, White Gold: California Farmworkers, Cotton, and the New Deal.* 1994.

Wollenberg, Charles. "Huelga, 1928 Style: The Imperial Valley Cantaloupe Workers' Strike." *Pacific Historical Review* 28 (February 1969): 45–68.

Zavella, Patricia. *Women's Work and Chicano Families: Cannery Workers of the Santa Clara Valley.* 1987.

4

WORKERS AND POLITICS

10   To Save the Republic

The California Workingmen's Party in Humboldt County

Daniel Cornford

EDITOR'S INTRODUCTION

By the mid-1850s, the prospects of a Californian striking it rich at the gold diggings were slim. Most of the prime mining sites were controlled by corporations. Nevertheless, thousands of people continued to migrate to California with great expectations of a better life in the Golden State.

While various studies have documented significant upward social and economic mobility after the gold rush, especially in San Francisco, California was still subject to the ups and downs of the national economy. Although some found riches on the Far West frontier, others experienced failure and disappointment. The opening of the transcontinental railroad in 1869 did not bring the prosperity and stability the railroad promoters had promised; indeed, its completion coincided with the onset of the "Terrible Seventies." An increased labor supply, the competition of cheap goods from the national market, and a national depression beginning in 1873 resulted in a sharp decline in wages and high levels of unemployment for most of the 1870s. All this came at a time when the Chinese population of San Francisco was growing rapidly, and inevitably the already strong anti-Chinese sentiment of many workingmen was fueled even further.

At the same time, farmers found that the railroad charged them exorbitant shipping fees, even as the prices of almost all their crops plummeted. Prospective California farmers discovered that much of the cultivatable land was still the subject of litigation dating back to the Mexican land disputes of the 1850s and that vast amounts of land had been engrossed by land speculators with the apparent connivance of the state government. In his pamphlet *Our Land and Land Policy* (1871), Henry George lamented: "In all of the new States of the Union land monopolization has gone on at an alarming rate, but in none of them so fast as California, and in none of them perhaps, are its evil effects so manifest."

By the early 1870s, growing economic and social discontent was finding expression in various third-party political movements. Many Californians believed that the problems were as much political as economic and that the woes of working people were attributable to the machinations and corruption of politics at all levels of government. In 1877, this political dissent came to a head in the wake of a massive railroad strike in the East. Under the leadership of Denis Kearney, the Workingmen's Party of California (WPC) was founded. Within months, it had become a major force, with branches in most California counties, and it elected many representatives. Most spectacularly, in 1878 it elected a third of the delegates to a state constitutional convention—only the collaboration of the Democrats and the Republicans prevented these delegates from controlling the convention.

These developments attracted the interest of many of the world's most illustrious political observers. Englishman Lord Bryce visited California in the 1870s and was so fascinated by the WPC that in his classic work *American Commonwealth* he devoted a chapter to "Kearneyism in California." In 1880, Karl Marx appealed to his American correspondent Friedreich Sorge for "something good (meaty) on economic conditions in California," and added, "California is very important to me because nowhere else has the upheaval shamelessly caused by capitalist concentration taken place with such speed."

Most studies of the WPC have focused on San Francisco and mainly on the role that anti-Chinese sentiment played in the WPC's founding. The following article by Daniel Cornford examines the WPC in Humboldt County, situated in northwest California, two hundred miles north of San Francisco. Although strong anti-Chinese sentiment existed in Humboldt County, other factors were more important in the rise of the WPC in that area.

Tracing the emergence of the WPC back to the late 1860s, this essay describes how a variety of local, state, and even national issues fueled dissenting movements in the county. Crucial to understanding why a dissenting tradition evolved in Humboldt County is the fact that the political culture of most residents was shaped by a cluster of values often referred to as a "democratic-republican" tradition. In essence, Humboldt County inhabitants believed that the American Revolution, and further struggles during the Jacksonian era, had established a republic in which "equal rights" for all should prevail. It is difficult to define this belief precisely, but to Humboldt County residents, developments after the Civil War—in particular, large concentrations of economic power, the perception that "class legislation" was being passed, and the belief that politics at all levels of government was riddled with corruption—violated their notion of what the republic was supposed to be. Viewing themselves as guardians of their cherished republic, a diverse group of farmers and workers united to form a workingmen's party.

Even when the WPC expired in 1880, these watchdogs of the democratic-republican tradition did not let down their guard. Their continued desire to purify the tainted republic was reflected in strong support for the Knights of Labor in the 1880s and the Populist party during the 1890s.

◆   ◆   ◆

Viewed from San Francisco, as it usually is, the California Workingmen's party appears as a reactive formation organized in response to the depression of the 1870s and the flood of Chinese immigrants released into the labor market by the completion of the Transcontinental Railroad.[1] Yet Workingmen's parties were founded in forty of California's fifty-two counties, and within less than a decade labor tickets or parties would appear in one hundred and eighty-nine towns and cities in thirty-four states.[2] Relatively little attention has been paid to dissenting third-party movements in the small towns and rural areas of Gilded Age America, although until 1900 two-thirds of the population lived in such places.[3] Historians of nineteenth-century radicalism have concentrated instead on events in major metropolitan areas. Furthermore, to the extent that the third-party insurgencies of the late 1870s and 1880s have been examined, their ideological and institutional antecedents have often been neglected.

In far northern California's Humboldt County, a radical democratic-republican tradition sustained a succession of dissenting third-party political and social movements, including the California Workingmen's party, the Greenback Labor party, the International Workingmen's Association, the Knights of Labor, and the Populists. Although none lasted more than a few years, the persistent reappearance of such movements indicates the vitality of the critical perspective which spawned them. In newspaper editorials, letters to the local press, diaries, sermons, correspondence to regional and national labor leaders, and in party platforms, Humboldt dissidents, from a wide variety of callings, clearly articulated an ideology shaped by the more radical elements of the values and rhetoric of the American Revolution and Jacksonian democracy.

The radical democratic-republican ideology drew on a cluster of ideas that embraced the notion of "equal rights" and the labor theory of value.[4] This progressive antebellum ideological legacy was sustained and reinforced by the acrimonious Civil War debates in which Union supporters characterized the conflict as one between the noble free laborer of the North and an autocratic slavocracy in the South. Embodied in the free-labor ideology was a deep faith that under a government founded and maintained on true democratic-republican principles the workingman could rapidly ascend the social ladder. A *Humboldt Times* editorial in 1864 argued that "if there is one thing in our government which more than commends it to the people it is the fact that the gate of honor is open to the poor and rich alike."[5] Moreover, any government that deprived a worker of the full product of his labor was guilty of "class legislation" and of fostering the interests of "monopolies" at the expense of the honest toiler. A government that adhered to true republican principles would result in a society in which, according to Humboldt pioneer James Beith, "none are very rich and none very poor."[6] While even the most radical upholders of the democratic-republican tradition did not believe in the feasibility or desirability of absolute social equality, nevertheless, as Beith put it, the principal aim of government should be "how to promote best the true social equality."[7]

As they scrutinized Gilded Age America, Humboldt County radicals were greatly alarmed by what they saw. They were convinced that economic power was becoming increasingly and dangerously concentrated and that the once pristine American political system was suffering from a serious affliction evidenced by a series of charges and revelations of corruption in local, state, and national government. Moreover, to the extent that the pioneers of Humboldt and other California counties expected to find a land of boundless opportunity and rough social equality in the Golden State, they were to be sorely disappointed. Within a decade of the Gold Rush, disparities of wealth were as marked as in many of the eastern communities from which the pioneers had come.[8]

Unlike the Eastern urban artisans who have been the focus of most of the important studies of nineteenth-century working-class radicalism, Humboldt's dissenters were not being "deskilled" or seriously affected by the advent of industrialization.[9] Twenty-five years after the Gold Rush had lured the first white settlers to Humboldt County, its economy was based primarily on lumber and agriculture. Humboldt County was on the verge of establishing itself as the heartland of the Redwood Empire's lumber industry. By 1876 there were twenty mills in the county and overall the county's lumber industry employed at least a thousand workers. At this time the lumber industry was centered primarily in Eureka and the vicinity of Arcata. Eureka was the county's "metropolis"; the city and its environs contained approximately a third of the county's 15,000 inhabitants in 1880. Throughout the county, and especially in the fertile Eel River Valley, farming also flourished.[10] The dissenters in Humboldt County constituted a broad coalition of lumber workers, farmers, artisans, and professionals.

Until the end of the Civil War, politics in Humboldt County was dominated by national issues. The county conventions and platforms of the major political parties hardly addressed local issues, and there is little evidence of divisiveness over them. The protracted sectional crisis probably helped subsume tensions, but there were other reasons for the consensus in local politics. Humboldt's pioneers were united by a desire to promote their community to outsiders. Highly conscious of their geographical isolation, they realized the need to attract outside capital and a larger population if the county was to become a viable economic entity. Accordingly, there was a widespread recognition of the need to use county revenues to lay the foundation of a basic economic infrastructure. At the same time, the possibility of discord over appropriations and expenditures was limited by their small scale. In addition, the transience of many early pioneers lessened the chances of polarization over local issues.

In the late 1860s, with the sectional conflict no longer the preeminent issue and with the county population growing and becoming more settled, important questions arose concerning county revenues that brought the consensus to an abrupt end. An increasing number of citizens began to feel that the county was going too deeply into debt to fund internal improvements and that the burden of taxation was falling disproportionately on small farmers and workers. A proposal in 1867 to build a hundred-mile road to link Humboldt County with the state road system raised a storm of protest amid charges of corruption and incompetence in the county government.[11] The bond issue to finance the project was defeated by a vote of 1,038 to 134 in the 1868 election.[12] In 1870, a bitter debate erupted over the extent of the county's indebtedness for expenditures financed by county warrants which no longer sold at anything like their par value. A year later, a plan to build a railroad from Eureka to the Eel River Valley encountered fierce opposition; voters repudiated a proposed $100,000 bond issue 899 to 143.[13]

The Republican party retained its ascendancy over the Democrats in Humboldt County for the immediate postbellum years, but its image was tainted and its support eroded by charges of corruption. A series of letters in the *Northern Independent* alleged that Republican candidate for the state assembly J. De Haven paid almost no local taxes and that the taxes paid by everyone on the 1869 Republican ticket amounted to "a mere pittance."[14] At the same time, H. L. Knight, the future secretary of the California Workingmen's party, charged that the vote at the Republican party convention had been blatantly manipulated to secure the renomination of Humboldt County sheriff W. S. Barnum and that Barnum was guilty of various forms of tax evasion.[15] Barnum's rebuttal was not convincing, and the *Humboldt Times*, which had supported the Republican party since the Civil War, endorsed several "independent" candidates while refraining from disputing the charges. At the election, the Republican party's traditional large majority was severely pruned, and Sheriff Barnum was not reelected.

Increasingly, the issues of taxation, public indebtedness, corruption, and political cliques became linked in the minds of many Humboldt County residents, a perception that was reinforced by their view of developments in state and national politics. To a growing number of people it seemed that, whether the symptom was a corrupt local sheriff or a national Crédit Mobilier scandal, a serious malaise had begun to afflict the American body politic. Numerous instances of actual or alleged corruption at all levels of government in the late 1860s and early 1870s shook people's faith in their political institutions. In Humboldt County, the Republican party had emerged from the Civil War with a large reservoir of moral and political credit that enabled it to buck the trend toward the Democratic party that occurred throughout most of California. But by the early 1870s, many Humboldters felt that the Republicans had exhausted their credit.

In 1871, Louis Tower, who had been an ardent supporter of the Republican party in the 1860s, eloquently expressed the growing sense of foreboding and disenchantment of many Humboldters in a series of articles entitled the "Next Irrepressible Conflict." Tower stated that it was his duty to "call the attention of my fellow laborers—the producers of wealth—to the consideration of our interests as treated in the policies and practices of our government." He asserted that "the tendency of our legislatures both national and state . . . is drifting in favor of capital" and mentioned specifically the growing wealth and power of corporations and railroads; the pervasiveness of corruption in politics; and the "absorption" of the public domain "into the hands of capitalists through Congressional action," which threatened the free laborer with "the fate that has befallen the workers of the older more densely populated countries." Tower spoke of the Republican party in its early days as representing "the rise, progress and culmination of the principle that labor should be free and that the soil, the great bank of labor exchange, should be free also." But, he argued, the conflict between labor and capital was not inevitable, and the "producers of wealth" should form a new party that would elect men of integrity.[16]

The *Humboldt Times* sensed the growing disaffection and entreated the "laboring classes" to retain their loyalty to the Republican party. The newspaper reminded readers that the Democratic party had supported slavery, "the very bane of free labor," had opposed the income tax, and had failed to provide public education in many states; the Republican party, in contrast, had abolished slavery, had thrown open the public lands to settlement, and had established a public educational system in many states.[17] Despite such pleas, disillusionment with the Republicans in Humboldt County mounted. In 1873, when Henry McGowan announced his candidacy for the state assembly as an independent, he expressed many of the same sentiments as Tower. He praised the Republicans for seeing the nation through the ordeal of the Civil War, but, he said, the party "has unfortunately allowed itself to be led by corrupt and designing men into a state of political depravity."[18]

On August 2, 1873, at a mass meeting at Ryan's Hall in Eureka, a Tax-Payer party was formed. The party's formation paralleled but apparently had no direct links with a Tax-Payer Independent party that was beginning to pick up momentum in California under Newton Booth.[19] Booth, the Republican governor of California, had been elected in 1871 with the strong support of the Grange, running on a platform that stressed opposition to railroad subsidies. In Humboldt County, many of the leading figures in the new party were former Republicans. The most notable among them was W. J. Sweasey, who had been chairman of the county's Republican party since the Civil War. Sweasey was elected president of the new party, and a full slate of candidates was chosen for upcoming elections. First among a long list of party resolutions was an expression of strong opposition to "giving lands or money or loaning the National credit to corporations or other persons, for the purposes of creating dangerous monopolies to oppress the people." Another resolution denounced corruption "whether by means of 'Credit Mobilier Frauds' in the East" or "Contract and Finance Companies in California." The Tax-Payer party declared its support for "equality of taxation, so that the burden of maintaining the government shall be borne by the rich in proportion to their wealth." Finally, it endorsed a measure to regulate "the carrying business of the country" by controlling railroad freight rates.[20]

The ensuing campaign was one of the most heated in the county's history. The Tax-Payer party faced difficulties from the outset. The Republican platform, although not quite as populist in tone, was almost indistinguishable from the Tax-Payer program in its planks on taxation, corruption, and monopoly. Several Republican candidates openly acknowledged that corruption and monopoly were serious problems. The Tax-Payer party also had to face the opposition of the county press and repeated allegations that party members were a group of "sore heads and broken down political hacks" who had been shunned by the Republican party, notwithstanding the fact that the Tax-Payer party held its convention before the Republicans.[21]

The Republicans fretted, in particular, about the allegiance of Humboldt's farmers. In 1872 and 1873, there were growing manifestations of their discontent. Farmers in various locales throughout the county began forming Farmers' Protective Unions in 1872 "for the purposes of reflecting the best interests of the farming community of the county and deriving some plan of action for mutual benefit."[22] In 1873, Humboldt County farmers affiliated with the California Grange.[23] While the Humboldt Grange did not make political endorsements, there can be no doubt that the organization reflected deep-seated discontents. Farmers complained repeatedly to the county press about low prices, and the *Humboldt Times* reported that for "several years" local farmers "have received but indifferent rewards for their labor" and that "in some instances it has taken nearly all . . . to pay commission and expenses of transportation."[24]

The overall performance of the Tax-Payer party was impressive. It succeeded in electing its candidate to the state assembly and lost most of the county contests by narrow margins. The extent of the county farmers' disaffection showed in the strong support the Tax-Payer party received in most rural precincts, equivalent to its showings in Eureka and Arcata.[25] The 1873 election was the first electoral expression of a rising tide of dissent in Humboldt County. Rumblings of discontent had been growing louder since the Civil War and were finally crystallizing into a coherent political movement. Several leading political figures in Humboldt County permanently severed their connections with the Republican and, to a lesser extent, Democratic parties. Sweasey emerged as the leading dissident in the county—a position he occupied for the next decade and that culminated in his nomination for the lieutenant governorship of California on the Greenback Labor party ticket in 1882. No one else in the county expressed with such lucidity and forcefulness the profound sense of disillusionment felt by many people.

Sweasey was born in London, England, in 1805. At age twenty-one, he captained a sea vessel engaged in trade with the West Indies. In 1837, he left "'perfidious Albion' to set out for the land of the free," and, shortly after arriving in America, he and his family joined Robert Owen's communitarian settlement in New Harmony, Indiana. For several years he was a "near neighbor" and employee of Owen, whom he described as "an old and valued friend." In the 1840s, Sweasey became involved with the Young America movement before taking the overland route to California in 1850. Soon after his arrival, he became a champion of settlers' rights in their battle with the Spanish land grant holders. He became known as the "Squatter King," and he lived on a ranch near Redwood City until he was evicted. He joined the Democratic party and in 1853 was elected to the California Assembly as a representative from San Francisco. In 1855 he moved to Hydesville, in southern Humboldt County, where he engaged in dairy farming. Within a year, he was chairman of the Humboldt County Democratic party, but shortly after the election of James Buchanan in 1856, he left the party. He helped found the county's Republican party and was its chairman from its inception until 1872.

Sweasey moved with his family to Eureka in 1862 and established a successful general store there.[26] By 1867, in spite of his prominent position in the county's Republican party, Sweasey had become highly critical of the Republican-dominated county administration. Just before the 1873 elections, he severed his ties with the party. He wrote frequent letters to the local press voicing his profound concern at the direction in which he believed America was heading, the most eloquent of which appeared a few months after the 1873 election.

> Look at the corruption and venality exposed in our late national councils. Look at the profligate disposal of our public domain, the noblest inheritance ever bequeathed to a people. Look at our swindling financial system, made and perpetuated to make the rich richer and the poor poorer. Look at the mass of misery and crime in our great cities; near 1,500 homicides in the city of New York alone in one year; thousands thrown houseless, breadless on the street. Why? Are they idle, unwilling to work? Has nature refused her support? Neither. Our harvests were never more bountiful. . . . A cen-

tury ago honesty and ability guided our national councils. Today can we say so? A few years more of this misrule of the weak minded and where will be the superiority of the condition of our people over the condition of the people of the monarchial governments of Europe? Already our taxes are greater than the taxes of any other people or nation. Our lands are held in quantities larger than German principalities; not by aristocracies of birth, but by aristocracies of wealth, by corporations who have no souls, who never die, who control the weak minded men, who fill our legislative halls, both National and State, while thousands upon thousands are suffering for food, shelter and the commonest necessaries of life.[27]

The depression of the late 1870s reinforced the fears of men like Sweasey and led to a revival of organized dissenting political activity. The dissidents were struck both by the social and political turmoil at state and national levels and by unprecedented social and economic dislocations in their own community. The destitution caused by the depression hit Humboldt County as early as January 1877. The *Humboldt Times* complained about the "insufferable nuisance" caused by the "professional beggar."[28] A few weeks later, the *Times* stated that "there seems to be a regularly organized band of ruffians in this city. Scarcely a day passes but what we hear of an assault being made upon some of our citizens."[29]

The depression severely affected the Humboldt County lumber industry as the price of redwood lumber plummeted. In 1876, prices stood at an all-time high of $30 per thousand board feet for clear lumber; by 1879, they had slumped to $18 per thousand feet.[30] Lumber workers' wages were cut by $5 to $25 a month in February 1877, a move that reportedly gave rise to "considerable complaint."[31] After the July 4 holiday that year, lumber employers closed their mills indefinitely. Hundreds of lumber workers lost their jobs, and there were grave predictions about the repercussions on the local economy.[32] Few mills resumed operations in 1877, and poverty and unemployment were widespread. The local press reported that many families were in dire straits. There were recurrent complaints about tramps and incidents of alleged arson.[33]

The press received a stream of anonymous letters that were indicative of growing social tensions. The *Democratic Standard*, which in 1877 came under the auspices of Greenback Labor party supporter William Ayres, provided a fresh outlet for expressions of discontent. In November 1877, it published a strongly worded letter from "Argonaut," insisting that a man had the right to work and warning that, while people prefer legal remedies, "men cannot be patient when they are hungry." He compared the plight of labor to a turtle "upon which the elephants of capital stand."[34] The *Hum-*

boldt Times received an equally strongly worded communication from "Justice":

> Dissensions, like contagions , seem to spread over the country. Even the little Hamlet of Arcata is not an exception. She has a few pioneers who have been fortunate enough to make a little money out of the Indians, the soldiers and the later immigrants, until they have acquired a few town lots and some tenantable housing. Not unlike the railroad kings they are the self-constituted aristocrats who claim the right to extort by law . . . all the blood money possible from the poorer classes.[35]

Another theme expressed in critical letters to the editor was suspicion that public land laws were being violated. One writer charged the county surveyor with long delays in filing plats for preemption claims and suggested that the delays were a conspiracy to aid the "land grabbers."[36] In fact, it was a common practice for large Humboldt County landholders to circumvent the 160-acre homestead limit by paying another person a fee to file the initial claim with the understanding that the land title would soon be transferred to the sponsoring landholder.[37]

Land fraud and the growing concentration of land ownership received considerable attention in the state press. Thus, in 1873 the *Sacramento Daily Record* published articles based on data from the State Board of Equalization which revealed that land distribution had become very skewed in many California counties. These findings were reported in many California newspapers, including the *San Francisco Chronicle* and the *Humboldt Times*.[38] In Humboldt, forty individuals or businesses owned over a thousand acres in 1873, and five owned more than five thousand. One individual owned 23,169 acres.[39] By the late 1870s, letters to the county press on the land question were frequent enough to suggest that sentiment on this issue contributed significantly to the discontent.

In the debates surrounding the election of delegates to the California constitutional convention in 1878, land monopoly and fraud were the most frequently discussed issues.[40] Sweasey wrote several long, impassioned letters on the subject. He asserted that unless reforms were undertaken to ensure a more equitable distribution of land, the result would be "serfdom and slavery or a bloody revolution."[41] He pointed to the turmoil in Ireland as proof of his argument and added that "what was done in Ireland by war and conquest was more successfully done in California by fraud under the pretense of law."[42] Sweasey described in great detail the fraudulent means by which much of California's land was acquired shortly after the Mexican-American War. He insisted that similar frauds were being used to obtain land in parts of California not covered by the Spanish land grants and alluded to one scheme to aggrandize "thirty square leagues, north of Cape Mendocino."[43] In another letter, Sweasey spoke of land monopoly as the "greatest evil," and recalled the day he had witnessed eighty families being evicted from their land under the English enclosure laws to make way for a deer park.[44] At the Franklin Society Debating Club in Eureka in 1878, a schoolteacher, George Sarvis, echoed many of Sweasey's arguments. Sarvis spoke in favor of a motion to limit the amount of land an individual or corporation might own on the grounds that "the holding of large and unlimited quantities of land by one individual or an association of individuals disturbs the unalienable right of each citizen and when carried out, destroys popular government."[45]

Humboldt County farmers were not immediately hit by the depression of the late 1870s. Harvests in 1877 and 1878 were bountiful, and prices for most crops held constant, although they began to fall slightly in 1879. Nevertheless, the county's Grange did not hesitate to join other dissidents in calling for far-reaching reforms. The Grange had become a strong force in the social and political life of the county by the late 1870s. There were at least six branches of the Grange in 1877. Complete lists of branches and membership figures are unfortunately hard to obtain, but the fact that the Ferndale Grange boasted a membership of 150 in 1877 (up from 90 in 1874) suggests that the Humboldt County Grange was flourishing.[46] The Grange performed important social and economic functions. The Table Bluff Grange built its own hall,[47] and all the Granges frequently held dances and other events. The Table Bluff Grange (and perhaps others) also established cooperative retail facilities.[48] In the political realm, Humboldt Grangers stressed the need for a stable and expanded money supply based on silver and greenbacks. And, in general, their prognosis for the American body politic was gloomy. In March 1878, the Ferndale Grange passed the following resolution:

> Whereas, a people view with alarm the growing tendency (by legislation) of a bourbon aristocracy, a system of landlordism such as exists in Germany, England and throughout Europe, and which if not checked soon will finally reduce the working classes of America to mere slaves and vassals. . . . The toiling masses of this country are today to the banks and corporations what the peons of Mexico are to the aristocracy of that so called Republic.
>
> Resolved, that we look upon this bourbon element with suspicion and distrust in their efforts to subvert that form of government bequeathed to us by our fathers, and to erect instead a semi-despotic government, controlled by a centralized aristocracy.[49]

A host of grievances that had been simmering for a decade surfaced in 1877–1878 in the context of the depression and the debate over the need for a new state constitution. Complaints included the costs of state government, inequitable tax laws, corruption in government at all levels, and the political power of the railroads in California and nationwide. This conjuncture of events and discontents led to the formation of a California Workingmen's party in Humboldt and thirty-nine other California counties. Humboldt voters expressed their growing disquiet in September 1877 when a statewide referendum was held on whether to call a convention to rewrite the 1849 California Constitution. In general, Californians content with the status quo were opposed to a convention. Humboldt County voted in favor of a convention by a margin of 10–1 (2,552 votes to 258);[50] voters statewide approved the measure by less than a 2–1 majority (73,400 to 44,200).[51]

In San Francisco, another issue gained prominence at this time. Anti-Chinese sentiment reached new heights during the depression of the late 1870s, a fact that historians have viewed as the most important element in the birth of the Workingmen's party there. The Chinese population of Humboldt County also increased, from 38 in 1870 to 242 in 1880,[52] and by the late 1870s Eureka possessed a Chinatown of sorts.[53] The local press commented occasionally on the alleged existence of opium dens and brothels in Eureka's Chinatown, and several attacks on Chinese people, usually by Eureka youths, took place. Notwithstanding this, and the fact that in 1885 Eureka achieved the dubious distinction of being one of the first western communities to expel its Chinese population, Sinophobia was not a major issue in county politics in the late 1870s for a number of reasons.[54] First, by 1880 the Chinese constituted only 1.5 percent of the county's population, whereas in San Francisco they made up 16.3 percent of the inhabitants, and they were 8.7 percent of the state population. Moreover, Humboldt's Chinese population was relatively dispersed. Eureka, with its so-called Chinatown, in 1880 contained only 101 Chinese people. Second, while competition from Chinese labor may have aroused some animosity, few Chinese were employed in the county's two principal industries, lumber and agriculture. Most worked as miners (66), laborers (62), cooks (37), and in the laundry business (23). Only 6 of the 228 Chinese employed in the county worked in the lumber industry.[55] Thus, the Chinese in Humboldt County did not threaten white labor as directly as they did in San Francisco and other parts of California. Significantly, when lumber employers tried to make more extensive use of Chinese labor in the early 1880s, anti-Chinese sentiment rose dramatically. Undoubtedly, most

Humboldters favored Chinese exclusion by the late 1870s, but a host of other grievances were far more important in the formation of the California Workingmen's party.

The Humboldt County Workingmen's party was organized in May 1878 to participate in elections to choose delegates to the California constitutional convention. Sweasey, the party's first chairman, was the candidate for the county delegate seat. J. N. Barton, a farmer from Ferndale, received the senatorial nomination for the 27th District. The party's convention passed a string of resolutions: Public officers convicted of bribery should be liable to a twenty-year jail sentence; taxes should be levied only "to meet the expenses of government"; and "taxation should be equal, so that the burden of maintaining government be borne by the rich in proportion to their wealth." Also, railroads should be taxed in relation to their "actual cash value," while the large landholdings of corporations and wealthy individuals should be taxed at the same rate per acre as small landholders. All legal means should be used to halt the immigration of the Chinese "and other inferior races who cannot amalgamate with us."[56] A few days after the convention, the party founded a newspaper, the *Workingman*, edited by Sweasey and Barton.

The county Democratic and Republican organizations joined forces to elect delegates to the constitutional convention. County judge C. G. Stafford applauded this cooperation, for "as matters now stand it is possible for the Communists to get control of the Convention."[57] The fusion plan aroused the ire of the Workingmen's party. The *Democratic Standard* asserted that "the managers of the two parties, under the direction of the monopolists, have joined hands . . . against the 'common enemy,' that is, the workingman."[58]

At the June 19 election, the Humboldt County Workingmen's party triumphed over the "nonpartisan" party. Both Sweasey and Barton were elected delegates to the constitutional convention. On the whole, the votes for the two men were remarkably evenly distributed over the county, with both candidates picking up approximately the same levels of support in Eureka as they did in the rural precincts. In Eureka, Sweasey and Barton won fifty-six percent and sixty percent of the vote, respectively. Outside Eureka, Sweasey's share of the vote in all precincts combined was slightly lower (fifty percent) and Barton's somewhat higher (sixty-seven percent). The consistency of the two men's performance throughout the county's twenty-three precincts indicates the breadth of support for the Workingmen's party.[59]

Barton proved an especially effective spokesman at the constitutional convention. He spoke with particular stridency on the issue of "land grabbing," calling for a state investigation and the repossession of fraudulently acquired lands. But he declared that he was pledged to no "agrarian measures" and that he was not at the convention "to disturb the rights of property." He advocated "equal taxation" as the best means to stop land grabbing. To this end, he introduced several resolutions calling for amendments to the state's tax system, including the adoption of a state income tax. He also spoke in favor of retrenchment in state expenditures and a reduction in the salaries of state officials.[60]

The Humboldt Workingmen's party was pleased with the outcome of the constitutional convention, unlike the San Francisco branch of the party, which split on the question of ratification. Within two weeks of the convention, the Humboldt party launched a vigorous campaign to ratify the new constitution, which promised strict regulation of railroads and other public utilities, a more equitable system of taxation, an eight-hour day on all public works projects, and a series of anti-Chinese provisions. The *Democratic Standard* was the only newspaper in the county to endorse ratification unequivocally. It denounced the California Democratic party for opposing ratification and accused the party of betraying "the true principles taught us by a Jefferson and a Jackson," and called on its readers to "remember General Jackson and his war upon the privileged classes."[61] In the ratification referendum on May 7, 1879, California voters endorsed the new constitution by a relatively small margin of 77,959 to 67,134 votes; but in Humboldt County the ratification majority was much more decisive, with 1,714 votes in favor and 1,051 against.[62]

The Humboldt Workingmen's party perceived the ratification as a triumph for the workingman, and the party's success encouraged the belief that the time was ripe for a basic realignment of political forces to regenerate a corrupt and decadent American body politic. With remarkable frequency, letters to local newspapers harkened back nostalgically to the days of Jefferson and Jackson when the American republic supposedly had true Democrats at the helm. As one voter, "Jeffersonian," put it: "We are upon the eve of a reorganization of political forces. The two old parties have had their day." The Democratic party represented democracy in name only and had "drifted far from its moorings," while the Republican party was dominated by corporations and pro-Chinese sentiment. He concluded that the Workingmen's party was the only true standard-bearer of pure democratic principles.[63]

The profound concern expressed about the peril to American democracy cannot be dismissed as partisan political rhetoric. "Is this a Republic?" asked the *Democratic Standard* at the head of its editorial column immediately after the ratification election. It recounted how, just before the election, workers at one lumber mill had found a ticket under their dinner plates marked "Against the Constitution." The *Standard* commented: "When the daily laborer can be intimidated and forced to vote against his judgement what is he but a slave," and the editorial concluded that "if we are to be a republic let it be so in fact. Our sires laid down their lives to establish one. We should be prepared to maintain it, if needs be with our lives."[64] A month later, the *Standard* reported that some employers in the county had dismissed workers who had voted for the new constitution.[65] Events at the local, state, and national levels produced profound disquiet on the part of many Humboldters, who saw themselves as defending a sacred democratic-republican legacy. Not surprisingly, they invoked the figureheads, symbols, and rhetoric of a supposedly golden age.

The Humboldt Workingmen's party began taking steps in the spring of 1879 to consolidate its organization to contest the forthcoming statewide and county elections. In March 1879, a convention was held to elect delegates to a state convention of the Workingmen's party and to encourage the establishment of workingmen's clubs. By June 1879, clubs were mushrooming throughout the county.[66] In the same month, a convention nominated candidates and drew up a platform. The platform extolled the new constitution, stressing in particular how it would reduce the burden of taxation. But it reiterated that the resolute implementation of the new constitution depended on electing "faithful friends" to all branches of the government.[67]

Who were the "faithful friends" nominated by the Workingmen's party?[68] Most of the candidates were in their forties or early fifties and had come to California in the 1850s. Almost all had resided in Humboldt County for at least ten years. A majority were natives of the New England and Middle Atlantic regions and came from relatively humble origins. Very few had held public office before, and only one had done so in Humboldt County. Two farmers, both Grangers, were on the ticket; one owned a "small farm" and the other a "comfortable farm." Thomas Cutler, the candidate for sheriff, was the only businessman on the ticket. He was, allegedly, one of only two merchants in Eureka who supported the Workingmen's party "against all the threats of the San Francisco wholesale merchants and railroad carriers." Two of the men on the ticket ran livery stables. One was Pierce Ryan, the senatorial candidate for the state's 27th

District; the other, John Carr, had spent most of his life as a miner and blacksmith. The nominee for county clerk was a carpenter, and the candidate for county treasurer had worked in the lumber mills for six years. Three professional people—two lawyers and a schoolteacher—rounded out the ticket. Their prospective offices of district attorney, superior court judge, and school administrator demanded at least a modicum of professional training and experience.

The Workingmen's party conducted a spirited campaign against the Republicans and Democrats in the county. Leaders of the new party berated the old-line forces for opposing ratification of the state constitution and portrayed themselves as the true standard-bearers of the American democratic tradition. J. D. H. Chamberlin, the Workingmen's party candidate for superior county judge, opened a speech at Ferndale by quoting at length from the Declaration of Independence.[69] The *Democratic Standard* warned that there are "vital principles involved in the election of the most unimportant officer. . . . The tory spirit has revived after 100 years of rest and today opposes the honest yeomanry of our country with all the oppressive bitterness that persecuted the heroes of American freedom."[70] On the evening before election day, the Workingmen's party staged a torchlight parade in Eureka that drew supporters from all over the county. The *Standard* described the procession as "composed entirely of farmers, laborers and mechanics."[71]

Although the Workingmen's party did not achieve the sweeping success it had in electing delegates to the constitutional convention, its performance was impressive. Every candidate for statewide office on the Workingmen's ticket got a majority of the vote in Humboldt County. Party candidates for the state senate and legislature were elected, and the party won half the county's executive positions, losing the remainder by only a few votes to the fusionist opposition. Precinct returns again indicated that the Workingmen's party received consistent support throughout the county, performing best in the burgeoning agricultural townships of Ferndale and Table Bluff. In most other rural precincts the party performed no better, and sometimes worse, than in Eureka, where it fell only a few votes short of a majority in almost all county and state contests. Statewide, the Workingmen elected the chief justice of the state supreme court, five of six associate justices, and sixteen assemblymen and eleven state senators. This result failed to give the party the hoped-for majority in the state legislature and was somewhat disappointing in view of its strong showing in the 1878 constitutional convention elections.

The ineffectual performance of many party representatives once in state and local office and persistent factionalism in the San Francisco branch led to a rapid decline of the party after the 1879 state elections. The gathering political momentum of the National Greenback party encouraged some members of the Workingmen's party, including Denis Kearney, leader of the San Francisco branch, to join the Greenbacks. In addition, the success of the Workingmen's party prompted California's Republican and Democratic parties (especially the latter) to become more responsive to the demands of the Workingmen's party on such issues as Chinese exclusion, land monopoly, and stricter regulation of railroads. Many Workingmen's representatives aligned with one of the two major parties, usually the Democrats, in a process that Alexander Saxton dubbed "the institutionalization of labor politics."[72]

The decline of the Workingmen's party in Humboldt County reflected its demise statewide. Supporters were discouraged by the overall performance of the party in the 1879 state elections and in municipal elections in Humboldt and other counties in early 1880. Throughout the 1879 campaign party leaders stressed that the new constitution was a dead letter unless the party obtained a majority in the state legislature. Thus, the Humboldt County Workingmen's party virtually turned the election into a referendum on the future of the party. Immediately after the election, the *Democratic Standard* declared that the new constitution had been "practically nullified." It lamented the well-publicized factionalism of the San Francisco branch and the fact that a considerable number of Workingmen's party representatives were moving into the old parties.[73] Humboldters who retained their faith in the new party after the elections became disillusioned with the performance of some representatives. In April 1880, the *Standard* reported "much talk of dissatisfaction among the workingmen of Eureka about the policy which some of the county officers elected on the Workingmen's ticket have chosen to pursue."[74] George Shaw, who had been elected county assessor on the party ticket, incurred the wrath of many people when he added an office clerk to his staff at a salary of $135 per month and selected a long-time enemy of the Workingmen's party as his main adviser.[75] By April 1880, Shaw was so unpopular that he required a bodyguard.[76]

Growing interest in the Greenback Labor party hastened the dissolution of the Humboldt County Workingmen's party. Greenback clubs sprang up throughout the county between 1878 and 1880. In fact, remnants of the Workingmen's party reconstituted themselves as the Humboldt Greenback Labor party. The Greenbackers' panaceas had a much stronger appeal in Humboldt County than they did in San Francisco and many other California counties.

By the late 1870s, a coherent dissenting tradition had emerged in Humboldt County. The evolution of this tradition owed much to the persistence of values associated with an antebellum democratic-republican ideology that stressed the superiority of the American political system. Chauvinistic and almost millennial assumptions engendered a profound set of beliefs and expectations about the nature of the American political economy. In particular, the free-labor tenet and its corollary, the labor theory of value, stressing as they did the immense contribution of the free laborer to America's progress, heightened expectations about the future, reinforced the workingman's sense of his moral worth, and endowed him with a civic responsibility to scrutinize the destiny of the republic. Between 1866 and 1880, developments at the local, state, and national levels convinced many Humboldters that pernicious economic and political events threatened the sanctity and purity of the American Republic and seriously threatened the free laborer's advancement.

Undeniably, contradictions and ambiguities existed in the democratic-republican legacy. Two contradictions, in particular, are worth noting. Both derived from a marked discrepancy between the dissenters' penetrating political analysis and their often superficial prescriptions. On the crucial question of land monopoly, for example, Sweasey took a radical stance in advocating a statutory limitation on the amount of land a person might own. Barton and the Ferndale Grange, for all their deeply felt anxieties about the concentration of land ownership and land fraud, could not countenance so direct an interference with the rights of private property.[77] Paradoxically, many dissenters railed against what they perceived as the dangers of unfettered capitalism but could not bring themselves to advocate far-reaching controls (with the possible exception of railroad regulation) over private property rights. This disparity between a keen perception of fundamental problems and a naïve faith in piecemeal solutions that ignored underlying structural problems stands out in the dissenters' faith that all could be rectified if only good, honest men were elected. Even a man as disenchanted as Sweasey could in one breath speak of the gravity of social and economic trends and the threat to the republic and in the next proclaim his belief in the ability of the "best men" to correct the situation.

Notwithstanding its ambiguous features, the democratic-republican tradition provided Humboldt's dissenters with an arsenal of ideas. Increasingly, they would jettison many (but not all) of the contradictory strands of the tradition and embrace reforms that entailed at least a measure of state control over private property. The Humboldt Workingmen's party bequeathed to the county a dissenting ideological legacy that the Greenback Labor party, the International Workingmen's Association, and the Knights of Labor were able to draw on in the 1880s, and that the Humboldt Populists relied on heavily in the 1890s. Many leaders of the Humboldt Workingmen's party played important roles in these movements. In 1886, the *Arcata Union* commented with alarm and derision on the growing strength of the People's party, the political arm of the Humboldt Knights of Labor, describing its leadership as "in the main the same old political fossils . . . that have monopolized every reform movement from the days of Kearney."[78]

NOTES

1. The fullest account of the California Workingmen's party is provided by Ralph Kauer, "The Workingmen's Party of California," *Pacific Historical Review* 13 (September 1944): 278–291. An important book on the California labor movement and reform politics in the late nineteenth century is Alexander Saxton, *The Indispensable Enemy: Labor and the Anti-Chinese Movement in California* (Berkeley: University of California Press, 1971). Also useful on the history of the California Workingmen's party are Royce D. Delmatier, Clarence F. McIntosh, and Earl G. Waters, *The Rumble of California Politics, 1848–1970* (New York: John Wiley & Sons, 1970), pp. 70–98; and Ira B. Cross, *A History of the Labor Movement in California* (Berkeley: University of California Press, 1935), pp. 88–129. These studies, however, focus mainly on the San Francisco branch of the California Workingmen's party and the anti-Chinese agitation.

2. Leon Fink, *Workingmen's Democracy: The Knights of Labor and American Politics* (Urbana: University of Illinois Press, 1983), p. 26. In an important review essay, David Montgomery has stressed the incidence of independent political activity in the Gilded Age and the need for further work in the field. David Montgomery, "To Study the People: The American Working Class," *Labor History* 21 (Fall 1980): 485–512.

3. Steven Hahn and Jonathan Prude, eds., *The Countryside in the Age of Capitalist Transformation: Essays in the Social History of Rural America* (Chapel Hill: University of North Carolina Press, 1985), p. 3.

4. Many historians of late eighteenth- and nineteenth-century American radicalism have noted the persistence of a democratic-republican tradition and have tried to define it, notwithstanding all its complexities. Among the most sophisticated efforts are: Leon Fink, *Workingmen's Democracy*; Eric Foner, *Free Soil, Free Men, Free Labor: The Ideology of the Republican Party Before the Civil War* (New York: Oxford University Press, 1970); Eric Foner, *Tom Paine and Revolutionary America* (New York: Oxford University Press, 1976); Sean Wilentz, *Chants Democratic: New York City and the Rise of the American Working Class, 1788–1850* (New York: Oxford University Press, 1984). In his book *The Indispensable Enemy*, Saxton also uses the concept to analyze the sources of radicalism in postbellum nineteenth-century California politics. See especially pp. 19–45.

5. *Humboldt Times*, March 26, 1864.

6. Letter Book of James Beith, January 24, 1862, p. 162. Bancroft Library, University of California, Berkeley.

7. Ibid.

8. See Robert A. Burchell, "Opportunity and the Frontier: Wealth-Holding in Twenty-Six Northern California Counties, 1848–1880," *Western Historical Quarterly* 18 (April 1987): 177–196; Daniel A. Cornford, "Lumber, Labor, and Community in Humboldt County, California, 1850–1920" (doctoral dissertation, University of California, Santa Barbara, 1983), pp. 37–40; and Ralph Mann, *After the Gold Rush: Society in Grass Valley and Nevada City, California, 1849–1870* (Palo Alto: Stanford University Press, 1982).

9. Besides the studies listed above, see Alan Dawley, *Class and Community: The Industrial Revolution in Lynn* (Cambridge: Harvard University Press, 1976); Paul Faler, *Mechanics and Manufacturers in the Early Industrial Revolution: Lynn, Massachusetts, 1780–1860* (Albany: State University of New York Press, 1981); Herbert G. Gutman, *Work, Culture, and Society in Industrializing America* (New York: Alfred A. Knopf, 1976); David Montgomery, *Labor and the Radical Republicans, 1862–1872* (New York: Alfred A. Knopf, 1967); Edward Pessen, *Most Uncommon Jacksonians: The Radical Leaders of the Early Labor Movement* (Albany: State University of New York Press, 1967); Howard B. Rock, *Artisans of the New Republic: The Tradesmen of New York City in the Age of Jefferson* (New York: New York University Press, 1979); Steven J. Ross, *Workers on the Edge: Work, Leisure, and Politics in Industrializing Cincinnati, 1788–1890* (New York: Columbia University Press, 1985); and Nick Salvatore, *Eugene V. Debs: Citizen and Socialist* (Urbana: University of Illinois Press, 1982).

10. For information on the early social and economic history of Humboldt County, see Lynwood Carranco, *Redwood Lumber Industry* (San Marino: Golden West Books, 1982); Cornford, "Lumber, Labor, and Community," pp. 24–106; Owen C. Coy, *The Humboldt Bay Region, 1850–1875* (Los Angeles: California State Historical Association, 1929); and *History of Humboldt County, California with Biographical Sketches* (San Francisco: W. W. Elliott & Co., 1881).

11. *Humboldt Times*, December 21, 1867 and January 4, 1868.

12. Ibid., November 14, 1868.

13. *Humboldt Times*, July 15, 1871; and *Northern Independent*, July 13, 1871.

14. *Northern Independent*, August 26 and September 1, 1869.

15. Ibid., August 19, 1869.

16. *Humboldt Times*, March 11, 1871.

17. Ibid., April 15 and August 26, 1871.

18. *West Coast Signal*, July 9, 1873.

19. This party is sometimes referred to as the Independent party or the Dollay Vardens. The secondary literature on it is sparse, but see Curtis E. Grassman, "Prologue to Progressivism: Senator Stephen M. White and the California Reform Impulse, 1875–1905" (doctoral dissertation, University of California, Los Angeles, 1970), pp. 17–22; and Walton E. Bean, *California: An Interpretive History* (New York: McGraw-Hill, 1978), p. 261.

20. *West Coast Signal*, August 6, 1873.

21. *Humboldt Times*, August 30, 1873.

22. Ibid., July 5, 1873.

23. Ezra Carr, *The Patrons of Husbandry on the West Coast* (San Francisco: A. L. Bancroft & Co., 1875).

24. *Humboldt Times*, September 20, 1873.

25. *West Coast Signal*, September 24, 1873.

26. Biographical information on Sweasey was obtained from T. J. Vivian and D. G. Waldron, *Biographical Sketches of the Delegates to the Convention* (San Francisco: Francis & Valentine, 1878), pp. 29–30; *West Coast Signal*, September 24, 1873; *Democratic Standard*, January 1, 1879; *Humboldt Times*, October 1, 1893; *Western Watchman*, October 7, 1893; and *Nerve*, October 7, 1893.

27. *Humboldt Times*, January 24, 1874.

28. Ibid., January 6, 1877.

29. Ibid., January 20, 1877.

30. *Pacific Coast Wood and Iron,* a trade journal of the Pacific lumber industry, published a review of redwood lumber prices for the previous thirty years in 1899, which was reprinted in the *Humboldt Standard,* December 13, 1899.

31. *Humboldt Times,* February 10, 1877.

32. *Daily Evening Signal,* July 3, 1877; *Humboldt Times,* July 7, 1877.

33. *Mendocino Democrat,* March 2, 1878; *Humboldt Times,* July 21, 1877. The *Humboldt Times* reported several acts of alleged arson in 1877 and 1878; *Humboldt Times,* July 21 and October 13, 1877, March 2, 1878. Saxton asserts that arson was quite frequent in San Francisco during the late 1870s, and implies that not uncommonly it was resorted to for political reasons: "Arson in California in those days was almost as commonplace as murder," *The Indispensable Enemy,* p. 149.

34. *Democratic Standard,* November 3, 1877.

35. *Humboldt Times,* August 25, 1877.

36. *Daily Evening Signal,* August 18, 1877.

37. Eugene F. Fountain, *The Story of Blue Lake* (n.p., n.d.), vol. 3, pp. 589–592. Manuscript in possession of the Humboldt State University Library. On fraudulent land acquisition practices in Humboldt County, see Howard Brett Melendy, "One Hundred Years of the Redwood Lumber Industry, 1850–1950" (doctoral dissertation, Stanford University, 1952), pp. 80–98. For an account of the dubious land acquisition practices of many lumber entrepreneurs in the United States, see Thomas R. Cox et al., *This Well-Wooded Land: Americans and Their Forests from Colonial Times to the Present* (Lincoln: University of Nebraska Press, 1985), pp. 138–142.

38. The study listed all landholders possessing 500 acres or more in every California county. The *San Francisco Chronicle* began serializing the findings on October 28, 1873, and the findings for Humboldt County were published in the *Humboldt Times,* November 8, 1873.

39. *Humboldt Times,* November 8, 1873.

40. See E. B. Willis and P. K. Stockton, *Debates and Proceedings of the Constitutional Convention,* 3 vols. (Sacramento: J. D. Young, Superintendent of State Printing, 1880).

41. *Humboldt Times,* April 27, 1878.

42. Ibid.

43. Ibid.

44. Ibid., May 11, 1878.

45. *Democratic Standard,* November 23, 1878.

46. *Humboldt Times,* May 9, 1874; *Pacific Rural Press,* July 14, 1877.

47. *Humboldt Times,* October 21, 1876.

48. Ibid., November 18 and December 2, 1876.

49. *Daily Evening Signal,* March 15, 1878.

50. *Humboldt Times,* September 22, 1877.

51. Delmatier et al., *Rumble of California Politics*, p. 83.

52. U.S. Bureau of the Census, *Statistics of Population of the United States at the Ninth Census, 1870* (Washington, D.C.: GPO, 1872), vol. 1, table 3, p. 90; U.S. Bureau of the Census, *Statistics of the Population of the United States at the Tenth Census, 1880* (Washington, D.C.: GPO, 1883), vol. 1, table 14, p. 498.

53. *Evening Star*, January 17, 1877.

54. Lynwood Carranco, "The Chinese Expulsion from Humboldt County," *Pacific Historical Review* 30 (November 1961): 329–340; Lynwood Carranco, "The Chinese in Humboldt County, California: A Study in Prejudice," *Journal of the West* 12 (January 1973): 139–162.

55. Data compiled from the Manuscript Census of Population for Humboldt County, 1880.

56. *Humboldt Times*, June 4, 1878; *Democratic Standard*, June 1, 1878.

57. *Humboldt Times*, May 11, 1878.

58. *Democratic Standard*, May 25, 1878.

59. *Humboldt Times*, July 6, 1878. In 1878, most lumber workers, as well as laborers, artisans, and business and professional people, resided in Eureka and, to a lesser extent, Arcata. Farmers constituted the majority of the electorate outside these precincts. Unquestionably, they made up a larger proportion of the registered voters in relation to their numbers than lumber workers and most other working-class occupational groups. Nevertheless, lumber workers and other workingmen made up a significant proportion of the registered voters. The geographic stability of a significant core of lumber workers and the relative leniency of residency requirements imposed by California election laws facilitated this. While farmers tended to "persist" longer on the voting registers than most other occupational groups, they too were a fairly transient bunch. On the above, see Burchell, "Opportunity and the Frontier," pp. 189–190.

60. Willis and Stockton, *Debates and Proceedings of the Constitutional Convention*, vol. 2, p. 1144.

61. *Democratic Standard*, May 3, 1879.

62. Ibid., May 24, 1879.

63. Ibid., April 5, 1879.

64. Ibid., May 10, 1879.

65. Ibid., June 7, 1879.

66. Ibid., April 12 and June 28, 1879.

67. Ibid., July 5, 1879.

68. Biographical sketches of the men on the Workingmen's party ticket appeared in the *Democratic Standard*, July 19, 1879.

69. *Democratic Standard*, August 16, 1879.

70. Ibid., July 5, 1879.

71. Ibid., September 6, 1879.

72. Saxton, *Indispensable Enemy*, p. 152.

73. *Democratic Standard*, March 13, 1880.

74. Ibid., April 24, 1880.

75. Ibid., May 15, 1880.

76. Ibid., April 17, 1880.

77. For critical responses to Sweasey's land-reform proposals, see the *Humboldt Times*, May 4, 11, and 18, 1878. Sweasey strongly defended his proposals in the *Daily Evening Signal*, June 12, 1878.

78. *Arcata Union*, August 14, 1886.

FURTHER READING

Barth, Gunther. *Bitter Strength: A History of the Chinese in the United States, 1850–1870.* 1964.

Bryce, James. *The American Commonwealth.* Vol. 2. 1889.

"The Chinese in California." Special issue. *California History* 57 (Spring 1978).

Cornford, Daniel. *Workers and Dissent in the Redwood Empire.* 1987.

Cross, Ira B. *A History of the Labor Movement in California.* 1935.

———, ed. *Frank Roney, Irish Rebel and California Labor Leader.* 1931.

Dancis, Bruce. "Social Mobility and Class Consciousness: San Francisco's International Workingmen's Association in the 1880s." *Journal of Social History* 11 (Fall 1977): 75–98.

Delmatier, Royce D., Clarence F. McIntosh, and Earl G. Waters. *The Rumble of California Politics, 1848–1970.* Chapter 3. 1970.

Ethington, Philip J. *The Public City: The Political Construction of Urban Life in San Francisco, 1850–1900.* 1994.

Gates, Paul W. *Land and Law in California: Essays on Land Policies.* 1991.

George, Henry. *Our Land and Land Policy.* 1871.

Griffiths, David. "Anti-Monopoly Movements in California, 1873–1898." *Southern California Quarterly* 52 (June 1970): 93–121.

Kauer, Ralph. "The Workingmen's Party of California." *Pacific Historical Review* 13 (September 1944): 278–291.

Kazin, Michael. "Prelude to Kearneyism: The 'July Days' in San Francisco." *New Labor Review* 3 (1980): 5–47.

Pisani, Donald J. "Squatter Law in California, 1850–1858." *Western Historical Quarterly* 25 (August 1994): 277–310.

Sandmeyer, Elmer C. *The Anti-Chinese Movement in California.* 1939.

Saxton, Alexander. *The Indispensable Enemy: Labor and the Anti-Chinese Movement in California.* 1971.

Shumsky, Neil Larry. *The Evolution of Political Protest and the Workingmen's Party of California.* 1991.

———. "Frank Roney's San Francisco—His Diary: April 1875–March 1876." *Labor History* 17 (Winter 1976): 245–264.

———. "San Francisco's Workingmen Respond to the Modern City." *California History* 55 (Spring 1976): 46–55.

11 Reform, Utopia, and Racism

The Politics of California Craftsmen

Michael Kazin

EDITOR'S INTRODUCTION

During the mid-1890s, the American labor movement fought to survive during one of the harshest depressions in the nation's history. Between 1897 and 1904, however, with the depression over, labor experienced a dramatic renaissance, with union membership growing from 440,000 to 2,067,000 nationwide.

In California, the growth of the labor movement was equally impressive. Between 1900 and 1904 alone, the number of unions increased from 217 to 805, and union membership rose from 30,000 to 110,000. While the trade union movement flourished in most of California's urban population centers, nowhere did it attain such power as in San Francisco. In 1904, muckraking journalist Ray Stannard Baker wrote an article about San Francisco entitled "Where Unionism Holds Undisputed Sway." Although Baker somewhat exaggerated the power of San Francisco labor in the early twentieth century, at least one-third of all of the city's workers belonged to unions at a time when less than 10 percent of the nation's industrial work force was unionized.

Unquestionably, San Francisco workers established the strongest labor movement in any American city during the early twentieth century. Teamsters, carpenters, iron molders, waitresses, seamen, and longshoremen, among others, benefited from the high wages and fixed hours that a virtual closed shop in their trades made possible. Moreover, economic power at the workplace translated into considerable political power. The Union Labor candidate for mayor was elected in 1901, 1903, and 1905. In the 1905 election, all eighteen members elected to the board of supervisors were Union Labor party nominees. In 1909, despite the exposure of corrupt practices on the part of two of its leaders, the Union Labor party elected its candidate mayor and obtained a majority on the board of supervisors.

In his book *Barons of Labor: The San Francisco Building Trades and Union Power in the Progressive Era*, Michael Kazin examines in-depth the most powerful component of the San Francisco labor movement. As early as 1901, the San Francisco Building Trades Council (BTC) boasted thirty-two locals with about fifteen thousand members. The administration and governance of the San Francisco BTC were dominated by Patrick Henry Mc-Carthy, an Irish immigrant who had worked as a carpenter in his youth. McCarthy and his henchmen had a major influence over both San Francisco labor matters and politics. McCarthy was president of the San Francisco BTC from 1898 to 1922, and in 1909 he was elected mayor of San Francisco under the banner of the Union Labor party.

In this selection, Kazin analyzes the political ideology of both the leaders and the membership of the San Francisco BTC and explains why it broke sharply with the national AFL policy of mistrusting political action. He also explores the relationship between the BTC and more radical organizations such as the Socialist party and the Industrial Workers of the World. Finally, Kazin looks at the important role of the San Francisco BTC in the Asiatic Exclusion League.

"A movement, however laudable and externally worthy, is bound to fail if it has no soul."
—Frank Roney, labor organizer in late nineteenth-century San Francisco[1]

"California is the white man's country and not the Caucasian graveyard."
—Olaf Tveitmoe, editor of *Organized Labor*, 1907[2]

In the years before World War I, Patrick McCarthy and his men yearned to govern San Francisco, but their aims went far beyond the filling of friendly pockets and the gratification of hungry egos. In every public arena, the craftsmen and former craftsmen who led the Building Trades Council expressed their desire for a society in which working people would both propose social reforms and play a large part in running the state which administered them. Inheritors of an "equal rights" tradition as old as the American republic itself, they argued that no government or corporation which excluded and patronized workers could be democratic in anything but name. For BTC men, the jostle for urban influence meshed continuously with the rhetoric of ideals. It would be naive to deny that they were fighting for themselves, but it would be equally myopic to miss the larger meaning of their struggle.

In their search for power, building trades unionists appealed to two overlapping constituencies. On the one hand, they spoke the language of class conflict and identified with wage-earners of all industries and nations. Their own redoubtable organizations seemed the perfect springboard for an army of workers that could—with the dual weapons of the labor vote and the closed shop—peacefully sweep aside all opponents. In 1910, sheet metal worker James Feeney grandiloquently described what he felt to be the *raison d'être* and ultimate objective of his San Francisco local:

> It is a grand thing to know you are one of an organization of progressive men, who see in every brother a fellow workman doing his best to maintain himself as a good citizen with the interest of his organization at heart at all times . . . we can ever press onward with charity in judgment of our Brother members, our hearts gladdened with the knowledge of duty well done, our spirits fired with the zeal of Argonauts as we fall in step with the grandest march civilization has ever known to that goal of industrial justice, the emancipation of the working class by and for themselves from the thraldom of competitive exploitation, strong in the hope and knowledge that, "We have nothing to lose but our chains, We have a world to gain."[3]

Publicly owned utilities, producer cooperatives, land reform, and state-financed welfare measures were all considered strides forward on this long march toward a glorious future for laboring men and women.

On the other hand, building tradesmen constantly affirmed their identity as *white* Americans who were engaged in a crusade to bar Asians from their blessed land. From the pioneer artisan-unionists of the Gold Rush era to McCarthy and Tveitmoe six decades later, California labor leaders believed they were carving a just and rational order out of the social chaos of America's last frontier. They branded Asians as threats to this nascent order, perpetual outsiders whose cultural distinctiveness and superior numbers (across the Pacific) made them a greater, more visceral threat than the frequent charge of "cheap labor" suggests. By scapegoating Chinese and Japanese and barring them from all areas of white working-class life, unionists affirmed, in their own minds, their ability to represent the common interests of the broad majority of Californians. The labor movement was thus not merely a device to press the economic demands of its members but a bulwark against the incursions of a hostile race.[4]

These two impulses—the inclusive, optimistic faith in class solidarity and the appeal to racial fears and hatred—did not pose an agonizing contradiction either for white labor leaders or for most of their followers. By the early twentieth century, the argument that the Western labor movement should defend the "productive" citizenry against "coolies" judged incapable of self-reliant work or thought had been echoed by the U.S. Congress in the Oriental Exclusion Act of 1882 and extensions passed in 1892 and 1902. In the South, "populist" Democrats like Senator Ben Tillman of South Carolina were carrying the day with similar arguments about Afro-Americans, and their words encouraged lynchings and other violent acts which surpassed anything that occurred in California.[5] Candid expressions of racism were completely legitimate features of America's political culture at the time. In fact, within the ranks of organized labor, the burden of proof rested heavily on those activists who called for a multi-racial movement. How could that ideal be realized in a world where nations and ethnic groups constantly warred over the division of scarce resources and territory?

Within the definition of the labor movement as a Caucasian preserve, self-defense was a cherished principle. The enemies of free white workers seemed to be everywhere: monopolistic corporations, anti-union judges, conservative politicians, and the Citizens' Alliance directed the attack, using "little yellow and brown men" as a flying wedge. To parry this challenge required a determination by all citizens to defend the rights and material conditions they had already won. But organized labor also had to enlarge its power in society more generally. So union spokesmen maintained that America's democratic civilization had no better guarantors of its survival and prosperity than the men and women who did its work. Thus, the BTC posed proudly as champion of both the majority class and the majority race. In so doing, it articulated a "common sense" about politics that was probably shared by most wage-earning Californians.[6]

Where did the men of the BTC fit within the broad ideological spectrum of labor in the Progressive era? On the right of labor opinion were the cautiously pragmatic leaders of most international craft unions, the members of the AFL Executive Council, and Samuel Gompers himself. In 1906, the AFL plunged into campaigns for Democratic candidates after lobbying Congress for a decade to pass an anti-injunction law and an eight-hour day for government workers. However, its governing philosophy was that of "voluntarism": an aversion to other than temporary ties with a political party and opposition to legislation such as unemployment insurance which would protect workers regardless of their union affiliation. The national AFL mistrusted political action because it might whet the desire for independent labor parties and other groups that could draw workers away from an exclusive reliance on the economic might of trade unions.[7]

Gompers and other longtime AFL officials also rejected the Marxian assumptions of their left-wing opponents who believed that capitalism brought only misery and a widening gap between the classes. Like American leaders in other fields at the turn of the century, the men who directed the AFL subscribed to many of the ideas of the "social Darwinist" Herbert Spencer, believing most government actions to be "interference" in a natural process which would inevitably bring amelioration of workers' lives.[8] Radicals not only opposed the policies that Gompers and his allies pursued. They also substituted the contentious and artificial mechanism of "class struggle" for the growing social harmony which the shared abundance of modern industry made possible. Thus, both practical and philosophical considerations led AFL leaders to say, "A true unionist could not be a socialist trade unionist."[9]

At the center of labor politics was a combination of reformist Marxists and nonsocialist advocates of industrial unionism. Men like Victor Berger of Milwaukee, Morris Hillquit of New York City, and Max Hayes of Cleveland as well as women like Rose Schneiderman and Helene Marot of the Women's Trade Union League composed the former group. Leaders of both the Socialist Party and powerful union federations in their home cities, they believed in a gradual transformation of capitalism through the ballot box and the universal organization of wage-earners. Until the United States entered World War I, Socialists formed a large bloc within the AFL and controlled several large unions such as the Brewery Workers and Tailors. At the party's apex in 1912, Max Hayes, running against Gompers, won almost a third of the votes for the presidency of the federation, while William Johnston, socialist head of the Machinists, took 40 percent of the total cast for the vice presidency.[10]

Less noted by historians but fully as important to their contemporaries were those boosters of industrial unionism who kept their distance from the Socialist Party. Men such as John Fitzpatrick of the Chicago Federation of Labor and Charles Moyer of the Western Federation of Miners learned the futility of craft-divided organization through the experience of jurisdictional squabbles and the rigors of strikes in company towns where disunity spelled certain defeat. At various points in their careers, Fitzpatrick and Moyer had worked closely with Marxists, but they always put the welfare of the unions they directed above the doctrines of radical spokesmen.

After the 1918 Armistice, Fitzpatrick and other unionists of his ilk founded the Independent Labor Party in hopes of attracting both socialists and unaffiliated militants. But both the Socialist Party and the AFL greeted the new organization with hostility, and it was soon crushed between the factional millstones of postwar America.[11]

The Industrial Workers of the World flamboyantly occupied the labor movement's revolutionary wing. Regarded with scorn as "dual unionists" by AFL members of every political stripe, Wobblies fought with much heroism but spotty success to organize unskilled proletarians regardless of race, sex, or immigrant status. The IWW took Gompers's mistrust of the state one gigantic step further. Denouncing Socialists for counseling workers to seek their liberation through the state, Wobblies prophesied that increased waves of resistance on the job would build to a future general strike and the takeover of the economy by the working class. The "One Big Union" embraced a variety of anarcho-syndicalism which was repugnant to mainstream socialists as well as to the vast majority of AFL members. The Wilson administration's wartime onslaught of propaganda and legal persecution against the IWW finally limited the group's core of support to those unafraid of serving a long jail term for their beliefs.[12]

The leaders of San Francisco building trades unionism drew in significant ways from and sustained a flexible relationship toward each of these national tendencies. As loyal members of the AFL, the BTC preserved separate craft unions at the same time as it required those unions to act together in a crisis. Like the reform socialists, the BTC called for organized wage-earners to "vote as they marched," viewing partisan politics and legislative action as the essential tools of an advancing labor movement. Together with the IWW, McCarthy and his men believed that their Council and others like it throughout the industrial world were the embryo of a more just, egalitarian, and prosperous society.

Until the United States entered World War I, the BTC was able to straddle a political divide that often bedeviled union activists elsewhere. On a daily basis, San Francisco construction unions operated within the norms of capitalist production. Any contractor who adhered to the closed shop and local trade rules was, in effect, protected by the BTC's virtual monopoly of the supply of skilled labor. But the BTC also mobilized voters and tried to shape public opinion to accept a state run by and for white wage-earners. While disclaiming any revolutionary intentions, these local leaders of the AFL pursued power through all the avenues which a capitalist democracy provided to a disciplined working-class organization.

Thus, the BTC gestured toward a combination of the Gompers brand of "business unionism" and a kind of syndicalism like that being advocated at the time by radical craftsmen in Western Europe. Syndicalists were a majority in the French General Confederation of Workers (CGT), and they were also a significant force in the labor movements of Italy, Spain, Sweden, and Great Britain. They preached that only industrial organizations steeled by "direct action" on the shop floor could win the trust of workers and represent them in the difficult contest for power against the bourgeois state. In 1915, Robert Michels described syndicalist aims in a way that also captured the aspirations of McCarthy and his men: "Syndicalism is to put an end to the dualism of the labour movement by substituting for the party, whose sole functions are politico-electoral, and for the trade union, whose sole functions are economic, a completer organism which shall represent a synthesis of the political and economic function."[13]

BTC spokesmen often chided Gompers and his associates for not confronting businessmen and the state. According to Olaf Tveitmoe, national unions needed "a little less petitioning and a little more show of teeth" in order to defeat industrial behemoths such as United States Steel. In 1913, after Gompers publicly attacked British syndicalist Tom Mann, BTC officials befriended and publicized the flamboyant organizer of London's stevedores. Welcomed to San Francisco by McCarthy, Mann preached the gospel of industrial unionism before large crowds at the Building Trades Temple and other local halls.[14] The barons of the construction trades were, to coin a phrase, "business syndicalists." While careful not to upset the equilibrium of their own industry, they were exuberant about the potential of a unified body of workers to transform society in their own image.

Reforms by and for the Working Class

To realize this potential, the BTC continuously participated in electoral politics. "United action by a million wage workers [then the membership of the AFL] in defining the policy of our national government," Tveitmoe wrote in 1900, "would be a factor that no party would dare to reckon without."[15] The BTC's leverage over one of San Francisco's most important industries and tutelage over a constituency that seldom numbered less than 15,000 men and their families made it formidable, as either friend or foe. The authoritarian style which provoked internal opposition also enabled the McCarthy machine to push its way into civic affairs and to negotiate on roughly even terms with members of the urban elite.

The BTC had several good reasons to follow an electoral strategy. First, the organization mobilized and represented a particularly avid bloc of voters. Building craftsmen tended to stay in San Francisco longer than other blue-collar workers, taking advantage of the high wage scales available in the metropolis.[16] Despite a large contingent of immigrants, construction unionists during the turn-of-the-century boom registered to vote in numbers far above their percentage in the work force as a whole. At the end of 1902, for example, 14 percent of all San Francisco registrants worked in an occupation represented by BTC unions, although construction workers were only 6 percent of the city's wage-earners. In 1916, building occupations registered about 8 percent of the total, still an important segment of the voting public. By this time, women could vote in California state elections, and they made up over a third of all registrants. Of course, there is no way to discover how many building workers actually voted, but if exhortations in *Organized Labor* (the official organ of the San Francisco BTC) and the diligent canvassing of business agents had any impact, it was a high percentage of those registered. Grant Fee, president of the Building Trades Employers' Association, testified to a healthy rate of labor participation when he told the Industrial Relations Commission in 1914 that "95 percent of men working for salaries attend to their civic duties," while less than half of businessmen bothered to vote.[17]

Moreover, building workers shared a personal interest in municipal decisions. A friendly administration and popularly elected judges would stand aside while the BTC enforced its boycott of nonunion materials and informally instruct police officers to deal lightly with cases of violence against "scabs." Lucrative public building contracts and appointments of union men to city posts also depended upon the inclinations of the mayor and Board of Supervisors. The municipal sector employed less than 5 percent of the San Francisco labor force during this period, but at least half of those approximately 12,000 jobs were in construction.[18]

In a larger sense, participation in local politics signified that the business of government should be a perpetual concern of the labor movement. Simply railing at capital's injustices had been fine for the late nineteenth century, when unions rode insecurely on the bucking horse of the economic cycle. However, permanent organization brought with it new power and new responsibilities. Leaders of the BTC wanted to prove they were at least as capable guardians of the welfare of the entire population as were the middle- and upper-class men who were accustomed to rule. By way of example, *Organized Labor* pointed to New Zealand and Australia where

national labor parties periodically controlled governments that passed legislation to protect the health and raise the wages of all workers. "We out-
number the capitalists ten to one," the BTC journal commented in appreciation of these achievements down under, "yet what say have we in regard
to the State laws?" [19]

The BTC placed the improvement of workers' lives highest on its reform
agenda. Unlike the national leaders of the AFL, San Francisco unionists
rarely opposed an expanded state role in the economy. In 1902, a BTC
committee drew up a bill to establish the eight-hour day on all public works
in California and convinced an assemblyman who was a former marble
cutter to introduce it. After the measure passed, both the BTC and California Federation of Labor urged the legislature to enact a "universal" eight-
hour law introduced by Socialist Assemblyman J. M. Kingsley. By 1915,
McCarthy was floating the idea of a six-hour day as a means of spreading
work to men whose jobs had been lost as a result of mechanization.[20]

The BTC also unsuccessfully championed a spate of measures that, if
enacted, would have made California the most advanced welfare state in
the nation. Lacking any trace of voluntarism, McCarthy and his men advocated the establishment of massive public works programs to absorb the
seasonally unemployed in the West and elsewhere. During World War I,
they energetically advocated "social" (public) health insurance, but attempts to pass such an amendment to the state constitution found few
backers outside the labor movement and a few left-wing progressives.[21]

Indeed, the only issue on which McCarthy's machine agreed with
Gompers's opposition to regulatory legislation was that of a minimum
wage for women. Sneering that some "bureaucratic commission" could
not be trusted to enforce the minimum, *Organized Labor* advised women
to join unions and rely on their own power at the workplace. Even in this
demurrer, however, the BTC did not hold consistently to an anti-statist
line. One of the original members of the California Industrial Welfare
Commission, formed in 1913 to set and enforce the female wage standard,
was McCarthy's close ally Walter Mathewson, longtime president of the
BTC in nearby Santa Clara County.[22]

Within San Francisco, the BTC and the rest of the local labor movement
usually achieved the reforms they demanded. From 1901 until after World
War I, mayors and boards of supervisors either genuinely sympathized
with labor's agenda or voted for it because they feared the potential wrath
of voters in the South of Market area and Mission District. However, outside the city, the belief that government should protect the interests of

property owners guided most legislators, who were themselves usually employers or professionals with close ties to business. Despite the presence of a full-time state lobbyist for the San Francisco Labor Council (SFLC), legislative measures banning child labor and work over eight hours on government projects were not enforced, and ones providing for factory inspections and workmen's compensation found few backers outside the Bay City. Moreover, at a time when corporations were increasingly using the courts to cripple strikes and boycotts, a series of anti-injunction bills failed to pass either house of the state legislature.[23]

The BTC welcomed aid from progressives who sincerely wanted to help workers, but McCarthy and his men never really warmed up to them. Republican reform Governor Hiram Johnson, who took office in 1911, had first gained recognition by serving as assistant prosecutor for the San Francisco graft trials, and his supporters regularly berated the BTC for acting like a "labor trust."[24] Progressives from Southern California also made several attempts to pass a state prohibition amendment. These initiatives received almost no votes from the union, Catholic, and immigrant precincts of the Bay Area.[25]

According to the BTC, cultural bigotry tainted the actions of middle-class reformers, most of whom were Anglo-Protestants or assimilated German Jews. Their attempt to stop workingmen from gathering at taverns was not so different from their eradication of a city administration that had been friendly to organized labor. Even some female unionists, who did not figure in the polling booth drama until they won the suffrage statewide in 1911, equated political progressivism with condescending social work. As a contemporary scholar put it, working-class women were "convinced that the laboring people themselves are more competent to work out a solution of their difficulties than any outsider could be."[26]

Labor and progressive activists also had divergent, competitive reasons for supporting the same reforms. Progressives wanted fair and efficient administrators to preside over a society free of class and partisan warfare. They were primarily concerned that the legal ground rules not favor business or labor. BTC leaders, on the other hand, viewed the state apparatus as a crucial arena in which the industrial conflict was being played out. It could not be separated from class interests.

The long campaign for municipal ownership of San Francisco's utilities, which both groups favored, illustrates their ideological differences. During the first third of this century, a complex battle raged over the control of resources upon which the city's economic life depended: water, telephones, natural gas and electricity, and streetcars. Firms which had earlier won lucrative long-term franchises under corrupt regimes clung to their properties and fought every official attempt to raise the funds to buy them out.[27]

The BTC agreed with urban progressives that public ownership would break the grip of greedy magnates over the city's future. "It will mean cheaper rates, better service, higher wages for the employees and far less political corruption," *Organized Labor* proclaimed in a 1901 editorial.[28] Disinterested bureaucrats would substitute altruistic principles for the seamy profit-mindedness which had resulted in poor maintenance, inadequate service, and frequent labor disputes. This was the heart of civic progressivism: anti-monopoly fervor harnessed to a rational, orderly solution.

However, when McCarthy's men connected municipalization to the enhancement of union power, they parted company with professional reformers. Olaf Tveitmoe argued that once cities owned their utilities, citizens would interest themselves more in the conditions of workers on the streetcars and in the pumping stations. With a faith in the public's pro-union attitudes that current labor officials could not share, Tveitmoe predicted that municipal ownership would bring steady improvements in wages and hours and a strict adherence to union standards. Thus, the interests of workers and the broader community would be equally served.[29]

The BTC's argument for public ownership exemplified the organization's general stance toward the reform temperament. While progressives cheered municipal trolleys and the Industrial Welfare Commission as steps away from the abyss of class warfare, San Francisco's most powerful unionists still spoke as trench soldiers slowly pushing back the army of capital. "The streets of this city belong to the people," *Organized Labor* declared in 1902, "and the transportation companies are common carriers and should be operated by the people."[30]

Reformers wanted both sides of the social cleavage to play fair by submitting their grievances to impartial, expert custodians of the public weal. They welcomed labor's support but mistrusted the class interest that kept slipping into the demands of even the most accommodating union leader. For their part, building trades unionists were convinced that only an increase of their own economic and political power would assure beneficial change. In moments of frustration, they would have echoed Eric Hobsbawm's assertion that "middle-class movements can operate as 'stage armies of the good'; proletarian ones can only operate as real armies with real generals and staffs."[31] While they energetically promoted legal solutions to workers' problems, McCarthy and his associates also shared the cynicism toward the state, even one controlled by progressives, that both Samuel Gompers and the revolutionary syndicalists of the IWW preached.

The emancipation of the working class depended, in the last analysis, on the strength of the labor movement.

Elements of a Vision

While engaged in the difficult struggle for reform, BTC leaders were aware that even the most successful trade unions could achieve only a partial and insecure solution to the woes of the industrial system. Behind the closed shop, the eight-hour day, and a friendly administration in City Hall lay the vision of a democratic society controlled by workers and small farmers, one which embodied both nostalgic and forward-looking notions of utopia. As editor of *Organized Labor*, Olaf Tveitmoe was the main architect of this idealistic project. However, most BTC unionists followed his lead, both rhetorically and materially. In their dreams, California could become a commoner's paradise, and they were willing to use the resources of the BTC to speed the transformation.

BTC leaders did not advocate socialism. They spoke instead of an "aristocracy" of businessmen who usurped the natural rights of workers through "artificial" means such as the courts and trusts. Their heroes were American statesmen like Jefferson and Lincoln who had stood for majority rule at times when democracy was imperiled. Testifying before the Industrial Relations Commission, McCarthy compared open-shop employers such as steel magnate Andrew Carnegie to the men "who threw the tea into the ship rather than from the battlement of the ship" in Boston harbor in 1773.[32] Even those leaders, like Tveitmoe, who hoped for a socialist future seldom discussed it with the membership. To do so would have created a major rift in the organization and with the national AFL. It would have also meant rejection of the BTC's claim to a share of civic responsibility. In early twentieth-century San Francisco, it was permissible for union leaders to make angry populist speeches and still have routine dealings with businessmen and politicians who did not share their views. Verbal allegiance to the creed of an international workers' order, however, would have relegated the BTC to a ghettoized existence.

The visionary aspect of BTC politics borrowed from a long, continuous tradition of working-class republicanism. Beginning in the cities and industrial towns of the Northeast in the 1820s and 1830s, labor activists castigated entrepreneurial manufacturers for making formerly independent men and women into tightly regulated drudges who had to operate machines for someone else's profit or risk starvation. "The time has arrived when the people of the United States must decide whether they will be a Republic in fact, or only a Republic in name," wrote George Henry Evans, a leader of the New York Workingmen's Party in the early 1830s. In essence, Evans and his many counterparts were condemning the elite for being anti-American, for sabotaging the egalitarian creed of the Revolution. Through the Gilded Age, such organizations as the National Labor Union and the Knights of Labor and individuals like Ira Steward and Henry George deepened this critique and popularized it among millions of native-born and immigrant workers who felt a similar gulf between the promise of American democracy and the powerless reality of industrial work. In addition to durable unions, they also advocated land reform, producer cooperatives, and a radical inflation of the money supply as ways to escape the tyranny of the wage system.[33] While BTC unionists took a pragmatic approach to such inherited proposals, they certainly did not reject them.

Producer cooperatives held a special attraction partly because they were something of a local tradition. Coopers, fishermen, and even underwear seamstresses had created at least a dozen such businesses in San Francisco between 1864 and 1900. In 1897, several hundred craftsmen had established a labor exchange, a system of distributing goods based on the quantity of labor expended on a particular product that had been pioneered in one of Robert Owen's utopian socialist colonies in the 1820s. The San Francisco exchange, one of over 300 that sprouted across the county during the depression of the 1890s, used "labor checks" redeemable for goods at a common warehouse or sympathetic retail stores. In San Francisco, the scheme lasted little more than a year, but the hundreds of mechanics and small businessmen who participated demonstrated that even an anachronistic cooperative plan could attract adherents.[34]

BTC leaders viewed mutualistic enterprises favorably, particularly when they enjoyed union sponsorship and were thus a salutary complement to normal activities. The union-operated planing mill which broke the back of the 1900–1901 lockout was the organization's most dramatic plunge into cooperation, but the BTC also extended financial and promotional assistance to other union enterprises, including a cooperative meat company and a brickmaking factory. For several years, the exclusionist Anti-Jap Laundry League operated laundries, managed and staffed by unionists under the guidance of BTC officials. Plans for a union-controlled bank, a cooperative building association, and a mattress factory to aid female strikers in that industry were promoted in the pages of *Organized Labor* but never bore fruit. Nevertheless, far from being a utopian notion which had died with the Knights of Labor, cooperation was a small but significant stone in the edifice of BTC strategy.[35]

McCarthy and his fellow leaders tempered their general support for mutualistic enterprise with a recognition of its ambiguous characteristics. Many building trades workers wanted to become individual employers or to enter into partnerships with other craftsmen. Calling such a business a "cooperative" insured it a degree of acceptance from the laboring population but ran afoul of union rules against members doubling as contractors. In 1914, a group of carpenters were fined for operating a building society which accepted both union and nonunion men as stockholders and mechanics. If operated under BTC auspices, the firm would have been welcomed. A delegate to the California BTC convention once even suggested that McCarthy and other officials should double as contractors and thus contribute to the relief of jobless unionists.[36]

Despite the gamut of enterprises which fell under the rubric of "cooperation," the concept retained an idealistic core. Building mechanics were well acquainted with the skills and responsibilities of contractors and material suppliers, and therefore viewed the separation between employer and employee with a degree of skepticism. "Why can we not assume the superintendency and couple the profits thereof to the wages we now receive," a craftsman named Cornelius Lynch asked in 1901, "and thus divert toward ourselves a larger share of the wealth that our labor creates?" Most cooperative firms led a short, debt-ridden life and failed to mount any real challenge to the contracting fraternity. However, the persistence of such efforts demonstrates that the republican dream of economic independence still struck a chord among white workers. As a cooperative activist wrote in 1921, "down in the heart and soul of every human being that works for a living [exists the feeling] that he is not free as long as he is compelled to work for another."[37]

San Francisco unionists believed that one major barrier to a democratic economy was the concentration of large holdings in land. Before the American conquest of California in the 1840s, a few Mexican *rancheros* had owned huge stretches of arable land on which they grew crops and grazed cattle. With the Gold Rush and statehood came wily speculators and such new corporations as the Central (later Southern) Pacific Railroad which swindled for and bought massive properties in the rich valleys which lie between the coast and the Sierra Nevada. In the 1870s, land speculators Henry Miller and Charles Lux acquired more than a million acres in California and the Pacific Northwest, effectively blocking ownership by prospective small farmers. Henry George's fierce indictment of "the land monopoly" in *Progress and Poverty* (published in 1879) drew its inspiration from the widespread disgust such holdings aroused in California.[38]

A quarter-century later, the unequal ownership of rural land continued to be an issue for urban-dwelling tradesmen. To BTC spokesmen, speculative holdings of unimproved property which could feed thousands seemed the quintessence of exploitation, the clearest indication that California was not being run in the interest of its people. When local employers accused San Francisco unions of hurting the state's economy with "unreasonable" demands, McCarthy shot back that "the heavy, the large, the tremendous bountiful grants of land associated with . . . few individuals" were the true culprits behind sluggish growth. *Organized Labor* ran numerous articles accusing financiers and real estate brokers of stealing public lands and monopolizing the irrigation funds which the U.S. Government had begun to provide under the Reclamation Act of 1902. These vehement attacks drew no distinction between the power of industrialists and that of wealthy landlords.[39] On a deeper, ancestral level, a Georgist diatribe may have appealed to unionists who were only a generation removed from the impoverished cotters of the West of Ireland or the tenant villages of Germany.

The BTC endorsed two solutions to the land problem, agricultural colonies and the "single tax." In 1910, Olaf Tveitmoe wrote, "the unions ought to have a tract of land where every striker could put in his labor in support of himself and his family." On the back page of the same issue of *Organized Labor*, a large advertisement announced the formation of a company offering land at twenty cents an acre in a virgin oil field near Bakersfield, California. As president of the firm, Tveitmoe had convinced sixteen union officials from both halves of the state to join him in a scheme which soon went bankrupt without selling a single plot. Five years later, the annual convention of the state BTC recommended that the organization purchase groves of apricot orchards as a self-supporting "land reserve" for injured, retired, and unemployed craftsmen.[40] With a unionist twist, the Jeffersonian ideal of agrarian democracy had sprouted in the unlikely soil of an urban federation of skilled workers.

The call to settle on the land revealed a subterranean dissatisfaction with the capital-labor nexus. Why, BTC leaders asked, should our horizons be limited to wages and work rules while other men engorge themselves on the bounty of crops or the profits of speculation? Unlike other "back-to-the-land" advocates of the period, BTC men did not perceive the city as a locus of social evil or uphold the family farm as a model to be emulated. They simply argued that collectively owned land could be "a harbor of refuge . . . a base of operations in times of industrial war." Union farms might also employ redundant workers whose lives were being wasted on the streets of San Francisco and other cities. If organized labor proved unable, the BTC was perfectly willing to let the state play the mobilizing role. The BTC even favored government ownership if that were necessary to break the stranglehold of the "land monopoly."[41]

The BTC also supported a campaign to enact Henry George's "single tax" in California. The former San Francisco journalist's idea to place a 100 percent levy on unimproved land had intrigued millions of readers and, together with his sympathy for workers' everyday grievances, almost got him elected mayor of New York in 1886. After George's death in 1897, "single tax" organizers switched from publicizing his plan internationally to attempting to put it into practice somewhere in the United States. In California, their tactic was to seek, through the initiative process, a constitutional amendment that would allow counties to write their own tax laws, hoping thereby to circumvent the statewide influence of large landholders. The campaign manager for the first initiative attempt in 1912 was Herman Guttstadt, a veteran leader of the West Coast Cigarmakers' Union and good friend of both Samuel Gompers and George himself. On several occasions, the BTC heard Guttstadt impart the gospel that "indolence and not industry should bear the burden of taxation."[42]

The local option initiative failed to gain a majority in three elections from 1912 to 1920, but it was not for lack of broad-based support. George had promised that enactment of the "single tax" would usher in an age of perpetual prosperity, "the Golden Age of which poets have sung and high-raised seers have told in metaphor," and California advocates of the proposal bridged the waters of political division. They included socialist minister J. Stitt Wilson, ex-Populist Congressman James Maguire, the State Federation of Labor and BTC, as well as liberal attorney Milton U'Ren and, at one point, a majority of both houses of the state legislature. All agreed that the strong medicine of the man Olaf Tveitmoe called "the immortal Henry George" might rid the world of a multitude of afflictions. Only a series of clever opposition campaigns that scared voters with predictions of economic disaster kept California from enacting the local option plan.[43]

The affection of BTC leaders for the "single tax," cooperatives, and agricultural colonies demonstrated both their romanticism and their pragmatism. The vision of a democracy of small producers receded ever further into historical myth, but it provided a rationale for political action which otherwise would have seemed simply a grab for power. On the other hand, utopian schemes could have utility, as the experience of Progressive Planing Mill Number One demonstrated. With Olaf Tveitmoe leading the charge, the men of the BTC moved comfortably in different arenas where their economic prowess was respected. While they lacked a deep commitment to any one cause, they affirmed a sustained interest in proposals which could soften or negate the inhumanity of American capitalism.

The BTC and the Left

This concern, joined with a desire to co-opt potential rivals, led the BTC to take an ambivalent stance toward the organized left. The IWW and the Socialist Party, the only groups which mattered, had members and sympathizers inside many San Francisco unions and a greater claim to the practice of class solidarity than the chieftains of the BTC could boast. Socialist and anarcho-syndicalist opinions circulated freely among the domestic and international migrants who populated the California labor movement. Acknowledging their appeal, BTC leaders never subjected radical *ideas* to serious criticism until the end of World War I. But, at the same time, they cooperated with radical *organizations* only on a limited, *ad hoc* basis. McCarthy's men felt more congenial with leftists than they did with middle-class progressives, but they were no more willing to compromise the strength of their federation for Big Bill Haywood than for Hiram Johnson. As always, the value of an alliance depended upon the size of the constituency each side brought to it.

BTC executives regarded the IWW with ideological warmth but organizational frigidity. The Wobblies were a rather inconsequential force in the Bay Area. They had a smattering of members among the unskilled laborers who passed through the Waterfront and South of Market districts but never mounted a strike in San Francisco. Left-wing Socialists admired the heroism of IWW organizers and shared their goal of industrial unionism, but they usually advocated "boring within" the AFL to achieve it. Thus, the men of the BTC confronted the Wobblies more as a state and national phenomenon than as a real threat to their local position.

At a number of critical points, the BTC did assist the organization which brazenly announced its intention to supplant the "labor fakirs" of the AFL. In 1907, eighty BTC and SFLC locals joined a defense league for IWW leader Big Bill Haywood and two officials of the Western Federation of Miners who were on trial for allegedly murdering an ex-governor of Idaho. In 1912, Olaf Tveitmoe traveled to San Diego to protest the brutal treatment which Wobbly free speech campaigners were receiving at the hands of local police and vigilantes. Across the front page of *Organized Labor*, Tveitmoe splashed photos of police using firehoses to disperse peaceful if boisterous "soap boxers." The BTC also praised the IWW for organizing polyglot industrial work forces in Lawrence, Massachusetts, and Paterson, New Jersey. "Syndicalist tactics have proven themselves wonderfully effective," enthused the BTC organ after the successful 1912 strike in Lawrence.[44]

While respecting their dedication, the BTC condemned the Wobblies for wanting to substitute themselves for the mainstream labor movement. Industrial unionism had always been popular in the West—among building workers as well as sailors, miners, and lumberjacks—but it could more easily be achieved through groups like McCarthy's which already wielded urban influence and had ample finances. Attacks on existing unions, a hostility to politics, and rhetorical bravado not supported by deeds only highlighted the fundamental weakness of the IWW's approach.[45] Even Big Bill Haywood deferred to the BTC's accomplishments. When the one-eyed veteran of minefield wars came to San Francisco in 1909, McCarthy invited him to speak at the Building Trades Temple. Haywood minimized any differences with his hosts and even lauded the BTC as "an organization that does things without talking and resolving and then adjourning to do nothing." Evidently, the confident use of power absolved the sins of business unionism.[46]

Relations with the Socialist Party were both more friendly and more complicated. The California branch, whose 6,000 members made it one of the nation's largest, was torn by a division of both regional and ideological dimensions. In the Los Angeles area, attorney Job Harriman led a faction of skilled workers, intellectuals, and feminists who advocated fusion with the Union Labor Party (ULP) to the north as well as woman suffrage and a host of other political reforms. But in the Bay Area, most activists were revolutionaries who followed the lead of labor organizers Tom Mooney and William McDevitt and the lawyer-theoretician Austin Lewis. They accused local craft union officials of committing "class collaboration" at the workplace and in politics.[47]

Both factions of the Socialist Party put up candidates for local and state office, but only the Harrimanites campaigned to *win*, tailoring their message to attract progressive-minded voters with pleas for municipal ownership and a more equitable tax structure. Successful "right wingers," like the Methodist minister Stitt Wilson who was elected mayor of Berkeley in 1911, were vociferously attacked by their internal rivals. In return, the "right" refused to sponsor Bill Haywood when he toured the state and even regarded Eugene Debs as too radical for the constituency they hoped to win over. The Harrimanites usually dominated the state organization, but factional bitterness was so great that each side often declined to recognize an intraparty victory by the other.[48]

BTC leaders were generally tolerant toward their radical brethren. Individual Socialists freely ran for local union office, and at least one affiliate (the Cabinetmakers) was controlled by Socialist Party faithful. BTC leaders had little use for the party's left-wing faction, but they worked with the Harrimanites in several political battles. A heretic within his own party, Harriman espoused amalgamation with the AFL under the umbrella of a national labor party. Only such an alliance, he believed, could realistically compete for public office and hope to transform America in the interests of the working class.[49]

Since they agreed on the need for a stronger AFL and a labor party, why didn't the BTC seek a permanent coalition with right-wing Socialists? The answer is that organizational integrity came first. Building trades workers must, their leaders believed, avoid entangling alliances which could jeopardize their fortunes. Socialists of the Harriman variety meant well and were certainly more trustworthy than self-righteous "good government" men who purported to treat labor and capital evenhandedly in circumstances where no equality of means existed. In a romantic moment, Tveitmoe could write that soon "we will see the workingmen of this Nation solidified as never before and marching under the banner of the party which looks alone to the workers of the world for its perpetuity."[50] However, even the most practical Socialists embroiled themselves too much in Marxist dogma, refusing to give up loyalty to a creed in favor of the less principled but more promising strategies of the labor movement. The BTC viewed itself as the capable vanguard of a better civilization that socialists could only proclaim.

Racism as Self-Defense

Ironically, the BTC's most successful political cause was one dedicated to preventing workers of a different race from taking any part in that civilization. From the 1860s to the 1920s, the demand for Asian exclusion bound together white wage-earners in a movement that spoke loudly and forcefully for a majority of Californians. Organized labor spearheaded the mobilization and thereby gained support from citizens who either could not or would not join a union. As economist Lucile Eaves wrote in 1910, "Much of the present strength of the California labor movement is due to the sense of common interests, and the habit of united action which were acquired in this great campaign." The anti-Japanese phase of the long racist march, beginning in the 1890s, drew inspiration from the earlier drive against the Chinese that had culminated with the passage of the nation's first immigration restriction law.[51]

However, a generation of trade union development had a marked effect on the campaign to restrict immigration in the Progressive era. From the 1860s to the 1880s, white workers inside and outside the fledgling unions had expressed their discontent through riots, "anti-coolie clubs," and votes for Denis Kearney's short-lived Workingmen's Party of California as well as for major party candidates who promised to "clean out the Chinese." By the twentieth century, strong locals and central labor federations were able to channel the frustration, managing the anti-Japanese campaign as they did strikes and boycotts against employers. Union officials handled the issue as one of several priorities which had to be balanced to further the interests of labor as a whole. The steady pressure of a lobbying group named the Asiatic Exclusion League largely replaced spontaneous violence and demagogic oratory. "Sandlot agitation is a thing of the past," wrote P. H. McCarthy in 1900, referring to the site of San Francisco's City Hall where Kearney's rhetoric had once inflamed thousands.[52]

The altered nature of the "enemy" also seemed to call for a more deliberate strategy. Unlike the Chinese who came earlier, immigrants from Japan did not accept a role at the bottom of society but, through diligent work, turned impressive profits in agriculture and commerce. Moreover, looming behind them was a government which had proved its military prowess and hunger for empire in two recent wars (against China in the 1890s and Russia in 1904 and 1905). White Californians felt a strong twinge of insecurity when they contemplated the pattern of Japanese success extended into the indefinite future. As Hiram Johnson candidly told Lincoln Steffens, "Their superiority, their aesthetic efficiency, and their maturer mentality make them effective in competition with us, and unpopular and a menace."[53]

Twentieth-century exclusion activists in California did not need to demonstrate their power in the streets; anti-Japanese sentiment was practically unanimous. Unionists began the movement but, within a decade, they were joined by the conservative *San Francisco Chronicle*, a large network of patriotic and fraternal groups, and even most leftists. Few white Californians even discussed the *rights* of Japanese. Instead, the dividing line was drawn between the great majority who favored an interventionist posture and a small minority which still clung to the laissez-faire policy of unrestricted immigration. Labor and progressive spokesmen both argued that a nation

which already suffered, in the South, the consequences of one "race problem" should not assume the burden of another. Leading San Francisco
merchants and manufacturers agreed. Socialists were torn, but most reluctantly favored exclusion. As Cameron King of the San Francisco Socialist
local wrote, "Our feelings of brotherhood toward the Japanese must wait
until we have no longer reason to look upon them as an inflowing horde of
alien scabs." Father Peter Yorke was merely echoing the attitudes of his
parishioners when he favored the ULP's segregation of Japanese school-
children. Only a few employers concerned about a labor shortage, some
Protestant missionaries, and, of course, Japanese immigrants themselves
dared stand against the tide.[54]

San Francisco labor launched the anti-Japanese campaign in 1900, a
year of rapid union growth. In May, both central councils passed resolutions calling for the total exclusion of Asian immigrants and invited
Mayor Phelan to help inaugurate the new crusade at a massive rally. One
of the orators, Stanford sociologist E. A. Ross, incurred the displeasure of
his university's administration by declaring that immigration restriction
served the same protective end as the high tariff. When Ross was fired, labor spokesmen claimed him as a martyr to "academic freedom." Olaf
Tveitmoe wrote in the professor's defense, "There is a jangle of rusty
shackles in Stanford's quad, and an odor of the medieval torture chamber
in the place where the dons sit in solemn conclave."[55] After this flurry of
attention to the Japanese issue, union officials concentrated on lobbying
Congress for a permanent Chinese exclusion law and managing their own
freshly won power at the workplace.

In 1905, labor returned to the anti-Japanese hustings with a vengeance.
On May 14, representatives of over one hundred local unions and a variety
of other groups formed the Japanese and Korean Exclusion League (JKEL)
(renamed, in 1907, the Asiatic Exclusion League [AEL]). The delegates
thanked the *Chronicle* for publishing a sensationalist series on the Japanese "threat," established a modest headquarters in a downtown office
building, and passed three resolutions which guided the organization's activities throughout its eight years of life: a demand that the Chinese Exclusion Act also cover Japanese and Koreans, a boycott of Japanese workers
and Japanese-owned businesses, and the advocacy of segregated public
schools. The BTC completely dominated the twenty-six-member executive board and the organization's staff. Olaf Tveitmoe was named president and major spokesman, John McDougald of the Marble Cutters served
as treasurer, and Abraham E. Yoell of the Electricians' Union was hired to
run the office.[56]

The AEL aspired to be the spearhead of a growing movement, but it served mainly as a propaganda center. Every week, Yoell sent out a thick packet of information to a mailing list of thousands, up and down the Pacific Coast. The publication both commented on progress being made toward the AEL's goals at various levels of government and supplied fuel for a wider racist perspective with articles on low wage rates, disease and sexual immorality among Japanese settlers, and warnings that many immigrants were actually spies for their emperor. The BTC financed the bulk of the AEL's restrained expenditures (which averaged about $4,500 a year), but the significance of the anti-Asian group transcended its meager material presence. As Alexander Saxton wrote, "its real function was to coordinate and *harmonize* the activities of an already existing organizational system—the trade unions."[57] Indeed, the AEL posed as the representative of all organized workers, on alert for their fellow citizens. Tveitmoe and Yoell publicized immigration statistics, monitored the activities of legislators and presidents, and supplied sympathetic officials with documentary ammunition to further the common end. Individual unions which conducted their own boycotts against employers of Japanese labor or Japanese-owned businesses received AEL advice and speakers. In October of 1906, the AEL enforced a ban against Japanese restaurants. The drive featured matchboxes with the slogan "White men and women, patronize your own race," and scattered incidents of violent coercion. In 1908, Tveitmoe helped union laundry workers *and* their employers to form the Anti-Jap Laundry League, which tried to convince local unions to impose fines of up to fifty dollars on members who took their soiled linen to Japanese-owned firms.[58]

The conjunction of the BTC and the AEL had political value for both groups. When Olaf Tveitmoe wrote to the Governor of California on behalf of the AEL, he also spoke as the representative of a body with influence which stretched from construction site to city hall. The San Francisco school crisis of 1906–1907, in which the segregation of ninety-three Japanese students set off a feverish bout of diplomacy between Tokyo and Washington, grew out of the ruling ULP's attempt to enact the AEL platform. Less than twenty delegates usually attended the AEL's monthly meetings, but the organization hosted mass election rallies at which scores of candidates declared their loyalty to the cause.[59]

From 1905 to 1910, the AEL was the core of a labor-based protest movement. Conservative Republicans then controlled the state government and routinely cited the swelling volume of trade with Japan to stymie discriminatory legislation. In Washington, President Roosevelt sought to pacify the anti-Asian sentiment of the West with a partial remedy while warning against provocations that could lead to war. That measure, the Gentleman's Agreement of 1908 between Tokyo and Washington, informally barred the future immigration of Japanese laborers but allowed those already in the country to send for their families. California Democrats denounced these moves as insubstantial, but only the AEL could criticize them without the taint of partisanship and in the name of all white workers.

While promoting a movement which enjoyed almost universal support in their region, BTC officials took a strangely defensive tone. "Let us give warning to the East and the South and the North," Olaf Tveitmoe told a labor convention in 1906, "that this nation cannot exist one-third yellow, one-third black, one-third Caucasian . . . any more than it could exist half free and half slave." In 1914, at a time when Asian immigration to the state was manifestly decreasing, P. H. McCarthy vowed, "I would rather see California without a solitary man within it . . . than to see California Japanized or Chinaized."[60]

Given the trickle of Japanese entering the United States and their scrupulously pacific attitude toward whites, such attitudes seem not just morally repugnant but absurdly irrational. Asian immigrants certainly posed no immediate threat to building tradesmen or other skilled urban workers. After disembarking at the port of San Francisco, Japanese typically went to work as domestic servants or in small businesses owned by their countrymen. Soon, a majority migrated to agricultural regions, especially near Los Angeles, where a young, efficient laborer could, according to historian Harry H. L. Kitano, "progress to contract farming, then to share tenancy and cash leasing, and finally to the outright purchase of land for his own truck farm." From rural backgrounds, few Japanese immigrants had been craft workers in their homeland, and they knew that any American union local would try to prevent them from picking up a tool. In 1910, less than 100 nonwhites were employed in *all* the building trades of San Francisco.[61] Why then did unionists regard the Japanese as such a serious threat?

The content of their fears demonstrates that a deep racial insecurity lurked behind economic strength. San Francisco's top labor leaders spoke as if their backs were to the wall with a force of enemy aliens attacking from all sides. The Japanese were simultaneously depicted as superhuman and totally repugnant. "I have learned," Walter MacArthur said at the founding convention of the AEL, "that a Jap can live on the smell of an oily rag." McCarthy told a union gathering, "That the Japanese is skilled and progressive must be admitted. Upon these qualities we must look with the greatest apprehension."[62] Like the Chinese before them, their efficiency and frugality made the Japanese "unfair" competitors. Moreover, they refused to accept discriminatory treatment and rushed to California courts with challenges to school segregation and restrictions on the ownership of land. In Tokyo, their parent government protested legal and vigilante attacks on its residents abroad. Such acts only heightened the fears of whites who had always assumed their self-evident superiority would make other races quake.

To labor activists, the assertiveness of the Japanese pointed up the fragile nature of their own status. A mere decade before the formation of the AEL, unions had struggled to survive against a united phalanx of employers. During the Progressive era, San Francisco remained the citadel of unionism in California, but the open shop was the rule elsewhere in the state. Japanese immigrants did not have to ally with Patrick Calhoun (owner of United Railroads, who had a virtual monopoly on San Francisco's streetcar business) to be considered enemies of labor. Their lack of interest in unions was assumed, despite some evidence to the contrary.[63] However, unlike in the days of Kearneyism, union spokesmen could not blame capitalists as a class for the influx of undesirable aliens; many wealthy farmers and businessmen also denounced the "Asiatic menace." So unionists identified a new danger: Japanese immigrants were the advance guard of a conquering army.

In the years immediately after the earthquake, the "Yellow Peril" occupied a significant place in the racial phobias of McCarthy and his associates. In 1906 and 1907, *Organized Labor* reported that Japanese contractors and mechanics had gained control of the Hawaiian building industry. The journal serialized a melodramatic novel by one John Dathan-Landor which predicted that a Japanese invasion force would launch an attack on the American mainland from facilities owned by their countrymen in Hawaii. Olaf Tveitmoe had once written, "Militarism is the laboring man's worst enemy," and BTC officials routinely opposed increasing funds for the armed services. But they made an exception in this case. *Organized Labor* urged citizens to gird themselves for an international race war. In the spring of 1908, Tveitmoe was positive that hostilities were about to begin. He even ran a front-page story warning the American fleet not to visit Tokyo on a world cruise expressly undertaken to demonstrate American naval prowess. Japanese "harbors are filled with mines and lined with guns," wrote the BTC secretary. "Her people have the cunning of the fox and the ferocity of a bloodthirsty hyena."[64] It was an attitude that led directly to the forced relocation of 112,000 Japanese aliens and their native-born children during World War II.

Repeated sentiments like Tveitmoe's exemplify an ideological slant which Richard Hofstadter once labeled "the paranoid style in American politics." Building tradesmen shared little else with the conservative, nativist WASPs whom Hofstadter discussed, but they did claim a genuine conspiracy was afoot to deprive white producers of their liberties.[65] Similar to other political paranoiacs, BTC leaders believed that the Japanese learned from and adapted to American society only in order to destroy it. The "superior" (white) civilization could be preserved only through the total elimination of "the enemy" from the Western Hemisphere. In the case of San Francisco unionists, however, a paranoid style still allowed the exercise of considered actions such as the establishment of the AEL or lobbying for limited victories in Sacramento. The catastrophic qualities of the anti-Asian movement did not diminish the political skills of its activists.

There was another, more conciliatory side to labor's anti-Asian ideology. As vehemently as Tveitmoe and his cohorts denounced the Japanese in racial terms, they did not forget their own position as leaders of a class-based movement.

Representatives of organized workers needed to explain their actions as derived from economic and political principles which were unselfish. "At this critical moment," wrote Tveitmoe in 1903, "when it is to be settled if America is to have what no other nation has ever had, namely, a common laboring class permanently earning more than a bare subsistence, our hope is to be blasted . . . by the invasion of cheap labor from the teeming Orient."[66] The invocation of a great cause, coupled with rhetorical support for Asian workers in their *own* countries, cast the racist appeal in a more altruistic, even fraternal mold.

On several occasions, *Organized Labor* acknowledged that Asians were capable of resisting the oppression of both state and capital. In 1909, the paper praised Japanese who were on strike against plantation owners on the Hawaiian island of Oahu and expressed horror at reports that the farmworkers toiled an average of fifteen hours a day. "Capitalists are the same the world over," was the curt analysis. Koreans and Filipinos both received sympathy for their struggles against Japanese and American imperialism, respectively. Sun Yat-sen, founder of the Chinese Republic, was hailed as an enlightened leader who believed in the "single tax" and the public ownership of utilities. Tveitmoe hoped the implementation of Sun's program in Asia would finally "settle the immigration question." In 1919, the BTC and SFLC jointly protested the deportation of Indian independence activists, although the labor press had earlier described "Hindoo" immigrants as "unspeakably filthy and in nearly every instance suffering from dangerous and incurable diseases." [67]

To straddle the line between bold-faced racist invective and more acceptable arguments about cheap labor required a nationalist version of workers' rights. Men and women who were allies when fighting for justice in their own countries became natural "scabs" once they touched American soil. State Federation of Labor leader Paul Scharrenberg, who remembered his anti-Asian activities with pride, also told an interviewer that he had twice traveled to Japan to aid union organizing. "As soon as you have our standard of living," he told the Japanese, "then you can move in at your leisure." His vision was of each race being confined to its continent of origin, where, unable to rely on the "safety valve" of immigration, it would have to create a better civilization suited to its unique needs. The only exception to this rule was the potential paradise of North America, reserved for those of European heritage.[68] Thus, the belief that equality necessitated racial purity dovetailed with a ritualistic expression of global solidarity. Exclusion might turn out to be a boon for the excluded!

An example of the clash between anti-Japanese paranoia and class principle took place on Labor Day, 1909. The main attraction for the San Francisco crowd of almost 50,000 was a lengthy address by Clarence Darrow. The celebrated radical lawyer surprisingly devoted most of his time to criticizing his working-class audience. "The great mass of trade unionists," said Darrow, "look upon the man who is willing to come here and toil, as his bitter enemy, and will strangle him or starve him because he proposes to do our work." When this statement was greeted with laughter and jeers, the attorney added that unions, by fearing foreign labor and limiting the number of men able to learn a trade, were turning their anger in the wrong direction. Tveitmoe responded in the next issue of *Organized Labor*. The exclusion of Asians was regrettable, wrote the editor, but necessary as a "war measure." In this case, the laudable ideal of international brotherhood had to be sacrificed in deference to "the real problems of life."[69] Protesting that the color line was immutable, unionists helped strengthen it by defining bigotry as the only rational policy.

The leaders of the San Francisco building trades were not systematic or original political thinkers. Their particular blend of civic reformism, egalitarian vision, romantic class consciousness, and anti-Asian fervor emerged from proposals that lay at hand to protect the wage-earners they represented. Land and utilities made huge profits for a corporate few; so they proposed a confiscatory tax on the first and wanted to buy out the other. Progressives in state government showed concern for the needs of workers; so unionists, somewhat warily, urged them to go further. Japanese threatened to undermine white standards; so the BTC led a movement to exclude them.

What united these disparate strands was a labor nationalism that looked two ways simultaneously. On the one hand, American workers as a class were sorely aggrieved, their status in the workplace and republic declining. Only strong unions could arrest the slide and put wage-earners once again on the road to power. On the other hand, a class identity did not capture the pride that skilled white workers felt in the accomplishments of their nation and the attendant fear that those accomplishments were fragile in a world ruled by "the law of self-preservation." Thus, BTC leaders regarded themselves as defenders of not just their own interests and those of other workers but of an entire people.

It is hardly surprising that the rhetoric of Tveitmoe, McCarthy, and their assistants resonated with populist themes, both when they condemned the venality of capital and the moral pretensions of reformers *and* when they cursed the Japanese. In American history, those who invoke the rights and interests of "the people" have usually been bound by a definition more ethnic than economic. Southern politicians from Tom Watson to George Wallace have proved particularly adept at striking vigorously democratic chords that were at the same time virulently racist.[70] But the same ideology could be applied nationally, and San Francisco unionists in the early twentieth century showed how. They posed as popular warriors with eyes set on a future of bounty and justice and with weapons of organization aimed at anyone who would threaten it. Stopping "hordes of coolies" from taking over white men's jobs and buying white men's land was a cause akin to stopping employers, judges, and legislators from destroying unions and defeating pro-labor politicians.

In one sense, the BTC's methods prefigured those employed by industrial unions during the upsurge of the 1930s and 1940s. A generation before the CIO successfully organized both inside factories and the halls of Congress, building tradesmen were operating in every possible arena. *Organized Labor* said of the BTC's dual strategy, "Labor is now fighting with both fists—politically and industrially. And in the language of the 'pug' [pugilist], it 'carries a knockout blow in each mitt.'" Yet, unlike their New Deal successors, the men of the BTC always assumed that their movement was the creation and property of one race. They would have sympathized with Jack London, who once, during an argument with Socialist comrades over Japanese exclusion, pounded his fist on a table and shouted, "What the devil! I am first of all a white man and only then a Socialist!"[71]

NOTES

1. Frank Roney, *Irish Rebel and California Labor Leader: An Autobiography*, ed. Ira B. Cross (Berkeley, 1931), 455.

2. *Organized Labor* (hereafter *OL*), Feb. 16, 1907.

3. Local Union No. 104, Amalgamated Sheet Metal Workers International Alliance, *Souvenir Pictorial History* (San Francisco, 1910), 119–121.

4. The most complete study of the anti-Asian politics of the labor movement is Alexander Saxton, *The Indispensable Enemy: Labor and the Anti-Chinese Movement in California* (Berkeley, 1971). However, Saxton slights the anti-Japanese aspects of the campaign.

5. On Tillman and other racialist "radicals" in the period from 1890 to 1915, see Joel Williamson, *The Crucible of Race: Black-White Relations in the American South Since Emancipation* (New York, 1984), 111–139.

6. The concept of a political "common sense" is drawn from the work of Antonio Gramsci. Anne Showstack Sassoon defines it as "the incoherent and at times contradictory set of assumptions and beliefs held by the mass of the population at any one time." *Approaches to Gramsci*, ed. Anne Showstack Sassoon (London, 1982), 13.

The following discussion is necessarily limited to the written records of the BTC and thus can only speculate on the degree to which leaders' views were shared by rank-and-file building workers. However, not until 1920 was the persistent resistance to McCarthy's *methods* of rule broadened into a *political* alternative. Before then, the leadership under McCarthy and Tveitmoe clearly initiated an engagement with issues larger than wages and the maintenance of the closed shop.

7. Michael P. Rogin, "Voluntarism: The Political Functions of an Antipolitical Doctrine," *Industrial and Labor Relations Review* 15 (July 1962), 532.

8. George B. Cotkin, "The Spencerian and Comtian Nexus in Gompers' Labor Philosophy," *Labor History* (hereafter *LH*) 20 (Fall 1979), 510–523.

9. Quoted in William M. Dick, *Labor and Socialism in America: The Gompers Era* (Port Washington, N.Y., 1972), 60.

10. For good descriptions of this tendency, see James Weinstein, *The Decline of Socialism in America, 1912–1925* (New York, 1967), 5–10, 29–53; Mari Jo Buhle, *Women and American Socialism, 1870–1920* (Urbana, 1981), 176–213.

11. For Fitzpatrick, see Weinstein, *The Decline of Socialism*, 222, 271, 279, 280; John H. Keiser, "John Fitzpatrick and Progressive Unionism, 1915–1925," Ph.D. diss., Northwestern University, 1965. For Moyer, see Melvyn Dubofsky, *We Shall Be All: A History of the IWW* (New York, 1969), 45–55, 80–81, 304–307; John H. M. Laslett, *Labor and the Left: A Study of Socialist and Radical Influences in the American Labor Movement, 1881–1924* (New York, 1970), 241–286. Also see Dick, *Labor and Socialism*, 63–68.

12. The best study of the IWW is Dubofsky, *We Shall Be All*.

13. For the history of syndicalism through World War I, see André Tridon, *The New Unionism* (New York, 1917); Robert Wohl, *French Communism in the Making* (Stanford, 1966), 21–42; Peter N. Stearns, *Revolutionary Syndicalism and*

French Labor (New Brunswick, N.J., 1971); Robert Michels, *Political Parties* (New York, 1959; orig. pub., 1915), 345 (quote).

14. *OL*, Aug. 6, 1910, Oct. 11, Nov. 1, 1913. On Mann's early thought and career, see Tridon, *New Unionism*, 126–147.

15. *OL*, Feb. 3, 1900.

16. Charles Stephenson claims this pattern held for other cities as well. "A Gathering of Strangers? Mobility, Social Structure, Political Participation in the Formation of Nineteenth-Century American Working Class Culture," in *American Workingclass Culture: Explorations in American Labor and Social History*, ed. Milton Cantor (Westport, Conn., 1979), 42–43.

17. San Francisco Board of Supervisors, Municipal Reports (hereafter SFMR) (1902–1903), 297–298; ibid. (1916–1917), 322, 462–463; U.S., Bureau of the Census, *Census of Occupations*, 1900. For the 1916 case, I did not compare building trades registrants to the proportion of construction workers in the next decennial census. Since there was far more construction in 1920 than in 1916, a comparison would not have been useful. Fee was certainly exaggerating, but his perception was common among businessmen. U.S., Congress, Commission on Industrial Relations, Final Report and Testimony (hereafter CIRR) (1912–1915), vol. 6, 5173.

18. Steven Erie, "Politics, the Public Sector, and Irish Social Mobility: San Francisco, 1870–1900," *Western Political Quarterly* 31 (June 1978), 281–282.

19. *OL*, March 30, 1901, Dec. 30, 1905, Aug. 27, 1910. On the attraction of the New Zealand example, see Peter J. Coleman, "New Zealand Liberalism and the Origins of the American Welfare State," *Journal of American History* 69 (Sept. 1982), 372–391.

20. *OL*, Nov. 1, Sept. 7, 1902, March 12, 1904, Aug. 15, 1914, July 3, Aug. 7, 1915. At the same time, both Gompers and Frank Duffy, General Secretary of the United Brotherhood of Carpenters, were opposing legislation to enforce an eight-hour day in private industry. Walter Galenson, *United Brotherhood of Carpenters: The First Hundred Years* (Cambridge, Mass., 1983), 165–166.

21. CIRR, vol. 6, 5191; *OL*, Mar. 30, Apr. 6, 20, Oct. 12, 19, June 26, 1920. The San Francisco Labor Council (SFLC) then opposed the proposal, and the California Federation of Labor did not take a position on it. Philip Taft, *Labor Politics American Style: The California State Federation of Labor* (Cambridge, Mass., 1968), 56. For working-class reformers in the East and Midwest, see John D. Buencker, *Urban Liberalism and Progressive Reform* (New York, 1973).

22. *OL*, Mar. 15, Apr. 24, 1915.

23. Lucile Eaves, *A History of California Labor Legislation with an Introductory Sketch of the San Francisco Labor Movement* (Berkeley, 1910), 440–441, 79–80.

24. George Mowry, *The California Progressives* (Berkeley, 1951), 92–96.

25. Gilman M. Ostrander, *The Prohibition Movement in California, 1848–1933* (Berkeley, 1957), 120–133.

26. Lillian Ruth Matthews, *Women in Trade Unions in San Francisco* (Berkeley, 1913), 92. The BTC took a generally positive attitude toward reforms, ranging from higher wages to suffrage to even birth control, that would benefit wage-earning women. See Michael Kazin, "Barons of Labor: The San Francisco Building Trades, 1896–1922," Ph.D. diss., Stanford University, 1983, 584–585.

27. On municipal water and streetcars, see Ray W. Taylor, *Hetch Hetchy, The Story of San Francisco's Struggle to Provide a Water Supply for Her Future Needs* (San Francisco, 1926); Morley Segal, "James Rolph, Jr. and the Early Days of the

San Francisco Municipal Railway," *California Historical Quarterly* (hereafter *CHQ*) 42 (March 1964), 3–18.

28. *OL*, Nov. 23, 1901.

29. Ibid., June 11, 1904.

30. Ibid., Nov. 29, 1902.

31. Eric Hobsbawm, *Workers: Worlds of Labor* (New York, 1984), 26.

32. *OL*, Feb. 13, 1909; CIRR, vol. 6, 5217. The BTC also organized a campaign to urge the city to reject the Carnegie Foundation's offer of a library or other major gift. Tveitmoe to San Francisco Labor Council, Oct. 25, 1912, Carton III, San Francisco Labor Council Papers, Bancroft Library, University of California, Berkeley (hereafter SFLCP).

33. For fine examples of the literature on labor republicanism, see Sean Wilentz, *Chants Democratic: New York City and the Rise of the American Working Class* (New York, 1984) (quote, 237–238); Alan Dawley, *Class and Community: The Industrial Revolution in Lynn* (Cambridge, Mass., 1976); Leon Fink, *Workingmen's Democracy: The Knights of Labor and American Politics* (Urbana, 1983); David Montgomery, "Labor and the Republic in Industrial America: 1860–1920," *Le Mouvement Social*, no. 111 (April-June 1980), 201–215.

34. Ira B. Cross, *A History of the Labor Movement in California* (Berkeley, 1935), 36, 44, 57, 145, 164, 172, 178, 213–214, 274, 339; on the Labor Exchange, see various articles in *Voice of Labor* (San Francisco) in 1897; H. Roger Grant, *Self-Help in the 1890s Depression* (Ames, Iowa, 1983), 41–58.

35. *OL*, Dec. 24, 1904, Mar. 23, Nov. 9, 1907, Apr. 9, 1910; *The Rank and File*, Nov. 3, 1920; Frederick L. Ryan, *Industrial Relations in the San Francisco Building Trades* (Norman, Okla., 1936), 137.

36. *OL*, Sept. 12, 1914, Apr. 1, 1916.

37. Ibid., Jan. 19, 1901; Albert Sonnichsen in *The Carpenter*, March 1921.

38. Walton Bean, *California: An Interpretive History*, 3d ed. (New York, 1978), 188–189. On the California origins of George's ideas, see John L. Thomas, *Alternative America: Henry George, Edward Bellamy, Henry Demarest Lloyd, and the Adversary Tradition* (Cambridge, Mass., 1983), 49–71.

39. CIRR, vol. 6, 5203; for examples, see *OL*, Nov. 28, Dec. 5, 1903, Sept. 23, 1905, Sept. 26, 1908, Dec. 27, 1913.

40. *OL*, July 9, 1910; Phillips Russell, "The Class Struggle on the Pacific Coast," *The International Socialist Review* (Sept. 1912), 238; State BTC of California, *Proceedings: Fifteenth Annual Convention, 1915* (San Francisco, 1915), 175–178.

41. Richard White, "Poor Men on Poor Lands," *Pacific Historical Review* 49 (February 1980), 105–131; *OL*, Mar. 18, 1905, Jan. 28, 1911, Sept. 20, 1913, Sept. 1, 1917.

42. Arthur Young, *The Single Tax Movement in the United States* (Princeton, 1916), 163–167; *OL*, Apr. 27, 1912; Cross, *History of the Labor Movement*, 172, 188–189; Samuel Gompers, *Seventy Years of Life and Labour* (New York, 1925), vol. 2, 231, 251, 304, 337; *OL*, Feb. 28, 1914. In 1902 Guttstadt and Gompers had co-authored an anti-Chinese pamphlet, entitled "Meat vs. Rice: American Manhood Against Asiatic Coolieism. Which Shall Survive?"

43. Henry George, *Progress and Poverty* (New York, 1961; orig. pub., 1879), 552; Commonwealth Club of California (San Francisco), *Transactions* 11 (October 1916); *OL*, June 14, 1913, June 24, 1916, Nov. 4, 1911 (quote). In 1916, the "single tax" itself was on the state ballot but lost badly. However, working-class assembly districts in San Francisco favored the proposal. SFMR (1916–1917), 487; Franklin

Hichborn, "California Politics, 1891–1939," typescript, Green Library, Stanford University, 1805–1806.

44. *OL*, Mar. 2, 1907, Apr. 27, May 4, 1912, June 14, 1913. Also see Paul Scharrenberg, "Reminiscences," an oral history conducted in 1954, Regional Oral History Office, Bancroft Library, University of California, Berkeley, 1954, 42; *Revolt*, Apr. 6, 1912.

45. On the IWW, *OL*, Feb. 25, 1905, Apr. 2, 1910, Dec. 6, 1913, Nov. 7, 1914; on organizing industrial workers, ibid., Dec. 18, 1909, Aug. 23, 1913.

46. Ibid., Apr. 3, 1909. The SFLC took a cooler attitude toward the IWW leader; see *San Francisco Examiner*, Oct. 12, 1907. According to Joseph Conlin, Haywood gradually came to the conclusion that the IWW should become "more like the old Western Federation of Miners, a union as highly organized and disciplined as the corporations it combatted." *Big Bill Haywood and the Radical Union Movement* (Syracuse, 1969), 171.

47. Ralph E. Shaffer, "A History of the Socialist Party of California," M.A. thesis, University of California, Berkeley, 1955; David Shannon, *The Socialist Party of America* (Chicago, 1967), 40–42; Bruce Dancis, "The Socialist Women's Movement in the United States, 1901–1917," senior thesis, University of California, Santa Cruz, 1973, 202–233.

48. Ira B. Cross, "Socialism in California Municipalities," *National Municipal Review* (1912), 611–619; Ralph E. Shaffer, "Radicalism in California, 1896–1929," Ph.D. diss., University of California, Berkeley, 1962, 166, 168; Ira Kipnis, *The American Socialist Movement, 1897–1912* (New York, 1952), 373.

49. On labor party sentiment within the national Socialist Party, see Dick, *Labor and Socialism*, 63–67. Harriman later founded a collective agricultural colony north of Los Angeles, which the BTC supported. See Kazin, "Barons of Labor," 339; Paul Kagan, "Portrait of a California Utopia," *CHQ* 51 (Summer 1972), 131–154.

50. *OL*, Nov. 9, 1912.

51. *Labor Clarion* (San Francisco) Sept. 2, 1910. The most complete study of the anti-Japanese campaign is Roger Daniels, *The Politics of Prejudice* (Berkeley, 1962). Also see Hichborn, "California Politics," 1200–1287; Frank P. Chuman, *The Bamboo People: The Law and Japanese Americans* (Del Mar, Calif., 1976), 18–103.

52. *OL*, Apr. 14, 1900.

53. Quoted in John Modell, "Japanese-Americans: Some Costs of Group Achievement," in *Ethnic Conflict in California History*, ed. Charles Wollenberg (Los Angeles, 1970), 104.

54. On business attitudes, see *OL*, Apr. 14, 1900; *Merchants' Association Review* (San Francisco), Sept., 1907; *San Francisco Chamber of Commerce Journal*, June, 1912; *San Francisco Business*, Oct. 15, 1920, Aug. 19, 1921. On the Socialist Party, Shaffer, "Socialist Party of California," 53–55; Aileen S. Kraditor, *The Radical Persuasion, 1890–1917: Aspects of the Intellectual History and the Historiography of Three American Radical Organizations* (Baton Rouge, La., 1981), 177–185. On Yorke, Joseph Brusher, S.J., *Consecrated Thunderbolt: A Life of Father Peter C. Yorke of San Francisco* (Hawthorne, N.J., 1973), 267–268.

55. *OL*, May 5, Nov. 24, 1900; Daniels, *Politics of Prejudice*, 21–22.

56. *OL* May 20, 27, Aug. 19, 1905.

57. The minutes of the Japanese and Korean Exclusion League (JKEL) and the Asiatic Exclusion League (AEL) were routinely reprinted in *OL*. Throughout its existence, over 90 percent of League affiliates were trade unions. See JKEL minutes, *OL*, Sept. 8, 1906; AEL minutes, *OL*, June 12, 1909, Mar. 12, 1910. Saxton, *Indispensable Enemy*, 252.

58. Daniels, *Politics of Prejudice,* 33; Matthews, *Women in Trade Unions,* 34–36.

59. David Brudnoy, "Race and the San Francisco School Board Incident: Contemporary Evaluations," *CHQ* 50 (September 1971), 295–312; *San Francisco Chronicle,* Sept. 17, 1906; *OL,* Sept. 28, 1907, Oct. 17, 1908, Mar. 12, 1910; Yoell to SFLC, Sept. 14, 1911, AEL File, Carton II, SFLCP.

60. *OL,* Jan. 20, 1906; CIRR, vol. 6, 5203.

61. Harry H. L. Kitano, "Japanese," in *Harvard Encyclopedia of American Ethnic Groups,* ed. Stephan Thernstrom (Cambridge, Mass., 1980), 563; Yamato Ichihashi, *Japanese Immigration: Its Status in California* (San Francisco, 1915), 11; Dennis K. Fukumoto, "Chinese and Japanese in California, 1900–1920: A Case Study of the Impact of Discrimination," Ph.D. diss., University of Southern California, 1976, 264–265.

62. *OL,* May 13, 1905, Jan. 13, 1906.

63. In the 1890s, Samuel Gompers had corresponded regularly with Fusatoro Takano, a union organizer who tried to apply the AFL model in his homeland. Philip S. Foner, *History of the Labor Movement in the United States,* 6 vols. (New York, 1947–1982), vol. 3, 274. In 1903, Japanese and Mexican agricultural workers waged a joint strike near Los Angeles and tried, unsuccessfully, to get the national AFL's support. Tomás Almaguer, "Racial Domination and Class Conflict in Capitalist Agriculture: The Oxnard Sugar Beet Workers' Strike of 1903," *LH* 25 (Summer 1984), 325–350 [Chapter 6 of this volume].

64. *OL,* Nov. 17, 1906, Dec. 6, 1907, Jan. 4, 1908, Aug. 18, 1900, May 16, July 25, 1908.

65. Richard Hofstadter, "The Paranoid Style in American Politics," in *The Paranoid Style in American Politics and Other Essays* (New York, 1967), 3–40.

66. *OL,* May 30, 1903.

67. On the 1909 Oahu strike, see Ronald Takaki, *Pau Hana: Plantation Life and Labor in Hawaii* (Honolulu, 1983), 153–164. For BTC views, see *OL,* July 24, Nov. 6, 1909; Tveitmoe to SFLC, Apr. 22, 1910, Carton III, SFLCP; *OL,* July 5, Nov. 22, 1919.

68. Scharrenberg, "Reminiscences," 63–64. On the "new immigrants" from Southern and Eastern Europe, both the BTC and SFLC were ambivalent. *OL* occasionally called the newcomers "ignorant tools of corporations" but vigorously advocated organizing all white wage-earners into unions.

69. *OL,* Sept. 11, 18, 1909.

70. Margaret Canovan, *Populism* (New York, 1981), 55–56.

71. *OL,* Sept. 9, 1911; Richard O'Connor, *Jack London: A Biography* (Boston, 1964), 220.

FURTHER READING

Bean, Walton. *Boss Ruef's San Francisco: The Story of the Union Labor Party, Big Business, and the Graft Prosecution.* 1952.

Burki, Mary A. M. "The California Progressive: Labor's Point of View." *Labor History* 17 (Winter 1976): 24–37.

Cornford, Daniel. *Workers and Dissent in the Redwood Empire.* Chapter 8. 1987.

Cross, Ira B. *A History of the Labor Movement in California.* 1935.

Daniel, Cletus E. "In Defense of the Wheatland Wobblies: A Critical Analysis of the IWW in California." *Labor History* 19 (Fall 1978): 485–509.

Deverell, William, and Tom Sitton, eds. *California Progressivism Revisited.* 1994.

Ethington, Philip J. *The Public City: The Political Construction of Urban Life in San Francisco, 1850–1900.* 1994.

Issel, William."Class and Ethnic Conflict in San Francisco Political History." *Labor History* 18 (Summer 1977): 341–359.

Issel, William, and Robert W. Cherny. *San Francisco, 1865–1932: Politics, Power, and Urban Development.* 1986.

Kazin, Michael. *Barons of Labor: The San Francisco Building Trades and Union Power in the Progressive Era.* 1987.

Knight, Robert E. L. *Industrial Relations in the San Francisco Bay Area, 1900–1918.* 1960.

McDonald, Terrence J. *The Parameters of Urban Fiscal Policy: Socioeconomic Change and Political Culture in San Francisco, 1860–1906.* 1986.

Perry, Louis B., and Richard S. Perry. *A History of the Los Angeles Labor Movement, 1911–1941.* 1963.

Rogin, Michael. "Progressivism and the California Electorate." *Journal of American History* 55 (September 1968): 305–334.

Saxton, Alexander. "San Francisco Labor and the Populist and Progressive Insurgencies." *Pacific Historical Review* 36 (November 1965): 421–437.

Shover, John. "The Progressives and the Working-Class Vote in California." *Labor History* 10 (Fall 1969): 584–602.

Stimson, Grace H. *Rise of the Labor Movement in Los Angeles.* 1955.

Taft, Phillip. *Labor Politics American Style: The California State Federation of Labor.* 1968.

Tygiel, Jules. " 'Where Unionism Holds Undisputed Sway'—A Reappraisal of San Francisco's Union Labor Party." *California History* 62 (Fall 1983): 196–215.

———. *Workingmen in San Francisco, 1880–1901.* 1992.

12   Mobilizing the Homefront
Labor and Politics in Oakland, 1941–1951

Marilynn S. Johnson

EDITOR'S INTRODUCTION

The 1930s witnessed the renaissance of the California labor movement. The membership of the California State Federation of Labor increased from slightly more than 100,000 in 1931 to 291,000 in 1938. The booming economic conditions created by World War II and sustained with but few interruptions through the 1940s provided the setting for an even more dramatic growth in trade union membership. In 1950, when the state took its first census of union members, there were 1,354,000 unionized employees, who made up 42 percent of California's wage and salary workers (excluding farmworkers). The greatly enhanced strength of the California labor movement enabled it to make gains at the workplace and also gave it more potential political power than at any time since the Progressive Era.

Although the jurisdictional disputes between the CIO and the AFL were as bitter in California as anywhere, the rival organizations sometimes forged alliances that made them a potent force in California local and state politics. The CIO had never been averse to political action. The California AFL was much more reluctant to enter the political fray directly by participating in electoral politics. But the gains that unions made in the late 1930s and early 1940s resulted in a legislative offensive against labor at the local, state, and national levels, which impelled the California AFL to switch its focus from legislative lobbying to actively engaging in electoral politics.

The resort to electoral activity was not solely a defensive move. It also reflected the fact that labor emerged during the war years with a new-found sense of its moral and political legitimacy. Many union leaders and rank-and-file union members were determined to forge a postwar social-democratic order fundamentally different from that of the 1930s, more akin to the political agenda of the labor movement in Western Europe.

Nowhere were the militancy and power of the California labor movement more apparent during the 1940s than in Oakland. In December 1946, a strike by retail clerks mushroomed into a general strike sanctioned by the Alameda County Central Labor Council and the Building Trades Council of the AFL. More than one hundred thousand workers took part. The strike was followed in the spring of 1947 by important municipal elections in which four labor candidates were elected on a progressive political platform.

Marilynn Johnson examines the factors that led to the Oakland general strike of 1946 and labor's subsequent political offensive. She shows how the defense boom helped to both cause and magnify a variety of urban social problems, which caused great discontent. The revolt was led by a coalition of labor, minorities, and workers from outside the trade union movement. The insurgents demanded such reforms as mayoral and district elections, public housing, rent control, and more money for schools. Johnson concludes that the labor movement's political challenge in Oakland (and other East Bay cities) foreshadowed progressive political revolts that would occur in later decades.

◆ ◆ ◆

On the eve of the 1947 municipal elections, an extraordinary event took place in Oakland, California. Starting from their respective flatland neighborhoods, hundreds of the city's working-class residents set out for the downtown district on foot, by automobile, and atop parade floats. They convened in a mass torchlight procession down Broadway, brandishing brooms and mops to dramatize the need for "municipal housecleaning." The most impressive float, constructed by the United Negro Labor Committee, showed American Federation of Labor (AFL) and Congress of Industrial Organizations (CIO) pallbearers lowering a casket labelled "The Machine" into the ground. Alongside the burial scene was a placard depicting two gloved fists—one black, one white—smashing the *Oakland Tribune* tower, headquarters of the city's conservative political machine. The fists were labelled "Oakland Voters," and the banner beneath read "Take the Power Out of the Tower."[1]

The election parade dramatized an urban political revolt that had been gaining momentum in Oakland and other California cities since the middle of World War II. While the defense boom accompanying the war created a spate of social problems and dislocations in these cities, such events also allowed political outsiders to challenge the status quo. Labor, black, and other progressive forces coalesced during the war and would become a major force in the municipal politics of the postwar era. In northern California, the city of Oakland became the site of the Bay Area's most dramatic and sustained political challenge. Cemented by a general strike in 1946, a labor-led coalition waged a mass electoral revolt against the business-oriented machine of *Oakland Tribune* publisher Joseph R. Knowland in 1947. Events there present a political dynamic different from the one that might be suggested by conventional wisdom.

Standard urban history accounts say little or nothing about wartime urban politics. In *The New Urban America,* one of the few works that address this issue, historian Carl Abbott argues that the war boom in southern and western cities laid the foundation for municipal political upheavals of the postwar era. Abbott describes these postwar political challenges as "G.I. revolts," led by returning veterans eager to build on wartime demographic and economic gains. This younger generation came to power by supporting a variety of middle-class reform measures aimed at promoting economic growth and municipal efficiency.[2]

In Oakland, however, it was not middle-class reformers who were the driving force in these struggles, but labor, minorities, and working-class people. Nor did these reformers seek to promote business-oriented municipal reform measures such as city manager government and nonpartisan elections (conservative forces had already instituted such practices in the prewar era). Instead, the labor insurgents called for an end to these practices, demanding an elected mayor, district elections, publicly owned mass transportation, public works projects, public housing, and increased funding for education and other social programs—in short, a broad-based liberal agenda. Middle-class business reformers, then, were not the only ones to take advantage of war-born opportunities; under the right conditions, labor and progressive forces also mounted effective political challenges to business-dominated city governments.

Furthermore, the Oakland experience suggests that municipal revolts in western cities were not strictly postwar affairs but had direct roots in wartime political arrangements. The wartime city, in fact, provided a crucible for progressives seeking to fulfill the social ideals of the 1930s. In this regard, the CIO was critical. Nearly all of the postwar issues and personalities can be traced back to the work of the newly formed CIO Political Action Committee (PAC) in 1944. Though initially a creation of the CIO's national executive board, the local PAC soon took on a life of its own and became the core of an insurgent political movement that united a wide array of community interests, including more liberal elements of the AFL. While this labor-led coalition did not survive the reactionary backlash of the 1950s, it foreshadowed progressive trends that would characterize the city in later decades.

Focusing mainly on the national level, labor historians have generally criticized wartime CIO political activity for fostering a rigid and ultimately detrimental relationship between labor, the federal government, and the Democratic Party.[3] When viewed at the grassroots level, however, the experience was far more open and fluid. By examining local politics in Oakland, we can begin to see how labor activists understood the war experience and why they chose to place their faith in the electoral system. Once in office, however, labor representatives found progress difficult. With the onset of the Cold War and domestic anti-Communism, Knowland forces were able to block labor initiatives and drove several progressive councilmembers from office. Indeed, just as the war had helped enhance labor's power in the mid-1940s, later national and international events contributed to labor's political demise. The Oakland experience thus speaks to both the potential and the limitations of electoral politics as a means of advancing workers' interests.

Located across the bay from San Francisco, Oakland had long been a thriving industrial center with a large blue-collar population. As a transcontinental railroad terminus and an active deep-water port, Oakland had become a key transportation and distribution center on the West Coast by the early twentieth century. As such, it attracted hundreds of manufacturing industries including automobile assembly, shipbuilding, canning and food processing, and electrical, chemical, and paint production. Despite the economic setbacks of the depression years, Oakland continued to grow through the 1930s, its population totalling 302,163 by 1940.

The city's industrial development attracted a diverse working-class population, many of whom settled in the flatland neighborhoods of East and West Oakland. In 1940, 14.1 percent of Oakland's population was foreign-born, while immigrants and their children accounted for approximately one-third of the population. The African-American community, though smaller than its counterparts in eastern cities, accounted for 2.8 percent. Centered in West Oakland, adjacent to the railroad yards that had long provided employment for many of its residents, Oakland's prewar black community was the largest in the Bay Area.[4]

Despite the city's blue-collar character, labor played only a minor role in Oakland politics prior to the war. Since the Progressive era, pro-growth business elites had dominated municipal government through the implementation of two major charter reforms. Sparked by a serious Socialist Party challenge in the 1911 municipal elections, local business elites worked to eliminate the ward system and replaced it with a nonpartisan commission form of government later that year. Even under the new system, however, competing business factions continued to fight among themselves. One of these factions, led by prominent Republican and *Oakland Tribune* publisher Joseph R. Knowland, began campaigning for a second round of charter reform in 1928. The subsequent establishment of a council-manager government in 1931 helped defeat Knowland's opponents and put his business machine in control of the city for the next fifteen years.[5]

The onset of the depression and the New Deal, however, enhanced labor's power by providing new organizing opportunities. The clearest sign of labor's revitalization was the eighty-three-day maritime strike of 1934, which culminated in a four-day general strike in both Oakland and San Francisco. Involving some 100,000 Bay Area workers, including members of over seventy Oakland locals, the dispute ended on an ambiguous note after AFL leaders agreed to government arbitration, over strong rank-and-file opposition. The "big strike," however, did galvanize support for labor and ushered in an era of union militancy in the Bay Area.[6]

The newly founded CIO was responsible for much of the renewed activism. In the late thirties, CIO activists in Oakland organized workers in a wide variety of manufacturing and service industries including auto plants, canneries, waterfront operations, newspapers, hospitals, and domestic service agencies. While the CIO sought to "organize the unorganized," local CIO dissidents also worked within existing AFL unions to form rival labor organizations. Such efforts outraged many local AFL leaders, who responded by purging CIO unions from the county's Central Labor Council, staging counter-raids on CIO unions, and supporting the use of city police against CIO pickets. Growing labor militance during these years also encouraged the Knowland machine to recruit Building Trades Council President James Quinn and several other AFL conservatives, offering them political patronage in exchange for labor's support of machine candidates and policies. Increasingly, AFL councilmembers backed the Knowland government in its efforts to suppress CIO organizing in the city.[7]

In-fighting between the AFL and the CIO ultimately hindered effective political action by labor during these years. While some liberal AFL members worked with the CIO through Labor's Non-Partisan League, a pro–New Deal political action group, the national and local AFL leadership remained staunchly opposed to any cooperation between the two groups. In Oakland, conservative AFL leaders formed a rival political organization that backed Knowland machine candidates against local CIO and Communist insurgents. In 1937–38, the two union federations would not even march in the same Labor Day parade, much less join forces politically.[8]

World War II, however, brought about cataclysmic changes in Oakland's economy, population, and physical development—changes that enhanced labor's role in the community. As one of the West Coast's major transportation and industrial centers, the metropolitan Oakland area received millions of dollars in federal defense contracts, including large outlays for shipbuilding, motor vehicle assembly, food processing, and military supply. To staff these operations, employers recruited local women, youth, and elderly workers and tapped distant labor markets in the South and Midwest as well. Consequently, Oakland's population grew from 302,163 in 1940 to 345,345 by mid-1944—a 14.3 percent increase in less than four years. Not surprisingly, the population boom severely strained housing, transportation, education, and other city services. To help alleviate these crowded conditions, the federal government provided funding for temporary war housing, expanded school facilities, and other community programs.[9]

The influx of civilian and military workers also altered Oakland's racial and class composition. Recruiting heavily in the southwest, defense employers drew many working-class families from Texas, Oklahoma, Arkansas, and Louisiana. Black families figured prominently among the southwesterners, and Oakland's black population mushroomed from 8,462 in 1940 to 21,770 in 1944 and to 47,562 by 1950. Making up less than 3 percent of the city's population before the war, black Oaklanders constituted 6.3 percent of the total by 1944 and 12.4 percent by 1950.[10] Assuming they remained in the city, black and working-class war migrants provided a potential new source of support for Oakland's embattled labor movement.

For most migrants, however, organized labor offered a hostile welcome at best. Since the shipbuilding industry absorbed the bulk of new workers, most newcomers found themselves within the jurisdiction of the Boilermakers Union and other conservative AFL trades. Outnumbered by wartime newcomers and alarmed at their potential power, the Boilermakers' leadership created special nonvoting auxiliaries to accommodate migrants, blacks, and other new workers. Conceived as a temporary wartime expedient, the second-class auxiliaries effectively squelched newcomers' participation in union activities and alienated them from the labor movement generally.[11]

By contrast, CIO unions and their more liberal AFL allies made serious attempts to address the needs of war migrants. Unable to organize most newcomers in the shipyards, CIO activists turned their attention to community problems. Such issues proved critical during the war as housing shortages, overcrowded transportation, inadequate social services, and increased racial tensions threatened productivity in Oakland and other important defense areas.

The unusual political arrangements of wartime cities also encouraged labor activists to adopt a community orientation. Specifically, the rhetoric and ritual of wartime unity offered labor, black, and other progressive forces an opportunity to participate on citywide committees and debate public policy issues. Following the example of federal agencies like the War Labor Board, local officials invited a wide range of community representatives to serve on ad hoc committees dealing with issues such as defense employment, housing, mass transit, public health, childcare, rationing, etc. Committee members included not only the conservative AFL building trades officials and black ministers traditionally appointed to represent the city's working class, but also left-leaning CIO and AFL members and black officials of the railroad brotherhoods. Organized labor embraced this opportunity to work with other community groups and praised Mayor John Slavich for "bringing labor spokesmen into committees and activity to further Oakland's war effort."[12]

Perhaps the most trenchant example of this urban corporatism was the Postwar Planning Committee convened by Mayor Slavich in 1943 to promote successful reconversion. Ostensibly representing all city residents, the committee was heavily business-dominated. Out of fifty members, thirty represented business and finance interests while only four spoke for organized labor. As an ad hoc group, the committee sidestepped formal planning bodies and developed projects that would make Oakland "the leading center of the New Industrial West." In an effort to provide long-deferred municipal improvements and to ease the transition to a peacetime economy, the committee developed an elaborate program of public works and civic projects. Their plans called for the repair or construction of roads, highways, sewers, schools, parks, pools, hospitals, and civic centers, many of which had languished since the depression. With fear of a postwar recession looming, such projects would create jobs for displaced veterans and defense workers—a key labor demand. For business interests, adequate facilities and services were prerequisites to industrial growth. "Immediate and postwar civic improvements will have a far-reaching effect on Oakland's industrial development," said the committee. "Eastern concerns are more likely to locate their plants in Oakland knowing that the city of Oakland is willing to provide the facilities required by industry."[13] But the business-labor unity symbolized by the Postwar Planning Committee proved illusory, and the execution of postwar plans would become a source of bitter and protracted conflict.

Even during the war, labor remained at best a junior partner in this experiment in urban corporatism. As Carl Abbott has pointed out, defense contractors and federal bureaucrats—who generally favored policies acceptable to the city's business elite—dominated ad hoc committees and decision-making. The important point, however, was not labor's lack of influence but the experience with and exposure to urban policy issues fostered by such participation.

During the war, labor moved from a relatively narrow focus on workplace organizing to a broad-based community orientation. Communist Party members, who were well represented in many West Coast CIO locals, had a long history of community organizing in the Unemployed Councils of the 1930s. In the full-employment context of wartime Oakland, such experience proved invaluable as the need for increased productivity to win the war provided a perfect rationale for linking community and workplace issues. In an effort to expand such activities, the Alameda County CIO Council urged every full-time union official to sit on at least one civic group or committee. The Council also endorsed a new course on community services offered by the Oakland-based California Labor School and urged union members to enroll. This growing concern and sophistication in dealing with community issues would not disappear at war's end.[14]

Labor not only gained experience in urban policymaking during the war but also developed an impressive organizational network. With the creation of the national CIO Political Action Committee in 1943, local PACs began forming in major industrial centers to support the reelection of Franklin Roosevelt and other pro-labor candidates. The passage of the anti-labor Smith-Connally Act in 1943 also served to galvanize labor forces nationwide in an effort to repeal the legislation. In California, a "right-to-work" initiative known as Proposition Twelve spurred especially enthusiastic PAC activity in the Los Angeles and San Francisco Bay areas in 1944 and helped bring the long-feuding AFL and CIO together in a united front. In Oakland, AFL and CIO members joined forces with the establishment of United Labor's Legislative Committee in 1944.[15]

The PACs conducted mass voter registration drives that summer and fall, enrolling a record number of voters statewide, including over 300,000 ballot applications from migrant defense workers. In Oakland, sound trucks patrolled working-class neighborhoods and war housing areas all day, every day, urging residents to register. The PAC appointed registrars in both the shipyards and war housing projects, while the Democratic Club led by black union leader C. L. Dellums concentrated on reaching new black voters in West Oakland. Defense migrants were popular targets for these campaigns, since working-class and Southern voters presumably voted Democratic. The PACs thus did extensive work in migrant neighborhoods, helping newcomers file for residency and explaining voting rights (including freedom from poll taxes and literacy tests). As a result of such efforts, Alameda County showed the greatest gains in voter registration in the Bay Area, rising from 225,000 voters before the primary election to 362,000 by late October.[16]

Labor groups made an equally impressive effort on election day. First, United Labor's Legislative Committee organized a mass distribution of slate cards in all major shipyards. Union members and their families then rallied voters via telephone and doorbell ringing, minded children while voters went to the polls, offered information on voting rights, and served as pollwatchers. When the returns were tallied, Oakland voters came in heavily for the triumphant Roosevelt and local pro-labor Democrats while defeating Proposition Twelve.[17]

Although it is hard to estimate the precise influence of PAC activity, the PAC's role as a nucleus of a progressive revolt in local politics is quite clear. As local shipyard worker and NAACP leader Joseph James observed in 1945, a progressive coalition had formed in the Bay Area "spearheaded by CIO-PAC in the 1944 elections. . . . The contacts made during the course of that political battle have remained intact to a surprising degree." In Alameda County, the origins of postwar progressivism were especially evident as local organizers of the 1944 campaign—Ruby Heide, J. C. Reynolds, C. L. Dellums, Earl Hall, and William Hollander—emerged as important figures in the grassroots revolt that first took shape in the 1945 Oakland elections.[18]

Once again, it was the CIO that spearheaded plans for an organized labor presence in the 1945 elections. In a meeting called by the CIO Council in December 1944, the PAC established four subcommittees to analyze the issues and candidates in the spring municipal elections in Oakland and other East Bay cities. The PAC hoped to identify progressive, pro-labor candidates who could defeat incumbents backed by local business machines. The present leadership was "obstructionist," said the PAC, and the region's future was being "stifled by selfish interests and machine politics." While the war had not yet ended, the era of wartime unity was clearly over.[19]

Labor's confrontational stance grew out of both changing economic conditions and disillusionment over the business community's failure to pursue postwar planning measures. By the winter of 1944–45, the slowdown of the war economy and the spectre of another depression gave labor reason for growing concern. Shipyard employment in the East Bay had begun contracting slowly in the fall of 1943. Job layoffs increased considerably over the next year, and by early 1945 unemployment claims were five times higher than in the previous year. At the same time, local urban leaders had shown little enthusiasm for inaugurating the postwar public works projects designed to cushion the shock of reconversion. City officials, labor contended, had taken no concrete action on the recommendations of the Postwar Planning Committee nor had they sought funding for any new projects. The issue, as one columnist put it, was whether the city "will go forward or backward. . . . It is prosperity versus the prewar status quo, which means a return to unemployment." [20]

The split between labor and business was not as sudden as it seemed; the rhetoric of wartime unity had merely obscured the longstanding animosity between the two groups. This is not to say that wartime rhetoric was entirely false, but rather that labor and business understood the meaning of the war experience differently. For much of the old-time business community, the war boom brought an unprecedented expansion of business, population, and economic growth accompanied by a temporary, but necessary, dose of federal intervention. Although excited about the economic potential of an expanded population, conservatives expressed concern that migrants had become dependent on government social programs. Business hoped to encourage continued economic growth in the postwar era, but under the control of the private sector.[21]

For labor, the collectivist experiments of the war years had a very different meaning. The mass mobilization of resources, personnel, and government services seemed to prove that business and government were capable of creating a humane capitalism that provided jobs, a decent standard of living, and fair treatment for all Americans. Wartime social programs such as health insurance, public housing, and childcare were not just temporary expedients, but models for the postwar future. Labor's vision, then, was not one of radical anti-capitalism, but of more moderate social-democratic reform based on the war experience.[22]

Organized labor also had a far more positive view of the areas's newcomers. Far from being disoriented and dependent, labor leaders argued, newcomers appreciated wartime social programs and merely wanted fair treatment from local housing authorities and other agencies. City leaders had "expressed hostility toward the problems of wartime inhabitants from outside areas," said one labor supporter. "The indifference . . . is rooted in the defeatist theory that such people are here only temporarily." To help overcome the nativist and racist sentiments that plagued the city, the PAC called for the creation of a civic unity committee that would bring different racial, occupational, and religious groups together to resolve community conflicts.[23]

The failure of elected officials to respond to such initiatives prompted the PAC to launch its own campaign in the spring of 1945. For the first time since the Progressive era, a unified opposition slate challenged local business rule, fielding candidates for city council, the school board, and other city offices. Calling themselves the United for Oakland Committee (UOC), the progressives campaigned for expanded industry and job opportunities, public works, slum clearance, public housing, a civic unity committee, increased pay for civil service employees, and expanded facilities and services for education, health care, childcare, recreation, and mass transit. In an effort to address the structural inequities of the council-manager system, UOC candidates also demanded district elections, an elected mayor, and other charter reform measures.[24]

The UOC's sweeping agenda attracted a broad-based alliance representing a diverse cross-section of the urban community. First, the coalition represented a solidly united AFL-CIO front unknown in prewar politics. Despite conservatives' efforts to split the labor vote by running machine-backed AFL candidates, the UOC remained united in support of its own candidates.[25] The labor coalition also forged links with forward-looking businesspeople who advocated aggressive postwar growth and opposed existing machines. UOC business supporters included former Postwar Planning Committee members Frank Belgrano, president of the Central Bank of Oakland and regional chairman of the Committee for Economic Development; liberal Republican Earl Hall, chairman of the Uptown Property Owners Association (rival of Knowland's Downtown Association); and Patrick McDonough, owner of defense-oriented McDonough Steel and chairman of the Alameda County Democratic Committee.

While both the Knowland machine and the UOC ostensibly supported industrial expansion, the labor group maintained that local machines jealously guarded their dominant position and created bottlenecks to discourage new businesses from locating in the city. Because of such attitudes, labor alleged, aircraft manufacturers like Lockheed chose to locate in southern California instead of Oakland. Other businesspeople, however, had "a sincere desire to take Oakland out of the rut it's been in," said PAC official Paul Heide. "These are the people we want to work with." Historian Carl Abbott has described these forward-looking businesspeople as the instigators of postwar "G.I. revolts." In Oakland, however, it was labor, not business, that played the dominant role in this new urban coalition.[26]

Most significant, labor forces worked hard to develop strong ties with the black community. Black labor leaders such as C. L. Dellums, business agent for the Brotherhood of Sleeping Car Porters, and Matt Crawford, former assistant director of the CIO Minorities Committee, provided key links between the labor movement and the larger black community. Dellums, in particular, represented a broad network of black interests in Oakland and helped deliver the support of the railroad brotherhoods, the local NAACP, and the Democratic Seventeenth District Citizens' League. The labor coalition's support for fair housing and employment practices, civic unity committees, and other civil rights measures made such interracial alliances possible.[27]

Finally, the labor coalition also drew support from middle-class white liberals, particularly those in progressive religious circles. Reflecting the social gospel tendencies of liberal Protestantism, members of the interracial war housing ministries and the local Council of Churches united with the UOC in support of fair labor practices and civil rights. As NAACP leader Joseph James explained, "There is a large group of prominent white persons who are outspokenly liberal on the question of racial equality." These people joined with "an overwhelming preponderance of working people, combined with the strength of the CIO," to form a truly broad-based progressive coalition in Bay Area cities.[28]

The UOC, however, was far less successful in actually turning out the vote on election day. With a dismally low turnout in the spring municipal elections, voters swept all of the incumbents back into office. Part of the problem was poor outreach; without the lure of Roosevelt and other high-profile national candidates, only 26 percent of the city's registered voters cast their ballots. In all likelihood, however, labor's message was as much a problem as its weak campaigning. By appropriating the pro-growth rhetoric of their opponents, liberal candidates were at times indistinguishable from machine incumbents. Future labor candidates would discover that a more frankly left-wing platform had more grassroots appeal than a watered-down reform agenda.[29]

Some last-minute concessions by Knowland forces may also have contributed to labor's defeat. Just prior to the elections, the city finally agreed to raise the wages of police and fire personnel, one of the UOC's campaign demands. At the same time, incumbent Mayor John Slavich announced the formation of a civic unity committee—another labor campaign plank—despite prior dismissals of the idea. Labor's defeat in 1945, then, was more than just a painful learning experience. The UOC had successfully pressured the Knowland machine into action on several key community issues and continued to win concessions afterward. In May of 1945, the city council finally presented a bond measure to provide modest funding for roads, sewers, libraries, swimming pools, parks, and a new hall of justice. The measure passed decisively with Knowland and UOC support. In a separate election in September, the city council offered a second bond measure to fund new school facilities. Heartened by these small victories, the UOC vowed to continue the fight by extending outreach and education efforts until the next election.[30]

In the meantime, the termination of hostilities between the U.S. and Japan virtually shut down Oakland's war industries. Local manufacturing operations had been contracting steadily since their peak in June 1943, when they employed nearly 1.2 million people statewide. By December of 1946, this figure had fallen to 730,000. The biggest losses occurred in the shipbuilding industry, which declined from 307,000 workers statewide in June 1943 to 25,000 by November 1946. As California's number one shipbuilding center, the East Bay felt these dislocations particularly hard, and the U.S. Employment Service reported increased unemployment claims for the area through 1946. Women, blacks, and other wartime newcomers faced the most severe layoffs, as employers sought to accommodate returning veterans whenever possible.[31]

Even those workers who kept their jobs after the war saw their living standards deteriorate. Despite record corporate profits in expanding consumer industries and services, the take-home pay of many workers declined as a result of reduced hours and the loss of overtime and bonus pay. With the termination of wartime price controls in the summer of 1946, consumer prices skyrocketed nationwide while real wages fell. Furthermore, the existence of a growing pool of unemployed benefitted local employers, who adopted an increasingly hostile stance toward organized labor. In Congress, Republican lawmakers attempted to roll back New Deal labor gains through open shop legislation and other anti-labor measures embodied in the Taft-Hartley Act. At the state level, California lawmakers initiated a similar anti-labor offensive. In reaction to these trends, labor discontent erupted in a nationwide strike wave in 1945–46.[32]

Oakland was one of six American cities that experienced a general strike in this tumultuous period. The conflict began in October 1946 when some four hundred members—mainly women—of the AFL Department and Specialty Store Employees Union walked off their jobs at Kahn's and Hastings downtown department stores. Demanding employer recognition of the union as a legitimate bargaining agent, striking workers picketed the stores throughout the month of November with the support of the Teamsters and other AFL trades. On December 1, Kahn's brought in nonunion drivers to deliver twelve truckloads of merchandise to the store under the protection of two hundred and fifty Oakland police.

Police involvement in the action triggered a sharp outcry against city officials, and on December 2 the Central Labor Council declared a "labor holiday." The next day, 142 unions with over 100,000 workers took to the streets, successfully shutting down streetcar and bus lines, factories, shipyards, stores, restaurants, hotels, and three local newspapers. After two and a half days, as the strike threatened to spread to adjoining Contra Costa County, leaders of the AFL Teamsters' and Machinists' internationals ordered their members back to work. With the loss of these critical unions, local leaders reluctantly accepted an agreement with the city manager to end the general strike in exchange for the city's pledge to observe workers' civil rights in the future. The general strike thus ended inconclusively while the store workers' strike continued as a separate dispute. Within weeks, however, the city again deployed police to protect scab workers at the downtown stores.[33]

Angry and betrayed, labor forces rebounded into the electoral arena in 1947. Outraged by the brazen pro-employer sentiments of the mayor and city council, the labor coalition of 1945 reorganized as the Oakland Voters League (OVL) and revitalized their efforts to build a unified urban movement. In the May elections, the OVL ran a slate of five candidates for city council on a platform reminiscent of the 1945 UOC campaign. As they had two years earlier, the OVL dubbed the Knowland machine "obstructionist" and demanded that postwar public works projects begin immediately. "Two years ago, $15,754,000 was voted for parks and playgrounds, swimming pools and recreational facilities, health services, street improvements, and other needed civic projects," the OVL asserted. "Where are they?"[34]

The 1947 platform also added some new planks, giving the OVL a more radical edge. Specifically, the OVL called for city council neutrality in all labor disputes; repeal of anti-picketing and anti-handbill ordinances often used against labor; investigation of police brutality against black residents; the restoration of rent control; repeal of the sales tax; and more equitable tax assessment procedures to eliminate unfair advantages for downtown property owners. The OVL also gave top priority to building public hous-ing, establishing a city fair employment commission, and constructing new school facilities. Disputing Chamber of Commerce data on industrial growth, the OVL noted that the majority of new industries had located in suburban areas outside the city. In contrast to 1945, though, Oakland progressives talked less about attracting new business; their main thrust was employment, community services, and social justice.[35]

As in 1945, the OVL represented a broad spectrum of community inter-ests—from Communists and left-wing CIO members to local veterans and church members. Labor remained the centerpiece of the coalition, and in the wake of the failed 1946 strike and the pending Taft-Hartley legisla-tion, union forces closed ranks as never before. The AFL, the CIO, and the railroad brotherhoods all endorsed the OVL, and in early April they held a mass support rally of over 10,000 union members at the Oakland Audito-rium. Labor support from West Oakland's black community was also strong; black unionists formed the United Negro Labor Committee, which played a particularly active and visible role campaigning for the OVL. Be-cause of labor's outspoken concern with providing housing for returning G.I.s, the OVL won support from veterans groups as well. By supporting housing and other pressing community concerns, labor built a broad-based urban coalition in support of the OVL.[36]

To combat the low turnout which hampered the UOC in the 1945 elec-tions, the OVL established a grassroots community network organized around neighborhood precincts. OVL precinct workers canvassed Oakland neighborhoods in the weeks prior to the election, distributing thousands of copies of the *Oakland Voters Herald*, an OVL newsheet designed to counter the meagre and often biased coverage of the organization by the *Oakland Tribune*. In West Oakland, the United Negro Labor Committee sponsored a street dance and other activities to help turn out the vote. The campaign culminated in the dramatic torchlight procession described earlier.[37]

On election day, the OVL's organizing efforts paid off. With a record turnout of 97,520 voters—65 percent of the city's registered voters—OVL candidates Vernon Lantz, Raymond Pease, Joseph Smith, and Scott Weak-ley defeated the Knowland-backed incumbents despite a bitter redbaiting campaign by the *Tribune*. The other OVL candidate, former Richmond shipyard worker Ben Goldfarb, lost by a margin of less than a thousand votes. Although no precinct voting records have survived, local news-papers agreed that the OVL's strongest support came from the working-class districts of East and West Oakland. The latter, inhabited predominantly by blacks and white migrants, contributed the strongest support with residents voting three-to-one in favor of the OVL. The landslide vote prompted the *Labor Herald* to chide that the "Old Guard's Waterloo was in West Oakland."[38]

The triumph of the four OVL candidates was an unprecedented event in Oakland that demonstrated the power of an interracial labor coalition. But Goldfarb's loss was a damaging blow. The new city council still stood five to four in favor of the Knowland forces. On nearly every progressive measure, the OVL councilmembers would find themselves narrowly outvoted and their initiatives stalled. Machine forces, however, did not always act as a coherent unit. When selecting a mayor a few months later, feuding Knowland councilmembers could not agree on a single candidate. As a result, OVL councilmembers elected their own favorite, Joseph Smith, in 1947.[39] As the mayoral contest indicated, OVL forces could win a council vote by trading favors with one of their opponents. This strategy would play a key part in what would become the defining issue of the postwar city—public housing.

Of all the troublesome legacies of World War II in Oakland, the housing problem topped the list. During the war, a severe housing shortage had prompted federal and local authorities to cooperate in building some 2,700 units of temporary war housing to accommodate incoming defense migrants. Under federal law, such housing was to be removed within two years of the war's end. The anticipated exodus of war workers, however, never occurred. Instead, the wartime phenomenon of chain migration continued, and thousands of veterans returned to the area, swelling the city's population to 384,575 in 1950. As an emergency measure, the city retained the temporary projects and added an additional five hundred temporary units for homeless veterans. In 1946, the Oakland Housing Authority estimated that at least 23,000 new units would be needed to accommodate families currently residing in temporary housing or sharing quarters with others.[40]

Minority and low-income families encountered the tightest housing conditions. While many middle-income white residents secured homes under G.I. loan programs in the suburbs, low-income families competed for a limited amount of older, central city dwellings. The housing options of black and Asian families of all income levels were also limited to certain urban areas because of racial covenants and biased lending practices. With the postwar institution of veterans' preferences and income ceilings, public war housing became the last refuge for what many city leaders saw as the area's least desirable residents—war migrants, minorities, and the poor. Increasingly, then, city officials targeted war housing for removal and redevelopment.[41]

As with other postwar planning issues, business and labor representatives found some common ground on the housing issue. Both agreed that temporary housing was overcrowded, badly deteriorated, and beyond salvage. They sharply disagreed, however, over the fate of the land and its inhabitants. Business leaders argued that housing lands were prime areas for industrial development and that the private market could accommodate displaced housing residents. Labor and other progressive community groups insisted that redeveloped land be used for new public housing to rehouse the displaced tenants. Their opponents, they claimed, were simply trying to force these unwanted refugees out of the city.

The housing fight came to a head in 1949–50 when new national housing legislation mandated the removal of war housing and provided federal funding for the construction of new projects. Labor representatives on the city council responded by drafting a request for three thousand units of federal public housing. With OVL forces occupying four of nine council seats, they needed only one defector to pass the measure. By trading their support for the mayoral candidacy of one of the Knowland-backed councilmembers in 1949, OVL forces gained the additional vote needed to pass the public housing resolution.[42]

In the meantime, the anti-housing Knowland forces found support for their cause from the newly formed Committee for Home Protection (CHP). Composed of the Oakland Real Estate Board, the Apartment House Owners Association, and other local development interests, the CHP had formed in 1948 to spearhead a drive for an anti–public housing referendum in Oakland. Attacking public housing as "socialistic," the CHP appealed to voters' patriotism, fiscal conservatism, and belief in free enterprise. In the midst of an economic upswing and growing anti-Communism, such rhetoric had strong appeal, particularly among the white middle class. The initiative won, defeating public housing in principle but without force of law. CHP forces were thus outraged when the city council later voted five to four in favor of three thousand new housing units on August 20, 1949.[43]

Infuriated, CHP leaders waged a fierce campaign designed to thwart pro-housing forces. Filing affidavits for the recall of three of the five pro-housing councilmembers (the other two had not yet served six months and were thus ineligible for recall), the CHP launched an elaborate media campaign associating the labor coalition with "socialized housing" and "CIO communism." While the use of redbaiting tactics had been largely unsuccessful in past elections, a rising tide of anti-Communism made the public more suspicious and susceptible to such appeals. In a special election held in February 1950, two members were reelected, but a third, Scott Weakley, was ousted. Losing his job as a radio announcer as a result of alleged employer blacklisting, Weakley committed suicide shortly thereafter. In a low turnout election the following year, OVL councilmembers Joseph Smith and Raymond Pease also lost to CHP-backed candidates running on an anti-housing, anti-Communist platform. The remaining OVL representative died in office.[44]

By 1951, then, the liberal challenge in Oakland had run its course—defeated over the housing issue that had come to symbolize the future of the city. Conservative forces regained firm control of the city government and rescinded the federal housing contracts signed by their predecessors. Between 1945 and 1965, the city constructed a total of only five hundred public housing units. During these same years, the city leveled one temporary housing project after another, displacing thousands of migrants, veterans, and low-income residents. While most white tenants managed to find housing in nearby suburbs, minority residents found themselves limited to deteriorating, overcrowded urban neighborhoods.[45]

What had happened between 1947 and 1951 to so shift the course of Oakland politics? Most critical, the pervasive climate of Cold War anti-Communism worked to the advantage of conservatives who used redbaiting to discredit liberal forces. But the internal divisions that wracked the labor coalition were even more damaging. Under the impact of Taft-Hartley loyalty oaths and the bitterness of the 1948 presidential election, CIO forces were torn by raids, ousters, and in-fighting. With the most progressive labor forces in disarray, the behind-the-scenes leadership of the labor coalition fell to the AFL contingent led by Central Labor Council Chairman J. C. Reynolds.

Reynolds' leadership was damaging to the coalition in several ways. Most obviously, Reynolds' 1951 federal indictment on bribery and conspiracy charges critically harmed the credibility of the labor coalition. The *Tribune*'s age-old cries of "labor bossism" now seemed disturbingly close to reality. In the political arena, Reynolds scorned any attempt to enlist the support of the local black community. From their perspective, black leaders had little cause to back labor candidates. Those elected in 1947 had not delivered on their campaign promises to pass a fair employment practices act and to deal with police brutality against minority citizens. Certainly, the conservative council majority had derailed their efforts to do so, but progressives had also defected on other issues such as the city sales tax increase.

In the conservative climate of postwar Oakland, labor representation was not the progressive panacea that many had hoped it would be. As the CIO *Labor Herald* explained, the defeat "was a tragic lesson in the cost of disunity and political opportunism." [46] Indeed, the internal effects of anti-Communism on the OVL proved more damaging than the external ones, as a feuding labor movement lost the ability to mobilize the community-wide coalition it had struggled so hard to build.

The devastating effects of postwar conservatism were by no means unique to Oakland. Particularly on the housing issue, progressive urban coalitions in many cities unraveled under redbaiting attacks by local conservatives. Under the coordination of the National Association of Real Estate Boards, local anti-housing groups formed around the country to fight public housing and its supporters. On the West Coast, where the fate of thousands of war housing tenants hung in the balance, anti-housing groups in Portland and Los Angeles launched successful referendum campaigns against public housing construction in the early fifties. On the heels of these victories, conservatives then used anti-housing appeals and redbaiting tactics to oust incumbent mayors Fletcher Bowron in Los Angeles and Dorothy Lee in Portland. As in Oakland, these cities then dismantled temporary war housing projects, displacing thousands of poor and minority residents into deteriorating, overcrowded neighborhoods. [47]

We should not, however, allow the bitter experiences of the 1950s to blind us to the accomplishments of progressives in the 1940s. In many ways, the activities of labor coalitions in the 1940s were a dress rehearsal for the urban liberalism of the 1960s and '70s. In Oakland and other Bay Area cities, labor demands such as civil rights legislation, district elections, rent control, and other urban social programs were eventually implemented. Public housing, with all its accompanying problems, would also reappear as a major urban program in the sixties and seventies. While many of these issues date back to the New Deal or before, it was World War II that was the springboard for an effective political mobilization on the municipal level.

The political arrangements of wartime cities offered labor representatives a new voice in municipal affairs and encouraged them to expand their political horizons from the workplace to the city at large. The formation of CIO-PACs gave this impulse an organizational coherence, while defense migrants provided an expanded working-class constituency. After the war, recessionary pressures served to galvanize labor and other progressive forces, helping them defeat business-backed incumbents. Labor unity, a willingness to build bridges to other community groups, and a commitment to grassroots organizing were the key ingredients in the success of these urban movements.

Labor's role in forging a progressive coalition was not limited to Oakland; labor forces in Los Angeles, San Francisco, Berkeley, and Richmond also spearheaded the organization of progressive community movements in the 1940s. As in Oakland, the Allied Berkeley Citizens, the Richmond Better Government Committee, and the San Francisco Voters League all grew out of wartime CIO activities, with many of their leaders drawn from the same unions. The Los Angeles Voters League, founded in 1948, was a direct descendant of the United AFL Committee for Political Action organized in 1943 as an AFL counterpart to the CIO-PAC. Like the OVL, the Los Angeles and San Francisco Voters Leagues worked to bring labor together with other progressive groups in the community to pursue a broad-based, multiple-issue program. Explicitly rejecting the role of political lobbying groups, the Voters Leagues organized from the precinct level up, stressing grassroots political participation and leadership development among rank-and-file union members and community activists.[48]

While further research is needed on labor politics in California cities, the early experience of the Oakland Voters League reveals an innovative and exciting experiment in grassroots democracy and urban coalition-building—an experience that contrasts favorably with labor's increasing rigidity and conservatism on the national level. The experience of the OVL in the 1940s also suggests a kind of organizational bridge between the class-based movements of the 1930s and the cultural or community-based social movements that have emerged since the 1960s (i.e., civil rights, women's liberation, community organizing, etc.). While the conservatism of the 1950s posed a historical chasm between these two types of movements, it is clear that the new social activism did not emerge full-blown in the sixties; the urban movements of the 1940s provided important precedents.[49] Unfortunately for the newer movements, the demise of the OVL and other labor-led coalitions in the 1950s caused later activists to distance themselves from their predecessors. In the process, they have had to relearn the difficult lessons of organizing, coalition-building, and ideological development that are essential to effective social action.

NOTES

I would like to thank Daniel Cornford, James Gregory, Thomas Knock, Susan Ware, and David Weber for their thoughtful reading and criticism of earlier drafts of this article.

364 / Marilynn S. Johnson

1. Edward C. Hayes, *Power Structure and Urban Policy: Who Rules in Oakland?* (New York: McGraw-Hill, 1972), 21; *CIO Labor Herald*, May 20, 1947; *Daily People's World*, May 7, 9, 1947.

2. Carl Abbott, *The New Urban America: Growth and Politics in Sunbelt Cities* (Chapel Hill: University of North Carolina Press, 1981), 120–142.

3. Proponents of this view include Nelson Lichtenstein, *Labor's War at Home: The CIO in World War II* (New York: Cambridge University Press, 1982); and James C. Foster, *The Union Politic: The CIO Political Action Committee* (Columbia, Mo.: University of Missouri Press, 1975).

4. Department of Commerce, Bureau of the Census, *Sixteenth Census of the United States, 1940: Reports on Population*, Vol. 2, *Characteristics of the Population*, Part I, "California"; Beth Bagwell, *Oakland: The Story of a City* (Novato, Calif.: Presidio Press, 1982), 62, 82, 90, 196; Lawrence P. Crouchett, Lonnie G. Bunch III, and Martha Kendall Winnacker, eds., *Visions Toward Tomorrow: The History of the East Bay Afro-American Community, 1852–1977* (Oakland: Northern California Center for Afro-American History and Life, 1989), 9–10, 37.

5. Hayes, *Power Structure and Urban Policy*, 10–14.

6. Bruce Nelson, *Workers on the Waterfront: Seamen, Longshoremen, and Unionism in the 1930s* (Urbana: University of Illinois Press, 1988), 127–129, 137, 219–221; Bagwell, *Oakland: Story of a City*, 218; *East Bay Labor Journal*, July 27, 1934.

7. *Labor Herald*, June 8, 15, August 24, September 22, October 6, 20, December 1, 29, 1937, March 31, May 19, October 27, 1938; Hayes, *Power Structure and Urban Policy*, 17–18.

8. *East Bay Labor Journal*, August 24, 1934; *Labor Herald*, July 27, 1937, May 5, July 7, August 4, 1938; Labor's Non-Partisan League of Alameda County, *Bring the New Deal to California* (Oakland, n.p., n.d.); Labor's Non-Partisan League of California, *Minutes and Report*, December 1937, June 1938, January 1939 (copies of League documents in Institute for Governmental Studies Library, University of California, Berkeley).

9. *Oakland Tribune Yearbook, 1943* (Oakland: Oakland Tribune Company, 1943), 29. Department of Commerce, Bureau of the Census, *Sixteenth Census of the United States, 1940: Reports on Population*, Vol. 2, *Characteristics of the Population*, Part 1, "California"; and *Population*, Series CA-3, No. 3, *Characteristics of the Population, Labor Force, Families and Housing, San Francisco Bay Congested Production Area, April 1944*. A general overview of the wartime transformation of West Coast cities is available in Gerald Nash's *The American West Transformed: The Impact of the Second World War* (Bloomington: Indiana University Press, 1985); a more specific account of the East Bay may be found in my book *The Second Gold Rush: Oakland and the East Bay in World War II* (Berkeley: University of California Press, 1993).

10. Commonwealth Club of California, *The Population of California* (San Francisco: Parker Printing Co., 1946), 127. Census Bureau, *U.S. Census of Population: 1950*, Vol. 2, *Characteristics of the Population*, Part 5, "California"; and *Population*, Series CA-3, No. 3, *Characteristics of the Population, San Francisco Area*, 14.

11. For a more complete account of labor organization in East Bay shipyards, see chapter three of Johnson, *The Second Gold Rush*.

12. *Labor Herald*, April 16, 1943. For specific examples of labor's involvement in citywide committees, see back issues of the *Labor Herald* for 1943–45.

13. Oakland Postwar Planning Committee, *Oakland's Formula for the Future* (Oakland: n.p., 1945); Hayes, *Power Structure and Urban Policy*, 145–146.

14. Carl Abbott, "Planning for the Home Front in Portland and Seattle, 1940–45, in *The Martial Metropolis*, ed. Roger Lotchin (New York: Praeger Publishers, 1984), 181–182; *Labor Herald*, December 12, 1944. For the shifting priorities of labor, see back issues of the CIO's *Labor Herald* for the war and prewar years.

15. Nelson Lichtenstein suggests that the founding of the CIO-PAC was also a reaction to the internal threat from left-wing CIO members (primarily in New York and Michigan) who supported a radical third-party alternative. I have found no evidence of a similar split in California CIO ranks. Lichtenstein, *Labor's War at Home*, 172–173; Robert H. Zeiger, *American Workers, American Unions, 1920–1985* (Baltimore: Johns Hopkins University Press, 1986), 115; Foster, *The Union Politic*, 14.

16. *Labor Herald*, June 20, 1944, October 6, 20, 1944, November 3, 1944; *Daily People's World*, October 23, 24, 1944. Local Republicans even suggested that a conspiracy was afoot to "colonize" California cities with Southern Democrats. Migrant war workers, said the editors of the local conservative weekly, "are being dragooned into California from the solid Democratic Southern states, where their votes are not needed . . ." *Oakland Observer*, June 17, 1944.

17. *Daily People's World*, November 4, 9, 1944. For an insider's view of PAC organizing in a war housing project, see Henry Kraus, *In the City Was a Garden* (New York: Renaissance Press, 1951).

18. James C. Foster argues that the CIO-PAC was not the effective vote-getting machine that contemporaries believed; see Foster, *The Union Politic*, 1–2; Joseph James, "Profiles: San Francisco," in "Race Relations on the Pacific Coast," ed. L. D. Reddick, *Journal of Educational Sociology* 19 (November 1945): 175; *Daily People's World*, November 10, 1944; *Oakland Tribune*, April 18, 1945. The organizational affiliations of the 1944 campaign coordinators were as follows: Ruby Heide, secretary of the Alameda County CIO Council; J. C. Reynolds, chair of the Alameda County Central Labor Council; William Hollander and Earl Hall, directors of the county Democratic and Republican campaigns to reelect Roosevelt; and C. L. Dellums, an official in the Brotherhood of Sleeping Car Porters and president of the Alameda County NAACP.

19. *Labor Herald*, December 22, 1944, February 16, March 2, 1945.

20. *Daily People's World*, March 17, 1945; Department of Labor, War Manpower Commission, "Summary of Monthly Narrative Reports, June 14, 1945," Labor Market Survey Reports, Box 27, Bureau of Employment Security, Record Group 183, National Archives, Washington, D.C.; *Labor Herald*, February 16, 1945.

21. For a more detailed articulation of this view, see William C. Mullendore. "What Price Prosperity?" (Oakland: Oakland Chamber of Commerce, 1946) (copy in Institute for Governmental Studies Library, University of California, Berkeley); and Gerald Nash, *World War II and the American West: Reshaping the Economy* (Lincoln: University of Nebraska Press, 1990).

22. My argument about the war years was influenced by my reading of Lizabeth Cohen, *Making a New Deal: Industrial Workers in Chicago, 1919–1939* (New York: Cambridge University Press, 1990).

23. *Daily People's World*, April 6, 13, 20, 1945; *Labor Herald*, February 16, 1945.

24. *Labor Herald*, February 16, 1945; *Daily People's World*, April 9, 13, 20, 1945.

25. In an attempt to split the labor vote, the Knowland forces pressured incumbent councilman James DePaoli to resign one month before the Oakland elections

of 1945. They appointed James D'Arcy, an official of the AFL Culinary Workers Union and a Knowland supporter, to replace him and then announced D'Arcy's candidacy as an incumbent. The United for Oakland Committee denounced D'Arcy, noting that his union had followed exclusionary and undemocratic policies during the war. Labor forces thus remained united behind their candidate, CIO steelworkers' shop steward Herman Bittman. *Labor Herald,* March 16, 1945; *Daily People's World,* March 15, 17, 1945.

26. *Labor Herald,* February 16, March 16, 1945; *Daily People's World,* March 15, April 6, 13, 1945; *Oakland Tribune Yearbook: 1944,* 45; Abbott, *The New Urban America,* 121.

27. *Labor Herald,* April 20, 1945; *Daily People's World,* March 16, 1945.

28. James, "Profiles: San Francisco," 175.

29. *Labor Herald,* April 13, 20, 1945; *Daily People's World,* April 19, 1945; *Oakland Tribune,* March 25, April 15, 18, 1945. Despite the moderate tone of the labor campaign, the pro-incumbent *Oakland Tribune* did not hesitate to redbait the UOC, highlighting the fact that the local Community Party supported the progressive slate. Such attacks, however, did not reach lethal potential until the peak Cold War years beginning in 1948.

30. Hayes, *Power Structure and Urban Policy,* 145; *Daily People's World,* April 19, 1945. The school measure was subsequently defeated; Hayes speculates that the separation of the bond measures indicated lukewarm business support for school funding.

31. M. I. Gershenson, "Wartime and Postwar Employment Trends in California," *Monthly Labor Review* 64 (April 1947): 577, 584; U. S. Department of Labor, War Manpower Commission, "Summary of Monthly Narrative Reports, June 14, 1945," Labor Market Survey Reports, Box 27, Bureau of Employment Security, Record Group 183, National Archives, Washington, D.C.; and "Monthly Area Statement, Richmond, California," October, November 1946, located in Box 20 of above collection.

32. Zeiger, *American Workers, American Unions,* 100–108; Philip Taft, *Labor Politics American Style: The California State Federation of Labor* (Cambridge, Mass.: Harvard University Press, 1968).

33. *Oakland Tribune,* December 2, 5, 1946; *San Francisco Chronicle,* December 4, 1946; Hayes, *Power Structure and Urban Policy,* 19–20. For the most detailed accounts of the Oakland general strike, see Philip J. Wolman, "The Oakland General Strike of 1946," *Southern California Quarterly* 57 (1975): 147–178; and Frank H. Douma, "The Oakland General Strike" (M.A. thesis, University of California, Berkeley, 1951).

34. Hayes, *Power Structure and Urban Policy,* 21–22; *Oakland Voters Herald,* May 9, 1947.

35. Hayes, *Power Structure and Urban Policy,* 21–22; *Labor Herald,* April 22, 29, May 6, 1947; Oakland Voters League circular, March 24, 1947 (copies in election files, Oakland History Room, Oakland Public Library).

36. *Labor Herald,* April 9, 1947; *Daily People's World,* May 6, 1947; Hayes, *Power Structure and Urban Policy,* 81–82. The only labor unions not participating in the OVL campaign were the fourteen locals of the Teamsters Union led by conservative Knowland supporter Charles Real. Real had been instrumental in getting the international to call off striking Oakland teamsters in 1946, thus breaking the general strike. *Oakland Voters Herald,* May 9, 1947.

37. *Labor Herald,* April 9, 1947; *Oakland Voters Herald,* May 9, 1947; *Daily People's World,* May 2, 6, 9, 12, 1947. The *Oakland Tribune, Post-Enquirer,* and

other mainstream newspapers were strangely mute about the electoral challenge. Except for some editorial redbaiting just prior to the elections (see, for example, April 1947 issues of the *Oakland Tribune*), the Knowland-owned *Tribune* and the Hearst-owned *Post-Enquirer* provided no sustained coverage. In ignoring their opponents, I suspect, the Knowland machine hoped to render them invisible and thus ineffective. By contrast, the labor and left press devoted extensive coverage to these events. Used carefully, these sources provide vital information on Oakland municipal politics unavailable elsewhere in the written record.

38. *Oakland Tribune*, May 14, 1947; *Labor Herald*, May 20, 1947; *Daily People's World*, May 14, 1947; Hayes, *Power Structure and Urban Policy*, 21. The *Labor Herald* claimed that Goldfarb's loss was a result of the misplacement of his name under the incumbents' column on the 1947 ballot. Alternatively, Hayes suggests that it was anti-Semitism which contributed to Goldfarb's defeat in this predominantly Protestant city.

39. *Labor Herald*, July 8, 1947.

40. Census Bureau, *Census of Population 1950*, Vol. 2, *Characteristics of the Population*, Pt. 5, "California"; Housing Authority of Oakland, "Analysis of the Oakland Housing Shortage as of January, 1946," 1 (located in Institute for Governmental Studies Library, University of California, Berkeley); Hayes, *Power Structure and Urban Policy*, 77–78.

41. For information on the changing composition of public housing projects, see Helen Smith Alancraig, "Codornices Village: A Study of Non-Segregated Public Housing" (M.A. thesis, University of California, Berkeley, 1953), 113; and Housing Authority of Oakland, *Annual Report, 1946–47*, 2–3. For a thorough explanation of the discriminatory functioning of federal loan programs, see Kenneth Jackson, *The Crabgrass Frontier* (New York: Oxford University Press, 1985).

42. Under the council-manager form of government, city councilmembers elected a mayor from among their own ranks. Several of the older conservative councilmembers were bidding for the position, which meant that liberals would cast the deciding vote. See Edward C. Hayes, "Power Structure and the Urban Crisis" (Ph.D. dissertation, University of California, Berkeley, 1968), 56–57.

43. California Housing Association, *Newsletter*, November 18, 1949; Alancraig, "Codornices Village," 82–83; *San Francisco Chronicle*, November 17, 1949.

44. *San Francisco Chronicle*, November 17, 1949, January 4, 1950; California Housing Association, *Newsletter*, December 27, 1949; Hayes, "Power Structure and the Urban Crisis," 59–60.

45. Alancraig, "Codornices Village," 85; Hayes, *Power Structure and Urban Policy*, 83. See also Housing Authority of Oakland, annual reports for 1948–49 through 1959–60.

46. Zeiger, *American Workers, American Unions*, 131; *Labor Herald*, May 22, 1951; *Daily People's World*, May 18, 1951; *Oakland Tribune*, May 11, 1951.

47. Richard Baisden, "Labor in Los Angeles Politics" (Ph.D. dissertation, University of Chicago, 1958), 359–378; Thomas S. Hines, "Housing, Baseball, and Creeping Socialism," *Journal of Urban History* 8 (February 1982): 137–140; Carl Abbott, *Portland: Planning, Politics, and Growth in a Twentieth Century City* (Lincoln: University of Nebraska Press, 1983), 156–158.

48. Baisden, "Labor in Los Angeles Politics," 309–314; James, "Profiles: San Francisco," 175; William Issel, "Liberalism and Urban Policy in San Francisco from the 1930s to the 1960s," *Western Historical Quarterly* 22 (November 1991): 431–450.

49. For an insightful analysis of "old" and "new" social movements, see Bob

Fisher and Joe Kling, "Popular Mobilization in the 1990s: Prospects for the New Social Movements," *New Politics* (Winter 1991): 71–84; and Robert Korstad and Nelson Lichtenstein, "Opportunities Lost and Found: Labor, Radicals, and the Early Civil Rights Movement," *Journal of American History* 75 (December 1988): 786–811.

FURTHER READING

Baisden, Richard. "Labor in Los Angeles Politics." Ph.D. dissertation, University of Chicago, 1958.

"Fortress California at War: San Francisco, Los Angeles, Oakland, and San Diego, 1941–1945." Special issue. *Pacific Historical Review* 63 (August 1994).

Douma, Frank Hartzell. "The Oakland General Strike." M.A. thesis, University of California, Berkeley, 1951.

Hayes, Edward C. *Power Structure and Urban Policy: Who Rules in Oakland?* 1972.

Issel, William. "Business Power and Political Culture in San Francisco, 1900–1940." *Journal of Urban History* 16 (November 1989): 52–77.

———. "Liberalism and Urban Policy in San Francisco from the 1930s to the 1960s." *Western Historical Quarterly* 22 (November 1991): 431–450.

Johnson, Marilynn S. *The Second Gold Rush: Oakland and the East Bay in World War II.* 1993.

"Labor and Labor Relations on the West Coast." Special issue. *Monthly Labor Review* 82 (May 1959).

Lotchin, Roger W. *Fortress California, 1910–1961: From Warfare to Welfare.* 1992.

———. "World War II and Urban California: City Planning and the Transformation Hypothesis." *Pacific Historical Review* 62 (May 1993): 143–172.

Nash, Gerald D. *The American West Transformed: The Impact of the Second World War.* Chapter 4. 1985.

Scobie Ingrid G. *Center Stage: Helen Gahagan Douglas, A Life.* 1992.

Taft, Philip. *Labor Politics American Style: The California State Federation of Labor.* 1968.

Verge, Arthur. *Paradise Transformed: Los Angeles During the Second World War.* 1993.

Weir, Stan. "American Labor on the Defensive: A 1940s Odyssey." *Radical America* 9 (July-August 1975): 163–185.

Wolman, Philip J. "The Oakland General Strike of 1946." *Southern California Quarterly* 57 (1975): 147–178.

5

WORKERS IN POST–WORLD WAR II CALIFORNIA

13 Cesar Chavez and the Unionization of California Farmworkers

Cletus E. Daniel

EDITOR'S INTRODUCTION

As the seemingly inexorable expansion of California agriculture progressed, its labor needs were met during World War II by the *bracero* program and after World War II by the program's successor, Public Law 78. In its peak year, 1957, the bracero program imported 192,000 Mexican workers. Along with Chicanos, the braceros soon became the most important component of the California agricultural work force after World War II.

Theoretically, the bracero program, at the insistence of the Mexican government, provided standard contracts covering wages, hours, transportation, housing, and working conditions. The American government guaranteed the provision of emergency medical care, workmen's compensation, and disability and death benefits. In reality, many of these provisions were never enforced, and it soon became clear that the bracero system perpetuated the tragic poverty of California's migratory laborers. Hispanic labor was used mainly on large farms, where growers regarded the workers as cheap and docile laborers, born to the hardship of agricultural work. The unlimited pool of labor available to the growers enabled them to keep wages down. Thus, between 1950 and 1960, the earnings of three million Mexican nationals employed in 275 important crop areas were effectively frozen; average annual wages in fact declined slightly, from $1,680 in 1950 to $1,666 in 1959.

In the 1930s and the 1940s, the Cannery and Agricultural Workers Industrial Union (CAWIU), the United Cannery, Agricultural, Packing and Allied Workers of America (UCAPAWA), and the National Farm Labor Union had all valiantly attempted to organize California's farmworkers. For many reasons—not the least of which was the bracero program itself, which was often used to import strikebreakers—these efforts eventually failed. In 1959, the AFL-CIO made another effort to organize farmworkers when it launched the Agricultural Workers Organizing Committee (AWOC).

The movement to organize California farmworkers during the 1960s came from more grassroots sources. No one played a more integral role than Cesar Chavez. In this article, Cletus Daniel evaluates the crucial role played by Chavez in the eventual founding of the United Farm Workers (UFW) and the struggle of the UFW to gain recognition and a strong foothold in California.

Daniel provides an interesting account of Chavez's social background, early influences, and political involvement before he began organizing farmworkers. Chavez founded the National Farm Workers Association in 1962. Throughout the 1960s and early 1970s, he and the UFW engaged in a bitter struggle with California agribusiness and the Teamsters. Chavez's nonviolent tactics and skillful political lobbying paid off when California's Agricultural Labor Relations Act was passed in 1975. Daniel concludes by noting the decline of the UFW in the late 1980s, attributing this in part to flaws in Chavez's leadership. Wherever the blame lies, when Cesar Chavez died in 1993, a union that once had had perhaps fifty thousand members had been severely reduced in numbers, in the face of a decline in the wages and working conditions of most farmworkers during the 1980s and early 1990s.

◆   ◆   ◆

It was, Cesar Chavez later wrote, "the strangest meeting in the history of California agriculture." Speaking by telephone from his cluttered headquarters in La Paz to Jerry Brown, the new governor of California, Chavez had been asked to repeat for the benefit of farm employers crowded into Brown's Sacramento office the farmworker leader's acceptance of a farm labor bill to which they had already assented. And as the employers heard Chavez's voice repeating the statement of acceptance he had just made to the governor, they broke into wide smiles and spontaneous applause.

That representatives of the most powerful special interest group in California history should have thus expressed their delight at the prospect of realizing still another of their legislative goals does not account for Chavez's assertion of the meeting's strange character. These were, after all, men long accustomed to having their way in matters of farm labor legislation. What was strange about that meeting on May 5, 1975, was that the state's leading farm employers should have derived such apparent relief and satisfaction from hearing the president of the United Farm Workers of America, AFL-CIO, agree to a legislative proposal designed to afford farmworkers an opportunity to escape their historic powerlessness through unionism and collective bargaining.

Beyond investing the state's farmworkers with rights that those who labored for wages on the land had always been denied, the passage of California's Agricultural Labor Relations Act (ALRA) was a seismic event, one that shattered the foundation upon which rural class relations had rested for a century and more. For the state's agribusinessmen, whose tradition it had been to rule the bounteous fields and orchards of California with a degree of authority and control more appropriate to potentates than mere employers, supporting the ALRA was less an act of culpable treason against their collective heritage than one of grudging resignation in the face of a suddenly irrelevant past and an apparently inescapable future. For the state's farmworkers, whose involuntary custom it had always been to surrender themselves to a system of industrialized farming that made a captive peasantry of them, the new law made possible what only the boldest among them had dared to imagine: a role equal to the employer's in determining terms and conditions of employment. Yet if the ALRA's enactment was a victory of unprecedented dimensions for California farmworkers as a class, it was a still greater personal triumph for Cesar Chavez.

More than any other labor leader of his time, and perhaps in the whole history of American labor, Cesar Chavez leads a union that is an extension of his own values, experience, and personality. This singular unity of man and movement has found its most forceful and enduring expression in the unprecedented economic and political power that has accrued to the membership of the United Farm Workers (UFW) under Chavez's intense and unrelenting tutelage. Indeed, since 1965, when Chavez led his then small following into a bitter struggle against grape growers around the lower San Joaquin valley town of Delano, the UFW has, despite the many crises that have punctuated its brief but turbulent career, compiled a record of achievement that rivals the accomplishments of the most formidable industrial unions of the 1930s.

While this personal domination may well be the essential source of the UFW's extraordinary success, it has also posed risks for the union. For just as Chavez's strengths manifest themselves in the character of his leadership, so, too, must his weaknesses. Certainly the UFW's somewhat confused sense of its transcending mission—whether to be a trade union or a social movement; whether to focus on narrow economic gains or to pursue broader political goals—reflects in some degree Chavez's personal ambivalence toward both the ultimate purpose of worker organization and the fundamental objective of his own prolonged activism.

Had his adult life followed the pattern of his early youth, Cesar Chavez need not have concerned himself with the task of liberating California farmworkers from an exploitive labor system that had entombed a succession of Chinese, Japanese, Filipino, Mexican, and other non-Anglo immigrants for more than a hundred years. Born on March 31, 1927, the second child of Librado and Juana Chavez, Cesar Estrada Chavez started his life sharing little beyond language and a diffuse ethnic heritage with the Chicano—Mexican and Mexican-American—workers who constitute nearly the entire membership of the United Farm Workers of America. Named after his paternal grandfather Cesario, who had homesteaded the family's small farm in the north Gila River valley near Yuma three years before Arizona attained statehood, Chavez enjoyed during his youth the kind of close and stable family life that farmworkers caught in the relentless currents of the western migrant stream longed for but rarely attained. And although farming on a small scale afforded few material rewards even as it demanded hard and unending physical labor, it fostered in Chavez an appreciation of independence and personal sovereignty that helps to account for the special force and steadfastness of his later rebellion against the oppressive dependence into which workers descended when they joined the ranks of California's agricultural labor force.

It is more than a little ironic that until 1939, when unpaid taxes put the family's farm on the auction block, Chavez could have more reasonably aspired to a future as a landowner than as a farmworker. "If we had stayed there," he later said of the family's farm, "possibly I would have been a grower. God writes in exceedingly crooked lines."

The full significance of the family's eviction from the rambling adobe ranch house that had provided not only shelter but also a sense of place and social perspective was not at once apparent to an eleven-year-old. The deeper meaning of the family's loss was something that accumulated in Chavez's mind only as his subsequent personal experience in the migrant stream disclosed the full spectrum of emotional and material hardship attending a life set adrift from the roots that had nurtured it. At age eleven the sight of a bulldozer effortlessly destroying in a few minutes what the family had struggled over nearly three generations to build was meaning enough. The land's new owner, an Anglo grower impatient to claim his prize, dispatched the bulldozer that became for Chavez a graphic and enduring symbol of the power that the "haves" employ against the "have-nots" in industrialized agriculture. "It was a monstrous thing," he recalled: "Its motor blotted out the sound of crickets and bullfrogs and the buzzing of the flies. As the tractor moved along, it tore up the soil, leveling it, and destroyed the trees, pushing them over like they were nothing. . . . And each tree, of course, means quite a bit to you when you're young. They are a part of you. We grew up there, saw them every day, and they were alive, they were friends. When we saw the bulldozer just uprooting those trees, it was tearing at us too."

The experience of the Chavez family fell into that category of minor tragedy whose cumulative influence lent an aura of catastrophe to the greater part of the depression decade. The scene became sickeningly familiar in the 1930s: a beleaguered farm family bidding a poignant farewell to a failed past; setting out for California with little enthusiasm and even less money toward a future that usually had nothing but desperation to commend it.

"When we were pushed off our land," Chavez said, "all we could take with us was what we could jam into the old Studebaker or pile on its roof and fenders, mostly clothes and bedding. . . . I realized something was happening because my mother was crying, but I didn't realize the import of it at the time. When we left the farm, our whole life was upset, turned upside down. We had been part of a very stable community, and we were about to become migratory workers."

Yet if Chavez's experience was in some ways similar to that of the dispossessed dustbowl migrant whose pilgrimage to California was also less an act of hope than of despair, it was fundamentally unlike that of even the most destitute Anglo—John Steinbeck's generic "Okie"—because of virulent racial attitudes among the state's white majority that tended to define all persons "of color" as unequal. For the Chavez family, whose standing as landowners in a region populated by people mainly like themselves had insulated them from many of the meanest forms of racism, following the crops in California as undifferentiated members of a brown-skinned peasantry afforded an unwelcome education. To the familiar varieties of racial humiliation and mistreatment—being physically punished by an Anglo teacher for lapsing into your native tongue; being in the presence of Anglos who talked about you as if you were an inanimate object—were added some new and more abrasive forms: being rousted by border patrolmen who automatically regarded you as a "wetback" until you proved otherwise; being denied service at a restaurant or made to sit in the "Mexican only" seats at the local movie house; being stopped and searched by the police for no reason other than that your skin color announced your powerlessness to resist; being cheated by an employer who smugly assumed that you probably wouldn't object because Mexicans were naturally docile.

But, if because of such treatment Chavez came to fear and dislike Anglos—*gringos* or *gabachos* in the pejorative lexicon of the barrio—he also came to understand that while considerations of race and ethnicity compounded the plight of farmworkers, their mistreatment was rooted ultimately in the economics of industrialized agriculture. As the family traveled the state from one crop to the next, one hovel to the next, trying desperately to survive on the meager earnings of parents and children alike, Chavez quickly learned that Chicano labor contractors and Japanese growers exploited migrants as readily as did Anglo employers. And, although the complex dynamics of California's rural political economy might still have eluded him, Chavez instinctively understood that farmworkers would cease to be victims only when they discovered the means to take control of their own lives.

The realization that unionism must be that means came later. Unlike the typical Chicano family in the migrant stream, however, the Chavez family included among its otherwise meager possessions a powerful legacy of the independent life it had earlier known, one that revealed itself in a stubborn disinclination to tolerate conspicuous injustices. "I don't want to suggest we were that radical," Chavez later said, "but I know we were probably one of the strikingest families in California, the first ones to leave the fields if anyone shouted 'Huelga!'—which is Spanish for 'Strike!' . . . If any family felt something was wrong and stopped working, we immediately joined them even if we didn't know them. And if the grower didn't correct what was wrong, then they would leave, and we'd leave."

Chavez had no trouble identifying the source of the family's instinctive militancy. "We were," he insisted, "constantly fighting against things that most people would probably accept because they didn't have that kind of life we had in the beginning, that strong family life and family ties which we would not let anyone break." When confronted by an injustice, there "was no question. Our dignity meant more than money."

Although the United Cannery, Agricultural, Packing and Allied Workers of America, a CIO-affiliated union, was conducting sporadic organizing drives among California farmworkers when Chavez and his family joined the state's farm labor force at the end of the 1930s, he was too young and untutored to appreciate "anything of the real guts of unions." Yet because his father harbored a strong, if unstudied, conviction that unionism was a manly act of resistance to the employers' authority, Chavez's attitude toward unions quickly progressed from vague approval to ardent endorsement. His earliest participation in a union-led struggle did not occur until the late 1940s, when the AFL's National Farm Labor Union conducted a series of ultimately futile strikes in the San Joaquin valley. This experience, which left Chavez with an acute sense of frustration and disappointment as the strike inevitably withered in the face of overwhelming employer power, also produced a brief but equally keen feeling of exhilaration because it afforded an opportunity to vent the rebelliousness that an expanding consciousness of his own social and occupational captivity awakened within him. Yet to the extent that unionism demands the subordination of individual aspirations to a depersonalized common denomination of the group's desires, Chavez was not in his youth the stuff of which confirmed trade unionists are made. More than most young migrant workers, whose ineluctable discontent was not heightened further by the memory of an idealized past, Chavez hoped to escape his socioeconomic predicament rather than simply moderate the harsh forces that governed it.

To be a migrant worker, however, was to learn the hard way that avenues of escape were more readily imagined than traveled. As ardently as the Chavez family sought a way out of the migrant orbit, they spent the early 1940s moving from valley to valley, from harvest to harvest, powerless to fend off the corrosive effects of their involuntary transiency. Beyond denying them the elementary amenities of a humane existence—a decent home, sufficient food, adequate clothing—the demands of migrant life also conspired to deny the Chavez children the educations that their parents valiantly struggled to ensure. For Cesar school became a "nightmare," a dispiriting succession of inhospitable places ruled by Anglo teachers and administrators whose often undisguised contempt for migrant children prompted him to drop out after the eighth grade.

Chavez's inevitable confrontation with the fact of his personal powerlessness fostered a sense of anger and frustration that revealed itself in a tendency to reject many of the most visible symbols of his cultural heritage. This brief episode of open rebellion against the culture of his parents, which dates from the family's decision to settle down in Delano in late 1943 until he reluctantly joined the navy a year later, was generally benign: *mariachis* were rejected in favor of Duke Ellington; his mother's *dichos* and *consejos*—the bits of Mexican folk wisdom passed from one generation to the next—lost out to less culture-bound values; religious customs rooted in the rigid doctrines of the Catholic church gave way to a fuzzy existentialism. In its most extreme form, this rebelliousness led

Chavez to affect the distinctive style of a *pachuco*, although he never really ventured beyond dress into the more antisocial ways in which that phenomenon of youthful rebellion manifested itself in the activities of Mexican gangs in urban areas like Los Angeles and San Jose. In the end, Chavez reacted most decisively against the debilitating circumstances of his life by joining the navy, a reluctant decision whose redeeming value was that it offered a means of escape, a way "to get away from farm labor."

The two years he spent in the navy ("the worst of my life") proved to be no more than a respite from farm labor. If Chavez had hoped to acquire a trade while in the service, he soon discovered that the same considerations of race and ethnicity that placed strict limits on what non-Anglos could reasonably aspire to achieve at home operated with equal efficiency in the navy to keep them in the least desirable jobs. Without the training that might have allowed him to break out of the cycle of poverty and oppression that the labor system of industrialized agriculture fueled, Chavez returned to Delano in 1946 to the only work he knew.

Finding work had always been a problem for farmworkers because of the chronic oversupply of agricultural labor in California. The problem became even more acute for migrant families after the war because agribusiness interests succeeded in their political campaign to extend the so-called *Bracero* program,[1] a treaty arrangement dating from 1942 that permitted farm employers in California and the Southwest to import Mexican nationals under contract to alleviate real and imagined wartime labor shortages.

For Chavez, the struggle to earn a living took on special urgency following his marriage in 1948 to Helen Fabela, a Delano girl whom he had first met when his family made one of its periodic migrations through the area in search of work. Being the daughter of farmworkers, and thus knowing all too well the hardships that attended a family life predicated upon the irregular earnings of agricultural work, did nothing to cushion the hard times that lay ahead for Helen Chavez and her new husband, a twenty-one-year-old disaffected farm laborer without discernable prospects.

Chavez met the challenge of making a living, which multiplied with the arrival of a new baby during each of the first three years of marriage, in the only way he knew: he took any job available, wherever it was available. Not until 1952, when he finally landed a job in a San Jose lumberyard, was Chavez able to have the settled life that he and Helen craved. The Mexican barrio in San Jose, known to its impoverished inhabitants as Sal Si Puedes — literally "get out if you can"—was a few square blocks of ramshackle houses occupied by discouraged parents and angry children who, in their desperation to do just what the neighborhood's morbid nickname advised, too often sought ways out that led to prison rather than to opportunity. Long before it became home to Chavez and his family, Sal Si Puedes had earned a reputation among the sociologists who regularly scouted its mean streets as a virtual laboratory of urban social pathology. In the early 1950s, however, the area also attracted two men determined in their separate ways to alleviate the powerlessness of its residents rather than to document or measure it. More than any others, these two activists, one a young Catholic priest, the other a veteran community organizer, assumed unwitting responsibility for the education of Cesar Chavez.

When Father Donald McDonnell established his small mission church in Sal Si Puedes, he resolved to attend to both the spiritual need of his destitute parishioners and their education in those doctrines of the Catholic church relating to the inherent rights of labor. To Cesar Chavez, the teachings of the church, the rituals and catechism that he absorbed as an obligation of culture rather than a voluntary and knowing act of religious faith, had never seemed to have more than tangential relevance to the hard-edged world that poor people confronted in their daily lives. But in the militant example and activist pedagogy of Father McDonnell, Chavez discovered a new dimension of Catholicism that excited him precisely because it was relevant to his immediate circumstances. "Actually," he later said, "my education started when I met Father Donald McDonnell. . . . We had long talks about farm workers. I knew a lot about the work, but I didn't know anything about economics, and I learned quite a bit from him. He had a picture of a worker's shanty and a picture of a grower's mansion; a picture of a labor camp and a picture of a high-priced building in San Francisco owned by the same grower. When things were pointed out to me, I began to see. . . . Everything he said was aimed at ways to solve the injustice." Chavez's appetite for the social gospel that McDonnell espoused was insatiable: "[He] sat with me past midnight telling me about social justice and the Church's stand on farm labor and reading from the encyclicals of Pope Leo XIII in which he upheld labor unions. I would do anything to get the Father to tell me more about labor history. I began going to the bracero camps with him to help with Mass, to the city jail with him to talk to prisoners, anything to be with him so that he could tell me more about the farm labor movement."

More than anyone else, Father McDonnell awoke Chavez to a world of pertinent ideas that would become the essential source of his personal philosophy; introduced him to a pantheon of crusaders for social justice (Gandhi among them) whose heroic exertions would supply the inspiration for his own crusade to empower farmworkers. Yet the crucial task of instructing Chavez in the practical means by which his nascent idealism might achieve concrete expression was brilliantly discharged by Fred Ross, an indefatigable organizer who had spent the better part of his adult life roaming California trying to show the victims of economic, racial, and ethnic discrimination how they might resist further abuse and degradation through organization.

Drawn to Sal Si Puedes by the palpable misery of its Chicano inhabitants, Ross began to conduct the series of informal house meetings through which he hoped to establish a local chapter of the Community Service Organization (CSO), a self-help group that operated under the sponsorship of radical activist Saul Alinsky's Chicago-based Industrial Areas Foundation. Always on the lookout for the natural leaders in the communities he sought to organize, Ross at once saw in Chavez, despite his outwardly shy and self-conscious demeanor, the telltale signs of a born organizer. "At the very first meeting," Ross recalled, "I was very much impressed with Cesar. I could tell he was intensely interested, a kind of burning interest rather than one of those inflammatory things that lasts one night and is then forgotten. He asked many questions, part of it to see if I really knew, putting me to the test. But it was much more than that." Ross also discovered that Chavez was an exceedingly quick study: "He understood it almost immediately, as soon as I drew the picture. He got the point—the whole question of power and the development of power within the group. He made the connections very quickly between the civic weakness of the group and the social neglect in the barrio, and also conversely, what could be done about that social neglect once the power was developed." "I kept a diary in those days," Ross said later. "And the first night I met Cesar, I wrote in it, 'I think I've found the guy I'm looking for.' It was obvious even then."

The confidence that Ross expressed in Chavez's leadership potential was immediately confirmed. Assigned to the CSO voter registration project in San Jose, Chavez displayed a natural aptitude for the work; so much in fact that Ross turned over control of the entire drive to him. And if his style of leadership proved somewhat unconventional, his tactical sense was unerring. While Ross had relied upon local college students to serve as registrars for the campaign, Chavez felt more could be gained by using people from the barrio. "Instead of recruiting college guys," he said, "I got all my friends, my beer-drinking friends. With them it wasn't a question of civic duty, they helped me because of friendship, and because it was fun." With nearly six thousand new voters registered by the time the campaign ended, Chavez's reputation as an organizer was established.

As exhilarated as he was by the challenge of organizing, Chavez was also sobered by the personal attacks that the local political establishment unleashed against anyone who presumed to alter the balance of power in the ghetto. Since it was the heyday of McCarthyism, the charge most frequently lodged against him was that he was a Communist. It seemed not to matter that such charges were preposterous. Even the vaguest suggestion of radicalism was enough to cause the more cautious members of the Chicano community to regard Chavez with growing suspicion. "The Chicanos," he said, "wouldn't talk to me. They were afraid. The newspaper had a lot of influence during those McCarthy days. Anyone who organized or worked for civil rights was called a Communist. Anyone who talked about police brutality was called a Communist."

> Everywhere I went to organize they would bluntly ask, "Are you a Communist?"
> I would answer, "No."
> "How do we know?"
> "You don't know. You know because I tell you."
> And we would go around and around on that. If it was somebody who was being smart, I'd tell them to go to hell, but if it was somebody that I wanted to organize, I would have to go through an explanation.

Before long, however, Chavez became an expert in turning the cultural tendencies of his Chicano neighbors to his own advantage. When his detractors wrapped themselves in the flag, Chavez countered, with the help of Father McDonnell and other sympathetic priests, by cloaking himself in the respectability of the Catholic church. "I found out," he recalled with apparent satisfaction, "that when they learned I was close to the church, they wouldn't question me so much. So I'd get the priests to come out and give me their blessing. In those days, if a priest said something to the Mexicans, they would say fine. It's different now."

In the course of raising the civic consciousness of others, Chavez broadened and deepened his own previously neglected education. "I began to grow and to see a lot of things that I hadn't seen before," he said. "My eyes opened, and I paid more attention to political and social events." And though his emergence as a trade union activist was still years away, Chavez the community organizer felt a sufficient affinity with his counterparts in the labor field that he adopted as texts for his self-education "biographies of labor organizers like John L. Lewis and Eugene Debs and the Knights of Labor."

After watching his protégé in action for only a few months, Fred Ross persuaded Saul Alinsky that the CSO should employ the talents of so able an organizer on a full-time basis. Becoming a professional organizer, however, was a prospect that frightened Chavez nearly as much as it excited him. Helping Fred Ross was one thing, organizing on his own among strangers was quite another. Yet in the end, his desire to oppose what seemed unjust outweighed his fears.

From the end of 1952 until he quit the organization ten years later to build a union among farmworkers, the CSO was Chavez's life. He approached the work of helping the poor to help themselves in the only way his nature allowed, with a single-mindedness that made everything else in his life—home, family, personal gain—secondary. For Chavez, nothing short of total immersion in the work of forcing change was enough. If his wife inherited virtually the entire responsibility for raising their children (who were to number eight in all), if his children became resentful at being left to grow up without a father who was readily accessible to them, if he was himself forced to abandon any semblance of personal life, Chavez remained unshaken in his belief that the promotion of the greater good made every such sacrifice necessary and worthwhile.

The years he spent as an organizer for the CSO brought Chavez into contact, and usually conflict, with the whole range of public and private authorities to which the poor were accountable and by which they were controlled. The problems he handled were seldom other than mundane, yet each in its own way confirmed the collective impotence of those who populated the Chicano ghettos that became his special province. "They'd bring their personal problems," Chavez said of his CSO clients. "They were many. They might need a letter written or someone to interpret for them at the welfare department, the doctor's office, or the police. Maybe they were not getting enough welfare aid, or their check was taken away, or their kids were thrown out of school. Maybe they had been taken by a crooked salesman selling fences, aluminum siding, or freezers that hold food for a month."

In the beginning, helping people to deal with problems they felt otherwise powerless to resolve was an end in itself. In time, however, Chavez saw that if his service work was going to produce a legacy of activist sentiment in Chicano neighborhoods, it was necessary to recast what had typically been an act of unconditional assistance into a mutually beneficial transaction. And, when he discovered that those whom he was serving were not just willing, but eager, to return the favor, Chavez made that volition the basis upon which he helped to build the CSO into the most formidable Mexican-American political organization in the state. "Once I realized helping people was an organizing technique," he said, "I increased that work. I was willing to work day and night and to go to hell and back for people—provided they also did something for the CSO in return. I never felt bad asking for that . . . because I wasn't asking for something for myself. For a long time we didn't know how to put that work together into an organization. But we learned after a while—we learned how to help people by making them responsible."

Because agricultural labor constituted a main source of economic opportunity in most Chicano communities, many of those whom Chavez recruited into the CSO were farmworkers. Not until 1958, however, did Chavez take his first halting steps toward making work and its discontents the essential focus of his organizing activities. This gradual shift from community to labor organization occurred over a period of several months as Chavez struggled to establish a CSO chapter in Oxnard, a leading citrus-growing region north of Los Angeles. Asked by Saul Alinsky to organize the local Chicano community in order that it might support the flagging efforts of the United Packinghouse Workers to win labor contracts covering the region's citrus-packing sheds, Chavez embarked upon his task intending to exploit the same assortment of grievances that festered in barrios throughout the state.

His new clients, however, had other ideas. From the beginning, whenever he sought to impress his agenda upon local citizens, they interrupted with their own: a concern that they were being denied jobs because growers in the region relied almost entirely on braceros to meet their needs for farm labor. It proved to be an issue that simply would not go away. "At every house meeting," Chavez recalled, "they hit me with the bracero problem, but I would dodge it. I just didn't fathom how big that problem was. I would say, 'Well, you know, we really can't do anything about that, but it's a bad problem. Something should be done.'" An apparently artless dodger, he was, in the end, forced to make the bracero problem the focus of his campaign. "Finally," he admitted, "I decided this was the issue I had to tackle. The fact that braceros were also farmworkers didn't bother me. . . . The jobs belonged to local workers. The braceros were brought only for exploitation. They were just instruments for the growers. Braceros didn't make any money, and they were exploited viciously, forced to work under conditions the local people wouldn't tolerate. If the braceros spoke up, if they made the minimal complaints, they'd be shipped back to Mexico."

In attacking Oxnard's bracero problem, Chavez and his followers confronted the integrated power of the agribusiness establishment in its most forceful and resilient aspect. While farm employers around Oxnard and throughout the state were permitted under federal regulations to employ braceros only when they had exhausted the available pool of local farmworkers, they had long operated on the basis of a collusive arrangement with the California Farm Placement Service that allowed them to import Mexican nationals without regard to labor market conditions in the region.

Although Chavez and the large CSO membership he rallied behind him sought nothing more than compliance with existing rules regarding the employment of braceros, the thirteen-month struggle that followed brought them into bitter conflicts with politically influential employers, state farm placement bureaucrats, and federal labor department officials. Yet through the use of picket lines, marches, rallies, and a variety of innovative agitational techniques that reduced the Farm Placement Service to almost total paralysis, Chavez and his militant following had by the end of 1959 won a victory so complete that farm employers in the region were recruiting their labor through a local CSO headquarters that operated as a hiring hall.

Chavez emerged from the Oxnard campaign convinced that work-related issues had greater potential as a basis for organizing Chicanos than any that he had earlier stressed. The response to his organizing drive in Oxnard was overwhelming, and he saw at once that "the difference between that CSO chapter and any other CSO up to that point was that jobs were the main issue." And at the same juncture, he said, "I began to see the potential of organizing the Union."

What Chavez saw with such clarity, however, the elected leadership of the CSO, drawn almost exclusively from the small but influential ranks of middle-class Chicanos, was unwilling even to imagine. Determined that the CSO would remain a civic organization, the leadership decisively rejected Chavez's proposal to transform the Oxnard chapter into a farm-workers' union. "We had won a victory," Chavez bitterly recalled, "but I didn't realize how short-lived it would be. We could have built a union there, but the CSO wouldn't approve. In fact, the whole project soon fell apart. I wanted to go for a strike and get some contracts, but the CSO wouldn't let me. . . . If I had had the support of the CSO, I would have built a union there. If anyone from labor had come, we could have had a union. I think if the Union of Organized Devils of America had come, I would have joined them, I was so frustrated."

Even though he remained with the CSO for two years following his defeat over the issue of unionism, Chavez's devotion to the organization waned as his determination to organize farmworkers increased. Finally, when the CSO once again rejected the idea of unionism at its annual convention in 1962, Chavez decided that he had had enough. He resigned as the convention ended and left the organization on his thirty-fifth birthday. "I've heard people say," he later explained, "that because I was thirty-five, I was getting worried, as I hadn't done too much with my life. But I wasn't worried. I didn't even consider thirty-five to be old. I didn't care about that. I just knew we needed a union. . . . What I didn't know was that we would go through hell because it was an all but impossible task."

Based on the often heroic, but inevitably futile, efforts of those who had earlier dared to challenge the monolithic power of industrialized agriculture in California—the Industrial Workers of the World before World War I; the Communist-led Cannery and Agricultural Workers Industrial Union during the early 1930s; the CIO in the late thirties; the AFL in the 1940s; and a rich variety of independent ethnic unions over the better part of a century—Chavez's assertion that organizing the state's farmworkers was "an all but impossible task" hardly overstated the case. Farm employers, assisted by a supporting cast representing nearly every form of public and private power in the state, had beaten back every attempt by workers to gain power while assiduously cultivating a public image of themselves as beleaguered yeomen valiantly struggling against the erosive forces of modernity, including unionism, to preserve the nation's Jeffersonian heritage.

To the task of contesting the immense power and redoubtable prestige of the agribusiness nexus, Chavez brought nothing more or less than an intensity of purpose that bordered on fanaticism. And while he would have rejected the disdain that the remark reflected, Chavez was in essential agreement with the cynical AFL official who declared in 1935: "Only fanatics are willing to live in shacks or tents and get their heads broken in the interest of migratory labor." In Chavez's view, nothing less than fanaticism would suffice if farmworkers were to be emancipated from a system of wage slavery that had endured for a century. When a reporter observed during one of the UFW's later struggles that he "sounded like a fanatic," Chavez readily admitted the charge. "I am," he confessed. "There's nothing wrong with being a fanatic. Those are the only ones that get things done."

In many ways, Chavez's supreme accomplishment as an organizer came long before he signed up his first farmworker. Attracting disciples willing to embrace the idea of a farmworkers' movement with a passion, single-mindedness, and spirit of sacrifice equal to his own was at once Chavez's greatest challenge and his finest achievement. By the fall of 1962, when he formally established the National Farm Workers Association (NFWA) in a derelict Fresno theater, Chavez had rallied to "La Causa"—the iconographic designation soon adopted by the faithful—an impressive roster of "co-fanatics": Dolores Huerta, a small, youthful-looking mother of six (she would have ten in all) whose willingness to do battle with Chavez over union tactics was exceeded only by her fierce loyalty to him; Gilbert Padilla, like Huerta another CSO veteran, whose activism was rooted in a hatred for the migrant system that derived from personal experience; Wayne Hartimire and Jim Drake, two young Anglo ministers who were to make the California Migrant Ministry a virtual subsidiary of the union; Manuel Chavez, an especially resourceful organizer who reluctantly gave up a well-paying job to join the union when the guilt his cousin Cesar heaped upon him for not joining became unbearable. Most important, there was Helen Chavez, whose willingness to sacrifice so much of what mattered most to her, including first claim on her husband's devotion, revealed the depth of her own commitment to farmworker organization.

Working out of Delano, which became the union's first headquarters, Chavez began the slow and often discouraging process of organizing farm laborers whose strong belief in the rightness of his union-building mission was tempered by an even deeper conviction that "it couldn't be done, that the growers were too powerful." With financial resources consisting of a small savings account, gifts and loans from relatives, and the modest wages Helen earned by returning to the fields, the cost of Chavez's stubborn idealism to himself and his family was measured in material deprivation and emotional tumult. Had he been willing to accept financial assistance from such sources as the United Packinghouse Workers or the Agricultural Workers Organizing Committee (AWOC), a would-be farmworkers' union established in 1959 by the AFL-CIO, the worst hardships that awaited Chavez and his loyalists might have been eased or eliminated. Yet, following a line of reasoning that was in some ways reminiscent of the voluntarist logic of earlier trade unionists, Chavez insisted that a farmworkers' union capable of forging the will and stamina required to breach the awesome power of agribusiness could only be built on the sacrifice and suffering of its own membership.

During the NFWA's formative years there was more than enough sacrifice and suffering to go around. But as a result of the services it provided to farmworkers and the promise of a better life it embodied, the union slowly won the allegiance of a small but dedicated membership scattered through the San Joaquin valley. By the spring of 1965, when the union called its first strike, a brief walkout by rose grafters in Kern County that won higher wages but no contract, Chavez's obsession was on its way to becoming a functioning reality.

Despite the studied deliberateness of its leaders, however, the struggle that catapulted the union to national attention, and invested its mission with the same moral authority that liberal and left-wing activists of the 1960s attributed to the decade's stormy civil rights, antipoverty, and anti-war movements, began in the fall of 1965 as a reluctant gesture of solidarity with an AWOC local whose mainly Filipino membership was on strike against grape growers around Delano. Given the demonstrated ineptitude of the old-time trade unionists who directed the AFL-CIO's organizing efforts among California farmworkers, Chavez had reason to hesitate before committing his still small and untested membership to the support of an AWOC strike. But the strike was being led by Larry Itliong, a Filipino veteran of earlier agricultural strikes and the ablest of the AWOC organizers, and Chavez did not have it in him to ignore a just cause. "At the time," he recalled, "we had about twelve hundred members, but only about two hundred were paying dues. I didn't feel we were ready for a strike—I figured it would be a couple more years before we would be—but I also knew we weren't going to break a strike." The formal decision to support AWOC, made at a boisterous mass meeting held in Delano's Catholic church on September 16 (the day Mexicans celebrate the end of Spanish colonial rule), produced twenty-seven hundred workers willing to sign union cards authorizing the NFWA to represent them in dealing with area grape growers.

The Delano strike, which soon widened beyond the table grape growers who were its initial targets to include the state's major wineries, was a painful five-year struggle destined to test not only the durability of agricultural unionism in California but also the wisdom and resourcefulness of Chavez's leadership. Because growers had little difficulty in recruiting scabs to take the place of strikers, Chavez recognized immediately that a strike could not deny employers the labor they required to cultivate and harvest their crops. Even so, picket lines went up on the first day of the strike and were maintained with unfailing devotion week after week, month after month. Chavez emphasized the need for picketing because he believed that no experience promoted a keener sense of solidarity or afforded strikers a more graphic and compelling illustration of the struggle's essential character. "Unless you have been on a picket line," he said, "you just can't understand the feeling you get there, seeing the conflict at its two most acid ends. It's a confrontation that's vivid. It's a real education."

It was an education, however, for which pickets often paid a high price: threats, physical intimidation, and outright violence at the hands of growers and their agents and arbitrary arrests and harassment by local lawmen who made no effort to mask their pro-employer sympathies. Yet, no matter how great the provocation, no matter how extreme the violence directed against them, strikers were sworn by Chavez not to use violence. Chavez's unwavering commitment to nonviolence was compounded from equal measures of his mother's teachings, the affecting example of St. Francis of Assisi, and the moral philosophy of Gandhi. In the end, though, it was the power of nonviolence as a tactical method that appealed to him. Convinced that the farmworkers' greatest asset was the inherent justice of their cause, Chavez believed that the task of communicating the essential virtue of the union's struggle to potential supporters, and to the general public, would be subverted if strikers resorted to violence. "If someone commits violence against us," Chavez argued, "it is much better—if we can—not to react against the violence, but to react in such a way as to get closer to our goal. People don't like to see a nonviolent movement subjected to violence. . . . That's the key point we have going for us. . . . By some strange chemistry, every time the opposition commits an unjust act against our hopes and aspirations, we get tenfold paid back in benefits."

Winning and sustaining public sympathy, as well as the active support of labor, church, student, civic, and political organizations, was indispensable to the success of the Delano struggles because the inefficacy of conventional strike tactics led Chavez to adopt the economic boycott as the union's primary weapon in fighting employers. Newly sensitized to issues of social justice by the civil rights struggles that reverberated across the country, liberals and leftists enthusiastically embraced the union's cause, endorsing its successive boycotts and not infrequently showing up in Delano to bear personal witness to the unfolding drama of the grape strike. Many unions—from dockworkers who refused to handle scab grapes to autoworkers, whose president, Walter Reuther, not only pledged generous financial assistance to the strikers but also traveled to Delano to join their picket lines—also supported the NFWA. Even the AFL-CIO, which had been sponsoring the rival Agricultural Workers Organizing Committee, ended up embracing the NFWA when Bill Kircher, the federation's national organizing director, concluded that the future of farmworker unionism lay with Chavez and his ragtag following rather than with the more fastidious, but less effective, AWOC. Kircher's assessment of the situation also led him to urge a merger of the UFWA and AWOC. And although their long-standing suspicion of "Big Labor" impelled many of the Anglo volunteers who had joined his movement to oppose the idea, Chavez and the union's farmworker membership recognized that the respectability and financial strength to be gained from such a merger outweighed any loss of independence that AFL-CIO affiliation might entail. With Chavez at its helm and Larry Itliong as its second-in-command, the United Farm Workers Organizing Committee (UFWOC) was formally chartered by the AFL-CIO in August 1966.

The public backing the farmworkers attracted, including that of Senator Robert F. Kennedy, who became an outspoken supporter of the union when the Senate Subcommittee on Migratory Labor held its highly publicized hearings in Delano during the spring of 1966, indicated that large segments of the American people believed that grape strikers occupied the moral "high ground" in their dispute with farm employers. To an important degree, however, public support for the farmworkers' cause also reflected a willingness among many Americans to believe and trust in Cesar Chavez personally; to see in the style and content of his public "persona" those qualities of integrity, selflessness, and moral rectitude that made his cause theirs whether or not they truly understood it. And if Chavez was more embarrassed than flattered by such adoration, he was also enough of an opportunist to see that when liberals from New York to Hollywood made him the human repository of their own unrequited idealism or proclaimed his sainthood, it benefited farmworkers.

"Alone, the farm workers have no economic power," Chavez once observed, "but with the help of the public they can develop the economic power to counter that of the growers." The truth of that maxim was first revealed in April 1966, when a national boycott campaign against its product line of wines and spirits caused Schenley Industries, which had 5,000 acres of vineyards in the San Joaquin valley, to recognize the farmworkers' union and enter into contract negotiations. For Chavez, who received the news as he and a small band of union loyalists were nearing the end of an arduous, but exceedingly well-publicized, 300-mile march from Delano to Sacramento, Schenley's capitulation was "the first major proof of the power of the boycott."

Chavez's tactical genius, and the power of a national (and later international) boycott apparatus that transformed an otherwise local dispute into a topic of keen interest and passionate debate in communities across the country, prompted one winery after another to choose accommodation over further conflict. For two of the biggest wine grape growers, however, the prospect of acquiescing to UFWOC's brand of militant unionism was so loathsome that they resolved to court a more palatable alternative: the giant International Brotherhood of Teamsters. And although they had no apparent support among farmworkers in the region, the Teamsters, under the cynical and opportunistic leadership of William Grami, organizing director of the union's western conference, eagerly sought to prove that theirs was indeed the type of "businesslike" labor organization which anti-union farm employers could tolerate. Yet as good as the idea first seemed to the DiGiorgio Fruit Corporation and then to Perelli-Minetti Vineyards, consummating such a mischievous liaison with the Teamsters proved impossible. In the end, neither the companies nor the Teamsters had the will to persist in the face of intensified UFWOC boycotts, angry condemnations by the labor movement, and a rising tide of public disapproval. The controversy was finally resolved through secret ballot elections, which resulted in expressions of overwhelming support for Chavez and UFWOC.

The victories won during the first two years of the Delano struggle, while they propelled the cause of farmworker organization far beyond the boundaries of any previous advance, left Chavez and his followers still needing to overcome table grape growers in the San Joaquin and Coachella valleys before the union could claim real institutional durability. The state's table grape industry, composed for the most part of family farms whose hardworking owners typically viewed unionism as an assault on their personal independence as well as a threat to their prerogatives as employers, remained unalterably opposed to UFWOC's demands long after California's largest wineries had acceded to them. Thus when Chavez made them the main targets of the union's campaign toward the end of 1967, table grape growers fought back with a ferocity and tactical ingenuity that announced their determination to resist unionism at whatever cost.

While the boycott continued to serve as the union's most effective weapon, especially after employers persuaded compliant local judges to issue injunctions severely restricting picketing and other direct action in the strike region, the slowness with which it operated to prod recalcitrant growers toward the bargaining table produced in farmworkers and volunteers alike an impatience that reduced both morale and discipline. It also undermined La Causa's commitment to nonviolence. "There came a point in 1968," Chavez recalled, "when we were in danger of losing. . . . Because of a sudden increase in violence against us, and an apparent lack of progress after more than two years of striking, there were those who felt that the time had come to overcome violence by violence. . . . There was demoralization in the ranks, people becoming desperate, more and more talk about violence. People meant it, even when they talked to me. They would say, 'Hey, we've got to burn these sons of bitches down. We've got to kill a few of them.'"

In responding to the crisis, Chavez chose a method of restoring discipline and morale that was as risky and unusual as it was revealing of the singular character of his leadership. He decided to fast. The fast, which continued for twenty-five painful days before it was finally broken at a moving outdoor mass in Delano that included Robert Kennedy among its celebrants, was more than an act of personal penance. "I thought I had to bring the Movement to a halt," Chavez explained, "do something that would force them and me to deal with the whole question of violence and ourselves. We had to stop long enough to take account of what we were doing." Although the fast's religious overtones offended the secular sensibilities of many of his followers, it was more a political than a devotional act; an intrepid and dramatic, if manipulative, device by which Chavez established a compelling standard of personal sacrifice against which his supporters might measure their own commitment and dedication to La Causa, and thus their allegiance to its leader. The power of guilt as a disciplinary tool was something Chavez well understood from his study of the life and philosophy of Gandhi, and he was never reluctant to use it himself. "One of his little techniques," Fred Ross said of Chavez's style of leadership, "has always been to shame people into doing something by letting them know how hard he and others were working, and how it was going to hurt other people if they didn't help too."

Those in the union who were closest to Chavez, whatever their initial reservations, found the fast's effect undeniably therapeutic. Jerry Cohen, the union's able young attorney, while convinced that it had been "a fantastic gamble," was deeply impressed by "what a great organizing tool the fast was." "Before the fast," Cohen noted, "there were nine ranch committees [the rough equivalent of locals within the UFW's structure], one for each winery. The fast, for the first time, made a union out of those ranch committees. . . . Everybody worked together." Dolores Huerta also recognized the curative power of Chavez's ordeal. "Prior to that fast," she insisted, "there had been a lot of bickering and backbiting and fighting and little attempts at violence. But Cesar brought everybody together and really established himself as a leader of the farm workers."

While a chronic back ailment, apparently exacerbated by his fast and a schedule that often required him to work twenty hours a day, slowed Chavez's pace during much of 1968 and 1969, the steadily more punishing economic effects of the grape boycott finally began to erode the confidence and weaken the resistance of growers. With the assistance of a committee of strongly pro-union Catholic bishops who had volunteered to mediate the conflict, negotiations between the union and the first defectors from the growers' ranks finally began in the spring of 1970. And by the end of July, when the most obdurate growers in the Delano area collapsed under the combined weight of a continuing boycott and their own mounting weariness, Chavez and his tenacious followers had finally accomplished what five years before seemed impossible to all but the most sanguine forecasters.

The union's victory, which extended to eighty-five percent of the state's table grape industry, resulted in contracts that provided for substantial wage increases and employer contributions to UFWOC's health and welfare and economic development funds. Even more important, however, were the noneconomic provisions: union-run hiring halls that gave UFWOC control over the distribution of available work; grievance machinery that rescued the individual farmworker from the arbitrary authority of the boss; restrictions on the use of pesticides that endangered the health of workers; in short, provisions for the emancipation of workers from the century-old dictatorship of California agribusiness.

After five years of struggle and sacrifice, of anguish and uncertainty, Chavez and his followers wanted nothing so much as an opportunity to recuperate from their ordeal and to savor their victory. It was not to be. On the day before the union concluded its negotiations with Delano grape growers, Chavez received the distressing news that lettuce growers in the Salinas and Santa Maria valleys, knowing that they would be the next targets of UFWOC's organizing campaign, had signed contracts providing for the Teamsters' union to represent their field workers. In keeping with the pattern of the Teamsters' involvement with agricultural field labor, no one bothered to consult the Chicano workers whose incessant stooping and bending, whose painful contortions in the service of the hated short-handle hoe, made possible the growers' proud boast that the Salinas valley was the "salad bowl of the nation."

Except for one contract, which the union acquired in 1961 through a collusive agreement with a lettuce grower scheming to break a strike by the Agricultural Workers Organizing Committee, the Teamsters had been content to limit their interest to the truck drivers, boxmakers, and packing-shed workers of the vegetable industry. The Teamsters' decision to expand their jurisdiction to include field labor was a frontal assault on UFWOC. Still weary from the Delano struggle and confronting the complex job of implementing the union's newly won contracts, Chavez and his staff rushed to Salinas in order to meet the challenge.

If William Grami and his Teamsters cohorts discovered that the specter of a UFWOC organizing drive put Anglo lettuce growers in an unusually accommodating frame of mind, they found that Chicano farmworkers in the Salinas and Santa Maria valleys were unwilling to accept a union other than of their own choosing, especially after Chavez launched his boisterous counterattack. As thousands of defiant workers walked off their jobs rather than join a union of the employers' choice, the Teamsters' hierarchy, inundated by a rising tide of liberal and labor criticism, decided that Grami's tactics were inopportune from a public relations standpoint, and therefore ordered him to undo his now inexpedient handiwork. Grami dutifully, if reluctantly, invited Chavez to meet with him, and the two men quickly worked out an agreement providing that the UFWOC would have exclusive jurisdiction over field labor, and that the Teamsters would renounce their contracts with lettuce growers and defer to the workers' true preference in bargaining agents. For a few of the largest growers in the Salinas valley, those who felt most vulnerable to the boycott Chavez had threatened, abandoning Teamsters' contracts in favor of agreements with UFWOC provided a welcome escape from a misadventure. Yet when the Teamsters asserted that they were "honor bound" to respect the wishes of 170 growers who refused to void their contracts, Chavez had no choice but to resume hostilities.

Although the more than five thousand workers who responded to UFWOC's renewed strike call brought great enthusiasm and energy to the union's rallies, marches, and picket lines, their capacity to disrupt the fall lettuce harvest declined as the influence exerted by a ready supply of job-hungry "green carders" (Mexican nationals with work permits) combined with aggressive strikebreaking by violence-prone Teamsters "guards," hostile police, politically influential employers, and injunction-happy local judges. As strike activities diminished and boycott operations intensified, employers obtained a court order declaring both types of union pressure illegal under a state law banning jurisdictional strikes.[2] Chavez later spent three weeks in jail for instructing his followers to ignore the order, but the publicity and additional support his brief imprisonment generated made it one of the few positive developments in an otherwise discouraging slide into adversity.

The challenge presented by the Teamsters-grower alliance in the lettuce industry forced UFWOC to divert precious resources into the reconstruction of its far-flung boycott network. It also distracted Chavez and his most competent aides at a time when the union was in the process of transforming itself from an organization expert in agitation into one equipped to administer contracts covering thousands of workers in the grape industry. Meeting the demands of the hiring hall and the grievance process, which were the union's greatest potential sources of institutional strength, also became its most worrisome and debilitating problem as ranch committees composed of rank-and-file members struggled against their own inexperience, and sometimes powerful tendencies toward vindictiveness, favoritism, and a residual servility, to satisfy the labor requirements of employers and to protect the contractual rights of their fellow workers.

Although Chavez instituted an administrative training program designed by his old mentor Fred Ross, he rejected an AFL-CIO offer of assistance because of his stubborn conviction that a genuinely democratic union must entrust its operation to its own members even at the risk of organizational inefficiency and incompetence. And when he shifted the union's headquarters fifty miles southeast of Delano to an abandoned tuberculosis sanitorium in the Tehachapi Mountains that he called La Paz—short for Nuestra Señora de la Paz (Our Lady of Peace)—Chavez claimed the move was prompted by a concern that his easy accessibility to members of the union's ranch committees discouraged self-reliance. "It was my idea to leave for La Paz," he explained, "because I wanted to remove my presence from Delano, so they could develop their own leadership, because if I am there, they wouldn't make the decisions themselves. They'd come to me." But the move intensified suspicions of internal critics like Larry Itliong, who left the union partly because Chavez's physical isolation from the membership seemed to enhance the influence of the Anglo "intellectuals" while diminishing that of the rank and file. The greatest barrier to broadening the union's leadership and administrative operation, however, was posed by neither geography nor the influence of Anglo volunteers, but by Chavez himself, whose devotion to the ideal of decentralization was seldom matched by an equal disposition to delegate authority to others. Journalist Ron Taylor, who observed Chavez's style of leadership at close range, wrote: "He conceptually saw a union run in the most democratic terms, but in practice he had a difficult time trying to maintain his own distance; his tendencies were to step in and make decisions. . . . Even though he had removed himself from Delano, he maintained a close supervision over it, and all of the other field offices. Through frequent staff meetings and meetings of the executive board, he developed his own personal involvement with the tiniest of union details."

If Chavez's deficiencies as an administrator troubled sympathetic AFL-CIO officials like Bill Kircher, they tended to reinforce the suspicion privately harbored by such trade union traditionalists as federation president George Meany that viable organization was probably beyond the compass of farmworkers, no matter how driven and charismatic their leader. Indeed, what appeared to be at the root of Meany's personal skepticism was Chavez's eccentric style of leadership and somewhat alien trade union philosophy: his well-advertised idealism, which uncharitably rendered was a species of mere self-righteousness; his overweening presence, which seemingly engendered an unhealthy cult of personality; his extravagant sense of mission, which left outsiders wondering whether his was a labor or a social movement; his apparently congenital aversion to compromise, which, in Meany's view, negated the AFL-CIO's repeated efforts to negotiate a settlement of UFWOC's jurisdictional dispute with the Teamsters. None of these reservations was enough to keep the AFL-CIO in early 1972 from changing the union's status from that of organizing committee to full-fledged affiliate—the United Farm Workers of America—but in combination they were apparently enough to persuade Meany that Chavez was no longer deserving of the same levels of financial and organizational support previously contributed by the federation.

Yet if trade union administration of an appropriately conventional style was not his forte, Chavez demonstrated during the course of several legislative battles in 1971 and 1972 that his talents as a political organizer and tactician were exceptional. When the Oregon legislature passed an anti-union bill sponsored by the American Farm Bureau Federation, Chavez and his followers, in only a week's time, persuaded the governor to veto it. Shortly thereafter, Chavez initiated a far more ambitious campaign to recall the governor of Arizona for signing a similar grower-backed bill into law. And while the recall drive ultimately bogged down in a tangle of legal disputes, Chavez's success in registering nearly one hundred thousand mostly poor, mostly Chicano voters fostered fundamental changes in the political balance of power in Arizona.

It was in California, however, that the UFW afforded its opponents the most impressive demonstration of La Causa's political sophistication and clout, and Chavez revealed to friends and foes alike that his ability to influence public debate extended well beyond the normal boundaries of trade union leadership. With the backing of the state's agribusiness establishment, the California Farm Bureau launched during 1972 a well-financed initiative drive—popularly known as Proposition 22—designed to eliminate the threat of unionism by banning nearly every effective weapon available to the UFW, including the boycott. Having failed the year before to win legislative approval for an equally tough anti-union measure, farm employers were confident that they could persuade the citizens of California, as they had so often before, that protecting the state's highly profitable agricultural industry was in the public interest. Aware that the UFW could not survive under the restrictive conditions that Proposition 22 contemplated, but without the financial resources needed to counter the growers' expensive media campaign, Chavez and his aides masterfully deployed what they did have: an aroused and resourceful membership. In the end, the growers' financial power proved to be no match for the UFW's people power. In defeating Proposition 22 by a decisive margin—58 percent to 42 percent—the UFW not only eliminated the immediate threat facing the union, but also announced to growers in terms too emphatic to ignore that the time was past when farm employers could rely upon their political power to keep farmworkers in their place.

The political battles that occupied Chavez and the UFW during much of 1972 involved issues so central to the union's existence that they could not be avoided. But even in the course of winning its political fights with agribusiness, the union lost ground on other equally crucial fronts. Organizing activities all but ceased as the UFW turned its attention to political action, and further efforts aimed at alleviating the administrative problems that plagued the union's operation in the grape industry and increasing the pressures on Salinas valley lettuce growers were neglected. At the beginning of 1973 the UFW was in the paradoxical situation of being at the height of its political strength while its vulnerability as a union was increasing.

Just how vulnerable the union was became apparent as the contracts it had negotiated in 1970 with Coachella valley grape growers came up for renewal. Chavez had heard rumors that the Teamsters were planning to challenge the UFW in the region, but not until growers made plain their intention to reclaim complete control over the hiring, dispatching, and disciplining of workers did he suspect that a deal was already in the making. The UFW retained the allegiance of a vast majority of the industry's workers, but neither the growers nor the Teamsters seemed to care. As soon as the UFW contracts expired, all but two growers announced that they had signed new four-year agreements with the Teamsters. Hiring halls, grievance procedures, and protections against dangerous pesticides disappeared along with the workers' right to a union of their own choice.

Unlike their earlier forays into agriculture, which reflected the opportunism of lower level functionaries interested in advancing their own careers, the Teamsters' move into the grape industry was only the leading edge of a grandiose new strategy by the union's top leadership to rescue farm employers from the UFW in return for the exclusive right to represent farmworkers. Teamsters president Frank Fitzsimmons, with the strong encouragement of the Nixon administration, had suggested such an arrangement late in 1972 when he appeared as the featured speaker at the annual convention of the American Farm Bureau Federation. The Teamsters provided further evidence of their revived interest in agriculture by announcing a few weeks later that the union had renegotiated contracts with 170 growers operating in the Salinas, Santa Maria, and Imperial valleys even though the existing five-year agreement still had nearly three years to run.

The Teamsters' special appeal to California's agribusiness community was obvious: while the UFW insisted that farm employers share power with their workers, Teamsters contracts required only a sharing of the industry's wealth in the form of higher wages and other economic benefits. That the Teamsters never contemplated a kind of unionism that would permit Chicano farmworkers to gain a measure of control over their own lives was confirmed by Einar Mohn, director of the Western Conference of Teamsters, who said shortly after the union announced its coup in the grape industry: "We have to have them in the union for a while. It will be a couple of years before they can start having membership meetings, before we can use the farm workers' ideas in the union. I'm not sure how effective a union can be when it is composed of Mexican-Americans and Mexican nationals with temporary visas. Maybe as agriculture becomes more sophisticated, more mechanized, with fewer transients, fewer green carders, and as jobs become more attractive to whites, then we can build a union that can have structures and that can negotiate from strength and have membership participation."

In the face of the Teamsters' onslaught, the UFW, reinforced by a familiar coalition of religious, student, liberal, and labor volunteers, resorted to its customary arsenal: picket lines, rallies, marches, boycotts, and appeals to the public's sense of justice. Yet with hundreds of beefy Teamster goons conducting a reign of terror through the region, and UFW activists being jailed by the hundreds for violating court orders prohibiting virtually every form of resistance and protest the union employed, the Chavez forces never had a chance of winning back what they had lost in the

Coachella valley, or of stopping the Teamsters when they later moved in on the UFW's remaining contracts with Delano-area table grape growers and the state's major wineries. George Meany, who described the Teamsters' raids as "the most vicious strikebreaking, union-busting effort I've seen in my lifetime," persuaded the AFL-CIO executive council to contribute $1.6 million to the UFW's support. But the money could only ease the union's predicament, not solve it. After five months of bitter struggle, more than thirty-five hundred arrests, innumerable assaults, and the violent deaths of two members—one at the hands of a deputy sheriff who claimed that his victim was "resisting arrest," the other at the hands of a gun-toting young strikebreaker who said he felt menaced by pickets—Chavez, his union in ruins, called off any further direct action in favor of the UFW's most effective weapon: the boycott. The UFW, which only a year before had more than one hundred fifty contracts and nearly forty thousand members, was reduced by September 1973 to a mere handful of contracts and perhaps one-quarter of its earlier membership.

In the wake of the UFW's stunning defeat in the grape industry, writing the union's obituary became a favorite pastime not only of its longtime adversaries but of some of its traditional sympathizers as well. Most acknowledged the irresistible pressures that a Teamsters-grower alliance unleashed against the union, but many also found fault with the leadership of Cesar Chavez, especially his real or imagined failure to progress from unruly visionary to orderly trade unionist. Chavez's "charisma," said one sympathizer, was no longer "as marketable a commodity as it once was." Another observer concluded that "the charisma and the cause are wearing thin." The "priests and nuns" were losing interest; "the radchics from New York's Sutton Place to San Francisco's Nob Hill are bored with it all." "I admire him," George Meany said of Chavez. "He's consistent, and I think he's dedicated. I think he's an idealist. I think he's a bit of a dreamer. But the thing that I'm disappointed about Cesar is that he never got to the point that he could develop a real viable union in the sense of what we think of as a viable union."

Yet if Chavez left something to be desired as a union administrator, his alleged deficiencies scarcely explained the UFW's precipitous descent. The union's battered condition was not a product of its failure to behave conventionally, or of Chavez's disinclination to abandon his assertedly quixotic proclivities in favor of the pure and simple ethic that informed the thinking and demeanor of the more typical trade union leader. Rather, the UFW's sudden decline was, for the most part, not of its own making:

grape growers had never resigned themselves to sharing power with their workers, and when the Teamsters proffered an alternative brand of unionism that did not impinge upon their essential prerogatives they happily embraced it.

It was precisely because Chavez was "a bit of a dreamer" that the idea of farmworker organization gathered the initial force necessary to overcome the previously insurmountable opposition of employers, and it was because he remained stubbornly devoted to his dream even in the face of the UFW's disheartening setbacks that those who had rushed to speak eulogies over the momentarily prostrated union were ultimately proven wrong. The resources available to him after the debacle of 1973 were only a fraction of what they had been, but Chavez retained both the loyalty of his most able assistants and his own exceptional talents as an organizer and agitator. As the nationwide boycotts he revived against grape and lettuce growers and the country's largest wine producers, the E. and J. Gallo Wineries, slowly gained momentum during 1974, Chavez reminded his Teamsters-employer adversaries in the only language they seemed to understand that the UFW was not going away no matter how diligently they conspired to that end.

The same message was communicated through the union's greatly intensified political activity in 1974. The union relentlessly lobbied the state assembly to win passage of a farm labor bill providing for secret-ballot union-representation elections. Although it later died in the agribusiness-dominated senate, Chavez still demonstrated that the UFW had lost none of its political prowess. The union also brought considerable pressures to bear on Democratic gubernatorial nominee Jerry Brown to win a promise that, if elected, he would make the passage of an acceptable farm labor bill one of his top legislative priorities. The UFW had no real hope of achieving its legislative aim as long as the anti-union administration of Governor Ronald Reagan dominated the state government, but in the youthful Brown, who had actively supported the UFW's grape boycotts while he was a seminary student, Chavez recognized a potential ally.

Because they could not have the kind of explicitly anti-union law they had promoted through their unavailing campaign in support of Proposition 22, the state's farm employers, in a significant reversal of their long-standing position, sought to undermine the UFW by joining with both the Teamsters and AFL-CIO in support of federal legislation extending the National Labor Relations Act (NLRA) to include farmworkers. Chavez, who had years before supported such an extension, strongly opposed

NLRA coverage for farmworkers both because of its diminished effectiveness in guaranteeing workers' rights and because it banned the secondary boycotts upon which the UFW had become so dependent.

With Brown's election in November 1974, a legislative solution to the conflict that had convulsed the state's agricultural labor relations for nearly a decade appeared to be at hand. But given the mutual rancor and distrust that existed between farm employers and Teamsters on the one hand and Chavez and his followers on the other, drafting legislation compelling enough in its composition to induce compromises required both unfailing patience and an uncommon talent for legerdemain. Brown, however, was persuaded that a combination of good will and resolve could produce such a "vehicle for compromise." The new governor recognized that almost ten years of constant hostilities had not only rendered the combatants less intransigent, but had also created public enthusiasm for legislation that might restore labor peace to California's fields and vineyards.

Though none of the parties affected by Brown's compromise bill was fully satisfied in the end, each found reasons to support it. For the Teamsters' union, whose reputation as labor's pariah was reinforced by its anti-UFW machinations, supporting the Agricultural Labor Relations bill was a belated act of image polishing. For the state's agribusinessmen, who were finally discovering that preemptive arrangements with the Teamsters would not protect them from the UFW's seemingly inexhaustible boycott organizers, accepting Brown's proposal promised to restore order to their long unsettled industry. For the UFW, whose leaders were hopeful that legislation might do for La Causa what it had earlier done for the civil rights movement, going along with the governor's bill was a calculated risk that had to be taken.

The Agricultural Labor Relations Act, which went into effect during the fall harvest season of 1975, established a five-member Agricultural Labor Relations Board (ALRB) to implement the law, the most important provisions of which guaranteed the right of farmworkers to organize and bargain collectively through representatives chosen by secret-ballot elections. The ALRB, which faced problems not unlike those confronted by the National Labor Relations Board forty years earlier, was forced to operate under exceedingly difficult circumstances, particularly after disgruntled growers provoked a bitter year-long political confrontation with the UFW by blocking the special appropriations the agency needed to support its heavier than expected workload. Yet despite attacks from all sides, an inexperienced staff, and the administrative miscarriages that inevitably attended the discharging of so controversial and exceptional a mandate, the ALRB doggedly pursued the law's essential intention of ensuring that farmworkers were free to decide questions of union affiliation without undue interference.

Whereas Chavez was often frustrated by the ALRB's plodding pace and periodic bungling, and at times criticized its operation in language as caustic and intemperate as that used by the most aggrieved farm employer, he considered the law a "godsend . . . without question the best law for workers—any workers—in the entire country." Chavez and the UFW, notwithstanding their sporadic fulminations, had good reasons to consider the ALRA in providential terms. Within two years of its passage, the UFW, with a membership approaching forty thousand, had regained its position as the dominant union in California agriculture. Even more important, the union's success persuaded the Teamsters, who had faltered badly in the heated competition for the allegiance of farmworkers, to sign a five-year pact that effectively ceded jurisdiction over agricultural labor to the UFW.[3] The ALRA became, in short, the means by which the UFW accomplished its own resurrection, the instrument by which Cesar Chavez redeemed his stewardship of La Causa.

But for the tenacious idealism and organizational virtuosity of Cesar Chavez, there is no reason to believe that the circumstances which fostered the ALRA's enactment would have arisen. Before he arrived on the scene, agribusinessmen in California were as secure in their power and authority as any employers in the country. Yet only ten years after Chavez and his followers first challenged their supremacy, farm employers were acquiescing to a law that augured the demolition of their one-hundred-year-old dominion over labor.

The law, however, imposed obligations as great as the benefits it promised. Beyond forcing the UFW to prove that the support it had always claimed to enjoy among farmworkers was actual rather than imagined, the ALRA had also challenged the capacity of Chavez and his lieutenants to take their organization into a new and different phase, one that rewarded abilities more closely associated with conventional trade union leadership than with the boycotting, marching, and other forms of social proselytism that the UFW had emphasized up to that time. Once the ALRA created the machinery whereby farmworkers might secure their rights to organize and bargain collectively, the conflicts that remained between themselves and employers had much less to do with elemental questions of justice than with arguable issues of economic equity and job control. The law enabled the UFW to make its presence felt in California's industrialized agriculture; it did not ensure that the union would either prevail in the short run or endure in the long run.

As from the beginning, the UFW's future as an organization is inextricably linked to Cesar Chavez's success as a leader. And since 1975 the union's record testifies to a mixed performance on Chavez's part. After reaching a membership of approximately fifty thousand by the late 1970s, the union has slowly dwindled in size, comprising roughly forty thousand members by the early 1980s, nearly all of whom, except for isolated outposts in Florida, Arizona, and a couple of other states, are confined to California. The union's continuing failure to make greater headway among the 200,000 farmworkers who are potential members in California alone is attributable, in part, to the growing sophistication of employers in countering the UFW's appeal to workers through voluntary improvements in wages and conditions; to the entry into the farm labor force of workers without strong emotional ties to or knowledge of the heroic struggles of the past; and to the inability of an increasingly politicized ALRB to enforce the letter and the spirit of its mandate in a timely fashion, especially following the election in 1984 of a governor allied with the union's fiercest opponents.

It is also the case, however, that the UFW's drift from vitality toward apparent stagnation is partially rooted in a web of complex factors related to the sometimes contradictory leadership of Cesar Chavez: a sincere devotion to democratic unionism that is undermined by a tendency to regard all internal dissidents as traitors at best and anti-union conspirators at worst; a professed desire to make the UFW a rank-and-file union governed from the bottom up that is contradicted by a strong inclination to concentrate authority in his own hands and those of close family members; a commitment to professionalize the administration of the UFW that is impeded by a reliance on volunteerism so unyielding as to have caused many of the union's most loyal and efficient staff members to quit.

In fairness, however, Chavez's performance must be assessed on a basis that encompasses far more than the normal categories of trade union leadership. For unlike most American labor leaders, who had stood apart from the traditions of their European counterparts by insisting that unionism is an end in itself, Chavez has, in his own somewhat idiosyncratic way, remained determined to use the UFW and the heightened political consciousness of his Chicano loyalists as a means for promoting changes more fundamental than those attainable through collective bargaining and other conventional avenues of trade union activism. In defining the UFW's singular mission, Chavez once declared: "As a continuation of our struggle, I think that we can develop economic power and put it in the hands of the people so they can have more control of their own lives, and then begin to change the system. We want radical change. Nothing short of radical change is going to have any impact on our lives or our problems. We want sufficient power to control our own destinies. This is our struggle. It's a lifetime job. The work for social change and against social injustice is never ended."

When measured against the magnitude of his proposed enterprise, and against his extraordinary achievements on behalf of workers who were among the most powerless and degraded in America prior to his emergence, Chavez's real and alleged deficiencies in guiding the UFW across the hostile terrain of California's industrialized agriculture in no way detract from his standing as the most accomplished and far-sighted labor leader of his generation. Whether or not he has it in him to be more than a labor leader, to turn the UFW into an instrument of changes still more profound and far-reaching than it has already brought about, remains to be proven.

The history of American labor is littered with the wreckage of workers' organizations—the Knights of Labor and the Industrial Workers of the World among them—that tried and failed to combine the immediate purposes of trade unionism with an ultimate ambition to alter the fundamental structure of American society. Indeed, in an era when many labor leaders are preoccupied with nothing so much as the survival of their organizations, Chavez's pledge before the UFW's 1983 convention to lead the union in new and even bolder assaults against the economic and political status quo seems distinctly unrealistic. Unrealistic, that is, until one recalls the implausibility of what he has already accomplished.

NOTES

EDITOR'S NOTE: This essay is reprinted as it appeared in Melvyn Dubofsky and Warren Van Tine, eds., *Labor Leaders in America* (Urbana: University of Illinois Press, 1987). In a bibliographic note at the end of the article Cletus Daniel lists important sources containing biographical material on Cesar Chavez. Some of the secondary sources he lists may be found in the further reading section at the end of this chapter. Daniel draws the reader's attention particularly to Jacques Levy's *Cesar Chavez: Autobiography of La Causa* (1975), which he describes as "an important and readily accessible source of personal recollections contributed by Chavez, and by many other individuals who participated in or otherwise influenced the union's [the United Farm Workers] development."

Daniel also points the reader to important primary sources on Chavez and the United Farm Workers (UFW), particularly the Archives of Labor and Urban

Affairs at Wayne State University. Various periodicals also provided good coverage of the life of Cesar Chavez and the struggles of the UFW. Among those he lists are the *Nation*, the *New Republic, Ramparts, Dissent*, as well as liberal religious periodicals such as *Christian Century, Christianity in Crisis, America*, and *Sojourners*. The attitudes of California farm employers toward Chavez and the UFW are reflected in the *California Farm Bureau Federation Monthly*, the *California Farmer*, and the *Farm Quarterly*. Newspapers such as the *Los Angeles Times*, the *Fresno Bee*, the *San Francisco Chronicle*, and *People's World* are another useful source of information for researchers, as is the UFW's newspaper, *El Macriado*.

1. The *Bracero* program—the word root means "arm" in Spanish—continued in force until the end of 1964, when political pressures finally led the federal government to abolish this "emergency" measure.

2. Two years later the California State Supreme Court overturned the order, citing the collusive relationship between the employers and the Teamsters and the latter's lack of support among farmworkers at the time the contracts were signed.

3. Early in 1982 the pact was extended for another five-year period.

FURTHER READING

Dunne, John G. *Delano: The Story of the California Grape Strike.* 1971.

Fodell, Beverly, ed. *Cesar Chavez and the United Farm Workers: A Selected Bibliography.* 1974.

Fogel, Walter, ed. *California Farm Labor Relations and Law.* 1985.

Garcia, Richard A. "Dolores Huerta: Woman, Organizer, Symbol." *California History* 72 (Spring 1993): 56–71.

Garcia, Richard A., and Richard Griswold del Castillo. *Cesar Chavez: His Life and Times.* Forthcoming.

Jenkins, J. Craig. *The Politics of Insurgency: The Farm Workers Movement in the 1960s.* 1985.

Levy, Jacques. *Cesar Chavez: Autobiography of La Causa.* 1975.

Loftis, Anne, and Dick Meister. *A Long Time Coming: The Struggle to Unionize America's Farm Workers.* 1977.

Majka, Linda C., and Theo J. Majka. *Farm Workers, Agribusiness, and the State.* 1982.

Matthiessen, Peter. *Sal Si Puedes.* 1969.

Rose, Margaret. "'From the Field to the Picket Line: Huelga Women and the Boycott,' 1965–1975." *Labor History* 31 (Summer 1990): 271–293.

Taylor, Ronald. *Chavez and the Farm Workers.* 1975.

14   Why Aren't High-Tech Workers Organized?

Lessons in Gender, Race, and Nationality from Silicon Valley

Karen J. Hossfeld

EDITOR'S INTRODUCTION

Since the 1930s, the character of the California economy has profoundly changed. The state had a significant manufacturing base by the 1930s, as Gerald Nash argues persuasively in his book *World War II and the West: Reshaping the Economy* (1990), but it was the Second World War that transformed California into a major manufacturing power. The Cold War further stimulated this transformation. Industries directly and indirectly tied to defense, especially aerospace, flourished, as did basic industries such as steel, oil, chemicals, clothing, and automobiles.

Employment in California grew rapidly. Between 1950 and 1980, while older regions of the country were suffering from severe structural unemployment, California's labor force grew by 250 percent. A key factor in this postwar economic prosperity was technical innovation. Waves of federal spending during World War II and afterward played a major role not simply in expanding the California economy but also in placing the state in the vanguard of the postwar high-technology revolution.

Since the end of World War II, the center of much of California's high-technology industry has been the Santa Clara Valley, now commonly called Silicon Valley. Largely as a result of the high-tech sector, employment in Santa Clara County doubled in the 1940s and 1950s. Between 1960 and 1980, four hundred thousand new jobs were created in Silicon Valley. By 1980, Silicon Valley was creating 20 percent of all high-technology jobs in the United States and contained more than two thousand high-tech companies.

Unlike most manufacturing industries in the United States, high-tech is almost entirely nonunion. Despite a few attempts by several unions, labor organizers estimate that fewer than 6 percent of production workers in Silicon Valley are organized. This failure is not unique to the region; the union movement has failed dismally at organizing a significant number of workers in any semiconductor or computer manufacturing firm anywhere.

In this selection, Karen Hossfeld examines the reasons for the failure of the union movement to take hold in Silicon Valley. Hossfeld's study is based on two hundred interviews with workers and their families, labor organizers, and employers, including in-depth interviews with more than eighty immigrant women workers from various Third World countries.

Hossfeld argues that the obstacles to union organizing efforts are formidable. The work force is divided by race, language, and nationality. Physically, the workers employed by a single company are often dispersed among several plants. Management threats to relocate or automate when faced with unionization have had a chilling effect. Furthermore, international unions have not demonstrated much commitment to organizing high-tech workers. Unions have not appreciated the importance to women of issues such as comparable worth, sexual harassment, domestic violence, and child care. Patriarchal ideology and structures are also obstacles: Union involvement is not encouraged by most male heads of households, and motherhood and domestic chores impose demands on women that leave little time for union involvement. Hossfeld argues that unions must alter their priorities and devise new strategies to have a reasonable prospect of organizing high-tech workers.

"We'll show a real interest in unions when they show a real interest in us."
   —Margarita, a Mexicana assembly worker in Silicon Valley

This article examines the problems of labor organizing in the high-tech manufacturing industry in Silicon Valley, California.[1] Microelectronics manufacturing is the largest and fastest-growing manufacturing industry in the world, and Silicon Valley is the industry's birthplace and reigning capital. An estimated two hundred thousand people work in the high-tech industry in California's Santa Clara County (Silicon Valley) region, approximately 20 percent of them in manufacturing production. Yet unions have paid little or no attention to organizing the industry's production workers. Working conditions for line operatives are notoriously dangerous and insecure, but Silicon Valley, like the high-tech industry worldwide, remains almost exclusively nonunionized. Unions do continue to wage organizing campaigns in older, more traditional industries such as auto and steel, despite the decreasing relative size and economic influence of these industries. So why aren't unions devoting more attention to an industry that is growing? In an era when the labor movement needs to bolster its declining membership in order to survive, why aren't high-tech workers being organized?

These questions are important both to Silicon Valley workers and to the labor movement in general, for Silicon Valley is viewed by global industrialists as a prototype, not only in terms of its new technologies but also in terms of labor arrangements. If organized labor is once again to become vital in the United States, it must come to grips with the types of challenges and failures it faces in Silicon Valley.

What are these challenges? Labor leaders have argued, quite legitimately, that the microelectronics industry's ability to easily "emigrate and automate" its production facilities is a strong deterrent to organizing efforts (although automation remains very costly, and workers in the "offshore" locations that the industry has favored are in many cases actually proving to be more likely to organize than workers in the United States).[2] Silicon Valley employers have also engaged in savvy union-busting strategies. But there are other major barriers to organizing that union leaders have not as readily acknowledged: namely, gender, race, and nationality dynamics, not only within the workplace but also outside it. Silicon Valley operatives, like their peers in high-tech assembly shops overseas, are predominantly Third World women.[3] The class concerns of these women workers are intricately entwined with their concerns based on gender, ethnic identity, and nationality, with their needs as wives, mothers, and members of ethnic and immigrant communities. Just as it is no coincidence that employers have focused on hiring this specific work force,[4] it is also no coincidence, my research suggests, that unions have been unable (and perhaps, in some cases, unwilling) to organize this work force.

This essay first provides an overview and a history of trade union organizing efforts in Silicon Valley and looks at management strategies to combat these efforts. It then focuses on how other dynamics affect the potential for labor organizing in the region's factories: sexism, racism, and national chauvinism within unions; gender arrangements in workers' households; and, finally, the ethnic and national identities of workers.

The discussion is based on data drawn from a larger field study of the lives and labors of Third World immigrant women workers in Silicon Valley.[5] Conducted between 1982 and 1993, the study includes more than two hundred interviews with workers, family members, union organizers, and employers. In-depth, open-ended interviews were conducted with eighty-four women workers who have emigrated from a total of twenty-one Third World countries. I also interviewed an additional group of workers, both immigrant and nonimmigrant, male and female, who were introduced to me by union contacts specifically because of their active union involvement. Although I present comments from this group, they are not included in my statistical references, as they were not representative of my target population, which was more randomly selected, consisted exclusively of immigrant women, and was decidedly less pro-union. The largest nationality groups both in my study and in the general production-line labor force in Silicon Valley are Mexican, Chinese, Filipino, Korean, and Vietnamese.

According to other researchers' estimates, Third World immigrant women account for between 68 and 90 percent of the operative labor force in Silicon Valley high-tech shops.[6] In the nineteen plants I observed (independent of conducting interviews with workers), the count averaged 90 percent. Collectively, the workers interviewed had been employed by more than thirty local microelectronics production companies, including large, well-known, vertically integrated firms, such as National Semiconductor and Advanced Micro Devices, and smaller, subcontracting assembly shops.

No trade union has ever won a shop floor vote in a Silicon Valley production firm, despite several past campaigns. Lockheed Missiles and Space Company, organized by the International Association of Machinists and Aerospace Workers, Lodge 508, and electronics distributor Wyle Labs, organized by the International Longshoremen's and Warehousemen's Union, Local 6, might be seen as exceptions, but they are not primarily engaged in semiconductor or computer manufacturing. In addition, these shops were organized before Santa Clara County's transformation into the high-tech-dominated Silicon Valley; the Machinists, for example, won their first contract with Lockheed in 1957. Organizers estimate that fewer than 6 percent of production workers in the local high-tech industry belong to unions. This situation is not specific to Silicon Valley: Nationwide, *no* merchant semiconductor or computer manufacturing firms are organized, in contrast to most manufacturing industries in the United States.

Two of the organizers I interviewed attribute this problem to the relative newness of the industry, with organizers and workers just beginning to get their bearings on a system still in formation. But several Silicon Valley manufacturing firms have now been around for twenty-five years—time enough for "newness" to be ruled out as the leading deterrent to organizing. Because high-tech has become a leading basic industry and is growing rapidly, it would seem logical for unions to target the industry as a high priority. Yet as of this writing in 1994, not one single full-time organizer was employed by a union to organize Silicon Valley high-tech production workers.[7] Have unions given up on the region and the industry? Have they temporarily retreated after a few important, but not historically atypical, setbacks? Are high-tech workers simply not "unionizable" compared to other workers?

The failure of Silicon Valley organizing drives must be located in the context of declining worker support for organized labor nationwide. In the American work force as a whole, union membership has been steadily declining since World War II. Between 1975 and 1985, it dropped from 29 percent of the total nonfarm work force to only 19 percent.[8] This decline has caused consternation among unions and other labor rights advocates and has sparked controversial debate about the future direction of and need for union activities.

The inability of traditional labor unions to organize Silicon Valley's workers is an important feature of the new international and gender division of labor within the high-tech industry. Whether this feature will persist or extend to other industries is not yet clear, but it is an important possibility for organized labor to consider. Union failure in Silicon Valley is not inevitable; unions have in the past dealt successfully with changes in the organization of work and the composition of the work force. In the 1930s, for example, American unions successfully adapted to the shift from craft to industrial work—although the adaptation came two decades after the shift in production began in the pre–World War I years.

The primary unions that in fact have tried to organize Silicon Valley shops are the Glaziers (Glaziers, Architectural Metal and Glassworkers Union), UE (United Electrical, Radio and Machine Workers), and the Machinists (International Association of Machinists and Aerospace Workers). Nationally, the Communication Workers of America (CWA) has also focused its sights on the high-tech manufacturing industry, conducting campaigns at companies located in Massachusetts's Route 128 region, such as Wang Laboratories, Digital Equipment, and Honeywell.[9] When I conducted my preliminary field research in the early and mid-1980s, UE was organizing worker committees at Signetics in Sunnyvale and National Semiconductor in Santa Clara, and the Glaziers were conducting a mass campaign at Atari. In addition, the Santa Clara County Central Labor Council, which coordinates 104 union locals and district councils, was involved in encouraging campaigns. Since the 1970s, at least seven concerted organizing drives have targeted specific plants in the valley. Union campaigns at Siliconix, Signetics, and National Semiconductor never reached the stage of elections. Campaigns that did hold elections—at Semimetals West, Xidex, Raytheon, and, most recently, Atari—failed to win a majority of worker votes.

The Glaziers' (Local 1621) campaign to organize Sunnyvale-based Atari's 3,000 employees in the early 1980s was one of the valley's most noted union drives. In 1982, the Glaziers announced that they had collected enough signature cards—from 30 percent of eligible employees, as required by law—to call an election. The company, which manufactures coin-operated video games and home computers, fought back in full force. Management circulated an anti-union petition, which supervisors pressured workers to sign, and began inviting production workers to unprecedented company-sponsored parties, according to workers and Glaziers organizer Ed Jones. Jones also collected signed affidavits from workers who were threatened by supervisors because of their union support. The union lost some support and had to cancel its petition for election with the National Labor Relations Board (NLRB), but the campaign continued.

In February 1983, while the Glaziers were gearing up for another election bid, Atari announced that it was laying off 1,700 employees and relocating production to Taiwan and Hong Kong. Atari spokesperson Bruce Entin claimed that the decision to relocate was based solely on cost considerations and had no connection to the union drive. Ed Jones and pro-union workers are convinced otherwise, according to interviews. Since the massive layoffs, the Glaziers have been unable to gain the required 30 percent of signatures from eligible workers on Atari's one remaining production line in the valley.

Typically in Silicon Valley, employers such as Atari argue that unions are unsuccessful because working conditions are already favorable to workers, making unions unnecessary and anachronistic. In contrast, organizers claim that unions are greatly needed in what is a very unfavorable work climate but that the industry's anti-union campaigns and its ability to relocate foil all attempts at organizing. Unions insist that they have a great deal to offer all workers, including women and immigrants, in terms of tangible benefits. According to Department of Labor statistics, women workers have even more to gain from union membership than males do in terms of wages. Male union members who worked full time earned an average of 18 percent more than their nonunion male peers in 1986 ($482 a week compared to $394), whereas female union members earned 25 percent more than their nonunion women peers ($368 a week compared to $274).[10] Women who work under union contracts also enjoy greater health care, retirement, and vacation benefits than those not under contract.[11]

Organizers in Silicon Valley stress that unions offer working parents their best chance for winning child care provisions and parental leave and also offer immigrants much-needed legal advocacy. They stress union commitment to protecting workers against problems to which high-tech manufacturing jobs are particularly prone: unsafe use of toxic chemicals in the work process, frequent layoffs, plant relocations, and automation. It is around these issues, as well as wages and benefits, that union organizers in Silicon Valley have tried to rally workers.

Yet national trade unions have not demonstrated a major commitment to or investment in organizing high-tech workers, according to frustrated local union activists. This is illustrated by the lack of commitment to the development of a full-time organizing staff. Without a greater allocation of resources, the hope of organizing high-tech workers locally or nationally remains slim. Lack of material support from union headquarters was a central problem pointed out by all the organizers with whom I talked. That unions have not focused more energy on the largest manufacturing industry in the United States is, in former UE organizer Mike Eisenscher's words, "a frightening condemnation of the labor movement."[12]

Local union activists justifiably argue that this limited show of sustained support dampens workers' confidence in the potential of unions. The high-tech production workers I interviewed do not consider unions capable of helping them achieve better working conditions or job security. In fact, the majority of those interviewed believe that union organizing drives *threaten* their jobs, for management's threats to automate or relocate if unions succeed have not been empty. Organizers consider Atari's decision to relocate overseas in the midst of a promising union campaign to be a prime example of management making good on its anti-union threats. When asked what they thought would happen if their manufacturing workers unionized, all of the employers I interviewed told me that they would probably relocate production. Whether or not all employers are actually prepared to follow through on this, relocation is financially and physically possible at most manufacturing facilities, and the threat is clearly articulated to workers. One of the comments I heard most frequently from workers was, "If we unionize, the company will move away."

But, in addition, an equally frequent comment was, "Unions don't improve anything, anyway."

It has been extremely difficult for unions to attempt to organize a labor force that is not only severely divided by language, race, and nationality but also often spatially and geographically spread out between multiple plants within one firm. Atari, for example, had several plants in Sunnyvale, Milpitas, and San Jose at the time of the Glaziers' organizing drive. Organizers point to these as key problems, along with the very real threats of plant relocation and automation.

Also important is the concerted effort Silicon Valley employers have mounted to keep the high-tech manufacturing industry union-free. Management has a strong vested interest in keeping unions out of the microelectronics industry. Chief among management's fears, undoubtedly, are wage increases and benefits. Wages in more organized industries are significantly higher than in high-tech: Steel and aerospace workers in the mid-1980s, for example, earned an average of approximately $12 an hour, autoworkers $12.50. The average hourly wage of skilled (nonassembly) workers at electronics equipment companies during the same period was only $9.62 [13]—and workers labeled "unskilled" and "semiskilled," such as the ones in subcontracted assembly work, usually earn half that.

Other concerns, not directly wage-related, are also central to employers' hostility toward unions. Tougher occupational health and safety standards; responsibility for the medical effects of occupational hazards; job security; input concerning the introduction of new technologies such as automation; grievance procedures; retraining and severance pay for laid-off workers—all these are issues that union campaigns have emphasized and that managers and employers complained about. "It's very simple," according to a subcontractor named Robert. "Unions cost too much, and they try to tell us what to do. I started this company because I wanted to do things my way. If they think their way is better, let them start their own companies." Steve, the production manager at a large assembly firm, commented: "If we made all the changes that [one union organizer] wanted, this would be a real cushiony place to work—and a lousy place to try to pull down an executive paycheck. The assemblers would be making as much as me!"

Several large high-tech firms, purportedly in connection with the American Electronics Association (AEA), have employed the services of union-busting law firms to combat union campaigns. Production supervisors and mid-level managers report that they have been shown training films and given lectures on such subjects as "keeping our company union-free," "dealing with outside agitation," and "the importance of an 'independent' work force." During my field research, managers at three firms invited me to "union prevention" seminars offered by their employers. Such in-house seminars have been common at larger firms, while smaller firms are more likely to send their managers out to attend similar courses offsite.

In 1983, the AEA published a report on union activity in the industry, crediting management tactics with stopping unionization. Workers and organizers also attest to management's large repertoire of anti-union tactics, from the simple to the costly. Several workers acknowledged that company spokespersons had warned them against unions. I saw newsletters from two companies telling employees that if they unionized, the companies would have no choice but to automate or relocate. Union organizers confirm that this is a standard tactic used by Silicon Valley employers. It is a tactic that is both ideological and pragmatic; whereas some companies only threaten, others, like Atari, actually move. Management does not tell workers that unions are harmful to profits because they lead to wage and benefit increases. Rather, they contend that unions lead to "bureaucratic overload and inflexibility that slows production," as one corporate leader told me, and "cut down on the company's ability to create [its] own set of benefits and type of work environment that are far better than any a union could provide."

Workers who have been identified with unionization drives report that they have been persecuted and fired. Although very few of the immigrant women operatives in my main sample had been involved with organizing drives, almost all had heard stories about other workers who were harassed or laid off when they got involved with unions. The comments made by Rui, a Chinese assembly worker, are typical of the attitudes these workers expressed:

> I could never risk my boss thinking I'm with [the union trying to organize her shop at the time]. They find a reason to fire you if they think you are involved. They say you're not doing good work anymore, or that they don't need so many people. Or they put you in a dangerous job, to try to make you quit. This already happened to two of the girls—and one was not even in the union, she was just friends with the girl who was. I can't afford that—I have three kids, and my husband is already out sick.

In one of the more extreme cases, a woman worker at Signetics was fired for her union organizing activities. Her co-workers protested and filed grievances. In 1984, the National Labor Relations Board ordered the laid-off worker reinstated (which she declined) and given back pay of $42,500.[14] Workers at other firms facing union drives also told me that organizers are routinely transferred and harassed, passed over for promotion, and fired first during layoffs. Immigrant workers at two assembly plants that do subcontracting work for "famous" large semiconductor companies told me that managers led them to believe that they could be deported for union activities—even if they were in the United States legally. Employers and managers generally deny these charges, but Ed, a Korean immigrant who works as a line supervisor at one of the large firms facing a union drive, told me, "It's standard policy to get rid of the troublemakers. If unions come in, it will hurt everyone—so we weed out the agitators, to protect the company and all of our jobs."

Management thus seems to take the union "threat" seriously, especially during periods of local union activism. While the campaign at Atari was going on, administrators at three other companies I visited were concerned that I was an undercover union organizer and denied me entrance to their plants. During the same period, employers at two other plants, when asked if they were aware of any union activities, took the opportunity to vilify Dave Bacon, a UE organizer who was well known for his radical activism. One employer said about Bacon: "He's a one-man, son-of-a-bitch troublemaker." Managers at firms that were not being targeted also knew the names and descriptions of individual organizers such as Ed Jones of the Glaziers and Mike Eisenscher of UE. "We do our homework," one executive told me. "Unions are one of the few things my competitors and I share information about."

There has been little optimism among union supporters in the valley for several years, at least until recently. But increasing job insecurity for industry employees at all levels, organizers argue, means that the time is ripe for renewed union efforts. The semiconductor and computer industries have continued their typically volatile up and down swings, accompanied by alternating layoffs and hirings. Even professional and skilled workers have come to realize the instability of their jobs, as they too face sudden layoffs without warning. Companies that supposedly had "no layoff" clauses, such as Hewlett-Packard and Advanced Micro Devices, reneged on their policies in the late 1980s and laid off hundreds of workers.

In order to circumvent the dissent and disruption that layoffs create, companies began to increasingly use temporary employment agencies in the mid-1980s. According to Janine, a personnel manager, "Temp agencies are the way of the future for large high-tech firms" because they allow expansion and contraction even more easily than subcontractors do. According to the director of one of the largest local temp agencies, Silicon Valley has a greater number of temporary agencies, relative to population size, than any other area in the country. More than half of these agencies were established in the 1980s. Electronics worker Pat Sacco reports that at one large firm, management told laid-off regular workers that they might try looking for work at a local temporary agency that had openings. The firm then hired back the same workers, through the agency, at lower wages. Because of this, these workers also lost their rights to unemployment benefits.[15]

The early 1990s have seen increased organizing activity in the valley. Several community groups, including ethnic, religious, and environmental organizations, have expanded their efforts to focus on workers' concerns. The Silicon Valley Toxics Coalition, for example, has initiated several educational campaigns about occupational hazards in the high-tech industry.[16] Labor unions have also increased their profile. In 1992, workers at Versatronex, a contract printed circuit board assembly plant in the city of Sunnyvale that employs predominantly Mexican women, struck for six weeks, the first time any Silicon Valley production workers have gone out on a concerted strike. The strikers went back to work when the National Labor Relations Board ruled in their favor that the company must reinstate Joselito Muñoz, a worker who had been fired for speaking out against poor working conditions and in favor of union organizing. The day they went back to work, the strikers filed with the NLRB for a union representation election. Versatronex management agreed to recognize the union, the United Electrical Workers, but as election arrangements were being made, the company announced that it was permanently closing down—and it did so soon after. Although the strikers' victory was bittersweet, it was not without impact on workers and employers elsewhere. Workers at other plants participated in sympathy hunger strikes and protests, rare events in the industry. In a letter of thanks to community supporters, the workers who participated in the strike wrote: "We are proud of our struggle, and we are proud to be part of the union movement."

Another historic first for Silicon Valley organizing occurred during the same time. The Service Employees International Union (SEIU) mounted a "Justice for Janitors" organizing campaign that may well have important ramifications for organizing in Silicon Valley. The union set out to pressure industry giant Apple Computer to hire only janitorial services that employ unionized workers. Investing more than one million dollars in a high-profile media campaign aimed at portraying image-conscious Apple in a critical light, the union won its goal in 1992.

The strategy of targeting the publicity-sensitive "big company" in order to accomplish change at the smaller companies it dealt with was effective, but expensive. SEIU's intent, according to one of the campaign's organizers, was to set a precedent and put other companies on notice. "We noticed, all right," a high-level executive at one of Apple's chief competitors told me. "We're all watching very carefully to see who they go after next." One of his colleagues added: "Most of us in this industry rely heavily on contracting work out. Unions could never touch the subcontractors—they're too small, and there are too many of them. They were very clever to go after it at our level." A local attorney and management consultant, who bills himself as "a professional union-buster," reports that his phones have been "ringing off the hook since this janitors thing."

Clearly, Silicon Valley employers have worked hard to keep unions out. But their efforts are not the only barriers to organizing. Also important are the dynamics of gender, race, and nationality, both within the unions and in the lives of immigrant women workers in general. The following sections examine some of these dynamics and also consider ways that unions might redirect their strategies to more fully incorporate and address the needs of a diverse work force.

Recent changes in the gender composition of the work force are important to labor organizations as well as to employers and to women. Most unions have traditionally had male leadership and a male membership drawn from male-dominated occupations. With women making up an ever-increasing proportion of the labor force, unions will have to redirect their membership focus.[17] At a time when total union membership in the United States is decreasing dramatically, female membership is actually increasing. This is partly explained by the unions' increased targeting of the state and service sectors, both of which have relatively high concentrations of women employees. But women are also being organized in the industrial sector, for example in textile plants and canneries.[18] Today, almost six million workers, 34 percent of all union members in the country, are women, double the percentage of 1960.[19] If unions are to survive, they must deal both with women workers' specific needs and with sexism in the union itself at all levels.

Historically, white male union members and leaders have often successfully campaigned to exclude immigrants, people of color, and women from the mainstream of labor through prejudice and discrimination.[20] Chris, a union organizer I interviewed, suggested that in recent years this exclusion has typically been more subdued, as unions have recognized its divisive and weakening effect on labor solidarity. Yet many unions still do not address the special situations and needs of immigrants, diverse ethnic and racial groups, and women. And even though in recent years union organizers have become more interested in and committed to these populations, 80 percent of the women immigrant workers I interviewed do not perceive traditional organizing movements as useful options for improving their work and life conditions in terms of their own priorities.

Approximately 50 percent of the women interviewed are also ideologically opposed to labor unions, although this varies by nationality, class background, and political affiliation. And, typically, even those women immigrant workers who are interested in union membership find it difficult to actively participate. They are constrained by the time demands of household responsibilities and "moonlighting" at jobs in the casual service sector to make ends meet. They also face resistance from male family members who do not approve of their womenfolk's involvement in "unchaperoned" activities with male "strangers" beyond paid work hours.[21]

In the past two decades, some unions have begun to organize around concerns targeted by women workers. Encouraged by the development of organizations such as the Coalition of Labor Union Women (CLUW), which was founded by women trade unionists in 1974, unions such as SEIU, the International Union of Electrical Workers (IUE), CWA, and others are active in the fight for pay equity, an end to sex and race discrimination, pregnancy benefits, and parental leave.[22] Only a few unions have given priority to these issues, however, and many are impeded by resentment from male union members who do not consider "women's issues" to be priorities, as illustrated by some of the testimony from my study. In Silicon Valley, I talked with union organizers who are clearly aware of and committed to these feminist workplace issues, but they agree that top union leadership still has not given full attention to such concerns. "The big unions are still completely male-dominated and male-defined at the top," a local organizer outside the high-tech industry told me. "That really hasn't changed, and it's killing the union movement."

Labor organizers and observers believe that part of the reason national union leadership has shown limited interest in organizing Silicon Valley is because Third World immigrant women are not a union priority. Linda, a Latina union organizer, reported:

> Sure, the big guys say they're interested in high-tech, but they give us only two or three organizers and a shoestring budget, and there's a couple hundred thousand workers out there. If this was steel, or auto, or any of the other traditional men's jobs, they'd give us a lot more attention. It's easy to get a sense that the union leadership really couldn't care less about

a bunch of minorities and women. The local leadership really does, but they don't control the resources.

Another woman organizer was so fed up with the low priority the national union gave her campaign that she quit in frustration. And a labor advocate in the immigrant community says that unions "still don't want to touch immigrant workers with a ten-foot pole, even though we're a permanent sector of the labor force."

Unions have traditionally had problems identifying with and appealing to the special needs of women, people of color, and immigrants. Luisa, a Chicana worker who supported an organizing drive at her plant, illustrates these problems:

> [The union organizers] kept asking me, "Why don't the other Mexican women come to the meetings? They have just as much to gain." I kept telling them—they're afraid of deportation, they can't afford the dues, they've got to take care of their kids, and their husbands won't let them. And they don't understand English good. And all [the organizers] said was, "But it's in their own best interests." . . . Eventually, they got Spanish-speaking organizers, but it's like they didn't even consider the other barriers. They kept asking me, "Why don't they come?"

Many organizers, leaders, and rank-and-file members of traditional industrial trade unions realize that women need to be integrated into the ranks of the organized. The problem for workers of both sexes who favor extending the brotherhood to sisters is how to create a "siblinghood" that is not based on exclusively male needs and definitions. SEIU is perhaps the best example of a union that has paid attention to the specific problems of its many women and immigrant members. Organizers targeting the high-tech industry agree that their unions have much to learn from the SEIU model—and a long way to go to implement the necessary changes.

Another significant barrier to women joining unions has been the discomfort and, in some cases, hostility expressed by male workers toward women workers and their perceived "petticoat encroachment," as one male rank-and-filer termed it. When asked by a friend what he thought of the feminization of his union, Bob, a U.S.-born member of a different union, responded, "That's an interesting term, 'feminization'—what you're really talking about is 'sissification' . . . and I'm against it."

What will it mean for the organizing strength of both women and unions if "female" is equated with low status and "sissification"? Both labor and women's organizations—as well as individual male workers—will have to contend with this problem if the feminization of the work force and labor unions continues. Although occupational sectors remain sex-segregated, unions are becoming more integrated, and male union members are being forced to face their own sexism within the ranks. Craig, a white male labor analyst I spoke with, went as far as blaming the current decline in the size, status, and power of unions on increased female membership, arguing that as women move in, men will move out. Historically this has certainly been the case with occupations such as secretarial work, but "blaming" women for their own devaluation is counterproductive. John, a Chicano union member, expressed the conflicts:

> It's strange having women at the meetings. I mean, the guys don't know how to act with ladies around. I know we were the ones complaining about declining membership, but we never thought the new "brothers" would be female. They're the ones getting the new jobs in this area, though, so if it comes down to women or no new members at all—well, I'm not sure *what* most of the guys would choose.

Women report that although many men have supported their membership, many others have reacted with none-too-subtle sexist hostility. Judy, an Afro-Caribbean woman who belongs to a union active in the high-tech industry, explained:

> The first time we [a group of women] showed up at the [union] meeting, we were a little bit nervous, so we drove over there together and all sat together in the back. Some of the guys got all upset and grumbled that the "cunt block" was taking over. Well, that broke down all the confidence we had built up in two of the girls just to come to the meeting, and they left right away. . . . Luckily, some of the guys have been real supportive of us—particularly the ones from our company—but a lot of them think we're "pinking up" their turf. What do they think we're going to do, put up lace curtains? This is a union, not a boys' club!

Not only do some of the men in Judy's union think that all the women want to do is put up lace curtains, but many also think that it is a woman's responsibility to do just that. When not actually relegated to coffee-making and interior decorating, women union members have found that they are expected to do secretarial work, make phone calls, and provide child care. Carla, one of the few Central American refugee women I met who is active in a union, told me that even though it was a man—a single father—who recommended that child care be provided during meetings, he assumed that women union members or the wives of other male members would organize, advertise, and provide the care. "How can I change diapers if I'm taking shorthand?!" protested Carla, who also takes minutes at the meetings. "I get to do drudge work on the line—that's not why I joined a union!"

My research indicates that male and female workers do not commonly see themselves as having generic, genderless needs as workers. Both men and women articulate the view that the two sexes have different styles of discussing, deciding on, and implementing policies and actions and also often tend to focus on different issues. Most of the men I interviewed devalue both the concerns of women workers and the women's style of presenting and processing their concerns. The women, in contrast, tend to acknowledge the men's concerns—although not always their presentation style and processing—as valuable. The following comment was made by Leonard, a white male trade union member in his thirties:

> [The women] just keep bringing up stuff that gets in the way of the union's real concerns. If it's going to turn into a ladies' bitch session or a coffee-klatsch, I'm not going to stick around.

And just what is the ladies' "stuff" that gets in the way of the union's "real concerns"?

> You know, all these new women's lib issues: wanting to spend our valuable time inventing a comparable worth program, instead of fighting for higher pay. And last meeting we had this whole program on sexual harassment. Christ, I'd like to have more sex at work, not less!

Leonard does not consider issues that affect primarily women at work to be workers' issues. He belittles and dismisses them as inappropriate union concerns because they do not affect men in the same way. But comparable worth and sexual harassment are of course labor issues: They affect workers on the job. Comparable worth means higher pay for a major sector of the work force, yet Leonard seems to view it as a struggle that will take energy away from increasing wages as he defines them, that is, male wages. Compare his attitudes with those of Clemintine, a Filipina in the same union:

> [The male shop steward] encouraged me to get more involved in union activities, and to get other women to join. He kept saying, "We really need more women—and the women could really benefit from the union." Well, I agree with him, but it's hard having to act like "just one of the guys." Of course, the issues they talk about are important to us—wages and close-downs and job security affect us, too. I even think it's fine that they spend a lot of time talking about, you know, "guy stuff," like sports, and fixing up their cars, and bragging about how much heavy equipment they can lift— and they organize social events around those things, and that's fine. But they get real annoyed when [the union leadership] brings up things that are important to the girls—like trying to get child care during meetings,

and counseling for domestic violence. They say *those* things are out of place at a union.

The problem Clemintine refers to is not simply that of men belittling women's social activities in comparison to their own. Gender-specific social concerns are frequently considered appropriate for union attention only if they are male, and inappropriate if they are female. Recreational activities that will improve men's quality of life, such as organizing male sports teams, are often deemed acceptable union business, whereas social change activities that will improve women's quality of life—such as providing child care and dealing with domestic violence—are seen as outside the bounds of union discussion. That child care and domestic violence are viewed by both men and women as female problems, while sports and cars are seen as men's interests, is of course one of the roots of the problem. Interestingly, these examples contradict male rank-and-filers' oft-voiced assumptions that women are more concerned with socializing and men more interested in "hard-core" work issues.

Conversations with both union and nonunion women workers indicate that for a woman to have the courage to enter an often hostile male union, the chances are that she is motivated by crucial work concerns. If she is looking for a social club or even a women's organization, she will likely turn to an organization less threatening than a male-dominated union to meet her needs. Certainly, men do not join a union merely because they want to play in its baseball league. But most unions are still places where men feel more comfortable than women, where males get more of their specific needs met than do women. Unions need to develop a better understanding of the gender biases of their own systems and processes, sensitizing workers to the reality that issues which primarily affect women workers are not "women's problems" and that male workers' definitions of issues are not necessarily the generic standard against which women workers should be measured. Unions must identify which work issues potentially unite and which divide male and female workers and learn how to deal with both. Otherwise, employers' tendency to devalue both work and women by creating more and more low-paid female jobs will be reproduced by unions and workers themselves.

For those immigrant women workers who are interested in and supportive of unions, gender ideologies and arrangements within the family can also be primary barriers to union involvement. In many families, males control and restrict women's time and access, meaning that women are heavily discouraged from engaging in union activities. This helps to explain why male immigrants are more likely to be involved in unions than their female family members. Maria Elena, a twenty-year-old Filipina worker, described her situation:

> I am in favor of unions. In Manila, my brother and my father worked for a clandestine union that the government was after. I used to work at National [Semiconductor], and the union was trying to organize there. But I could never go to the meetings because my father would not let me. It is true for my friends, too. Girls are not allowed to go to any meetings or places without a relative.

Workers I talked with from a wide spectrum of national backgrounds, including European American, reported that males frequently discourage or forbid female family members from participating in unions. Some of the men believe that unions are a male preserve and prerogative, and not a place for women; some are simply anti-union and expect their womenfolk to act accordingly. Others are fearful of company or state retribution and want to protect their family. Still other men, as well as a few women, think that it is inappropriate for females to "mix" with males in an unchaperoned environment, particularly with men of different ethnic, national, and religious backgrounds. ("Mixing" on the job site was considered chaperoned or simply unavoidable; then, too, the workplace is highly sex-segregated.)

Many women, and some men, disagree with these gender-based assumptions, and some immigrant women workers do indeed become involved in unions. More than 95 percent of those I interviewed, however, do not. Even those women who wished to get involved have little leverage in disobeying male authority when their life and survival are intricately connected to family and household. The women who do get involved in unions tend either to have familial support for doing so or to live in households without men. In my main informant group, however, fewer than 10 percent of the women workers lived in households with no adult male present. Approximately 70 percent of the women interviewed believed that their menfolk would stand in their way if they wanted to become involved in unions.

Another central ideological barrier to immigrant women's involvement in organizing involves the women's own consciousness about their jobs. Many immigrant women in Silicon Valley shops view their current occupations as both temporary and secondary.[23] Although they are critical of the low wages, the lack of job security, and the high-risk occupational hazards, they are typically hesitant to organize because they believe that they will stay at these jobs only for a short time, while they are "helping" their menfolk become established in the United States. They also consider their primary identity to be as a family caregiver, and they view their wages as secondary to male family members' wages. In reality, however, in 1993, the large majority of women in my study were still employed in the same industry—if not by the same employer—as they were when I started interviewing them in the early 1980s. In addition, 80 percent of the women have consistently been the primary source of steady income in their households throughout the course of my study, even when adult males are present. Nonetheless, they continue to perceive themselves as temporary workers and secondary earners, identities that mitigate against investing energy in workplace organizing.

In addition to gender ideology, hierarchical gender structures—in particular, the unequal sexual division of labor within the home—often constrain women's union involvement. Libby, a white thirty-six-year-old divorced mother of two, who works in high-tech processing, commented:

> Union meetings? Who has the time? The commute [to work] is over an hour each way—I get home, pick up my kids, and then try to spend some time with them before they go to bed, when I do the laundry. And I'm trying to find time to go back to school. Even if I had the time, I can't afford to pay a sitter while I'm off saving the world.

Women who live in households with other adults, as do most of the women in my formal sample, have the same constraint. Said Marta, a Mexicana assembly worker who is married and lives with her in-laws:

> I would really like to get involved with the union, but there is no time to go to meetings or help recruit after work. I have too much to do when I come home, with the kids, the apartment, and so forth. I need to relieve my mother-in-law, who has taken care of everything all day while I'm at work—I would feel bad asking her to stay longer. *My husband, of course, doesn't have this problem,* so he gets involved for the both of us and brings me home reports of the meetings and things. [emphasis added]

That her husband "doesn't have this problem" of working a double shift, first on the job and then in the household, is not something she questions; she later agreed that it is perhaps unfair, but she is resigned that "God did not make men and women equal." Her sentiments are not unique: Family responsibilities are cited as barriers to labor organizing by most of the women who are at all interested in unions.

Historically, many union leaders have viewed this situation as a failure of women themselves to adjust and give priority to traditional union platforms and practices. Donald, an African American union organizer who works outside the high-tech industry, told me that "any worker who truly recognizes the importance of having a say over his [sic] job can make time to get involved. It's like anything else; you make time for your top priorities." He added that "for whatever the reasons," women workers are not as committed to gaining control over their jobs as are males:

> Most of the gals would *rather* spend more time at home, doing domestic things, than get involved with the union. There's not much we can do about that. . . . Everyone likes to spend more time with their kids, of course, but all we need is one night a week. The fellas are willing to give that, but not the ladies. [emphasis added]

It did not seem relevant to Donald that women workers usually have no choice about working this double shift. Male workers may be more "willing" to devote time to unions because, in most cases, they in fact have more time—a situation that should not be news to union activists who are familiar with women's lives.

Several of the women I interviewed who were familiar with union activities expressed dissatisfaction with what unions have to offer people who must handle the double shift of work and household demands. Charo, a Mexicana semiconductor processor, noted:

> Why should we pay money to the unions? We already have the supervisors telling us what to do—we don't need someone else to do it, too. My major problem is that I can't find good child care, and I don't have any time to study English. Will the union keep my kids off of the streets? Will they keep [my husband] from drinking? No.

Her friend Mila, who was sitting in on this interview, added: "What you need is a wife, not a union!"

Another factor that greatly influences the relationship of immigrant workers to the U.S. labor movement is their earlier experience with politics and organizing in their country of origin. This section provides some limited anecdotal information that may help to explain why immigrants of different nationalities tend to view unions differently. Not all the nationalities represented in my study are discussed here; the findings are preliminary, but they convey a sense of the magnitude of multicultural understanding that must be developed by anyone wishing to effectively organize a diverse immigrant labor force.

According to Thu, a Vietnamese community leader and union advocate, many Vietnamese immigrants to the United States equate unions with communism. If they are anti-communist, as are the vast majority who have fled to America, they tend to be anti-union. For example, 90 percent of Vietnamese refugees with U.S. citizenship are registered in and vote regularly for the Republican party,[24] which traditionally supports business interests when they conflict with organized labor. Vietnamese immigrants, across classes, strongly favor Republican candidates and policies because they perceive Republicans as more staunch opponents of communism and greater supporters of military defense than Democrats. Only one of the Vietnamese workers I interviewed claimed to have had any involvement with labor unions in Vietnam. Most would not discuss their families' direct involvement in political activities, except to specify that they were vehemently anti-Vietcong. None of the Vietnamese immigrant workers or their family members claim membership in any U.S. labor union, and most speak of unions in either a derogatory or a wary tone.

In contrast, local Filipino immigrant communities have a tradition of labor militancy that is tied to labor and resistance movements in the Philippines. Under former president Ferdinand Marcos, outlawed labor unions were clandestine and were part of the insurgency against the regime. The majority of working-class Filipino immigrants in Silicon Valley are anti-Marcos, according to community members interviewed; many of them came to the United States to escape political persecution by the Marcos regime. Many Filipino immigrants have remained in close contact with political groups in their homeland and have been influenced by the rising tide of labor militancy there. Compared to Vietnamese immigrants, fewer Filipinos who immigrated during the Marcos days have sought American citizenship, and thus voting rights, because they expected that Marcos would soon be overthrown and that they would return home. Since Marcos has fallen, however, relatively few have returned to the Philippines.

Among the Filipino immigrants I interviewed, most politically support U.S. labor unions in theory, but their own organizing energy in recent years has been directed toward conditions in the Philippines. During the time of my earlier interviews, before Corazon Aquino took office, anti-Marcos Filipinos in the United States, like those in the Philippines, had to remain clandestine and low-profile in all of their political activities, for fear of retaliation by pro-Marcos forces. Informants claimed that wealthy Marcos supporters in the San Francisco Bay Area maintained a "hit squad" that targeted local anti-Marcos activists. Sympathizers on both sides of the struggle expressed fear of reprisals.[25] Although Marcos supporters in the

United States feared retaliation from the numerically stronger anti-Marcos forces, the pro-Marcos sector wielded much greater financial and political power. Anti-Marcos activists claim that before Aquino's victory they were harassed by both the FBI and its Filipino equivalent and that their activities in the United States led to severe persecution of family members in the Philippines. Because of these conditions, many Filipino workers I talked with before the ouster of Marcos were understandably reticent to discuss their political involvement. Those who did were overwhelmingly anti-Marcos. In an interview I conducted in 1983, Tito, a Filipino janitor and the husband of a high-tech production worker, commented:

> Of course we are all anti-Marcos; that is why we came here. If we liked what he was doing, if we were not afraid for our lives, would we have left the homes we love? . . . The only ones here who are for the regime are Imelda's rich cronies—they come here to invest their money safely—but they still fly back to see her all the time.

His teenage daughter told me that it was easy to distinguish which of her compatriots were pro-Marcos: "They're the ones you see shopping; we're the ones you see working."

In the post-Marcos period, more wealthy, pro-Marcos Filipinos have immigrated to the Bay Area. A pro-Marcos position is generally equated with a pro-Republican stance, whereas those who are anti-Marcos range from being pro-Democrat to having left-wing sympathies. Working-class Filipino immigrants tend to be anti-Marcos and pro-labor. Only two of the Filipina workers I interviewed claimed to have been active in labor unions in the Philippines, but 40 percent reported that male family members had been actively involved. In several of the Filipino households I visited, family members engaged in impassioned discussions about labor and liberation movements in the Philippines when I asked them about their homeland. Similarly, although only two Filipina workers (one of whom was also a trade unionist in the Philippines) reported that they had been involved in U.S. unions, approximately 30 percent of their adult male family members reported that they were unionists.

Institutional barriers to women's participation are very real, yet women have nevertheless been active in the local labor movement. And Filipinos of both sexes have been at the forefront of collective organizing efforts that have taken place in Silicon Valley. In 1985, a group of twelve workers from chip-maker giant National Semiconductor Corporation came before Santa Clara County's Human Rights Commission to publicly testify about their employer's racially discriminatory labor practices. Most of these workers were Filipino. And during the drive to organize National Semiconductor, the single largest group of workers to join the union were Filipinas. Organizers note that the involvement of these women coincided with one of the major nationalist upsurges against Marcos in the Philippines. Local organizers report that National Semiconductor is aware of the connection between politics in the Philippines and Silicon Valley organizing; according to rumor, the company has even sent management representatives to the Philippines to investigate and lobby against labor unions.[26]

Most of the immigrants I talked with from the Philippines, El Salvador, Indochina, and other regions torn by civil war essentially came to the United States as political refugees, whether or not the U.S. government granted them official refugee status. The factors that push other groups to immigrate to America are less frequently tied to individuals' particular political affiliations, although in the broader sense all immigration occurs in a political context. Within nonrefugee communities, there tends to be a greater diversity of political histories and labor sympathies, much of which seems to be tied to previous experiences with organizing and to class background. This was the case with Mexican workers I interviewed. Mexican informants and their family members tend to have been either unemployed or underemployed in rural or urban labor before coming to the United States. Although few workers—less than 10 percent of the women and just over 10 percent of their male family members—reported involvement in unions or other labor groups in Mexico, 10 percent of the women and 30 percent of the men reported attending at least one union meeting in the United States. Two of the Mexican women had joined a union in the United States, and more than 20 percent had male family members who belong to a union.

Recent labor insurgencies in South Korea, such as the widespread strikes at Hyundai and other plants, might suggest that Korean immigrants, like their Filipino co-workers, would also be inclined to labor militancy. This was not the case for the Korean workers I talked with. Half of these workers were nonunionized professional or semiprofessional workers before immigration. Only one claimed that she or any family member had ever been involved in union activities in Korea. None of the Korean women is involved in a union in the United States, although a few female family members are. Approximately 8 percent of the male family members interviewed have been involved in unions since their arrival.

Most of the immigrant women workers I interviewed were aware of union organizing drives in the valley during the course of their employment, yet fewer than 10 percent knew which unions were involved, what union membership entails, or the issues on which unions were focusing. Fewer still expressed any interest in participating in union activities. One reason that the women were relatively uninformed about union specifics is the language barrier; another is fear of persecution by the Immigration and Naturalization Service and other government agencies.

My findings indicate that the large majority of immigrant women in Silicon Valley high-tech manufacturing jobs are alienated from the trade union movement. That does not mean, however, that they do not understand the value of collective organizing. Irma, a Filipina immigrant, an undocumented high-tech production worker and a young mother, told me this story. After a hard day on the job, she cooks dinner and puts the kids to bed. Late at night, when she is done helping her husband get off to his night job and her sister go through the job ads, she sometimes goes over to her neighbor's apartment "to watch TV." Her neighbor is a Mexican woman who works at the same plant. They sit around drinking coffee while their kids are asleep, and though they are exhausted, they talk about their dreams and goals and how to achieve them:

> When I think about it, we don't really dream of fortunes or kingdoms or things like that very often. We mainly dream about our real lives. . . . And so much of what we want for ourselves and our families is conditioned by our jobs, even though we don't think of our jobs as something that we care about, because they're pretty depressing. . . .
>
> We dream that when we work hard, we'll be able to clothe our children decently, and still have a little time and money left for ourselves. And we dream that when we do as good a job as other people, we get treated the same, and that nobody puts us down because we're not like them. We dream that our jobs are safe, and secure, and when we're really on a roll— we even imagine that they're interesting and enjoyable! . . .
>
> Then we ask ourselves, "How could we make these things come true?" And so far we've come up with only two possible answers: win the lottery, or organize. What can I say, except I have never been lucky with numbers. So tell them this in your book: Tell them it may take time that people don't think they have, but they have to organize! It doesn't have to be through a union, because God knows unions have problems. So you can do it anywhere—but organize! Because the only way to get a little measure of power over your own life is to do it collectively, with the support of other people who share your needs.

For immigrant women workers, a successful organizing movement will be one that addresses the intersections of class, gender, race, and nationality in their lives, a movement recognizing that for women such as Irma a work life means not only wage work but household and community labor, and often includes the struggles associated with being undocumented. What is needed is an interethnic labor and community movement that challenges gender and racial oppression as well as dangerous, unstable working conditions in the high-tech industry. And because of the global scope and mobility of the industry, such a movement must also have an international component.

These are, of course, very tall orders. But Third World women workers such as the ones interviewed for this study constitute a major and growing force in the modern international division of labor. A labor movement that wishes to remain viable must therefore make the problems presented in these pages a primary focus. To paraphrase Margarita, the Mexicana assembler quoted in the opening of this article, today's new workers will take an interest in labor movements—or any social movement—only when those movements demonstrate a real interest in them.

NOTES

1. An earlier, shorter version of this article appears in *Common Interests: Women Organising in Global Electronics,* ed. Women Working Worldwide (London: Women Working Worldwide, 1991), pp. 37–51.

2. For accounts of organizing efforts among women high-tech workers in other countries, see Women Working Worldwide, *Common Interests.*

3. I agree with Chandra Mohanty, Ann Russo, and Lourdes Torres, among others, that the term *Third World* is problematic but perhaps less so than *developing countries, postcolonial,* and other terms currently in use. See Mohanty, Russo, and Torres, eds., *Third World Women and the Politics of Feminism* (Bloomington: Indiana University Press, 1991), for discussion.

4. See Karen J. Hossfeld, "Hiring Immigrant Women: Silicon Valley's Simple Formula," in *Women of Color in U.S. Society,* ed. Bonnie Thornton Dill and Maxine Baca Zinn (Philadelphia: Temple University Press, 1994), pp. 65–93.

5. Karen J. Hossfeld, *"Small, Foreign, and Female": Profiles of Gender, Race, and Nationality in Silicon Valley* (Berkeley: University of California Press, forthcoming).

6. Lenny Siegel and Herb Borock, *Background Report on Silicon Valley,* prepared for the U.S. Commission on Civil Rights (Mountain View, Calif.: Pacific Studies Center, 1982).

7. Michael Eisenscher, "Organizing the Shop in Electronics" (paper presented at the West Coast Marxist Scholars Conference, Berkeley, Calif., November 14, 1987).

8. "Beyond Unions," *Business Week,* July 8, 1985, p. 72. *Business Week's* cover story on declining union strength makes no mention, however, of increasing female membership and its potential ramifications.

9. David Sylvester, "Atari Workers Don't Mince Words on State of the Union," *San Jose Mercury News*, July 25, 1983, p. 1E.

10. U.S. Department of Labor, Bureau of Labor Statistics, *Employment and Earnings*, vol. 34 (Washington, D.C.: Government Printing Office, January 1987), Table 61, p. 221.

11. Ibid.

12. Eisenscher, "Organizing the Shop in Electronics."

13. Ray Alvatorres, "Unionizing High Tech," *San Jose Mercury News*, August 3, 1986, p. 4F.

14. Ibid.

15. Pat Sacco, "The View from the Shop Floor" (paper presented at the West Coast Marxist Scholars Conference, Berkeley, Calif., November 14, 1987).

16. For information, contact the Silicon Valley Toxics Coalition, 760 N. First St., San Jose, Calif., 95112.

17. For discussion of the history of the relationship between unions and women workers, see Ruth Milkman, ed., *Women, Work, and Protest: A Century of U.S. Women's Labor History* (Boston: Routledge and Kegan Paul, 1985).

18. The Mexicana and Chicana workers who engaged in a long and bitter union-coordinated strike at canneries in Watsonville, California, in 1986–1987 are a case in point. They are also a case in point that immigrant women workers can and do organize in labor unions.

19. U.S. Department of Labor, Bureau of Labor Statistics, *Employment and Earnings*, vol. 34, Table 59, p. 219.

20. Milkman, *Women, Work, and Protest*; Ruth Milkman, "Organizing the Sexual Division of Labor: Historical Perspectives on 'Women's Work' and the American Labor Movement," *Socialist Review* 49 (1980): 95–150; Margaret Cerullo and Roslyn Feldberg, "Women Workers, Feminism, and the Unions," *Radical America* 18 (September-October 1984): 2–5; Alice Kessler-Harris, *Out to Work: A History of Wage-Earning Women in the United States* (New York: Oxford, 1982); Barbara Wertheimer, *We Were There: The Story of Working Women in America* (New York: Pantheon, 1977); Richard Freeman and James Medoff, *What Do Unions Do?* (New York: Basic Books, 1984); Rosalyn Teborg-Penn, "Survival Strategies Among African-American Women Workers: A Continuing Process," in Milkman, *Women, Work, and Protest*, pp. 139–155.

21. The church is perhaps the only potential organizing arena in which large numbers of Silicon Valley's immigrant women of all nationalities participate both because of their own choice and because of family approval. Church involvement is thus an important reality to recognize in any discussion of how, where, and in what forms this group of workers might organize. See Hossfeld, "Hiring Immigrant Women."

22. Barbara M. Wertheimer, "The United States of America," in *Women and Trade Unions in Eleven Industrialized Countries*, ed. Alice H. Cook, Val R. Lorwin, and Arlene Kaplan Daniels (Philadelphia: Temple University Press, 1984), pp. 286–311.

23. Karen Hossfeld, "'Their Logic Against Them': Contradictions in Sex, Race, and Class in Silicon Valley," in *Women Workers and Global Restructuring*, ed. Kathryn Ward (Ithaca: ILR Press, 1990), pp. 149–178.

24. *San Jose Mercury News*, July 19, 1987, p. 23A.

25. Ibid. Reports were also confirmed by informants.

26. The management representative at National Semiconductor contacted about this report was unable to confirm or deny it.

FURTHER READING

Chapkis, Wendy, and Cynthia Enloe. *Of Common Cloth: Women in the Global Textile Industry.* 1983.

Colclough, Glenna, and Charles M. Tolbert. *Work in the Fast Lane: Flexibility, Divisions of Labor, and Inequality in High-Tech Industries.* 1992.

Fernandez-Kelly, Maria Patricia. *For We Are Sold, I and My People: Women and Industry in Mexico's Frontier.* 1983.

Friaz, Guadalupe Mendez. "Employment Security in a Nonunion Workplace: A Study of Blue Collar Workers in a High-Tech Firm." Ph.D. dissertation, University of California, Berkeley, 1989.

Green, Susan S. *Silicon Valley's Women Workers: A Theoretical Analysis of Sex-Segregation in the Electronics Labor Market.* 1980.

Gregory, Kathleen. "Signing-Up: The Culture and Careers of Silicon Valley Computer People." Ph.D. dissertation, Northwestern University, 1984.

Hayes, Dennis. *Behind the Silicon Curtain: The Seductions of Work in a Lonely Era.* 1989.

Hossfeld, Karen J. "Hiring Immigrant Women: Silicon Valley's Simple Formula." In *Women of Color in U.S. Society,* edited by Bonnie Thornton Dill and Maxine Baca Zinn, pp. 65–93. 1994.

———. *"Small, Foreign, and Female": Profiles of Gender, Race, and Nationality in Silicon Valley.* Forthcoming.

———. "'Their Logic Against Them': Contradictions in Sex, Race, and Class in Silicon Valley." In *Women Workers and Global Restructuring,* edited by Kathryn Ward, pp. 149–178. 1990.

Katz, Naomi, and David S. Kemnitzer. "Women and Work in Silicon Valley: Options and Futures." In *My Troubles Are Going to Have Trouble with Me: Everyday Trials and Triumphs of Women Workers,* edited by Karen Bodkin Sacks and Dorothy Remy, pp. 209–218. 1984.

Keller, John Frederick. "The Production Workers in Electronics: Industrialization and Labor Development in California's Santa Clara Valley." Ph.D. dissertation, University of Michigan, 1981.

Muller, Thomas, and Thomas J. Espenshade. *The Fourth Wave: California's Newest Immigrants.* 1985.

Olson, Lynne. "The Silkwoods of Silicon Valley." *Working Woman* 8 (July 1984).

Saxenian, AnnaLee. "Contrasting Patterns of Business Organization in Silicon Valley." *Environment and Planning D: Society and Space* 10 (1992): 377–391.

———. "In Search of Power: The Organization of Business Interests in Silicon Valley and Route 128." *Economy and Society* 18 (1989): 25–70.

———. "Urban Contradictions of Silicon Valley: Regional Growth and Restructuring of the Semiconductor Industry." *International Journal of Urban and Regional Research* 7 (June 1983): 237–261.

Siegel, Lenny, and John Markoff. *The High Cost of High-Tech: The Dark Side of the Chip.* 1985.

Storper, Michael, and Richard Walker. *The Capitalist Imperative: Territory, Technology, and Industrial Growth.* 1989.

U.S. Commission on Civil Rights. *Women and Minorities in High Technology.* 1982.

Walker, Richard. "The Playground of U.S. Capitalism: The Political Economy of the San Francisco Bay Area in the 1980s." In *Fire in the Hearth: The Radical Politics of Place in America,* edited by Mike Davis et al., pp. 3–82. 1990.

Winner, Langdon. "Silicon Valley Mystery House." In *Variations on a Theme Park: The New American City and the End of Public Space,* edited by Michael Sorkin, pp. 31–60. 1993.

15   Fontana

Junkyard of Dreams

Mike Davis

EDITOR'S INTRODUCTION

In 1920, Upton Sinclair wrote that California was "a parasite upon the great industrial centers of other parts of America." Beginning during World War II, however, a set of basic industries emerged in California that provided the state with a manufacturing base comparable to that in most of the industrialized states of the East and the Midwest. Southern California was the primary location of this industrial expansion, with growth centered in the greater Los Angeles conurbation. Between 1940 and 1944, more than $800 million was invested in five thousand new industrial plants in southern California, and the value of Los Angeles's manufacturing output during the war rose from $5 billion to $12 billion.

The growth continued after the war. Manufacturing payrolls increased from $1.3 billion in 1947 to $4.4 billion in 1956, with southern California accounting for 71 percent of the total factory payrolls of the state. More than 90 percent of the state's aircraft and parts, rubber and tire, and scientific industries were located in southern California in 1956, while approximately 80 percent of the apparel, furniture, electrical machinery and equipment, and motor vehicle industries were based in the southland.

Federal government expenditures for defense and aerospace played a significant role. By a conservative estimate, the federal government spent $100 billion in California between 1940 and 1970, far more than in any other state. During the 1980s, the Los Angeles area alone accounted for 17 percent of all U.S. defense spending. Little wonder that between the early 1970s and the early 1980s the Los Angeles region generated a quarter of a million jobs.

But this phenomenal growth masked underlying problems that existed in some of southern California's manufacturing industries long before the

433

devastating impact of the recession that began in 1989 took effect. Certain basic industries were falling victim to the pressures of international competition. From 1978 to 1982, ten of the twelve largest nonaerospace plants in East Los Angeles laid off more than fifty thousand workers, many of them African Americans and Chicanos.

All was not well in the "Inland Empire" (San Bernardino and Orange counties) either. During World War II, Henry Kaiser built the first steel mill in the Pacific Coast states at Fontana, fifty miles east of Los Angeles. For more than two decades, Fontana flourished. By the late 1960s, however, a series of events occurred that would ultimately doom this blue-collar community.

In this extract from his book *City of Quartz: Excavating the Future in Los Angeles*, Mike Davis returns to Fontana to tell the history of his birthplace and analyze the profound social, cultural, and environmental changes and tensions produced over the years. He examines how the Kaiser steel plant transformed pastoral Fontana during World War II, bringing jobs but also social dislocation and a high crime rate, including vigilantism against African Americans.

During the late 1960s and early 1970s, Kaiser ignored the competition from more profitable Asian and European steel plants. Efforts to modernize the plant in the 1970s were too little too late. In 1983, the plant closed, and six thousand workers lost their jobs. But Fontana did not turn into a ghost town. A group of ambitious real estate developers converted it into a suburban bedroom community. The new middle-class and upper-class residents of Fontana, in alliance with developers, then killed industrial redevelopment plans, arguing that they would have an adverse environmental impact on a densely populated residential suburb.

◆　　◆　　◆

Mental geographies betray class prejudice. In the trendy-chic *L.A. Weekly*'s "Best of Los Angeles" guide, one of the "Ten Best of the Best" is the Robertson Boulevard off-ramp of the Santa Monica Freeway near Beverly Hills: where the air starts to clear of smog and the true heaven of the Westside begins. In Yuppie deli-map consciousness, landscapes tend to compress logarithmically as soon as one leaves the terrain of luxury lifestyles. Thus Fairfax is the near Eastside, while Downtown is the far horizon, surrounded by dimly known zones of ethnic restaurants. Even if the

Westsider is vaguely familiar with the old concentrations of Wasp wealth marooned in Pasadena, Claremont, or Redlands, the eastbound San Bernardino Freeway (the I-10)—traversed at warp speed with the windows rolled up against the smog and dust—is merely the high road to Palm Springs and the Arizona Desert. The "Inland Empire" of western San Bernardino and Riverside counties is little more than a blur.

One of the few modern writers to venture thither, Joan Didion, on her way to a San Bernardino murder trial, found the landscape "curious and unnatural":

> The lemon groves are sunken, down a three- or four-foot retaining wall, so that one looks directly into their dense foliage, too lush, unsettlingly glossy, the greenery of nightmare; the fallen eucalyptus bark is too dusty, a place for snakes to breed. The stones look not like natural stones but like the rubble of some unmentioned catastrophe.[1]

Rising from the geological and social detritus that has accumulated at the foot of the Cajon Pass sixty miles east of Los Angeles, the city of Fontana is the principal byproduct of this "unmentioned catastrophe." A gritty blue-collar town, well known to line-haul truckers everywhere, with rusting blast furnaces and outlaw motorcycle gangs (the birthplace of the Hell's Angels in 1946), it is the regional antipode to the sumptuary belts of West L.A. or Orange County. "Designer living" here means a Peterbilt with a custom sleeper or a full-chrome Harley hog. A loud, brawling mosaic of working-class cultures—Black, Italian, hillbilly, Slovene, and Chicano—Fontana has long endured an unsavory reputation in the eyes of San Bernardino County's moral crusaders and middle-class boosters.

But Fontana is more than merely the "roughest town in the county." Its indissoluble toughness of character is the product of an extraordinary, deeply emblematic local history. Over the course of the seventy-five years since its founding, Fontana has been both junkyard and utopia for successive tropes of a changing California dream. The millions of tourists and commuters who annually pass by Fontana on I-10, occasionally peeking into the shabbiness of its backyards and derelict orchards, can little imagine the hopes and visions shipwrecked here.

In its original, early-twentieth-century incarnation, Fontana was the modernized Jeffersonian idyll: an arcadian community of small chicken ranchers and citrus growers living self-sufficiently in their electrified bungalows. Then in 1942 the community was abruptly reshaped to accommodate the dream of a Rooseveltian industrial revolution in the West. The Promethean energies of Henry Kaiser turned Fontana overnight into a mighty forge for war, the only integrated steel complex on the Pacific Slope. In the early 1980s, with equally brutal swiftness, the milltown was shuttered and its workers and machines reduced to scrap. Yet, phoenix-like, a third Fontana—the "affordable suburb"—has arisen from the ruins of Kaisertown. In the new economic geometry of the Southern California "metrosea," where increasing masses commute three or more hours daily to reconcile paychecks with mortgages, Fontana—and its sister communities of San Bernardino County's "West End"—are the new dormitories of Southern California's burgeoning workforces.

If violent instability in local landscape and culture is taken to be consti-tutive of Southern California's peculiar social ontology, then Fontana epit-omizes the region. It is an imagined community, twice invented and pro-moted, then turned inside-out to become once again a visionary green field. Its repeated restructurings have traumatically registered the shifting interaction of regional and international, manufacturing and real-estate, capitalism. Yet—despite the claims of some theorists of the "hyperreal" or the "depthless present"—the past is not completely erasable, even in Southern California. Steelmaking in the shadow of the San Bernardinos— the transposed culture of Pennsylvania millworkers on a horticultural semi-utopia on the edge of the desert—have left human residues that defy the most determined efforts of current developers to repackage Fontana as a vacant lot. To this extent the Fontana story provides a parable: it is about the fate of those suburbanized California working classes who cling to their tarnished dreams at the far edge of the L.A. galaxy.

Fontana Farms

It was just the type of place they often had talked of. Ten acres of level land . . . rich, fertile. On it were 200 fine walnut trees, young, but sturdy. And on four sides was a beautiful fringe of tall, graceful eucalyptus, through which they glimpsed the lofty crests of the San Bernardinos.

"It would be wonderful, if we just had money enough," said she. "At least," said he, "we have enough to make a start. We can pay down what we can spare and stay in the city for a while. There'll be enough to put up a little garage house, and we'll have a place of our own to come to weekends and holidays."

And so, much sooner than they had hoped, their dream of a place all their own, out in the country, came true. Every weekend, every holiday, found them on their Fontana farm, planting things, culti-vating their walnut trees, watching things grow. And their farm returned their affection in full measure. Never did the walnut trees thrive so. Never did berry bushes and fruit trees do better. Each week they carried back with them some of the products of their farm.

Then there came a day when they could build the farm home they always had planned. A roomy, rambling house, with a world of windows. A broad green lawn, and trees in front, and at the back equipment for 2,000 chickens, a rabbitry for 240 full-blooded New Zealand Whites, and, just for the fun of it, pens for Muscovy and Peking ducks, turkeys . . .

And so, the first of the year, they moved in. Each week brings an egg check of $40 to $50 or more. There is a ready market for every rabbit they can produce. The walnut trees will be in production soon, and in full bearing they will add another $2,000 per year net to the profits of the place. In all Fontana there's no farm that's finer, no couple that is happier, and it's proved so easy . . . after they found their Fontana farm.

Fontana Farms ad, 1930[2]

Fontana Farms was the brainchild of A. B. Miller, San Bernardino contractor and agriculturalist. All but forgotten today, Miller was one of the hero-builders of a unique civilization of affluent agricultural colonies in what was once known as the "Valley of the South,"[3] stretching from Pomona to Redlands. Like the more widely known George Chaffey, whose Ontario colony had decisive influence on the technology of Zionist settlement in Palestine, Miller was a visionary entrepreneur of hydroelectric power, irrigated horticulture, cooperative marketing, and planned community development. Which is to say, he was a brilliant real-estate promoter who fully grasped the combination of advertising and infrastructure required to alchemize the dusty plains of the San Bernardinos into gold. If Chaffey, along with L.A. water titan William Mulholland, far surpassed the hydraulic accomplishments of Miller, the latter was unique in the thorough planning and complementary agricultural diversity that made Fontana such a striking realization of the petty-bourgeois ideal of withdrawal into Jeffersonian autonomy. Only the failed Socialist utopia of Llano del Rio, in the Mojave Desert north of Los Angeles, aspired to a more ambitious integration of civility and self-sufficiency.

In 1906 Miller, flush with construction profits from the new Imperial Valley, took over the failed promotion of the Semi-Tropic Land and Water Company: twenty-eight square miles of boulder-strewn plain west of San Bernardino. Incessantly raked by dust storms and desiccating Santa Ana winds, the alluvial Fontana–Cucamonga fan for the most part retained the same forlorn aspect—greasewood, sage, and scattered wild plum trees— that had greeted the original Mormon colonists sent by Brigham Young in

1851 to establish San Bernardino as Deseret's window on the Pacific. Raising capital from prominent Los Angeles bankers, Miller undertook the construction of a vast irrigation system (tapping the snows of Mount Baldy via Lytle Creek) and the planting of half a million eucalyptus saplings as windbreaks. By 1913 his Fontana Company was ready to begin laying out a townsite between Foothill Boulevard (an old wagon road soon to become part of famous US 66) and the Santa Fe tracks. At the inaugural barbecue, Miller's friend and sponsor, Pacific Electric Railroad President Paul Shoup, promised that his Red Cars would soon bring thousands of daytrippers and prospective homesteaders to see the future at work in Fontana.[4]

Other famous irrigation colonies of the day—Pasadena, Ontario, Redlands, and so on—thrived by franchising citrus growing as an investment haven for wealthy, sun-seeking Easterners. The cooperative, "Sunkist" model (later so influential in shaping Herbert Hoover's vision of self-organized capitalism) provided newcomers with a network of production services, a coordinated labor pool, and a national marketing organization with a common trademark.[5] On the other hand, the arcadian life of a Southern California orange, lemon, or avocado grower required substantial startup capital (at least $40,000 in 1919) and outside income to sustain the operator until his trees became fruit-bearing.[6] Ready access to capital was also necessary to tide growers over between the seasons and periodically to absorb the costs of crop-killing frosts. Seduced by the siren song of fabulous profits in the foothills, thousands of undercapitalized citrus ranchers lost their life savings in a few seasons.[7]

Miller's concept of Fontana was presented as an alternative to aristocratic citrus colonies like Redlands as well as to the more speculative settlements in the eastern San Gabriel Valley. Fontana was envisioned as an unprecedented combination of industrialized plantation (Fontana Farms) and Jeffersonian smallholdings (subdivided by Fontana Land Company). Fontana Farms was a futuristic example of vertically integrated, scientifically managed, corporate agriculture. Its primary input was the City of Los Angeles's garbage, which, from 1921 to 1950, it received in daily gondola car shipments by rail. (The garbage contract was so lucrative that Miller was forced to make large payoffs to corrupt city councilmen—igniting a 1931 municipal scandal.) The five or six hundred daily tons of garbage fattened the sixty thousand hogs that made Fontana Farms the largest such operation in the world. When the hogs reached full weight, they were shipped back to Los Angeles for slaughter, recycled garbage thus providing perhaps a quarter of the region's ham and bacon. The coincident accumulation of manure was no less valued: it was either utilized as fertilizer for Miller's citrus grove (also the world's largest) or peddled to neighboring ranchers. Fontana Farms even made a small profit reselling the silverware it reclaimed from restaurant garbage.[8]

Meanwhile the Fontana Company was busy subdividing the rest of the Miller empire into model small farms. With an enthusiasm for mass marketing and production that clearly prefigured Henry Kaiser's, Miller aimed his promotion at precisely that middling mass of would-be rural escapists who had previously been cannon-fodder for Southern California's most ill-fated land and oil speculations. His "affordable" Fontana farm idyll, by contrast, was designed to be assembled on lay away with combinations of small semi-annual installments and lots of sweat equity. For bare land prices of $300–500 (for the minimum 2.5 acre "starter farm" in 1930), the prospective Fontanan was offered a choice of bearing grapevines or walnut trees (corporate Fontana Farms maintained a vast nursery of a million saplings). Starting with "vacation farming" on weekends (Los Angeles was only an hour away by automobile or Red Car), the purchaser could gradually add on living quarters, which the Fontana Farms Company offered in a complete range from weekend cabins to the ultimate "charming, redtile Spanish Colonial farmhouse." Examples of these are still widely visible throughout Fontana.

What was supposed to make the whole endeavor ingeniously self-financing, however, was Miller's formula of combining tree crops (walnuts and mixed citrus) or vineyards with poultry, supported by cheap inputs from Fontana Farms' industrial economies of scale (fertilizer, saplings, water, and power). Colonists were urged to install chicken coops as soon as possible to generate reliable incomes. This famous "Partnership of Hens and Oranges" was intended to stabilize the small tree rancher through the vagaries of frost and cashflow, while simultaneously guaranteeing the Fontana Company its installment payments. Ideally, it was supposed to allow the retired couple with a modest pension, the young family with rustic inclinations, or the hardworking immigrant the means to achieve a citrus-belt lifestyle formerly accessible only to the well-to-do.[9]

Miller's dream sold well, even through the early years of the Depression. By 1930 the Fontana Company had subdivided more than three thousand homesteads, half occupied by full-time settlers, some of them immigrants from Hungary, Yugoslavia, and Italy. The ten pioneer poultry plants of 1919 had grown to nine hundred, making the district the premier poultry center of the West. Fontana Farms, meanwhile, had expanded to a full-time workforce of five hundred Mexican and Japanese laborers—comparable to the largest cotton plantations in the Mississippi Delta. In the early thirties Miller joined forces with the Swift dynasty from Chicago to buy out the historic Miller (no relation) and Lux cattle empire in the San Joaquin Valley. His rising stature in California agriculture, together with his contributions to making it into a genuine "agribusiness," were acknowledged by Republican Governor Rolph, who appointed Miller president of the State Agricultural Society and, ex officio, a regent of the University of California.

Even if Fontana Farms was ultimately little more than a real-estate promotion cleverly, and extravagantly, packaged as semi-utopia, it retains considerable historical importance as the most striking Southern California example of the "back to the land" movement in the inter-war years. Originally a yeoman's version of the irrigation colony ideal (exemplified by both Chaffey's Ontario and the Socialists' Llano del Rio), Fontana grew to share many of the qualities of Frank Lloyd Wright's "Broadacres" project and the 1930s anti-urban experiments. Skimming through old advertising brochures for Fontana Farms, one is struck by the ideological congruence—however inadvertent—between Miller's declared aims and the Henry Georgian program which Giorgi Ciucci has claimed infused Wright's Broadacres: "labor-saving electrification, the right of the average citizen to the land, the integration of the city and the countryside, cooperation rather than government, and the opportunity for all to be capitalists." If, as Ciucci sarcastically observes, "Wright's ideal city would be realized only in the grotesque and preposterous form of Disneyland and Disney World,"[10] Miller's more practical version of the Broadacres ideal had a brief, but real tenure. All the more ironic, then, that pastoral Fontana Farms would be upstaged, and eventually uprooted, by Henry Kaiser's "satanic mill."

Miracle Man

The "Miracle Man" Comes to Fontana

1942 headline[11]

In 1946, after two years of criss-crossing all the old forty-eight states ("my ideal day was to spend all morning with the First National Bank and the afternoon with the CIO"), John Gunther published *Inside USA*—his vast (979-page), Whitmanesque snapshot of the domestic political scene on the threshold of the postwar era.[12] For Gunther, the most popular journalist of his generation, World War Two was comparable to the Revolution or the Civil War as a watershed of American character. From the standpoint of an onrushing "American Century," he was concerned to distinguish the progressive from the reactionary, the visionary from the backward-looking. Although later journalists, albeit only by team effort, eventually duplicated the scale of his canvas (that is, the entire US political universe), none has ever matched the astuteness or piquancy of his characterizations of an entire generation of public figures. Unsurprisingly, in the gutter bottom of national political life, Gunther identified the representatives of Mississippi, the Hague machine of New Jersey, and other avatars of domestic fascism. Conversely, at the very pinnacle of his new American pantheon, rising above even Governors Warren and Stassen (perennial Gunther favorites), was "the most important industrialist in the United States . . . the builder of Richmond and Fontana," Henry J. Kaiser.[13]

Forty-five years later, with the mighty Kaiser empire now dismantled, Gunther's panegyric to Kaiser (he was given an entire chapter to himself) requires some explanation.[14] In essence, Gunther, like many contemporary observers, saw Kaiser as the exemplary incarnation of the Rooseveltian synthesis of free enterprise and enlightened state intervention. Kaiser of the 1930s and 1940s is heroically entrepreneurial—Gunther compares him to nineteenth-century empire-builders like the Central Pacific's "Big Four"—yet, unlike the old-fashioned "railroad corsairs," Kaiser "has great social consciousness and conscience." A lifelong registered Republican, he avidly supports the New Deal. "As to labor Kaiser's friendly relations are well known. He wants to be able to calculate his costs to the last inch, and he never budges without a labor contract."[15] Although his early background was as a small-town salesman, lacking any formal training in engineering or manufacturing, Kaiser by the mid 1940s had become the great problem-solving magician of the war economy: mass-producing Liberty ships in four days and achieving other productivist feats worthy of Edison or Ford. Even better than Ford himself (who represented an earlier era of authoritarian engineer-capitalism), Kaiser personified the spirit of the war-generated high-productivity, high-wage economy that later economic historians would refer to as "Fordism." But "Kaiserism" would have been a more apt name for the postwar social contract between labor and management:

> Production in the last analysis depends on the will of labor to produce . . .
> you can't have healthy and viable industry without, first, a healthy labor
> movement, and second, social insurance, community health, hospitalization

plans, and decent housing. "To break a union is to break yourself." *The "Kaiser Credo"*[16]

Kaiser was also a hero of the West. Denounced by Wall Street as the "economic Antichrist" and "coddled New Deal pet," he was welcomed west of the Rockies as a self-made frontier capitalist who, against incredible odds, had triumphed over William Jennings Bryan's "cross of gold."[17] To Western economic nationalists, like A. G. Mezerik, Kaiser was a "new kind of industrialist," an incarnation of the "trust-busting Second New Deal" and a pioneer of the "independent industrialization of the West."[18] In fact, Kaiser, accumulating a small fortune in the corrupt street-paving business during the auto-crazy 1920s, was transformed into an industrial giant during the 1930s by virtue of strategic (and sometimes secretive) business and political alliances. In the late 1920s, Kaiser became a favorite of the legendary Amadeo Giannini, founder of the Bank of Italy (later Bank of America) and the West's major independent financier.[19] With Giannini backing, Kaiser assumed de facto leadership over the coalition of construction companies building Hoover Dam and became the Six Companies' Washington lobbyist. In the capital Kaiser hired consummate New Deal "fixer" Tommy Corcoran to represent his interests in the White House, while cultivating his own special relationship to powerful Interior Secretary Harold Ickes.[20]

Most important, Kaiser, together with Giannini and other local allies, was able to recognize the extraordinary "window of opportunity" for Western economic development opened up by the political crisis of the "First" New Deal in 1935–36. To be fair, it was actually Herbert Hoover, the first president from California, who had launched the industrialization of the Pacific Slope by authorizing construction of both the Hoover Dam and the Golden Gate Bridge. But the big chance for Western (and Southern) businessmen came in the interregnum between the Banking Act of 1935 and the beginning of Lendlease, when relations between the White House and Wall Street reached their twentieth-century nadir. As Eastern finance capital (including many key supporters of FDR in 1933) turned against the New Deal, Kaiser and Giannini, together with Texas oil independents and Mormon bankers (led by Six Companies partner and new Federal Reserve chairman Mariner Eccles), politically and financially shored up the Roosevelt Administration, preventing the insurgent labor movement from dominating the national Democratic Party.[21] In his epic *Age of Roosevelt*, Arthur Schlesinger describes the convergence of interests that supported the "Second" ("anti-trust") New Deal of the late 1930s:

> It included representatives of the "new money" of the South and West, like Jesse Jones, Henry J. Kaiser and A. P. Giannini, who . . . were in revolt against the *rentier* mentality of New York and wanted government to force down interest rates and even supply capital for local development. It included representatives of new industries, like communications and electronics [including Hollywood]. . . . It included representatives of business particularly dependent on consumer demand, like Sears Roebuck. And it included speculators like Joseph P. Kennedy, who invested in both new regions and new industries.[22]

The modern "Sunbelt" was largely born out of the political rewards of this Second New Deal coalition. Billions of dollars in federal aid (representing *net* tax transfers from the rest of the country) laid down an industrial infrastructure in California, Washington, and Texas. And nearly $110 million in major construction contracts—including the Bay Bridge, the naval base on Mare Island, and Bonneville, Grand Coulee, and Shasta dams—fueled the breakneck expansion of the Kaiser Company. Long before Pearl Harbor, Kaiser was already discussing with Giannini and a select group of Western industrialists (Donald Douglas, Stephen Bechtel, and John McCone) strategies for maximizing the role of local capital in a war economy. Recognizing that a Pacific war would make unprecedented demands on the under-industrialized California economy, Kaiser proposed to adapt Detroit's assembly-line methods to revolutionize the construction of merchant shipping. Although critics initially scoffed at the idea that a mere "sand and gravel man" could master the art of shipbuilding, Kaiser, with the support of his high-level New Deal connections, became the biggest shipbuilder in American history. In four years his giant Richmond, Portland, and Vancouver (Washington) yards launched a third of the American merchant navy (80 per cent of "Liberty Ships") as well as fifty "baby flat-top" aircraft carriers: nearly 1,500 vessels in all.[23]

In Richmond, where 747 ships were build, Kaiser was able to create a social and technological template for postwar capitalism. To simplify welding, huge deckhouses were assembled upside-down and then hoisted into place, helping reduce the traditional six-month shipbuilding cycle to a week. In the absence of a skilled labor force, Kaiser "trained something like three hundred thousand welders [at Richmond alone] out of soda jerks and housewives."[24] But his real genius was the systematic attention he focused on maintaining labor at high productivity with minimum time lost to sickness or turnover—the nightmares of other military contractors. Back in 1938, while trying to meet deadlines on the Grand Coulee, Kaiser experimented with transforming indirect medical costs into a direct, calculable industrial input by subscribing his workers to the pre-paid health plan pioneered by Dr. Sidney Garfield. This Permanente Health Plan—to be the most enduring part of the Kaiser legacy—was adapted with union collaboration to the massive Richmond workforce, together with active company intervention to construct war housing, organize recreation, and rationalize overloaded public transport (Kaiser imported cars from the old Sixth Avenue El in New York).[25]

But Kaiser's Richmond shipyards had a critical bottleneck: a persistent shortage of steel plate. An industrial colony of the East, the West Coast had always imported steel at high markups ($6–$20 per ton); now, in the midst of a superheated war economy, the Eastern mills could not supply, nor could the railroads transport, enough of this high-cost steel to meet the demands of Pacific shipyards. Although US Steel's Benjamin Fairless claimed that "abstract economic justice no more demands that the Pacific Coast have a great steel industry than that New York grow its own oranges,"[26] the war shortage prompted the corporation to propose a new integrated (ore to steel) mill on a Utah coalfield. Arguing, however, that the postwar Western market would not justify the extra capacity added by the mill, US Steel demanded that the Defense Production Corporation pay the cost of construction.

Kaiser countered with his own, characteristically audacious proposal to borrow the money from the government to build on his own account a tidewater steel complex in the Los Angeles area, using Boulder (Hoover) Dam power. From the outset this was treated by all sides as a Western declaration of independence from Big Steel, provoking rage in Pittsburgh in equal measure to the enthusiasm it generated in California. In any event, Washington tried to satisfy all sides by allowing US Steel to operate the government-built mill in Geneva, Utah, while loaning $110 million to Kaiser via the Reconstruction Finance Corporation.[27] The War Department, however, whether acting from post–Pearl Harbor hysteria or secretly lobbied by Big Steel (as Mezerik believed), insisted that the Kaiser facility had to be located at least fifty miles inland, "away from possible Japanese air attack."[28] This locational constraint was widely thought to preclude postwar conversion of the facility to competitive production. Rule-of-thumb wisdom held that an integrated complex could operate at a profit only if dependence on rail transport was confined to one "leg" of its logistical "tripod" of iron ore, coking coal, and steel product. A Southern California tidewater plant was accorded but a slim chance of survival in the postwar market; an inland location, dependent upon coal and iron rail shipments from hundreds of miles away, was considered an economic impossibility.[29]

But Kaiser believed that "problems were only opportunities with their work clothes on" and refused to be daunted. He calculated that radical economies in steel-making and mining technology, together with the vast promise of the postwar California market (drastically underestimated by Big Steel), would allow him to convert profitably to peacetime production. Accepting the War Department's disadvantageous conditions, he sent his engineers in search of a suitable inland location. They quickly fixed their sights on Fontana.

The De Luxe War Baby

From Pigs to Pig Iron!
Fontana Steel Will Build a New World!
Kaiser Slogans, 1940s [30]

In that Indian summer before Pearl Harbor, Fontana's destiny seemed fixed forever on hogs, eggs, and citrus. While locals debated the hot prospects in the annual "Hen Derby" or fretted over rising mortality on "Death Alley" (Valley Boulevard), Fontana Farms publicists were boasting that the 1940 Census "Proves Fontana, Top Agricultural Community in the United States!" [31] A. B. Miller, now in partnership with giant Swift and Company, waxed more powerful than ever in state agribusiness circles and conservative Inland Empire politics. Then, with chilling punctuality, death struck down Fontana's founders: Miller (April 1941), followed within months by leading businessman Charles Hoffman, water system founder William Stale, and Fontana Farms Citrus Director J. A. McGregor. [32]

With the passing of the pioneer generation, and the growing awareness that California would soon become the staging ground for a vast Pacific war, boosters in spring 1941 began a xenophobic promotion of Fontana as an ideal location for war industry. Miller's Fontana Farms successor, R. E. Boyle, joined local supervisor C. E. Grier and congressman Henry Sheppard in cajoling Fontanans into accepting that their "patriotic duty . . . based on real American principles" was to create the new "Partnership of Agriculture and [War] Industry." [33] But six months of aggressive advertising and patriotic bombast yielded not a single munitions plant or aircraft factory. Instead, the hysteria that followed Pearl Harbor, when Japanese aircraft were daily "sighted" over Long Beach and Hollywood, prompted a sudden rush for "safe," inland residences. In the early weeks of 1942 Fontana Farms was selling two ranches per day to anxious refugees from Los Angeles. [34] Even supervisor Grier, chief advocate of the military industrialization of the Inland Empire, was forced to admit that Fontana would contribute "in great measure to winning the war by the productivity of its poultry."[35] Then came the great bolt from Kaiser headquarters in Oakland.[36]

Prevented from building at tidewater, Kaiser was attracted to Fontana for two different reasons. On the one hand, his engineers and their military counterparts added up the ready-made advantages of Miller's infrastructural investments: cheap power from Lytle Creek (now augmented by Boulder Dam), excellent rail connections near two major railyards (San Bernardino and Colton), and, most important in a semi-desert, an autonomous, low-cost water supply.[37] The weak claims of local government over the unincorporated Fontana area were also considered an asset. San Bernardino was a "poor rural county" with an unusually large relief load, and Kaiser clearly preferred to deal with, and if necessary overawe and intimidate, its unsophisticated officials, desperate for any type of industrial investment, than face more powerful and self-confident public bureaucracies elsewhere.

On the other hand, Kaiser was personally captivated by Miller's utopia. As in Richmond, he placed social engineering on par with the priorities of production engineering, figuring that hens and citrus might mitigate the class struggle.

> He saw advantages to building in a rural community. Workers at the steel mill had the opportunity to raise chickens on the side or plant gardens. Kaiser believed these "hobby farms" created a more relaxed atmosphere and the workers would be more content. It was something that could not be found in the Eastern steel towns [and, therefore, a comparative advantage].[38]

On the first anniversary of A. B. Miller's interment, Kaiser broke ground on a former Miller ranch a few miles west of Fontana township, his bulldozers literally chasing the hogs away.[39] Under the supervision of veterans of Grand Coulee and Richmond, the construction shock-brigades made breathtaking progress. By 30 December 1942 the acrid smell of coke hung over the citrus groves, and, as local radio announcer Chet Huntley officiated, Mrs. Henry J. Kaiser threw the switch that fired the giant, 1,200-ton blast furnace named in her honor ("Big Bess"). An even more elaborate ceremony in May 1943 celebrated the tapping of the first steel. Surrounded by Hollywood stars and top military brass, Kaiser—with typical bravado—announced that Fontana was the beginning of the "Pacific Era" and "a great industrial empire for the West." Fleets of diesel trucks began the long shuttle of Fontana-made plate to the steel-hungry shipyards of Richmond and San Pedro.[40]

The vast, mile-square plant—Southern California's "de luxe war baby"[41]—seemed to erupt out of the earth before Fontanans had a chance to weigh the impact on their small rural society. Perhaps because of the rapidity of the transition, or because of patriotic consensus, there was no recorded protest against the plant construction. Kaiser spokesmen reassured residents that the plant "could be erected in the middle of an orange grove and operated continuously without the slightest damage to trees."[42] By the end of the first year, however, disturbing evidence to the contrary had become obvious. The coking coal first employed at Fontana had high sulfur content, producing acidic vapors that withered saplings and burnt the leaves off trees. Ranchers across from the mill picked grapefruit from their trees for the last time in the fall of 1942.[43] This was the beginning of the end of Miller's Eden, as well as the start of a regional pollution problem of major proportions.

While Fontanans were watching their trees die, Kaiser was shattering the illusion of starry-eyed San Bernardino County supervisors that the plant would be an enormous tax windfall. Assessed at normal rates in July 1943, the Company rejected the County's bill out of hand, warning that they "might be forced to close the plant." Although reporters scoffed at the obviously absurd threat to shutter the brand-new, $110 million mill, overawed supervisors obediently reduced the assessment to a small fraction of the original.[44] Their concession set a precedent that allowed Kaiser officials to protest any prospective tax increase as undercutting the economic viability of the plant. As a result, San Bernardino County saw its major potential tax resource evolve into a net tax liability (a fact that helps explain official apathy to the plant's closure a generation later).

As the experts had foreseen, the major difficulty in producing steel in Fontana was the organization of raw material supply. Kaiser could purchase limestone and dolomite flux from local quarries, but it had no alternative but to develop its own network of captive mines to source iron and coal. Although geologists reassured Kaiser that the nearby Mojave Desert contained enough iron ore within a three-hundred-mile radius to supply the plant for several centuries, exploitation of the richest deposits required costly investments in rail-laying and mining technology. Initially Fontana was supplied with ore from the Vulcan Mine near Kelso; after the war, the company developed the great Eagle Mountain complex in Riverside County with its own rail line and mining workforce of 500. Coking coal—the most difficult supply variable—had to be imported 800 miles from Price, Utah (in 1960 Kaiser Fontana switched to new mines in New Mexico). Overall, Fontana was refining low-cost iron ore with the nation's highest-cost coal, an equation that left its furnace costs well above other integrated mills (including US Steel's coalfield plant in Utah).[45]

Despite the burden of these supply costs, Kaiser by 1944 was making steel more efficiently than anyone had expected, to build ships in greater tonnage than anyone had dreamt possible. He was also smelting aluminum, assembling bombers, mixing concrete, even producing the incendiary "goop" with which the Army Air Corps was systematically immolating Tokyo and Osaka. At the pinnacle of his popularity, he was widely rumored to be Roosevelt's favorite choice for a fourth-term running-mate. Meanwhile, his alliance with the New Deal had catapulted the Kaiser companies to the top ranks of privately owned firms, and, unlike the California aircraft industry, his operations were totally independent of Wall Street and Eastern banks. (When he was not borrowing government money, his old ally Giannini made available the Bank of America's largest single line of credit.)[46] Buoyed by the successes of his shipyards and steel and aluminum mills, Kaiser surveyed a bold, coordinated expansion into postwar markets for medical care, appliances, housing, aircraft, and automobiles. In his wartime speeches, Kaiser was fond of adding a fifth "freedom" to Roosevelt's original four: "the freedom of abundance."[47]

He recognized, with singular prescience, that the conjuncture of rising union power (which he supported) and wartime productivity advances was finally going to unleash the mass consumer revolution that the New Deal had long promised. He also calculated that the pent-up demand for housing and cars, fueled by the fantastic volume of wartime forced savings, created an explosive market situation in which independent entrepreneurs like himself might find the opportunity of the century to compete with the Fortune 500. Everything depended on the speed of reconversion/retooling and the ability to offer the kind of streamlined products that Americans had been dreaming about since the 1939 New York World's Fair.

With characteristic hubris, Henry J. attempted to expand into all markets simultaneously. His venture into experimental aviation was short-lived, when he abandoned to the obsessive Howard Hughes the further development of their prototype super-transport, the notorious "Spruce Goose."[48] In the field of mass-produced housing, on the other hand, Kaiser had substantial success. For two decades he had been building homes for his dam and shipyard workers, even master-planning entire communities. He had also been discussing the national housing crisis with such seminal thinkers as Norman Bel Geddes, the designer of the famous Futurama exhibit at the 1939 World's Fair. Shortly after V-J Day Kaiser dramatically announced a "housing revolution": "America's answer to the so-called accomplishments of Communists and Fascists." Creating "a nearly 100 mile plant-to-site assembly line" in Southern California (where he predicted that immigration would reach a million per year in the immediate postwar period), he launched construction of ten thousand prefabricated homes in the Westchester, North Hollywood, and Panorama City areas. Defying an acute shortage of ordinary building materiel, Kaiser engineers innovated with fiberglass board, steel, aluminum siding, and sheet gypsum, while "applying Richmond methods" to train armies of construction workers whom Kaiser promptly unionized.[49]

But Kaiser Homes, however important in demonstrating the feasibility of postwar "merchant homebuilding," were only a sideshow for their master. Henry J.'s real ambition was to challenge the Eastern corporate establishment on its own turf. Unfortunately, he chose to fight Detroit and Pittsburgh at the same time. "Tilting at the most dangerous and dramatic of American windmills,"[50] he launched Kaiser-Frazer Motors in a giant reconverted bomber plant in Willow Run, Michigan. Simultaneously, he brought Fontana steel into direct competition with Big Steel for control of Western markets.

Only one capitalist from the West had ever attempted such a brazen invasion of the East: Giannini in the late 1920s. For the impudence of staking a seat on Wall Street, Giannini was temporarily deposed in his own house, as J. P. Morgan mounted a retaliatory raid on Transamerica, the Giannini bank holding company.[51] (As a Morgan director told Giannini: "Right or wrong, you do as you're told down here.")[52] It was poetic justice, therefore, that Giannini was allied to Kaiser's postwar schemes, introducing him to Joseph Frazer, the rebel Detroit capitalist, as well as supporting the campaign to refinance Fontana steel.

The "debacle" of Kaiser-Frazer has been recently retold in Mark Foster's scholarly biography of Henry J. Fearing postwar layoffs as well as an anti-union backlash by the major automakers, the United Auto Workers had begged Kaiser to convert the Willow Run assembly lines (scheduled for closure after V-J Day) to auto production. Teamed up with Frazer, the former head of Willys-Overland, and cheered on by the unions, Kaiser and his engineers tried to duplicate the miracle of Richmond. Within a year of taking over Willow Run, they had built 100,000 cars and recruited an impressive national network of dealerships. The 1947 Kaiser-Frazer shock wave rattled nerves in the executive suites of Dearborn Park and the Chrysler Building. But, endemically undercapitalized in the face of the auto majors' billion-dollar plant expansions and model changes, the new company sank deep into the red. In the meantime Giannini had died, Wall Street had boycotted Kaiser's offerings, and Frazer had resigned. After the failure of a last-ditch remodeling in 1954–55, Willow Run was sold off to

General Motors and the dies were shipped to South America, where Kaiser-body cars were still being assembled as late as the 1970s. Although Kaiser continued for another decade to build Jeeps at his Willys-Overland subsidiary in Toledo, the Western invasion of Detroit was over.[53]

Fontana, by contrast, was an untrammeled success, despite bitter opposition from Big Steel and financial problems comparable to Kaiser-Frazer's. In the immediate reconversion period of steel shortages and turbulent industrial relations (1945–46), Kaiser's friendship with the CIO exempted Fontana from the bitter national steel strike. Expanding into new product markets, especially construction, Kaiser Steel strained at capacity during the steel drought, even briefly exporting to Europe. But, once the steel strike was settled and capacity had begun to adjust to demand, Fontana's inherent logistical and financial problems seemed to signal doom.[54]

Fortunately, Kaiser metallurgists produced the kind of technical breakthrough at Fontana that eluded the design teams at Willow Run. Just as Henry J. had brashly promised, his engineers offset their high coal costs by radically reducing coke loads and increasing blast furnace efficiency. Similarly at Eagle Mountain, Kaiser mining engineers pioneered new economies in ore extraction, reducing their iron costs even further below Eastern averages. By the mid 1950s Fontana was an international benchmark of advanced steelmaking, keenly studied by steelmasters from Japan and other high raw-material-cost countries.[55]

A more intractable problem was repaying the Reconstruction Finance Corporation (RFC) loan that had built Fontana. With Congress recaptured by the Republicans in 1946, and his New Deal allies leaving the Truman Administration in droves, Kaiser was politically isolated. Under fire in Congress for alleged profiteering on his wartime shipbuilding contracts (a calumny, he charged, that was spread by his Eastern corporate enemies), he was unable to persuade the RFC to discount or refinance any of his 1942 loan. Despite liberal support (the *New Republic* denounced the RFC for betraying the West's "attempts to build its own steel mills and free itself from control by the East"), and innumerable resolutions from chambers of commerce, Kaiser had exhausted his political IOUs. To rub salt in his wounds, the War Assets Administration auctioned the Geneva, Utah, mill to US Steel (the *lowest* bidder) for a mere twenty-five cents on the dollar of its cost.[56]

If steel demand had softened at this precarious point, Fontana might have floundered. Instead a big transcontinental gas pipeline deal provided

Kaiser Steel with invaluable collateral, while the sudden outbreak of the Korean War revived the West Coast shipbuilding industry. Following the advice of the Giannini family (who also extended Fontana's credit), Kaiser made his steel operations public. The Los Angeles business elite, led by *Times* heir Norman Chandler (who became a Kaiser Steel director) and old friend John McCone, rallied to the initial stock offering, allowing Henry J. to retire the RFC loan in 1950.[57]

With increased access to private capital, and with a Southern California market booming beyond all expectations, Kaiser Steel expanded and diversified. Two postwar expansions added a second blast furnace as well as new tinplate, strip, and pipe mills; a revolutionary pellatizing plant was installed at Eagle Mountain; and in 1959 Governor Brown joined Henry J. for the dedication of a state-of-the-art basic oxygen furnace. With a workforce of eight thousand, and plans on the drawing board for doubling capacity, Kaiser Steel was a national midget, but a regional giant. In 1962, in a move that "was a big step in the direction of eliminating that historic phrase 'prices slightly higher west of the Rockies,'" Kaiser Steel sharply reduced its prices. Eastern steel was virtually driven from the market, leaving Fontana, together with US Steel at Geneva, to co-monopolize the Pacific Slope.[58]

Equally reassuring, Kaiser Steel seemed to continue in the forefront of enlightened industrial relations. Although, unlike in 1946, Fontana was closed down during the long 1959 steel strike, it broke ranks with Big Steel to embrace the United Steel Workers' proposals for a gains-sharing plan to integrate technological change into the collective bargaining framework. First a tripartite committee, with a public member, was established to study conflicts between local work rules and the introduction of automation. Then in 1963 the company and union, with considerable ceremony, formalized the landmark Long Range Sharing Plan (loosely based on the so-called "Scanlon plan"), whose complex formulae and provisions were supposed to fairly compensate workers for accepting rapid productivity advance. The Plan, whose original backers had included the elite of academic industrial relations specialists and two future Secretaries of Labor (Goldberg and Dunlop), became the Kennedy Administration's prototype for New Frontier—era collective bargaining and was soon cited as such in every industrial relations textbook.[59]

This was the golden age of Kaiser Steel, Fontana—flagship of the West's postwar smokestack economy. Neither the captain on the deck nor the crew below could see the economic icebergs ahead.

Holocaust in Fontana

Whites from the South compose the majority of the population of
Fontana. They have brought to that community their backward
community mores, their hate-mongering religious cults . . .

O'Day Short, murdered by Fontana vigilantes, 1946[60]

For hundreds of Dustbowl refugees from the Southwest, still working in
the orchards at the beginning of World War Two, Kaiser Steel was the
happy ending to the Grapes of Wrath. Construction of the mill drained the
San Bernardino Valley of workers, creating an agricultural labor shortage
that was not relieved until the coming of the *braceros* in 1943. Kaiser originally believed that he could apply his Richmond methods to shaping the
Fontana workforce: leaving the construction crews in place and "training
them in ten days to make steel" under the guidance of experts hired from
the East. But he underestimated the craft knowledge and folklore, communicated only through hereditary communities of steelworkers, that were
essential to making steel. Urgent appeals, therefore, were circulated through
the steel valleys of Pennsylvania, Ohio, and West Virginia, recruiting draft-
exempt steel specialists for Fontana.[61]

The impact of five thousand steelworkers and their families on local
rusticity was predictably shattering. The available housing stock in Fontana and western San Bernardino County (also coveted by incoming military families) was quickly saturated. With few zoning ordinances to control
the anarchy, temporary and substandard shelters of every kind sprouted
up in Fontana and neighboring districts like Rialto, Bloomington, and Cucamonga. Most of the original blast furnace crew was housed in a gerry-
built trailer park known affectionately as "Kaiserville." Later arrivals were
often forced to live out of their cars. The old Fontana Farms colonists came
under great pressure to sell to developers and speculators. Others converted their chicken coops to shacks and rented them to single workers—a
primitive housing form that was still common through the 1950s.[62]

Although areas of Fontana retained their Millerian charm, especially
the redtiled village center along Sierra with its art-deco theater and prosperous stores, boisterous, often rowdy, juke joints and roadhouses created
a different ambience along Arrow Highway and Foothill Boulevard.
Neighboring Rialto—presumably the location of Eddie Mars's casino in
Chandler's *The Big Sleep*—acquired a notorious reputation as a wide-open
gambling center and L.A. mob hangout (a reputation which it has recovered in the 1990s as the capital of the Inland Empire's crack gangs). Meanwhile the ceaseless truck traffic from the mill, together with the town's

adjacency to Route 66 (and, today, to Interstates 10 and 15), made Fontana a major regional trucking center, with bustling twenty-four-hour fuel stops and cafes on its outskirts.[63]

Boomtown Fontana of the 1940s ceased to be a coherent community or cultural fabric. Instead it was a colorful but dissonant *bricolage* of Sunkist growers, Slovene chicken ranchers, gamblers, mobsters, over-the-road truckers, industrialized Okies, *braceros*, the Army Air Corps (at nearby bases), and transplanted steelworkers and their families. It was also a racial frontier where Black families tried to stake out their own modest claims to a ranch home or a job in the mill. Although, as the war in the Pacific was ending, there was an optimistic aura of sunshine and prosperity in the western San Bernardino Valley, there were also increasing undertones of bigotry and racial hysteria. Finally, just before Christmas eve 1945, there was atrocity. The brutal murder (and its subsequent official cover-up) of O'Day Short, his wife, and two small children indelibly stamped Fontana— at least in the eyes of Black Californians—as being violently below the Mason-Dixon line.

Ironically Fontana had been one of the few locations in the Citrus Belt where Blacks had been allowed to establish communities. Every week during the 1940s, the *Eagle*—Los Angeles's progressive Black paper—carried prominent ads for "sunny, fruitful lots in the Fontana area."[64] For pent-up residents of the overcrowded Central Avenue ghetto, prevented by restrictive covenants ("L.A. Jim Crow") from moving into suburban areas like the San Fernando Valley, Fontana must have been alluring. Moreover, Kaiser's Richmond shipyards were the biggest employer of Black labor on the coast, and there was widespread hope that his new steel plant would be an equally color-blind employer. The reality in Fontana was that Blacks were segregated in their own tracts—a kind of citrus ghetto—on the rocky floodplain above Baseline Avenue in vaguely delineated "north Fontana." Meanwhile in the mill, Blacks and Chicanos were confined to the dirtiest departments—coke ovens and blast furnaces (a situation unchanged until the early 1970s).

O'Day Short, already well known in Los Angeles as a civil rights activist, was the first to challenge Fontana's residential segregation by buying land in town (on Randall Street) in fall 1945. Short's move coincided with the Ku Klux Klan's resurgence throughout Southern California, as white supremacists mobilized to confront militant returning Black and Chicano servicemen. In early December, Short was visited by "vigilantes," probably Klansmen, who ordered him to move or risk harm to his family. Short stood his ground, reporting the threats to the FBI and the county sheriff, as well as alerting the Black press in Los Angeles. Instead of providing protection, sheriff's deputies warned Short to leave before any "disagreeableness" happened to his family. The Fontana Chamber of Commerce, anxious to keep Blacks above Baseline, offered to buy Short out. He refused.[65]

A few days later, on 16 December, the Short house was consumed in an inferno of "unusual intensity." Neighbors reported hearing an explosion, then seeing "blobs of fire" on the ground and the family running from their home with clothes ablaze. Short's wife and small children died almost immediately; unaware of their deaths, he lingered on for two weeks in agony. According to one account, Short finally died after being brutally informed by the district attorney of his family's fate. (The D.A. was later criticized for breaking the hospital's policy of shielding Short from further trauma.)[66]

The local press gave the tragedy unusually low-key coverage, quoting the D.A.'s opinion that the fire was an accident.[67] That a coroner's inquest was held at all (on 3 April 1945) was apparently due to pressure from the NAACP and the Black press. "Contrary to standard practice in such cases," District Attorney Jerome Kavanaugh refused to allow witnesses to testify about the vigilante threats to the Short family. Instead Kavanaugh read into the record the interview he had conducted with Short in the hospital, "in which the sick man repeatedly said he was too ill and upset to make a statement, but yielded to steady pressure and suggestion by finally saying that the fire seemed accidental 'as far as he was concerned.'" Fontana fire officials, conceding they had no actual evidence, speculated that the holocaust might have been the result of a kerosene-lamp explosion. The coroner's jury, deprived of background about the vigilante threats, accordingly ruled that the Shorts had died from "a fire of unknown origin." The sheriff declined an arson investigation.[68]

The Black community in Fontana—many of whom "themselves had been admonished by deputy sheriff 'Tex' Carlson to advise the Shorts to get out"—was "unanimous in rejecting the 'accident' theory." Fontana's most famous Black resident, Shelton Brooks (composer of the *Darktown Strutter's Ball*), demanded a full-scale arson investigation. J. Robert Smith, crusading publisher of the *Tri-County Bulletin,* the Black paper serving the Inland Empire, decried an official cover-up of "mass murder"—a charge echoed by Short's friends Joseph and Charlotta Bass, publishers of the Los Angeles *Eagle.*[69]

The case became a brief national *cause célèbre* after the Los Angeles NAACP, led by Lorenzo Bowdoin, hired renowned arson expert Paul T.

Wolfe to sift through the evidence. Noting that the supposed cause of the fire, the kerosene lamp, had actually been recovered intact, he found compelling evidence that the Short home had been deliberately soaked in quantities of coal oil to produce an explosive blaze of maximum ferocity. He concluded that "beyond a shadow of a doubt the fire was of an incendiary origin." In the meantime, the *Tri-County Bulletin* discovered that the original sheriff's report on the fire had "mysteriously" disappeared from its file, while the *Eagle* raised fundamental doubts about Short's purported testimony to D.A. Kavanaugh. Mass demonstrations were held in San Bernardino and Los Angeles, as scores of trade-union locals, progressive Jewish organizations, and civil rights groups endorsed the NAACP's call for a special investigation of "lynch terror in Fontana" by California's liberal attorney general Robert Kenny (another Gunther favorite). Catholic Interracial Council leader Dan Marshall pointed out that "murder is the logical result of discrimination," while Communist leader Pettis Perry described the Short case as "the most disgraceful that has ever occurred in California."[70]

But it was hard to keep the Short holocaust in focus. Attorney General Kenny succeeded in temporarily banning the Ku Klux Klan in California, but made no attempt to reopen the investigation into the Short case or expose the official whitewash by San Bernardino officials. The Los Angeles NAACP, spearhead of the campaign, quickly became preoccupied with the renewed struggle against housing discrimination in Southcentral Los Angeles.[71] The Trotskyist Socialist Workers' Party continued its own sectarian campaign through the spring of 1946, but used the Short case primarily to polemicize against Kenny (Democratic nominee for governor) and his Communist supporters.[72] In the end, as protest faded, the vigilantes won the day: Blacks stayed north of Baseline (and in the coke ovens) for another generation, and the fate of the Short family, likely victims of white supremacy, was officially forgotten.[73]

However, early postwar Fontana found it difficult to avoid notoriety. If the press downplayed the Short case, it sensationalized the murder trial of Gwendelyn Wallis—a local policeman's wife who confessed to shooting her husband's mistress, a pretty young Fontana schoolteacher named Ruby Clark. At a time when countless Hollywood films in the Joan Crawford vein were beginning to sermonize against wartime morals and gender equality, the Wallis trial became a lightning rod for contending values. Girls argued with their mothers, husbands fought with wives, marriages reportedly even broke up over Gwendelyn's justification for killing Ruby: that she was a "scheming, single, working woman." Her surprise acquittal in March 1946 was greeted across the country with both anger and cele-bration. At the courthouse in San Bernardino she was "mobbed by sympa-thetic women"—mostly long-suffering housewives like herself, who had become her adoring fans in the course of this real-life soap opera.[74]

Finally, to permanently reinforce the new Fontana's wild image, 1946 was also the year that the original nucleus of the Hell's Angels began to coalesce in the area. According to legend, the founders were demobbed bomber crewmen, right out of the pages of Heller's *Catch-22*, who re-jected the return to staid civilian lives. Whatever the true story, members of the Fontana-based gang were surely participants in the infamous Hol-lister (July 1947) and Riverside (July 1948) motorcycle riots that were im-mortalized by Brando in *The Wild One* ("the bike rider's answer to the *Sun Also Rises*").[75] When the beleaguered American Motorcycle Associa-tion denounced an "outlaw one per cent," the proto-Angels made that label their badge of honor. At a "One-Percenters" convention in Fontana in 1950 the Hell's Angels were formally organized; the "Fontana-Berdoo" chap-ter became the "mother" chapter with exclusive authority to charter new branches. The founding philosophy of the group was succinctly ex-plained by a Fontana member: "We're bastards to the world, and they're bastards to us."

Although "Berdoo" continued through the 1960s as the nominal capital of outlaw motorcycledom, power within the Angels shifted increasingly toward the ultra-violent Oakland chapter led by Sonny Barger, who also launched the group into big-time narcotics dealing.[76] As Hunter Thomp-son put it, "the Berdoo Angels made the classic Dick Nixon mistake of 'peaking' too early." There are two different versions of the story of their decline. According to "Freewheelin' Frank," the acidhead Nazi secre-tary of the San Francisco chapter, "Berdoo" was ruined by the seduction of the movie industry and a lawyer-huckster named Jeremiah Castelman, who convinced them that they would become rich selling Hell's Angels T-shirts.[77]

In the other version of the story, they were driven off the streets by po-lice repression. After the lurid publicity of a rape and two violent brawls, the Berdoo Angels became the *bête noire* of LAPD Chief William Parker, who organized a posse of law enforcement agencies to crush the chapter. Establishing police checkpoints on favorite motorcycle itineraries like the Pacific Coast Highway and the Ridge Route, he generated "such relentless heat that those few who insisted on wearing the colors [Angel jackets] were forced to act more like refugees than outlaws, and the chapter's rep-utation withered accordingly." By 1964, when Thompson was slumming with the Oakland chapter, Fontana—"heartland of the Berdoo chapter's turf"—had been essentially pacified. Local Angels "couldn't even muster a quorum" for an outlaw motorcycle scene in a Sal Mineo movie: "some were in jail, others had quit and many of the best specimens had gone north to Oakland."[78] Despite its eclipse, however, the Berdoo chapter never collapsed. A generation after Thompson's account, mother Angels are still bunkered in their Fontana redoubt, raising enough hell to force the cancellation of a major motorcycle show in Downtown Los Angeles (in February 1990) after a violent collision with another gang.[79]

Milltown Days

For Abel to win the nomination at Fontana, the public relations pivot of the McDonald administration, would be a definite psychological victory.

John Herling[80]

After the turbulent, sometimes violent, transitions of the 1940s, Fontana settled down into the routines of a young milltown. The Korean War boom enlarged the Kaiser workforce by almost 50 per cent and stimulated a new immigration from the East that reinforced the social weight of traditional steelworker families. The company devoted new resources to organizing the leisure time of its employees, while the union took a more active role in the community. The complex craft subcultures of the plant intersected with ethnic self-organization to generate competing cliques and differential pathways for mobility. At the same time, the familiar sociology of plant-community interaction was overlaid by lifestyles peculiar to Fontana's Millerian heritage and its location on the borders of metropolitan Los Angeles and the Mojave Desert. Although locals continued to joke that Fontana was just Aliquippa with sunshine, it was evolving into a *sui generis* working-class community.

This is not to deny that there was a lot of Aliquippa (or Johnstown or East Pittsburgh) in Fontana. Mon Valley immigrants ended up as the dominant force in United Steel Workers Local 2869. Dino Papavero, for instance, who was president of the local in the early 1970s, moved out from Aliquippa in 1946 because his father was worried about a postwar slump at Jones and Laughlin. It was widely believed amongst Pennsylvania steelworkers that Kaiser, in booming California, was recession-proof. John Piazza—Papavero's vice-president and current leader of the Fontana School Board—first came to San Bernardino County (from Johnstown, PA) as one of Patton's "tank jockeys" training for the Sahara in the Mojave. While hitchhiking Route 66 to the Hollywood USO he was intrigued by a billboard boasting of the opening of Kaiser Steel. After the war, he found himself trapped in an apparently hopeless cycle of layoffs and rehiring at Bethlehem which seemed to preclude any advancement up the seniority ladder. Together with other Johnstowners, he headed out to Fontana—initially living in one of the converted chicken coops—because Kaiser advertised itself as a frontier of opportunity for younger workers.[81]

These young Mon Valley immigrants quickly discovered that mobility within the plant or union in Fontana, as in Aliquippa or Johnstown, depended upon the mobilization of ethnic and work-group loyalties. The oldest and most visible of local ethnicities were the Slovenes. Their community core—a group of Ohio coal miners who had amassed small savings—had come to Fontana in the 1920s as chicken ranchers, establishing a prosperous branch of the Slovene National Benevolent Society, a large meeting hall and retirement home. Some of their children worked in the mill. Although only informally organized, the "Roadrunners" from West Virginia and the Okies constituted distinctive subcultures within both the plant and the community. But it was the local Sons of Italy chapter—attracting streetwise and ambitious young steelworkers like Papavero and Piazza—that ultimately generated a whole cadre of union leaders during the 1960s and 1970s.

Although the Southern California District of the USW in the 1950s and early 1960s, under Director Charles Smith and his henchman Billy Brunton, was a loyalist stronghold of international president Donald McDonald, Local 2869 with its Mon Valley transplants became a hotbed of discontent. Many Kaiser workers resented Smith's and Brunton's proconsular powers and ability to bargain over their heads in a situation where Local 2869 was far and away the largest unit in the District. In 1957 the rank and file dramatically registered their dissent by electing Tom Flaherty, local spokesman for the national anti-McDonald movement (the Dues Protest Committee), as president of 2869. After several wildcat strikes, the Kaiser management demanded that McDonald intervene to force the local "to discharge its contractual obligations." Obligingly the international imposed an "administratorship" on 2869 and deposed Flaherty and his followers.[82]

Although "law and order" were now officially restored within Fontana by the international's police action, the opposition was simply driven underground. By 1963–64 the older dues protesters (led by Joe and Minnie Luksich) had been joined by younger workers embittered by the wage inequalities generated by the new "fruits of progress" plan. To rub salt in rank-and-file wounds, the Committee of Nine who administered the plan virtually ignored Local 2869 and Fontana, preferring to conduct their deliberations in the more congenial setting of a Palm Springs resort. As a result, "the situation deteriorated so badly in the summer of 1964 that the members picketed the union hall. Their signs read: 'USWA Unfair to Organized Labor' and 'Equal Pay for Equal Work.'" At this point, Ronald Bitoni, former chairman of the plant grievance committee, began to unify the different opposition factions around the national insurgency of I. W. Abel, a dissident official supported by Walter Reuther. In his history of the successful Abel campaign, John Herling described Fontana as both the "gem of McDonald's achievement in labor-management cooperation" and the Achilles heel of his power in the West. On election day, 9 February 1965, tens of thousands of pro-Abel steelworkers in the oppositional heartland of the Ohio and Monogahela valleys nervously watched to see how Fontana, two thousand miles away, would vote. Abel's commanding 2,782 to 1,965 victory within Local 2869 announced the end of the *ancien régime*.[83] But at the same time it warned of profound rank-and-file discontent with the "textbook" gains-sharing model. Within a few years many Kaiser unionists would be as alienated from the "reformist" administration of Abel as they had been from the absolutism of McDonald.

While Local 2869 was fighting to increase local control over the gains-sharing plan, the relationship between the company and the town was evolving in a very curious way. Despite the stereotype of being a Kaiser "company town," Fontana was no such thing. When Fontana incorporated in 1952, the mill was left outside the city limits in its own, low-tax "county island." Not contributing directly to the town's budget, Kaiser lacked the despotic fiscal clout that Eastern steelmakers conventionally exercised over their captive local governments. Nor did a majority of Kaiser management ever live in the Fontana area. Unlike Bethlehem or Johnstown, no corporate suburb or country-club district projected the social and political power of management into the community. Managers, instead, commuted from genteel redtile towns like Redlands, Riverside, and Ontario. The dominating presence in Fontana was, rather, the huge union hall on Sierra. Local merchants and professionals were left in relatively unmediated dependence upon the goodwill of their blue-collar customers and neighbors. Although never directly controlled by labor, Fontana government, as a result, tended to remain on the friendly side of the union.

Yet while eschewing direct control, the Company still played a ubiquitous role in communal life. The location of the mill, far from big city lights, stimulated the organization of leisure time around the workplace.

Kaiser's 1950s–60s personnel director, Vernon Peake, managed one of the most extensive corporate recreation programs west of the Mississippi. The internal structure of plant society was vividly reproduced in the composition of Kaiser's six bowling leagues during the kegling craze of the 1950s. While Hot Metal battled Cold Roll in the no-nonsense Steelers League, white-collar Bulb Snatchers traded spares with Pencil Pushers in the Fontana League, and Slick Chicks edged Pinettes in the Girls' (*sic*) League. Like other steel towns, Fontana prided itself on Friday night "smokers," and there were usually half a dozen pros and scores of amateurs training in the mill's boxing club. "Roadrunners" and Okies were especially active in the plant's various hunting and gun clubs, while others joined the popular fishing club.[84]

But blue-collar Fontana also enjoyed recreations that were usually management prerogatives in the more rigid caste order of Eastern steel towns. Golf was popular in some production departments, and leading union activists were frequently seen on the fairways. Other steelworkers took up tennis, joined the toastmasters, became rockhounds, rehearsed with the excellent local drama society, or even moonlighted as stuntmen in Hollywood. Others raced stockcars, dragsters, and motorcycles, or simply spent weekends plowing up the Mojave in their dune buggies.[85] Whatever the avocation, the point was that Fontana tended to see itself differently—as more egalitarian and openminded (at least for white workers)—than the steel cultures left behind in the valleys of the Ohio.

Drivin' Big Bess Down

The Fontana plant has the potential to be competitive with any in the world. (1980)
You can't melt steel in the middle of a residential valley profitably. (1981)

Elliot Schneider, steel industry "expert"[86]

Like every decline and fall, Kaiser Steel's was an accumulation of ironies. One was that the future began to slip away from Fontana not in the midst of a recession, but at the height of the Vietnam boom. Kaiser was forced out of a rapidly expanding market. Another irony was that, although Kaiser executives in the last days would complain bitterly that Washington had abandoned them in the face of Japanese competition, the company had collaborated avidly with that very same competition in a vain attempt to restructure itself as a steel resource supplier. Kaiser was literally hoisted on its own corporate petard.

After firing up its first Basic Oxygen Furnace (BOF) in 1959, Kaiser

Steel neglected plant modernization for almost fifteen years. Having wrested the West from Pittsburgh, it ceased looking over its shoulder at the competition. In the meantime Asian and European steelmakers were rapidly moving ahead with a technological revolution that included full conversion to BOF and the introduction of continuous casting. Kaiser fought the Japanese, its erstwhile protégés and main competitors (whose original plants Kaiser-made "goop" had incinerated in 1945), with Pearl-Harbor era technology that included obsolete open-hearth furnaces, old-fashioned slab casting, thirty-five-year-old blast furnaces, and dinosaur, over-polluting coke ovens. Although Kaiser protested that the Japanese steel industry enjoyed "unfair" state subsidies, this hardly explains why its own investment program (the company was in the black until 1969) failed to sustain technological modernization. If Kaiser Steel squandered its once formidable technical leadership, it was because, unlike the more single-minded Japanese, it purposely diverted its cashflow into alternative accumulation strategies.

In truth, Fontana and the other fifty-odd Kaiser enterprises were an unwieldy legacy. After Henry J.'s retirement to Hawaii in the mid 1950s, Kaiser Industries evolved as a family holding company with decreasing hands-on affinity for the world of production. Orthodox financial management, not heroic technical problem-solving, became the order of the day. From this basically rentier perspective, Kaiser Aluminum, with its consistently high profit margins, became the family's darling. Kaiser Industries' long-range planning focused on how to complement aluminum sales to the Pacific Basin with other primary product exports. When, in the early 1960s, the Japanese demand for steel began to soar (as a result of the first stages of a "Fordist," home-market-led expansion), Kaiser Industries (the major shareholder in Kaiser Steel) was more concerned about sourcing this demand with raw materials than with the future implications of expanded Japanese capacity for international competition. Specifically for Kaiser Steel this entailed a fateful diversion of its plant modernization budget to purchase export-oriented iron ranges in Australia and coal mines in British Columbia. Eagle Mountain was also expensively remodeled, with an elaborate pellatizing plant added to process iron ore for export to Japan. Thus, years before US Steel's notorious acquisition of Marathon Oil with funds coerced from its basic steel workforce in the name of "modernization," Kaiser Steel was restructuring itself, with diverted capital improvements, to export resources to its principal competitor, while allowing its own industrial plant to become obsolete.[87]

The Vietnam War—which jump-started the Japanese export offensive—dramatically transformed economic relationships around the Pacific Rim. In 1965 Japanese steel imports claimed a tenth of the US West Coast market; by the war's end, a decade later, nearly half the steel in California was Asian-made and the state was officially included in the Japanese steel industry's definition of "home market." Kaiser Steel made large profits exporting iron and coal to the Japanese only to see these raw materials shot back at them in the form of Toyotas and I-beams for skyscrapers. Together with US Steel's Geneva mill (still entirely open-hearth, since USS's plant modernization had been concentrated in the East), Kaiser Fontana could supply barely half of Western demand, and they were constrained from adding capacity because of their technological inability to compete at cost with the foreign steel. Thus the Japanese, and increasingly the Koreans and the Europeans as well, were able to confiscate all the Vietnam-boom growth in Western steel demand. The so-called "trigger price mechanism," adopted by the Carter Administration at Big Steel's urging, only worsened the situation on the West Coast. Trigger prices were too low to prevent Japanese imports and, because they were calibrated higher in the East, they actually encouraged EEC producers to dump steel in California.[88]

In the meantime Kaiser's vaunted labor peace was beginning to erode. Over the years relations between workers and managers had calcified at the shop level—a situation that was exacerbated by the recruitment of truculent managers from Big Steel during the 1970s. At the same time the incredibly complex formulae of the Long Range Sharing Plan continued to generate pay inequalities that had already sparked protest in 1964–65. Workers retaining membership in the older incentive scheme were winning pay increases at a dramatically higher rate than participants in the general savings scheme (a trend which also aggravated inter-generational tension within the union). Likewise LRSP remuneration seemed arbitrarily detached from individual productivity efforts.[89]

Faced with a new wave of rank-and-file discontent, the recently elected president of Local 2869, Dino Papavero, called a strike vote in February 1972. The resulting 43-day walkout was the first "local issues" strike—apart from the two 1957 wildcats—in the plant's history. Papavero, who clearly visualized the import threat, hoped that the strike would be a safety-valve, releasing accumulating tensions and paving the way for a new labor-management detente. With the encouragement of the company, he launched a plant-wide "quality circle" movement in a last-ditch effort to raise productivity to competitive levels. Although workers cooperated in hundreds

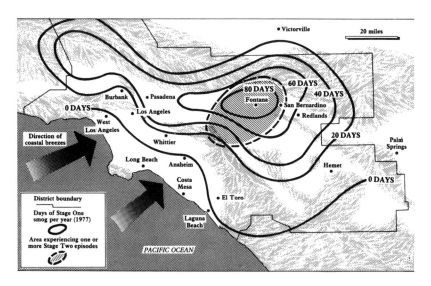

FONTANA, CAPITAL OF THE SMOG BELT

of improvements, management appeared to go along for a free ride, refusing to implement the broad capital modernization program that was necessary to save the plant. Moreover there was the traditional dissonance between Local 2869's priorities and the international's goals. USW Regional Director George White—as always, concerned about the impact of Kaiser innovations upon Big Steel—opposed the work-rule-weakening precedent of the quality circles. He was supported, moreover, by Fontana rank-and-filers embittered by the long walkout and fearful of the loss of hardwon seniority rights and clearcut job boundaries. In 1976 Papavero, the main advocate of cooperativism in the historic spirit of the LRSP, was defeated by a more confrontationist slate.[90]

The year 1976 was indeed one of bad omens. Steel profits had entirely collapsed, and Kaiser Steel's net earnings were exclusively sustained by profits from resource exports. The long delayed modernization program, aiming at full conversion to BOF and continuous casting, was finally launched, only to immediately encounter complaints about the plant's role as chief regional polluter. Since the 1960s Fontana had emerged as the literal epicenter of air pollution in Southern California, and Kaiser Steel's huge plume of acrid smoke became indissolubly linked in the public mind with the smog crisis in the Inland Empire.[91] (See map.)

The actual situation was considerably more complex: aerial photographs taken by Kaiser during the 1972 strike, when the plant was entirely shut down, showed no abatement in air pollution.[92] Moreover many ex-steelworkers still vehemently believe that the Kaiser pollution scare was purposely manufactured by developers who regarded the plant—smog-spewing or not—as a huge negative externality to residential construction in the Cucamonga-Fontana area. As San Bernardino County's West End fell under the "urban shadow" of Los Angeles and Orange County, developable property values came into increasing conflict with the paycheck role of the mill as leading local employer. Inevitably the pollution debate reflected these divergent material interests. While developers became strange bed-partners with environmentalists in demanding a huge cleanup at Fontana, the Kaiser workforce joined with its management to protest the costs of abatement. As one ex-steelworker put it, "Hell, that smoke was our prosperity."[93]

In any event, Kaiser was forced to sign a consent decree with the Southern California Air Pollution Control Board that mandated $127 million for pollution reduction. This was more than half of the modernization budget.[94] Partly as a result—from 1975 to 1979 while "modernization" was being implemented—the union was forced to accept painful triage. Capacity was ruthlessly pared as older facilities were scrapped, including the open hearth, the cold weld, pipe and cold roll mills, and, finally, the original BOF. The inefficient and polluting coke ovens, on the other hand, were deemed too expensive to replace and were left intact. Fontana, in quiet anguish, began to bleed away its future. Four thousand younger workers—sons, brothers, and a few daughters—were laid off by seniority. With the company reassuring them that the new technology would restore price competitiveness, Local 2869 accepted partial decimation as a necessary sacrifice to save the plant and the community of steelworkers.[95]

When, at last, the new Kaiser Steel chief, Mark Anthony, launched the modernized facilities in an elaborate ceremony on 9 February 1979, he proclaimed the company's "rededication to making steel in the West."[96] But the new technology—including BOF 2, the continuous caster, and state-of-the-art emission controls—proved cruelly disappointing. Startup costs were staggeringly over budget, and pollution from the antiquated coke ovens continued to embroil the plant in battles with local and federal air quality control agencies. In the face of this deteriorating situation, and with the vaunted modernization program near shambles, Anthony was removed, and Edgar Kaiser, Jr., personally took the helm, advised by experts from his family's investment bankers, First Boston. Although company publicists extolled the return of "Kaiser magic" to active management, most workers were skeptical.[97] Henry J.'s grandson was widely viewed as a "playboy," more interested in his toys, like the Denver Broncos, than in saving California's ailing steel industry.[98]

Mistrust became rampant as the Kaiser family's real strategy was gradually revealed. Years later Edgar Jr. confessed to an interviewer that, despite all the promises to the contrary, he had been sent to Fontana in 1979 by his father as a liquidator:

> We were both in tears. I knew what it meant. Nobody else saw it, but I knew what I had to do . . . break up a lot of Steel. I sold off a lot of divisions of Steel. My first day on the job was the prodigal son returning. I had to go out after 30 percent of the workforce at Fontana. . . . It sure wasn't fun.[99]

The Kaiser family had in fact been engaged in negotiations with Nippon Kokan KK, the world's fifth largest steelmaker.[100] The Kaisers wanted the Japanese to take over Fontana while they restructured Kaiser Steel as Nippon Kokan's resource supplier. This was, perhaps, the inevitable consequence of the company's long-term bias toward resources rather than steel products. But to Oakland's consternation Nippon Kokan did not take the bait as expected. Instead, following detailed technical inspections of Fontana by its engineering teams, the Japanese giant politely declined Kaiser's offer.[101]

As Kaiser Steel ran out of cash and its stock plummeted on the exchanges, a second merger deal was hastily confected and put on offer to Dallas-based LTV. The negotiations collapsed in the face of the Volcker-Reagan recession, which plunged the US steel industry into its worst crisis since 1930.[102] On the West Coast, local branch-plant manufacture was swept away by a typhoon of Asian imports. At the very moment when Fontana's fate depended on an iron will to survive—as during Henry J.'s fight to pay off the RFC loan after World War Two—the Kaiser heirs reached for the financial ripcord. The cherished goal of a resource-oriented restructuring was abandoned in favor of a staged liquidation of Kaiser Steel.

In order to keep Fontana temporarily afloat as an attraction to potential buyers, and to drive stock values up to assuage panicky stockholders, the Kaisers sold off the Australian ore reserves, the British Columbia coal mines, and the Liberian ore shipping subsidiary.[103] Edgar Jr. withdrew as CEO in 1981 after, as promised, "breaking up a lot of Steel."[104] The new managerial team, after a few months of bravado about a "crusade" to save the blast furnaces, stunned the survivors of previous cutbacks with the announcement that ore mining at Eagle Mountain and primary steelmaking at Fontana would be phased out, while the modernized fabrication facilities were put up for sale. Barely two years after their ceremonious "rededication," BOF 2 and the continuous caster were being written off as scrap, a $231 million loss.[105]

Local 2869 mustered for a last stand, as best it could, but it had tragically few friends or resources. A desperate move to trade wage and work-rule concessions for job-protection guarantees was cold-shouldered by the company before being vetoed altogether by the international.[106] As horrified members watched another two thousand pink slips being readied, the Local clutched at the final straw of an employee buyout, an "ESOP."[107] British Steel, long interested in finding a stable market on the West Coast for its unfabricated steel slabs, signaled that it was ready to consider a liaison with a restructured Fontana mill under ESOP ownership. Local 2869 retained the Kelson Group as advisors and sent representatives to Sacramento to lobby Governor Brown and the Democratic leadership.[108] In any event, however, Kaiser's intransigence about the ESOP frightened off British Steel, while government intervention on behalf of Fontana—or, for that matter, of any of California's floundering heavy industrial plants— was ruled out by Jerry Brown's new *entente cordiale* with the California Business Roundtable.

Meanwhile, San Bernardino County leaders were divided over the implications of the closure of Kaiser Steel. Having boasted for years that Kaiser pumped nearly a billion dollars annually into the local economy, they were anxious about the loss of so many paychecks. But apprehension was balanced by delight at the thought of rising real-estate values and the removal of the county's principal environmental stigma. As a result, with the exception of pro-union Democratic Congressman George Miller, the local elites and politicos sat on their hands.

In the face of this inertia in the local power structure, Local 2869's only remaining hope might have been a militant community-labor mobilization against shutdowns that allied Fontana with similarly threatened factories and communities like Bethlehem–Maywood, General Motors–South Gate, or US Steel–Torrance.[109] Unfortunately there was no tradition of communication or mutual support between Southern California's big smokestack workforces. Moreover the international unions and the county federations of labor tended to oppose any rank-and-file or local union initiative that threatened their prerogatives. When the rudiments of such a united front— the Coalition Against Plant Closures—finally emerged in 1983 it was too little and too late to save Fontana. At best, some of the survivors managed to float a life raft: the Steelworkers' Oldtimers Foundation, which has helped unionists deal with the bitter aftermaths at Fontana and Bethlehem.

The Unscrupulous Suitors

How Kaiser Steel arrived at this sorry state is an American tragedy.

Forbes[110]

While Local 2869 was fruitlessly searching for friends in high places, Kaiser Steel was like Ulysses' wife Penelope: haplessly pursued by a hundred unscrupulous suitors. Despite the reluctance of other steelmakers to assimilate Fontana to their operations, there was no shortage of corporate predators eager to stripmine the company's financial reserves. Following the sale of the offshore mineral properties, the company was temporarily awash in liquidity—by one estimate, almost one-half billion dollars.[111] Many Wall Street analysts believed that the plant was undervalued. With shrewd management, they guessed that the modernized core could be reconfigured as a profitable "minimill," fabricating imported slabs or local scrap.[112]

While the new CEO (the sixth in seven years), Stephen Girard, feuded with the Kaiser family over the terms of sale, desperate unionists and stockholders looked toward San Francisco investor Stanley Hiller, who was rumored to represent billionaire speculators Daniel Ludwig and Gaith Pharaon. Hiller's offer of $52 per share appeased the Kaiser family, but Girard, trying to retain control over a cash hoard still estimated at $430 million, broke off negotiations. The Kaisers, backed by the union (which believed it could interest the Hiller group in its ESOP concept), rallied other large stockholders to override Girard.[113] By March 1982, however, when Girard resumed talks with Hiller, the write-down costs of phased-out steel facilities, originally estimated at $150 million, were admitted to be nearly $530 million, including $112 million in employee termination costs. The contingent liabilities in health and benefits for the laid-off workforce seemed especially to overawe the Hiller group, who, to the consternation of unionists and stockholders, abruptly retreated from the field on 11 March.[114]

The company promptly moved to claim tax write-offs by auctioning its primary steelmaking equipment for scrap: a final blow that killed any hope of an ESOP-based resurrection.[115] In late October 1983 the last heat of Eagle Mountain iron ore was smelted into steel; for another month a skeleton crew of 800 (out of a workforce that once numbered 9,000) cold-rolled the remaining slabs into coils, sheets, and plate. At 4 P.M. on Saturday, 31 December, Kaiser Steel Fontana died.[116]

While thousands of Kaiser workers and their families mourned the sinking of California's industrial flagship, sharks in grey flannel suits circled around the undervalued assets of Kaiser Steel, no longer hemorrhaging $12 million per month in operating deficits. The first to strike was corporate raider Irwin Jacobs of Minneapolis—known in the trade as "Irv the Liquidator"—who had become the leading shareholder after the withdrawal of Hiller.[117] Scared that he would simply "gut" the company, Kaiser Steel management swung behind the rival bid of Oklahoma investor J. A. Frates. Then, as *Forbes* later reported, "Monty Rial suddenly appeared, uninvited and unknown," swaggering like a corporate Butch Cassidy and brandishing the high-powered law firm of Wachtell, Lipton, Rosen and Katz. Posing as a coal baron from Colorado (though his holdings had never actually produced a ton of coal), Rial dealt himself into the Kaiser Steel takeover game by boasting that he could profitably restructure the company around its billion tons of high-grade coal reserves in Utah and New Mexico.

What Jacobs and Frates didn't realize, or bother to find out, was that Rial was simply bluffing. While laying siege to Kaiser's half-billion-dollar equity, Rial's "Perma Group" was itself less liquid than some of the Fontana bars in which the ex-steelworkers groused. According to *Forbes*, the "Perma Group couldn't even pay its copying bills. A local copy shop was pursuing the company to collect a past-due $1,200, which Perma paid in twelve monthly installments." No matter: an impressed and incredibly gullible Frates admitted Rial ("it rhymes with smile") as a fifty-fifty partner. In February 1984 they outbid Jacobs to take control of Kaiser Steel, offering $162 million in cash and $218 million in preferred stock.

The most viable sections of the Fontana plant were immediately sold off—for $110 million (exactly the amount that Kaiser had borrowed from the RFC in 1942)—to a remarkable consortium that included a Long Beach businessman, Japan's giant Kawasaki Steel, and Brazil's Campanhia Vale Rio Doce Ltd. In a mindbending demonstration of how the new globalized economy works, California Steel Industries (as the consortium calls itself) employs a deunionized remnant of the Kaiser workforce under Japanese and British supervision to roll and fabricate steel slabs imported from Brazil to compete in the local market against Korean imports. Derelict Eagle Mountain, whose iron ores are five thousand miles closer to Fontana than Brazil's, has meanwhile been proposed as a giant dump for the nondegradable solid waste being produced by the burgeoning suburbia of the Inland Empire.

While Fontanans were trying to absorb these strange economic dialectics, Rial—the guy who couldn't pay his Xerox bill ten months before—was wresting control of the company from Frates (and transferring its headquarters to Colorado). His method of financing the takeover was ingenious: he sold to Kaiser Steel, at incredibly inflated prices, additional coal reserves which he owned and which it scarcely needed. The impact of the two back-to-back leveraged buyouts was little short of devastating. The original half-billion-dollar cash hoard was reduced to $500,000 as the raiders ran away with their spoils.[118] Moreover the company was hopelessly saddled with new, and utterly unnecessary, debt. As the rest of the business press was celebrating the contribution of corporate raiders to making the economy "leaner and greener," two *Forbes* journalists saw a different moral in the story of Frates and Rial looting Kaiser Steel without spending a penny of their own money:

> Frates staged a classic, no-money-down, 1980s takeover. Kaiser Steel changed hands for $380 million. Where did the money come from? Not from the pockets of the people doing the takeover. The Frates Group used $100 million borrowed from Citibank and $62 million of Kaiser's own cash to pay $22 a share to Kaiser's stockholders, and gave them $30 [face value] of preferred stock for the rest of the price. Thus, for $162 million that wasn't his and $218 million of paper in the form of Kaiser Steel preferred, Frates took over the company. Naturally, Frates took millions of dollars in fees and expenses, so his net cash investment was less than nothing.
> [To buy out Frates] Rial traded illiquid assets to Kaiser for land and cash. . . . Kaiser shelled out $78 million for the same Perma assets Frates valued 18 months earlier at only $65 million. What's more, because the SPS [coal contract] was valued at only $12.2 million this time around, the value of Rial's coal properties must have risen to $65.8 million—a 65% increase. . . . When the dust settled Frates had $20 million of cash, a $5 million near-cash receivable . . . and $15 million of Kaiser land. . . . Rial hasn't stinted himself, however. He took $2.4 million in salary last year.[119]

Rial's swashbuckling depredations finally provoked a backlash from Kaiser Steel's preferred stockholders, who allied themselves with Bruce Hendry, the famous scrapdealer in distressed companies (he had previously picked over the remains of Erie-Lackawanna and Wickes).[120] Forcing Rial aside as CEO in 1987, Hendry proposed to rescue the stockholders' equity at the expense of the ex-Kaiser workforce. Borrowing a leaf from Frank Lorenzo, Hendry plunged Kaiser Steel into a chapter-eleven proceeding in order to liquidate worker entitlements.

During the shutdown in 1983, workers had taken some solace in the assurance that cash-rich Kaiser, unlike some bankrupted Eastern steelmakers, would always be able to honor its obligations. Now, four years later, six thousand outraged former employees watched as Hendry cancelled their medical coverage and pension supplements, while transferring part of the burden of their pension funding to the federal Pension Benefit Guarantee Corporation. In order to deflect worker anger, he also initiated lawsuits to recover the $325 million in Kaiser reserves allegedly "stolen" by Frates and Rial through their buyouts.[121] At the moment of this writing, three years further on, most of the benefits remain unrecovered, the various lawsuits have disappeared in a judicial logjam, and thousands of ex-steelworkers and their families have endured further, unexpected hardships.

The Mirage of Redevelopment

Nothing Is As Nice As Developing Fontana
    Current official slogan

Fontana Headed For Economic Catastrophe
    Headline, 1987[122]

Even as the "Reagan Boom" was taking off in 1983, steel towns were still dying across the country, from Geneva (Utah) to Lackawanna (New York), Fairfield (Alabama) to Youngstown (Ohio). Aliquippa, from which so many Fontanans had emigrated in the 1940s and 1950s, was amongst the hardest hit. The shutdown of the immense, seven-mile-long Jones and Laughlin (LTV) complex, and the layoff of twenty thousand workers, was the equivalent of a nuclear disaster. A third of the population fled; of those left behind, more than half were still jobless four years after the closure. The Salvation Army became the town's leading employer. A 1986 study of three hundred Aliquippa families revealed that 59 per cent had difficulty feeding themselves, 49 per cent were behind in their utility bills, and 61 per cent could not afford to see a doctor.[123]

Driving through the Valley on Thanksgiving Day 1988, on the way to lay a wreath at the union martyrs' monument in Homestead, I found little improvement or new hope. For miles along the Ohio River the sides of the great mill had been stripped away by demolition crews, exposing the rusting entrails of pipework and machinery. Downtown Aliquippa, tightly wedged in its abrupt valley, was boarded up and as empty as any Western ghost town. At the old main gate, through which ten thousand Aliquippans had once daily streamed to work, a forlorn lean-to and some fading picket signs announced "Fort Justice," the site of a futile, two-year vigil by local unionists to save the plant from demolition.

By any standard Fontana should have suffered the same fate as Aliquippa.

Studies in the early and late 1970s confirmed that almost half of the town worked for Kaiser and nearly three-quarters drew paychecks dependent upon the mill.[124] Yet when the final shutdown came in December 1983, Fontana was a boom-, not a ghost-town. Side by side with the defeated milltown, a new community of middle-class commuters was rapidly taking shape. In the last years of the plant's life the population began to explode: doubling from 35,000 to 70,000 between 1980 and 1987, with predictions of 100,000–150,000 by the year 2000. In an interview with the *Times* as the last slabs were being rolled out at Kaiser, Fontana's Mayor Simon exulted about the city's new-found prosperity as the housing frontier of Southern California. "Nobody expected what's been happening here. When Kaiser closed, everybody thought the town was going to go kaput, but that hasn't happened."[125]

The recycling of Fontana had begun in the mid 1970s after a clique of local landowners and city officials, led by City Manager Jack Ratelle, recognized that residential redevelopment was a lucrative alternative to continued dependence upon the waning fortunes of Kaiser Steel and its blue-collar workforce. Unlike Aliquippa they had the dual advantages of being the periphery of a booming regional economy and having access to an extraordinary tool of community restructuring—California's redevelopment law. Created by a liberal legislature in the late 1940s to allow cities to build public housing in blighted areas, the law had become totally perverted by the 1970s. Not only was it being employed for massive "poor removal" in downtown San Francisco and Los Angeles, but "blight" was now so generously interpreted that wealthy cities and industrial enclaves—from Palm Springs to City of Industry—were using the law to build luxury department stores, convention centers, and championship golf courses with "tax increments" withheld from general fund uses.

Fontana's particular riff on these redevelopment strategies was its creation of an open, some would say "golden," door for developers. Ratelle and the other city fathers fretted about their ability to compete with Rancho Cucamonga to the west—a "greenfield" city concocted out of several thinly populated, agricultural townships. In order to eventually become like Orange County, they started out by acting like Puerto Rico. To compensate for gritty Fontana's "image problem," and to give it a comparative advantage in the Inland Empire's landrush, they bent redevelopment law to offer "creative financing" for large-scale developers: tax-increment and tax-exempt bonds, waiver of city fees, massive tax rebates, and, unique to Fontana, direct equity participation by the redevelopment agency. Application and inspection processes were drastically streamlined to accelerate groundbreaking in the city that aspired to become the "developer's best friend."

Fontana's pioneer redevelopment project was an expensive—many would say unnecessary—facelift of Sierra Avenue begun in 1975. David Wiener, whom the local paper likes to call the "dean of Fontana developers," was given tax-exempt financing and sales-tax rebates to construct four new shopping complexes. A little later the Fontana Redevelopment Agency (FRA) began to uproot vineyards south of Interstate 10 to build the Southwest Industrial Park. But the big Orange County and West L.A.–based developers, already heavily involved in Ontario and Rancho Cucamonga, refused to consider Fontana until it was clear that Kaiser Steel was doomed and that the milltown onus could be removed.

Fontana's first megaproject, initiated in 1981, was the Village of Southridge, located in the Jurupa Hills redevelopment area south of I-10 and projected for a build-out of nine thousand homes by the year 2000. Creative Communities, the Huntington Beach–based developers of Southridge, seduced Fontana's civic leaders by giving them a tour of Irvine, the famous master-planned city in southern Orange County. They convinced the starstruck Fontanans that a simulacrum of Irvine could be developed in Fontana's own south end if the city were willing to provide adequate infrastructure and financing. As Mayor Simon later recalled, "the city fathers wanted the project so bad that they could taste it." Accordingly, with visions of Fontana-as-Irvine dancing before their eyes, they signed a far-reaching agreement with Creative Communities that pledged the FRA to reimburse most of the infrastructural costs normally borne by developers.[126]

In 1982, one year after the groundbreaking in Southridge, Fontana annexed a huge triangle of boulder-strewn fields north of the city, abutting Interstate 15 (then under construction). The completion of I-15 through western San Bernardino and Riverside and northern San Diego counties has created one of the nation's most dynamic growth corridors. (One of the corridor's boomtowns is "Ranch California," a 100,000-acre project originated by Kaiser Development Co. in Temecula.) Three hundred thousand new residents are expected in western San Bernardino County alone.[127] Fontana, sitting at the strategic intersection of I-15 and I-10 (the San Bernardino Freeway), has superb linkages to this rapidly expanding commutershed. The North Fontana Project Area, which incorporates the old Fontana "ghetto" (an area of ironically exploding land values), is the largest redevelopment project in California (fourteen square miles), encompassing a series of prospective master-planned communities. Largest is the upscale Village of Heritage, directly competitive with Rancho Cucamonga's Terra Vista, and Victoria, which is being developed by BD Partners of West Los Angeles (Richard Barclay and Joseph Dilorio), with heavy equity participation from FRA. Heritage will provide four thousand of the eighteen thousand new homes that the FRA wants to add in North Fontana over the next generation.[128]

By the time the demolition crews got around to dismantling Big Bess, Fontana's leaders had managed to put 20,000 new homes in the $60,000-and-up range on the drawing boards in Southridge and North Fontana.[129] Within four years of Kaiser Steel's closure, raw land prices in Fontana had doubled.[130] This remarkable achievement garnered national accolades and much talk of a paradigmatic "Fontana miracle." The Los Angeles *Times*, for example, downplayed the impact of the Kaiser shutdown and resulting 15 per cent local unemployment (which it misreported as 9 per cent) in order to emphasize the city's "bright future" under its redevelopment strategy.[131] Journalists uncritically reproduced city officials' claims that Fontana would soon be wealthy from its soaring tax bases and profits on its equity position in different developments. Just as Kaiser industrial relations had once been studied as a textbook model, now Fontana's resilience was presented as laboratory confirmation of the Reagan Administration's claim that deindustrialization was only a temporary and marginal cost in the transition to postindustrial prosperity based on services, finance, and real estate.

The first symptom that all was really not so well in Fontana *redux* was the sharp increase in white supremacist agitation and racial violence after the layoffs at the mill. During the course of 1983 the local Ku Klux Klan—about two dozen strong—crawled out from under their rock and began distributing leaflets in the high schools, holding public rallies, and even offering to "assist" the Fontana police. The Klan revival seems to have exercised a certain charisma upon a periphery of skinhead youth. In a savage October 1984 attack, a twenty-year-old Black man, Sazon Davis, was left paralyzed from the chest down after being beaten by three skinheads on Sierra Avenue—Fontana's main street. The Black community was further outraged—shades of O'Day Short—when the San Bernardino County district attorney refused to prosecute the white youths, one of whose mothers was the dispatcher for the Fontana police. (The reaction of Fontana development director Neil Stone to this local precursor of Howard Beach was to moan that "image has been our main problem.")[132]

Worse problems lay soon ahead. By Christmas 1986 the Fontana bubble had burst. City Finance Director Edwin Leukemeyer resigned in the face of charges that he had embezzled public funds and sold off city-owned vehicles to his friends and relatives. Within six months the stream of resignations and indictments prompted one paper to claim that "police detectives and auditors [are] almost as common a sight in City Hall as file clerks."[133] Amongst the new casualties—a list that included the city treasurer, the motor pool director, the redevelopment director, and the development director—was City Manager and ex officio FRA chief Jack Ratelle, the chief architect of the "third Fontana." The city council forced Ratelle to resign after published reports of gratuities from leading developers made his position untenable.[134]

Demoralization in Fontana City Hall was turned into panic in August 1987 by the release of an independent audit of the city by the regional office of Arthur Young. The Young report was devastating: the FRA was in a "chaotic state of disarray" and the city was on the edge of bankruptcy.[135] The Young analysts discovered that the FRA had pawned Fontana's future in order to seduce developers. With 60 per cent of its tax base located in redevelopment areas, and obligated as payments or rebates to developers, the city could not afford to meet the needs of its expanding population. No tax revenue was left over to pay for the additional load that the new suburban population placed on its schools or public services.

Southridge alone, which Ratelle had always portrayed as a municipal gold mine, threatened to drive the city into bankruptcy as the FRA faced $10,000 per day in new interest charges accumulating on the unreimbursed principal which it owed Creative Communities. Official estimates of the total tax revenue that will be absorbed in debt service to Southridge run as high as *$750 million* by 2026 when the agreement expires.[136] It is unlikely that the principal will ever be repaid. Like a miniature Mexico or Bolivia, Fontana is a debtor nation held in thrall to its Orange County and West L.A. creditor-developers. With its suburban property tax streams diverted to debt service, the city has had to impose both austerity (in the form of overcrowded schools and degraded services) and (as in Southridge) special fee assessments on unhappy new arrivals. The alternative of raising additional city income from existing commerce is excluded by the FRA's profligate rebates of sales taxes and municipal fees to the owners of the new shopping centers.

The release of the Young report (which also included sensationalist details of financial mismanagement and the destruction of records in City Hall) emboldened local journalists to muckrake through the FRA's records, untangling the circumstances of the agency's incredible profligacy. Mark Gutglueck of the *Herald-News* eventually exposed in detail how various redevelopment schemes had pauperized the city.[137] The older mom-and-dad businesses along Sierra Avenue, for instance, were starved of redevelopment funds by FRA policies that favored chain-store "K-Marti-zation." Thus the FRA, in a typical example, gave tax-exempt financing and a $750,000 tax rebate to induce National Lumber to move into one of David Weiner's new shopping centers, itself financed by tax givebacks. The net result for the city was a large tax deficit and the closure of Ole's Hard-ware, an oldtime Fontana institution.[138]

Likewise, in the case of Southridge, Gutglueck revealed how City Man-ager Ratelle and redevelopment lawyer Timothy Sabo (accused in the Young report of raking off excessive fees) overrode the strong objections of the city attorney to provide Creative Communities (later Ten-Ninety Ltd.) with whatever they demanded: hiked-up interest rates on FRA's obliga-tion, forgiveness for their failure to build schools on time per contract, and so on. Moreover, the developers were repeatedly allowed to modify the community's specific plan, successively reducing the quality of housing and local amenities. The developers, in turn, pampered officials (like plan-ning chief Neil Stone) with "finders fees," gratuities, and the use of a lake-side resort, while Southridge—which Mayor Simon liked to call "the Bev-erly Hills of Fontana"—evolved into misery.[139] One planner who worked there has described it as "rabbit hutches with two-car garages, without ad-equate schools or public services."[140] Not surprisingly the Young report and the Gutglueck revelations fueled a revolt by embittered Southridge residents who demanded a moratorium on further growth, the recall of the council majority, and a system of district elections.[141]

Given the enormity of Fontana's suddenly exposed problems—the venality of its officials, its Andean-sized debt and the lien on its tax base until the next millennium, its underfunding of essential services, a grow-ing mismatch between housing and jobs, and so on—the voter revolt was strangely muffled. Closure of Kaiser had dispersed much of the political base once organized by Local 2869, while the new commuter citizens had little time or focus for civic engagement. As a result the growth coali-tion—minus a few leaders in jail or exile—handily dispersed its chal-lengers.[142] The Southridge-instigated recall campaign was easily defeated, while the demand for a growth moratorium was harmlessly converted into a 45-day temporary freeze on building permits. The council did scale back a few development plans in North Fontana and gave lip service to the Young report's two hundred recommendations. But the most symptomatic reaction to the crisis came from Mayor Simon (then under investigation for making unlawful personal investments in one of the redevelopment areas), who simply urged Fontanans "to just keep smiling."[143]

Since then the city fathers have tried to escape bankruptcy by tacking their sails to various, sometimes countervailing, winds. Like the rubes they are, they have ended up buying back into schemes virtually identical to those that Bolivianized Fontana in the early 1980s.

First, they have searched high and low for some commercial *deus ex machina* to generate a compensatory tax flow for their fiscal deficit. Mayor Simon's own pet-rock scheme—contrived during a Canadian vacation from his legal problems—was to induce a multi-billion-dollar investor to build the California version of the Edmonton supermall in Fontana.[144] In the absence of responses from Donald Trump or the Sultan of Brunei, the city teamed up instead with Alexander Haagen, Southern California's major mall builder, in a scheme to build a combination mall-entertainment complex in South Fontana. Just like Southridge, Haagen's Fontana Empire Center (scheduled for completion in 1995) was sold to local officials in a blaze of Orange County imagery: "Fontana's answer to the South Coast Plaza." Lest any of the Fontanans stop to ponder the absurdity of a Sears-anchored mall competing with the nation's wealthiest regional center anchored by Gucci and Neiman-Marcus, Haagen anesthetized opposition by generously donating to all ten candidates vying for the two vacant seats on the council.[145] (Recently Haagen has started to backtrack on his original promises, proposing to develop one-half of the mall site for luxury homes instead of commerce.)[146]

Meanwhile, Fontana leaders have tried to scrub the city clean of its blue-collar, "felony flats" image by drastically limiting the development of apartments and low-income units.[147] The revised Fontana masterplan even de-emphasizes "starter homes"—the meat and potatoes of the previous plan—to favor more expensive "move-up" or second homes.[148] Salesmen of Fontana's "new look," however, were immediately embarrassed by a recrudescence of the old Fontana in 1988. Millions of television viewers nationwide watched as celebrants of Martin Luther King's birthday had to be escorted down Sierra Avenue by a hundred and twenty police as acrid little knots of Fontana Klansmen shouted, "Long live the Klan. Long live the white boys." Subsequent "Death to the Klan" counter-rallies by the Jewish Defense League contributed yet more unwanted notoriety.[149]

The campaign for an upscaled Fontana also collided with plans for a reindustrialized Fontana. With an unerring sense for courting contradiction, as one group of Fontana planners was trying to increase residential exclusivity, another was simultaneously kicking out the jambs for breakneck factory and warehouse construction. Offering contractors the state's fastest track for industrial development, they guarantee building starts six days after application, rather than the nine months normal elsewhere.[150]

As angry homeowners have pointed out, combining poorly monitored industrial development—much of it highly toxic—with dense residential development is like mixing oil with water. This point was vividly illustrated in 1988 when more than 1,500 Southridge residents had to be evacuated after a nearby chemical spill.[151]

The final irony, however, is Fontana's ardent courtship of Kaiser Steel's residuum: Kaiser Resources. Left with a mile-long slag mountain and seven hundred acres of polluted wasteland, KR in partnership with Lusk-Ontario Industries has maneuvered brilliantly to get Fontana to foot the bill for the clean-up. By coyly flirting with Ontario and Rancho Cucamonga, then suddenly throwing kisses to advocates of independent cityhood for Fontana's unincorporated westside ("Rancho Vista"), KR drove Fontana officials into a jealous frenzy. As a result, debt-hobbled Fontana is offering a memorandum of understanding to KR and Lusk that would guarantee $190 million in public funds to renovate the ex–Kaiser Steel site. In particular Fontana would help clean up the still spreading plume of soil and groundwater contamination that is the legacy of forty years of steelmaking, and which has replaced the smoke-cloud from Kaiser's coke ovens as the symbol of environmental distress in San Bernardino County. KR and Lusk, in turn, would accept annexation by Fontana and agree to develop a high-tech industrial park. But a centerpiece of KR's plan is a perverse environmental joke: importing Silicon Valley's toxic waste for processing in Kaiser Steel's still extant treatment facility.[152]

So What's Left?

It's tacky, very, very tacky. But, maybe I should be grateful. People tell me it used to be worse.

New Fontana commuter-resident[153]

Eat shit and die.

Reaction of old Fontana "homeboy"

After so many schemes, scandals, and sudden upheavals, what is Fontana today? Begin, arbitrarily, with its Wild West, unincorporated fringe. Follow the fire-engine-red Kenworth K600A "Anteater" pulling its shackled double reefers into the lot of "Trucktown" off the Cherry Street exit of I-10, just south of the Kaiser ghost plant. There are more than one hundred and twenty independent trucking companies based in the Fontana area, and this is their central fuel stop and oasis. Around midnight Trucktown really bustles, and rigs are often backed up to the Interstate waiting for a fuel-stop or parking berth. The biggest truckstop in the country is just a few miles further west in Ontario, but drivers resent Union 76's private police force and stale pie.

Cherry Avenue is clearly, as they say, "west of the Pecos," and it is easier to make deals of all kinds here. Inside the cafe the counter is occupied by an apparition of Lee's Army after Appomattox: lean, bearded, hollow-eyed, and taciturn. There is more animation in the booths. Owner-operators wrestle with logbooks and second-driver problems; husband-wife teams have family arguments; brokers with questionable loads wrangle for haulers; outlaw bikers peddle old ladies and "Black Molly" (speed). The Cherry Avenue fringe has always accommodated illicit but popular activities. Until its recent closure by the Highway Patrol, the adjacent rest area on I-10 functioned as a girls-and-dope drive-in for morning commuters in Toyotas and tourists in Winnebagos.

Now the entire Fontana periphery (including the incorporated northside and Rialto as well as the Cherry Street area) has become the Huallaga Valley of Southern California. Long the "speed capital of the world," its meth labs have recently diversified into the mass manufacture of "ice" (crystal, smokable speed) and "croak" (a smokable combination of speed and crack). For the most part this is grassroots narco-patriotism: drug addiction made-in-America by small-town good old boys and distributed throughout the heartland by a vast network of motorcycle gangs and outlaw truckers. From the standpoint of free enterprise economics it is also a textbook example of small entrepreneurs filling the void left by the collapse of a dinosaur heavy industry. Speed not steel is now probably Fontana's major export.

Which is not to deny that a lot of steel is still being hauled out of Fontana even if Big Bess herself was long ago melted for scrap. The multinational hybrid of California Steel Industries, just up Cherry Avenue, continues to roll Brazilian slabs into a variety of products for local markets (although the Japanese, and increasingly the Koreans, dominate the big-ticket structural items). The United Steel Workers recently attempted to organize CSI, but the campaign ended in disaster. Whether out of fear of losing their jobs again, or in resentment against the international's failure to come to their aid eight years earlier, the ex–Local 2869 men at CSI resoundly voted the union down (88 per cent to 12 per cent).

The former primary steelworks itself looks like Dresden, Hiroshima, or, perhaps the most fitting image, Tokyo in April 1945 after three months of concentrated fire-bombing with Kaiser-made "goop" had burnt the city down to the ferroconcrete stumps of its major buildings. The wreckers long ago picked the plant clean of any salvageable metal—some of which, reincarnated in Toyotas and Hyundais, zooms by on I-10. Meanwhile, the towering smokestacks, once visible for thirty miles, are collapsed into rubble, while only the skeletal concrete cores of the blast furnaces remain. Around the heavily guarded perimeter, Kaiser Resources leases land to a series of "mom-and-dad" scrapyards, who, having run out of Kaiser wreckage, are now happily crushing and shredding derelict automobiles. The whole scene looks like *Mad Max:* a post-apocalyptic society of industrial scavengers and metal vultures.

Across the road lie shadows of Fontana Farms. A ghostly vintage chicken ranch is overgrown with weeds but otherwise kept intact by its octogenarian owner who recalls the great plague of Newcastle's disease in 1971 that killed millions of Fontana hens. A few miles away in South Fontana a handful of chicken ranchers have managed to hang on and modernize their operations. Near the corner of Jarupa and Popper stands an astounding automatic chicken plant that works by conveyor belts, where one man can easily tend 250,000 hens. But the resulting accumulation of chicken manure is so vast that it has to be pushed around the ranch by bulldozers. Nearby commuter homeowners—no longer beguiled by the romance of chicken shit—are circulating petitions to close down this successful survival of the Millerian age. When the last trace of the chickens, pigs, and orchards has been removed, Fontana's remaining link to its agrarian past will be its thousands of dogs. We are not talking about manicured suburban house dogs, but old-fashioned yard dogs: snarling, half-rabid, dopey, friendly, shaggy, monstrous, and ridiculous Fontana dogs.

Fontana probably also has more wrecked cars per capita than anywhere else on the planet. The nearby Southern California Auto Auction is considered by some aficionados to be the eighth wonder of the world. More impressive to me is the vast number of dismantled or moribund cars deliberately strewn in people's yards like family heirlooms. I suppose it is a sight that blights Fontana's new image, but the junkyard sensibility can grow on you after a while (at least it has on me). The Fontana area—or rather the parts of it that are not named "Heritage" or "Eagle Pointe Executive Homes"—is a landscape of randomly scattered, generally uncollectable (and ungentrifiable) debris: ranging from Didion's creepy boulders to the rusting smudge-pots in phantom orchards, to the Burma-Shave–era motel names (like "Ken-Tuck-U-In") on Foothill Boulevard. Even crime in Fontana has a random surreality about it. There is, for instance, the maniac who has murdered hundreds of eucalyptus trees, or Bobby Gene Stile ("Doctor Feldon"), the king of obscene phone calls, who has confessed to fifty thousand dirty phone conversations over the last twenty-three years.

"Doctor Feldon" had, perhaps, wandered too far and too freely in the fleshpots of Fontana's Valley Boulevard (still, as in 1941, "Death Alley"). Just east of Cherry Avenue the boulevard is a boring repetition of adult bookstores and used truck dealerships. Closer to Sierra, however, there is a gathering sense of a *mise en scène* by a downhome Fellini. On one corner a hardluck cowboy is trying to sell his well-worn Stetson hat to the patriarch of a family of road gypsies—or are they Okies circa 1990?—who pile out of their converted Crown bus home. They have just left the Saturday swap meet at the nearby Belair Drive-In. Inside a lobster-faced desert "flea" from Quartzite is haggling with a trio of super-bag-ladies from the San Fernando Valley over the value of some "depression" glass saucers and an antique commode. Some local kids with "Guns and Roses" gang-bang T-shirts are listening to another grizzled desert type—this one looking like Death Valley Scotty—describe his recent encounter with aliens. A Jehovah's Witness in a maroon blazer kibbitzes uncomprehendingly.

A block away is an even more improbable sight: a circus wrecking yard. Scattered amid the broken bumper cars and ferris wheel seats are nostalgic bits and pieces of Southern California's famous extinct amusement parks (in the pre-Disney days when admission was free or $1): the Pike, Belmont Shores, Pacific Ocean Park, and so on. Suddenly rearing up from the back of a flatbed trailer are the fabled stone elephants and pouncing lions that once stood at the gates of Selig Zoo in Eastlake (Lincoln) Park, where they had enthralled generations of Eastside kids. I tried to imagine how a native of Manhattan would feel, suddenly discovering the New York Public Library's stone lions discarded in a New Jersey wrecking yard. I suppose the Selig lions might be Southern California's summary, unsentimental judgment on the value of its lost childhood. The past generations are like so much debris to be swept away by the developers' bulldozers. In which case it is only appropriate that they should end up here, in Fontana—the junkyard of dreams.

NOTES

1. Joan Didion, *Slouching Towards Bethlehem*, New York 1968, p. 5. Her reaction to the Fontana area was a symptomatic premonition of her very revulsion to the landscape of El Salvador twenty years later.

2. ". . . and then they found Fontana Farms"—1930 advertising brochure in Fontana Historical Society collection. Fontana Farms Company was headquartered at 631 S. Spring St. in Downtown Los Angeles.

3. At least this was the name given by geographers to the intermontane basin which includes the Pomona, Chino, and San Bernardino valleys, as well as the Riverside Basin and the great Cucamonga Fan. (See David W. Lantis, *California:*

Land of Contrast, Belmont, Calif. 1963, p. 226.) The current appellation of "Inland Empire" loosely encompasses the Perris Valley and the San Jacinto Basin as well.

4. See Karen Frantz, "History of Rural Fontana and the Decline of Agriculture," typescript, no date, in Fontana Public Library.

5. See Richard Lillard, "Agricultural Statesman: Charles C. Teague of Santa Paula," *California History*, March 1986.

6. By 1895 Riverside was supposedly "the richest city per capita" in the United States. See Vincent Moses, "Machines in the Garden: A Citrus Monopoly in Riverside, 1900–31," *California History*, Spring 1982.

7. See Charles Teague, *Fifty Years a Rancher*, Santa Paula (private printing) 1944.

8. See Silver Anniversary issue, *Fontana Herald-News*, 10 June 1938.

9. Frantz, "History of Rural Fontana." According to Mr. Barnhold, who still lives in his 1927 Fontana Farms bungalow just east of Cherry Street: "One thousand chickens and two-and-a-half acres did not make a good living. Miller's propaganda was untrue, and many Fontanans had a hard, uphill struggle to survive the Depression especially." (Interview, June 1989.)

10. Giorgio Ciucci, "The City in Agrarian Ideology and Frank Lloyd Wright: Origins and Development of Broadacres," in Ciucci et al., *The American City: From the Civil War to the New Deal*, Cambridge, Mass. 1979, pp. 358, 375.

11. *Fontana Herald-News*, 31 July 1942.

12. John Gunther, *Inside USA*, New York 1946, p. xiv.

13. Ibid., p. 68.

14. By the 1951 revised edition of *Inside USA*, however, Gunther's infatuation with Kaiser had clearly waned, and the Kaiser chapter was abridged into a short subsection.

15. Quotes from "Life and Works of Henry Kaiser," ibid., pp. 64, 70.

16. Ibid., p. 70. On the other hand, Kaiser became a patron of labor only *after* he had become a leading beneficiary of lucrative New Deal contracts. Earlier, during the construction of Hoover Dam, he and his partners had systematically violated labor standards and health and safety regulations. When, after a series of appalling industrial accidents and deaths from heat prostration, the dam workers struck under IWW leadership in 1931, they were crushed by the Six Companies. See Joseph Stevens, *Hoover Dam: An American Adventure*, Norman 1988, pp. 69–78.

17. Gunther, *Inside USA*, p. 64.

18. A. G. Mezerik, *The Revolt of the South and West*, New York 1946, p. 280.

19. A major disappointment of Mark Foster's recent biography of Kaiser (*Henry J. Kaiser: Builder in the Modern American West*, Austin 1989) is its failure to shed new light upon the Kaiser-Giannini relationship.

20. Ibid., pp. 58–59.

21. Cf. Marquis and Bessie James, *Biography of a Bank: The Story of Bank of America*, New York 1954, pp. 389–92; Arthur Schlesinger, *The Age of Roosevelt: The Politics of Upheaval*, Cambridge, Mass. 1960, pp. 121, 297, 411. In 1934 Giannini made a last-minute intervention on FDR's behalf to buy out Upton Sinclair's radical bid for governor on the Democratic ticket. (See Russell Posner, "A. P. Giannini and the 1934 Campaign in California," *Journal of California History* 34, 2, 1957.) Although unsuccessful in coopting Sinclair, Giannini went on to play a crucial role in winning California for Roosevelt in 1936. His support for the New Deal, however, waned after 1938 as he perceived the consolidation of the power of a "Jewish cabal" led by his old enemy Eugene Meyer and Secretary of the Treasury

Morgenthau. See Julian Dana, *A. P. Giannini: Giant in the West*, New York 1947, pp. 315–17, 322–23.

22. Schlesinger, *Age of Roosevelt*, p. 411.

23. Gunther, *Inside USA*, pp. 71–72; Foster, *Henry J. Kaiser*, Chapter 5, "Patriot in Pinstripes—Shipbuilding," pp. 68–89.

24. Gunther, *Inside USA*, p. 71.

25. The Kaiser model of the expanded or complex wage agreement, including a medical component (cheapened by an economy of scale), was a potent influence upon the collective bargaining system ultimately hammered out by the CIO unions and the major industrial employers in the late 1940s.

26. Quoted in Mezerik, *Revolt*, p. 265.

27. Gerald Nash is quite mistaken, of course, in asserting that Fontana was built "largely at government expense." (See *The American West Transformed: The Impact of the Second World War*, Bloomington, Ind. 1985, p. 28.)

28. Ibid., p. 264.

29. See the discussion in John E. Coffman, "The Infrastructure of Kaiser Steel Fontana: An Analysis of the Effects of Technical Change on Raw Material Logistics," M.A. thesis, Department of Geography, UCLA, Los Angeles 1969, pp. 1–2, 5, 25–29.

30. Frantz, "History of Rural Fontana," p. 25; *Fontana Herald-News*, 7 January 1943.

31. *Fontana Herald-News*, 14 and 21 January 1941.

32. Ibid., 18 April (Miller obituary), 16 May, and 19 September 1941.

33. Ibid., 6 June 1941.

34. Ibid., 29 May 1958 (recollections of the war years).

35. Ibid., 2 and 30 January 1942. The critical role of poultry in the national defense had been avidly discussed by Fontanans the previous fall. (See ibid., 19 September 1941.)

36. The "bolt" appeared in local papers on 6 March 1942 (see ibid.).

37. Frantz, "History of Rural Fontana," p. 26.

38. Ibid.

39. *Fontana Herald-News*, 3 and 10 April 1942.

40. Cf. *Business Week*, 21 November 1942; *Fontana Herald-News*, 30 December 1942, 7 and 14 January 1943. Cal-Ship in San Pedro was operated by Kaiser's old partners, Stephen Bechtel and John McCone (the future CIA chief).

41. Gunther, *Inside USA*, p. 72.

42. Ibid., 3 April 1942.

43. Interview with Barnhold family, early residents of the Cherry Street area across from the Kaiser plant. See also Frantz, "History of Rural Fontana," p. 27.

44. *Fontana Herald-News*, 22 July 1943.

45. *Steel Magazine*, 25 September 1944. On the other hand, Kaiser Steel in its early years was able to take advantage of the informal tariff barrier erected around California by the railroad's exorbitant shipping rates and Pittsburgh's own monopoly surtax.

46. James and James, *Biography of a Bank*, p. 468.

47. See Henry J. Kaiser, Jr.'s exposition of his father's views in *Fontana Herald-News*, 10 December 1942.

48. See Foster, *Henry J. Kaiser*, pp. 1–2, 179–82.

49. *Fontana Herald-News*, 26 February and 19 September 1946; Foster, *Henry J. Kaiser*, pp. 132–34.

50. Gunther, *Inside USA* (1951 revised ed.), p. 47.

51. See Book Four, "Transamerican Titan," in Dana, *Giannini*.

52. Dana, *Giannini*, p. 163.

53. Cf. Gunther, *Inside USA*, pp. 73–74; and Foster, *Henry J. Kaiser*, pp. 142–64.

54. *Iron Age*, 7 October 1948.

55. Cf. Coffman, "Infrastructure"; J. S. Ess, "Kaiser Steel—Fontana," *Iron and Steel Engineer* 31, February 1954; and C. Langdon White, "Is the West Making the Grade in the Steel Industry?" *Stanford Business Research Series* 8, 1956.

56. White, "Is the West Making the Grade?" pp. 102–3; and Mezerik, *Revolt*, p. 266.

57. White, "Is the West Making the Grade?" pp. 103–5; and James and James, *Biography of a Bank*, pp. 493–94; and Robert Gottlieb and Irene Wolt, *Thinking Big: The Story of the Los Angeles Times*, New York 1977, p. 244.

58. Cf. Neil Morgan, *Westward Tilt: The American West Today*, New York 1963, p. 29; and Kaiser Steel Company, *Annual Reports*, 1959 and 1965.

59. For the history of the agreement, see William Aussieker, "The Decline of Labor-Management Cooperation: The Kaiser Long-Range Sharing Plan," IRRA, *35th Annual Proceedings*, pp. 403–9. For typical textbook celebrations of the Plan, see James Henry, ed., *Creative Collective Bargaining*, Englewood Cliffs, N.J. 1965; and Herbert Blitz, ed., *Labor-Management Contracts and Technological Change*, New York 1969.

60. Quoted in *Eagle*, 20 December 1945.

61. Frantz, "History of Rural Fontana," pp. 27–30; *Fontana Herald-News*, 12 August 1943.

62. Interviews with pioneer Barnhold family, steelworker veterans, John Piazza and Dino Papavero, and my own family (residents of Fontana from 1941 to 1949). Also see *Fontana Herald-News*, 31 December 1942, and 22 July and 12 August 1943, as well as the recollections in the 29 May 1955 issue.

63. Ibid.

64. See virtually any issue of the *Eagle* on file at the Southern California Library for Social Research.

65. Cf. *Eagle*, 20 December 1945; Charlotta Bass, *Forty Years: Memoirs from the Pages of a Newspaper*, Los Angeles (privately printed) 1960, pp. 135–36; and *The Militant*, 2 February 1946.

66. Bass, *Forty Years*; *The Militant*, 2 February and 23 March 1946.

67. *Fontana Herald-News*, 3 January 1946.

68. *Eagle*, 3 January 1946; *Daily World*, 2 January 1946.

69. Bass, *Forty Years*; *Eagle*, 17 and 31 January 1946; *The Militant*, 2 February 1946.

70. *Daily World*, 6 and 14 February 1946; *Eagle*, 7 February 1946; *The Militant*, 11 February 1946.

71. The period from V-J Day 1945 to Fall 1946 witnessed a rising arc of white resistance to civil rights in Los Angeles: riots by white high-school students, unwarranted police shootings, cross burnings at USC, a judicial verdict in support of restrictive covenants, and, on 7 May 1946, a Klan bombing of a Black home in Southcentral. See the *Eagle* file; and Bass, *Forty Years*.

72. *The Militant*, 23 March 1946.

73. However, the civil rights fight in Fontana continued. For example, in early 1949 ministers of the local AME church sued a Fontana cafe for lunch-counter discrimination. (See *Eagle*, 13 January 1949.)

74. See *Fontana Herald-News,* 14 March 1946.

75. Hunter Thompson, *Hell's Angels: A Strange and Terrible Saga,* New York 1966, p. 90.

76. For an insider's account of the Oakland chapter's rise, see George Wethern (with Vincent Colnett), *A Wayward Angel,* New York 1978.

77. Frank Reynolds (as told to Michael McClure), *Freewheelin' Frank,* New York 1967, pp. 7, 110–11.

78. Thompson, *Hell's Angels,* pp. 59–62. Thompson makes an interesting case that the harassment tactics used against the Berdoo Angels were the precedent for police "street cleaning" efforts against the 1960s peace movement (p. 60).

79. Los Angeles *Times,* 15 February 1990 (hereafter cited as *Times*).

80. John Herling, *Right to Challenge: People and Power in the Steelworkers Union,* New York 1972, p. 207.

81. Interviews with Dino Papavero and John Piazza, Steelworkers' Oldtimers Foundation, Fontana, May 1989.

82. Herling, *Right to Challenge,* pp. 198–212.

83. Ibid., pp. 207–11, 265–66, 280. The essence of Local 2869 alienation was summarized by a McDonald supporter: "Dissatisfaction developed because of the wage discrepancy between those who were paid under the sharing plan and those under the incentive plan [older workers]. Added to this, the Committee of Nine had not consulted the local union leadership. . . . All the local leadership got was a decision handed down to them by the big boys on top" (p. 212).

84. From a cuttings album of the Kaiser Personnel Department in the 1950s, retrieved from trash during the plant dismantling in 1985 by Dino Papavero. Most historical records of plant society were wantonly discarded.

85. Ibid.

86. *Times,* 6 September 1980 and 4 November 1981.

87. KSC *Annual Report,* 1961, 1963, 1964, 1966, and 1971.

88. Cf. retrospective analysis in KSC (Form 10-K) *Annual Report* 1980; and *Times,* 31 July 1977, 24 April 1978, 9 February 1979.

89. See Aussieker, "Decline," pp. 403–9.

90. Interview with Dino Papavero, May 1989; also see Aussieker, "Decline," pp. 405–6; *Times,* 2 February 1972, 28 March 1972.

91. KSC *Annual Report,* 1976, 1977; *Times,* 25 December 1976.

92. "And the Smog Stayed On," pamphlet issued by Kaiser Steel, 1972.

93. "Bill," in discussion at Steelworkers' Oldtimers Foundation, Fontana, May 1989. See also *Times,* 30 May 1978.

94. KSC (Form 10-K) *Annual Report* 1980.

95. *Times,* 6 and 10 September 1980.

96. *Times,* 9 February 1979.

97. *Times,* 27 September 1979.

98. Interview with Papavero and Piazza, May 1989.

99. Interviewed in *Times,* 4 August 1985.

100. KSC *Annual Report* 1979.

101. KSC (Form 10-K) *Annual Report* 1980; *Times,* 24 October and 22 November 1979.

102. Cf. KSC; and *Times,* September 1980.

103. *Times,* 2 June 1979.

104. KSC *Annual Report* 1981.

105. *Times,* 4 November 1981.

106. *Times,* 27 August 1980 and 13 February 1982.

107. The ESOP (Employee Stock Ownership Plan) divided Local 2869 into bitterly opposed factions with president Frank Anglin in favor and Ralph Shoutes leading the opposition. The last Local election was narrowly won by Anglin in April 1982. (See *Fontana Herald-News,* 8 April 1982.)

108. See Aussieker, "Decline," p. 408; *Times,* 14 August 1982.

109. In the Volcker-Reagan recession of 1979–83 nearly 20,000 jobs were lost in California's steel and iron products sector, and the state membership of the United Steel Workers fell by 41 percent. See Anne Lawrence, "Organizations in Crisis: Labor Union Responses to Plant Closures in California Manufacturing, 1979–83," Dept. of Geography, University of California, Berkeley 1985, pp. 55–57.

110. Allan Sloan and Peter Fuhrman, "An American Tragedy," *Forbes,* 20 October 1986.

111. On the accumulation of this cash hoard, see *Times,* 18 October 1979, 6 September 1980, 4 November 1981.

112. Ibid.

113. *Times,* 5 February 1982.

114. *Times,* 16 March 1982.

115. The *People's World,* 7 January 1984, marveled at the tax laws that make it so "profitable" to scrap the plant. "Net profits from the destruction of the only basic 'integrated works' in the West may exceed all the profits made on the corporation's activities since the end of World War Two."

116. *Fontana Herald-News,* 2 January 1984; *Times,* 4 August 1985.

117. *Times,* 27 May 1983.

118. *Sun,* 18 January 1988.

119. Sloan and Fuhrman, "An American Tragedy," pp. 32–33; see also *Times,* 25 September 1987.

120. *Times,* 9 February 1987.

121. *Times,* 27 January, 9 and 13 February 1987, 10 and 31 August 1988. Ex–Local 2869 President Frank Anglin expressed the following opinion of Hendry's management: "I haven't seen him do anything but lose money" (*Sun,* 18 January 1988).

122. *Sun,* 19 August 1987.

123. See "Horse Dies in One-Horse Steel Town," *Times,* 1 September 1986.

124. *Times,* 30 January 1971; 23 June 1978 (Urbanomics Research Associates study); and 1 September 1985. 3,200 Kaiser workers lived in Fontana (population 21,000), 2,600 in Rialto/San Bernardino, and 3,200 in the rest of the Inland Empire.

125. *Times,* 15 August 1985.

126. See Joe Bridgman, "Southridge Village: Milestone or Millstone for Fontana?" *Sun,* 16 February 1986.

127. *San Bernardino County General Plan Update,* 1988.

128. *Times,* 1 September 1985; *Sun,* 23 January 1986.

129. Cf. "Southridge Village Specific Plan," FRA, n.d.

130. *Times,* 25 September 1988.

131. *Times,* 30 December 1983.

132. *Times,* 15 August 1985.

133. *Times,* 24 June 1987.

134. *Fontana Herald-News,* 14 December 1987.

135. Arthur Young International, Inland Empire Office, *Management Audit of*

the City of Fontana, six volumes, 18 August 1987 (public copy of volume one in Fontana Library); *Sun,* 19 August 1987; and *Fontana Herald-News,* 19 August 1987.

136. *Sun,* 16 February 1986; debt estimate updated, 5 September 1987. In fact the FRA was so "informal" in dealings with developers that it never bothered to accurately record or report its burgeoning debt. As the Arthur Young auditors noted: "Although the Redevelopment Agency is highly leveraged, a definitive assessment on the exact amount of its obligations has not been made. . . . a determination of the Agency's total financial obligation has been frustrated by a lack of adequate record-keeping and file maintenance in the Agency, resulting in missing documents that are essential in quantifying the dollar amounts committed by the Agency to various developers" (p. II–7).

137. *Fontana Herald-News,* 15 September, 26 and 29 October 1987.

138. Ibid., 26 and 29 October 1987. See also *Sun,* 17 August 1986.

139. *Fontana Herald-News,* 15 September 1987; also *Sun,* 16 February 1986.

140. Interview with "P.C.," former Fontana planner, September 1989. It is questionable whether Southridge will ever be finished; phase three is officially described as "in limbo." (See *Fontana Herald-News,* 9 January 1990.)

141. The Fontana School Board also sued because of the developers' failure to build desperately needed schools.

142. The dissipation of the union political base was emphasized by John Piazza, May 1989.

143. *Sun,* 18 September 1987.

144. Ibid., 13 August 1987.

145. *Fontana Herald-News,* 1 November 1988.

146. Ibid., 9 January 1990.

147. On "image," see *Sun,* 13 August 1978.

148. *Fontana Herald-News,* 8 December 1987; 26 October 1988.

149. Ibid.

150. Ibid., 24 August 1988.

151. Ibid., 26 October and 13 December 1988.

152. Cf. *Fontana Herald-News,* 3 November 1988; 11 January and 19 April 1989; and 16 January 1990.

153. *Times,* 6 August 1989.

FURTHER READING

Center on Budget and Policy Priorities. *A Tale of Two Futures.*1994.

Clark, David L. "Improbable Los Angeles." In *Sunbelt Cities: Politics and Growth Since World War II,* edited by Richard M. Bernard and Bradley R. Rice, pp. 268–308. 1983.

Clayton, James. "The Impact of the Cold War on the Economies of California and Utah, 1946–1965." *Pacific Historical Review* 36 (November 1967): 449–453.

Collins, Keith E. *Black Los Angeles: The Making of the Ghetto, 1940–1950.* 1980.

Davis, Mike. "Chinatown Revisited? The 'Internationalization' of Downtown Los Angeles." In *Sex, Death, and God in L.A.,* edited by David Reid, pp. 19–53. 1992.

———. *City of Quartz: Excavating the Future in Los Angeles.* 1990.

———. "The Empty Quarter." In *Sex, Death, and God in L.A.,* edited by David Reid, pp. 54–71. 1992.

————. "Fortress Los Angeles: The Militarization of Urban Space." In *Variations on a Theme Park: The New American City and the End of Public Space*, edited by Michael Sorkin, pp. 154–180, 244–245. 1993.

————. "The Los Angeles Inferno." *Socialist Review* 22 (January-March 1992): 58–80.

————. "Who Killed L.A.? A Political Autopsy." *New Left Review* 197 (January-February 1993): 3–28.

————. "Who Killed Los Angeles? Part Two: The Verdict Is Given." *New Left Review* 199 (May-June 1993): 29–54.

DeLeon, Richard Edward. *Left Coast City: Progressive Politics in San Francisco, 1975–1991.* 1992.

Delgado, Hector L. *New Immigrants, Old Unions: Organizing Undocumented Workers in Los Angeles.* 1993.

"Envisioning California." Special issue. *California History* (Winter 1989/1990).

Fishman, Robert. *Bourgeois Utopias: The Rise and Fall of Suburbia.* Chapter 7. 1987.

Fogelson, Robert. *The Fragmented Metropolis: Los Angeles, 1850–1930.* 1967.

"Fortress California at War: San Francisco, Los Angeles, Oakland, and San Diego, 1941–1945." Special issue. *Pacific Historical Review* 63 (August 1994).

Foster, Mark S. *Henry J. Kaiser: Builder in the Modern American West.* 1989.

Hartman, Chester. *The Transformation of San Francisco.* 1984.

Hazen, Don, ed. *Inside the L.A. Riots.* 1992.

Jackson, Bryan O., and Michael B. Preston, eds. *Racial and Ethnic Politics in California.* 1991.

Klein, Norman M., and Martin Schiesl, eds. *Twentieth-Century Los Angeles: Power, Promotion, and Social Conflict.* 1990.

Kotkin, Joel, and Paul Grabowicz. *California Inc.* 1982.

"Los Angeles—Struggles Toward Multiethnic Community." Special issue. *Amerasia Journal* 19 (Spring 1993).

Los Angeles Times. Understanding the Riots: Los Angeles Before and After the Rodney King Case. 1992.

Lotchin, Roger W. *Fortress California, 1910–1961: From Warfare to Welfare.* 1992.

Markusen, Ann, et al. *Rise of the Gunbelt.* Chapter 5. 1991.

Ong, Paul, ed. *The Widening Divide: Income Inequality and Poverty in Los Angeles.* 1989.

Rieff, David. *Los Angeles: Capital of the Third World.* 1991.

Schiesl, Martin J. "Airplanes to Aerospace: Defense Spending and Economic Growth in the Los Angeles Region, 1945–60." In *The Martial Metropolis: U.S. Cities in War and Peace*, edited by Roger Lotchin, pp. 135–149. 1984.

————. "City Planning and the Federal Government in World War II: The Los Angeles Experience." *California History* 59 (Summer 1980): 126–143.

Scott, Mel. *The San Francisco Bay Area: A Metropolis in Perspective.* 1985.

Sonenshein, Raphael. *Politics in Black and White: Race and Power in Los Angeles.* 1993.

Walker, Richard. "The Playground of U.S. Capitalism: The Political Economy of the San Francisco Bay Area in the 1980s." In *Fire in the Hearth: The Radical Politics of Place in America*, edited by Mike Davis et al., pp. 3–82. 1990.

Walters, Dan. *The New California: Facing the 21st Century.* 1992.

Wiley, Peter, and Robert Gotlieb. *Empires in the Sun: The Rise of the New American West.* 1982.

Wollenberg, Charles. *Golden Gate Metropolis: Perspectives on Bay Area History.* 1985.

Contributors

TOMÁS ALMAGUER is associate professor of sociology and American culture at the University of Michigan. He is the author of *Racial Fault Lines: The Historical Origins of White Supremacy in California* (1994).

SUCHENG CHAN is professor of history and Asian American studies at the University of California, Santa Barbara. She is the author of *This Bittersweet Soil: The Chinese in California Agriculture, 1860–1910* (1986), *Asian Americans: An Interpretive History* (1991), *Asian Californians* (1991), and editor of several other books.

DOROTHY SUE COBBLE is associate professor in the labor education department at Rutgers University. She is the author of *Dishing It Out: Waitresses and Their Unions in the Twentieth Century* (1991) and editor of *Women and Unions: Forging a Partnership* (1993).

DANIEL CORNFORD is associate professor of history at San Jose State University. He is the author of *Workers and Dissent in the Redwood Empire* (1987), associate editor of the *Emma Goldman Papers,* microfilm edition (1992), and co-editor of *American Labor in the Era of World War II* (1995).

CLETUS E. DANIEL is professor of American labor history in the School of Industrial and Labor Relations at Cornell University. He is the author of *Bitter Harvest: A History of California Farmworkers, 1870–1941* (1981), *The ACLU and the Wagner Act: An Inquiry into the Depression-Era Crisis of American Liberalism* (1980), and *Chicano Workers and the Politics of Fairness: The FEPC in the Southwest, 1941–1945* (1991).

MIKE DAVIS is the author of *City of Quartz: Excavating the Future in Los Angeles* (1990) and *Prisoners of the American Dream* (1986). He is co-editor of *Reshaping the U.S. Left: Popular Struggles in the 1980s* (1988) and *Fire in the Hearth: The Radical Politics of Place in America* (1990).

JAMES N. GREGORY is associate professor of history at the University of Washington, Seattle. He is the author of *American Exodus: The Dust Bowl Migration and Okie Culture in California* (1989).

KAREN J. HOSSFELD is associate professor of sociology at San Francisco State University. She is the author of several articles on high-tech workers in Silicon Valley and the book *"Small, Foreign, and Female": Profiles of Gender, Race, and Nationality in Silicon Valley* (forthcoming).

MARILYNN S. JOHNSON is assistant professor of history at Boston College. She is the author of *The Second Gold Rush: Oakland and the East Bay in World War II* (1993).

MICHAEL KAZIN is associate professor of history at American University. He is the author of *Barons of Labor: The San Francisco Building Trades and Union Power in the Progressive Era* (1987).

DOUGLAS MONROY is associate professor of history at Colorado College. He is the author of *Thrown Among Strangers: The Making of Mexican Culture in Frontier California* (1990).

BRUCE NELSON is associate professor of history at Dartmouth College. He is the author of *Workers on the Waterfront: Seamen, Longshoremen, and Unionism in the 1930s* (1988).

VICKI RUIZ is professor of history at the Claremont Graduate School. She is the author of *Cannery Women, Cannery Lives: Mexican Women, Unionization, and the California Food Processing Industry, 1930–1950* (1987). She is co-editor of *Women on the U.S.–Mexican Border: Responses to Change* (1987), *Western Women: Their Land, Their Lives* (1988), and *Unequal Sisters: A Multicultural Reader in U.S. Women's History* (1990).

DEVRA WEBER is assistant professor of history at the University of California, Riverside. She is the author of several articles on California farmworkers and the book *Dark Sweat, White Gold: California Farmworkers, Cotton, and the New Deal* (1994).

CHARLES WOLLENBERG is an instructor in history at Vista College, Berkeley. He is the author of *All Deliberate Speed: Segregation and Exclusion in California Schools, 1855–1975* (1976), *Golden Gate Metropolis: Perspectives on Bay Area History* (1985), and *Marinship at War: Shipbuilding and Social Change in Wartime Sausalito* (1990). He is also the editor of *Ethnic Conflict in California History* (1970).

Credits

Douglas Monroy's "Brutal Appetites: The Social Relations of the California Mission" is extracted from chapters 1 and 2 of his book *Thrown Among Strangers: The Making of Mexican Culture in Frontier California* (Berkeley: University of California Press, 1990). Reprinted with permission from the University of California Press.

Sucheng Chan's "Chinese Livelihood in Rural California: The Impact of Economic Change, 1860–1880" appeared in *Pacific Historical Review* (53) 1984. Reprinted with permission from the University of California Press.

Dorothy Sue Cobble's "Dishing It Out: Waitresses and the Making of Their Unions in San Francisco, 1900–1941" is extracted from chapters 3 and 4 of her book *Dishing It Out: Waitresses and Their Unions in the Twentieth Century* (Urbana: University of Illinois Press, 1991). Reprinted with permission from the University of Illinois Press.

James N. Gregory's "Okies and the Politics of Plain-Folk Americanism" is a reprint of chapter 5 of his book *American Exodus: The Dust Bowl Migration and Okie Culture in California* (New York: Oxford University Press, 1989). Reprinted with permission from Oxford University Press.

Charles Wollenberg's "*James v. Marinship:* Trouble on the New Black Frontier" was published in *California History* 60 (Fall 1981). Reprinted with permission from the California Historical Society.

Tomás Almaguer's "Racial Domination and Class Conflict in Capitalist Agriculture: The Oxnard Sugar Beet Workers' Strike of 1903" was published in *Labor History* 25 (1984). Reprinted with permission from *Labor History.*

Devra Weber's "Raiz Fuerte: Oral History and Mexicana Farmworkers" is reprinted from *Oral History Review* 17 (1989). Reprinted with permission from the *Oral History Review.*

Bruce Nelson's "The Big Strike" is a reprint of chapter 5 of his book *Workers on the Waterfront: Seamen, Longshoremen, and Unionism in the 1930s* (Urbana: University of Illinois Press, 1988). Reprinted with permission from the University of Illinois Press.

Vicki Ruiz's "A Promise Fulfilled: Mexican Cannery Workers in Southern California" was first published in *Pacific Historian* 30 (1986). Reprinted with permission from Sally M. Miller.

Daniel Cornford's "To Save the Republic: The California Workingmen's Party in Humboldt County" was published in *California History* 66 (1987). Reprinted with permission from the California Historical Society.

Michael Kazin's "Reform, Utopia, and Racism: The Politics of California Craftsmen" is a reprint of chapter 6 of his book *Barons of Labor: The San Francisco Building Trades and Union Power in the Progressive Era* (Urbana: University of Illinois Press, 1987). Reprinted with permission from the University of Illinois Press.

Marilynn S. Johnson's "Mobilizing the Homefront: Labor and Politics in Oakland, 1941–1951" is based mainly on chapter 7 of her book *The Second Gold Rush: Oakland and the East Bay in World War II* (Berkeley: University of California Press, 1993). Reprinted with permission from the University of California Press.

Cletus E. Daniel's "Cesar Chavez and the Unionization of California Farmworkers" is reprinted from *Labor Leaders in America,* edited by Melvyn Dubofsky and Warren Van Tine (Urbana: University of Illinois Press, 1987). Reprinted with permission from the University of Illinois Press.

Karen J. Hossfeld's "Why Aren't High-Tech Workers Organized? Lessons in Gender, Race, and Nationality from Silicon Valley" was written for this volume and presages parts of her forthcoming book *"Small, Foreign, and Female": Profiles of Gender, Race, and Nationality in Silicon Valley.*

Mike Davis's "Fontana: Junkyard of Dreams" is reprinted from chapter 7 of his book *City of Quartz: Excavating the Future in Los Angeles* (London: Verso, 1990). Reprinted with permission from Verso.

Compositor:	G&S Typesetters, Inc.
Text:	10/13 Aldus
Display:	Aldus
Printer:	Haddon Craftsmen, Inc.
Binder:	Haddon Craftsmen, Inc.